Cloud Networking and Resilience

Designing Scalable, Fault-Tolerant, and Highly-Available Cloud Network Architectures

Cristian Critelli

Apress®

Cloud Networking and Resilience: Designing Scalable, Fault-Tolerant, and Highly-Available Cloud Network Architectures

Cristian Critelli
Geneva, Geneve, Switzerland

ISBN-13 (pbk): 979-8-8688-2435-7   ISBN-13 (electronic): 979-8-8688-2436-4
https://doi.org/10.1007/979-8-8688-2436-4

Managing Director, Apress Media LLC: Welmoed Spahr
Acquisitions Editor: Celestin Suresh John
Editorial Assistant: Gryffin Winkler

Cover designed by eStudioCalamar

Cover image provided by the author

Distributed to the book trade worldwide by Springer Science+Business Media New York, 1 New York Plaza, New York, NY 10004. Phone 1-800-SPRINGER, fax (201) 348-4505, e-mail orders-ny@springer-sbm.com, or visit www.springeronline.com. Apress Media, LLC is a Delaware LLC and the sole member (owner) is Springer Science + Business Media Finance Inc (SSBM Finance Inc). SSBM Finance Inc is a **Delaware** corporation.

For information on translations, please e-mail booktranslations@springernature.com; for reprint, paperback, or audio rights, please e-mail bookpermissions@springernature.com.

Apress titles may be purchased in bulk for academic, corporate, or promotional use. eBook versions and licenses are also available for most titles. For more information, reference our Print and eBook Bulk Sales web page at http://www.apress.com/bulk-sales.

Any source code or other supplementary material referenced by the author in this book is available to readers on GitHub. For more detailed information, please visit https://www.apress.com/gp/services/source-code.

If disposing of this product, please recycle the paper

To Ade (2017–2022)

Your presence taught me what resilience is in life.

You were joy when I could not find it, calm when the world felt loud,
and company when silence felt heavy.

You taught how saving another life can save your own in return.

Your image is on the cover, but your imprint lives far deeper.

Adei (2017–2022)

Buvimas su tavimi mane išmokė kas gyvenime yra stiprybė.

Tu buvai džiaugsmas, kai jo negalėjau rasti, ramybė, kai pasaulis
atrodė pernelyg triukšmingas ir mano palaikymas, kai tyla atrodė
per sunki.

Tu mane išmokei, kad išgelbėdamas kitą gyvybę, gali išgelbėti
ir savąją.

Tavo atvaizdas yra ant knygos viršelio, o tavo palikimas kažkur giliai
širdyje.

Per Ade (2017–2022)

La tua presenza mi ha insegnato cosa significa davvero essere resilienti
nella vita.

Sei stato gioia quando non la trovavo più, calma quando il mondo era
troppo rumoroso,

e compagnia quando il silenzio pesava troppo.

Mi hai insegnato che salvare una vita significa salvare anche la
propria.

La tua immagine è sulla copertina, ma la tua impronta vive molto più
in profondità.

Table of Contents

Chapter 5: Implementing Resilience Throughout the OSI Model with AWS Examples 259

About the Author

 **Cristian Critelli** is a cloud networking and resilience specialist with deep expertise in network engineering, multi-region architectures, traffic engineering, and large-scale network fault tolerance. As the EMEA Lead for Networking and Resilience at Amazon Web Services (AWS), he works with enterprise customers, financial institutions, global partners, and cloud practitioners to design and operate scalable, highly available, and fault-tolerant cloud solutions.

With a background spanning network engineering, cloud networking, and reliability, Cristian has authored technical blogs, white papers, and enablement content widely used by cloud professionals. He is an industry speaker and trusted expert on topics such as resilient network design, cross-region architectures, and regulatory operational resilience (including DORA and NIS2).

Cristian also holds more than 57 professional certifications across AWS, CISCO, Microsoft, Riverbed, IBM, and Wireshark—reflecting a career-long commitment to mastery in network engineering and cloud architecture. He is a strong advocate for building systems that withstand failures gracefully and continue delivering value while affected by service impairments.

About the Technical Reviewer

Venkat Kondepati is a seasoned technology leader with over two decades of experience driving digital transformation and cloud architecture initiatives across global enterprises. As former Director of Software Engineering at S&P Global, he led multi-million dollar modernization projects, including the migration of 60+ applications to AWS cloud infrastructure and the development of AI-driven data platforms that delivered 70% cost savings. Currently serving as Manager of Data Architecture and Engineering at Ascentt, Venkat specializes in cloud-native architectures, generative AI implementation, and building high-performance engineering teams across distributed global organizations. He holds multiple certifications including AWS Solutions Architect and PMP and has completed advanced studies in Data Science and Generative AI for Business Transformation.

Acknowledgments

This book would not exist without the love, patience, and support of the people—and the cats—who have walked beside me throughout this journey and over the years that shaped it.

To **Rasa**, my fiancée—thank you for your patience, your strength, and for standing by me through every day, every late night, every doubt, and every empty page. Your belief in me gave me the courage to keep writing.

To **my parents**, who gave me everything long before I had anything to give back. If I am here today, it is because of the values, resilience, and love you placed in me from the beginning.

To the **partners, customers, and colleagues** I've had the privilege of working with—this book is shaped by the real challenges we faced together. Every conversation, every design session, every failure and recovery has taught me more than any course or certification ever could. You helped turn theory into reality.

And of course, the most important and quiet acknowledgment belongs to **Ade**. His presence taught me what resilience feels like in lived experience—silent, gentle, unwavering. Though this book is written in the language of technology, its spirit was shaped in part by him.

Finally, to every reader who believes that networks, like living beings, should endure, adapt, and recover—I hope these pages serve you well.

Introduction

Resilience is no longer a luxury—it is an imperative. In today's cloud-native era, where digital services span time zones and serve users around the clock, the question is not whether failure will occur, but when. From widespread outages like the CrowdStrike global incident to subtle, hard-to-detect degradations in complex distributed systems, resilience has emerged as the defining characteristic of trustworthy, enduring cloud architectures.

Cloud Networking and Resilience is the result of years spent working closely with some of the world's leading organizations, helping them design, implement, and sustain cloud systems that can withstand disruption and adapt in the face of uncertainty. In my role as the EMEA Lead for Networking & Resilience at Amazon Web Services (AWS), I've had the privilege of supporting enterprises of all sizes as they grapple with the realities of high availability, operational continuity, and architectural rigor. What I've learned is that the greatest challenges to resilience are rarely technical—they are conceptual. Too often, resilience is misunderstood, deprioritized, or approached as an afterthought.

This book is an attempt to change that.

While many of the technical examples and reference architectures throughout this book are drawn from AWS—reflecting my current professional focus—the principles and strategies presented are cloud-agnostic. Whether you work with Microsoft Azure, Google Cloud Platform, or another provider, the foundational patterns of resilient design remain consistent. My aim is to make those patterns practical, portable, and actionable.

Rather than centering purely on application-layer recovery or generalized high-level guidance, this book focuses on what is often the most underestimated yet critical layer: cloud networking. Networks are the lifelines of distributed systems. They connect services, users, regions, and environments. And they are often the first point of failure—and the last to be understood.

Through deep technical exploration, this book examines how to build resilient networks at every layer—from DNS and routing to traffic engineering, hybrid connectivity, fault isolation, and disaster recovery. Each chapter is crafted to build upon the last, guiding you from fundamental concepts to advanced architecture patterns, practical tools, and real-world deployment insights.

Although the book begins by introducing resilience and foundational principles, it is written with the expectation that readers are already familiar with core cloud technologies and networking concepts. The primary focus is not on teaching the basics, but on exploring where cloud networking and resilience intersect—and how that intersection shapes robust, production-grade architectures.

Whether you are a cloud architect, network engineer, site reliability engineer (SRE), or DevOps practitioner, my hope is that this book becomes a trusted guide in your pursuit of building systems that are not only available, but truly resilient—systems that can absorb, adapt to, and recover from the unexpected with minimal disruption.

On a personal note, this book carries a deeper meaning for me. It is dedicated to *Ade* (Hades in English), my beloved Bengal cat and gentle companion, whose quiet strength and resilience were a source of comfort and inspiration during difficult times. His memory lives on—not only in spirit but also on the cover of this book, where his image stands as a reminder of love, calm, and the quiet power of connection.

Finally, I wish to share something very close to my heart: all personal proceeds I receive from this book will be donated to charitable organizations that support cats in distress, particularly those specializing in the treatment and rehabilitation of trauma-affected felines. This commitment is mine alone—any revenue or royalties retained by the publisher remain separate and unaffected. It is a small way to give back, and to honor the very spirit of resilience that inspired this work.

Thank you for joining me on this journey. May it empower you to think critically, design intentionally, and advocate for resilience—not only in systems, but in the teams and communities that build them.

Prerequisites and Recommended Background

This book assumes a foundational understanding of networking concepts commonly encountered in modern IT environments. Readers are expected to be familiar with basic principles such as IP addressing, routing, DNS, load balancing, and the OSI or TCP/IP models. Prior exposure to cloud computing concepts—such as virtual networks, regions, and availability zones—will be beneficial.

For readers who are new to networking or would like a refresher, the following resources are recommended before proceeding:

- General networking fundamentals (IP addressing, routing, BGP, and DNS)

- Basic cloud networking constructs (virtual networks, subnets, and security boundaries)

- Introductory material on distributed systems and fault tolerance

These prerequisites are intentionally lightweight; the book focuses on resilience and network design patterns rather than introductory networking theory. Readers without this background may still follow the material but are encouraged to review foundational resources alongside the early chapters.

Companion Repository

This book is accompanied by a GitHub repository containing diagrams, reference architectures, and supporting material related to the topics discussed throughout the book.

The repository is available at
https://github.com/crcritel/cloud-networking-resilience
or https://github.com/Apress/Cloud-Networking-and-Resilience

CHAPTER 1

What Is Resilience in the Cloud Era

The cloud has transformed the way we connect, communicate, and operate globally. At its heart, networking is what makes the cloud possible—stitching together data centers, services, and users into a seamless experience. But with this interconnection comes complexity: networks must not only perform but also withstand failures, adapt to demand, and recover quickly when disruptions occur. This book is dedicated to exploring how resilient cloud networking is designed, built, and operated.

Section 1.1 sets the stage by defining cloud computing in broad strokes, but always with networking in mind. We explore how abstraction, elasticity, and global reach depend on the underlying network, and why resilience is not a luxury but a necessity. By grounding ourselves in these fundamentals, we establish the context for the advanced networking and resilience patterns that will unfold in the chapters ahead.

While the principles of cloud resilience discussed in this book apply across all major cloud platforms, Amazon Web Services (AWS) is used as the primary reference for terminology, services, and architectural examples throughout the book. This reflects the author's professional focus and allows concepts to be illustrated using concrete, production-grade implementations. Where helpful, equivalent services in Microsoft Azure and Google Cloud Platform (GCP) are briefly referenced to aid cross-platform understanding, while keeping the emphasis on underlying resilience principles rather than provider-specific features.

C. Critelli, *Cloud Networking and Resilience*, https://doi.org/10.1007/979-8-8688-2436-4_1

Section 1.1: Introduction to Cloud Computing and Resilience

Cloud computing has redefined the way we design, deploy, and manage technology. What once required racks of servers, fixed networks, and long procurement cycles is now delivered instantly through virtualized, elastic services available at a global scale. Yet this shift also changes the nature of risk: infrastructure is no longer static, and failures can emerge from many layers—applications, networks, regions, or third-party dependencies. The critical question is no longer *if* something will fail, but *how* your system will respond when it does. This chapter introduces the fundamentals of cloud computing and resilience, showing how resilience extends beyond availability and disaster recovery to become a continuous discipline of anticipating, isolating, and recovering from disruption. It sets the foundation for the networking and architectural patterns explored throughout the book. So, let's start with the basics; let's define what cloud computing is.

Cloud computing is the on-demand delivery of compute, storage, database, networking, and higher-level IT resources over the internet with pay-as-you-go pricing, as offered by major cloud platforms such as AWS, Microsoft Azure, and Google Cloud Platform. Unlike traditional on-premises data centers, where infrastructure is statically provisioned and tightly coupled with physical assets, cloud computing abstracts hardware into virtualized, scalable, and elastic services.

At its core, cloud computing introduces a fundamental shift in how we architect, deploy, and manage IT resources:

- **Abstraction and Virtualization**: Compute resources (e.g., CPUs, RAM), storage volumes, and networks are abstracted from the physical hardware. Virtual machines (VMs), containers, and functions (serverless computing) are dynamically provisioned and managed by orchestration layers.

- **Elasticity and Auto-Scaling**: Infrastructure can scale horizontally or vertically based on demand. This allows systems to automatically add or remove compute nodes, adapt storage throughput, and adjust networking capacity to maintain performance and cost-efficiency.

- **Consumption-Based Pricing**: Resources are billed based on usage. This model eliminates the need for upfront capital expenditures and enables experimentation, scaling, and right-sizing without over-provisioning.

- **Global Accessibility and Low Latency**: Cloud providers maintain regional and edge infrastructure that reduces latency by bringing workloads closer to end users. Services like content delivery networks (CDNs), edge locations, and local zones enhance performance.

From a networking perspective, cloud computing redefines the perimeter. Unlike on-premises networks with rigid firewalls and static IPs, cloud networks are software-defined, policy-driven, and inherently distributed. Key aspects include:

- **Software-Defined Networking (SDN)**: Cloud networks are configured via APIs or infrastructure-as-code tools rather than physical cabling or CLI-based interfaces. Routing, subnets, NAT, and firewalls are dynamically managed by platform-level controllers.

- **Isolation Through Virtual Networks**: Customers operate in logically isolated environments such as Virtual Private Clouds (VPCs), where subnets, route tables, gateways, and ACLs mimic traditional network topologies with cloud-native elasticity.

- **Service-Oriented Access Models**: Instead of IP-based perimeter access, cloud environments rely on identity-aware access (IAM), security groups, and endpoint policies to control communication.

- **Network-As-a-Service Models**: VPNs, Direct Connectivity, Transit Hubs, and Global Load Balancing are offered as managed services that abstract complexity and provide rapid connectivity without manual provisioning.

Moreover, cloud computing introduces the concept of **shared responsibility**. The cloud provider secures the underlying infrastructure (hardware, facilities, and physical network), while customers are responsible for securing their workloads, data, access control, and configuration. This model requires a new approach to designing and securing networks that are both dynamic and externally exposed.

Cloud computing is not simply a technical evolution—it is an operational paradigm shift. It enables faster innovation, reduces the time to market, improves resiliency through redundancy and automation, and creates opportunities to implement failover and recovery mechanisms that were impractical in traditional IT environments.

Let's now address resilience and its meaning in this context.

What Is Resilience?

Resilience in cloud computing refers to the ability of workloads and systems to maintain functionality and recover gracefully from infrastructure failures, service impairments, or unexpected spikes in demand. It's not just about staying online—it's about delivering consistent service levels, even when parts of your system are degraded. In cloud-native environments, resilience is both an engineering objective and a cultural practice.

The cloud changes the very nature of how we think about failure. In traditional infrastructure, a failed server might take days to replace. In the cloud, infrastructure is ephemeral and programmatic—meaning systems can detect issues, react, and reconfigure within seconds. This shift allows architects to design systems that expect and embrace failure and use it as a signal to heal and adapt.

As Werner Vogels, CTO of Amazon.com, puts it: "Everything fails, all the time." Cloud resilience starts from this axiom. Whether the disruption stems from faulty hardware, misconfigurations, software bugs, or natural disasters, resilient systems are designed to minimize the impact and maintain user experience through isolation, failover, automation, and rapid detection.

Resilience of the Cloud vs. Resilience in the Cloud

Cloud providers—AWS, Microsoft Azure, and Google Cloud Platform (GCP)—all approach resilience across two complementary dimensions, even if terminology and service names differ.

Resilience of the Cloud:

This dimension refers to the built-in redundancy, scalability, and automation provided by the cloud platform itself. All major providers design their regions using multiple isolated fault domains to limit blast radius and absorb infrastructure-level failures.

- **AWS**: Regions are composed of multiple physically isolated Availability Zones (AZs), enabling services such as Amazon S3, EC2, and RDS to distribute workloads and replicate data for high availability.

- **Azure**: Regions are built using Availability Zones and fault/update domains, allowing services like Azure Virtual Machines, Azure SQL Database, and Azure Storage to operate in zone-redundant configurations.

- **GCP**: Regions are divided into zones with independent power, cooling, and networking, and services such as Compute Engine, Cloud Storage, and Spanner are designed to leverage zonal and regional redundancy.

These platform-level capabilities form the fault-tolerant foundation upon which customer workloads run, but they do not, by themselves, guarantee end-to-end resilience.

Resilience in the Cloud:

This is the customer's responsibility and depends on how workloads are architected and operated using cloud-native primitives.

- **AWS**: Deploying application tiers across multiple AZs using Auto-Scaling Groups and Elastic Load Balancers, and replicating data across regions using services such as Route 53 failover routing, Aurora Global Database, or DynamoDB Global Tables.

- **Azure**: Distributing workloads across Availability Zones behind Azure Load Balancer or Application Gateway and implementing regional recovery using Azure Site Recovery, Traffic Manager, or Front Door.

- **GCP**: Spreading instances across zones using Managed Instance Groups (MIGs), routing traffic with global HTTP(S) Load Balancing, and replicating data using multi-regional Cloud Storage or Spanner.

Cloud providers supply the building blocks, but resilience only emerges when those components are deliberately combined, automated, and continuously tested.

A resilient application leverages both dimensions: it builds on the provider's fault-tolerant infrastructure while implementing workload-specific resilience strategies at the application, data, and network layers. In an ideal design, infrastructure or service impairments may occur, but the user experience remains unchanged—or degrades gracefully without interruption.

Throughout this book, AWS services are used as concrete examples of these concepts. However, the underlying principles apply equally to platforms such as Microsoft Azure and Google Cloud Platform, which expose comparable constructs for fault isolation, scaling, and recovery.

Categories of Failure for Resilience

So, what are the possible failures a workload or application can be affected by?

Failures in cloud systems can be categorized using resilience frameworks that group disruptions based on their origin and impact. In AWS, this is formalized through the Resilience Analysis Framework (RAF); Microsoft Azure and Google Cloud Platform (GCP) address equivalent failure modes through constructs such as fault domains, availability zones, regional services, and dependency modeling. Understanding these categories helps teams prioritize mitigations and plan effective response strategies across platforms.

Application Failure: Failures originating from software bugs, memory leaks, unhandled exceptions, or logic errors in application code. Mitigations include auto-healing deployments, container restarts, retries, and graceful degradation. For example, for AWS: Auto-Scaling and ECS/EKS restarts; for Azure: App Service auto-heal and AKS pod restarts; for GCP: GKE pod restarts and managed instance group (MIG) healing.

Infrastructure Failure: Issues related to physical or virtual infrastructure, such as VM termination, host failures, or hardware malfunctions. These are mitigated using auto-scaling mechanisms, redundant deployments, and managed service redundancy. For example, for AWS: EC2 Auto-Scaling; for Azure: Virtual Machine Scale Sets; for GCP: Managed Instance Groups with regional distribution.

Availability Zone/Fault Domain Failure: Occurs when an entire fault boundary becomes unavailable due to loss of power, networking, or cooling. Designs must avoid single-zone deployments and distribute workloads across independent fault domains. For example, for AWS: Availability Zones with ALBs and multi-AZ databases; for Azure: Availability Zones and fault domains with Azure Load Balancer or Application Gateway; for GCP: multi-zone and regional services behind global load balancers.

Region Failure: A rare but high-impact event affecting all fault domains within a region. Mitigations involve multi-region architectures, global traffic management, and cross-region data replication. For example, for AWS: Route 53 failover and global databases; for Azure: Traffic Manager or Front Door with paired regions; for GCP: global HTTP(S) Load Balancing with multi-region backends and geo-replicated data stores.

Dependencies and Third-Party Failures: Failures in external systems or managed dependencies, such as DNS providers, identity platforms, or payment processors. Mitigations include caching, circuit breakers, timeouts, and fallback logic. This category applies in the same way across AWS, Azure, and GCP.

Deployment and Configuration Failures: Failures caused by incorrect configuration changes, infrastructure-as-code errors, or faulty CI/CD pipelines. Mitigations include change management, version control, staged deployments (blue/green or canary), and automated rollback mechanisms. For example, on AWS: CloudFormation/CDK and deployment strategies; on Azure: ARM/Bicep, deployment slots; on GCP: Deployment Manager/Terraform with progressive rollouts.

Operational Failures: Human errors such as accidental deletion, incorrect permissions, or misconfigured network rules. Mitigations include least-privilege access, approval workflows, and comprehensive audit logging. For example, for AWS: IAM and CloudTrail; for Azure: Azure RBAC and Activity Logs; for GCP: IAM and Cloud Audit Logs.

Cybersecurity Events: Includes DDoS attacks, malware, credential compromise, or unauthorized access attempts. Mitigations rely on layered security controls, traffic filtering, and incident response automation. For example, for AWS: Shield and WAF; for Azure: Azure DDoS Protection and WAF; for GCP: Cloud Armor and security incident response tooling.

Desired Resilient Properties

Let's define resilience as a system's ability to recover from disruptions and continue to deliver acceptable levels of performance. This capability hinges on several desired system properties, each targeting a specific aspect of resilience engineering. Let's focus on how AWS uses the RAF (Resilience Analysis Framework). Below are the key properties an application should leverage in order to continue serving users even when affected by service impairments:

- **Redundancy**: Redundancy removes single points of failure by deploying multiple instances of a system component across fault boundaries such as Availability Zones. Redundancy must account for dependencies as well—whether it's storage (e.g., Amazon S3), data platforms (e.g., DynamoDB), or compute (e.g., AWS Lambda), each must be deployed with failover in mind.

- **Sufficient Capacity**: Systems must be provisioned with adequate resources (CPU, memory, IOPS, bandwidth) to perform their expected function, even under peak load. Insufficient capacity can result in throttling, increased latency, or outright denial of service.

- **Timely Output**: The system should perform within acceptable time bounds. Customers' tolerance for latency is typically shaped by median or P50 expectations. Violations of latency SLAs or SLOs can erode user experience and reflect degraded resilience.

- **Correct Output**: It's not enough to respond fast—systems must return valid and accurate results. Misconfigurations, logic bugs, and stale dependencies can all lead to functional correctness failures, resulting in improper behavior despite apparent uptime.

- **Fault Isolation**: When a failure occurs, it should be contained within a limited blast radius. Isolating failures prevents cascading faults across system boundaries or tenant workloads. AWS promotes fault isolation through practices like cell-based architecture, account-level separation, and VPC boundaries.

These principles are used to evaluate and categorize common resilience violations, which AWS refers to using the SEEMS model:

- **Single Point of Failure (SPOF)**: This occurs when a critical component lacks redundancy and its failure causes the entire system to become unavailable. A resilient design must eliminate SPOFs by deploying components across fault-tolerant boundaries like Availability Zones or Regions.

- **Excessive Load**: A failure mode triggered when a resource (e.g., EC2 instance, database connection pool) is overwhelmed due to unexpected demand, leading to throttling or degraded performance. This is typically a result of insufficient capacity planning or a poor auto-scaling strategy.

- **Excessive Latency**: Even if a system responds, if it does so outside acceptable latency thresholds (SLOs/SLAs), the perceived availability is compromised. Latency-based failures can cascade into timeout errors and retry storms.

- **Misconfiguration and Bugs**: Software bugs or incorrect configurations can lead to invalid system behavior, degraded output, or security vulnerabilities. These faults may be introduced through CI/CD pipelines, IaC (Infrastructure as Code), or manual changes.

- **Shared Fate:** A fault that breaches intended fault isolation boundaries and affects multiple tenants, components, or systems. For example, a common identity provider failure can prevent access across otherwise unrelated applications.

By proactively designing for these five categories and enforcing the five properties, cloud architects can identify hidden risks in their systems before failures occur. As we move into later chapters, you will see how AWS services like Auto-Scaling, Route 53, VPC segmentation, and multi-region replication directly map to these desired properties, forming the backbone of production-grade cloud resilience. and will be explored in detail across subsequent chapters, where we'll map them directly to network architecture patterns, service-level objectives, and automated remediation pipelines.

Different cloud providers offer comparable features, but their implementations reflect subtle differences in how resilience is achieved.

AWS:

- **Availability Zones (AZs):** Independent data centers within each region, fault-isolated and interconnected via low-latency links.

- **Elastic Load Balancers (ELB) and Auto-Scaling Groups:** Dynamically distribute load and replace unhealthy instances.

- **Aurora Multi-AZ, DynamoDB Global Tables, and Route 53 Failover Routing:** Data-layer and routing-layer resilience patterns.

- **AWS Resilience Hub:** Automates the assessment and improvement of resilience posture.

- **Fault Injection Service (FIS):** Enables chaos engineering directly on AWS resources.

Azure:

- **Availability Sets and Availability Zones:** Offer fault domain and update domain separation.

- **Azure Site Recovery:** Provides replication and automated failover for DR.

- **Zone-redundant services** like Azure SQL Database and Application Gateway support HA natively.

Google Cloud Platform (GCP):

- **Global Load Balancing**: Allows frontends to shift traffic across regions based on health and latency.

- **Regional Managed Instance Groups (MIGs)**: Automatically distribute instances across zones.

- **Cloud Monitoring and Operations Suite**: Enables detailed observability and alerting.

Each provider emphasizes distributed deployment and automated healing but differs in the maturity and integration of tooling. AWS has the broadest coverage of chaos engineering and resilience-by-design practices.

Principles of Architecting Resilient Systems

Designing for resilience involves a multifaceted approach that extends beyond simple redundancy. While adding backup components and failover paths is crucial, truly resilient systems are architected around principles that ensure fault isolation, real-time insight, graceful degradation, and autonomous recovery. Below are the core principles, elaborated with technical depth and practical considerations:

> **Modular Isolation**: At the heart of fault-tolerant design is the idea of minimizing the blast radius. Modular isolation segments the system into independently functioning units—whether these are functional modules (e.g., microservices), tenancy domains (e.g., customer shards), or geographic partitions (e.g., cells, regions). Cell-based architectures are especially effective: each cell is a self-contained unit that can fail without impacting others. For example, a multi-region SaaS platform may isolate each tenant into a dedicated VPC (VNET for Azure, VPC Network for GCP) or Kubernetes namespace to ensure that failures in one tenant's environment do not cascade.

> **Static Stability**: A resilient system should continue serving its core functions even when parts of the control plane are degraded or unavailable. This is known as static stability. In practical terms, this might mean ensuring your data plane (traffic handling,

API serving) operates independently from the control plane (infrastructure provisioning, configuration changes). For instance, storage systems like object stores or databases should be able to read and serve data even when write operations or management APIs are impaired. This principle supports operational continuity during outages and planned maintenance.

Automated Recovery: Manual intervention increases downtime. Resilient systems detect failures automatically and initiate recovery workflows without human input. These workflows can include restarting services, spinning up new instances, rerouting traffic, or isolating compromised zones. Auto-Scaling, health checks, and lifecycle hooks are typical enablers in cloud-native environments. Self-healing logic often uses readiness probes and failure thresholds to trigger state-aware automation.

Observability: Observability provides the data required to understand, debug, and act on system behavior under both normal and degraded conditions. This includes metrics (e.g., latency, CPU, error rates), logs (structured and unstructured), and distributed traces. Tools like Prometheus, Grafana, and OpenTelemetry can be used to instrument applications and infrastructure. High-cardinality metrics and structured logs with correlation IDs enable root cause analysis and are essential for detecting silent failures and degraded states.

Chaos Engineering/Resilience Testing: To validate resilience assumptions, failures must be simulated. Chaos engineering is the deliberate injection of faults—such as shutting down nodes, introducing latency, or corrupting network paths—to observe how a system reacts. Practices can be automated with tools like Gremlin or integrated chaos platforms. Engineers often define steady-state metrics and assess whether injected faults cause unacceptable drift. This is especially effective when combined with canary deployments or blue/green infrastructure to minimize risk.

Decoupling: Loose coupling ensures that dependencies between components do not cause system-wide failure. Techniques like event-driven design, asynchronous messaging, and API gateway abstraction can help isolate services. For example, using SQS or Kafka as a buffer between producers and consumers allows systems to tolerate transient spikes or downstream slowness without backpressure.

Idempotency and Retry Logic: Network disruptions and partial failures require that clients retry failed requests safely. Idempotent operations return the same result when repeated— essential for database writes, provisioning APIs, and payment flows. Clients must implement exponential backoff and circuit breakers to avoid flooding systems under stress. Combined with distributed transaction models like Saga patterns or compensating transactions, retries ensure data consistency and operational integrity.

Together, these principles guide the construction of systems that are not only robust against failure but also actively engineered to detect, isolate, recover, and learn from it. They form the core of resilient networking, compute, and application layers and will be referenced throughout this book in the context of practical architecture, service selection, and operational readiness. A critical distinction in resilience design is between the **control plane** and the **data plane**:

- The **control plane** manages configuration, orchestration, and resource management (e.g., launching EC2 instances, updating security groups).

- The **data plane** handles traffic and business-critical operations (e.g., serving web content, processing messages).

Resilient services separate these planes to limit the scope of failures. For example, Simple Storage Service (S3)'s data plane can serve objects even if you can't modify bucket policies during a control plane disruption. This principle—**static stability**— means your application can continue functioning even if you lose access to the management API.

This separation should be mirrored in your architecture. For example, an internal API might store data to S3 and queue events in SQS—both data plane operations—while deferring configuration changes until stability returns.

Real-World Failure Examples and Lessons Learned

Public cloud outages offer concrete insights into the practical application—or lack—of resilience principles. These high-profile disruptions serve as cautionary tales, reinforcing why resilient architecture is critical.

Amazon S3 Outage (February 28, 2017—us-east-1): One of the most significant early cloud disruptions occurred when a technician debugging the S3 billing system accidentally entered a command that removed a larger set of servers than intended, which included critical components of the S3 control plane. As a result, the S3 service in the us-east-1 region became severely impaired, affecting many dependent services, including EC2, Lambda, and even the AWS Service Health Dashboard. Since S3 acts as a foundational storage layer for hosting assets such as CSS, JavaScript, images, and web applications, thousands of websites and SaaS platforms experienced loading failures.

Lesson Learned: This outage underscored the importance of separating control and data planes, implementing strong change management and validation tools, and using content delivery networks (CDNs) or local caching strategies to reduce dependencies on remote objects during runtime.

Microsoft Azure DNS Outage (April 1, 2021): A widespread outage occurred when Azure's DNS infrastructure suffered a service degradation. The issue was linked to a code defect triggered during a system update to the DNS edge cache. The impact was global, affecting multiple services such as Azure App Services, Azure Storage, and authentication endpoints.

Lesson Learned: Centralized DNS creates a single point of failure if not properly isolated or diversified. Organizations using private DNS, split-horizon DNS models, or hybrid DNS forwarding via services like Route 53 Resolver or custom BIND instances experienced less downtime. The incident emphasized the need for layered DNS resolution strategies and tighter canary testing for updates.

Google Cloud Networking Outage (November 12, 2020): Google Cloud experienced packet loss across multiple regions due to a configuration error in its internal traffic engineering system, which manages BGP advertisements. The fault affected inter-service communication and API endpoints, disrupting applications that required access to core networking functions.

Lesson Learned: Even minor changes in routing policy can create wide-reaching effects. Organizations that were designed with multi-region resilience, automated traffic failover, and intelligent retry logic were better able to maintain uptime. The outage also highlighted the importance of route health checks, diversified ingress paths, and isolated fault domains.

These incidents highlight that resilience is not just about technology—it's about culture, testing, and assumptions. Each scenario points to common principles: minimize blast radius, diversify dependencies, validate changes in production-like environments, and always design for failure.

What's Next?

Resilience is the intersection of architecture, automation, observability, and organizational philosophy. It assumes failure, designs for recovery, and rewards those who test and verify.

As we move forward, keep in mind:

- You're not designing to avoid failure. You're designing to embrace failure and recover fast.

- The cloud provides tools—but your architecture defines the outcome.

- Resilience is not achieved once. It's maintained continuously; it is not a one-day job but continuous iteration.

In the next section, we will explore the nuanced differences between resilience, availability, and disaster recovery. Understanding these distinctions is crucial to framing how resilience fits within the broader landscape of high availability and business continuity planning. We will then transition into how these concepts influence the design of networking constructs in cloud architectures.

Section 1.2: Resilience vs. Availability vs. Disaster Recovery

Your system will fail, eventually, so embrace the failure. In modern cloud architecture, the terms **resilience**, **availability**, and **disaster recovery (DR)** are often used interchangeably. However, each represents a distinct discipline within the broader context of system continuity and fault tolerance. A nuanced understanding of how these concepts differ—and work together—is essential for designing robust and dependable cloud-native systems. In the following sections, we will explore what the main differences are and how they work together to support our workloads.

Availability

Availability refers to the system's ability to operate normally and successfully respond to user requests during standard conditions. It is commonly measured as a percentage of uptime over a specific period—such as "three nines" (99.9%) or "four nines" (99.99%)—and is closely tied to minimizing service interruptions caused by predictable events like instance failures, software crashes, or planned maintenance.

To achieve high availability (HA), architects distribute workloads across fault boundaries and incorporate automated failover mechanisms. In practice, this often involves:

- **Redundant Deployment Across Multiple Failure Domains** (e.g., availability zones or physical data centers)

- **Health-Checked Load Balancers** to detect and reroute away from unhealthy nodes

- **State Decoupling**, using managed databases and stateless application tiers

High availability strategies aim to prevent service degradation during minor disruptions but do not, by themselves, guarantee graceful handling of severe or systemic failures.

So how do we measure availability? To understand the how, we need to dive deeper into the following concepts:

> Resilience in distributed systems can be quantified using a series of time-based reliability indicators that describe not only how often failures occur but also how quickly they are detected, mitigated, and recovered from. The most common are **MTBF**, **MTTD**, and **MTTR**.

Mean Time Between Failures (MTBF) represents the average operational duration between two consecutive failures of a system or component. It measures inherent reliability and is derived from observing a statistically significant number of failures over time. A higher MTBF indicates fewer disruptions and better design durability.

Mean Time to Detect (MTTD) quantifies how long it takes to *discover* that a fault or outage has occurred. Detection includes monitoring latency, alert thresholds, and the efficiency of incident response automation. Modern observability stacks—metrics, logs, traces, and health checks—directly influence MTTD. In many cases, improving detection speed has a greater impact on resilience than hardware redundancy, because unobserved failures silently erode availability.

Mean Time to Recover (MTTR) extends beyond repair alone— it encompasses the total time from failure detection to full service restoration. This includes detection (**MTTD**), diagnosis, escalation, remediation, validation, and return to steady state.

Reducing MTTR requires not just technical automation (self-healing infrastructure, auto-scaling, failover orchestration) but also process maturity: clear escalation paths, tested playbooks, and pre-validated recovery environments.

The classical availability formula:

$$A = \frac{MTBF}{MTBF + MTTR}$$

Even a system with a high MTBF can exhibit poor availability if its MTTR is excessive. Conversely, rapid detection and recovery can compensate for more frequent, smaller faults. In practice, resilience engineering focuses on minimizing **MTTD** and **MTTR**, as MTBF is often constrained by external dependencies and statistical uncertainty.

Ultimately, improving resilience is not just about preventing failure but about *reducing the time you spend unaware and unresponsive.* Detection is part of recovery, and measuring it explicitly within MTTR provides a more accurate reflection of operational readiness and real-world availability.

Resilience

Going back to resilience in a more general way now, resilience is a broader and more dynamic property. It defines a system's ability to anticipate, withstand, recover from, and adapt to unexpected disruptions—whether they are infrastructure failures, misconfigurations, cascading errors, or external attacks.

We discussed in detail how to measure availability, but resilience includes but surpasses availability. A system may maintain "availability" (respond to requests) but still fail to meet performance objectives or deliver correct results if it's not resilient. Resilient systems are engineered with the expectation that components will fail—and that such failures must not lead to systemic collapse.

Some key attributes of resilient systems include

> **Graceful Degradation**: Instead of failing entirely, the system sheds load, disables non-essential features, or reduces functionality while maintaining core services.

> **Automated Recovery and Retry Mechanisms**: Leveraging retries with exponential backoff, circuit breakers, or self-healing infrastructure.

> **Observability**: Integrated metrics, logs, and traces that expose latent errors and enable root-cause analysis.

> **Fault Isolation**: Using patterns like cell-based architecture, service segmentation, and dependency containment to prevent blast radius expansion.

Resilience is both an engineering and an operational discipline. It requires continuous validation through game days, fault injection experiments, and failure-mode analysis. In this context, principles and methodologies emerging from platforms like AWS, Azure, and GCP have matured to enable simulation of faults and resilience scoring without waiting for real-world disasters to occur.

Disaster Recovery (DR)

Disaster recovery is a distinct subset of resilience, focused on restoring operations following catastrophic events—such as a regional service outage, data corruption, or ransomware attack. DR planning answers the question, *"What happens if an entire zone or region becomes unavailable?"*

Whereas availability assumes the system remains operational, and resilience assumes the system can recover dynamically from most events, disaster recovery is concerned with **worst-case scenarios** that require separate environments or systems to resume service.

Key metrics in DR planning include:

- **Recovery Time Objective (RTO)**: The maximum allowable downtime after an incident.

- **Recovery Point Objective (RPO)**: The maximum amount of data loss (in time) the system can tolerate.

Now that we defined the policy in terms of RTO and RPO, let's look in detail at what the strategies we can leverage in the cloud are with the next paragraph.

As shown in Figure 1-1, disaster recovery strategies range from backup and restore to multi-site active/active, with progressively lower RPO/RTO targets and higher cost and complexity.

Disaster Recovery Strategies in the Cloud

Strategy	Deployment	Typical RPO	Typical RTO	Infrastructure State (before event)	Cost Profile	Complexity	Suitable For
Backup & Restore	Passive	Hours	Hours or Days	No compute running; backups stored in secondary Region	$	Low	Non-critical workloads, archival systems, internal tools
Pilot Light	Active/Passive	Tens of Minutes	Tens of Minutes	Core infrastructure (databases, minimal services) running; application tier scaled down or off	$$	Medium	Important workloads with moderate downtime tolerance
Warm Standby	Active/Passive	Minutes	Minutes	Fully functional but scaled-down environment running continuously	$$$	Medium-High	Business-critical applications requiring rapid recovery
Multi-Site (Active/Active)	Active/Active	Near Zero	Near Zero	Fully active production environments in multiple Regions	$$$$	High	Mission-critical systems requiring zero downtime and minimal data loss

Figure 1-1. *DR Strategies*

Disaster Recovery Strategies in the Cloud

Disaster recovery (DR) strategies vary widely in complexity, cost, and recovery performance. Each approach represents a trade-off between Recovery Time Objective (RTO), Recovery Point Objective (RPO), operational effort, and resource consumption. In cloud environments—where automation, elasticity, and geographic distribution are native capabilities—DR design becomes more powerful but also more nuanced. Defining recovery topologies through code, distributing workloads across regions, and automating failover workflows enables far more dynamic recovery than traditional models, while increasing the impact of architectural missteps if these patterns are poorly understood.

Backup and Restore

The most basic DR strategies are Backup and Restore. Application data, configuration, and state are periodically backed up and stored in durable, low-cost storage such as Amazon S3 Glacier or Azure Cool Blob Storage. In the event of a failure, infrastructure is reprovisioned, data is restored, and traffic is rerouted.

This approach is attractive due to its simplicity and low cost, but it comes with significant drawbacks. Because environments must be rebuilt from scratch, both RTO and RPO are typically high. Restoring large datasets—such as analytics pipelines storing terabytes of data—can take hours, during which the business remains disrupted. Teams often pair this model with infrastructure-as-code templates using tools like AWS CloudFormation, Terraform, or Azure Bicep to reduce provisioning time. Even so, Backup and Restore is best suited for non-critical workloads, archival systems, or dev/test environments where downtime is acceptable.

Pilot Light

The Pilot Light strategy keeps only the most critical components—such as databases, identity services, or configuration stores—running in a secondary region at minimal capacity. The remainder of the infrastructure exists as templates or powered-down resources. When a failure occurs, orchestration pipelines deploy and scale the remaining components in the standby region.

This model significantly reduces RTO compared to Backup and Restore while avoiding the cost of a fully active replica. However, it introduces operational challenges: stateful components must replicate data continuously, and infrastructure definitions in the standby region must remain in sync with the primary environment. Services such as

Aurora Global Database, DynamoDB Global Tables, or Azure SQL Active Geo-Replication help address data replication, but regular validation of deployment pipelines is essential to ensure successful recovery during real incidents.

Warm Standby

For workloads that require faster recovery, Warm Standby offers a balanced approach. A scaled-down but fully functional version of the production environment runs continuously in a secondary region. All services are deployed, albeit with reduced capacity. When the primary region fails, the standby environment scales up through auto-scaling or deployment orchestration.

Because services are already instantiated, recovery is much faster than with Pilot Light. Data consistency is maintained via continuous replication, and traffic can be redirected quickly using latency-based DNS or global traffic management services such as Amazon Route 53 or Azure Traffic Manager. Warm Standby is well suited for customer-facing applications and SaaS APIs that must meet strict RTO targets but cannot justify the cost of a full active-active deployment. Cost optimization techniques—such as downscaled compute or spot capacity in the secondary region—are commonly used to control expenses.

Active-Active

The most advanced DR strategy is Active-Active, where two or more fully operational environments run simultaneously and share production traffic. This model delivers the lowest RTO and RPO, often enabling near-zero downtime and continuous availability. However, it also introduces the highest complexity and cost.

Active-Active architectures require distributed state management, global traffic routing, and multi-writer data synchronization. For example, a globally distributed retail platform might use Route 53 latency-based routing with DynamoDB Global Tables or Azure Front Door with Cosmos DB multi-region writes, combined with stateless application tiers behind regional load balancers. Failover becomes an automatic consequence of health-aware routing rather than a manually orchestrated event.

This model demands careful consideration of data consistency. The CAP Theorem becomes central: in the presence of inevitable network partitions, systems must trade strong consistency for availability. Most cloud-native databases used in Active-Active designs favor availability and partition tolerance, relying on eventual consistency. As a result, applications must be designed with idempotency, conflict resolution, and robust retry logic. While platforms such as DynamoDB Global Tables, Cosmos DB, or Firestore provide primitives to support this behavior, correctness ultimately remains the application's responsibility.

Operational and Regulatory Considerations

DR strategies are not chosen based on technical criteria alone. They reflect an organization's risk posture, business continuity objectives, and regulatory obligations. Under regulations such as the EU's Digital Operational Resilience Act (DORA), organizations are required to regularly test DR capabilities and demonstrate failover readiness. This regulatory pressure has increased adoption of Pilot Light and Warm Standby models, which balance compliance requirements with cost control.

Regardless of strategy, several principles remain constant: DR must be automated, observable, and tested regularly. Mean Time to Recover (MTTR) should be measured empirically through failover drills and game days, not assumed. Observability pipelines must detect failures, trigger recovery actions, and provide feedback loops to continuously refine recovery behavior.

Blended Models and Evolution

In practice, organizations often combine DR strategies. A common pattern is to use Warm Standby for user-facing services, Active-Active for critical data stores, and Backup and Restore for less time-sensitive workloads such as reporting or analytics. As systems mature and risk profiles evolve, these models may change—Pilot Light environments may grow into Warm Standby, and Warm Standby may evolve into Active-Active when justified by scale or business impact.

Ultimately, disaster recovery is not an add-on—it is an architectural commitment. Each strategy must be selected with a clear understanding of its implications for performance, complexity, and sustainability. In later chapters, we will explore how to automate these models using CI/CD pipelines, health-aware routing, infrastructure-as-code, and observability frameworks—transforming disaster recovery from a static checklist into a continuously validated capability.

Key Differences Resilience vs. Availability vs. Disaster Recovery

Here, Table 1-1 summarizes what we've discussed so far.

As Table 1-1, shows, availability, resilience, and disaster recovery all contribute to system reliability, but they serve different purposes and operate at different layers of architecture and operational response.

- **Availability** is about uptime during expected scenarios.

- **Resilience** is about surviving and adapting to the unexpected.

- **Disaster Recovery** is about recovering from the unthinkable.

By understanding the distinctions and interdependencies between them, cloud architects and engineers can build systems that are not only "always on" but also *always ready*. Let's discuss in the next section why and how network meets resilience and why it matters.

Table 1-1. *Key differences between availability, resilience, and disaster recovery*

Property	Focus	When It Applies	Key Metrics
Availability	Uptime during normal operations	During regular workloads	Percentage uptime (e.g., 99.99%)
Resilience	Continuity through failure	During partial/system failures	Fault tolerance, degradation handling
Disaster Recovery	Recovery after major failures	Post-catastrophic events	RTO, RPO

Section 1.3: Why Network Resilience Matters: From Downtime to Brand Damage

Now that we've established the foundations regarding resilience, availability, and disaster recovery, let's discuss how this applies to networking.

In cloud computing, networking is far more than a background function—it's the nervous system of your digital infrastructure. Every API call, web request, database connection, and service-to-service interaction depends on reliable network pathways to function. While compute and storage often receive the spotlight in architecture discussions, networking is the foundation that silently enables—or disables—everything above it.

The Technical Stakes

Cloud-native networking is fundamentally more dynamic and complex than traditional static infrastructures. It spans global backbones, multiple Availability Zones (AZs), Virtual Private Clouds (VPCs), edge locations, and increasingly hybrid links into on-premises environments. It integrates routing protocols like Border Gateway Protocol (BGP), DNS-based routing decisions, NAT traversal, and transit architectures that must scale and adapt to rapidly changing traffic patterns.

This programmable flexibility introduces new risks. A single misconfigured route, an unanticipated DNS TTL, or a misconfigured route can interrupt traffic across environments. Often, these failures aren't massive outages but subtle degradations—dropped packets, asymmetric routing, or service latency—that silently damage reliability and user experience until they escalate.

For example, overly permissive BGP advertisements can propagate invalid routes and blackhole production traffic. Similarly, a minor change to a security group or network ACL can isolate an entire subnet. These are not theoretical risks—they happen routinely in large-scale production systems.

From Uptime to Business Continuity

Network resilience isn't just a matter of uptime—it's the cornerstone of business continuity. A resilient application may recover gracefully from degraded backend services, but without a functioning, secure, and performant network path, none of that matters.

When a network breaks down, the consequences escalate quickly:

> **Downtime:** Services become unreachable. SLAs are breached. Customers lose access.

> **Revenue Loss:** For digital-native companies, minutes of downtime can mean millions in lost transactions.

> **Brand Damage:** Public-facing outages—especially recurring ones—erode trust and affect long-term customer retention.

Operational Paralysis: Internal tools and back-office systems often rely on network paths to communicate. A network partition can freeze operations across departments.

As application architectures evolve into microservices, service meshes, and multi-region deployments, the dependency on network resilience only grows. Without proper design, a network disruption in one zone or service tier can propagate across dependencies—violating the core principle of **fault isolation**. This leads to **shared fate** scenarios, where what was meant to be a localized issue cascades across the stack, affecting unrelated services, regions, or tenants. In distributed systems, failure domains must be explicitly defined and enforced at the network layer to prevent blast radius expansion and maintain service continuity at scale.

Network Resilience in Practice

A resilient cloud network is built on architectural principles that go beyond basic connectivity. These principles are designed to prevent downtime, minimize blast radius, and ensure consistent service delivery—even in the face of unpredictable failures. We have already discussed the desired resilience properties for an application; let's see what should be taken into consideration when designing resilient network infrastructures in the cloud.

Redundant Paths and Transport Diversity

The foundation of resilient networking is **redundant transport**. At a minimum, this means provisioning multiple network paths across **Availability Zones (AZs)** and, where applicable, across **regions**. In the cloud, you achieve this by distributing critical services across subnets tied to different AZs and routing traffic through **multi-AZ load balancers** (e.g., the Application Load Balancer or Network Load Balancer in AWS).

For hybrid environments, where traffic flows between on-premises data centers and AWS, **AWS Direct Connect** offers private, constant performance connectivity. To enhance resilience, AWS recommends two key models:

- **High Resiliency Model**: Two physical Direct Connect connections in a single location, ideally on separate devices.

- **Maximum Resiliency Model**: At least four connections—two at each of two separate Direct Connect locations. This protects against failures in both the facility and the device.

These setups are typically backed by **site-to-site VPNs** configured over the public internet as failover paths. When paired with **BGP**, these links allow for automatic route convergence and failover when a primary Direct Connect link becomes unreachable. VPNs serve not only as failover options but also as short-term bridges during onboarding or disaster recovery events.

Failover Mechanisms and Routing Policy

A resilient network must detect degradation and respond dynamically. Failover mechanisms range from simple **health checks** to intelligent **routing policies** that steer traffic away from degraded nodes or paths. In AWS, this can be achieved through

- **Route 53 Health-Checked DNS Failover**, which allows for region-based or latency-aware redirection

- **BGP with Path Preference Manipulation**, using AS path prepending or BGP communities to influence route selection

While the full configuration of these mechanisms will be covered in later chapters, it's important to recognize that **automated routing changes**, not just link redundancy, are what turn a "highly available" architecture into a resilient one.

Segmentation and Fault Domains

One of the most overlooked aspects of network resilience is **segmentation**. When a network is not properly segmented, faults propagate. This is a direct violation of the **fault isolation** property we introduced earlier, and it increases the risk of **shared fate** incidents—where one failure impacts otherwise unrelated services or tenants.

In AWS, segmentation can be enforced through

- **Separate VPCs** per environment or tenant

- **Transit Gateways** to centralize routing and isolate shared services

- **Network ACLs and Security Groups** to control traffic flows and prevent lateral movement

- **Cell-Based Architectures**, where each cell contains its own compute, storage, and network boundaries, minimizing the impact radius of any single failure

This strategy ensures that even if a specific workload, AZ, or network path fails, the issue is contained.

Distributed Control Planes

Cloud-native networks rely heavily on control planes for provisioning, scaling, and configuration. However, a single control plane outage—such as those involving API failures or IAM propagation delays—can paralyze operations.

A resilient network ensures that control planes are either

- **Distributed Across Regions**, where feasible, or

- **Separated from the Data Plane**, so that even if orchestration or automation tools are unavailable, the network can continue to serve traffic

In AWS, many services are built with this separation by default. For instance, S3's data plane (object retrieval) continues operating even during control plane issues (e.g., inability to update policies or create new buckets).

Dynamic Reconfiguration and Infrastructure as Code

Finally, resilience is not just about preventing failure—it's about recovering from it **quickly and predictably**. This is only possible with **dynamic reconfiguration**, enabled by **Infrastructure-as-Code (IaC)** tools like AWS CloudFormation, CDK, or Terraform.

IaC allows teams to:

- Rebuild environments rapidly

- Roll back faulty deployments

- Automate traffic re-routing during failure events

In the context of networking, this includes pushing new **route table updates**, reconfiguring **Transit Gateway attachments**, or modifying **Route 53 records** in response to a detected issue—all via automated pipelines triggered by observability data.

However, these capabilities are only as effective as their observability; let's see how.

Observability: The Foundation of Resilience

Resilient networks are observable networks. Without meaningful, continuous visibility into traffic behavior, configuration states, and anomaly patterns, it's nearly impossible to detect and diagnose degradation before it becomes user-facing.

In a resilient architecture, observability goes beyond basic monitoring—it becomes the central nervous system that powers proactive defense, root cause analysis, and automatic recovery. As best practice, a well-observed system supports the **detection, correlation, alerting, and analysis** of both anticipated and emergent issues across both control and data planes.

The Three Pillars of Observability

Metrics: Quantitative indicators such as traffic throughput, packet drop rates, BGP update rates, and interface utilization. These are essential for establishing baselines and triggering threshold-based alerts (e.g., AWS CloudWatch Metrics).

Logs: Context-rich records of system activity. For network observability, AWS VPC Flow Logs provide granular insight into traffic that is accepted or rejected across Elastic Network Interfaces (ENIs), enabling audit trails and forensic analysis.

Traces: End-to-end visibility into the journey of a request or packet. While typically used in application-level tracing, traces also apply to network path validations—for example, with **Reachability Analyzer**, which simulates network paths to validate connectivity and security posture.

AWS Observability Services for Networking in AWS

VPC Flow Logs: Capture IP-level metadata for all traffic within and between subnets, interfaces, and endpoints. Critical for tracing communication issues, identifying misconfigured security groups or NACLs, and profiling normal vs. abnormal flows.

Reachability Analyzer: Validates the end-to-end path between network resources (e.g., EC2 instance to RDS DB) and surfaces any misconfigurations that block traffic. Useful during change validation and pre-deployment reviews.

CloudWatch Metrics and Logs: Provide infrastructure-wide observability with alarms on custom KPIs, including VPN tunnel health, interface drops, connection states, and Transit Gateway throughput.

AWS Network Manager: Particularly useful for global WAN and hybrid environments, offering topology maps, telemetry integration with SD-WAN, and real-time link state awareness.

Route 53 Health Checks: While primarily used for DNS failover, they also serve as synthetic traffic probes, enabling application-level observability across network tiers.

Why Observability Enables Resilience

Effective observability in networking helps answer the following questions:

- *Is traffic reaching the right destination through the right path?*

- *Can we detect increased packet latency before it causes an outage?*

- *Is our DNS failover working correctly?*

- *Have our route tables drifted from the intended configuration?*

- *Are all VPN tunnels active and routing traffic as expected?*

Without these answers, resilience cannot be validated—only assumed. The above questions focus on networking concepts but of course observability is a main pillar of the operational resilience model and should be implemented across all layers, not just networking.

Observability Design Principles

So, what are the design principles, and how can they help us in designing resilient networks?

- **Proactive Testing**: Observability enables proactive validation through synthetic testing (e.g., continuous ping, route health, simulated failovers).

- **Blast Radius Assessment**: Logs and flow records allow quick identification of scope—who is affected, where, and to what extent.

- **Recovery Triggers**: Observability metrics often act as automation inputs, triggering AWS Lambda, Step Functions, or runbooks that initiate reconfiguration or mitigation.

- **Contextual Alerting:** Instead of simple threshold alarms, modern observability integrates with SLOs and provides contextual insights—e.g., not just "latency is high," but "latency increased 30% for all requests passing through AZ-b."

Observability Is a Lifecycle

Like resilience, observability is not a one-day job; it is not a one-time investment; it must evolve with your architecture. As your topology, routing logic, and failover mechanisms change, your telemetry must adapt. Regular resilience testing, log audits, and connectivity simulations ensure that observability remains tightly coupled with actual failure domains.

The Business Case

We discussed technicalities, business continuity, observability, and monitoring, but what about the business? The financial and reputational cost of a poorly designed network with limited resilience in mind can far outweigh the engineering investment required to improve it. Proactive design—redundancy, automation, observability, and testing—prevents cascading failures and ensures customer trust.

For regulated industries, network resilience is not optional. Frameworks such as DORA (Digital Operational Resilience Act), PCI-DSS, and ISO 27001 explicitly require demonstrable network failover capabilities, secure segmentation, and incident response planning.

Moreover, organizations increasingly run **chaos experiments** on networking components, validating BGP pathing, DNS failover, and control plane resilience in production-like environments. These exercises, combined with active monitoring and runbook automation, shift network reliability from aspiration to discipline.

As we move forward in this book, we will explore how resilience principles translate into architectural patterns and real-world implementations—starting with how to design Virtual Private Clouds (VPCs), subnets, routing layers, and service-to-service communication in a resilient, fault-tolerant way.

Because at the end of the day, I often say, "**If the network fails, everything fails.**"

Section 1.4: Understanding Resilient Architectures in the Cloud

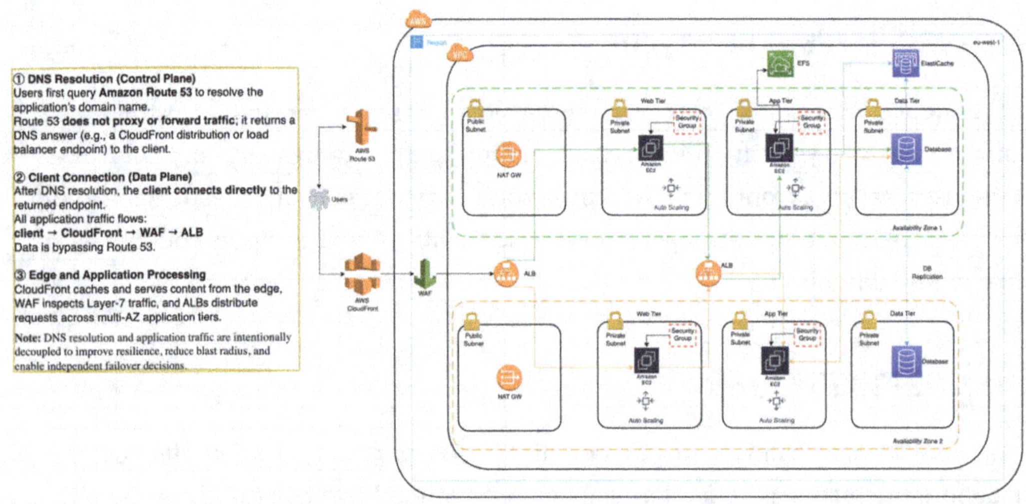

Figure 1-2. *Multi-AZ Architecture*

Resilience in Action: Applying Properties to the Architecture

So, we have mentioned the SEEMS model adopted by AWS in the previous sections; let's apply AWS's five desired resilience properties and the SEEMS failure categories to this design.

Redundancy:

The workload is distributed across two Availability Zones, ensuring that no single zone failure (a common fault domain) will bring down the application. Each tier (web, app, and DB) is deployed in both AZs, with the ALBs performing health checks to route traffic to healthy targets. Additionally, redundant NAT gateways in public subnets ensure outbound connectivity remains operational even if one gateway becomes unavailable. This explicitly eliminates **Single Points of Failure (SPOFs)** across the network path.

Sufficient Capacity:

Auto-Scaling Groups (ASGs) for EC2 instances in the web and application tiers ensure that the system can elastically respond to load increases or failover events. Each AZ can independently scale up in response to failure in its peer zone, assuming that headroom has been allocated properly. This mitigates **Excessive Load** by planning for surge capacity and avoiding tight coupling between scaling groups.

Timely Output:

ALBs provide real-time health checks to avoid routing to degraded instances, maintaining application responsiveness. Placement across two AZs, combined with CloudFront's caching layer and Route 53's latency-based routing, ensures low latency by always directing users to the optimal entry point. This protects against **Excessive Latency**, especially under partial failure conditions.

Correct Output:

By isolating web, app, and DB functions into dedicated tiers and segmenting them across subnet boundaries with strict **Security Groups** and NACLs, the architecture minimizes the risk of incorrect output due to misconfiguration or unauthorized access. Version-controlled infrastructure deployments, using IaC tools like CloudFormation or Terraform, further protect against errors. These guardrails mitigate **Misconfiguration and Bugs.**

Fault Isolation:

This architecture is explicitly designed with **cell-based principles** in mind—each AZ functions as a fault-isolated cell. Should one zone fail, traffic seamlessly flows to the healthy peer, while database replication ensures data continuity. Additionally, Route 53 and CloudFront operate from AWS's global edge locations, providing fault containment at the DNS and CDN layers. This limits the blast radius of failures and protects against **Shared Fate**, ensuring that one degraded component doesn't take down unrelated services.

A Narrative Walkthrough

Here's how resilience plays out in this architecture when a fault occurs.

Imagine a scenario where AZ1 suffers from a partial outage or service impairment, affecting the EC2 instances in the App Tier. The ALB health checks detect these failures and immediately redirect traffic to AZ2, where healthy EC2s continue serving requests. Auto-Scaling in AZ2 may trigger to compensate for lost capacity. The Web Tier in AZ1 is unaffected and continues serving static assets, while the NAT gateway in AZ2 takes over outbound traffic responsibilities.

Meanwhile, the DB tier in AZ1 replicates data to AZ2's database instance asynchronously. Thanks to well-architected **DB replication and failover configurations**, the app continues reading from a consistent replica or uses reader endpoints to minimize disruption. Since DNS is decoupled from AZ-specific resources, clients accessing the service via Route 53 remain unaware of the failure and experience uninterrupted service.

From a resilience perspective, this example showcases **blast radius containment**, **fault recovery**, and **graceful degradation**. No user-visible downtime occurs, and business continuity is maintained without human intervention.

Control Plane vs. Data Plane: The Hidden Layer of Risk

We briefly introduced the concepts of control plane and data plane earlier; here, we examine why this distinction is critical in resilient cloud architectures. Although the two planes operate independently, they interact closely to support modern cloud systems. The data plane often receives the most architectural attention because it directly impacts application performance and uptime. The control plane, however—less visible but equally critical—can represent a deeper and more insidious risk, particularly in network resilience design.

The data plane is responsible for handling application traffic. It processes packets, forwards requests, delivers content, and performs compute and storage operations. This is the layer users interact with directly through API calls, object retrievals, or database queries. In the earlier multi-AZ architecture example (Figure 1-2), we saw how distributing workloads across Availability Zones preserves data plane continuity, allowing traffic to flow, application tiers to remain responsive, and databases to fail over gracefully during localized failures.

The control plane, by contrast, governs orchestration, configuration, and state propagation. It manages actions such as updating route tables, registering instances with load balancers, applying security group rules, or provisioning new resources through auto-scaling. In cloud-native environments, these functions are abstracted behind provider APIs. While the data plane handles real-time traffic, the control plane determines how that traffic is routed, filtered, and scaled.

This separation introduces a subtle but significant risk. During regional degradation events or periods of high operational load, control plane APIs may be throttled, delayed, or temporarily unavailable. The data plane may continue serving traffic, but the system loses its ability to react, adapt, and recover. At precisely the moment when change is required, the architecture becomes operationally static.

Consider an auto-scaling group attempting to replace failed instances during a zonal outage. If the control plane responsible for provisioning or instance registration is impaired, scaling actions may fail silently. Similarly, delayed route table updates during a traffic reroute can send traffic into a black hole—even when healthy failover targets exist.

A common manifestation of this risk appears in large-scale network topologies built around AWS Transit Gateway (TGW). Hub-and-spoke designs often rely on dynamic route propagation and attachment updates. During a control plane event, TGW route propagation may be delayed or blocked entirely. Architectures that depend on real-time route changes during failover or blue/green deployments can therefore experience broken communication paths and misrouted traffic, directly violating resilience objectives.

The concept of static stability provides a design response to this challenge. Static stability means that data plane operations remain functional even when the control plane is degraded or unavailable. Amazon S3 is a well-known example: during rare control plane impairments, existing GET and PUT operations often continue to succeed, even if bucket configuration changes are temporarily unavailable. This separation allows applications to continue serving users despite orchestration limitations.

Architects should apply the same principle to network design. Route tables required for failover should be pre-populated and validated in advance, not generated dynamically during an incident. Security groups must include all necessary rules ahead of time, and load balancer target groups should already contain healthy endpoints, avoiding reliance on runtime registration. Infrastructure-as-code (IaC) tooling—such as Terraform or AWS CloudFormation—should reflect this mindset: deploy once, validate often, and minimize runtime mutations.

Control plane degradation must also be considered in deployment workflows. If a CI/CD pipeline fails to update a load balancer due to API throttling, it should not leave the system in an inconsistent state. Rollbacks must be automatic, auditable, and reversible, covering changes to routing, IAM policies, DNS records, and endpoint configurations.

From a networking perspective, control plane dependencies appear in many critical operations: registering VPC endpoints, modifying BGP advertisements during Direct Connect failover, or pushing updated firewall rules. If these actions are embedded in time-critical response paths and the control plane is unavailable, the architecture may fail to meet its RTO and RPO targets—not because traffic cannot flow, but because the system cannot adjust itself.

This is especially evident in hybrid networking scenarios using AWS Direct Connect or Azure ExpressRoute. High-resiliency designs rely on redundant physical connections, often paired with VPN tunnels for fallback. While data plane path diversity is essential, successful failover also depends on timely control plane actions such as BGP convergence, route activation, and attachment updates. If these steps depend on impaired APIs or manual intervention, failover may not occur in time.

The same principle applies to newer service networking layers such as VPC Lattice. Although Lattice simplifies service-to-service communication across VPCs, its behavior is governed by control plane constructs. In resilience-oriented designs, service discovery and routing policies must be pre-applied and validated, rather than updated dynamically during incidents.

Ultimately, resilience to control plane failures requires a shift in architectural thinking. It is not enough to build systems that survive outages; they must also behave predictably when reconfiguration is impossible. Designing for static stability and minimizing control plane dependencies during active traffic conditions are key to achieving this goal.

Throughout the rest of this book, we will revisit this theme in the context of BGP convergence, DNS failover, automation pipelines, and resilience testing. In each case, we will examine where control plane dependencies introduce risk and how sound architectural and operational practices can mitigate it.

Resilience is not defined solely by uptime metrics or SLA guarantees. It is defined by the predictability of a system under unpredictable circumstances—and few layers challenge that definition more subtly than the control plane.

Looking Ahead

Now that we defined the main differences and examples between the Control Plane and Data Plane, let's go back to the architecture we used as our example. This tier 3 application architecture represents a **resilient, multi-AZ workload** that leverages AWS primitives to isolate, absorb, and recover from faults. However, it is important to note that **multi-AZ ≠ multi-region**. In future chapters, we will explore what happens when an entire region fails and how to evolve this pattern into an **active-active regional deployment**.

But the fundamentals remain the same: isolate, detect, recover. Build redundancy not only into the design but also into your thinking. Architect for uncertainty, and verify your assumptions continuously through testing.

Let's have a look at how all this applies to the hybrid network connectivity example.

The Hybrid Angle: Beyond the VPC

While cloud-native applications are often the focal point of modern architecture, a significant portion of enterprise workloads operate in **hybrid environments**— where mission-critical systems span both cloud and on-premises data centers. These topologies require a different class of resilience design, as failure domains extend beyond the cloud provider's boundaries. Network resilience, in this context, must accommodate multiple layers of risk, including physical fiber cuts, BGP misconfigurations, and control-plane failures at the edge.

Figure 1-3 illustrates a **high-resiliency hybrid connectivity model** using **AWS Direct Connect (DX),** a service that enables private, constant performance connections between on-premises networks and AWS. This example reflects a setup that follows the AWS **Resiliency** recommendation: two dedicated connections provisioned across two separate Direct Connect locations, terminating in independent AWS edge devices and ultimately converging at a Transit Gateway (TGW) in the cloud. We can have BGP helping in redirecting traffic accordingly or ECMP (Equal Cost Multi Path) depending on how we configure the routers. We will in the next chapters when we will go deeper into routing manipulation for enabling resilient networks. For now let's see how this architecture will behave in case of service impairment, like we did for the tier-3 application architecture at the beginning of this section.

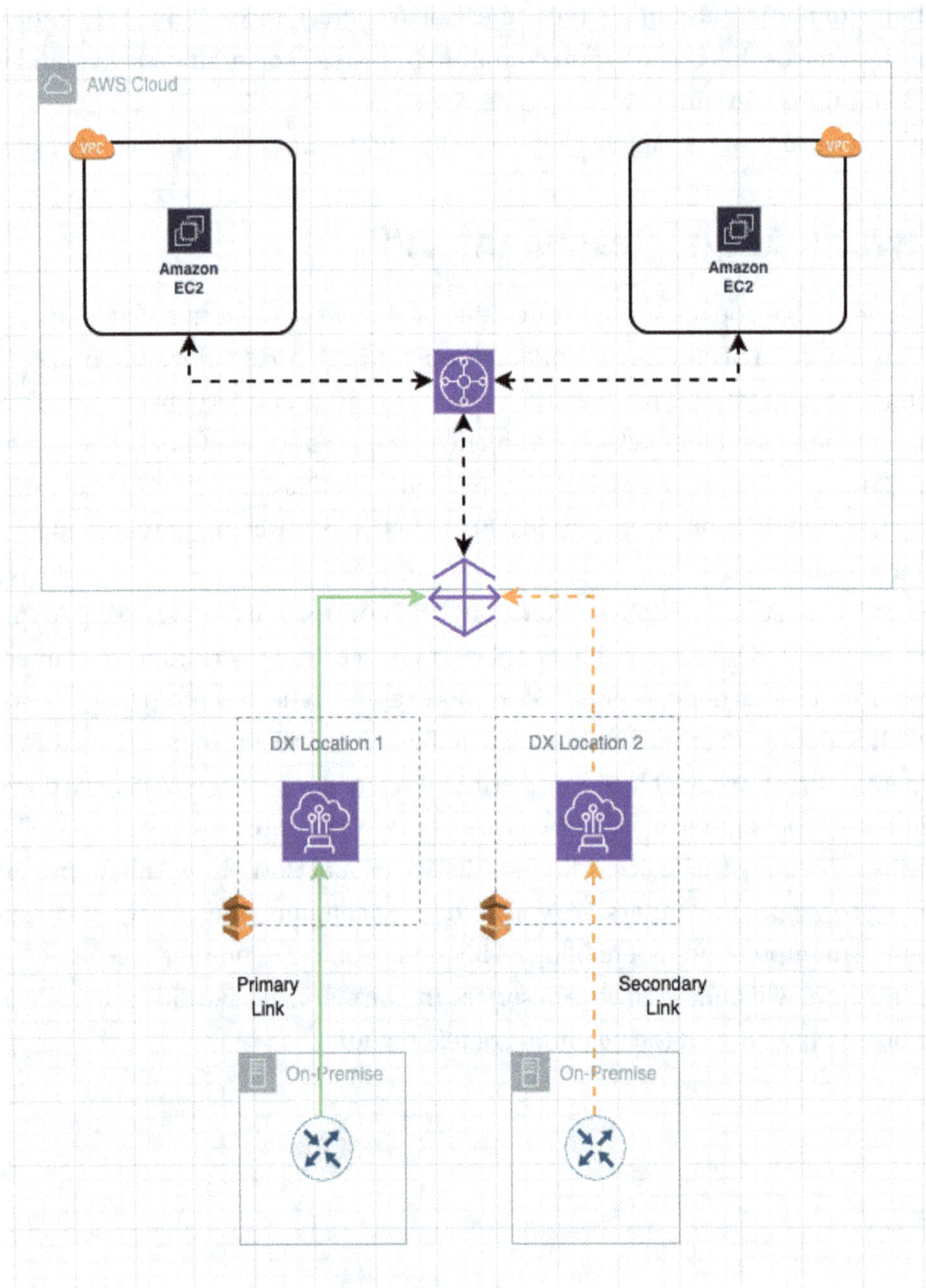

Figure 1-3. *Hybrid Resilient Connectivity*

Observability and Validation

Let's apply what we learned about observability here and see how it ties the architecture together. Without **VPC Flow Logs**, **Reachability Analyzer**, **Route 53 health checks**, and metrics piped into **CloudWatch**, the best failover logic cannot be trusted. Observability closes the loop by validating assumptions, exposing misconfigurations, and providing real-time context when things go wrong.

Teams should test this architecture regularly using **Resilience Hub assessments**, **chaos simulations with FIS (Fault Injection Service)**, or scripted AZ isolation tests. Only by proving that this system survives simulated failures can we claim it is resilient.

Let's now analyze how this architecture behaves in case of service disruption.

Anatomy of the Hybrid Resilience Design

At a high level, the architecture includes:

- **DX Location 1 (Primary)**: Connected to AWS via a green path, terminating at a TGW.

- **DX Location 2 (Secondary)**: Provides a failover route via an orange dashed path.

- **Transit Gateway**: Aggregates the connections and enables routing into one or more VPCs hosting workloads (e.g., EC2 instances).

- **On-Premises Routers**: Participate in BGP routing for dynamic path selection and failover control.

This design introduces **redundancy at multiple levels**—from fiber path to device, DX location, and even the on-prem infrastructure. It also enables **active/passive** or **active/active** failover models, controlled via BGP policy configuration and monitored using keepalives and health-check timers.

Applying Resilience Principles

Let's evaluate this setup through the lens of the **five resilience properties we discussed before**:

- **Redundancy**: There are two physically separated links through distinct colocation facilities (DX Location 1 and 2). Each uses different AWS devices and fiber carriers, reducing the likelihood of correlated failure. This eliminates a **single point of failure** in the connectivity path.

- **Sufficient Capacity**: Both primary and secondary circuits should be provisioned with enough bandwidth to handle failover load, assuming full traffic migration in an outage scenario. In an **active/active** model, traffic should be balanced without saturating either link. Failing to plan for capacity could result in **excessive load** or dropped packets when failover occurs.

- **Timely Output**: BGP route timers and health checks must be tuned to allow fast but stable failover—often in the range of seconds. Slower failover can cause **latency spikes**, timeouts, or degraded end-user experience. The transit gateway and route propagation rules must be optimized for low convergence time.

- **Correct Output**: Misconfigured BGP communities or incorrect route filtering can lead to **route leaks**, blackholing, or asymmetric routing—all of which compromise functional correctness. Infrastructure-as-Code (IaC) and automated validation pipelines can help prevent such **misconfiguration and bugs**.

- **Fault Isolation**: The separation between DX locations ensures that even a catastrophic facility-level failure (e.g., fire, flood, power outage) will not affect the secondary path. Isolation continues into the cloud via TGW route tables and VPC-level segmentation. This design helps prevent **shared fate**, where a single fault propagates across the entire network stack.

Failure Scenarios and Mitigation

Let's consider several real-world failure scenarios and how this architecture mitigates them:

1.   **DX Location 1 Fiber Cut**: The primary path is severed. BGP detects link failure and routes traffic via DX Location 2. This transition is seamless if both links participate in route advertisements and are health-checked appropriately. The architecture isolates the failure and preserves continuity.

2.   **Transit Gateway Route Table Misconfiguration**: An incorrect static route or attachment misalignment prevents one of the VPCs from receiving traffic. Here, observability is critical. Tools like **VPC Reachability Analyzer** can help trace route propagation and expose the root cause. Infrastructure templates should undergo validation prior to deployment.

3.   **Overloaded Secondary Link**: If the secondary DX circuit has insufficient bandwidth to handle production workloads during failover, service degradation ensues. This highlights the importance of planning for **excessive load** and aligning provisioning with **RTO/RPO** targets.

4.   **Asymmetric Routing Due to Route Preference Misalignment**: If BGP attributes (e.g., AS Path Prepend, MED, Local Preference) are incorrectly configured, return traffic may flow over the wrong link, violating expected traffic patterns and making troubleshooting difficult.

5.   **Configuration Drift Between Sites**: On-prem firewalls or routers might have diverged ACL rules or NAT behavior, which could result in inconsistent application responses. This is a **shared fate** scenario, where systems fail not because of core path issues but due to poor coordination.

Control Plane Resilience and Observability

In this design, **control plane resilience** is essential. For instance, if a configuration update to the Transit Gateway fails to propagate due to a permission or API rate-limit error, the data plane may remain healthy, but new routes won't function. Separating lifecycle operations (e.g., route attachment updates) from runtime traffic helps enforce **static stability**.

Observability plays a pivotal role. AWS-native tools include:

- **VPC Flow Logs**: Reveal traffic visibility at the subnet and ENI level.

- **Network Manager**: Provides a topology-aware view of your entire hybrid WAN.

- **CloudWatch Alarms**: Track BGP status, interface health, and packet drops.

- **Reachability Analyzer**: Allows synthetic tracing of route paths between components.

A resilient hybrid architecture doesn't stop at failover. It includes alerting when both DX links flap, monitoring BGP session timers, and validating that both paths are actually forwarding traffic as expected.

The Foundation of Hybrid Resilience

This hybrid connectivity model exemplifies the broader philosophy of resilient cloud architecture—**designing for failure, not hoping to avoid it**. With fault-isolated Direct Connect locations, dynamic route control via BGP, VPN failover paths, and end-to-end observability, organizations can confidently extend their enterprise footprint into the cloud while meeting stringent business continuity goals.

At the same time, this architecture builds on the foundation laid in our earlier example: a **multi-AZ application deployment** using layered redundancy across tiers, zones, and services. In both scenarios—whether regional and cloud-native or hybrid and enterprise-integrated—the principles of resilience remain the same:

- **Isolate**: Boundaries must exist to contain the blast radius—across zones, regions, network segments, and service domains.

- **Detect**: Real-time telemetry, health checks, and route tracing provide the early warning systems required for timely intervention.

- **Recover**: Redundant paths, scalable infrastructure, and policy-driven failover allow for graceful, automated restoration of service.

But it's important to emphasize: **multi-AZ ≠ multi-region**. While the architecture described here tolerates a zone failure or Direct Connect outage, it does not account for complete regional disruption, nor does it guarantee continuity in case of cross-region

DNS or routing anomalies. Those are challenges we'll address in later chapters as we evolve these patterns into **active-active multi-region topologies**, **cross-cloud failover models**, and **zero-trust global overlays**.

What you've seen so far are not isolated design patterns—they're **composable building blocks**. As this book progresses, we'll revisit these same foundations in the context of DNS-based failover, resilient routing using BGP and Anycast, control plane decoupling, and automation pipelines that verify the resilience posture at every deployment.

Ultimately, **resilience is not an attribute—it's a discipline**. One that requires forethought, validation, and continuous refinement. These architectures are a starting point, but your mindset is the multiplier.

This is how resilience is achieved—not by chance, but by choice.

Section 1.5: Common Challenges in Achieving Resilience

Designing for resilience in cloud environments—especially cloud networking—is a multidimensional discipline. It's not just about enabling failover mechanisms or deploying redundant resources. Resilience requires deliberate architectural choices, process maturity, and constant validation across all planes of operation. While many of the challenges are well-documented, in practice they are often overlooked, misunderstood, or underestimated. This section outlines key, but by no means exhaustive, obstacles in achieving operational resilience, accompanied by real-world examples and potential mitigations.

I will now list a series of possible challenges and how they could be mitigated using AWS services as an example.

1. Misalignment Between RPO/RTO Expectations and Operational Realities

Recovery Point Objective (RPO) and Recovery Time Objective (RTO) are foundational in resilience planning. RPO measures acceptable data loss, while RTO defines acceptable downtime. In theory, they are easy to define. In reality, they are difficult to meet consistently. A system that claims to support zero RTO and RPO but runs health checks every 10 minutes and triggers failover through a manual process will never achieve its stated goals.

Example: A fintech company wants zero RPO/RTO but lacks real-time monitoring and uses manual DNS updates to switch regions. Despite having an active-passive architecture, failover may take hours.

Mitigation:

- Deploy low-latency observability pipelines using Amazon CloudWatch Metric Streams or Azure Monitor diagnostic settings.

- Use EventBridge, Step Functions, or Azure Logic Apps to automate escalation paths.

- Leverage Route 53 health checks tied to API responsiveness, not just EC2 instance status.

2. The Complexity of Multi-region and Multi-cloud Designs

Multi-region deployments promise regional fault tolerance, but they introduce a host of problems: data consistency, policy synchronization, asymmetric routing, latency divergence, and more.

Multi-cloud takes this further—each provider has its own API conventions, routing semantics, encryption mechanisms, and observability stacks. Ensuring consistency becomes a nightmare.

Example: An e-commerce platform running on AWS and GCP faces DNS failover timing mismatches and duplicated IAM roles. Security groups are inconsistently applied, and backend data synchronization lags by minutes.

Mitigation:

- Leverage infrastructure-as-code (Terraform, Pulumi) with CI/CD pipelines to ensure repeatable deployments.

- Use globally distributed datastores like DynamoDB Global Tables, Spanner, or Cosmos DB where eventual consistency is tolerable.

- Adopt BGP communities and policy-based routing to direct traffic based on region availability and latency.

3. CAP Theorem and Data Integrity Trade-Offs

The CAP theorem explains the trade-off between consistency, availability, and partition tolerance. In distributed systems, you can only pick two:

- **CA (Consistency + Availability)** systems fail during partitions.

- **AP (Availability + Partition Tolerance)** systems allow inconsistency.

- **CP (Consistency + Partition Tolerance)** systems may delay availability.

Example: A news aggregation service chooses high availability across regions using AP mode with eventual consistency. During a network partition, two readers see different article versions.

Mitigation:

- Choose consistency models based on business needs. Use quorum-based replication where conflict resolution is difficult.

- Architect applications with idempotency, retries, and version tracking.

- Document data consistency guarantees and educate application teams on behavior under failure.

4. Over-Reliance on Manual Recovery

Despite automation tools, many organizations rely on playbooks and human intervention for failover. DNS changes, ACL edits, or route updates are handled manually.

Example: A regional outage occurs, and the network team must initiate failover by editing Transit Gateway routes and NAT gateway policies. Human delays cause prolonged outages.

Mitigation:

- Use Route 53 failover records with health checks that validate application endpoints.

- Implement Lambda or Cloud Functions to automate response to health check failures.

- Integrate AWS Systems Manager Automation runbooks for standardized recovery steps.

5. Lack of End-to-End Observability

Resilience depends on detecting not just outages but degradation. Network faults often manifest as increased latency or partial connectivity issues—too subtle for traditional monitoring.

Example: An app is unreachable from one continent due to a BGP route flap. Standard service monitoring shows no alerts.

Mitigation:

- Use Reachability Analyzer and VPC Flow Logs in AWS to trace paths.

- Enable regional probes using Route 53 Resolver endpoints and CloudWatch Synthetics.

- Implement anomaly detection for packet loss and latency distributions.

6. Budget Constraints and Partial Resilience Implementations

True resilience incurs cost—redundant services, data replication, observability, and automated recovery require financial investment. When budgets tighten, resilience often becomes the first sacrifice.

Example: A startup deploys an active-passive architecture with standby infrastructure never tested or validated. During a failover event, the secondary environment fails due to misconfiguration.

Mitigation:

- Use cost visibility tools like AWS Cost Explorer or Azure Cost Management to track resource ROI.

- Design critical services with full resilience, while less critical systems follow tiered recovery plans.

- Periodically test passive failover paths using disaster recovery drills and gamedays.

7. Change Management and Deployment Risk

In dynamic environments, changes to routing, IAM, or service topology can introduce unplanned failures. Resilience means understanding the risk surface and validating changes before production.

Example: A route table propagation change in AWS breaks access between tiers. The change was rolled out without simulation.

Mitigation:

- Implement canary deployments for infrastructure with tools like AWS CloudFormation StackSets or Terraform Workspaces.

- Use pre-deployment validations with configuration analysis (e.g., AWS Config, Azure Policy).

8. Limited Control in Managed Services

Public cloud users delegate parts of infrastructure control to the provider. This improves scalability but constrains low-level fault recovery options.

Example: An S3 control plane throttling event delays lifecycle policy updates. Applications relying on timely deletions hit storage limits.

Mitigation:

- Design for static stability: applications must operate on cached or stale data when the control plane is impaired.

- Separate control/data plane logic. Don't embed provisioning logic in the critical path of your application.

9. The New Regulatory Mandate: Testing and DORA

As of January 17, 2025, the Digital Operational Resilience Act (DORA) mandates financial institutions operating in the EU to perform operational resilience testing. This elevates resilience from a best practice to a legal requirement.

Example: A bank must demonstrate that it can failover its trading platform across AWS regions in under 15 minutes while maintaining audit trails and RTO compliance.

Mitigation:

- Use Resilience Hub or Fault Injection Service to simulate failures and generate compliance artifacts.

- Integrate test outcomes with compliance documentation and incident response protocols.

10. The Missing Discipline: Testing As the Cornerstone of Resilience

Architecting for resilience without actively testing is akin to installing fire alarms that have never been checked. They may exist on paper—diagrams, templates, or even compliance reports—but without simulation, validation, and iterative improvement, they provide little assurance when failure strikes.

Despite the availability of tools and frameworks to simulate failures, many organizations still fear or avoid resilience testing. Some worry that injecting faults might disrupt production workloads. Others lack clear accountability—unsure whether testing belongs to application teams, network engineering, platform teams, or compliance. In some cases, the avoidance is psychological: *"We've never had an issue"* becomes a justification for skipping proactive tests. But the absence of recent outages is not evidence of resilience; it may simply mean your failure conditions haven't been fully exercised yet.

Why Testing Matters

A well-architected design defines Recovery Time Objective (RTO) and Recovery Point Objective (RPO). But *how* do you know these objectives can be met? Can you prove it repeatedly under changing conditions?

Consider the following scenario: an enterprise configures Route 53 failover between two AWS Regions and sets an RTO of 5 minutes. However, failover is triggered by an ALB health check, which only polls every 30 seconds. The health check is configured to wait for five consecutive failures before marking the region as unhealthy. Meanwhile, DNS TTLs are set to 180 seconds. Theoretically, this system cannot fail over in under five minutes—and that's before any routing propagation or client-side DNS caching is factored in.

Testing helps surface these *configuration mismatches* and operational assumptions. Without it, organizations can find themselves in breach of their own service-level commitments without even realizing it.

Types of Testing and What They Reveal

There are multiple layers of testing, each mapping to different resilience properties and failure categories (as discussed earlier):

- **Control Plane Impairment Testing**: Simulate failures in provisioning workflows—e.g., throttling of API calls, IAM misconfigurations, or route table propagation delays. These tests validate whether your application can operate in the absence of real-time updates.

- **Data Plane Fault Injection**: Drop traffic between AZs, simulate degraded cross-region bandwidth, or block access to a critical service endpoint. This validates latency handling, retry behavior, and fault isolation.

- **Service Dependency Chaos**: What happens when your logging, DNS, or identity provider goes down? Many workloads fail not due to core functionality loss, but because auxiliary systems aren't resilient.

- **End-to-End Resilience Drills**: Full regional failover with DNS switchover, traffic steering, and observability validation. These are difficult but necessary to validate disaster recovery objectives.

- **Resilience Regression**: Ensure that new deployments do not degrade resilience posture. For example, a recent update to BGP route prioritization may accidentally remove backup paths that were essential for failover.

Each test should answer one fundamental question: "Can we detect, contain, and recover from this failure within our RTO/RPO?"

Barriers to Testing

Even when the will exists, several barriers make resilience testing hard in practice:

- **Cost and Risk**: Running chaos tests in production environments carries operational risk. Creating staging environments with full parity is expensive.

- **Cultural Resistance**: Teams worry about blame, incident generation, or customer impact. Testing is often deprioritized in favor of feature delivery.

- **Tooling Complexity**: Injecting faults across distributed systems (especially multi-cloud or hybrid architectures) requires orchestration across multiple layers—networking, compute, storage, and application.

- **Lack of Metrics**: Without clear definitions of *success* (e.g., "failover within 2 minutes," "90% of users unaffected"), it's difficult to quantify results and take action.

How to Overcome Them

Despite the hurdles, testing must become a first-class citizen in the resilience lifecycle. The following strategies can help embed it as an operational norm:

1. **Automate Testing with Guardrails**: Use tools like AWS Fault Injection Service (FIS), Azure Chaos Studio, or Gremlin to inject failure in controlled, incremental ways. Start small—test ALB failover, DNS TTL impact, or NAT gateway saturation.

2. **Make Testing Non-Disruptive**: Start in lower environments, but don't stop there. Use canary chaos (limited scope), simulate network partitions between AZs, or drop non-critical paths before expanding to full failure modes.

3. **Integrate into CI/CD Pipelines**: Incorporate resilience validation as a stage in your infrastructure deployment lifecycle. Use tools like AWS Resilience Hub to detect gaps based on configuration and generate remediation recommendations.

4. **Quantify MTTR and MTTD**: Track Mean Time To Detect and Mean Time To Recover as first-class metrics. These show whether your observability stack and automation pipelines are effective.

5. **Tie Testing to Regulatory and Business Outcomes**: Use DORA, ISO 22301, or internal compliance requirements as drivers. Map test outcomes directly to audit controls or SLA commitments.

6. **Test for Degradation, Not Just Outage**: Simulate slow DNS responses, increased cross-AZ latency, or partial loss of availability zone services. Many failures aren't binary—they degrade performance before disabling functionality.

Strategic Example: Simulating Hybrid Link Failure

In a hybrid AWS + on-prem architecture using AWS Direct Connect and Site-to-Site VPN backup, you might simulate the following:

- Disable BGP advertisements over Direct Connect and observe VPN failover

- Trace traffic flow via Reachability Analyzer to validate path shifts

- Measure time between path failure, DNS propagation, and restored service for external clients

- Confirm firewall rules, IAM permissions, and application-level dependencies are properly scoped to avoid blocking traffic on the failover path

This single scenario touches the **control plane**, **network layer**, **IAM**, and **observability**. Without regular simulation, your hybrid network's resilience is theoretical—not verified.

From Optional to Essential

Historically, resilience testing has been a *"nice to have."* In today's regulatory, always-on, interconnected environments, it's a necessity. Whether driven by customer SLAs, internal risk mitigation, or DORA requirements, the absence of testing is the absence of assurance.

Every automated backup, multi-region deployment, or traffic steering policy is just a hypothesis—until it is tested.

As we continue in this book, you'll see resilience not only as a design principle but also as an operational behavior. Building is one thing. Proving it works under stress is where true resilience begins.

What's Next?

These challenges are not exhaustive. Every architecture brings its own nuances based on business goals, technical stacks, compliance requirements, and operational maturity. However, common themes emerge:

- Detection precedes response.

- Automation outperforms manual intervention.

- Cost must be weighed against impact.

- Complexity must be abstracted and continuously validated.

- Testing is always a challenge.

In this chapter, we established the foundations of cloud computing and why resilience is a core design discipline rather than an afterthought. We defined cloud computing as the on-demand, pay-as-you-go delivery of virtualized compute, storage, networking, and higher-level services, highlighting its key characteristics such as abstraction, elasticity, global reach, and shared responsibility. We explored how resilience differs from but complements availability and disaster recovery: availability keeps systems running under normal conditions, resilience enables graceful recovery and adaptation to unexpected failures, and DR prepares for worst-case regional or systemic outages. Using AWS's Resilience Analysis Framework, we examined common failure modes (SEEMS), desired system properties (redundancy, capacity, timely and correct output, fault isolation), and real-world outage lessons that underscore the need for fault isolation, observability, and testing. We introduced core principles— like modular isolation, static stability, automated recovery, decoupling, and chaos engineering—and showed how they map to practical architectures such as multi-AZ deployments and hybrid connectivity with Direct Connect. We also distinguished control plane vs. data plane risks, emphasized the role of observability (metrics, logs, traces), and reviewed common resilience challenges, including CAP-theorem trade-offs, misaligned RTO/RPO, cultural resistance to testing, and regulatory drivers like DORA. Above all, readers should take away that resilience is an ongoing practice:

design for failure, validate assumptions continuously, and treat network reliability as a business-critical capability. These concepts form the basis for the networking and architecture patterns explored in later chapters.

As we progress to the next chapters, these challenges will guide our design decisions—whether building a resilient Virtual Private Cloud, engineering global DNS failover, or fine-tuning BGP routes for optimal failover. The path to resilience is iterative, but by understanding its obstacles early, we increase our chances of building systems that don't just survive failure—but thrive in spite of it.

CHAPTER 2

Fundamentals of Cloud Networking and Network Topologies

In Chapter 1, we explored what cloud computing is and how resilience is intertwined with its foundational principles. Now, in Chapter 2, we take a deep dive into the networking layer of cloud systems, because networking is the invisible thread connecting every cloud service. This chapter will explore three major pillars that underpin modern cloud networking:

Virtualization and Network Functions Virtualization (NFV): How hardware-based networking evolved into software-defined, virtualized components, enabling elasticity and agility that were impossible with traditional appliances.

Software-Defined Networking (SDN): The architectural shift that separates control planes from data planes, bringing programmability and automation to networks at hyperscale.

Cloud Network Architectures and Topologies: How these virtualized, software-defined building blocks are composed into resilient, scalable cloud network designs, including patterns like hub-and-spoke, service meshes, and zero-trust architectures.

In Section 2.1, we begin by examining virtualization and NFV, exploring how traditional network hardware (routers, firewalls, load balancers) has transformed into software instances running on commodity hardware and orchestrated dynamically. We'll see how this transformation enabled cloud providers to deliver services at a global scale and how enterprises can leverage NFV to build resilient multi-cloud and hybrid solutions.

In Section 2.2, we'll analyze SDN, the architectural paradigm shift that enables centralized control, intent-based networking, and APIs to configure and monitor networks, unlocking automation and innovation at hyperscale.

Finally, in Section 2.3, we'll synthesize these technologies into cloud-native network topologies, exploring how enterprises design resilient networks leveraging NFV and SDN principles. We'll also cover multi-region designs, edge architectures, and the trade-offs involved.

Together, these sections will not just define terms; they will uncover why these technologies emerged, how they solve real problems, and what lessons they hold for building resilient cloud systems.

Section 2.1: Virtualization and Network Functions Virtualization (NFV)

The Evolution from Hardware to Virtualization

The early days of networking were defined by "physicality." To connect systems together, you needed boxes—routers, switches, and firewalls—each with a fixed identity and function. These devices were built with painstaking engineering, often around custom silicon, to do one thing very well. A Cisco router in the late 1990s was designed to forward packets at wire speed, nothing more, nothing less. I still have three of those connected at home; I used to practice and study on them when I was a kid. A Check Point firewall was engineered with proprietary operating systems and ASICs optimized for deep packet inspection. These appliances had personalities; a data center was a "zoo of specialized creatures," each contributing to the functioning of the whole. But while this world had a certain elegance for those who mastered it, it was also inflexible. A network could not change faster than the rate at which steel, copper, and silicon could be ordered, shipped, racked, and powered.

This rigidity was not a problem at first. In the client–server era, change was measured in years. Businesses planned IT infrastructure in long cycles, often buying ahead of demand and living with inefficiency as the cost of stability. The internet changed all that. Suddenly, traffic patterns were unpredictable. A new product launch could double traffic overnight. Viral growth meant that networks could not be planned in neat five-year increments. Enterprises began to discover that their carefully purchased hardware was either overbuilt and underused or catastrophically underprovisioned when demand spiked. Hardware's physical nature clashed with the internet's dynamism.

Consider the example of an international bank in the early 2000s. Its IT staff might have forecasted branch growth and transaction volume to size firewalls accordingly. A conservative forecast meant buying hardware rated for five times the expected load, ensuring room for expansion but locking up millions in unused capacity. An aggressive forecast risked undersizing the devices, forcing costly emergency procurements. In both cases, resilience depended on physical redundancy: for every critical router, there was a "twin" sitting idle, waiting for the day its partner failed. This was resilience by duplication, a model that worked but scaled poorly.

The mismatch between agility and hardware was particularly stark in the telecom industry. Carriers were expected to handle exploding mobile data traffic as smartphones proliferated. To keep pace, they would have needed to deploy armies of new packet core devices, load balancers, and session border controllers. Each device was expensive, each required space, power, and cooling, and each came with vendor-specific management systems that did not talk to one another. Scaling networks this way was like trying to grow a modern city using medieval construction methods—possible, but painfully slow.

Virtualization offered a way out. When compute virtualization took off in the mid-2000s, first through VMware and later through open-source hypervisors like KVM, it changed the assumptions of IT. A single physical server could now host multiple operating systems, each isolated and each thinking it owned the hardware. Virtual machines could be created and destroyed in minutes, transforming server utilization from 10–15% to 70–80%. This was not just incremental efficiency—it was a step change. IT teams could suddenly think in terms of workloads rather than servers, applications rather than boxes.

Networking lagged behind at first, and this lag exposed the limits of the traditional model. You could spin up a virtual server in five minutes, but then you had to wait for a network engineer to provision a VLAN, configure a firewall, and maybe even install a physical load balancer to make the application accessible. In a sense, virtualization created an asymmetry: compute became fast and flexible, while networking remained slow and rigid. This bottleneck frustrated enterprises and inspired a search for solutions.

The concept of Network Functions Virtualization (NFV) emerged out of this search. The idea was radical yet intuitive: if servers and storage could be virtualized, why not network functions? Why should a firewall be a box when it could be a piece of software running on a virtual machine? Why should WAN optimization require a proprietary appliance when it could be deployed as code? NFV proposed decoupling the "brains" of networking from the "bodies," allowing the same functions to run on generic, commodity hardware. The physical appliance would no longer be the anchor of networking. Instead, the network would become a malleable, software-defined service layer.

Telecommunications companies were among the first to champion NFV, formalizing it through ETSI's Industry Specification Group in 2012. Their motivation was clear: without virtualization, scaling mobile networks for 4G and beyond would have bankrupted carriers. By moving packet cores, IMS systems (IP Multimedia Subsystems), and firewalls into virtualized environments, carriers could use elastic pools of commodity servers rather than endlessly purchasing bespoke boxes. This transition also made it possible to orchestrate network functions dynamically. A surge of traffic in one region? Spin up more virtual EPC instances (Evolved Packet Core) in that data center. A firewall failing in another? Launch a replacement in seconds without waiting for a technician.

For cloud providers, virtualization was not optional—it was existential. When AWS began its meteoric rise in the mid-2000s, it faced the challenge of building a global network to support millions of customers. Physical appliances simply could not scale to meet the demand of a hyperscale cloud. There was no way to ship firewalls to every region at the pace required, nor any way to manage them consistently. AWS, Google, and Microsoft instead bet everything on software. Their load balancers, NAT gateways, and firewalls were designed as virtualized, distributed functions from day one. To customers, these looked like simple services—"Elastic Load Balancer," "Azure Firewall"—but under the hood they were vast fleets of virtualized functions running on commodity hardware, orchestrated with efficiency.

The resilience implications of this shift were profound. In the hardware world, resilience was fragile because it depended on a small number of expensive boxes. If a firewall failed, the failover box took over, but there was always a single point of failure in the switchover process. Mean time to recovery was measured in minutes, sometimes hours if human intervention was required. In the virtualized world, resilience became intrinsic. Instead of two firewalls, you might run twenty instances spread across availability zones. If one failed, traffic was instantly rerouted to the others. Recovery was not an event; it was a property of the architecture. Elasticity became resilience.

Performance was the one area where hardware seemed to maintain an edge. Proprietary appliances were built with custom ASICs capable of handling packets at wire speed with minimal latency. In the early days of NFV, virtual appliances running on x86 servers could not match this efficiency. Critics dismissed NFV as a poor substitute, good only for test environments or small workloads. Yet technology advanced rapidly. Multi-core CPUs, kernel-bypass networking stacks, and technologies like Intel DPDK (Data Plane Development Kit) closed the performance gap. Later, the rise of SmartNICs and Data Processing Units (DPUs) brought hardware acceleration into the virtualized realm, offloading packet processing from CPUs and enabling virtual firewalls and routers to operate at near line rate. By the 2020s, the performance argument against NFV had largely evaporated, especially in the cloud, where horizontal scaling compensated for individual limits.

This improvement in performance was not just about speed—it was about resilience. A VNF that collapses under heavy load is as dangerous as a failed hardware box. By accelerating packet processing and allowing workloads to keep pace with surges in demand, NFV became a reliable foundation for resilient architectures. The guarantee that virtualized functions could scale without choking gave enterprises confidence to move mission-critical workloads into the cloud. In other words, performance was not a luxury; it was a prerequisite for resilience.

Resilience, however, is not only about throughput. It is also about **state**. Stateless VNFs, such as proxies or simple NAT devices, are easy to scale horizontally—drop in another instance, and the system absorbs the load. Stateful VNFs, such as firewalls or session border controllers, are different. They maintain session tables, user contexts, and transaction states. If one of these fails, all the active sessions risk being lost, causing visible outages. True NFV resilience required solving this challenge: replicating state across instances, ensuring session stickiness, and synchronizing tables so that traffic could continue seamlessly even in the face of failure. Cloud providers took this lesson seriously. For example, AWS Network Firewall replicates state across availability zones, ensuring continuity if an instance fails. In this way, NFV resilience matured from simple elasticity to a sophisticated handling of stateful services.

Another resilience innovation that NFV enabled was **service chaining**. In the hardware era, functions like firewalling, intrusion detection, and load balancing were physically chained together—cabled in sequence. If one appliance in that chain failed, the chain broke, and resilience was lost (resilience category of failure—shared fate from Chapter 1). NFV and orchestration changed this model entirely. Virtualized functions could be dynamically linked, and if one failed, the chain could reroute traffic to a healthy instance. In the cloud, this is embodied in services like AWS Gateway Load Balancer, which lets customers run fleets of virtual firewalls and automatically directs flows only through healthy appliances. Service chains became not brittle physical constructs but resilient, self-healing logical paths.

The transition was not just technological but cultural. Networking engineers, long accustomed to racking and stacking boxes, now had to think in terms of virtual machines, APIs, and orchestration platforms. Their jobs, my job, shifted from manual configuration to automation, from physical deployment to logical design. I remember when, for the first time, I captured network traffic on a VM hosted in the cloud, and I was shocked by seeing multiple MAC addresses assigned to the same NIC! This cultural change was challenging, but it also empowered engineers to operate networks at an unprecedented scale. No longer constrained by shipping lead times and vendor contracts, they could respond to business needs in hours instead of months.

Real-world examples illustrate the transformative impact. Netflix, for instance, famously migrated its infrastructure to AWS to achieve global scale and resilience. Doing so required abandoning reliance on hardware appliances and embracing virtualized networking. Instead of deploying physical load balancers and firewalls, Netflix leveraged software-based equivalents in AWS, orchestrating them as code. This allowed Netflix to expand into new regions rapidly, spinning up entire network stacks without ever shipping a box. The same story played out in enterprises across industries: banks deploying virtual firewalls for compliance, retailers adopting virtual load balancers for seasonal traffic spikes, and governments running virtual VPN concentrators to handle remote work during crises like the COVID-19 pandemic.

The evolution from hardware to virtualization is often compared to the transition from horse-drawn carriages to automobiles. At first, automobiles were less reliable and slower than horses, but they offered a path to scalability and flexibility that horses never could. Similarly, early NFV lacked the polish and raw performance of hardware appliances, but its trajectory was unstoppable because it aligned with the fundamental needs of modern business: agility, elasticity, and resilience. Over time, just as automobiles replaced horses, NFV and virtualized networking functions supplanted hardware in critical infrastructures worldwide.

In my opinion, what makes this story so compelling is not just the technological shift but the philosophical one. In the hardware era, networks were static, brittle, and vendor-defined. In the virtualized era, networks are dynamic, resilient, and programmable. Resilience is no longer something purchased by doubling appliances; it is something designed into the very nature of the system.

This shift sets the stage for the next section of this chapter, the next layer of transformation: Software-Defined Networking (SDN), which takes the virtualization of functions and extends it into the centralization of control, enabling networks to be managed with the same agility as the workloads they serve.

Section 2.2: Software-Defined Networking (SDN)

When virtualization and NFV reshaped networks, they addressed many long-standing problems. Functions that once depended on proprietary boxes could now be spun up in minutes as virtual appliances. Firewalls, load balancers, and VPN concentrators became elastic, programmable, and infinitely reproducible. Yet this transformation carried a hidden limitation: each function was still configured, monitored, and healed individually. NFV made the pieces agile, but the system as a whole remained fragmented. For a network to be truly resilient, it needed something more. It needed an overarching nervous system capable of orchestrating all those functions, ensuring they worked together, recovered together, and evolved together. That nervous system is software-defined networking (SDN).

Defining SDN

Software-Defined Networking is the architectural model that separates the control plane from the data plane. In traditional networks, both planes lived inside the same device. A router not only forwarded packets but also made decisions about the best path for those packets, based on its routing protocols. A firewall not only inspected and blocked traffic but also stored the entire policy set locally. Each device was its own brain and muscle, an island with its own perspective.

SDN disrupts that assumption. The "brain"—the control plane—is pulled out of the device and centralized in a controller, or often a cluster of controllers. These controllers hold a global view of the network, compute paths, apply policies, and then push instructions down into the devices. The devices, stripped of their autonomy, become streamlined data planes. Their role is no less vital, but it is simplified: move packets according to the forwarding state they receive. This fundamental separation allows the network to be programmed as a unified system rather than as a patchwork of individually managed boxes.

The result is profound. In SDN, a network can be treated like software: consistent, testable, and reproducible. Failures can be responded to centrally and in milliseconds. Misconfigurations are reduced because policies are expressed once, not typed in repeatedly across hundreds of devices. For resilience, this is a leap forward: instead of relying on each device to react in its own way, the system responds as a coordinated whole.

Control Plane and Data Plane

We briefly talked about this concept in the previous chapter, and you will see me bringing it up quite often. To understand why this matters, one must unpack the distinction between the control plane and the data plane in greater detail.

The control plane is the layer of intelligence. In traditional networking, routers exchange reachability information with protocols like OSPF or BGP. They gossip, they compute shortest paths, and they install forwarding entries into their tables. Each router holds only a slice of the global picture, limited to what its neighbors have told it. Firewalls maintain their own local rules. Load balancers decide their own pool memberships. In this world, every device has its own opinion, its own limited view of reality.

The data plane, by contrast, is the fast path. It simply moves packets. Once the control plane has installed a forwarding entry, the data plane is a high-speed assembly line: header lookups, policy checks, and forwarding actions. It operates in silicon, ASICs or NPUs, engineered for performance.

In SDN, the control plane is removed from the individual devices and consolidated. Controllers hold the topology, the policies, and the real-time view of failures. When a device joins, it does not independently decide what to do. It asks the controller: what flows should I install, and what rules should I enforce? The data plane continues to forward, but now its instructions come from a single, coherent source.

This has immediate implications for resilience. In a traditional distributed control plane, when a link fails, each router independently runs its convergence algorithm. They send updates, recompute paths, and after a while, the system stabilizes. During that time, packets may loop, be dropped, or follow suboptimal routes. In SDN, the controller sees the failure once, recomputes the new paths, and installs them deterministically across the fabric. The recovery is faster, more predictable, and less prone to compounding errors.

Static Stability in the Cloud

Cloud providers like AWS have taken the SDN principle and embedded within it a powerful concept known as **static stability.** This is one of the most important resilience principles in the modern era, and it's important in the networking field too. Static stability means that the **data plane continues to function even if the control plane is degraded or offline.**

In AWS's design philosophy, the control plane is acknowledged to be the more complex, fragile element. It is composed of orchestration systems, distributed databases, and APIs—all of which, by their very nature, have many dependencies. The data plane, on the other hand, is streamlined and engineered to forward packets without needing constant intervention. Static stability dictates that once a forwarding state is installed in the data plane, it should persist.

This means that if the AWS VPC control plane becomes temporarily impaired—if, for instance, the API to modify a security group or update a route table is delayed—existing applications continue operating as if nothing happened. Packets are forwarded along established flows. Sessions remain intact. Your workload does not grind to a halt waiting for the control plane to recover.

This principle profoundly enhances resilience. It eliminates a dangerous class of outages: those where the management system is unavailable but the network itself is otherwise healthy. Customers' applications, which depend on predictable packet forwarding, remain unaffected. Control-plane impairments are absorbed silently. The philosophy is clear: build for the assumption that control planes fail more often than data planes, and ensure that applications are insulated from those failures. Of course the principle of static stability applied not only to the networking layer but also to the application layer as well. Here the focus is on networking, but I wanted to mention that this is also applied to the way you architect your applications in the cloud.

From Distribution to Centralization

This centralization of the control plane challenges traditional ideas of resilience. For decades, networking wisdom held that distribution was resilience: if one router failed, others continued. But as networks grew, distribution became fragile. Each device needed to be configured, updated, and monitored separately. Each device ran its own control protocols, with no one in charge of global consistency. Outages often originated not from device failures but from the unpredictable interactions of distributed brains.

SDN inverted this. By consolidating control, networks became more predictable. The trade-off was philosophical: put more responsibility into the controller, but make the data plane robust through static stability. In other words, shift resilience from distribution to determinism.

Layers of SDN

In practice, SDN can be understood as three interlocking layers. At the top, the application layer is where intent is expressed. Administrators declare desired outcomes: "encrypt all traffic between these subnets," "prioritize video packets over bulk data," or "reroute traffic away from this region if latency exceeds 100 ms."

Beneath that, the control layer translates intent into specific forwarding instructions. It maintains topology maps, tracks health, computes failover paths, and orchestrates changes. In large systems, controllers themselves are distributed and hierarchical, both to scale and to remain resilient.

Finally, the infrastructure layer consists of the switches, routers, and virtual network elements that carry out instructions. These devices no longer need to run heavy control logic. Their mission is streamlined: forward packets according to rules.

This architecture has proven itself in hyperscale cloud. When you update an AWS route table or Google Cloud firewall rule, you are not configuring a box. You are declaring intent at the application layer. The cloud's control plane computes and distributes the necessary rules. The infrastructure layer enforces them at scale.

Case Study: Google B4 Backbone

A vivid example of SDN's role in resilience is Google's B4 backbone. This private WAN interconnects Google's data centers worldwide and carries a massive share of traffic, including YouTube and Gmail. Traditional routing protocols could not allocate bandwidth efficiently across such a backbone. If one link failed or traffic surged in a region, Border Gateway Protocol (BGP) convergence would be too slow and too crude.

Google built B4 as a centrally controlled SDN fabric. Controllers allocate bandwidth across links based on global demand. If a transpacific cable degrades, B4 reroutes traffic instantly, shifting flows across other links. If demand spikes in Europe, capacity is rebalanced in seconds. This dynamic traffic engineering prevents congestion and ensures applications remain available even during failures.

The technical detail is striking: B4 uses OpenFlow to program switches directly, with the controller dynamically splitting elephant flows across multiple paths, a technique called multi-path forwarding. The controller continuously monitors utilization and adapts. The resilience is not reactive but continuous—Google customers never notice when cables fail, because B4 heals invisibly.

Case Study: Netflix on AWS

Netflix, one of the largest consumers of AWS networking, relies heavily on SDN-driven resilience. Its global streaming platform cannot tolerate outages measured in minutes. To achieve this, Netflix uses AWS's Global Accelerator, an SDN-based service that directs user requests to the healthiest available endpoints. If a region becomes degraded, traffic is instantly shifted to another.

Under the hood, this works because AWS's controllers operate with global visibility. DNS responses are steered via Anycast IPs, and data planes enforce forwarding rules across regions. Netflix applications don't need to know about link failures or control-plane delays. The resilience comes from the static stability of the data planes combined with SDN's centralized intelligence.

Netflix engineers have described how this model allows them to run "chaos tests" in production—intentionally disabling regions to confirm traffic reroutes smoothly. Without SDN, such experiments would be reckless. With SDN, they are routine, proving the system's resilience by design.

Case Study: Financial Services

Banks and financial institutions face not only availability demands but also strict compliance requirements. Firewalls, segmentation, and logging are non-negotiable. In traditional networks, each firewall or switch needed its own configuration. Drift was inevitable, and outages were often caused not by failures but by inconsistent policies.

With SDN, financial institutions moved to fabrics where segmentation policies are defined once and enforced globally. If a workload moves between data centers or into the cloud, its policies follow. This dramatically reduces human error, which is the single largest cause of outages. It also provides resilience by reducing blast radius: if one segment is compromised, SDN-enforced boundaries contain it.

The technical mechanism often involves micro-segmentation: virtual switches at the hypervisor layer enforce rules provided by the controller. If a VM migrates, the rules migrate with it. The result is not only compliance but also operational resilience.

The Future of SDN

SDN is not static. It is evolving toward **intent-based networking**, where administrators no longer configure policies at all but instead declare outcomes: "This service must only talk to these backends." "This subnet must have 99.99% availability." The SDN system then ensures those intents are met, continuously adjusting the network state to maintain compliance.

Cloud providers are layering AI and machine learning onto SDN telemetry. These systems analyze flows, predict congestion, and preemptively reroute before performance degrades. The shift is from resilience as recovery to resilience as anticipation.

Edge computing will extend SDN further, bringing centralized control and static stability principles into distributed, latency-sensitive environments. IoT devices, 5G base stations, and autonomous vehicles will all depend on SDN's ability to enforce consistent policy and heal dynamically.

What's Next?

If NFV made network functions virtual, SDN made the network programmable, consistent, and resilient. Together they form the foundation of cloud networking. But resilience is not only a property of components; it is a property of architectures. In the next section, we will explore how NFV and SDN combine into real-world topologies: hub-and-spoke, service meshes, and zero-trust architectures. These patterns illustrate resilience not just in theory but in global practice.

Section 2.3: Cloud Network Architectures and Topologies Examples

In the first two sections of this chapter, we examined the transformation of networking from a world of specialized hardware appliances to **Network Functions Virtualization (NFV)** and then into programmable, centrally orchestrated fabrics through **Software-Defined Networking (SDN)**. These two shifts established the technological foundation for resilience in the cloud. Yet resilience does not emerge solely from the capabilities of individual network functions or from the intelligence of a control plane. It is defined most clearly by the way these elements are arranged and interconnected—the **network topology**.

Topology determines how traffic flows, how failures are isolated, and how recovery unfolds. A robust topology can contain disruptions and allow workloads to continue operating despite localized issues. A poorly designed topology, on the other hand, can amplify small faults into large-scale outages.

In this section, we will explore some of the **architectures and topologies of cloud networking**, with a particular focus on how they shape resilience. We will begin by looking at the transition from traditional on-premises topologies to cloud-native designs, comparing their underlying assumptions and trade-offs. From there, we will examine canonical cloud topologies in detail, analyzing their resilience properties and identifying best practices that make them reliable at scale.

Where appropriate, we will reference examples from AWS and principles from the **Well-Architected Reliability Pillar**. However, our aim is not to catalogue services tied to a single provider. Instead, our focus is on **universal design principles** that apply across all clouds—principles that advanced practitioners can adopt to build resilient networks regardless of platform.

From On-Premises to Cloud: A Paradigm Shift in Topologies

For decades, enterprise networks were built around **physical data centers** and followed a highly standardized three-tier model of **core, distribution, and access**.

- **Core routers** provided high-speed connectivity to external networks and between data centers.

- **Distribution switches** aggregated connections from the access layer and enforced policy boundaries.

- **Access switches** connected servers, storage, and end-user devices.

The **wide-area network (WAN)** mirrored this structured hierarchy. Most enterprises deployed **hub-and-spoke topologies** over **MPLS (Multi-protocol Label Switching)** circuits, where branch offices terminated into a central hub at headquarters. The hub was the entry and exit point for the internet and inter-data center traffic, secured by **DMZ (Demilitarized Zone)** firewalls, intrusion detection and prevention systems (IDS/IPS), and HTTP proxies. In this design, **centralized inspection tiers** processed nearly all north–south traffic.

Resilience in this environment relied on **hardware redundancy**. Core routers were usually deployed in pairs, distribution switches included dual supervisors, firewalls operated in active–standby/active-active clusters, and MPLS circuits were provisioned with primary and backup links. This design certainly addressed **infrastructure failures** (Chapter 1) by providing duplication of hardware. However, it left other categories unaddressed. **Deployment and configuration failures** were common: misconfigurations were often applied to both members of a redundant pair, turning resilience into synchronized fragility. **Dependencies and third-party failures** occurred when multiple branches relied on a single MPLS provider or fiber path—if the carrier failed, entire enterprises were impacted. **Operational failures** by administrators, such as mispatching or misapplying ACLs, were frequent contributors to downtime. Finally, **scale-induced failures** often translated into **infrastructure failures**: centralized inspection devices would hit throughput ceilings, and scaling required manual procurement cycles, leaving businesses exposed until new hardware arrived.

As workloads began migrating to the cloud, many enterprises attempted to extend these familiar patterns directly. They built "cloud DMZs" with virtual firewalls serving as centralized inspection tiers, or interconnected Virtual Private Clouds (VPCs) in full-mesh patterns to mimic the any-to-any reachability of MPLS. Yet these topologies often clashed with the fundamental nature of cloud networking. Cloud infrastructure is **region-based, availability zone (AZ)–oriented, and API-driven**. Designs that simply replicated static, centralized inspection tiers or WAN meshes introduced fragility and negated the cloud's intrinsic resilience properties.

Fault Domains: From Data Centers to Availability Zones

In the previous subsection, we examined how enterprises attempted to extend familiar on-premises models into the cloud, often replicating centralized inspection tiers or full-mesh WANs. These designs clashed with the cloud's very nature because they ignored its most fundamental concept: **fault domains.**

In traditional data centers, fault domains were limited in scope. For most enterprises, the unit of failure was a **rack**, a **row of racks**, or at most the **entire building**. Resilience was achieved by clustering hardware within the same site or by maintaining a secondary site nearby, often in active–passive disaster recovery mode. This provided protection against **infrastructure failures** (Chapter 1)—like hardware loss or localized power issues—but struggled to address broader-scale events. A fire or extended outage of an entire data center represented what we now classify as an **Availability Zone Failure**, and many enterprises lacked the automation or capacity to recover quickly.

Cloud providers redefined fault domains to address these limitations. An **Availability Zone (AZ)** is a physically independent facility with its own power, cooling, and network connectivity. AZs within a **Region** are engineered to avoid correlated failures, meaning that the loss of one AZ does not impact others. Regions, therefore, represent a broader fault domain, composed of multiple AZs working together.

Here it is important to distinguish carefully:

- Deploying across multiple AZs within a single region provides strong protection against **Availability Zone Failures**. This is the baseline resilience strategy for most workloads.

- However, workloads confined to a single AZ—even inside a region— still inherit the fragility of traditional on-premises designs. In this case, a localized AZ outage can result in downtime.

Some architects assume that resilience always requires **multi-region** deployments, but this is not accurate. Multi-region is only necessary when specific business requirements demand it—for example, compliance obligations, sovereignty rules, global latency needs, or tolerance of **Region Failures** (Chapter 1). For the majority of workloads, **multi-AZ within one region**, combined with **static stability principles** (introduced in Section 2.2), already provides resilience against both **infrastructure failures** and transient **service/control plane impairments** without the operational burden of multi-region complexity.

The key lesson is that cloud topologies must be deliberately mapped to fault domains. Multi-AZ should be treated as the minimum deployment pattern for production workloads. Multi-region should not be seen as a universal requirement for resilience but as a specialized architecture that should only be pursued when the risk profile and requirements explicitly justify it. We will expand on these considerations later in the book when we analyze **multi-region architectures for resilience**, but for now it is enough to recognize that resilience in the cloud is first and foremost achieved by aligning architectures with **AZ fault isolation** and reinforcing them with **static stability**.

The WAN Reimagined

In the previous subsection, we discussed how cloud providers redefined fault domains, shifting resilience boundaries from racks and buildings to Availability Zones and Regions. This same redefinition applies to the **wide-area network (WAN)**, which has undergone one of the most dramatic transformations in the move from on-premises to cloud.

Traditionally, the WAN was a **carrier-managed service**. The dominant design was **MPLS (Multi-protocol Label Switching)** deployed in a hub-and-spoke pattern, where branch offices and remote sites terminated into the headquarters hub. The hub served as the convergence point for security inspection, internet access, and inter-data center connectivity. Enterprises chose MPLS for predictable latency and carrier-grade service-level agreements.

Resilience in this model depended heavily on the carrier. Enterprises typically purchased dual MPLS circuits, often from different providers, or used **IPSec VPN (Internet Protocol Security Virtual Private Network)** tunnels as encrypted overlays for redundancy. In some advanced deployments, **MACsec (Media Access Control Security)** was implemented to provide Layer 2 encryption for sensitive traffic traversing carrier links. While this protected against **Infrastructure Failures** (Chapter 1), other failure categories remained problematic. A core outage in the carrier network was a classic **Dependencies and Third-Party Failure**. Centralizing all branch traffic at headquarters exposed the entire organization to **Deployment and Configuration Failures**, since an ACL or firewall misconfiguration at the hub could take down every spoke. Moreover, **Operational Failures**, such as administrator mistakes in managing hub routers, often had a global impact.

Cloud networking reimagines the WAN as an **elastic, software-defined fabric** rather than a static carrier product. Instead of waiting months for an MPLS circuit to be provisioned, enterprises can interconnect workloads dynamically using constructs such as **AWS Transit Gateway (TGW)**, **AWS Cloud WAN**, **Azure Virtual WAN**, or **Google Cloud Interconnect**. These act as policy-driven hubs that can elastically scale to connect hundreds or thousands of environments. Within those environments, workloads run inside **VPCs (Virtual Private Clouds, AWS and GCP)** or **VNets (Virtual Networks, Azure)**, and these in turn are stitched together by cloud WAN fabrics to form enterprise-wide overlays.

Hybrid connectivity extends this further. **Direct Connect (AWS)**, **ExpressRoute (Azure)**, and **Cloud Interconnect (GCP)** provide dedicated, high-bandwidth private links to on-premises networks. These are typically complemented by IPSec VPN tunnels as encrypted backups. In more advanced designs, **MACsec** is enabled on physical circuits to ensure confidentiality and integrity at the data-link layer, reducing reliance on overlay encryption alone. Together, these options offer redundancy across both logical and physical planes.

The resilience trade-offs here are important. On the positive side, cloud WANs reduce reliance on a single carrier backbone, mitigating **Dependencies and Third-Party Failures**. They enable routing and segmentation policies to be applied consistently across a global footprint. On the negative side, the responsibility for resilience now shifts more toward the architect. Policy changes are made through APIs and control planes. If misapplied, these can cause **Deployment and Configuration Failures** at scale; for example, a misconfigured route propagation in AWS Cloud WAN or Transit Gateway can instantly blackhole traffic across dozens of VPCs. This risk is amplified compared to on-premises WANs, where a misconfiguration often affected only a single site or hub.

Recovery mechanisms also behave differently. MPLS networks depended on routing protocol convergence (OSPF, BGP), which could take seconds or even minutes. In cloud WANs, failover relies on **software-defined controllers** updating the data plane programmatically. In **ideal conditions**, failover can be measured in **hundreds of milliseconds**, delivering a much tighter recovery objective. However, this is not guaranteed: convergence times depend on topology size, service health, and propagation of control-plane changes. Architects should therefore plan for variation and avoid assuming instantaneous recovery.

This shift underscores a broader theme: in the cloud, the WAN is no longer something purchased as a static service from a carrier. It is a **programmable design element** that must be deliberately architected for resilience. Where resilience in the MPLS era was outsourced to a provider's backbone, resilience in the cloud era is determined by how well you design policies, align with fault domains, and mitigate the new failure categories identified in Chapter 1.

DMZs and the Evolution of Centralized Inspection Tiers

In the previous subsection, we looked at how the WAN has been reimagined in the cloud, shifting from static MPLS backbones to programmable, software-defined fabrics. This same transformation also extends to how enterprises handle security inspection and traffic control.

In on-premises architectures, security was built around the **DMZ (Demilitarized Zone)**. All ingress and egress traffic was funneled through a **centralized inspection tier** consisting of firewalls, IDS/IPS (Intrusion Detection and Prevention Systems), and web proxies. This made sense in a client–server era where applications were static and data centers served as the network's focal point. Resilience was achieved primarily by deploying appliances in redundant active–standby pairs, a strategy that addressed **Infrastructure Failures** (Chapter 1) but often failed against other categories. A failed firewall upgrade is a classic **Deployment and Configuration Failure**; a misaligned rule set between appliances is an **Operational Failure**; and saturated inspection appliances created bottlenecks that turned into **Application Failures** through latency and dropped sessions.

Cloud networking challenges this centralized model. Workloads are distributed across **Availability Zones (AZs)** and even across regions. Routing all traffic through a single, appliance-centric inspection cluster undermines the cloud's fundamental resilience properties. That said, **centralized inspection is not entirely obsolete**. Many enterprises implement **VPC inspection models**, where north–south and even east–west traffic is routed through dedicated inspection VPCs. This approach remains valid, but resilience depends on how it is implemented. If inspection VPCs are built as monolithic tiers, they replicate the fragility of the on-premises DMZ. If they are deployed elastically across AZs and integrated into the topology as scalable services, they become enablers of resilience rather than barriers. We will return to this when we discuss **inspection topologies in best practices** later in this section.

A key distinction in cloud architectures is between **centralized inspection** and **distributed inspection**. In centralized models, all traffic—north–south and east–west— is forced through a limited set of inspection nodes. This simplifies policy management but creates concentrated failure domains. In distributed models, inspection capacity is spread across multiple AZs and scaled horizontally. Policies are enforced consistently through orchestration, while resilience improves because no single failure can disrupt the entire path.

This intersection highlights an important principle: **security and resilience travel in parallel**. Both must be designed into the topology, and both must scale together. If security controls become bottlenecks, they reduce resilience; if resilience bypasses controls, it undermines security. In the cloud, inspection must evolve into a **resilient service layer**—elastic, distributed, and aligned with AZ fault domains—rather than remaining an appliance-centric dependency.

Pros and Cons Revisited Through Failure Categories

In the previous subsection, we examined how inspection models have evolved from centralized DMZ tiers to more distributed, service-based approaches in the cloud. That shift illustrates a broader truth: resilience cannot be evaluated in abstract. It must be assessed against the **categories of failure** introduced in Chapter 1. By mapping traditional on-premises topologies and modern cloud topologies against these categories, the trade-offs become clearer.

Application Failures:

On-premises architectures rarely accounted for application-level failures in their topology design. The assumption was that if the network delivered packets, the application would handle the rest. In reality, centralized inspection tiers often amplified application fragility by introducing latency, asymmetric routing, or session drops under load. Cloud topologies, by contrast, integrate application resilience into the network fabric. Distributed inspection fleets, elastic load balancers, and service meshes are explicitly designed to absorb or isolate application faults. Still, poorly designed service chaining in the cloud can create subtle application failures—latency amplification and inconsistent policies remain risks.

Infrastructure Failures:

Traditional networks mitigated infrastructure risks through hardware redundancy: paired core routers, active–standby firewalls, and dual MPLS circuits. These solutions addressed local hardware loss but provided limited coverage for data center-wide outages. In the cloud, **Availability Zones (AZs)** redefine infrastructure resilience. An AZ is a **fault-isolated collection of one or more physical data centers within a metropolitan area, each with independent power, cooling, and connectivity, and interconnected with low-latency, high-bandwidth links**. By default, services can be deployed across multiple AZs, ensuring that a router or hypervisor failure in one location does not affect workloads elsewhere. Topologies that remain confined to a single AZ, however, inherit the same fragility as on-premises data centers.

Availability Zone Failures:

This category did not exist in on-premises thinking, because enterprises usually did not operate multiple fault-isolated facilities within a single metropolitan region. The equivalent was an entire data center outage. Cloud topologies mitigate AZ failures by distributing workloads across zones. A hub-and-spoke topology with inspection tiers in every AZ, for example, can continue forwarding traffic even if an AZ becomes unavailable. The caveat is that AZ resilience must be designed in—placing all firewalls or NAT gateways in one AZ collapses resilience back to the on-prem model.

Region Failures:

On-premises networks often had secondary data centers for disaster recovery, but these were usually manual failover sites with limited capacity. Cloud regions formalize this concept, but multi-region architectures come with trade-offs. They address the rare but catastrophic Region Failure category, but they add complexity in routing, data consistency, and operational overhead. As discussed in the previous subsection on fault domains, multi-region should be reserved for workloads with explicit requirements; for most, multi-AZ deployments within a single region provide sufficient resilience.

Dependencies and Third-Party Failures:

On-premises WANs depended heavily on carriers, with MPLS or leased-line providers representing external dependencies. Failures in a carrier backbone could cripple global connectivity. Cloud topologies reduce this risk by leveraging provider-operated backbones that span continents, often with built-in redundancy. However, new dependencies emerge: reliance on a cloud provider's control plane or managed services. A misconfiguration in a Transit Gateway or Cloud WAN route table can act as a systemic dependency failure if not isolated properly.

Deployment and Configuration Failures:

On-premises, changes were manual and device-specific. Misconfigurations often affected a single site or appliance. Cloud topologies, by contrast, are API-driven: a single command or misapplied template can affect hundreds of VPCs simultaneously. This increases the blast radius of deployment errors. Resilience therefore depends on disciplined change management, infrastructure as code, and the use of automation pipelines with guardrails. The topology itself should enforce boundaries—segmented hubs and distinct route domains reduce the chance of a misconfiguration propagating globally.

Operational Failures:

Operator mistakes—accidental ACL deletions, mis-patched cables, or overlooked failover tests—were common in on-premises designs. In the cloud, the nature of operational failures shifts. Direct console access is replaced with API-driven changes, and physical errors vanish, but mismanagement of IAM roles, insufficient monitoring, or neglected automation can produce equally impactful outcomes. Cloud topologies that isolate environments (e.g., spoke VPCs segmented by workload or team) reduce exposure to operator errors by localizing their impact.

Cybersecurity Events:

Centralized DMZs on-prem provided clear enforcement points but also clear targets. DDoS attacks, for example, often overwhelmed firewalls that were never designed for volumetric defense. In the cloud, topologies are designed with distributed edge protection—provider-operated DDoS mitigation, WAFs deployed at scale, and inspection fleets across AZs. This provides stronger defense in depth, but as mentioned previously, security and resilience must evolve in parallel. An insecure topology is not resilient, and a resilient topology that ignores security creates a different kind of failure risk.

By revisiting the categories of failure, we see the progression clearly. On-premises designs focused heavily on **Infrastructure Failures** and attempted to solve them through hardware duplication. Cloud designs emphasize **fault domain awareness**, **distribution**, and **automation**, addressing a broader set of categories: from **Availability Zone Failures** to **Deployment and Configuration Failures**. Yet the cloud also introduces new risks: misconfigurations propagate faster, dependencies shift from carriers to control planes, and operational practices require new disciplines.

The net effect is that resilience in the cloud cannot be assumed; it must be consciously designed. Topologies act as the scaffolding that determines whether failures are isolated or amplified. In the next subsection, we will look at **canonical cloud topologies**—hub-and-spoke, mesh, hybrid, multi-region, and others—and evaluate how each addresses or exposes these categories of failure in practice.

Commonly Used Cloud Topologies

Single VPC/Flat Topology

In the previous subsection, we assessed how different categories of failure—application, infrastructure, configuration, operational, and others—manifest differently in on-premises and cloud topologies. To bring that analysis into practice, we now turn to the **concrete topologies** used in cloud networking. The simplest of these is the **single VPC (Virtual Private Cloud, AWS and GCP) or VNet (Virtual Network, Azure)** design, often referred to as a **flat topology**.

In this model, all workloads—application tiers, databases, and supporting services—reside in a single logical network construct. **Subnets** are used for segmentation, but it is important to note that in AWS, a subnet is bound to a **single Availability Zone (AZ)**. Subnets cannot span multiple AZs. To design for resilience, each tier must be deployed in multiple subnets distributed across different AZs.

As shown in Figure 2-1, a single VPC or flat topology places subnets across multiple Availability Zones within the same VPC, allowing a load balancer to distribute traffic across zonal resources while maintaining a simple network design.

Figure 2-1. *Single VPC/Flat Topology*

This flat topology has obvious appeal. It is easy to deploy, fast to set up, and suitable for small environments or proof-of-concept workloads. It mirrors the simplicity of early on-premises networks, where VLANs provided logical separation but everything remained within one large domain.

From a **resilience perspective**, however, the limitations are significant:

- **Infrastructure Failures**: If all workloads are placed in a single subnet (and therefore in a single AZ), an AZ outage will take down the entire application. To mitigate this, architects must deploy workloads across multiple subnets in multiple AZs. Supporting infrastructure requires careful consideration. **NAT Gateways** and **firewall endpoints** are AZ-scoped, meaning you must provision one in each AZ for redundancy. By contrast, **Elastic Load Balancers (ALBs, NLBs, and Gateway Load Balancers)** are designed to scale horizontally and operate across AZs automatically, routing traffic only to healthy targets.

- **Deployment and Configuration Failures**: Flat topologies often centralize routing and security into a small number of control points. A misconfigured route table, security group, or network ACL can inadvertently affect the entire environment. With no isolation between application domains, the blast radius of a single error is far larger than in segmented designs.

- **Operational Failures**: Because everything resides in one VPC, operator mistakes, such as an accidental IAM policy change or an unintended deletion of a shared resource, can impact every workload simultaneously. On-premises, VLAN segmentation sometimes contained these mistakes; in flat cloud topologies, there are no such boundaries.

- **Dependencies and Third-Party Failures**: When hybrid connectivity is introduced—via **Direct Connect (AWS)**, **ExpressRoute (Azure)**, or **Cloud Interconnect (GCP)**—a flat topology often relies on a single private link. This becomes a critical external dependency. AWS provides specific resiliency patterns for Direct Connect, including the **High Resiliency Model** and the **Maximum Resiliency Model**, which use multiple independent connections to avoid single points of failure. These models should be considered even in small topologies to mitigate external dependency risks.

For these reasons, the single VPC/flat topology is best understood as a **starting point**. It is sufficient for small-scale deployments, test environments, or applications where failure domains can be tolerated. But as soon as scale, compliance, or resilience requirements grow, its limitations become clear.

The key takeaway is that while a flat topology maximizes simplicity, it also maximizes blast radius. Subnets, NAT Gateways, and firewalls are tied to single AZs; workloads must be explicitly deployed across zones to gain resilience. Elastic Load Balancers provide some relief by scaling across zones automatically, but they do not remove the need for thoughtful multi-AZ design. In practice, most enterprises evolve quickly from flat designs toward **hub-and-spoke** or **segmented multi-VPC architectures**, which we will examine next.

Hub-and-Spoke Topology

As organizations outgrow the limitations of flat designs, the most common next step is the **hub-and-spoke topology**. In this model, multiple VPCs (Virtual Private Clouds, AWS/GCP) or VNets (Virtual Networks, Azure) act as "spokes" that connect into a central **hub**. The hub functions as the transit domain for inter-VPC communication, shared services, and often centralized inspection. AWS **Transit Gateway (TGW)**, AWS **Cloud WAN**, Azure **Virtual WAN**, and GCP's **Cloud Interconnect/Cloud Router** are typical hub constructs, providing scalable policy-driven routing across many spoke environments.

For smaller deployments, many organizations start with **VPC Peering**. This allows direct connectivity between two VPCs without requiring a hub construct. Peering is simple and performant, but it does not scale well for enterprise needs: it is non-transitive, meaning each VPC pair requires a dedicated connection. As the number of VPCs grows, this results in a management overhead known as **"peering sprawl."** To avoid this fragility, most enterprises evolve toward hub-based designs using TGW, Cloud WAN, or equivalent constructs.

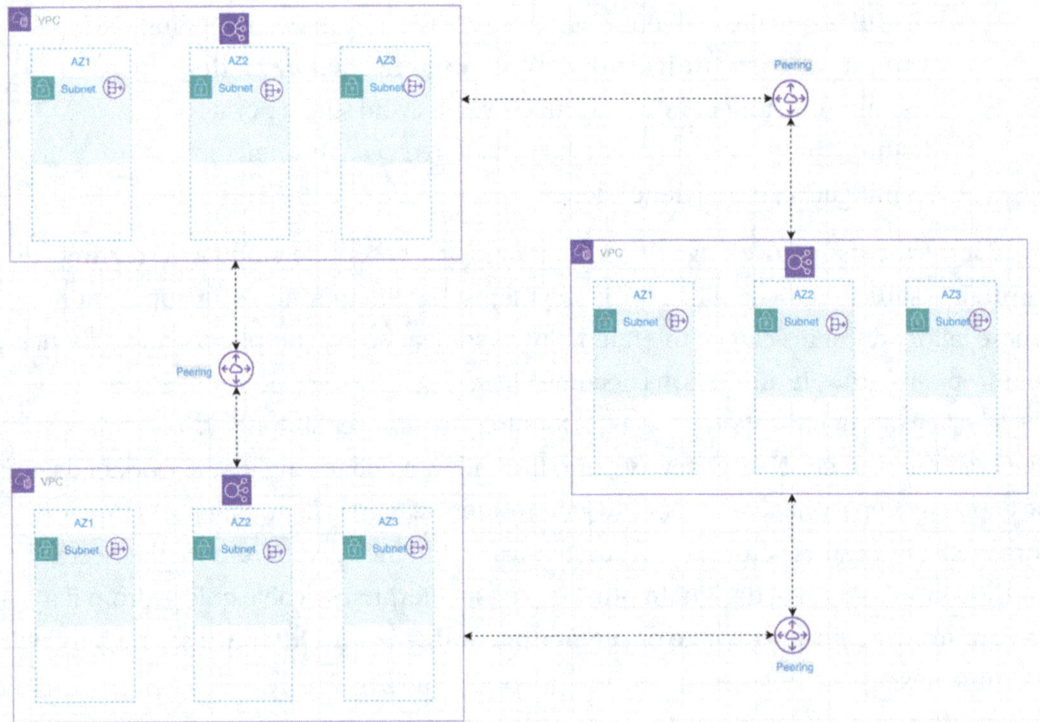

Figure 2-2. *VPC Peering with Hub&Spoke*

In **AWS**, the hub-and-spoke pattern is usually implemented with **Transit Gateway (TGW)**. A common approach is to designate a **hub VPC** that hosts shared services such as Active Directory, DNS resolvers, logging collectors, or security appliances. This VPC can also serve as an **inspection VPC**, where firewalls are deployed to enforce north–south and east–west policies. Spoke VPCs attach to TGW and route inter-VPC or hybrid traffic via the hub, where policy and inspection are applied consistently.

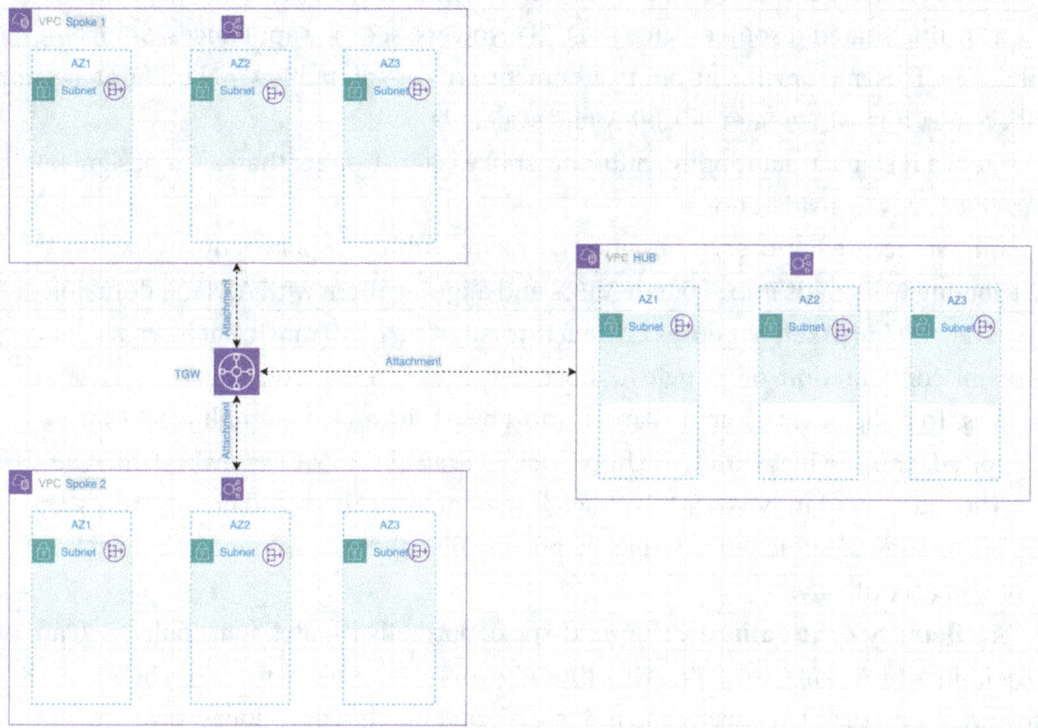

Figure 2-3. *Transit Gateway Hub&Spoke*

In **Azure**, the design looks different. There is no direct equivalent of TGW, and **VNet peering is not transitive**. To build hub-and-spoke, the hub VNet must include an **IP forwarder** that relays traffic between spokes. This can be implemented using **Azure Firewall**, which natively supports packet forwarding, or by deploying a **Linux VM router** to perform forwarding. While this achieves the same logical outcome, it introduces additional **operational burden**: appliances must be patched, scaled, and monitored, which increases complexity compared to AWS TGW's managed approach.

In **GCP**, hub-and-spoke can be achieved with **shared VPCs** and **Cloud Router**, leveraging the global VPC model. Although routing is more flexible, enterprises still designate hub projects for shared services, with spokes tied to specific workloads or business units.

The value of hub-and-spoke lies in **segmentation and policy centralization**. Each spoke VPC or VNet can represent an environment (e.g., dev, test, prod), a business unit, or a workload domain. The hub enforces connectivity and inspection policies, often hosting shared resources such as DNS resolvers, security appliances, or logging collectors. This mirrors the on-premises practice of consolidating WAN traffic at a central data center, but with greater flexibility and scale.

From a resilience standpoint, hub-and-spoke is far stronger than a flat design, but it introduces new considerations:

Infrastructure Failures. If designed correctly, hub-and-spoke reduces fragility by distributing workloads into separate VPCs and aligning them with AZ fault domains. However, the **hub itself becomes critical infrastructure**. A Transit Gateway or Cloud WAN misconfiguration, or a single AZ hosting the hub appliances, can create systemic outages. To mitigate this, hub constructs must be deployed across multiple AZs where supported, and services within the hub (such as firewalls or NAT gateways) must be provisioned redundantly. AWS TGW itself is regionally resilient and not tied to a single AZ, but appliances attached to it (like inspection fleets) are AZ-scoped and must be deployed accordingly.

Availability Zone Failures: Hub-and-spoke naturally isolates some failures. If an AZ within a spoke fails, workloads in other AZs (or other spokes) remain reachable. However, centralizing inspection in a single AZ of the hub reintroduces fragility. This is where **distributed inspection across multiple AZs** is essential; otherwise, an **Availability Zone Failure** at the hub layer creates an outage for all spokes. Below you can see examples of centralized vs. distributed inspection architectures.

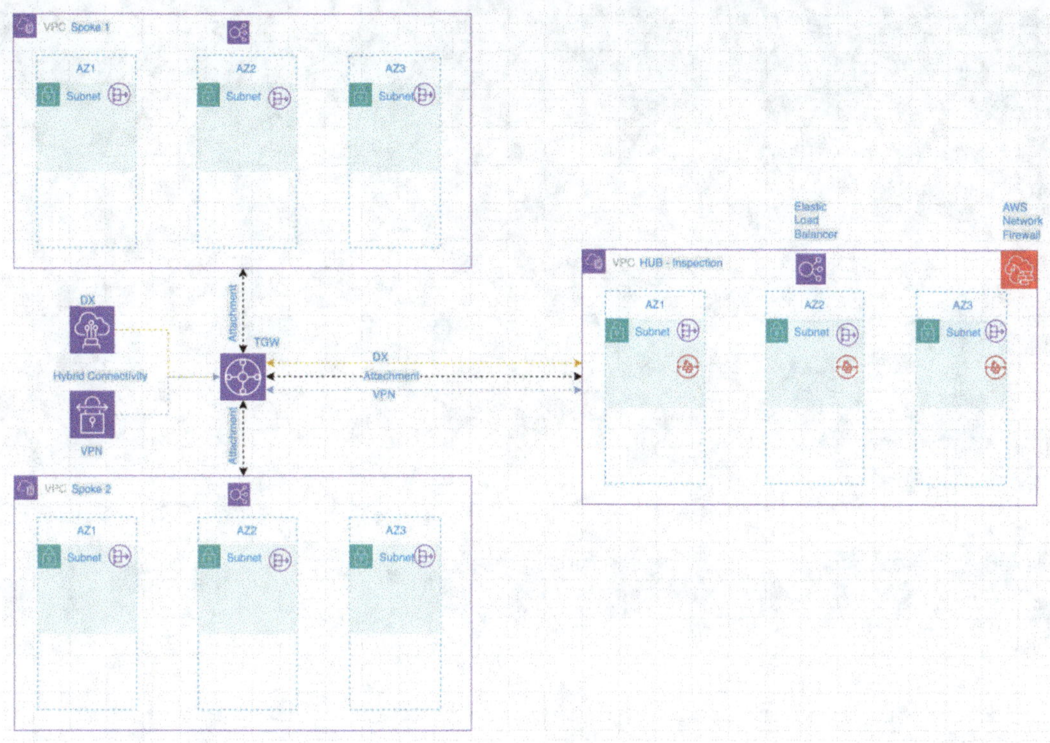

Figure 2-4. *Centralized Inspection Hub&Spoke*

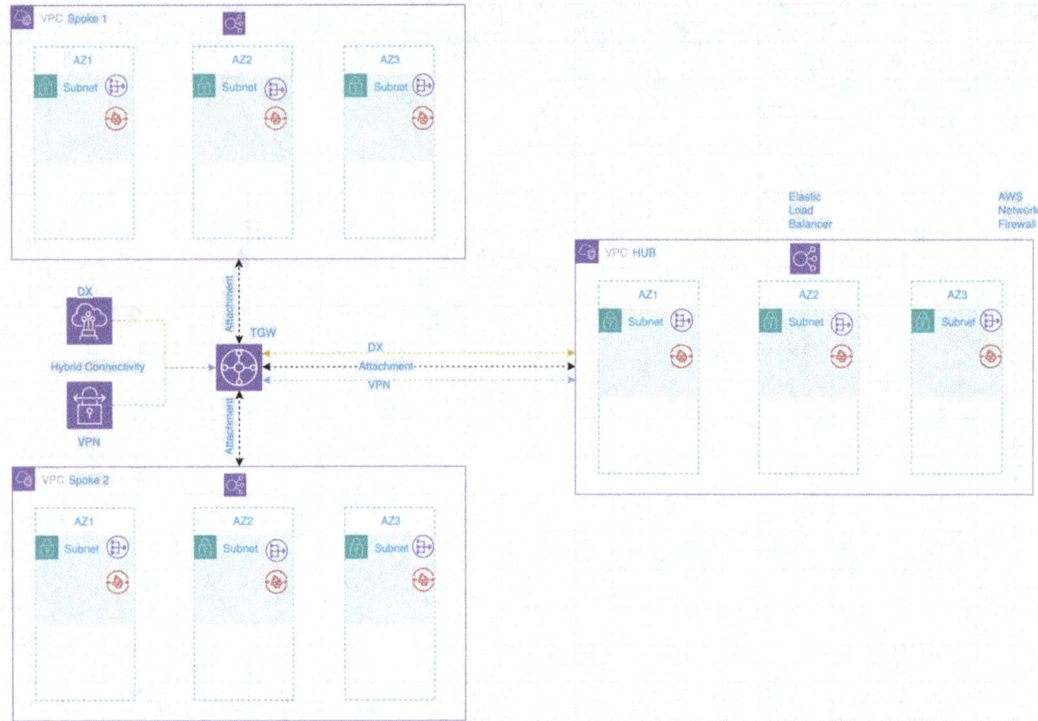

Figure 2-5. *Distributed Inspection Hub&Spoke*

Region Failures: A single-region hub-and-spoke design cannot protect against a full **Region Failure**. If the hub resides in only one region, all spokes depending on it lose connectivity when that region is impaired. For enterprises with multi-region requirements, dual hubs in separate regions—with DNS-based or Global Accelerator-based failover—are necessary. This introduces complexity in routing and traffic steering but is the only way to protect against rare but catastrophic regional events.

It is important to add distinction on centralized vs. distributed. In AWS hub-and-spoke architectures, network inspection can be implemented using two primary patterns: **centralized inspection**, where all traffic funnels through a single inspection layer in the hub, and **distributed inspection**, where each Availability Zone (AZ) hosts its own inspection path. Both rely on AWS Network Firewall's zonal endpoint model, but they differ significantly in how traffic flows, how resiliency is achieved, and how operational complexity scales.

Centralized inspection places all traffic through a single set of firewalls in the hub, simplifying policy management but creating a chokepoint. All spoke VPCs hairpin through the same inspection layer, increasing cross-AZ traversal, latency, and blast radius. Because Network Firewall endpoints are zonal, centralizing inspection requires routing traffic from multiple spokes into the same AZ-bound endpoint fleet, which can cause asymmetric routing or unintended bypass if not carefully engineered. *Pros:* simpler governance, fewer endpoints to deploy, and consistent policy in one place. *Cons:* higher latency, potential cross-AZ charges, larger blast radius, and reduced resilience if the inspected AZ becomes impaired.

Distributed inspection removes this bottleneck by deploying AWS Network Firewall endpoints in each Availability Zone and steering traffic locally within the spoke or through per-AZ hub attachments. This pattern preserves AZ boundaries, avoids cross-AZ hairpinning, and ensures that firewalling survives a single-AZ impairment. *Pros:* improved resilience, deterministic routing, and optimal latency due to local inspection paths. *Cons:* more endpoints to manage, increased configuration overhead across multiple AZs, and the need for consistent policy replication to maintain a uniform security posture. Overall, distributed inspection aligns more closely with AWS best practices for high availability and zonal isolation, particularly for mission-critical or regulated workloads.

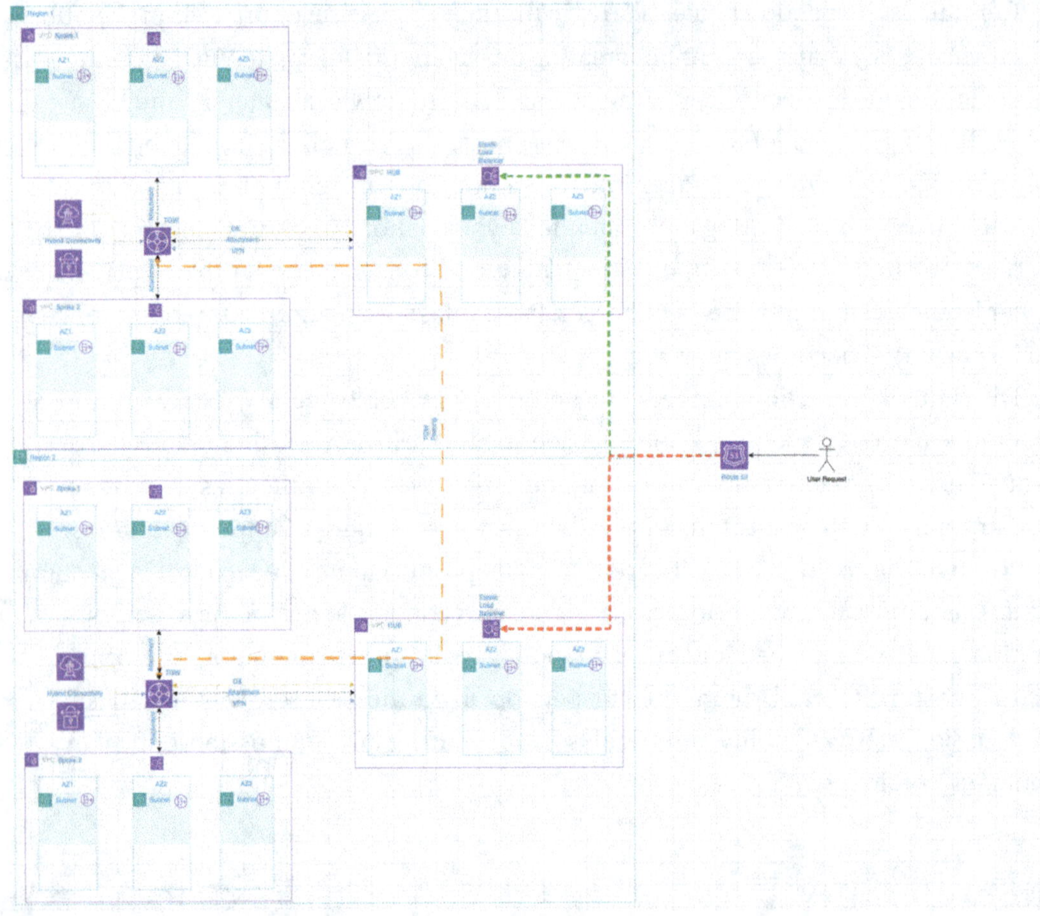

Figure 2-6. *Multi-region Hub&Spoke with Route 53*

Dependencies and Third-Party Failures: Hybrid connectivity is usually terminated at the hub, making it the enterprise's bridge to on-premises networks. A single Direct Connect circuit into the hub becomes a critical dependency. AWS offers resiliency models (**High Resiliency, Maximum Resiliency**) to mitigate this, using multiple diverse links and locations. Similar strategies apply with ExpressRoute or Cloud Interconnect. Without them, the hub becomes an external dependency bottleneck.

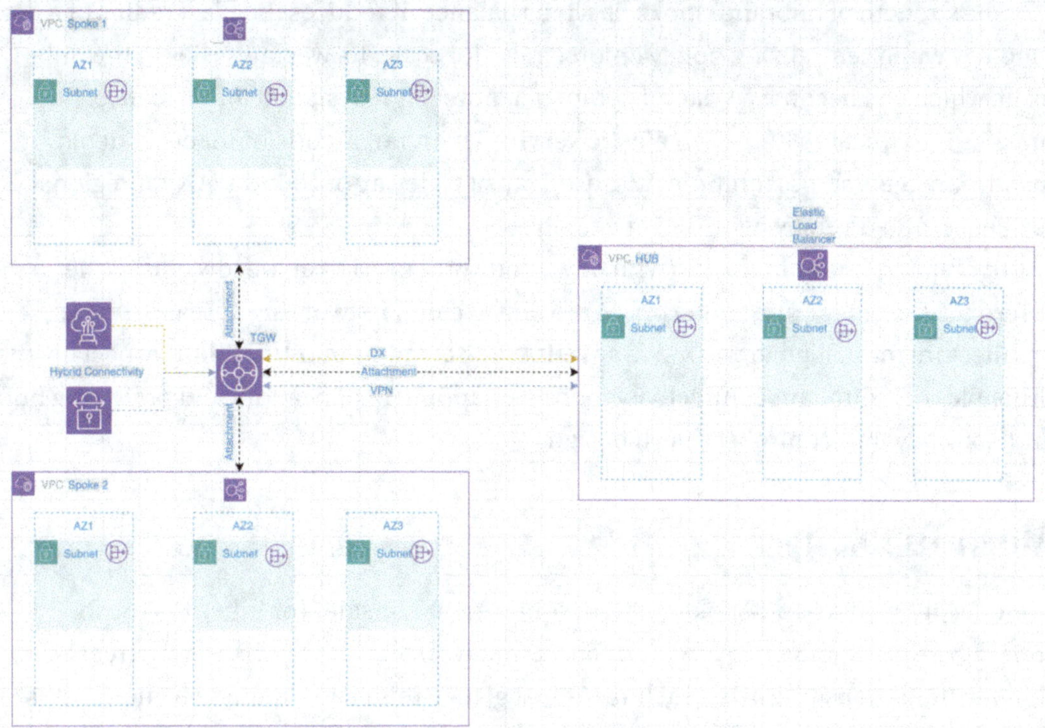

Figure 2-7. *Hub&Spoke with Hybrid Connectivity Example*

Deployment and Configuration Failures: Centralizing routing and policy at the hub improves consistency but also increases blast radius. A single misapplied route propagation in Transit Gateway can disrupt dozens of spokes simultaneously. Resilience therefore requires careful segmentation of route domains, scoped route tables per environment, and guardrails in the CI/CD pipeline to prevent untested changes from applying globally.

Operational Failures: In on-premises WANs, operational mistakes often remained localized. In hub-and-spoke, mistakes at the hub can impact every spoke at once. To mitigate this, strong IAM separation should be enforced so that operators of individual spokes cannot alter hub-level policies. Additionally, operational playbooks must explicitly cover failure testing at the hub layer, since this is the new systemic risk.

Cybersecurity Events: The hub is an attractive target: compromise of hub inspection appliances or misconfiguration of hub routing exposes the entire network. Resilient hub-and-spoke designs therefore enforce least-privilege access, logging, and often defense-in-depth by layering distributed controls at the spoke level as well. Security and resilience again move in parallel—one without the other undermines both.

The strength of hub-and-spoke lies in its balance: it reduces the blast radius of a flat topology while centralizing policy enforcement for scale. Its weakness lies in the hub itself, which can become a systemic point of failure if not designed for resilience. Best practice is to treat the hub as an **elastic service layer**, not a static bottleneck: deploy inspection fleets across multiple AZs, use Transit Gateway or Cloud WAN for regional resilience, and diversify hybrid connectivity.

In practice, hub-and-spoke (with or without VPC Peering at the low end) is the **reference design** for most enterprises moving to cloud networking at scale. It is the architecture most aligned with AWS's **Well-Architected Reliability Pillar**, especially the principles of redundant connectivity, non-overlapping IP allocation, and preferring hub-and-spoke over uncontrolled mesh designs.

Mesh Topology

Building on the hub-and-spoke pattern, some teams consider (or inherit) a **mesh topology**—interconnecting environments directly so that any VPC/VNet can reach any other without transiting a central hub. At first glance this seems attractive: more paths, no single "hub" dependency, and potentially lower latency between certain pairs of workloads. In practice, at cloud scale, a mesh very often **trades structural resilience for operational fragility**.

In **AWS**, meshes typically start as a series of **VPC Peering** links. Peering is performant (it uses the provider backbone) and simple to enable, but it is **non-transitive**: VPC-A↔VPC-B and VPC-B↔VPC-C do **not** imply A↔C. To give A and C reachability, you must create an additional A↔C peering, then update **route tables** in both VPCs. Specifically, you must add a route in the subnet route tables of VPC-A pointing to the CIDR of VPC-C with the target set to the **VPC Peering Connection ID**, and vice versa in VPC-C. As the number of VPCs grows, this results in dozens—or even hundreds—of manual route table entries. This is the origin of what practitioners call **"peering sprawl."**

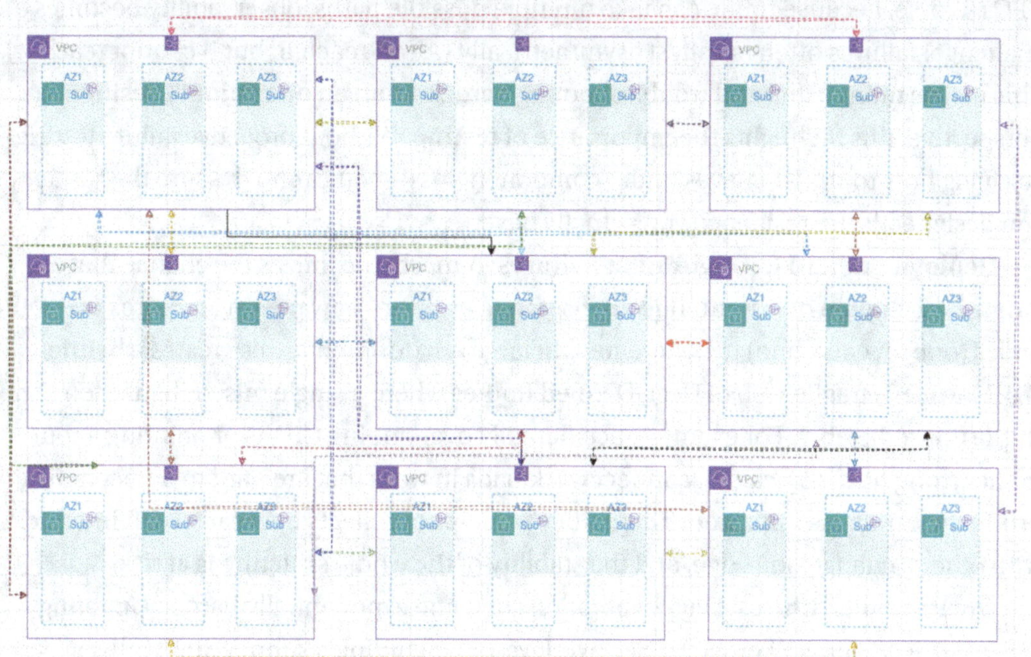

Figure 2-8. *Peering Sprawl Example*

In **Azure**, we already discussed in the hub-and-spoke subsection that there is no equivalent of TGW and that **VNet peering is not transitive**. The same limitation applies in a mesh: to pass traffic between VNets that are not directly peered, you need to insert an **IP forwarder** into the topology. This is usually an **Azure Firewall** acting as a packet forwarder, or in some cases a **Linux VM router**. While it enables mesh-like reachability, the operational burden is high—more appliances to patch, more UDRs (User-Defined Routes) to configure, and more moving parts that can fail.

In **GCP**, a mesh is constructed with **VPC Network Peering**. Like AWS and Azure, it is non-transitive, so full reachability requires multiple peerings and explicit routing configuration. GCP's global VPC model reduces the number of peerings somewhat but still relies on manual route management and consistent policy enforcement across projects.

From a **resilience** standpoint, the mesh's promise is path diversity without a central hub dependency. The reality is more nuanced:

Infrastructure Failures: While each peering path rides the provider backbone, every new link increases the number of infrastructure dependencies. A single misconfigured or failed NVA (Network Virtual Appliance) can silently blackhole traffic between specific

VPCs. Worse, because traffic can take multiple possible paths, observability becomes a challenge: failures often manifest asymmetrically (A can reach B, but B cannot reach A). This makes monitoring and troubleshooting harder. From an **operational resilience** perspective, this highlights the importance of **testing**. Without proactive failure testing—verifying how routing behaves under component loss—you cannot be sure the resilience you designed is the resilience you actually have.

Deployment and Configuration Failures: A mesh maximizes the chance that a **single bad change** has unintended consequences. Every new peering requires two route tables (one on each side) to be updated. In large environments, this creates a **brittle UDR lattice**: a fragile web of User-Defined Routes where a single misconfiguration can ripple unpredictably. For example, accidentally overlapping CIDRs or pointing a route to the wrong next hop can disconnect workloads in ways that are hard to detect until production traffic is impacted. The "lattice" metaphor reflects how each UDR interlocks with others: change one edge, and the stability of the whole structure is at risk.

Operational Failures: Day-2 operations become exponentially harder. Updating firewall rules, rotating keys for IPSec overlays, or expanding a subnet CIDR must all be coordinated across dozens of independent peerings. Because ownership is often fragmented across teams, an **Operational Failure** in one corner (for example, a missed route update or a firewall misconfiguration) can cause a partial outage that no single team has full visibility into. Mean-time-to-detect grows, and mean-time-to-recover suffers accordingly.

Dependencies and Third-Party Failures: A mesh reduces reliance on a single hub but increases reliance on multiple smaller constructs: peering connections, UDRs, NVAs, and VPNs. In hybrid deployments, "mesh to on-prem" often means many IPSec tunnels or private circuits, each a separate third-party dependency. Compared to a hub, where Direct Connect resiliency can be engineered with AWS's **High Resiliency** or **Maximum Resiliency Models**, a mesh spreads dependencies thinly, making them harder to manage consistently.

Application Failures: Meshes could introduce **asymmetric routing**: ingress traffic flows over one peering, while return traffic flows over another. Stateful firewalls or inspection devices often drop asymmetric flows, and telemetry systems may misreport performance because they only see one half of the conversation. Latency can also vary, as there is no central mechanism to enforce traffic engineering.

Cybersecurity Events: A mesh magnifies the risk of **policy inconsistency**. Every new peering must be secured with route tables, security groups/NSGs, and ACLs. Missing one rule creates a path for lateral movement. Distributed peering also complicates **service insertion**. For example, forcing all inter-VPC traffic through an **AWS Gateway Load Balancer** endpoint or an **Azure Firewall** requires **manual per-link route table modification**, which is operationally intensive.

Where a mesh **does** fit:

- Very small environments (two or three VPCs/VNets) with limited, well-defined flows.

- Latency-sensitive pairings where a direct connection is justified.

- Temporary migration bridges—if tightly controlled and well-documented.

Techniques to reduce fragility if a mesh is unavoidable:

1. **Constrain the graph.** Avoid full mesh; use partial meshes that connect only the minimum required pairs.

2. **Codify intent.** Express all peerings and routes as **infrastructure-as-code**, with automated checks for overlapping CIDRs or missing inspection paths.

3. **Centralize policy logic.** Even if the data plane is pairwise, keep route intent consistent by using shared route modules or templates.

4. **Ensure path symmetry.** Design routing so that traffic in both directions follows the same path (important for stateful firewalls and observability).

5. **Bound the blast radius.** Separate environments by account/subscription/project and tightly control who can create peerings.

6. **Prefer managed transit as you scale.** In AWS, move to **Transit Gateway** or **Cloud WAN**; in Azure, move to **Virtual WAN** or hub VNet with Azure Firewall/Linux forwarder; in GCP, use **Shared VPC with Cloud Router**.

Bottom Line: while a mesh may look resilient because there is no central node, the **operational and configuration blast radius grows quadratically**. At scale, it becomes a major source of **Deployment/Configuration Failures** and **Operational Failures**, while also complicating security and monitoring. Meshes should be kept **small, codified, and temporary**, with a transition plan to a managed transit domain for long-term resilience.

Hybrid Topologies

In the previous subsection, we examined the mesh model and saw how its promise of path diversity is often undermined by configuration fragility and operational complexity. Hybrid topologies bring the discussion back into the real world of most enterprises: cloud rarely exists in isolation. Applications, teams, and compliance constraints mean that on-premises and cloud must interoperate. This intersection is where hybrid architectures emerge—and where resilience must be engineered across two very different domains.

Most enterprises do not move directly from on-premises to all-cloud overnight. They operate in a **hybrid topology**, where workloads are distributed across on-premises data centers and one or more cloud providers. Hybrid designs are essential during migration phases, but many organizations remain hybrid indefinitely for regulatory, latency, or sovereignty reasons.

At the simplest level, hybrid is built with **VPN tunnels**—typically IPSec tunnels over the internet—that connect on-prem routers or firewalls to cloud gateways (AWS Virtual Private Gateway, Azure VPN Gateway, GCP Cloud VPN). VPNs are quick to deploy and flexible, but their resilience depends on commodity internet links, making them susceptible to congestion, packet loss, variable performance, or, like I like to say, susceptible to the internet weather.

Enterprises needing predictable connectivity typically adopt **private circuits**: AWS **Direct Connect (DX)**, Azure **ExpressRoute**, or GCP **Cloud Interconnect**. These extend on-premises networks directly into the cloud provider backbone, bypassing the internet. Unlike VPNs, the strength of private links lies in **constant latency and consistent performance**, combined with a secure, dedicated path where traffic does not traverse the internet and therefore is not affected by the unpredictability the internet path offers. They also **might offer higher throughput** than commodity broadband—but this depends on the bandwidth ordered.

AWS explicitly defines resiliency models for Direct Connect in its **Resiliency Toolkit** (`https://docs.aws.amazon.com/directconnect/latest/UserGuide/resiliency_toolkit.html`).

These include the following:

High Resiliency Model: Redundant DX connections at multiple locations with a single router.

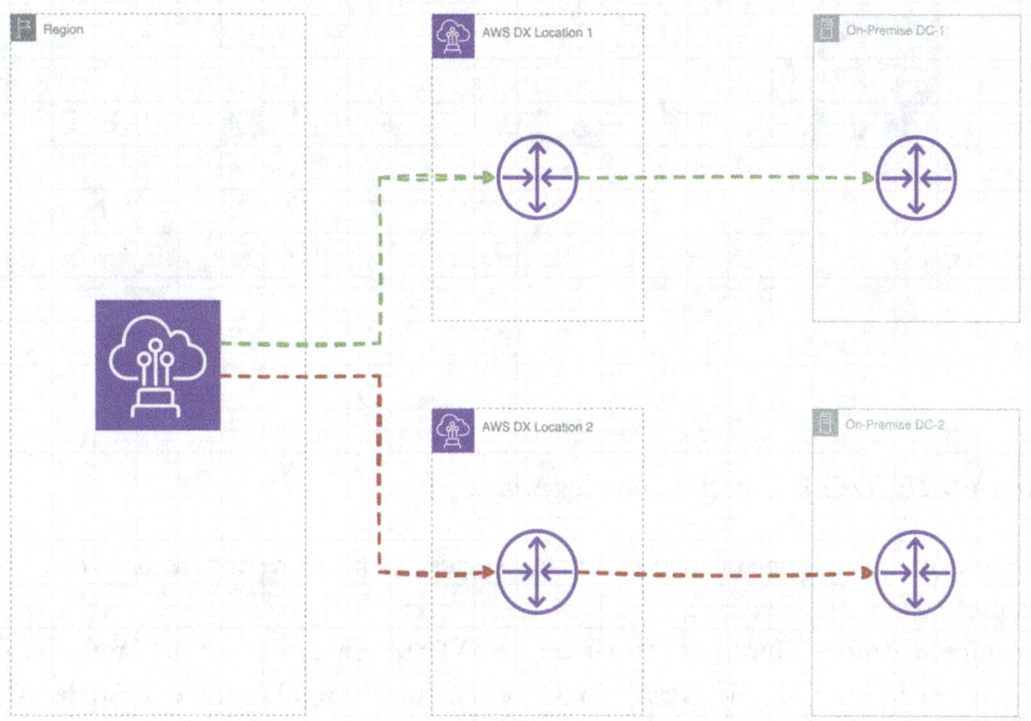

Figure 2-9. *DX High Resiliency Model*

Maximum Resiliency Model: redundant DX connections at multiple geographically diverse locations, with diverse carrier paths and redundant routers.

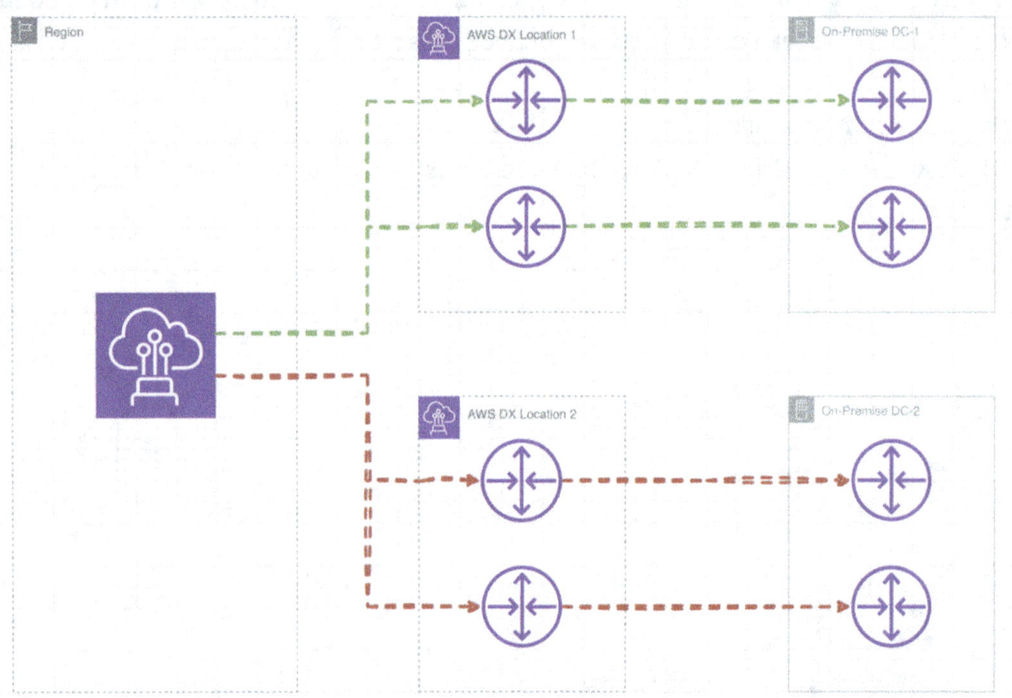

Figure 2-10. *DX Maximum Resiliency Model*

From a resilience perspective, hybrid topologies highlight several categories of failure:

Infrastructure Failures: Private circuits and VPNs terminate on physical routers, cross-connects, and edge devices. A **single CE (Customer Edge) router or a single circuit** represents a textbook **single point of failure** as defined in Chapter 1. Resilience requires redundancy across devices, facilities, and carriers. Just as important, enterprises need to measure **KPI patterns** during failover testing: how long does BGP take to converge? How does packet loss behave during switchover? Without testing, you cannot know how the network will behave when a link fails.

Availability Zone Failures: Hybrid topologies must ensure that traffic from on-prem does not funnel into a single AZ in the cloud. If all VPN tunnels or DX virtual interfaces terminate into one AZ, an AZ outage severs hybrid connectivity. Instead, gateways (Transit Gateways, Virtual Private Gateways, or equivalent) must be deployed across multiple AZs, and routing must be designed to automatically steer traffic around impaired zones.

Region Failures: Private connectivity is regional: DX, ExpressRoute, and Interconnect circuits land in specific metros tied to a region. If the region becomes impaired, connectivity is lost unless additional regions and locations are provisioned. AWS supports a feature called **Direct Connect SiteLink**, which allows enterprises to interconnect multiple on-premises data centers via the AWS backbone using their DX connections, bypassing the need for hairpinning traffic through a region. Resilient designs can also terminate DX connections in multiple regions or metros, enabling failover between them. In such designs, **BGP Communities, AS-Path Prepending, and traffic engineering policies** become essential to steer routing predictably. We will explore these mechanisms in more depth in Chapter 7.

Dependencies and Third-Party Failures: Hybrid connectivity relies on carriers, exchange providers, and colocation facilities. A single carrier outage has caused many enterprise-wide outages. Designing for diversity means ensuring truly independent providers and conduits—not just "two circuits" that actually share the same trench or carrier backbone.

Deployment and Configuration Failures: Hybrid routing depends on **BGP (Border Gateway Protocol)** policies. A misconfigured prefix advertisement, or accidentally advertising the default route, can create blackholes or traffic leaks that impact both cloud and on-premises. The blast radius of these failures is large because hybrid links are often the only bridge between environments. Infrastructure-as-code, staged route testing, and careful prefix filtering are essential.

Operational Failures: Hybrid deployments bring together two worlds: cloud teams and traditional networking teams. Lack of coordination often leads to outages—for example, the cloud team provisioning a new VPC attachment without informing the on-prem routing team. Operational resilience requires joint playbooks, shared monitoring, and coordinated change control across both domains.

Cybersecurity Events: Hybrid links are high-value targets: compromise gives attackers lateral movement into both environments. IPSec VPNs provide encryption; Direct Connect and ExpressRoute can use **MACsec (Media Access Control Security)** at Layer 2 for data confidentiality and integrity. Inspection VPCs or on-premises firewalls should enforce segmentation and policy on hybrid flows to avoid blind spots.

The strength of hybrid topologies lies in enabling gradual cloud adoption and ensuring workloads in both worlds interoperate. Their weakness lies in **external dependencies (carriers, facilities)** and the complexity of coordinating routing, failover, and operational processes. Hybrid resilience therefore depends on both **redundancy (routers, links, locations, carriers, regions)** and **discipline (BGP policy design, testing, monitoring, and joint operations)**.

The key lesson is that hybrid topologies extend resilience beyond cloud constructs. A well-architected hybrid network must plan for both **cloud fault domains** and **physical connectivity fault domains**. Without redundancy and continuous testing, hybrid links risk becoming the weakest part of the design.

Multi-region Topologies

In the previous subsection, we explored **hybrid topologies**, where resilience depends as much on physical circuits, carriers, and BGP design as on cloud constructs. The logical extension of hybrid thinking is **multi-region topologies**. If hybrid ensures workloads can span on-premises and one cloud region, multi-region ensures they can span *across cloud regions*. This is the ultimate test of resilience: surviving a complete **Region Failure** (Chapter 1), one of the rarest but most impactful events in the resilience analysis framework.

It is important to clarify that **multi-region is not the default answer to resilience**. For most workloads, multi-AZ deployments inside a single region already provide strong protection against infrastructure and AZ-level failures. Multi-region becomes relevant only when specific requirements demand it: regulatory or sovereignty constraints, ultra-low latency delivery across continents, or mission-critical systems where even the loss of a region is unacceptable. We will examine multi-region strategies and trade-offs in much greater detail in Chapter 6. Here, our focus is on positioning multi-region within the broader set of cloud topologies and understanding its resilience properties.

Multi-region designs come in two primary forms:

> **Active/Passive (Standby)**: Workloads are fully deployed in one region, with another region serving as a cold or warm standby. Failover requires DNS or routing changes and often a data synchronization step. This reduces cost but increases recovery time. Please note that Route 53 in the diagram is not part of the data path. It is included to represent name resolution, and for the purposes of this exercise, it has been positioned in this way to simplify the illustration.

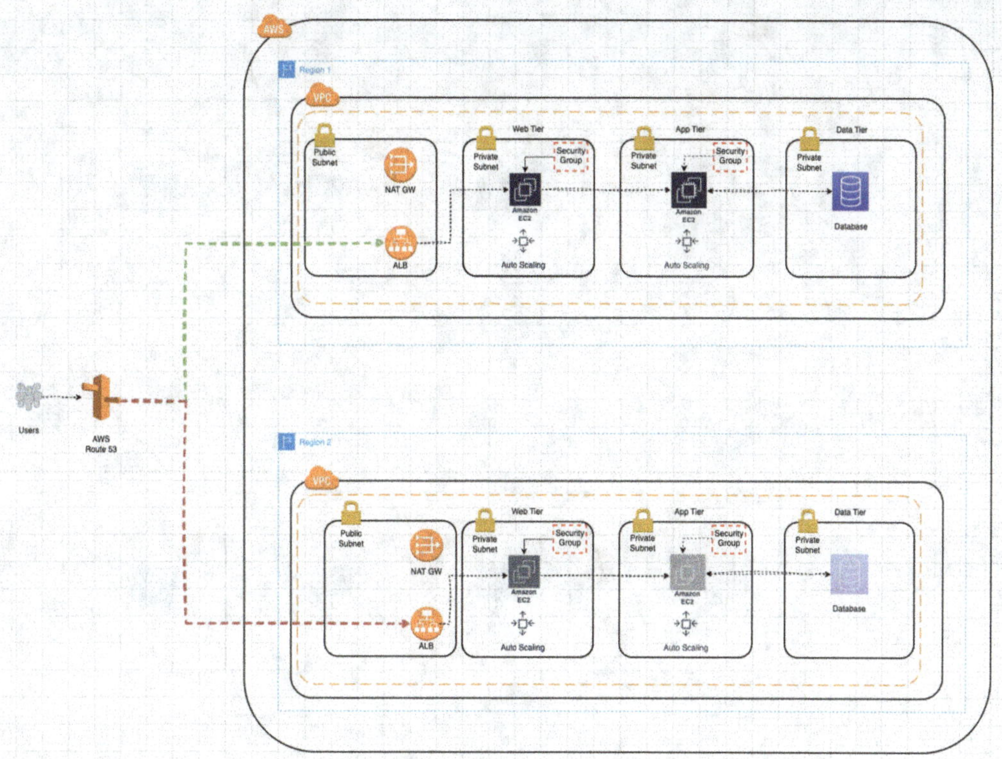

Figure 2-11. *Multi-region Active/Passive*

Active/Active: Workloads are deployed simultaneously in multiple regions, serving traffic concurrently. This minimizes recovery time but requires advanced routing control, data replication strategies, and conflict resolution mechanisms. Please note that Route 53 in the diagram is not part of the data path. It is included to represent name resolution, and for the purposes of this exercise, it has been positioned in this way to simplify the illustration.

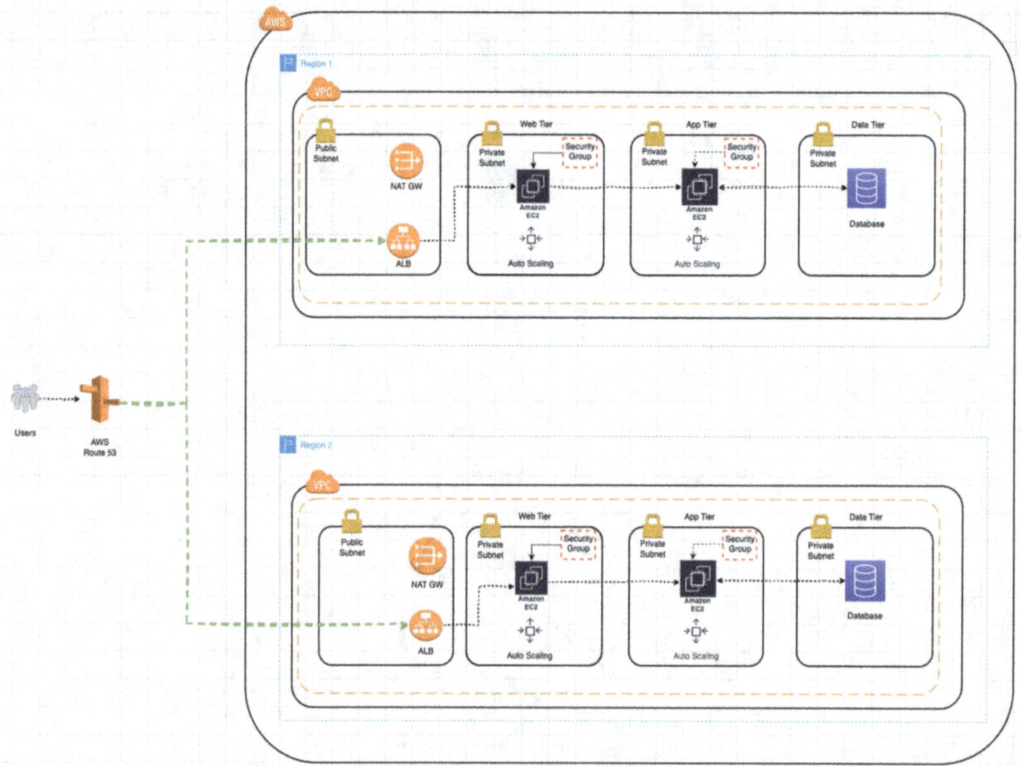

Figure 2-12. *Multi-region Active/Active*

From a resilience standpoint, multi-region topologies address the **Region Failure** category directly. But they also interact with other categories:

> **Infrastructure and AZ Failures**: Multi-region designs assume these are already mitigated within each region by deploying workloads across multiple AZs. Without strong intra-region resilience, multi-region adds complexity without solving the more common failure domains.
>
> **Dependencies and Third-Party Failures**: Multi-region connectivity often relies on inter-region cloud backbones and sometimes third-party interconnects. Dependencies must be evaluated carefully; a misconfigured global routing policy can blackhole traffic at a global scale.

Deployment and Configuration Failures: A misapplied change in one region can propagate inconsistencies across regions if infrastructure as code or automation pipelines do not enforce guardrails. The blast radius of configuration errors increases in multi-region because every region must stay in sync while also preserving isolation.

Operational Failures: Operating in multiple regions requires a higher level of organizational maturity: monitoring, playbooks, and on-call coverage must be duplicated. Without disciplined operations, the added surface area of a second region becomes a liability rather than a safeguard.

Cybersecurity Events: Multi-region designs reduce the risk of a single compromised region bringing down all workloads, but they expand the attack surface. Global routing, DNS failover mechanisms, and inter-region replication links all become targets that must be protected.

An additional factor unique to multi-region designs is traffic steering. When multiple regions can serve the same application, user traffic must be distributed intelligently. DNS, for example through AWS Route 53 latency-based or failover routing, is one of the most common mechanisms for this. Global Accelerator, or equivalent services, can also provide more deterministic routing with health checks. This naturally leads us into the next chapter, where we will examine the basics of DNS to set the stage for more advanced DNS resilience techniques. In the preceding diagram, Route 53 is included to represent traffic steering and name resolution, but it is not part of the application data path.

What's Next?

With multi-region, we close the exploration of **cloud network architectures and topologies**. In this chapter, we saw the progression from flat designs that maximize blast radius to hub-and-spoke architectures that balance segmentation and policy control, to mesh designs that promise path diversity but often create fragility, to hybrid topologies where physical connectivity resilience is paramount, and finally to multi-region topologies that address the most extreme failure category.

The central theme is clear: resilience is not an attribute of individual services but of the **topology as a whole**. How you arrange VPCs, VNets, hubs, spokes, peerings, and regions determines how failures propagate—or are contained.

In the next chapter, **DNS Fundamentals**, we will start setting the base concepts that will allow us to dive deep in Chapter 4, where we will connect these topologies to the mechanisms that direct user traffic into them. DNS becomes the bridge between resilience in the network and resilience as experienced by the user.

CHAPTER 3

DNS Fundamentals

In the previous chapter, we explored cloud network architectures and topologies. We saw how workloads are arranged into VPCs and VNets, how traffic flows between hubs and spokes, meshes, and hybrid environments, and how multi-region topologies push resilience to its highest level. But as those topologies scale, one question becomes unavoidable: **how do users and systems find the services they need inside those networks?**

No matter how resilient a topology is, if clients cannot locate endpoints, resilience collapses at the first hurdle. This is where the **Domain Name System (DNS)** becomes central. DNS is the invisible directory of the internet and the cloud, mapping human-readable names to IP addresses and service identifiers. Every connection begins with a name lookup, which means DNS is not only critical but also a potential single point of failure.

That is why this chapter is dedicated to DNS fundamentals. We will cover the building blocks of DNS: what it is, how resolution works, what records exist, how the hierarchy is structured, and the distinction between recursive and authoritative servers. Each section will not simply describe mechanics; it will highlight **resilience considerations specific to that part of DNS**. By the end of this chapter, you will not only understand DNS deeply but also know where and how DNS designs succeed—or fail—under stress.

To guide the reader, the chapter is organized as follows:

Section 3.1: What Is DNS?

We will explain the role of DNS in modern networking, why it was invented, and how it evolved from simple hosts files into the distributed, hierarchical system we use today. We will also discuss why DNS is considered a foundational element of cloud resilience.

© Cristian Critelli 2026

C. Critelli, *Cloud Networking and Resilience*, https://doi.org/10.1007/979-8-8688-2436-4_3

Section 3.2: The DNS Resolution Process.

We will walk step by step through how a client resolves a name, from stub resolver to recursive resolver, through root, TLD, and authoritative servers. At each stage, we will examine potential failure points and how caching and redundancy mitigate them.

Section 3.3: Types of DNS Records.

We will cover record types such as A, AAAA, CNAME, MX, TXT, and beyond. Each record type has different resilience implications, from multi-value A records for distribution to TXT records for authentication.

Section 3.4: DNS Hierarchy and Root Servers.

We will look at the DNS tree, from the root zone down to individual domains. We will highlight how the global root infrastructure provides resilience through Anycast and distribution, and why this matters for both enterprises and cloud providers.

Section 3.5: Recursive vs. Authoritative DNS.

We will differentiate between recursive resolvers (such as ISP resolvers or public DNS services) and authoritative servers (which actually hold the records). Each has unique resilience challenges, from recursive cache poisoning to authoritative outages.

Section 3.6: DNS in the Cloud Context.

Although fundamentals are the focus here, we will end this chapter by bridging to the cloud context. In the next chapter, we will analyze DNS techniques for resilience, where we connect these building blocks to topologies like hub-and-spoke, hybrid, and multi-region.

In short, this chapter takes DNS from **definition to design relevance**. Each section will include a dedicated discussion of resilience:

- What happens when this part of DNS fails?

- How do we design against those failures?

- What best practices emerge from decades of DNS operations, and how can we apply them in cloud contexts?

DNS may appear to be "just name resolution," but in practice it is one of the most important control planes in distributed systems. History has shown repeatedly—major DNS outages at large providers have disrupted entire swaths of the internet—that without resilient DNS, resilient networking is not achievable.

Section 3.1: What Is DNS?

When we concluded Chapter 2, we saw how resilient topologies can distribute workloads across fault domains—across Availability Zones, even across Regions. But a topology, no matter how carefully designed, cannot serve users if clients don't know *where to connect*. The very first question in resilience is not "can the workload recover?" but "can the client find the workload at all?" This is where the **Domain Name System (DNS)** enters the picture.

The role of DNS is deceptively simple: it translates a name like `www.example.com` into an IP address. Humans need memorable, portable names; machines need numerical identifiers. Without DNS, we would be forced to memorize and type something like *192.0.2.10*—or, in its binary representation, *11000000.00000000.00000010.00001010*. Imagine doing that across hundreds of services. DNS was created to solve this basic mismatch between human and machine needs.

But to dismiss DNS as "just a phonebook" is to miss its significance. It is a globally distributed, hierarchical, query-driven system—an **essential control plane** for the internet and for the cloud. The moment you type a URL, open an app, or launch a cloud service, the very first operation that occurs is a DNS lookup. If that lookup fails, nothing else matters: the most resilient topology in the world becomes invisible.

Domains, Zones, and Delegation

The DNS namespace is structured as a hierarchy, an inverted tree with the **root** at the top. Below the root are **Top-Level Domains (TLDs)** such as *.com*, *.org*, or country codes like *.uk*. Responsibility for each portion of the tree is divided into **zones**, managed by authoritative servers. A **domain** is simply a position in this namespace—for example, *example.com*—while a **zone** is the operational slice that contains records and is served by specific authoritative servers.

A crucial concept here is **delegation**. Delegation is how responsibility flows down the hierarchy. For example, the *.com* TLD name-servers do not contain the records for *example.com*. Instead, they delegate responsibility to the authoritative servers for *example.com*, telling resolvers, "If you want this name, go ask those servers." Delegation provides **isolation**: a misconfiguration in *example.com* will not impact *.org* or any other zone. It is also a resilience mechanism: authority can be spread across operators, avoiding global single points of failure.

DNS As a Distributed Database

Unlike a central phonebook or a single *HOSTS.TXT* file (how the ARPANET began), DNS is a **distributed database**. Each zone's authoritative servers manage only their slice of the namespace, and no single server has knowledge of the entire internet. Queries are resolved through referrals, with resolvers walking down the delegation chain from the root to the TLD to the domain's authoritative servers.

This distributed model is both a strength and a challenge. It means no one failure takes down the entire namespace—root servers are replicated worldwide, and each zone publishes multiple name servers—but it also means queries traverse multiple layers, introducing latency and more potential points of failure. In resilience terms, DNS is built on **redundancy and delegation**, but its **failure modes are unique**: stale caches, misconfigured records, or broken delegations can create outages that are subtle and far-reaching.

DNS As a Control Plane: AWS Route 53 Example

The distinction between **control plane** and **data plane**—introduced in Chapter 2 when we discussed SDN—is critical here. DNS is a control plane: it tells clients where to go, but it doesn't carry the application traffic itself. This makes it both powerful and fragile.

Take AWS **Route 53** as an example. Route 53 hosts authoritative DNS zones and answers client queries. If Route 53's control plane (the console or APIs) experiences an outage, you may not be able to add or edit records. But because DNS resolution operates from the **data plane**, existing queries still succeed. The design aligns with AWS's principle of **static stability**: applications should keep working even if control planes are impaired.

Best practice in Route 53 is to integrate **health checks** that probe endpoints directly. Instead of requiring operators to intervene during failures, DNS failover policies automatically remove unhealthy IPs from DNS responses. This ensures the DNS data plane continues to direct clients' queries correctly even if the control plane is unavailable. The lesson is simple but profound: resilience depends on designing DNS not just as a name system but as an *automated failover mechanism.*

DNS and Dynamic Cloud Workloads

In traditional enterprise networks, IP addresses were relatively stable. Applications could hard-code addresses or rely on DHCP reservations. In the cloud, this is no longer true. Virtual machines, containers, and serverless functions are **ephemeral**: they spin up and down on demand, often receiving new IP addresses when they do.

Elastic Load Balancers (ELBs) illustrate this perfectly. AWS **Application Load Balancers (ALB)** and **Network Load Balancers (NLB)** are fronted by DNS names. Their **IP addresses can change** when scaling events occur or when AWS shifts infrastructure. Customers are explicitly told not to hard-code ELB IPs but to always resolve the DNS name. Only in the case of **NLBs with static IP mode enabled** do addresses remain fixed. This reliance on DNS as the indirection layer—more precisely, as the **abstraction layer between services and underlying IPs**—is one reason DNS is indispensable in the cloud.

DNS in Troubleshooting: "The Internet Is Down"

One of the most common reports in IT is *"The internet is down."* As an escalation engineer, I learned quickly that this often translates to *"DNS resolution is failing."* A simple test can reveal this: if you can't reach `www.example.com`, try connecting directly to its IP address—assuming you know it. If the IP works but the name does not, the problem is DNS resolution, not the application or the network path.

This matters for resilience because it illustrates DNS's position in the failure chain. Users don't distinguish between "DNS resolution is broken" and "the service is down." To them, both look the same. Resilient DNS design is therefore not an afterthought; it is the first layer of user experience.

Why DNS Is Foundational for Cloud Resilience

DNS's true importance is that it enables **service discovery across fault domains**. Multi-AZ and multi-region designs (Chapter 2) rely on DNS to steer clients away from failures and toward healthy endpoints. Without DNS, these topologies cannot function. DNS is the connective tissue that ties resilience in infrastructure to resilience as *experienced by users*.

In short:

- DNS exists to decouple naming from addressing.

- It achieves resilience through delegation, distribution, and redundancy.

- In the cloud, it underpins every resilient topology, from a simple ALB failover to global active/active routing.

- It is also a frequent point of failure—and must be treated as a first-class citizen in resilience planning.

Now that we understand what DNS is, why it exists, and why it is central to cloud resilience, we can move on to how it works in practice. In the next section, we will trace the journey of a query through the DNS resolution process, analyzing each step and its potential failure points.

Section 3.2: The DNS Resolution Process in Depth

When a user types *www.cool-network.com* into their browser, the response feels almost magical. Within milliseconds, a website begins to load, an API responds, or a video stream starts. Yet behind that apparent simplicity lies a remarkably sophisticated distributed system. The **Domain Name System (DNS)** does not merely "look up" names; it executes a carefully orchestrated resolution process across multiple fault domains, relying on delegation, caching, and layers of authority to answer the question: *Where should I send this traffic?*

For engineers designing resilient cloud networks, understanding this process in detail is not optional. Resolution is the very first step of resilience. Like I mentioned before, no matter how well a service is designed across **Availability Zones (AZs)** or **Regions**, if the client cannot discover its endpoint, the service is effectively down. DNS resolution, therefore, is both a foundation of reliability and one of its greatest vulnerabilities.

In this section, we will walk step by step through the DNS resolution process: from stub resolver to recursive resolver, from root servers to **Top-Level Domain (TLD)** servers, and finally to the authoritative servers that hold the records. At each stage, we will explore how resilience is designed in, how it can fail, and what real-world events teach us about the fragility and strength of this system.

From Flat Files to Distributed Resolution

Resolution was not always this complex. In the earliest days of ARPANET, name-to-address mappings were stored in a single file called *HOSTS.TXT*. Every host periodically downloaded this file from a central server at Stanford Research Institute.

At first, this worked. With a few hundred machines, the file was manageable. But as networks expanded, the limitations became obvious. Updates propagated slowly, creating inconsistencies across the network. Collisions between hostnames were frequent. And most importantly, resilience was nonexistent: if the master file became corrupted or the distribution server went offline, the entire network lost name resolution.

In today's terminology, *HOSTS.TXT* was a catastrophic **single point of failure**—an example of an **Infrastructure Failure** from Chapter 1's categories. A single administrative or operational mistake could bring the network to a halt.

The introduction of DNS in 1983 solved these problems by decentralizing resolution. Instead of one flat file, DNS introduced a hierarchical, distributed model. Authority could be delegated down the tree: from the root to the TLD to individual domains. Responsibility was fragmented, and with it, resilience improved. A misconfiguration in *cool-network.com* would no longer impact *.org*. Outages became compartmentalized.

This shift—away from centralized fragility and toward distributed delegation—is the essence of DNS's resilience story. To appreciate it fully, we must examine how resolution unfolds in practice. Here is a diagram that will help you go through the below steps.

As shown in Figure 3-1, DNS resolution begins with the stub resolver querying a recursive resolver, which then follows the DNS hierarchy through the root, TLD, and authoritative name servers before returning the final answer to the client.

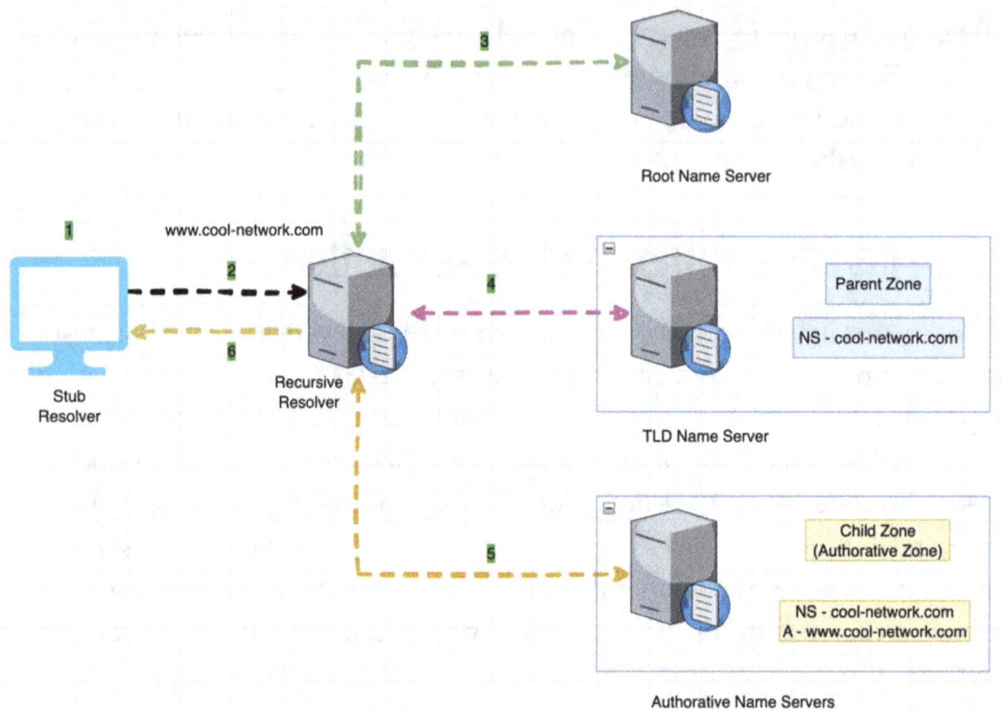

Figure 3-1. *DNS Resolution Process*

Step One: The Stub Resolver

Every DNS query begins at the **stub resolver**, a lightweight component embedded in the operating system of every device: laptop, smartphone, server, or IoT sensor.

When an application requests a connection to `www.cool-network.com`, the stub resolver first checks its **local cache**. If an answer exists and has not expired, resolution completes instantly. The user experiences no delay, no external queries, and—most importantly—no dependency on upstream infrastructure.

This caching mechanism is a powerful resilience feature. It shields users from transient upstream failures. If the authoritative servers for *cool-network.com* are temporarily offline, a cached answer may allow users to continue accessing the service uninterrupted.

But caches can also be dangerous. If the cached entry points to an unhealthy endpoint—for instance, an IP address that no longer belongs to the load balancer—clients continue attempting connections until the **Time to Live (TTL)** expires. In resilience terms, this creates an **Application Failure**: the application is alive, but DNS directs traffic to a dead end. Cache poisoning attacks exploit this weakness, inserting false answers into local caches that persist long enough to cause damage.

Even at this first stage, DNS resolution illustrates resilience trade-offs: caching improves availability but risks staleness; short TTLs improve agility but increase dependency on upstream servers. So how do we solve this? The answer is not immediate, but keep this question in mind. Later in this chapter, and especially in the next one, we will return to it and see how resilience is achieved in practice.

Step Two: The Recursive Resolver

If the stub resolver lacks an answer, it forwards the query to a **recursive resolver**. Here the real work begins.

The recursive resolver is responsible for walking the DNS hierarchy on behalf of the client. It queries the root, the TLD, and eventually the authoritative servers, collecting referrals along the way until it finds the answer. Once found, it caches the result and returns it to the stub resolver.

Recursive resolvers are provided in many forms:

- ISPs run them for customers.

- Enterprises deploy them internally for policy enforcement.

- Public providers like Google DNS (8.8.8.8), Cloudflare (1.1.1.1), and Quad9 (9.9.9.9) offer globally distributed resolvers optimized for speed and resilience.

Most modern resolvers are deployed with **Anycast**, meaning the same IP address is advertised from multiple data centers around the globe. Clients are routed to the nearest healthy node, improving latency and insulating users from localized failures.

Yet recursive resolvers are also one of the most fragile dependencies in DNS. If your chosen resolver fails—due to misconfiguration, overload, or attack—your entire resolution chain collapses, even if the authoritative servers are healthy. This is a textbook **Dependency and Third-Party Failure**.

A dramatic example occurred in June 2019. A small ISP leaked incorrect **Border Gateway Protocol (BGP)** routes, which were accepted and propagated by Verizon. The leak redirected massive volumes of internet traffic through a misconfigured network with insufficient capacity. Among the affected services was Cloudflare, whose resolvers suddenly became unreachable. For millions of users, DNS resolution stopped cold. From the outside, it appeared as if "the internet was down." In reality, this was a routing failure, not a DNS failure—but because DNS is the first step in almost every connection, the symptom was universal.

The lesson is clear: resilience at the recursive layer requires diversity. Enterprises should configure multiple resolvers from different providers, ensuring that a single dependency failure does not cascade into total outage.

Step Three: The Root Servers

If the recursive resolver has no cached entry, it begins at the very top of the hierarchy: the **root servers**.

The root is the anchor of DNS. There are 13 named root server identities, labeled A through M, each operated by independent organizations. But they are not thirteen machines. Each identity is replicated globally across hundreds of sites, deployed with Anycast routing. When a resolver queries the root, it is automatically directed to the nearest healthy instance.

When asked about `www.cool-network.com`, the root does not return an IP address. Instead, it provides a **referral**: "I don't know this name, but here are the authoritative servers for the *.com* TLD. Ask them."

This referral mechanism illustrates the core principle of DNS: delegation. No single server knows everything, but each server knows where to point the resolver next. Authority is compartmentalized, and with it, resilience improves.

The design of the root is deliberately robust. Attacks against the root have occurred—most notably the 2002 and 2007 DDoS attempts—but never caused a full outage. The combination of Anycast distribution, independent operators, and global replication makes the root one of the most resilient layers of the internet.

Still, fragility exists. If a resolver is unable to reach the root—for example, due to national firewalling, routing errors, or infrastructure partitioning—resolution fails immediately. This is an **Infrastructure Failure** cascading into **Application Failures**: services remain healthy but unreachable.

Step Four: TLD Servers

The next stop is the authoritative servers for the relevant **Top-Level Domain (TLD)**. In our example, the root directs the resolver to the *.com* TLD servers.

The TLD servers do not contain the answer for `www.cool-network.com`. Instead, they provide another referral: "The authoritative servers for *cool-network.com* are located here."

Again, delegation both scales and isolates. If the *.com* servers are unavailable, all .com domains are impacted, but *.org* or *.net* remain unaffected. Failures are contained within fault domains.

But misconfigurations at this layer can have a severe impact. If **Name Server (NS)** records for a domain are incorrect or missing, resolution fails completely for that domain. NS records specify which servers are authoritative for a domain. We will explore them in more detail in the next section, but here it is enough to say that they are the glue holding delegation together. Misconfigured NS records are a classic **Configuration Failure**. Unlike infrastructure outages, which may be masked by caching, configuration errors persist until corrected.

Steps Five and Six: Authoritative Servers

Finally, the resolver reaches the **authoritative servers** for the target domain. These are the sources of truth. They contain the actual records: A records mapping names to IPv4 addresses, AAAA records to IPv6, MX records for mail, and CNAMEs for aliases.

For `www.cool-network.com`, the authoritative server might respond: `www.cool-network.com` ➤ *1.2.3.4* The recursive resolver caches this answer and returns it to the stub resolver (step 6), and the client connects to the service.

From the user's perspective, the process is invisible. From the engineer's perspective, the entire hierarchy has just been traversed successfully; a distributed system spanning continents has just cooperated to answer a single query.

But authoritative servers are also where most outages occur. This is where configuration errors, expired domains, or provider outages manifest most acutely.

Before diving into case studies, it is worth setting the stage. The resolution chain is robust by design, but it is not immune to failure. Outages in recent years have shown us exactly how resolution can collapse in practice. They also provide some of the most vivid illustrations of resilience—of how containing blast radius and embracing failure can allow systems to continue functioning even under stress.

Case Study: The 2016 Dyn DDoS

Dyn was a major DNS provider operating authoritative servers for many large websites. On October 21, 2016, Dyn was targeted by a massive Distributed Denial of Service (DDoS) attack launched by the Mirai botnet. Mirai had compromised hundreds of thousands of poorly secured IoT devices—cameras, routers, DVRs—turning them into a coordinated flood of traffic.

The attack generated unprecedented volumes of traffic, overwhelming Dyn's infrastructure. For hours, major websites including Twitter, GitHub, Reddit, Netflix, and Spotify were unreachable. Not because their servers were down, but because their names could not be resolved. DNS had become the single point of failure.

From a resilience perspective, this was a **Cybersecurity Event**, and it raised the larger issue of **cyber resilience**. It also demonstrated a **Dependency and Third-Party Failure**. Enterprises had placed all their DNS with one provider: Dyn. When Dyn fell, so did they.

What could have been done differently? Secondary DNS providers could have mitigated the blast radius. Shorter TTLs could have improved failover responsiveness. More fundamentally, the event demonstrated that DNS must be treated as critical infrastructure. It is not a commodity; it is a control plane dependency. Enterprises learned painfully that DNS resilience cannot be outsourced without conscious design.

Case Study: Cloudflare 2019 Outage

On July 2, 2019, Cloudflare experienced a global outage lasting approximately 30 minutes. The cause was not a DDoS, but a software deployment. A new Web Application Firewall (WAF) rule containing a poorly optimized regular expression was deployed globally. The regex consumed excessive CPU resources across Cloudflare's edge servers, leading to saturation.

The result was widespread HTTP 502 errors. A 502 error means a server acting as a gateway or proxy received an invalid response from an upstream server. In this case, the edge machines could not even reach their own backend processes, collapsing the ability to answer user requests.

From a resilience perspective, this was a **Deployment and Configuration Failure**. The key insight was not simply "test better," but that failure must be embraced and its blast radius contained. A single rule should never have been able to cripple the entire global fleet. Cloudflare's response included implementing stricter canary release processes and building better "kill switches" to disable faulty rules instantly. These are lessons in operational resilience: design so that failure is expected, contained, and survivable.

Case Study: AWS Route 53 2019 DDoS

In late 2019, AWS Route 53 experienced an impairment in the **us-east-1 Region** due to a large-scale DDoS attack. The control plane—used for creating and managing records—was degraded. However, the **data plane continued serving existing DNS queries without interruption**.

This demonstrated the AWS principle of **static stability**. Even if the control plane is impaired, the system is designed to keep operating. Queries were answered correctly, and applications continued functioning, even though administrators could not make changes. This assumed the infrastructure architects built on AWS was leveraging the principle of static stability, of course. If not, and if they had to modify DNS records manually, their applications would have been affected.

The resilience comes from automation and data-plane health checks, not manual intervention. Best practice is to design DNS failover with health checks that operate independently of the control plane, ensuring applications continue to resolve without operator action.

From a resilience perspective, this was an **Infrastructure Failure** absorbed by resilient design. The blast radius was contained, and users were unaffected.

Caching, TTLs, and Trade-Offs

Throughout the resolution process, caching plays a central role. Each resolver caches answers for the duration of the TTL specified in the DNS record. This reduces the sload on authoritative servers and speeds up queries.

But TTLs are also resilience levers. Short TTLs improve agility: if an endpoint fails, updating DNS quickly propagates. But short TTLs also increase dependency on upstream servers, raising the risk of failure if authorities are down. Long TTLs improve stability, insulating clients from outages, but risk staleness—directing users to dead endpoints during failovers.

Finding balance is the art of resilience, but it is also always a trade-off. Too short, and you risk fragility; too long, and you risk inflexibility.

DNS in the Cloud

In cloud environments, DNS resolution is even more critical. Endpoints are dynamic. AWS **Application Load Balancers (ALBs)** and **Network Load Balancers (NLBs)** may change IP addresses as infrastructure scales. AWS explicitly warns customers not to hard-code IPs but to use DNS names instead. Only NLBs with static IP mode enabled are exceptions.

At a global scale, DNS also enables multi-region routing. Services like AWS Route 53 offer latency-based routing and failover policies that depend entirely on DNS responses. Here, DNS is not just a directory; it is the traffic controller of resilience.

Without reliable resolution, even the most carefully designed multi-AZ or multi-region topology is affected.

Troubleshooting Resolution

For engineers, troubleshooting DNS often begins with a simple question: *"Can you reach the service by IP?"* If yes, the problem is DNS, not the application.

Tools like dig +trace allow step-by-step observation of the resolution process. One can see the referral from the root, the referral from the TLD, and the authoritative answer. Walking the chain reveals precisely where the failure lies.

As an escalation engineer, I often encountered the phrase "the internet is down." In reality, it was almost always DNS. A misconfigured delegation, an expired domain, a poisoned cache—these are invisible to users but devastating in effect. That is why observability into the resolution path is therefore not optional for resilience; it is mandatory.

Summary

The DNS resolution process is more than a lookup. It is a distributed choreography involving stub resolvers, recursive resolvers, root servers, TLD servers, and authoritative servers. Each stage is a potential point of failure but also a point of resilience. Delegation, caching, and redundancy are what make the system robust.

Real-world outages—from the 2016 Dyn DDoS to the 2019 Cloudflare regex bug to the 2019 Route 53 impairment—remind us that DNS is fragile when mismanaged and resilient when designed consciously. These cases show us how failure must be contained, the blast radius minimized, and automation leveraged to sustain operations so that users continue without feeling affected.

So how do we solve the inherent trade-offs in caching, TTLs, and delegation? The answer lies in the details of record types, DNS policies, and resilient architectures. That is where we now turn.

Section 3.3: The DNS Data Model—Records and Zones

In the previous section, we traced how a DNS query travels across the global hierarchy—from stub resolvers to recursive resolvers, through the root servers, into the Top-Level Domain (TLD) servers, and finally down to the authoritative servers. That description gave us the choreography—the sequence of interactions that must occur before a name can be translated into an address.

But choreography alone does not explain the story. DNS resolution is only useful if there is meaningful data waiting at the end of the chain. The actual answers live in DNS records. These records are the atomic units of DNS. They are small, deceptively simple lines of text that tell the world where services live, which servers should handle mail, which machines are authoritative for a domain, or which Certificate Authorities (CAs) are permitted to issue TLS certificates. On their own they may look trivial, but collectively they are among the most consequential configuration objects in networking. A misplaced record can render a service invisible, direct millions of queries to a dead end, or block the renewal of certificates, crippling secure connections.

Understanding DNS records in detail is therefore critical to building resilience. Every record type embodies both functionality and fragility. Each solves a problem, but each also opens new avenues for failure. In this section, we will take a deep dive into the major record types—A, AAAA, CNAME, MX, NS, TXT, PTR, SRV, and CAA—examining what they do, why they exist, how they fail, and how to design them for resilience. Along the way, we will explore real-world incidents where records were the weak link in otherwise robust infrastructures.

A Records: IPv4's Fundamental Construct

The most basic DNS record is the A record, short for "Address." It maps a hostname to an IPv4 address. If you resolve *www.cool-network.com* and receive 1.2.3.4, that mapping was created by an A record. This may appear trivial, but the A record is the fundamental construct of the entire system. Without it, a name has nowhere to go.

An A record represents a 32-bit IPv4 address. Written in dotted decimal form, the address is easy enough to parse, but underneath it is just binary: 1.2.3.4 translates to 00000001.00000010.00000011.00000100. This binary is what routers and operating systems actually use when forwarding packets. DNS is a layer of indirection that spares humans from memorizing these binary or decimal numbers.

From a resilience standpoint, A records illustrate the tension between stability and agility. A record's values are cached for the duration of their Time to Live (TTL). A long TTL improves efficiency and shields clients from transient upstream outages, but it risks staleness: if the service's IP changes, users may continue pointing to a dead address until caches expire. A short TTL improves agility by enabling rapid failover, but it increases dependency on authoritative availability. This is the same question we raised in Section 3.2—*which one should you pick?*—and it remains one of the hardest resilience trade-offs to balance.

A vivid case study comes from an e-commerce giant in 2012. During a migration, its load balancer IPs changed. DNS was updated promptly, but many of the company's applications had hard-coded the old IP addresses instead of resolving names dynamically. For hours, those applications continued sending traffic to addresses that no longer accepted connections. From the perspective of DNS, everything was functioning correctly—the A records were valid and propagated. The outage was entirely self-inflicted by bypassing DNS indirection. This incident became an industry proverb: DNS is only resilient if you actually use it.

AAAA Records: IPv6 in Action

As the internet grew and IPv4 addresses began to run out, the need for a larger address space drove the introduction of IPv6. DNS adapted with the AAAA record, which maps hostnames to 128-bit IPv6 addresses. For example, where the A record points to something like 1.2.3.4, an AAAA record might return 2001:db8:85a3::8a2e:370:7334.

The size of IPv6 addresses makes them impossible to manage without DNS. Written in hexadecimal, they can already be daunting; in binary, they are nearly incomprehensible strings of digits. DNS is not just a convenience here—it is a necessity.

From a resilience perspective, AAAA records introduce both opportunities and risks. They create diversity: if clients and applications support dual-stack (both IPv4 and IPv6), they can fail over between protocols. An IPv4 outage does not necessarily impact IPv6, and vice versa. This is an additional fault domain. At the same time, AAAA records double the surface area for misconfiguration. Many enterprises deploy IPv6 inconsistently, leaving some services unreachable via IPv6 even though they work via IPv4. Clients that prefer IPv6 may silently fail in these cases.

In 2019, a SaaS provider enabled AAAA records for its global infrastructure. IPv4 routing was stable, but IPv6 advertisements in parts of Europe were misconfigured, leading to black-holing of traffic. Dual-stack clients defaulted to IPv6 and failed, while IPv4-only clients saw no issue. The monitoring systems, unfortunately, were IPv4-only. For hours, operators saw all green dashboards while customers complained of outages. The lesson was stark: publishing AAAA records means you are now responsible for monitoring and validating IPv6 paths just as carefully as IPv4. Resilience cannot be one-sided. This is also an example of grey failures, where your dashboard still shows services as green, but in reality, the users cannot use such services.

CNAME Records: Aliases and Abstraction

The CNAME (Canonical Name) record introduces indirection. It does not provide an address itself but points one name to another. For instance, api.cool-network.com might be a CNAME for service.cool-network.com, which finally resolves via an A record to 1.2.3.4.

CNAMEs are essential in cloud networking. When AWS creates an Application Load Balancer (ALB), it exposes a DNS name such as my-alb-my-region.elb.amazonaws.com. Customers alias their own domain to that name with a CNAME. CDNs rely heavily on this pattern: cdn.cool-network.com might point via CNAME to a provider-controlled domain that changes IP addresses frequently as infrastructure scales. The abstraction allows providers to reconfigure their infrastructure without exposing those changes directly to customers.

But CNAMEs are double-edged. Each additional indirection adds latency and another opportunity for failure. Long chains of CNAMEs can exceed resolver depth limits, resulting in failures. A misconfigured CNAME pointing to a retired or nonexistent name is effectively a dead end. And because CNAMEs are often used to point to third-party services, they transfer dependency: your resilience is now partially determined by the provider's health.

In 2020, a major CDN outage illustrated this vividly. An operator accidentally introduced a loop in its CNAME configuration: cdn1.cool-network.com pointed to cdn2.cool-network.com, which pointed back to cdn1.cool-network.com. Recursive resolvers dutifully followed the chain until they exceeded their maximum depth, at which point they returned errors. For users, media assets on thousands of websites failed to load worldwide. The fragility was not in infrastructure capacity or routing; it was a simple CNAME misconfiguration, amplified by the recursive nature of resolution.

MX Records: The Lifeline of Email

If A and AAAA records connect users to services, the MX (Mail Exchange) record connects mail servers to each other. It specifies which servers should accept email for a domain. Without MX records, mail has nowhere to go.

An MX record consists of a domain name and a priority. For example:

cool-network.com MX 10 mail1.cool-network.com
cool-network.com MX 20 mail2.backup-mail.net

Here, mail servers try mail1 first, and if it is unavailable, they fall back to mail2. The priorities create ordered redundancy.

MX records are particularly sensitive to resilience. A single MX record pointing to a dead host results in total mail loss. Multiple MX records add resilience, but only if the backup servers are genuinely operational. All too often, enterprises treat backups as placeholders rather than live systems. Worse, backup MX servers are sometimes hosted by third parties with weaker security, exposing opportunities for attackers to intercept or tamper with mail.

A dramatic example occurred in 2016 when a Fortune 500 company accidentally deleted its primary MX record during a DNS cleanup. Mail servers dutifully attempted delivery to the backup MX, but that server was a non-production system configured only for testing. It could not accept the load, and mail bounced globally. For nearly 24 hours, employees could not send or receive email. The outage was not in the mail servers themselves—they were perfectly healthy—but in the DNS records that directed traffic. This was a textbook configuration failure, with resilience undone by a single misapplied change.

The lesson is simple: redundancy on paper is not resilience in practice. Backup MX servers and every architecture out there must be live, tested, and secured, or they are worse than useless. Without testing, you will never know if the resilience of your architecture will actually sustain a service impairment.

NS Records: The Glue of Delegation

While A and MX records map services, NS (Name Server) records determine who is authoritative for a domain. They are the glue of delegation.

If you query the *.com* TLD for cool-network.com, it will return a set of NS records—perhaps ns1.provider.net and ns2.provider.net. These tell the resolver where to go next. Without NS records, delegation collapses.

NS records are unique in that they appear both in the child zone (the domain itself) and in the parent zone (the TLD). If the NS records in those two places disagree, resolution becomes unstable. Additionally, if the NS servers reside inside the domain they are authoritative for (e.g., ns1.cool-network.com), the parent zone must publish glue records—A or AAAA records that provide the IP addresses of those name servers. Without glue, resolution loops infinitely: to find ns1, you must resolve cool-network.com, but to resolve cool-network.com, you need ns1.

Resilience requires distributing NS servers across different networks and geographic locations. If all NS servers reside in one data center or one Availability Zone, an outage there makes the domain unreachable.

In 2021, a SaaS provider suffered intermittent outages because half its NS records still pointed to a decommissioned DNS host. Recursive resolvers alternated between the healthy and unhealthy NS entries. Users experienced flapping resolution: sometimes the site loaded instantly and sometimes it timed out. This was worse than a clean outage because it was unpredictable. The incident illustrates the fragility of NS misconfigurations: they are not always binary failures but often degrade service into inconsistency, which is far more damaging to user trust.

TXT Records: Flexibility, Authentication, and Risk

The TXT (Text) record was originally intended for free-form descriptive text, but it has since become one of the most heavily used record types in modern DNS. Its flexibility has made it the vehicle for many authentication and verification systems.

TXT records underpin email authentication through SPF (Sender Policy Framework), which specifies which servers are authorized to send mail on behalf of a domain; DKIM (DomainKeys Identified Mail), which publishes public keys for verifying message signatures; and DMARC (Domain-based Message Authentication,

Reporting and Conformance), which defines how receiving mail servers should handle unauthenticated mail. TXT records are also widely used for domain ownership verification, such as proving to a cloud provider or a certificate authority that you control a domain.

Resilience risks abound. A single syntax error in an SPF record can invalidate the entire policy, causing receiving servers to reject all mail. DKIM records that are too long for resolvers to handle can break validation. TXT records often tie directly to third-party dependencies—for instance, when you integrate with a SaaS provider that requires specific verification strings. If the provider changes its requirements and you fail to update, services silently fail.

In 2018, a European bank updated its SPF record to restrict outbound mail servers. A minor syntax mistake rendered the record invalid. Receiving servers worldwide treated all mail as unauthorized and rejected it. For several hours, employees were unable to communicate with customers by email. This was a configuration failure in its purest form: a single misplaced character in a TXT record collapsed a critical communication channel.

The lesson is that TXT records, while flexible, are not forgiving. They are security and resilience controls disguised as text.

PTR Records: Reverse DNS

The PTR (Pointer) record performs the reverse of an A record. Instead of mapping a name to an address, it maps an address back to a name. For example, 1.2.3.4 might map back to `www.cool-network.com`. These records live in special reverse-mapping domains such as in-addr.arpa.

PTR records are particularly important for mail servers. Many receiving servers reject connections from IPs without valid reverse DNS entries as a defense against spam. Missing PTR records may not break web traffic, but they quietly sabotage email deliverability.

From a resilience perspective, PTR records often represent operational failures. Administrators set up new mail servers but forget to configure reverse DNS, leading to silent rejections. The result is maddening for operators: servers show green, connections succeed, but mail disappears downstream.

SRV Records: Service Discovery

The SRV (Service Locator) record allows services to advertise not only their hostname but also the port and protocol on which they operate. A typical example might be:

sip.tcp.cool-network.com SRV 10 60 5060 sip1.cool-network.com

This indicates that the SIP service for cool-network.com runs over TCP on port 5060 at the host sip1.

SRV records are widely used in VoIP and in DNS-based service discovery frameworks. They provide resilience by allowing multiple targets with priorities and weights, enabling clients to fail over smoothly. But misconfigured SRV records can direct clients to the wrong port or a dead server, creating outages that are difficult to diagnose because the DNS resolution itself appears to succeed.

CAA Records: Controlling Certificate Authorities

The CAA (Certificate Authority Authorization) record is a newer addition to DNS. It specifies which Certificate Authorities are permitted to issue TLS certificates for a domain. For instance:

cool-network.com CAA 0 issue "letsencrypt.org"

This means only Let's Encrypt may issue certificates for the domain.

CAA records enhance security, but misconfigurations can have resilience consequences. If the allowed CA is incorrect or incomplete, legitimate certificates cannot be renewed. When certificates expire, HTTPS traffic fails. What looks like an application outage is actually a DNS record error.

In 2020, a SaaS provider inadvertently restricted its CAA record to exclude its chosen CA. When renewal time came, certificates could not be issued. Overnight, HTTPS endpoints began failing. The outage was not in infrastructure but in a DNS misconfiguration that blocked certificate issuance.

Bringing It Together

Each record type plays a unique role, but together they form the backbone of internet resilience. A records point to services, AAAA records extend them to IPv6, CNAMEs provide abstraction, MX ensures email continuity, NS holds delegation together, TXT governs authentication and verification, PTR secures mail reputation, SRV supports discovery, and CAA enforces certificate security.

From a resilience lens, every record type is a potential fault domain. A stale A record directs users to a dead service. An inconsistent NS set creates intermittent failures. A malformed SPF TXT entry silences an organization's mail. An over-restrictive CAA record blocks certificate renewal. The root cause of many high-profile outages has not been failing hardware or overwhelmed servers, but fragile records.

So, at the end of the section, I would like to say that, in my opinion, DNS records are the "DNA" of resilience. They are not "just text files," but the instructions that determine whether services are reachable, secure, and robust. They must be engineered, tested, and monitored with the same rigor as servers, routers, and cloud networks.

In the next section, we will zoom out from the records themselves to the larger DNS hierarchy and root servers. There we will examine how records are organized globally, how authority is delegated at each level, and how the system is made robust against failures that could otherwise undermine the entire internet.

Section 3.4: DNS Hierarchy and Root Infrastructure

In the previous section, we examined individual DNS record types—the atomic data that directs clients to services. But records alone do not ensure resolution. What truly gives DNS its resilience is its **hierarchy**: the tree structure that dictates how responsibility is delegated, where authority resides, and how queries are answered across fault domains. Understanding this hierarchy is crucial for networking and resilience, because failures at different levels propagate differently.

The DNS Tree Structure

The DNS namespace is organized as an **inverted tree**. At the very top sits the **root zone**, represented by a dot in fully qualified domain names (FQDNs). Below the root are **Top-Level Domains (TLDs)** such as .com, .org, .net, or country-code TLDs like .uk or .jp. Each TLD may delegate authority further to second-level domains such as cool-network. com, and those domains can delegate subdomains like api.cool-network.com.

As shown in Figure 3-2, the DNS namespace is organized as an inverted hierarchical tree, starting at the root zone and delegating authority downward to top-level domains, second-level domains, and subdomains.

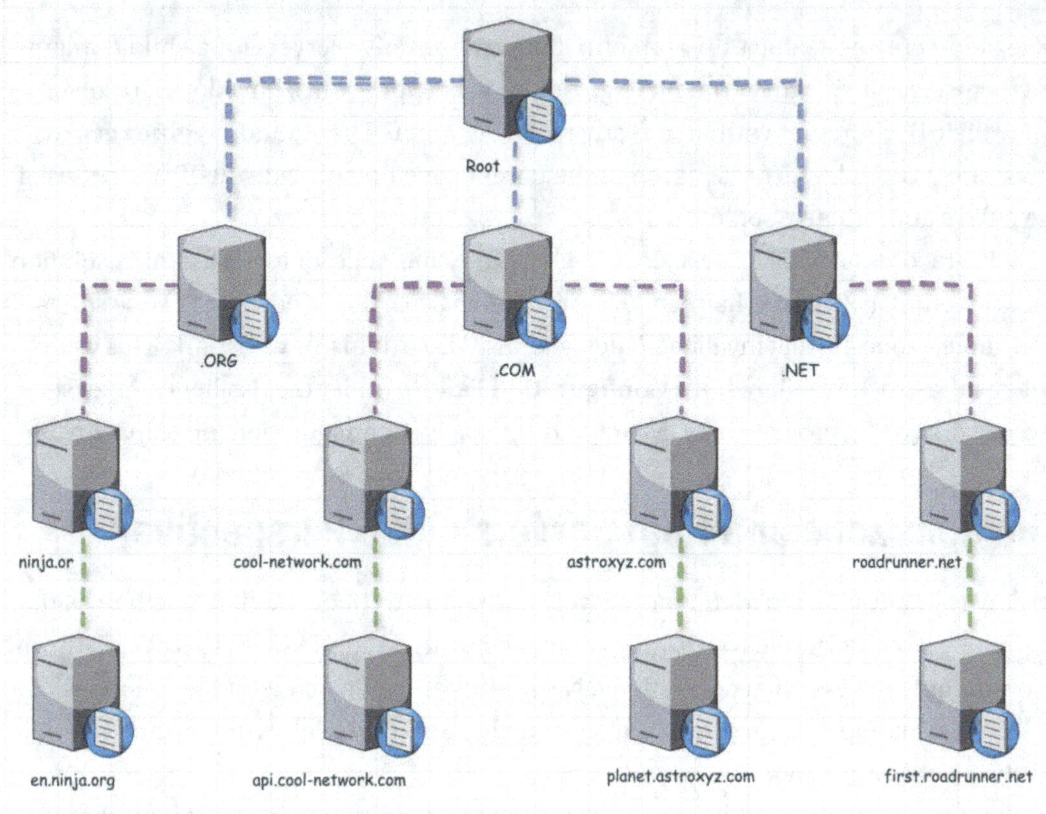

Figure 3-2. *DNS Tree Structure*

The distinction between a **domain** and a **zone** is essential. A domain is simply a position in the namespace, while a zone is an operational portion of that namespace managed by authoritative servers. A single zone may cover one or many domains, depending on delegation.

Authority flows through the tree via **delegation**. Parent zones do not contain all records for their children; instead, they point to authoritative name servers for those children using **NS (Name Server) records**. This delegation is what allows DNS to scale globally and to contain failures. A misconfiguration in one zone, such as cool-network. com, does not affect .org or .net.

Delegation and Glue

Delegation creates a bootstrap problem: if the authoritative servers for a child domain are themselves inside that domain (e.g., ns1.cool-network.com), how does a resolver know their IP addresses without already resolving them? The solution is **glue records**. These are A or AAAA records placed in the parent zone that provide the IP addresses of the child's authoritative servers.

Glue records are vital for resilience. If glue is missing, stale, or inconsistent, resolution loops indefinitely. This has happened in practice. In 2009, the Swedish ccTLD .se suffered a corrupted zone file that invalidated delegations. All .se domains went dark. This was not an infrastructure failure but a **Configuration Failure** under the Resilience Analysis Framework (RAF), proving that DNS fragility often lies in configuration, not capacity.

The Root Zone and Root Servers (2026 Perspective)

We have already referred to the root servers earlier in this book, but it is worth revisiting them here in context. The **root zone** is managed by IANA, under ICANN's oversight, and contains only the essential delegations: NS records and glue for every TLD, along with DNSSEC signatures. Its simplicity reduces fragility but makes it the single anchor point for the global namespace.

Root information is published through the **root servers**. There are 13 logical root server identities, labeled A through M, each operated by independent organizations such as Verisign, RIPE NCC, and ICANN. These are not 13 machines; each identity is replicated globally using **Anycast**, meaning the same IP address is advertised from multiple geographic locations. Resolvers are automatically directed to the nearest healthy instance.

As of 2026, there are more than **1,600 physical instances of root servers worldwide**, reflecting growth since earlier years. This vast distribution is what makes the root remarkably resilient. A failure or attack on one instance is absorbed by others.

History has shown the importance of this design. In 2002 and again in 2007, root servers were targeted by large DDoS attacks. Several instances became unreachable, but the system held. Anycast distribution, independent operators, and resolver caching ensured continuity. These incidents were classic **Cybersecurity Events** under the RAF. They did not cause global outages, but they underscored the importance of operational resilience and of maintaining **brand trust and impact**: headlines claimed "the internet nearly broke," even though most users saw no disruption.

TLD Servers and National Outages

Beneath the root are the **TLD servers**. Generic TLDs (gTLDs) like .com and .org are generally robust, operated by large registries with global Anycast networks. Country-code TLDs (ccTLDs) are more varied. Some are highly professional, others more fragile.

Failures at this level have had dramatic effects. In 2009, .se was taken offline by a broken zone file, invalidating all delegations beneath it. In 2012, .cl (Chile) experienced a DNSSEC key rollover failure, causing resolvers that required DNSSEC validation to reject all .cl domains. Both incidents were **Configuration Failures** and **Operational Resilience** breakdowns, showing how a single administrative error can cascade to millions of users.

The lesson is clear: TLD resilience varies, and enterprises must design around the fragility of the zones they rely on.

Walking the Hierarchy: Why Again?

Earlier in this chapter, we traced the DNS resolution process from stub resolver to authoritative servers. Why walk it again now? The difference is perspective. Before, we looked at resolution as mechanics. Now, we look at it as **hierarchy**: a system of delegation and authority, where each step is a potential failure domain.

Consider api.cool-network.com:

- The resolver queries the root, which points to .com servers.

- .com responds with NS records for cool-network.com and glue for its name servers.

- The resolver queries those authoritative servers, which return the A or AAAA records for api.cool-network.com.

The difference now is that we evaluate resilience at each stage. If .com is unreachable, every .com domain fails. If cool-network.com is misconfigured, only that domain is affected. Understanding hierarchy is therefore about **fault containment**: knowing where failures will be scoped and how to mitigate them.

Failure Mapping with the Resilience Analysis Framework (RAF)

Using the RAF, we can classify hierarchical failures and their mitigations:

Infrastructure Failures: A root server instance goes offline. Mitigation: Anycast and distribution ensure queries reroute. Best practice: diversify recursive resolver paths to avoid reliance on a single operator.

Availability Zone Failures: At the global root/TLD level, AZs are abstracted. In private DNS hierarchies, however, deploying authoritative servers in a single AZ creates fragility. Best practice: deploy across multiple AZs to preserve resilience.

Region Failures: Some ccTLDs concentrate infrastructure regionally. If that region suffers an outage, the TLD fails. Mitigation: geo-distribution of servers. Enterprises should prefer TLDs with a robust, multi-region presence.

Configuration Failures: Misconfigured glue or corrupted zone files. Best practice: pre-deployment validation, automated checks, DNSSEC.

Operational Failures: Human errors, expired domains, or incorrect delegations. Mitigation: strict change management, monitoring, and renewal automation.

Dependency and Third-Party Failures: Relying on a single DNS provider. Mitigation: multi-provider DNS, secondary DNS arrangements.

Cybersecurity Events: Cache poisoning, BGP hijacks, or DDoS. Mitigation: DNSSEC (RFC 4033–4035), Anycast, RPKI for routing security, and DDoS protection.

By mapping failures this way, resilience is not abstract. It becomes measurable, with clear best practices tied to each failure mode.

Split-Horizon DNS

I can't miss talking about split-horizon, one common enterprise strategy for DNS resolution. In this model, the same domain name resolves differently depending on the querying client's location or network. For example, app.cool-network.com might resolve to a private IP for internal users and a public IP for internet clients.

Split-horizon enables flexibility but introduces fragility. Inconsistent answers between internal and external views can create application failures. If monitoring only observes one view, failures in the other may go unnoticed. Split-horizon must therefore be managed carefully, with consistency testing and explicit policies.

Hybrid Resolution

We talked about hybrid architectures previously, so we need to talk about hybrid resolution. Modern architectures rarely operate with a single namespace. Enterprises run hybrid environments where on-premises resolvers forward queries to cloud DNS zones, or cloud workloads query on-premises authorities. This hybrid resolution introduces new dependencies. If conditional forwarders are misconfigured, resolution can loop endlessly. If cloud zones are unreachable, on-premises applications stall.

Resilience in hybrid resolution requires redundancy, consistent delegation, and explicit failover strategies. These principles mirror those we've already seen in other areas of networking: avoid single points of failure, monitor continuously, and test under load.

We will examine hybrid resolution strategies in greater detail in later sections of this chapter.

Best Practices for Hierarchical DNS Resilience

Distribute authoritative NS servers across diverse geographies and networks.

Validate glue records continuously to prevent delegation loops.

Monitor delegation chains end-to-end with trace tools.

Adopt DNSSEC to ensure authenticity and integrity.

Use multiple DNS providers for critical zones to avoid dependency failures.

Simulate failures (resilience testing) (e.g., TLD outage, NS misconfiguration) to understand blast radius.

Maintain split-horizon consistency with dual-view testing.

Ensure hybrid forwarding chains are redundant and avoid circular dependencies.

What's Next?

The DNS hierarchy—root, TLD, second-level domains, and subdomains—is the structural backbone of name resolution. Delegation provides scalability, glue resolves dependencies, and distribution ensures resilience. Yet the system is not immune to fragility. Outages in .se and .cl, DDoS attacks on the root, and misconfigured delegations have all shown that resilience is as much about operational discipline as it is about infrastructure.

For enterprises and cloud architects, the lesson is direct: design DNS hierarchies with distribution, testing, validation, and redundancy. Monitor the delegation chain, test failure modes, and always consider DNS a first-class element of resilience.

In the next section, we turn to the operational engines of DNS: **recursive resolvers** and **authoritative servers**. Recursive resolvers walk the hierarchy, asking on behalf of clients; authoritative servers answer with truth. Together, they form the dynamic interface between names and addresses. Understanding how they work—and how they fail—is the next step in mastering DNS resilience.

Section 3.5: Recursive vs. Authoritative DNS—Roles and Responsibilities

In Section 3.4, we examined how the DNS hierarchy structures responsibility, from the root to Top-Level Domains (TLDs) and down to zones. But hierarchy itself does not resolve a name; it is simply the framework. Resolution requires servers that play distinct roles. These are **recursive resolvers (RDNS)** and **authoritative name servers (ANS)**. Their functions are complementary but fundamentally different, and resilience in DNS depends on understanding those differences in depth.

Iterative vs. Recursive Queries: Protocol-Level Mechanics

The foundation of this division lies in the protocol itself, as defined in **RFC 1034** and **RFC 1035**. When a client issues a DNS query, it can request either **recursive** or **iterative** behavior.

In a **recursive query**, the server is expected to return a final answer. If it does not know, it must pursue the answer by querying other servers until it can reply definitively. Stub resolvers—the DNS components embedded in every operating system—typically send recursive queries to their configured resolvers. As a reminder, this process can be observed below as per the previous section.

As shown in Figure 3-3, recursive DNS resolution relies on the recursive resolver to query the DNS hierarchy on behalf of the client, following referrals from the root name server to the TLD name server and then to the authoritative name server before returning the final answer.

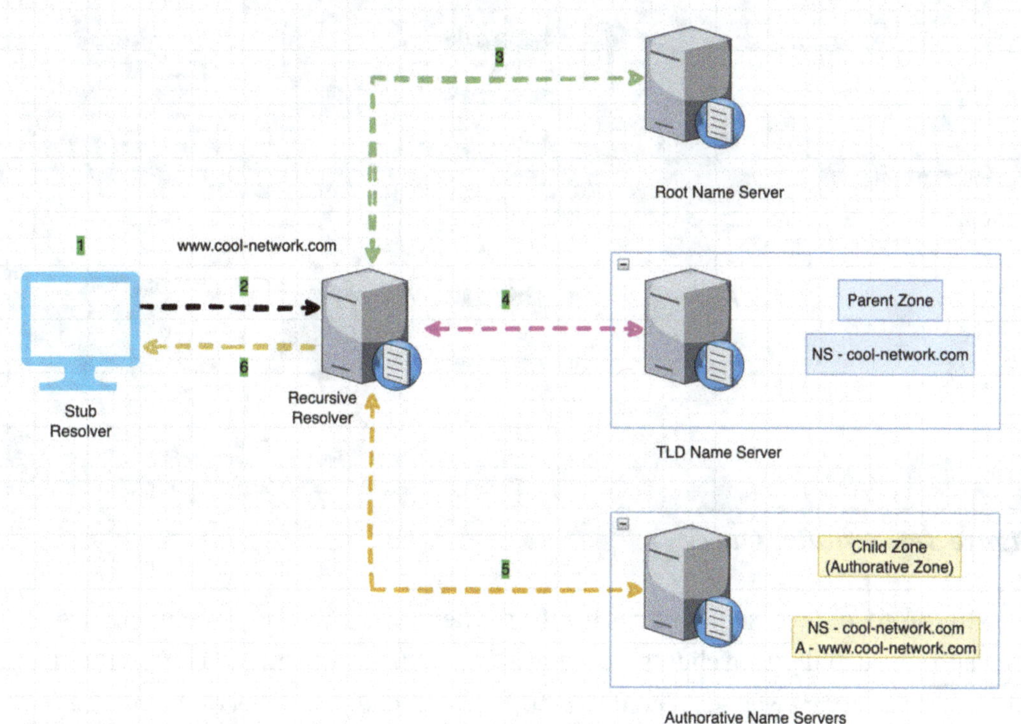

Figure 3-3. *Recursive Query*

In an **iterative query**, the server responds with the best answer it has, often a referral. For example, if asked about api.cool-network.com, a root server responds with a referral to the .com Top-Level Domain (TLD) servers rather than the final IP address. The recursive resolver then continues the process by querying the TLD and eventually the authoritative servers for cool-network.com.

As shown in Figure 3-4, iterative DNS resolution allows the recursive resolver to query each layer of the DNS hierarchy in sequence, receiving referral answers from the root and TLD name servers before obtaining the final answer from the authoritative name server.

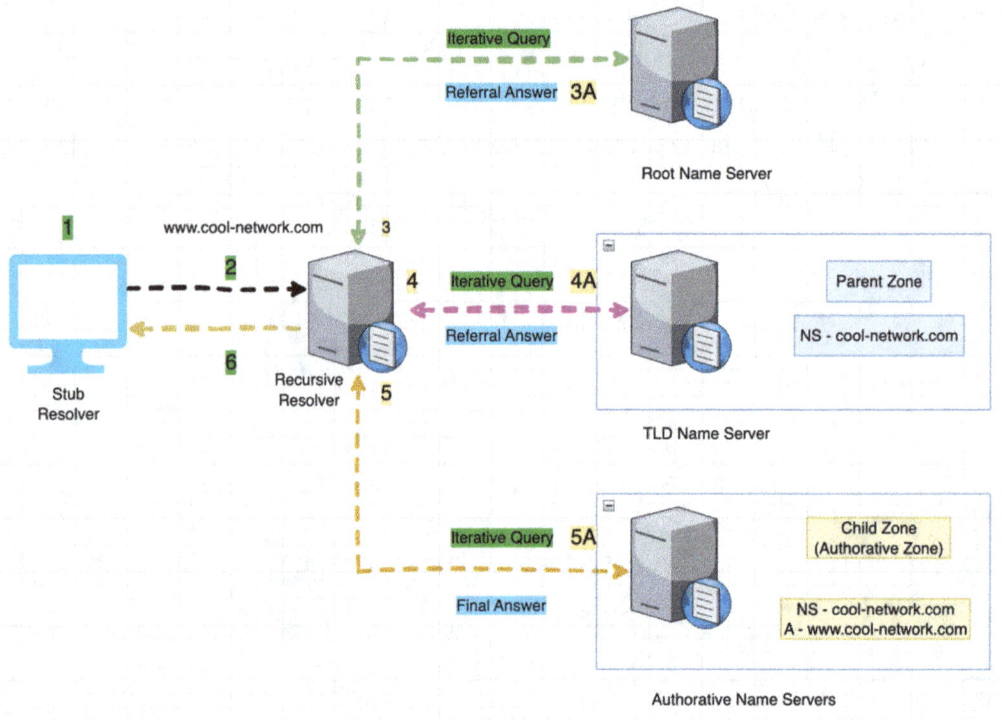

Figure 3-4. *Iterative Query*

This protocol-level separation is itself a resilience mechanism. If recursion were not centralized, billions of clients would overwhelm the root and TLD infrastructure. If authoritative servers were expected to recurse, their load would become unsustainable. By assigning recursion to resolvers and authority to name servers, DNS achieves scalability and reduces fragility.

Recursive Resolvers: Fault Domains and Risks

Recursive resolvers act as the intermediaries between clients and the global hierarchy. Their greatest strength is **caching**. Once a resolver learns the IP address for api.cool-network.com, it stores that answer for the duration of the Time to Live (TTL). This reduces latency for users, lowers the load on authoritative servers, and provides a buffer during transient upstream failures.

Yet caching introduces fragility. If a resolver caches an incorrect entry—whether due to misconfiguration or a malicious injection—millions of clients can be misdirected until the TTL expires. The 2008 Kaminsky attack exposed this weakness. By predicting DNS transaction IDs, attackers injected false responses into recursive caches, effectively hijacking domains at scale. This was not a failure of authoritative servers but a **cybersecurity event** at the recursive layer. The lesson from this event was the need for cryptographic validation, leading to widespread adoption of **DNSSEC (Domain Name System Security Extensions, RFC 4033–4035)**.

Recursive resolvers also represent a critical dependency. An enterprise relying on a single resolver provider risks a **dependency and third-party failure**. In June 2019, an ISP leaked incorrect Border Gateway Protocol (BGP) routes, which were propagated by Verizon. As traffic was misdirected, resolvers such as those operated by Cloudflare became unreachable. From a user perspective, the internet appeared to be down, even though authoritative servers were unaffected. The failure mode was not at the source of truth but at the recursive layer.

Authoritative Servers: Source of Truth and Fragility

Authoritative servers provide definitive answers. They do not recurse. If they host the zone for cool-network.com, they can respond with the IP address of `www.cool-network.com` or state that no such name exists (NXDOMAIN). Their role is narrower than recursion but more fundamental: without authoritative servers, recursive resolvers have nothing to deliver.

Authority is structured around **primary servers**, where zone data is maintained, and **secondary servers**, which replicate data using zone transfers (AXFR/IXFR, RFC 5936). Best practice is to publish multiple authoritative servers across diverse networks and geographies.

Fragility arises when this principle is ignored or misapplied. In 2012, a DNSSEC key rollover in Chile's .cl TLD was mishandled. Resolvers worldwide began rejecting records as invalid, rendering domains under .cl unreachable. This was a **configuration failure**, where a misstep in cryptographic management led to a regional-scale outage.

In 2021, a registrar error deleted NS (Name Server) records for several high-profile domains. While cached answers persisted temporarily, once TTLs expired, the domains effectively vanished. This was an **operational failure**, a human error at the registrar's control plane. The incident highlighted that authoritative DNS is not only about infrastructure but also about disciplined operational practices.

Resilience Trade-Offs and the AWS Resilience Analysis Framework

Resilience in DNS can be mapped directly to the categories of the **AWS Resilience Analysis Framework (RAF).**

> **Application Failures**: If a resolver caches stale data pointing to an unhealthy backend, applications appear down even though infrastructure is healthy. Best practice is to align TTLs with backend health check intervals so DNS can adapt to failures at application speed.

> **Infrastructure Failures**: A recursive cluster crash or a DDoS against authoritative servers halts resolution. Mitigation requires distributed Anycast deployment for resolvers, multiple authoritative providers, and health checks integrated with services like Route 53.

> **Availability Zone Failures**: For internal DNS in AWS, endpoints must be deployed across multiple Availability Zones (AZs). A single-AZ deployment introduces fragility identical to a traditional single data center.

> **Region Failures**: Hosting all DNS authority in one AWS Region risks total unreachability during a regional event. Multi-region deployments, combined with latency-based or failover routing, protect against this rare but high-impact category.

> **Configuration Failures**: Misconfigured NS records or DNSSEC errors immediately invalidate a zone. Automated pipelines, pre-deployment validation, and active monitoring reduce the likelihood of these failures.

> **Operational Failures**: Expired domains or misapplied changes at registrars can silently disrupt entire organizations. Auto-renewal, strict access controls, and resilience testing are critical.

> **Cybersecurity Events**: Cache poisoning, amplification abuse, and registrar hijacking target DNS directly. Mitigation involves DNSSEC, Anycast architectures, and layered defenses.

Dependency and Third-Party Failures: Over-reliance on a single resolver or DNS provider magnifies blast radius. Designing for resilience requires diversity across providers and geographies.

By explicitly mapping recursive and authoritative roles against RAF categories, it becomes clear that both layers are fault domains in their own right. Each requires tailored strategies for resilience.

AWS Perspective: Route 53 and Resolver

In AWS, the distinction between recursion and authority is made concrete. **Amazon Route 53** provides authoritative DNS with globally distributed Anycast servers, DNSSEC support, and automated health checks. Critically, these health checks operate from the **data plane**, meaning that DNS failover continues to function even if the control plane is degraded. This design embodies AWS's principle of static stability: applications should continue functioning without human intervention even during control plane impairments.

For recursion, **Route 53 Resolver** provides DNS services inside Amazon VPCs. It offers inbound endpoints for on-premises clients and outbound endpoints for VPC workloads to resolve external domains. Resolver endpoints are deployed across multiple AZs, ensuring that infrastructure failures do not create blind spots. This tight integration reduces query latency, ensures hybrid resolution, and provides observability into the resolution path.

When combined, authoritative Route 53 and recursive Resolver services illustrate a layered approach to DNS resilience. Authority ensures the truth is globally available, while recursion optimizes access and insulates clients from upstream disruptions. Both are necessary.

Hybrid Resolution and Split Horizon

Hybrid environments, where enterprises use on-premises recursive resolvers alongside cloud-hosted authoritative zones, introduce additional resilience considerations. Forwarding rules in Route 53 Resolver allow internal and external queries to be directed consistently, but errors here can create loops or outages. Split-horizon DNS, where the same name resolves differently depending on the source of the query, is common in hybrid networks. It enables separation between internal and external service discovery, but it also doubles the risk of misconfiguration. A split-horizon failure can cause clients to receive private IPs externally or stale external IPs internally, undermining both security and resilience. Designing these systems requires rigorous validation, monitoring, and failover testing.

What's Next?

Recursive resolvers and authoritative servers are distinct systems with different responsibilities, failure modes, and resilience strategies. Recursive resolvers aggregate, cache, and optimize queries but are vulnerable to poisoning and third-party dependency. Authoritative servers publish definitive records but can fail through misconfiguration, operational error, or targeted attack. Both layers are essential, and neither can substitute for the other.

Resilience is built by treating them as complementary fault domains: caching protects clients during outages, authority provides cryptographic integrity, and both require diversity and redundancy. The trade-offs between long and short TTLs, between centralized and distributed authority, and between reliance on one or many providers define how DNS behaves under stress.

In the next and final section of this chapter, we will synthesize these principles into **DNS techniques for resilience and apply what we learned to cloud context**, where recursion, authority, hierarchy, and record management converge into architectures built to withstand failure at scale.

Section 3.6: DNS in the Cloud Context

By now, hopefully, the pieces should align. Chapter 1 (Section "Categories of Failure for Resilience") gave us the taxonomy of what can go wrong. Chapter 2 (Sections "Cloud Network Architectures and Topologies" and "Software-Defined Networking and Static Stability") showed how we use fault domains—Availability Zones (AZs) and Regions—to contain blast radius and keep data planes operating when control planes are impaired. Chapter 3 established DNS fundamentals: what DNS is, how resolution proceeds hop by hop, how records behave under stress, how the hierarchy constrains failure propagation, and how recursive and authoritative roles divide responsibility.

This is the architectural turning point: in cloud architectures, DNS is the control-plane fabric that makes those topology and fault-domain ideas work at runtime. All the redundancy you built into compute, storage, and networking is useful only if clients are continuously steered to healthy endpoints by resilient name resolution. At the same time, let's keep in mind the shared responsibility model for resiliency at AWS: the provider, in this case AWS, is responsible for the resilience **of** the cloud, hardware and services, compute, storage, database, networking, and AWS global infrastructure (Availability Zones and Regions), while you are responsible for resilience **in** the cloud, testing, workloads architecture, observability, failure management, etc. Your design choices around DNS are squarely in that second category.

Why Resilient DNS Resolution Is the First Success Condition in the Cloud

In traditional environments, hostnames often pointed to long-lived servers or static IP addresses, and the infrastructure rarely moved beneath them. In the cloud, elasticity and change are constant. Instances terminate and relaunch with new addresses, container tasks reschedule, and front doors such as load balancers scale horizontally and may change IPs. DNS is the abstraction layer that decouples client identity from that churn. If DNS experiences service impairments, every layer above it appears broken.

Viewed through Chapter 1's lens, weak DNS design manifests across several failure categories at once. Stale answers convert a localized application fault into a widespread client-perceived outage. Single recursive clusters, single forwarding paths, or single resolver endpoints create dependency and third-party failures. Authorities and resolvers confined to one AZ undermine your AZ-isolation strategy and effectively re-centralize risk. Region-scoped designs without cross-region authority and steering trap clients during a regional impairment. Misapplied rules, unassociated private zones, and expired domains are configuration and operational failures that silently sever reachability. The goal of resilient cloud DNS is to make these failure modes survivable by design— distributing resolver capacity across fault domains, making forwarding deterministic and minimal-privilege, centralizing authoritative truth while decentralizing recursion, and biasing toward data-plane automation so the system remains stable even when a control plane is degraded.

How Thinking Changes in the Cloud

On-premises practice often revolved around boxes: a pair of recursive servers, a pair of authoritative servers, perhaps a forwarding chain through a DMZ, and this, assuming the network architect had enough budget to allocate to eliminate single points of failure. I remember when I was working as a network architect for on-prem DC; when designing for resilience, the common practice was to at least deploy two "boxes" per switch/router and so on.

When in the cloud, things are different. In the context of DNS, it is a native control-plane capability of the virtual network. That changes the engineering conversation:

> **Resolvers are VPC-scoped services.** On AWS, every Virtual Private Cloud (VPC) exposes a highly available resolver reachable at the second IP of the VPC CIDR (e.g., 10.0.0.2 in 10.0.0.0/16) and at 169.254.169.253. It scales with the VPC and preserves AZ isolation.

> **Hybrid resolution is a first-order design primitive.** Route 53 Resolver inbound and outbound endpoints are elastic network interfaces placed in your subnets. You deploy multiple IPs across different AZs for availability, and you control forwarding with rules rather than device-local configuration.

> **Authority can be decoupled from tenancy.** Private Hosted Zones (PHZs) can be associated with one or many VPCs, even across accounts, so you can centralize authoritative truth while keeping workloads isolated.

In other words, you shift from managing appliances to composing cloud services. The right questions now are: are these services distributed across AZs and regions in ways that match failure boundaries; are forwarding decisions deterministic and least-privilege; do we have diversity for every external dependency; and, if an impairment occurs, will clients still resolve and reach healthy endpoints without operator intervention, without users knowing that our application is suffering a service impairment? If those questions make you curious, keep reading—this section turns them into concrete patterns you can build.

Implementing Resilient Resolution in AWS: Scope and Assumptions

At this point I would assume the reader is already comfortable with the foundations laid in this and previous chapters and with core AWS networking concepts. We will not restate the basics. Instead, we will focus on how to compose resilient building blocks and where the sharp edges are. The examples use AWS because that is my operating context and where I can offer field-tested guidance; the patterns themselves translate closely to other clouds with equivalent services.

The In-VPC Resolver and DHCP Option Sets

Let's start with how we resolve IP in DNS names within Virtual Private Cloud constructs (VPCs). Every VPC exposes a managed recursive resolver at VPC-CIDR+2 and 169.254.169.253. Leave your VPC's DHCP option set pointing at this Amazon-provided resolver so instances, container tasks, and managed services use it by default. This preserves AZ isolation, removes per-instance bottlenecks, and keeps recursion close to the workloads. Overriding DHCP to point at a pair of virtual machines running DNS may seem familiar, but it typically introduces latency hotspots, erodes AZ isolation, and pushes packet-rate limits onto individual elastic network interfaces. Here you can see how the resolution occurs in AWS VPC, its processing order, and how to implement fault isolation. In Figure 3-5, Route 53 is classifying queries. The first thing it checks is if there is a private hosted zone for that specific domain name. If there is not, it checks the VPC DNS, and finally, if no answers are returned, it sends the query to public DNS.

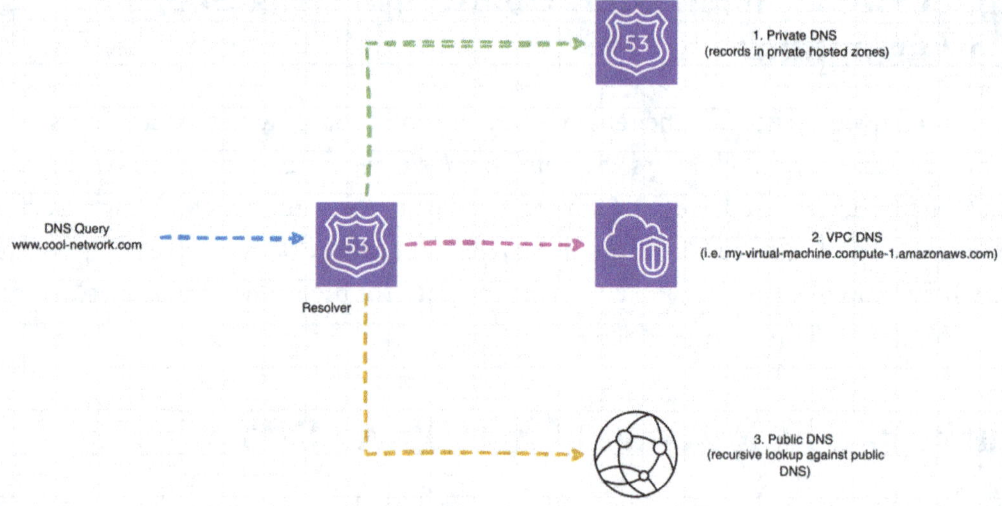

Figure 3-5. *AWS VPC Resolution Process*

Now, let's look at how the same design behaves when we enforce Availability Zone isolation as a fault-containment strategy for networking and resilience.

Note   Authoritative Route 53 for public DNS is global/Anycast—not AZ-scoped—so AZ isolation applies to VPC-internal resolution; internet clients reach the nearest Route 53 edge regardless of AZ.

In Figure 3-6, VPC-internal DNS queries are served by AmazonProvidedDNS (".2" in each subnet) and/or Route 53 Resolver endpoints that we deploy across multiple subnets/AZs. This keeps resolution zonal, so workloads in one AZ don't rely on DNS infrastructure in another.

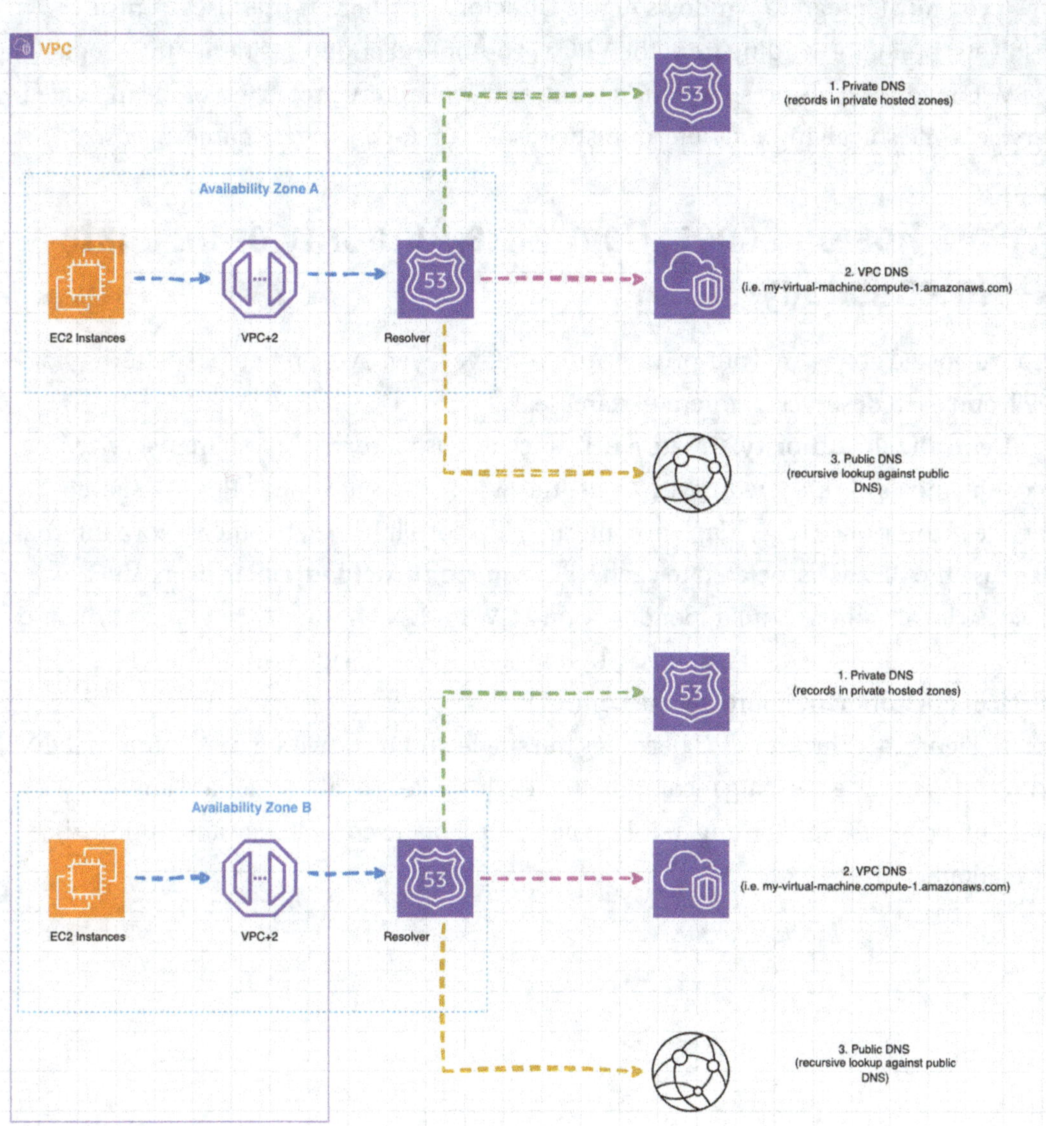

Figure 3-6. *Resolution with AZ Isolation*

This alignment of DNS resolution with AZ boundaries preserves fault containment: an impairment in one zone neither prevents name resolution in healthy zones nor forces cross-zone dependencies, which is exactly what we want for resilient, blast-radius-aware designs.

If you must integrate Windows Active Directory or other on-premises-centric resolvers, prefer forwarding from the VPC via outbound endpoints rather than replacing the VPC resolver. This preserves the scaling and availability properties of the managed service while still giving you deterministic resolution for corporate namespaces.

Private Hosted Zones: Centralize Authority or Delegate It—Intentionally

Private hosted zones are your private authoritative layer. Two archetypal patterns work well, and each deserves a concrete example.

Centralized authority. Create a PHZ such as corp.internal in a shared-services account and associate it with every consumer VPC across accounts. Publish shared service records once (e.g., ldap.corp.internal, idp.corp.internal, telemetry.corp.internal). Because the PHZ is associated to each VPC, **AmazonProvidedDNS** in every VPC answers locally; there is no dependency on TGW for DNS traffic. This reduces drift and eliminates split-brain, and it aligns with hub-and-spoke designs where the shared-services environment is already the control locus.

In Figure 3-7, the hub VPC becomes the single authoritative source for internal DNS, with associations extending resolution into each spoke. Local queries are answered without cross-VPC forwarding, reinforcing control plane consistency and minimizing operational risk.

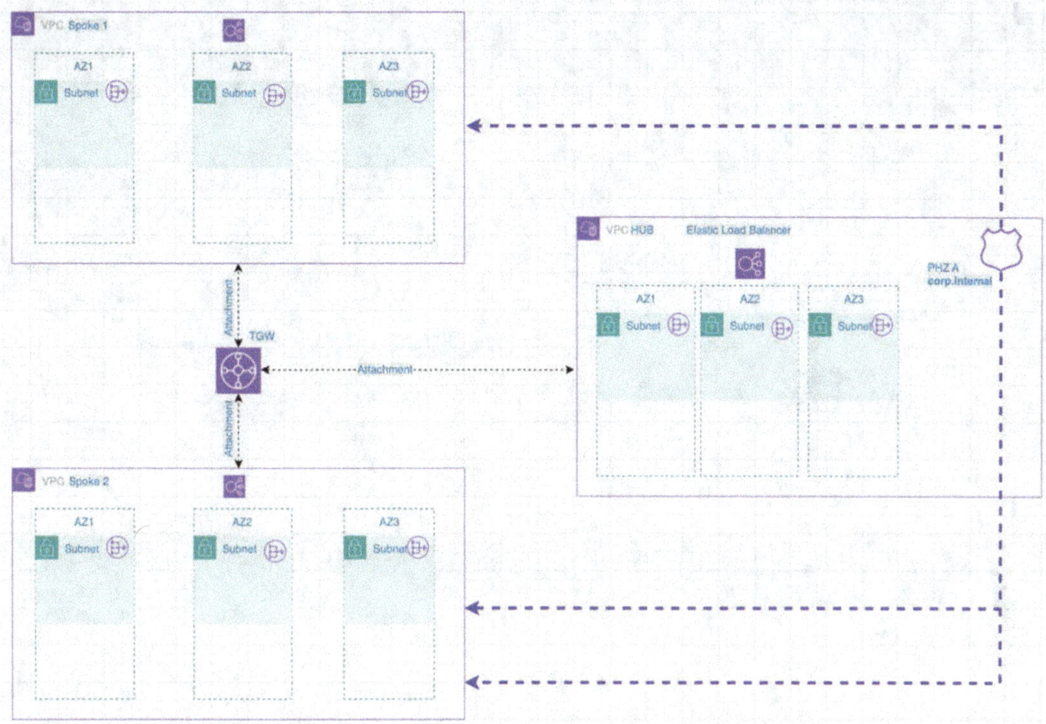

Figure 3-7. *Centralized Authority*

Decentralized authority. Keep PHZs per workload or per environment (e.g., payments.prod.internal, payments.dev.internal) to maximize autonomy and isolate change. Consumers can either associate the owning PHZ into their VPCs or use Route 53 Resolver with outbound rules and inbound endpoints to reach the VPC that owns the zone. This avoids cross-team coupling but requires a disciplined naming plan so zones do not overlap and, if forwarding is used, redundant endpoints in multiple subnets/AZs.

In Figure 3-8, each VPC owns its own private hosted zone (*dev.internal, test.internal, prod.internal*). This maximizes autonomy and isolates risk but requires strict naming discipline and forwarding rules to prevent overlaps and resolution failures.

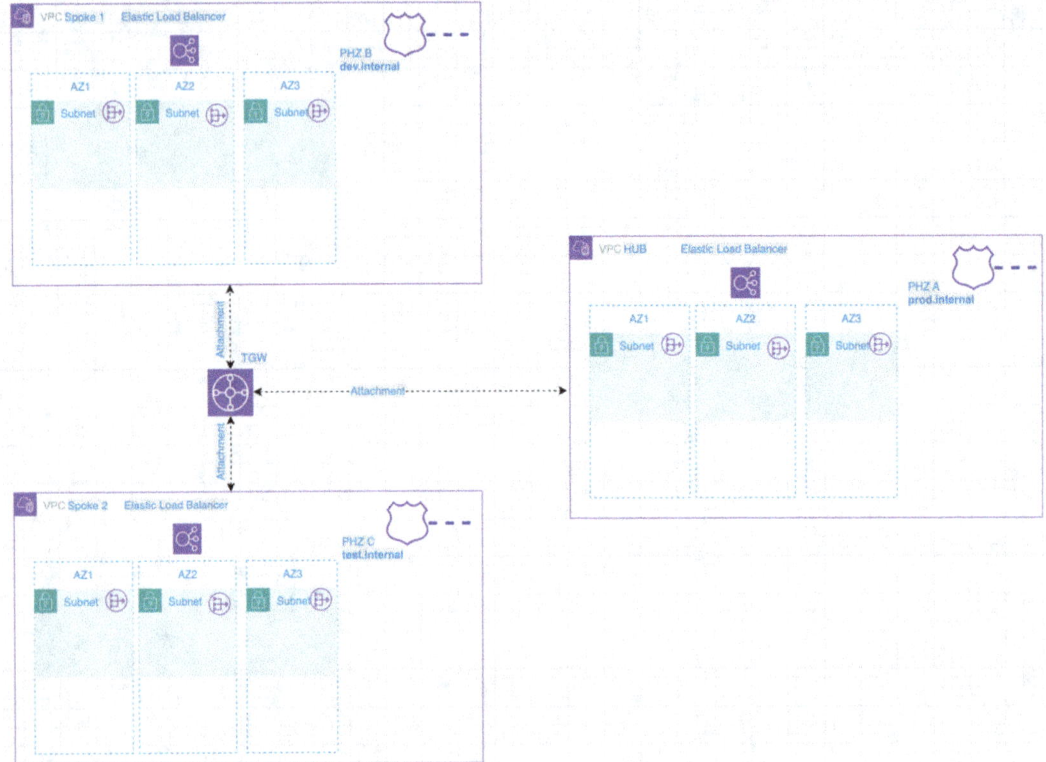

Figure 3-8. *Decentralized Authority*

Whichever model you choose, maintain one authoritative publisher per name.
Duplicate authority for the same name, even unintentionally, is a common source of
intermittent failures and maps directly to the *Configuration Failure* category defined in
Chapter 1.

Hybrid Resolution with Route 53 Resolver Endpoints

Hybrid name resolution has two directions. Engineer both.

From AWS to On-Premises

In Figure 3-9, an EC2 instance in a VPC asks for `www.on-prem.internal.example`. The
instance's stub resolver sends the query to **AmazonProvidedDNS** (the VPC resolver at
VPC-CIDR+.2, shown as **172.16.0.2**). Because a **Route 53 Resolver FORWARD rule**
exists for the domain on-prem.internal.example, the VPC resolver forwards the query

via a **Route 53 Resolver outbound endpoint**. The outbound endpoint sends the query over your private underlay (**Direct Connect or VPN**) to the designated on-premises DNS server(s)—for example, **10.0.0.171**—which are authoritative for the on-prem private zone. The on-prem name server returns the final answer; the outbound endpoint relays it back to AmazonProvidedDNS, which responds to the EC2 instance.

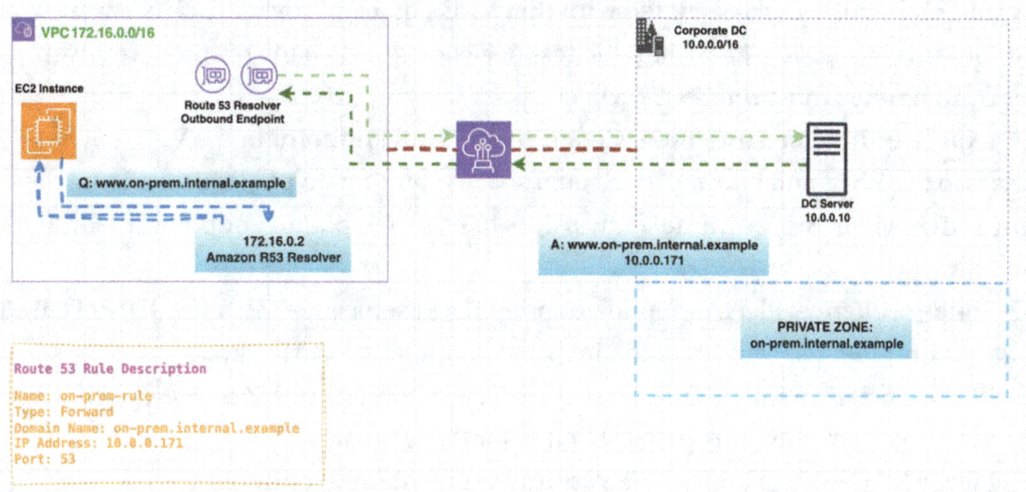

Figure 3-9. *AWS to On-Prem Resolution*

Design notes (AWS ➤ on-prem):

Forward rules are precise. Create **FORWARD** rules for each internal namespace (e.g., corp.internal, on-prem.internal.example) and required reverse zones (e.g., 10.in-addr.arpa, 16.172.in-addr.arpa, 168.192.in-addr.arpa, or ip6.arpa segments). The most specific match wins; keep rules narrow so you don't siphon unrelated names off-platform.

Endpoint resilience. Place outbound endpoint IPs in **at least two subnets across distinct AZs**. Size for throughput: each endpoint IP handles **on the order of ~10k QPS (queries per second)**, and capacity scales linearly with additional IPs.

Network and policy. Ensure underlay redundancy (diverse DX/VPN) and routing reachability, and allow **UDP/TCP 53** in the endpoint security groups and on-prem firewalls.

From On-Premises to AWS

An on-prem application needs `www.aws.internal.example`. Your on-prem resolver is configured to **forward** aws.internal.example to the **Route 53 Resolver inbound endpoint** IPs in the VPC. The inbound endpoint receives the query and passes it to **AmazonProvidedDNS** inside the VPC. Because a **Private Hosted Zone (PHZ)** aws.internal.example is **associated with that VPC**, AmazonProvidedDNS answers authoritatively (e.g., A 3.4.5.6), and the response flows back to the on-prem resolver.

Design notes (on-prem ➤ AWS):

Expose only what's intended. Create an **inbound endpoint** in the VPC that has access to the PHZs and internal AWS namespaces you want to publish. Configure the **on-prem resolver's conditional forwarders** to use the inbound endpoint IPs for those domains.

Zonal resilience. Place inbound endpoint IPs in **separate AZs**; allow **UDP/TCP 53** from the on-prem resolver IPs in the inbound endpoint's security group.

PHZ association is key. Queries resolve locally only if the PHZ is **associated** with the VPC; no Transit Gateway path is needed for those names.

Figure 3-10—On-prem ➤ AWS resolution via inbound endpoint.

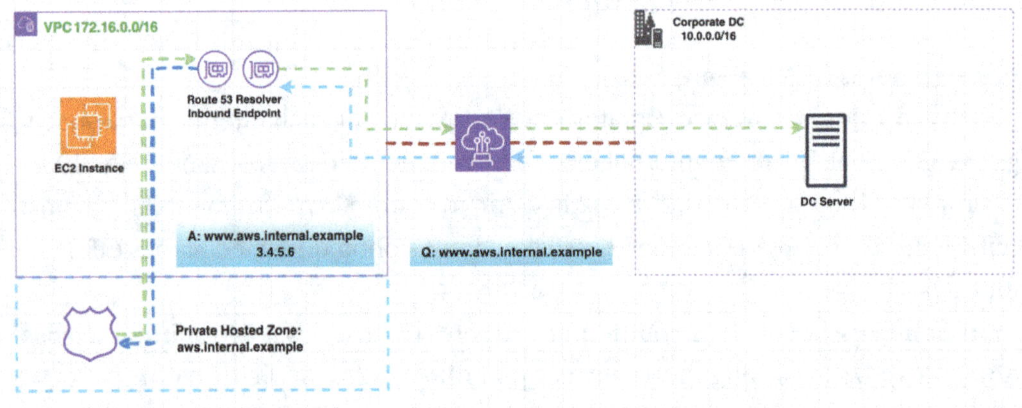

Figure 3-10. *On-Prem to AWS Resolution*

On-prem DNS forwards aws.internal.example to a Route 53 Resolver **inbound endpoint**; AmazonProvidedDNS in the VPC answers from the **associated PHZ** and returns the record to on-prem.

Rule Precedence, Scope, and Sharing

Rule types. Route 53 Resolver supports **SYSTEM** rules (let the VPC resolver perform normal resolution) and **FORWARD** rules (send matching names to specific target IPs). The **longest/most specific suffix match wins**. Keep FORWARD domains tight; don't forward broad suffixes that could capture cloud-internal names unintentionally.

Regional boundaries. Endpoints and rules are **Regional** resources. If you need identical behavior in multiple regions, **create regional copies** of endpoints and rules. This preserves fault-domain isolation and avoids hidden inter-region dependencies in your resolution path.

Multi-account estates. You can **share FORWARD rules** with other accounts with AWS Resource Access Manager so VPCs in those accounts can **associate with the shared rule** and use the **outbound endpoint** in the owning account/region. Manage associations per VPC to keep the blast radius small.

Observability and testing. Log queries with **Route 53 Resolver query logs**, measure end-to-end health, and periodically disable individual paths to verify that failover behaves as expected. Track convergence and error patterns as KPIs so you know your resolution SLOs under link or device failure.

Security and Observability at the Resolver Layer

Operational resilience depends on seeing real behavior and constraining it when needed. Remember what I mentioned earlier in the previous chapters: the best resilience model without testing is ineffective, testing is important to verify that the resilience you put in place works as intended.

In the case of DNS and Route 53, you can enable Route 53 Resolver query logging to CloudWatch Logs, Amazon S3, or Kinesis Data Firehose so you can trace resolution paths during incidents, validate that clients actually follow intended routes during failover tests, and build detectors for anomalies such as sudden spikes in NXDOMAIN or SERVFAIL. Apply DNS Firewall policies to block known malicious domains and to enforce allow-lists where regulatory or security controls require them. Keeping these controls at the resolver edge of every VPC ensures they scale with your estate and remain close to the workloads they protect.

Regional Scope, Multi-account Design, and Shared Rules

Route 53 Resolver is regional. Endpoints terminate inside subnets of a single region, rules live in that region, and VPC association to rules is regional. In practice, that means:

- If consumers in two regions need the same hybrid resolution behavior, create endpoints and rules in both regions rather than hairpinning queries across regions.

- In multi-account environments, share rules across accounts in the same region so one outbound endpoint fleet in a shared services VPC can serve many VPCs. This reduces operational surface area without introducing hidden cross-region coupling.

- Treat endpoint fleets as regional capacity pools. Scale endpoint IPs per region according to observed QPS and latency. Monitor per-IP utilization and error codes and add capacity before saturation becomes user-visible.

This approach keeps your resolution path aligned with fault domains and avoids surprises during AZ or region-scoped events.

Operational Best Practices for VPC and Hybrid DNS

Here is a list of the best practical examples of how to manage DNS within VPC and when hybrid connectivity is in place.

Keep the VPC resolver as the default path via the DHCP option set. It is built to be highly available and AZ-aware, and it removes per-instance scaling concerns.

Use Private Hosted Zones as single sources of truth, either centralized or decentralized, and avoid creating two authoritative views for the same name.

Deploy inbound and outbound endpoints with multiple IPs across AZs and size them to expected load in QPS.

Keep FORWARD rules as narrow as possible and prefer SYSTEM resolution for cloud-native namespaces so you do not route those names through on-premises resolvers.

Turn on query logging and enforce DNS Firewall policies consistently.

Automate associations of VPCs to PHZs and attachment of rules as part of your VPC and account provisioning pipelines so configuration drift does not become an intermittent production fault.

Reference Architecture Examples

In the last part of Section 3.6, the focus shifts from fundamentals to **reference architectures** that demonstrate how resilient DNS resolution is implemented in the cloud. The following scenarios—**Single-Region, multi-AZ application with a private entry point, Hub-and-Spoke with centralized DNS and hybrid connectivity, Cross-Region private resolution**, and **Multi-account estates without endpoint sprawl**—illustrate how theory translates into working topologies. Each example shows how DNS underpins resilience, ensuring workloads remain discoverable and reachable across fault domains. These patterns are introduced here, in the fundamentals chapter, because they build directly on the resolution process, record behavior, and hierarchical fault domains covered earlier. At the same time, they act as a bridge into the next chapter, where advanced techniques—routing policies, failover, and multi-provider strategies—extend these foundations into global-scale resilience.

Single-Region, Multi-AZ Application with a Private Entry Point

In the first example, all workloads resolve names through the VPC's AmazonProvidedDNS at the VPC-CIDR+.2 address, which is authoritative for the Private Hosted Zone (PHZ) that contains api.service.internal. The PHZ is associated with the workload VPC, so lookups are answered locally without transiting a transit domain. The private entry point spans multiple Availability Zones with per-AZ load balancer nodes and per-AZ target groups. Health checks continuously evaluate targets; when a target or an AZ degrades, the entry point withdraws those endpoints and continues serving only healthy targets. Record time-to-live (TTL) is set in line with the application's health-check cadence—short enough to converge during an impairment, long enough to benefit from resolver caching—so clients keep receiving usable answers even while capacity shifts.

In Figure 3-11, workloads resolve api.service.internal via AmazonProvidedDNS, which is authoritative for the associated Private Hosted Zone (PHZ). Each Availability Zone hosts its own load balancer node and target group. Health checks prune unhealthy targets, TTLs control how quickly clients adapt, and AZ-local resolution ensures that clients continue receiving answers scoped to healthy fault domains. Cross-zone load balancing is disabled here to preserve AZ isolation and reduce inter-AZ dependencies.

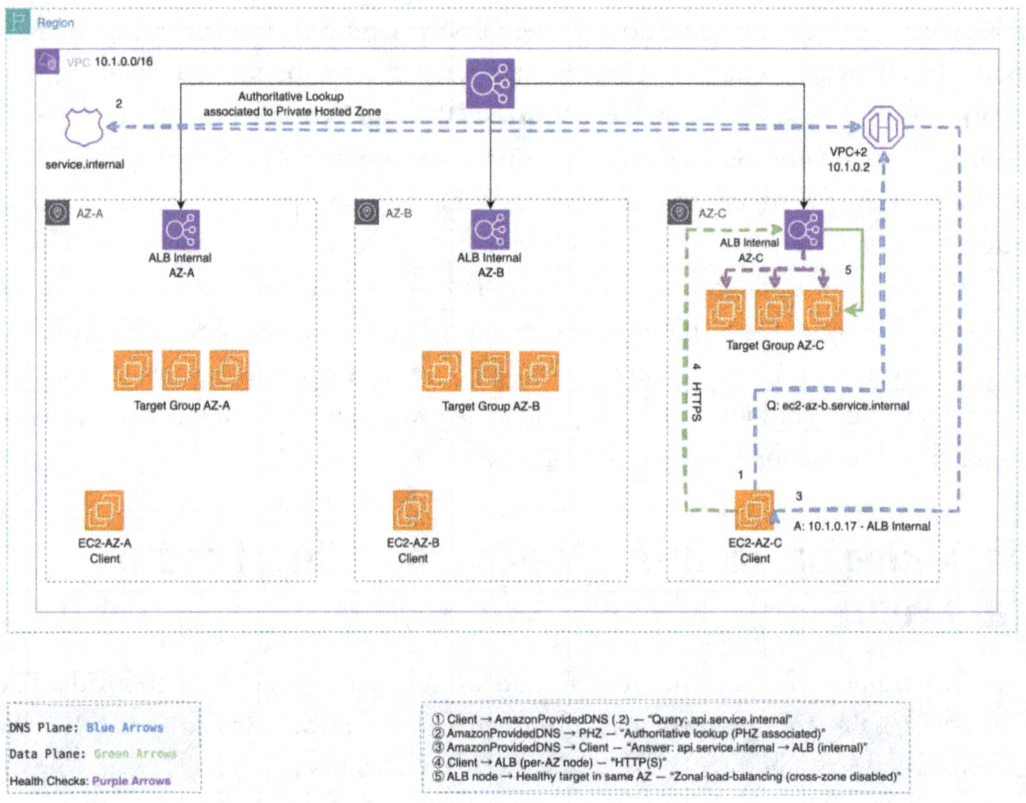

Figure 3-11. *Single Region/Multi-AZ and Private Endpoint*

Cross-zone load balancing—when to enable vs. disable: At Layer 7, an internal Application Load Balancer (ALB) always performs cross-zone load balancing by default. This maximizes availability and helps smooth traffic during uneven AZ capacity, but it can also introduce inter-AZ data transfer. When strict AZ locality and fault containment are the priority, however, consider shifting the private entry point to an internal Network Load Balancer (NLB) with cross-zone load balancing disabled and with targets registered in every AZ. In this model, clients in each AZ are served by the load balancer node and targets within the same AZ, reducing the blast radius and inter-AZ traffic while still allowing the service to operate if one AZ fails. The design shown here adopts this "AZ-local" approach to emphasize fault-domain isolation and predictable data-path locality: the PHZ keeps resolution local, the entry point removes only the impaired AZ's targets, and healthy AZs continue to serve traffic without control-plane intervention.

Hub-and-Spoke with Centralized DNS and Hybrid

In this design, a shared services VPC acts as the central authority for DNS resolution in the cloud. It hosts Private Hosted Zones (PHZs) such as *aws.internal.example* and provides both inbound and outbound Route 53 Resolver endpoints. Spoke VPCs continue to use their local AmazonProvidedDNS (always available at VPC CIDR+2) as their default resolver. When a workload in a spoke needs to resolve an on-premises namespace—for example, *on-prem.internal.example*—its query is sent to the local resolver, which applies a shared FORWARD rule and forwards the request to the outbound endpoint in the hub. The hub relays the query to the on-premises resolver across the hybrid transport (Direct Connect or VPN). The answer is then returned to the spoke via the same path.

Resolution in the opposite direction follows the same pattern. On-premises resolvers forward AWS private domains to the inbound endpoint in the hub. From there, queries are passed to the AmazonProvidedDNS in the shared services VPC, which responds using the PHZ or internal AWS zones. This ensures that both cloud and on-premises clients can resolve each other's namespaces consistently and securely, without duplicating authority across environments.

Figure 3-12 illustrates these flows: **Q1/A1** shows AWS-to-on-premises resolution, while **Q2/A2** shows on-premises-to-AWS resolution. The hub becomes the single place to enforce forwarding logic and audit authority, while recursion remains distributed and Availability Zone (AZ)-isolated in the spokes.

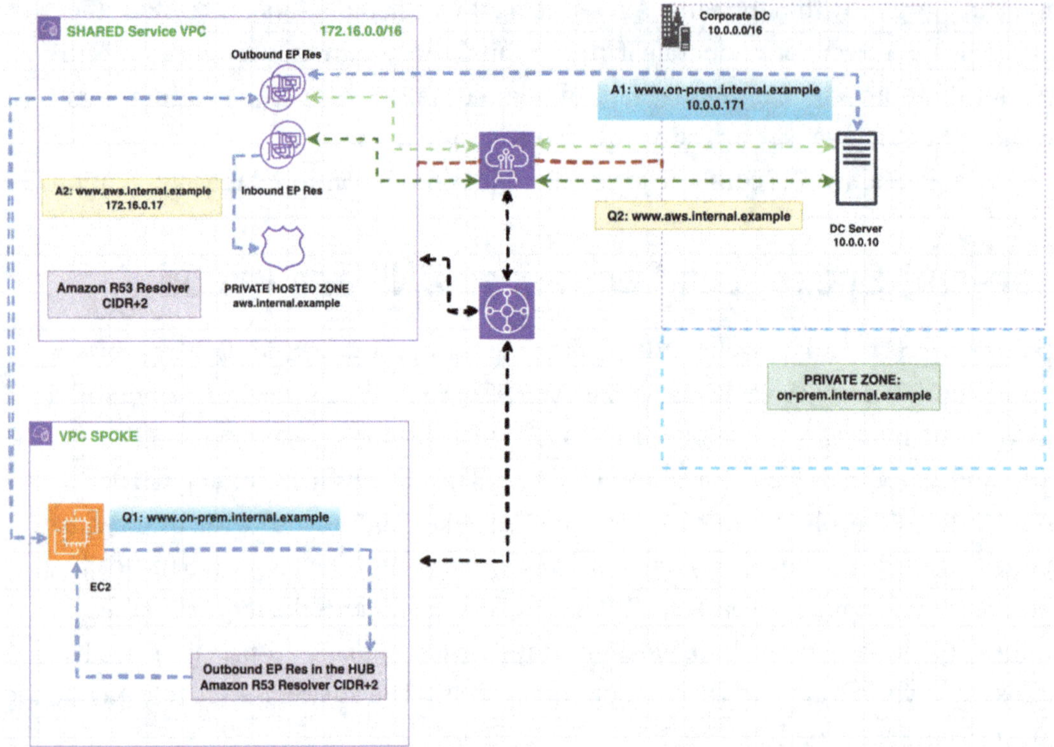

Figure 3-12. *H&S with Centralized DNS and Hybrid Connectivity*

Some of the best practices related to Figure 3-12 I have learned while designing solutions are:

> **AmazonProvidedDNS**: Always reachable at VPC base address + 2 (e.g., 172.16.0.2). Each VPC resolver remains local; DNS queries do not cross the TGW to reach the outbound endpoint.

> **Resolver Endpoints**: Deploy inbound and outbound endpoints with two or more IPs across different subnets/AZs to maintain Availability Zone isolation and high availability.

> **Rule Scope**: Route 53 Resolver rules are regional. Share FORWARD rules with spoke VPCs using AWS Resource Access Manager (RAM) so each spoke can forward specific domains (e.g., on-prem.internal.example) to the shared outbound endpoint. Replicate rules and endpoints in additional regions if required.

Hybrid Transport: Queries forwarded to on-prem resolvers traverse redundant underlay connectivity. AWS Direct Connect supports high resiliency and maximum resiliency models, or you can combine Direct Connect with VPN for diverse failover paths.

On-Prem Forwarders: Configure on-premises resolvers to forward AWS private namespaces (e.g., aws.internal.example) to the inbound endpoint IPs in the shared-services VPC.

Additionally, resilience depends on specific design considerations. Endpoint IPs must be deployed across multiple subnets and AZs so that an AZ failure does not impact resolution. Resolver rules are regional resources, so they must be created per region and replicated consistently across multi-region deployments. Hybrid transport must be redundant, with at least two Direct Connect circuits in separate facilities or a combination of Direct Connect and VPN. Without these measures, the hybrid DNS path itself becomes a single point of failure.

This approach centralizes DNS authority without centralizing recursion. It preserves the blast-radius isolation of spoke workloads while providing enterprises with one authoritative place to govern hybrid resolution. The result is a balance of scalability, manageability, and resilience.

Let's have a look at the two examples for the Route 53 Rules we should implement here:

AWS ➤ On-Premises Resolution

Route 53 Rule Description
Name: on-prem-rule
Type: Forward
Domain Name: on-prem.internal.example
IP Address: 10.0.0.171
Port: 53

On-Premises ➤ AWS Resolution

Route 53 Rule Description
Name: aws-rule
Type: Forward
Domain Name: aws.internal.example
IP Address: 172.16.0.17
Port: 53

Note on Rule Directionality: forwarding rules are directional. A rule that forwards *on-prem.internal.example* queries from AWS to on-premises resolvers does nothing for the opposite flow; a second rule must be explicitly created for *aws.internal.example* to enable on-premises-to-AWS resolution. Overlapping or overly broad rules—for example, forwarding ".internal" as a whole—can silently break resolution by diverting queries that should be answered within AWS to an external resolver. Best practice is to scope rules as narrowly as possible and test both directions under failure scenarios to validate resilience.

Cross-Region Private Resolution

The default posture for multi-region architectures is local resolution in each region. Associate your private hosted zones (PHZs) with the VPCs that need them in each region, and let every workload query its AmazonProvidedDNS (the reserved VPC base address + 2) inside its own region and Availability Zone (AZ). This keeps latency low, preserves AZ/Region fault-domain isolation, and avoids concentrating query load in a single place. Route 53 PHZs can be associated across accounts and regions, so you can keep identical names reachable locally without hairpinning across regions.

There are cases, however, where conditional cross-region forwarding is required (e.g., a region-specific private namespace that must remain authoritative only in Region B). In that pattern

> **Region B (Authority)**: Deploy a Route 53 Resolver inbound endpoint in subnets across at least two AZs. Ensure the PHZ (e.g., region-b.example) is associated only with the VPCs in Region B that should serve as the source of truth.

> **Region A (Clients)**: Deploy a Resolver outbound endpoint and create a FORWARD rule for the Region B private namespace (e.g., svc.region-b.example) that targets the IP addresses of the inbound endpoint in Region B. Share the rule with any VPCs in Region A that need it. Resolver endpoints and rules are regional resources.

> **Underlay Connectivity**: Provide private IP reachability between the two endpoints using inter-region Transit Gateway (TGW) peering (or inter-region VPC peering). Permit UDP/TCP 53 in security groups/NACLs for the endpoint ENIs.

This is exactly what Figure 3-13 shows: blue arrows depict in-region lookups answered locally by AmazonProvidedDNS; the red dashed path labeled "Conditional Forward: svc.region-b.example" shows Region A's outbound endpoint forwarding only that subdomain to Region B's inbound endpoint over TGW inter-region peering, where Region B's VPC/PHZ returns the Region B private IP. Because the endpoints and rules are regional, this design stays aligned to fault domains and avoids creating an implicit dependency on a third region.

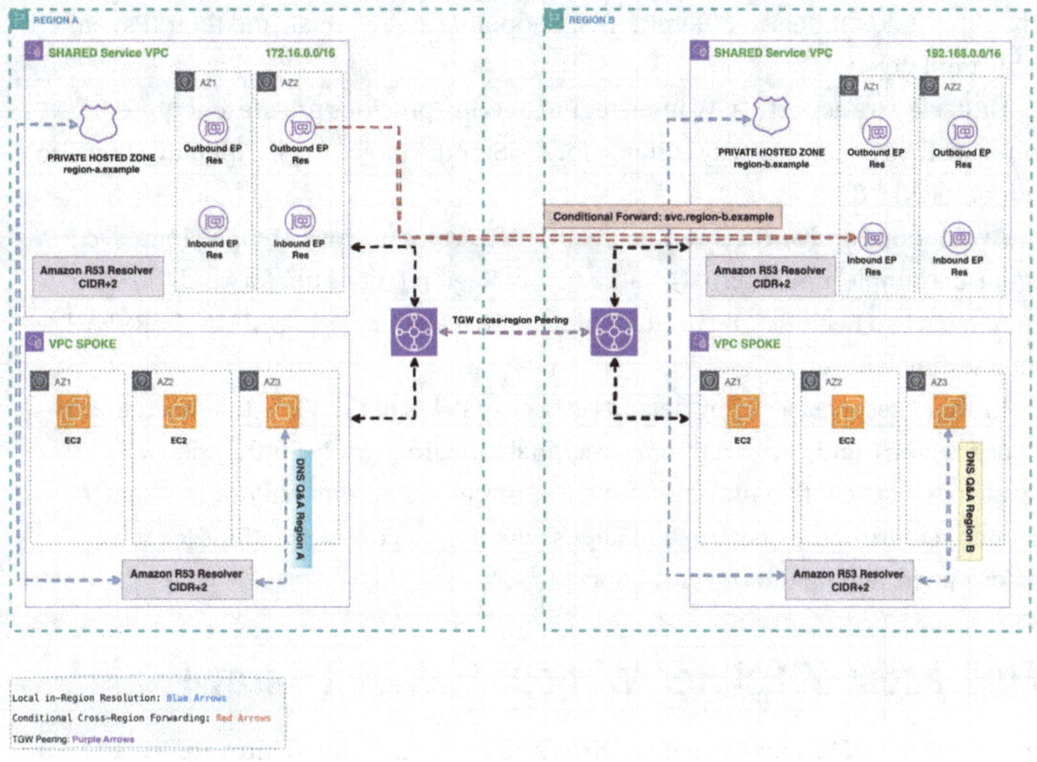

Figure 3-13. *Cross-Region Private Resolution*

Why Prefer Local Resolution—And When to Forward

AWS guidance cautions against centralizing DNS through a small number of resolver endpoints as a general pattern. Keep answers local via the PHZ association; use forwarding only for well-scoped, necessary namespaces. This reduces blast radius, avoids needless inter-region round trips, and helps stay within per-endpoint QPS (queries per second) limits ($\approx$10K QPS per endpoint IP; scale by adding IPs across subnets/AZs).

Implementation Notes That the Diagram Implies

PHZ scope beats forwarding. If a PHZ is associated with a VPC in Region A, the local VPC resolver will answer and the query will not forward. Only create the FORWARD rule in Region A for names that are not locally authoritative there.

Regional sharing. Share FORWARD rules with spoke VPCs in the same region using AWS RAM; replicate rules and endpoints per region if both directions are required.

High availability per fault domain. Place inbound and outbound endpoint IPs across multiple subnets in different AZs. Endpoints are regional, and their IPs remain stable until deletion.

Underlay transport. TGW inter-region peering provides private, encrypted, non-transitive IP connectivity suitable for DNS; route tables must explicitly allow the endpoint ENI CIDRs.

Avoid loops and surprises. Keep FORWARD rules narrowly scoped (e.g., svc. region-b.example, not .internal). Validate that Region B does not forward the same domain back to Region A. Be mindful of negative caching (NXDOMAIN/SERVFAIL) when testing failover.

In short: resolve locally by default (associate PHZs to the VPCs that need them in each region), and use conditional, regional forwarding only for the specific private namespaces that must remain authoritative in another region. This matches the architecture in the diagram and aligns with AWS recommendations for scale, performance, and operational resilience.

Multi-account Estates Without Endpoint Sprawl

Finally, in large AWS environments, DNS resolution can balloon into duplicated infrastructure and management friction. A scalable best practice is to keep **authoritative zones decentralized (also previously discussed in this chapter)**—each team controls its own Private Hosted Zones (PHZs) in its account and uses local recursion via AmazonProvidedDNS (VPC base address + 2).

For non-local namespaces (e.g., on-prem.internal), a **single outbound Route 53 Resolver endpoint fleet per region in a shared-services account** provides forwarding. These FORWARD rules are then shared to consumer accounts through AWS Resource Access Manager (RAM), avoiding redundant endpoints in every VPC. Resolver endpoints are regional resources, and endpoint IPs should be deployed across multiple subnets/ AZs to align with fault-domain isolation.

Figure 3-14 illustrates the flow. Workloads in Spoke VPCs begin resolution by querying their local VPC resolver (blue arrows). If the query matches a locally authoritative PHZ—e.g., dev.internal or test.internal—the local resolver answers directly (blue dashed flow). If instead the query matches a FORWARD rule shared via RAM—for example, on-prem.internal—the local resolver forwards the query to the **outbound endpoint ENI** in the shared-services VPC (orange dashed arrows). From there, the query leaves AWS over the **private underlay (DX/VPN)** to the on-premises DNS server, which responds with the authoritative answer. The response flows back through the outbound endpoint, to the VPC resolver, and finally to the workload that issued the query. TGW attachments (purple arrows) continue to carry application traffic but do not carry the DNS queries themselves.

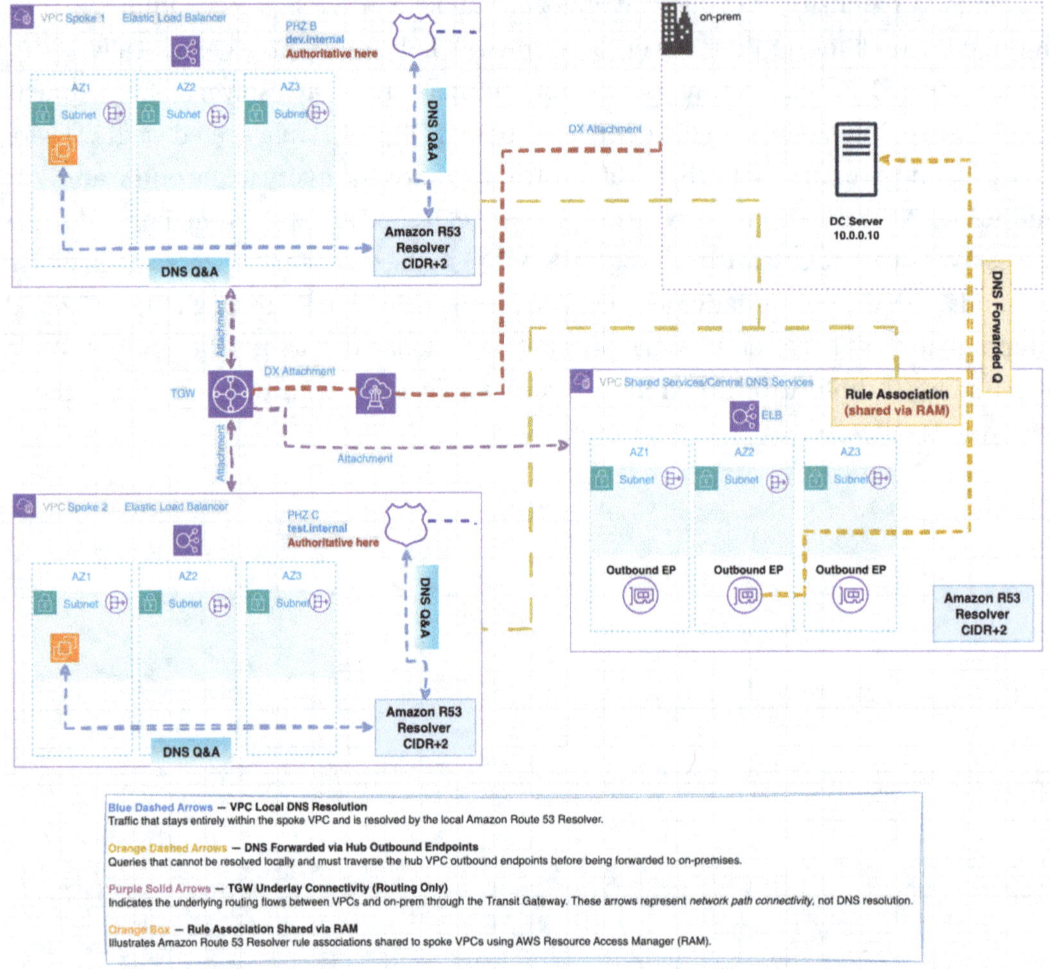

Figure 3-14. *Multi-account Estate Without Endpoint Sprawl*

This design centralizes **forwarding** while leaving **authority local**, minimizing sprawl and operational burden. Teams retain ownership of their PHZs, while the shared-services account provides a single outbound fleet per region for efficient and resilient forwarding. By default, workloads resolve locally; only when a query matches a shared forwarding rule does it traverse the outbound path. The result is a balance of cost efficiency, separation of duties, and resilience across large multi-account estates.

These reference architectures illustrate how DNS resolution underpins resilience across a variety of deployment models: single-region, multi-AZ workloads; hub-and-spoke estates with hybrid resolution; cross-region designs; and multi-account organizations. Each shows that the placement of resolvers, the scope of forwarding rules, and the handling of fault domains determine whether failures are absorbed or amplified. By analyzing these patterns now, the reader is equipped to see DNS not just as an ancillary service but as an active design primitive for resilience. With this foundation, it becomes possible to address more demanding scenarios—how DNS behaves during disaster recovery and how to recognize and avoid its common failure modes—which we will examine in the following subsections.

Coordinating DNS During Disaster Recovery Events

When failures exceed what high availability can absorb—an AZ impairment that becomes systemic or a regional disruption—DNS becomes the steering mechanism for recovery. Amazon Route 53 Application Recovery Controller (ARC) turns disaster recovery from a static runbook into an operational capability.

ARC models the deployment as cells (e.g., AZs and regions) and groups resources into recovery groups. **Readiness checks** continuously validate that the target cell has the capacity, configuration, quotas, and dependencies required to accept traffic—preventing the classic surprise of "the standby can't actually take load." **Routing controls** are highly available data-plane switches that shift traffic between cells even when parts of a control plane are degraded, aligning with the static-stability principle from Chapter 2. There is also a new feature called "region switch" in ARC, which helps orchestrate large-scale and complex recovery tasks for your application. We will touch upon this feature in the next chapters. **Safety rules** also enforce guardrails so operators cannot route traffic into an unready cell or create unsafe combinations of states during an incident.

A practical pattern is to use the availability tactics from Chapter 2 to absorb AZ-scoped turbulence and reserve ARC routing controls for deliberate, quickly executed region shifts. With readiness already proven, moving traffic becomes a controlled, low-risk change rather than an improvised rescue.

Common Failure Modes and How to Avoid Them

It is now time to go through different failure modes and learn what the best ways to avoid them are, or rather, how to architect resilient DNS resolution mechanisms.

Replacing AmazonProvidedDNS with custom DNS by default. Pointing instances at IaaS DNS VMs erodes AZ isolation, introduces ENI bottlenecks, and adds operational load. Keep the VPC-native resolver as the default; integrate on-premises resolution through outbound Resolver endpoints when required. Use IaaS DNS only for clearly justified, application-specific requirements.

Overbroad forwarding. A "dot" FORWARD rule that sends every name off the platform creates a single point of failure and unnecessary latency. Forward narrowly for domains you own or must resolve on-premises; keep SYSTEM resolution for cloud-native names.

Duplicate authority for the same name. Publishing a private name from multiple PHZs causes intermittent answers and flapping. Maintain exactly one authoritative publisher per private name; associate that PHZ to all consumer VPCs.

Unassociated VPCs or missing rules. New VPCs that lack required PHZ associations or rule attachments fail in opaque ways. Treat PHZ associations and rule attachments as part of the VPC creation pipeline; automate them.

Under-sized resolver endpoints. Endpoint fleets that cannot meet peak load will intermittently drop queries. Monitor per-endpoint traffic and errors; scale horizontally by adding endpoint IPs across multiple subnets/AZs.

No resolvability telemetry. Without query logs, there is no ground truth during incidents and no way to verify client behavior after a failover. Enable query logging early and use it in drills. Observability underpins RTO/RPO compliance and prevents policy drift.

Each failure maps to Chapter 1's taxonomy—configuration, operational, dependency, or infrastructure—and the mitigations above keep their blast radius contained.

Closing Chapter 3: Turning DNS design into day-to-day resilience

The earlier sections established how DNS works; this section has shown how to make it work **for** resilient cloud networking. You now have a concrete model that connects Chapter 1's failure categories to design choices inside a VPC, across accounts, and into hybrid networks—and you have tied those choices to cloud fault domains so name resolution does not recentralize risk that the network topology distributed.

At this point, it should be possible to trace any workload's resolution path end-to-end: where recursion occurs, where authority lives, which rules govern forwarding, and where blast radius is introduced or contained. The Amazon-provided resolver is the default recursive substrate that preserves AZ isolation; private hosted zones are the internal sources of truth; inbound and outbound resolver endpoints are the bridges for hybrid resolution, and observability and policy at the resolver edge turn DNS from a blind spot into an auditable system. Finally, Amazon Recovery Controller (ARC) elevates disaster recovery from a document to an executable control system, so DNS can steer safely on the worst day—not just the best.

Equally important is what **not** to do. Forcing all queries through a pair of VMs destroys AZ isolation. Forwarding "everything" off-platform turns a private-WAN hiccup into a company-wide outage. Publishing the same private name from multiple zones invites intermittent failure no monitor will cleanly catch. Under-sizing endpoint fleets virtually guarantees that DNS becomes the bottleneck during an incident. These are avoidable configuration, operational, dependency, or infrastructure failures.

Use the material in this section as a **design flow**, not a grab bag of tips:

- **Establish the Default Recursion Path**: Keep the VPC resolver as a baseline via DHCP options. This anchors resolution to the same AZ/ regional fault domains as the workloads.

- **Decide Authoritative Ownership Up Front**: Centralize private authority where names are shared; decentralize where teams need autonomy—but never publish the same name from two places. Associate PHZs to every VPC that must see them and automate those associations.

- **Make Hybrid Resolution Explicit**: Place inbound endpoints close to the names you expose; place outbound endpoints where workloads live. Write narrow, specific FORWARD rules; prefer SYSTEM resolution for cloud-native namespaces.

- **Align with Regions on Purpose**: Resolver is regional. Build regional copies of endpoints and rules rather than hairpinning queries across regions. Treat each region as its own capacity and failure domain.

- **Instrument First, then Optimize**: Turn on query logging and, where appropriate, DNS Firewall policy. Use real query data to right-size endpoint fleets and verify that clients follow intended paths during failover drills.

- **Rehearse Recovery**: Use ARC readiness checks to prove the standby cell is genuinely ready, and use routing controls to practice safe, fast traffic shifts. Tie drills to the TTL and health-check behavior defined earlier so the control plane and data plane agree under pressure.

If each of those steps can be affirmed for a workload, DNS has moved from prerequisite to **capability**—repeatable across accounts and regions, auditable with consistent logs and guardrails.

Common DNS Misconfigurations and How to Avoid Them

Even well-architected DNS environments often fail for the simplest reasons. Many outages attributed to "network issues," "application failures," or "hybrid connectivity problems" can be traced back to misconfigurations at the DNS layer. The following is a summary of the most frequent issues observed in cloud and hybrid environments, along with practical guidance to avoid them. Although this uses AWS nomenclature, these are applicable to any cloud provider.

- **Over-broad forwarding rules**

    A common anti-pattern is forwarding overly generic suffixes such as .internal, .corp, or entire TLDs to an on-premises resolver. This causes the VPC resolver to offload names that should be resolved locally, creating hidden dependencies, extra latency, and single points of failure across Direct Connect/VPN.

    Mitigation: Forward narrowly and intentionally. Create per-namespace rules such as on-prem.internal.example, not wildcard patterns. Use SYSTEM resolution for all cloud-native names.

- **Duplicate authority for the same private name**

    Publishing a domain-like service.internal from multiple Private Hosted Zones (PHZs), or mixing PHZ authority with on-premises zones, results in flapping, intermittent resolution, and inconsistent client behavior.

    Mitigation: Establish one authoritative owner per private name. Associate the PHZ to all VPCs that need it, or delegate subdomains explicitly (e.g., dev.internal, test.internal) to avoid overlaps.

- **Missing PHZ associations or missing rule attachments**

  New VPCs are created, workloads deploy successfully, and then
  DNS fails because they weren't attached to the PHZ or to the shared
  FORWARD rule. This is one of the most common—and opaque—
  failure modes in multi-account estates.

  Mitigation: Treat PHZ associations and rule attachments as part
  of the VPC creation process. Enforce them through CI/CD or
  organizational automation so they cannot be skipped.

- **Replacing AmazonProvidedDNS with custom DNS servers**

  Pointing DHCP options to on-premises resolvers or EC2-hosted DNS
  VMs erodes availability zone isolation increases latency and pushes
  per-ENI packet-rate limits into the data path. Under load, this design
  collapses.

  Mitigation: Use AmazonProvidedDNS as the baseline resolver.
  Integrate on-premises DNS only via outbound resolver endpoints,
  leaving recursion distributed and AZ-local.

- **Under-sized resolver endpoints**

  Resolver endpoint ENIs have finite throughput (~10k QPS per IP).
  Undersizing leads to intermittent SERVFAILs and unpredictable
  behavior during peak load or hybrid failover events.

  Mitigation: Deploy endpoints with multiple IPs across at least
  two AZs. Monitor per-IP utilization and scale horizontally before
  saturation affects workloads.

- **Overly long TTLs masking unhealthy endpoints**

  Long TTLs improve cache hit rates but can trap clients pointing to
  dead IPs during failover, delaying RTO and prolonging outages even
  when infrastructure is healthy.

  Mitigation: Tune TTLs to match the health-check cadence of the
  application. Keep them long enough for stability but short enough to
  support your recovery objectives.

- **Direct Connect/VPN dependency for internal names**

  Forwarding large internal namespaces off-platform ties DNS availability to hybrid connectivity. A trivial DX interruption can suddenly make cloud workloads appear down.

  Mitigation: Prefer local PHZ authority for cloud-hosted services. Forward only the minimal set of names that truly live on-premises.

- **Confusing search paths and host-level DNS overrides**

  In hybrid fleets, OS-level DNS overrides (multiple resolvers, search paths, or custom resolv.conf entries) often cause resolution to diverge from intended VPC behavior.

  Mitigation: Standardize resolver configuration. Use the VPC-native resolver as the first hop and avoid manual per-host DNS unless absolutely required by an application.

- **No DNS query observability**

  Without query logs, it becomes nearly impossible to analyze resolution failures, understand client behavior during failover, or detect forward loops.

  Mitigation: Enable Route 53 Resolver query logging early. Use logs to audit forwarding paths, detect anomalies, and validate behavior during resilience testing.

- **Forwarding loops or circular delegation**

  Misconfigured forwarders (AWS ➤ on-prem ➤ AWS) or overlapping subdomains create loops that only surface under load or after caches expire.

  Mitigation: Keep forwarding directional and specific. Validate that no resolver forwards a namespace back into the source environment.

Summary

The majority of DNS outages are not caused by infrastructure failures but by configuration drift, overly broad forwarding, ambiguous authority, and missing associations. Treating DNS as a first-class part of resilience—complete with clear ownership, automation for consistency, and observability—prevents these issues from turning minor misconfigurations into organization-wide incidents.

Why DNS Deserves a Touch of Automation

Many of the misconfigurations we discussed in the previous section share a common root cause: they arise not from architectural misunderstandings, but from the accumulated effect of small, manual steps carried out inconsistently across environments. DNS is deceptively simple to modify and dangerously easy to drift. This is why even a modest amount of automation can transform DNS from a fragile control plane into a consistently reliable one.

In many organizations, DNS changes still happen by hand—someone adds a private hosted zone, someone else updates a forwarding rule, and a third person associates a new VPC "when they get to it." These tasks seem trivial in isolation, but in cloud environments they accumulate into one of the most common sources of resilience issues: configuration drift. What makes DNS particularly unforgiving is that mistakes rarely fail loudly. A missing PHZ association or an absent forwarding rule might only affect a single workload, in a single account, in a single region—until the day traffic shifts during an incident and those gaps suddenly turn into an outage.

This is where a small amount of automation goes a long way. I am not referring to elaborate pipelines or full-blown DNS-as-code frameworks. Even lightweight Infrastructure as Code—using Terraform, CloudFormation, or an internal provisioning workflow—can eliminate the silent fragility that emerges when DNS is managed manually. When new VPCs are created, automation can automatically associate the correct private hosted zones. When teams need access to hybrid namespaces, the relevant forwarding rules can be attached consistently. When inbound and outbound endpoints are deployed, automation ensures they land across multiple AZs, sized for load and aligned with fault domains. And crucially, automated templates can prevent accidental duplication of authority, which is one of the easiest ways to create intermittent resolution failures.

The goal is not to remove humans from DNS entirely but to remove the repetitive steps that humans are most likely to overlook—steps that introduce fragility precisely because DNS is a control plane. Automating these small pieces ensures that names resolve the same way everywhere, that new environments inherit correct behavior by default, and that resilience does not depend on whether someone remembered to click through a console screen. In practice, a modest amount of automation often makes the difference between DNS that quietly supports an estate and DNS that quietly undermines it.

Key Takeaways

- DNS is the control-plane fabric of cloud resilience; availability is only as strong as the answers clients receive.

- Fault domains matter at the name layer; keep recursion, authority, and endpoints distributed across AZs and aligned with regions.

- Authority must be unambiguous; one publisher per private name, associated everywhere it's needed.

- Forwarding is a scalpel, not a net; prefer local resolution for cloud-native names and forward narrowly by intent.

- Observability and policy are part of resilience; query logs and DNS Firewall contain blast radius and verify behavior.

- Most DNS outages stem from configuration drift, not infrastructure failures; misconfigurations in forwarding, authority, PHZ associations, and endpoint sizing are the primary real-world causes of resolution incidents.

- Consistency is a resilience feature. Treat PHZ associations, forwarding-rule attachments, and resolver endpoint deployment as part of the environment's lifecycle—not ad-hoc tasks.

- Light automation dramatically reduces DNS fragility. Even minimal IaC—Terraform, CloudFormation, or internal workflows—prevents silent misconfigurations from accumulating and turning into outages during failover.

- Small, manual DNS steps create large, unexpected blast radii; automating the repetitive ones ensures predictable resolution behavior across accounts, regions, and fault domains.

- Recovery is a practiced operation; Amazon Recovery Controller (ARC) turns failover into a controlled data-plane action with readiness verified in advance.

- TTL settings are critical. Stale records caused by overly long TTLs can derail failover during a disaster, keeping users pointed to unhealthy endpoints when you most need agility. TTLs must be tuned to balance stability with the recovery objectives you defined.

With these foundations in place, we can now move into Chapter 4, where DNS evolves from resilient resolution to advanced routing policies, multi-provider strategies, and global scale techniques that build on everything we have established here.

CHAPTER 4

Resilient DNS Architectures and Techniques

In the previous chapter, we examined the fundamentals of DNS—how names are resolved, how records are structured, and how recursive and authoritative systems collaborate to make the Internet and the cloud navigable. We also saw that DNS is not just a directory but a control plane that can strengthen or break an architecture's resilience depending on how it is designed and operated.

Now that we understand *how* DNS works, this chapter turns to *how we build it to survive failure*. When a single lookup underpins every connection, even a small fault in DNS propagation or availability can cascade across entire applications. The goal of this chapter is therefore to transform DNS from a potential single point of failure into a multi-layered system of resilience—capable of absorbing outages, shifting load, and maintaining integrity across regions, networks, and providers.

We will explore the architectural techniques and mechanisms that make DNS truly resilient: from the **Anycast networks** that keep authoritative servers reachable worldwide, to the **routing policies** that distribute traffic intelligently, to **failover and redundancy strategies** that keep services alive even during widespread disruptions. We will also look at how **multiple DNS providers** can be used in tandem for diversity, how **DNSSEC (Domain Name System Security Extensions)** safeguards trust, and how **private and hybrid DNS** extend reliability into internal environments.

To guide the reader, the chapter is organized as follows:

© Cristian Critelli 2026

C. Critelli, *Cloud Networking and Resilience*, https://doi.org/10.1007/979-8-8688-2436-4_4

Section 4.1: Anycast Routing for DNS High Availability

We begin by examining the foundation of DNS resilience: Anycast routing. We will explain how Anycast uses BGP to make authoritative DNS globally reachable, how it reacts to failures, and why all major clouds rely on it.

Section 4.2: Routing Policies for Global Load Distribution

We will explore weighted, latency-based, geolocation, and IP-based policies that shape where users are directed once DNS resolution succeeds.

Section 4.3: DNS Failover Strategies

We will compare how AWS Route 53, Azure Traffic Manager, and Google Cloud DNS detect health, trigger failover, and maintain service continuity.

Section 4.4: Using Multiple DNS Providers for Redundancy

We will discuss cross-provider replication, consistency challenges, and how multi-signer DNSSEC models keep integrity intact across platforms.

Section 4.5: DNSSEC for Security and Integrity

We will explain how cryptographic signing protects against tampering and why operational discipline is essential to avoid key or chain-of-trust failures.

Section 4.6: Private DNS and Hybrid Cloud Considerations

We will extend resilience into private and hybrid domains, covering resolver endpoints, split-horizon architectures, and integration with on-premises networks.

By the end of this chapter, we will have evolved DNS from a conceptual component into an *operational shield*—a system designed not just to resolve names, but to persist through loss of infrastructure, network partitions, and even provider-level failures.

It is here that DNS stops being a background service and becomes a cornerstone of cloud resilience.

Section 4.1: Anycast Routing for DNS High Availability

Anycast is a simple idea with profound implications for Internet reliability. It allows multiple, geographically distributed servers to announce the same IP address using the **Border Gateway Protocol (BGP)**. To the outside world, that single address represents a logical service endpoint. In reality, dozens or even hundreds of physical nodes across the globe respond to it. When a client issues a query, Internet routers automatically direct the packet to the nearest available node according to routing policy and network topology.

Unlike **unicast addressing**—where one IP corresponds to a single server—Anycast creates a stateless collective. Each node advertising the Anycast prefix can independently serve requests, and if one becomes unreachable, the routing announcement for that node is withdrawn. The network converges, and subsequent packets find the next reachable destination, often in a matter of seconds. No manual failover is required, no DNS record changes are made, and clients remain blissfully unaware that anything happened at all.

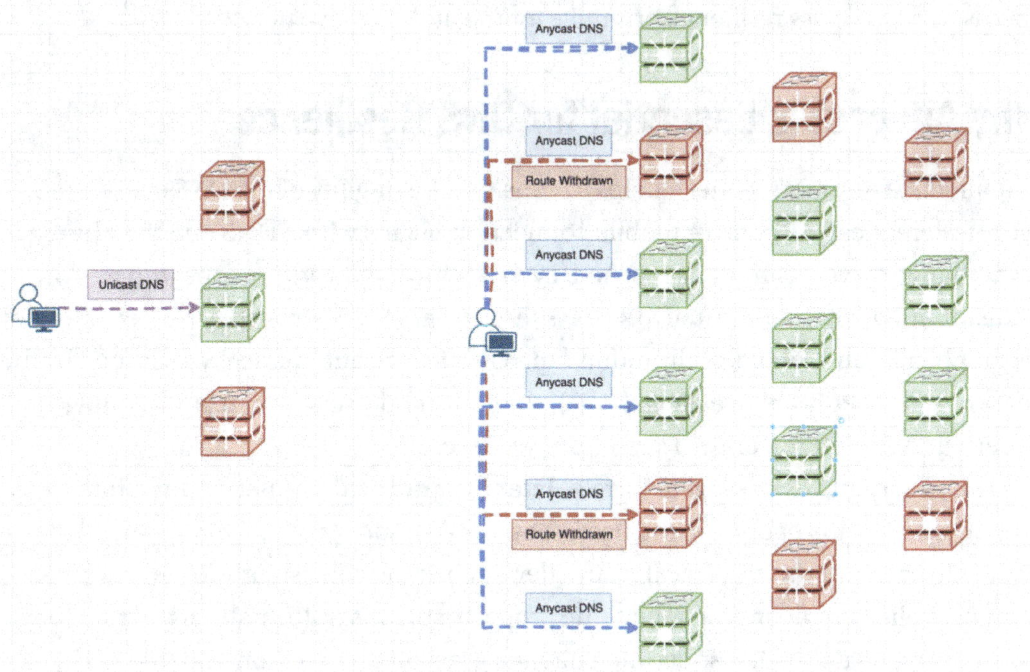

Figure 4-1. *Unicast DNS vs. Anycast DNS*

In Figure 4-1, we can see an example of a unicast model (left), where a single server answers all queries for a given IP address. If that server or its network path fails, resolution halts until a new server is manually selected. In an Anycast model (right), the same IP address is advertised from multiple edge nodes. When a node becomes unreachable, its BGP route is withdrawn, and queries are automatically routed to the nearest healthy node. This network-layer convergence occurs transparently to users and applications, preserving DNS availability even during regional outages.

This behavior makes Anycast uniquely suited to the authoritative DNS layer, which must answer queries reliably even when large segments of the Internet experience instability. It provides a **self-healing data plane** for DNS availability.

The practice of serving authoritative DNS via Anycast is not a fashion of the cloud era; it is a well-established operational pattern with **IETF** guidance behind it. Early operational advice for authoritative servers appears in **RFC 3258**, which describes distributing a single named server across multiple sites, and **RFC 4786**, which codifies best current practice for running Anycasted services at Internet scale. Together, they capture a simple rule: keep the service stateless and consistently configured at every node so the network can move clients freely without breaking semantics. DNS fits that rule particularly well—short, idempotent transactions tolerate path changes—making Anycast is a first-class resilience primitive for the authoritative tier.

Why Anycast Is Essential for DNS Resilience

To appreciate Anycast's value, it helps to consider the fragility of the DNS ecosystem. Every web request, API call, or mobile connection begins with a DNS query. If the authoritative servers cannot be reached, even healthy applications appear to be down. By distributing those authoritative servers through an Anycast mesh, DNS becomes both geographically and topologically redundant. Queries are automatically absorbed by the nearest healthy **Point of Presence (PoP)**, shielding end users from regional outages, undersea cable failures, or data center power losses.

This also provides an elegant form of **latency optimization**. Because the Internet's routing fabric sends packets to the nearest available node, users in Tokyo, Frankfurt, and São Paulo each interact with local responders, achieving consistently low query times without explicit configuration. The same property spreads traffic naturally across the global fleet, preventing hot spots and enabling graceful degradation under load.

Another by-product is **defense-in-depth against denial-of-service (DoS) attacks**. Instead of overwhelming a single origin, attack traffic is dissipated across the entire Anycast footprint. Localized scrubbing or rate-limiting at the edge can neutralize spikes before they reach critical control systems. In this way, Anycast not only keeps DNS online—it also forms the first defensive perimeter of a resilient Internet presence.

The global DNS root has used Anycast for years, and measurements from **RIPE NCC** and **CAIDA** show why: distributing instances across many sites reduces packet loss and tail latency for most clients and limits the blast radius of attacks or regional faults. Studies of **K-root** and other root letters observed clear improvements in resilience and user-perceived performance once Anycast was deployed and expanded. This is not anecdote; large-scale data sets consistently demonstrate that *more nodes, more widely dispersed*, translates into better continuity under stress.

How Cloud Providers Implement It

All major public clouds rely on Anycast for their DNS reachability. **Amazon Route 53** operates its authoritative name servers on a global Anycast network distributed across AWS edge locations. Each hosted zone is served by four unique name servers mapped to separate clusters, ensuring that even a complete regional isolation does not affect the overall service.

Microsoft Azure DNS and **Traffic Manager** follow a similar pattern: authoritative name servers and routing endpoints are advertised from multiple Azure edge sites across continents.

Google Cloud DNS, running on the same backbone that supports Search and YouTube, pushes this model to an extreme, serving each zone from more than two hundred locations worldwide. In each case, BGP convergence rather than manual intervention restores accessibility when a node disappears from the routing table. The result is a globally distributed DNS layer that operates independently of any single data center or control-plane region.

Cloud providers explicitly lean on Anycast for their authoritative DNS fleets. Google Cloud DNS documents Anycasted name servers for high availability and proximity routing; Azure notes Anycasted name servers for both Azure DNS and Traffic Manager; AWS Route 53 confirms answering queries from the optimal Anycast location based on current network conditions. When you consume a managed authoritative service, you inherit these Anycast properties by default, which is why DNS remains reachable even during large-scale regional events.

Behavior During Failures

When an Anycast node fails—whether due to power loss, maintenance, or network isolation—the route it advertises is withdrawn. Border routers remove it from their tables, and the Internet reconverges. Clients whose queries would have been routed to the failed node automatically discover a new, reachable one. The transition happens at the routing layer, not within DNS itself. Typical reconvergence times range from several tens of seconds to a couple of minutes, depending on how quickly upstream providers detect and propagate the change.

Operators pair Anycast with **fast failure detection** on the edge so routes are withdrawn promptly when a node is unhealthy. At the routing layer, **Bidirectional Forwarding Detection (BFD)** can accelerate detection of link or path failure to sub-second ranges, triggering BGP to converge faster than relying on hold timers alone. For planned work, **BGP Graceful Shutdown (RFC 8326)** allows a node to signal its intent to drain traffic before a hard withdrawal, minimizing dropped queries during maintenance windows. These techniques move Anycast from *eventually consistent reachability* toward **predictable recovery behavior**, which is what resilience **Service-Level Objectives (SLOs)** ultimately measure.

From a user's perspective, this looks like continuous availability. Queries that would have timed out in a unicast model are simply answered by another nearby responder. The system achieves fault isolation: a local incident never scales into a global outage. This is precisely the kind of **graceful degradation** that resilient architectures aim for.

Design Discipline Behind the Scenes

Operating an Anycast network requires balancing reachability, stability, and responsiveness. Advertising too many small prefixes can create unnecessary complexity, while advertising too few can make withdrawal events too coarse-grained. Most operators announce **/24 prefixes (IPv4)** and **/48 prefixes (IPv6)**—the smallest routable blocks that avoid filtering. Continuous monitoring of BGP announcements and round-trip latency helps detect route leaks or hijacks before they affect end users. Mature providers integrate this telemetry into their SLOs, tracking metrics such as *regional query success rate (QSR)* and *median authoritative latency* as first-class indicators of DNS health.

Because Anycast's resilience depends on the integrity of its control plane, many operators now adopt **Resource Public Key Infrastructure (RPKI)** and **Mutually Agreed Norms for Routing Security (MANRS)** to authenticate and filter BGP announcements. Publishing **Route Origin Authorizations (ROAs)** and validating "invalid" prefixes at the edge materially reduces the risk of route hijacks that could divert DNS traffic—a subtle but vital aspect of operational resilience.

Another subtlety is the interaction between Anycast and caching. While Anycast ensures queries reach an available name server, it cannot refresh stale responses already cached by resolvers. **Time-to-Live (TTL)** values therefore remain a strategic parameter of resilience, a topic we will return to later in this chapter when discussing failover and recovery timing.

Putting It All Together

Consider a financial-services firm that hosts its transaction portal on AWS. Its DNS zones are served through Route 53's Anycast fleet. One morning, a fiber break isolates the Frankfurt and Paris edge locations. Within seconds, their BGP announcements vanish from the Internet, and resolvers throughout Europe begin querying London and Dublin instead. Users continue trading, unaware that half of the regional DNS infrastructure has just gone dark. Later, **ARC routing controls** detect the degraded cell and redirect application traffic accordingly—but the crucial detail is that DNS never stopped answering. The network healed itself before the recovery controller had to act.

This is the invisible power of Anycast: it guarantees the reachability of the steering mechanism itself. Without it, every upper-layer automation we build—ARC, health checks, blue-green deployments (see Chapter 3)—would rest on a fragile foundation.

What's Next?

With Anycast securing global access to authoritative servers, the next challenge is to determine what those servers should *answer* when queried. Resilience no longer depends solely on reachability but on the intelligence of routing decisions. In the following section, we will explore how **DNS routing policies**—weighted, latency-based, geolocation-aware, and IP-based—translate business intent into traffic distribution, ensuring that user requests land where capacity, compliance, and health conditions are optimal.

Section 4.2: Routing Policies for Global Traffic Management and Load Distribution

In the previous section, we saw how **Anycast routing** provides the foundation of DNS resilience by ensuring that authoritative servers remain reachable even when entire regions or networks experience degradation. Yet reachability alone does not guarantee that users will connect to the *right* place once DNS responds. The question now becomes: *what answer should DNS give?* Which endpoint is closest, healthiest, or compliant with local regulations? How does DNS decide between two available regions when one is busy, or when you want to slowly release a new version of your service?

This is the realm of **routing policies and global traffic management**—the logic that transforms DNS from a passive directory into an active participant in resilience. Routing policies are the decision-making layer that determines *where* traffic goes once Anycast has guaranteed that DNS itself can be reached. They convert network topology, latency, compliance, and operational intent into deterministic name-resolution outcomes.

In this section we will explore the major routing policies offered by **Amazon Route 53**, using them as our reference model. While the book's focus remains general, Route 53's design provides an excellent baseline because it mirrors how other cloud providers—**Microsoft Azure Traffic Manager** and **Google Cloud DNS**—implement similar techniques. Along the way, we will highlight where equivalence exists, where it does not, and what resilience trade-offs emerge in each case.

The Philosophy of DNS-Level Routing

Routing at the DNS layer operates one step before network transport. Each DNS answer is effectively a *traffic decision* cached by resolvers across the Internet. Because of that cache, DNS routing cannot change instantly—unlike a dynamic load balancer that responds to each connection in real time—but it scales effortlessly. No inline appliances, no per-connection overhead, and near-zero latency. The trade-off is that the **Time-to-Live (TTL)** of records governs agility: the longer the TTL, the slower new decisions propagate.

This tension—between *speed of adaptation* and *query load*—runs through every routing policy. As you read through each type, consider how TTL, health-check cadence, and resolver behavior shape the effectiveness of the policy.

Simple Routing—The Straight Path

Simple routing is the default, the baseline against which all others are measured. In **Route 53**, a simple policy returns a single record set: one IPv4 (A) or IPv6 (AAAA) address, or one alias target. Every client receives the same response, regardless of geography or latency.

This model suits endpoints that are themselves highly available—such as **Amazon CloudFront** distributions, **Elastic Load Balancers (ELB)**, or **Global Accelerator** endpoints—because those systems already perform health-based distribution at lower layers. The DNS layer in that case merely provides a stable name.

However, when used directly with static servers or region-specific endpoints, simple routing introduces brittleness. A power failure or fiber cut that isolates that single endpoint translates immediately into a service outage until operators manually update the record or automation triggers a failover.

For internal environments—private zones inside **Amazon VPC (Virtual Private Cloud)** or **Azure VNet (Virtual Network)**—simple routing can still be valuable. Internal applications often depend on service discovery through **AWS Cloud Map** or **Consul**, where health monitoring occurs elsewhere. In those cases, the "simplicity" of this policy is actually resilience by delegation: DNS defers availability decisions to a more agile subsystem.

Failover Routing—The Safety Net

Failover routing transforms DNS from a passive directory into an **active resilience mechanism**. Rather than always returning the same static answer, **Amazon Route 53** associates each DNS record with a **health check** that continuously monitors the target's reachability and responsiveness. As long as the primary endpoint remains healthy, Route 53 responds with that record's value. When the health check fails, the DNS layer automatically promotes the secondary (standby) record, redirecting traffic toward the next available endpoint—typically another AWS Region, Availability Zone, or backup site.

In practice, failover routing functions as a **DNS-level heartbeat**. Route 53 health checks operate from multiple AWS Regions, ensuring that local network noise or transient path issues do not trigger false alarms. These checks are performed directly against the **data plane**—the path users actually traverse—through continuous HTTP(S) requests, TCP socket probes, or custom metrics integrated with **Amazon CloudWatch**. This distinction between **control plane** and **data plane**, introduced in Chapter 2 and expanded in Chapter 3, is fundamental to AWS's design philosophy: the control plane governs orchestration and configuration, while the data plane governs real-time reachability. By placing health checks in the data plane, Route 53 ensures that failover decisions are based on actual user experience rather than on the assumed state of an abstract control system.

When a quorum of health checkers detects consistent failure across regions, Route 53 marks the record as unhealthy and removes it from subsequent DNS answers. Because DNS relies on caching, the transition propagates as resolvers expire old entries according to their **Time-to-Live (TTL)** values. A high TTL can delay failover by minutes; a short TTL accelerates recovery.

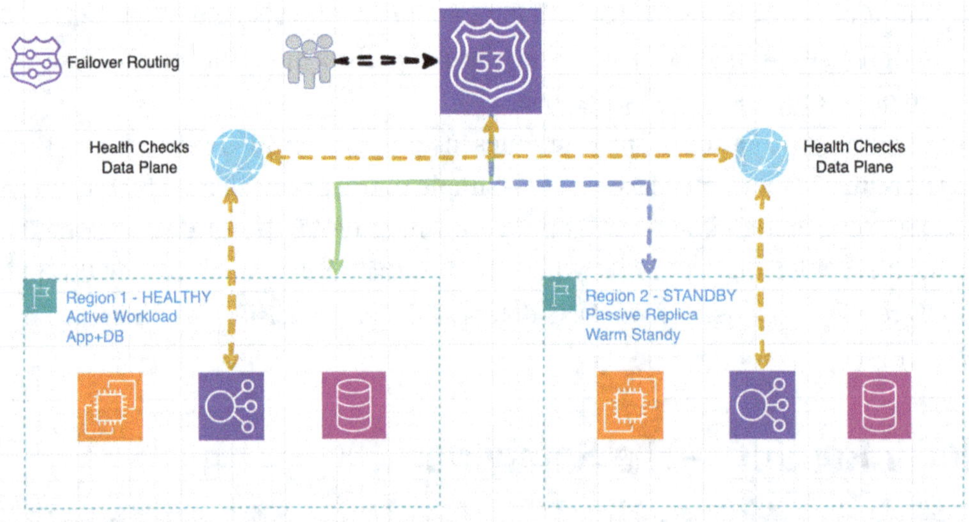

Figure 4-2. *Failover Routing (Healthy State)*

In the configuration illustrated in Figure 4-2, Amazon Route 53 performs continuous health checks from multiple global locations (the data plane) against both primary and standby regions. As long as Region 1 remains healthy, Route 53 responds to DNS queries with its endpoint, directing user traffic to the active workload. Health check results are evaluated independently of the control plane, ensuring that DNS decisions reflect the true user experience rather than the configuration state. Region 2, configured as a warm standby, remains ready but inactive until a failure is detected. This setup demonstrates how failover routing maintains reachability by coupling data-plane health visibility with automated DNS redirection, providing seamless continuity without manual intervention. When service impairment occurs, failover routing helps make sure that user requests are redirected to the newly promoted active record, which corresponds to the region that is not active.

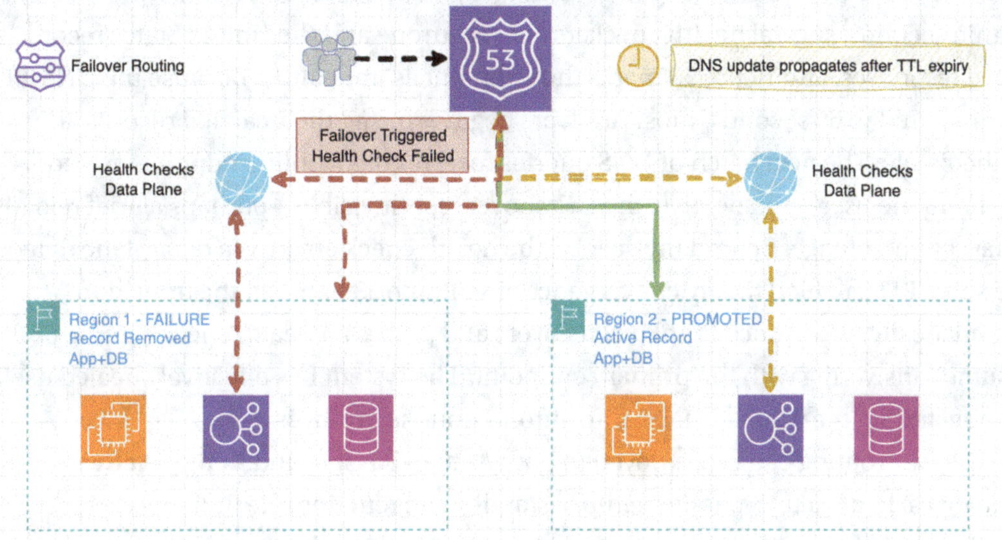

Figure 4-3. *Failover Routing (After Failover)*

As shown in Figure 4-3, when Route 53 health checks detect persistent failure in the primary region, the record is withdrawn from DNS responses, and users are automatically redirected to the standby region. The failover occurs after cached entries expire based on their TTL value, ensuring traffic continuity with no manual intervention. Once the primary region recovers, health checks restore it as active, completing the self-healing cycle.

Lastly, it's very important to align TTL values with your **RPO (Recovery Point Objective)** and **RTO (Recovery Time Objective)** targets. If your architecture is designed for an RTO of five minutes but your DNS TTL is set to 300 seconds, the DNS layer alone may consume the entire recovery window, preventing users from reaching the healthy endpoint within the intended timeframe. In resilient DNS design, TTL is not just a caching parameter—it's a **time boundary of recovery**. Always ensure that TTL values are shorter than, or at least proportional to, the system's defined RTO so that failover and recovery goals remain achievable.

Example:

Consider a financial-services company operating a web platform across **eu-central-1 (Frankfurt)** as the primary region and **eu-west-1 (Dublin)** as the standby. Route 53 continuously probes the Frankfurt front-end using both HTTP and TCP health checks. Late one evening, Frankfurt begins returning high latency and intermittent 500 errors. Within seconds, several health checkers across Europe and the United States record failed responses, and Route 53 marks the endpoint as unhealthy. Because the DNS TTL is configured to 60 seconds, most resolvers begin expiring their cached records almost immediately. The next batch of DNS queries receives the Dublin endpoint instead.

From the user's perspective, the switchover feels invisible—perhaps a brief reload delay, but no outage. Behind the scenes, the health check acted as a data-plane detector, the short TTL enabled timely convergence, and Route 53 handled the transition automatically. Later, once Frankfurt recovers and passes all health checks, Route 53 resumes answering with the primary endpoint. The system has effectively healed itself, demonstrating the value of DNS as an autonomous safety layer.

Failover routing can be deployed in both **Active–Passive** and **Active–Active** topologies. In an active–passive setup, a standby site remains idle until needed, providing predictable failover at the expense of resource utilization. In an active–active design, multiple regions handle live traffic simultaneously, each acting as the other's fallback. This model increases availability and throughput but demands tighter synchronization of state and health metrics across sites. We will be discussing multi-region deployments later in this book with all their pros/cons and requirements.

This capability directly complements the **Application Recovery Controller (ARC)**, which we introduced at the end of Chapter 3. ARC represents the **control-plane orchestration**—it determines *when* failover should occur and validates that the target environment is ready to receive traffic. Route 53, on the other hand, enforces **data-plane continuity**—it executes those routing changes in real time based on the health signals it observes. ARC can integrate with Route 53 health checks to verify readiness conditions before DNS redirection begins, ensuring that traffic is only steered toward fully provisioned and healthy infrastructure.

Together, ARC and Route 53 form the two halves of an integrated resilience system: the control plane **decides** and validates, and the data plane **detects** and executes. This layered approach prevents premature or unnecessary failover while guaranteeing that, once a transition is justified, users continue to receive valid answers without interruption. We will explore this relationship in greater detail in the next section, where we examine how health checks, routing logic, and automation combine to create a DNS failover strategy that is both predictable and self-healing.

Weighted Routing—Controlled Distribution

Weighted routing introduces probability into the equation. Each record receives a numeric weight, and Route 53 serves answers proportionally to those weights. This is the DNS-layer equivalent of a load balancer's traffic distribution algorithm—but without maintaining per-request state.

Weighted routing is invaluable for **blue/green** and **canary deployments**, two operational techniques that enhance resilience during change. In a *blue/green* deployment, two identical environments—"blue" (active) and "green" (idle or staging)—exist in parallel. New versions of an application are deployed to the green environment first; once validated, DNS weights are shifted to progressively direct more traffic there until it becomes the new production environment. In a *canary* deployment, only a small, controlled portion of traffic (e.g., 5–10%) is sent to the new version to observe its behavior under real workloads before committing the change globally.

By adjusting weights in **Amazon Route 53**, operators can control the proportion of DNS queries that resolve to each environment. This allows rapid rollback by simply restoring the previous weighting if issues arise—no redeployment or DNS zone reconfiguration is needed. Weighted routing therefore becomes not just a balancing mechanism but a **change-resilience strategy**, letting teams validate releases in production conditions while maintaining service continuity and user trust.

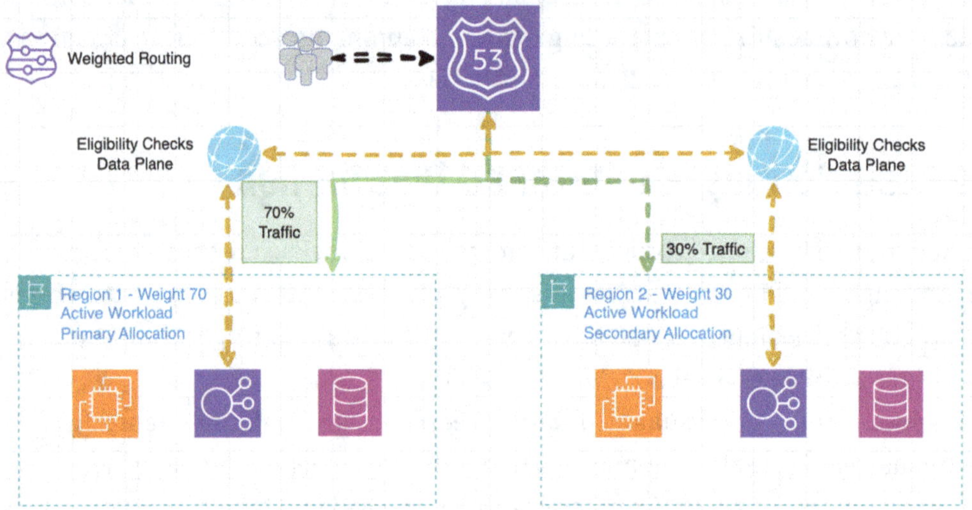

Figure 4-4. *Weighted Routing*

In Figure 4-4, Amazon Route 53 distributes DNS responses across multiple healthy endpoints based on configured weights. In this example, Region 1 receives 70% of traffic, and Region 2 receives 30%. Both regions remain active and eligible as long as their health checks succeed. Weighted routing enables controlled distribution for A/B testing, gradual rollouts, or proportional load sharing while maintaining DNS-layer resilience through continuous data-plane eligibility checks.

Example:

A global e-commerce application deploys a new checkout service. The team creates two records—checkout.example.com—one pointing to version 1 in **us-east-1**, another to version 2 in **us-west-2**. By setting weights of 95 and 5, they divert only 5% of DNS queries to the new stack. If telemetry shows no anomalies, weights are adjusted gradually until version 2 absorbs all traffic.

Because DNS operates on cache expiry, weighted transitions take effect over minutes rather than seconds. Yet for systems where immediacy is not critical, this provides a simple, cost-free release mechanism.

Azure offers an identical **weighted routing** mode, and Google Cloud DNS supports **weighted round robin**. The shared caveat: clients behind recursive resolvers that reuse cached answers may not observe precise percentages. For that reason, use weighted routing for gradual exposure and load spreading, not for precise quota enforcement.

Latency-Based Routing—Performance As a Policy

Latency-based routing is **Amazon Route 53's** mechanism for performance-driven steering. Behind the scenes, AWS operates a vast measurement system that continuously records round-trip times between its **edge locations**—the same global network used by **CloudFront** and **Global Accelerator**—and every AWS Region. These measurements form a constantly refreshed **latency map**, allowing Route 53 to make data-driven decisions rather than relying solely on geography.

When a DNS query arrives, Route 53 evaluates the regions for which you've created **latency records** and answers with the region that provides the **lowest latency** to the user's resolver network, based on AWS's latency measurements. The returned DNS answer reflects observed performance rather than geographic distance, and—because decisions use aggregated measurements rather than per-query probes—clients avoid "flapping" between regions during transient network spikes.

If the recursive resolver provides an **EDNS0 (Extension Mechanisms for DNS) client subnet** field, Route 53 can further refine this decision based on the user's actual network prefix instead of the resolver's address—making the selection even more precise. (We will examine EDNS0 in detail later in this section when discussing how Route 53 estimates user location.)

In practical terms, latency-based routing ensures that a customer in Paris connects to the Frankfurt region, while a user in Sydney reaches Sydney, and one in Chicago reaches Ohio—all without any manual configuration. The result is a **self-optimizing DNS layer** that continuously directs users to the lowest-latency, highest-performing endpoint available, turning the global DNS system into an intelligent performance engine.

This policy is conceptually similar to Azure Traffic Manager's **Performance** method and to Google Cloud DNS's **health-checked routing with geographic fallback**.

Example:

A SaaS provider hosts identical API stacks in **us-east-1**, **eu-central-1**, and **ap-southeast-1**. A customer in Singapore issues a DNS query through a local ISP resolver. Route 53's latency table indicates that ap-southeast-1 averages 45 ms to that resolver, while eu-central-1 averages 200 ms. The DNS response therefore points to the Singapore region. The user experiences faster first-byte times and, indirectly, higher application availability because latency and packet loss correlate under network stress.

Accuracy, however, depends on where the resolver sits. If the user's enterprise tunnels DNS queries through a remote data center, the lookup may be associated with that location instead. AWS mitigates this limitation by leveraging **EDNS0 (Extension Mechanisms for DNS) client-subnet (ECS)** data, described later, which allows authoritative servers to see a truncated prefix of the user's IP and make a more accurate decision.

For workloads requiring deterministic placement, such as compliance-bound data flows, latency policies should be combined with **geolocation** or **IP-based** routing to override unexpected resolver behavior.

Geolocation Routing—Serving by Geography

Geolocation routing enables DNS to tailor its answers based on where a user originates, not merely on which endpoint happens to respond fastest. While latency-based routing optimizes for performance, geolocation routing optimizes for intent—directing users to endpoints that comply with legal, linguistic, or business boundaries.

When Amazon Route 53 receives a DNS query, it first inspects the source IP address of the recursive resolver that issued the request. Using global IP-to-location mapping databases, Route 53 determines the resolver's geographic region—typically at the country or continent level. If the resolver supports **EDNS0 Client Subnet (ECS)**, the DNS query includes a truncated prefix of the actual client's IP address. This allows Route 53 to infer geography more accurately by seeing a fragment of the user's real network rather than the resolver's alone. *(We will cover EDNS0 in depth later in this chapter, including its role in improving location precision.)*

Once the user's location is inferred, Route 53 searches for a geolocation record set defined for that country, region, or continent. The service evaluates these from most specific to least specific—for example, a record defined for *France* takes precedence over one defined for *Europe*. If no explicit match exists, Route 53 uses the default record, which acts as a universal fallback to prevent resolution failures.

This mechanism enables architects to design **region-aware DNS behavior**. Consider a global e-commerce company maintaining infrastructures in North America, Europe, and Asia Pacific. Using geolocation routing, North American users are directed to a front end hosted in *us-east-1*, Europeans to *eu-central-1*, and Asians to *ap-southeast-1*. Each region can display local currencies, comply with data-residency laws such as the GDPR, and operate within appropriate latency boundaries.

From a resilience perspective, geolocation routing provides **fault containment**: an outage in one region doesn't ripple globally, because users outside that geography aren't directed there. If the European infrastructure degrades, only European users are affected; others remain fully operational. This segmentation reduces the blast radius of incidents and allows staggered recovery actions per region.

Geolocation routing also reinforces **compliance resilience**. Many regulated sectors—financial services, healthcare, and the public sector—must ensure that data belonging to specific countries never leaves their jurisdiction. By defining geolocation-based DNS responses, architects can guarantee that French users always land on servers located in France or within the EU, while U.S. users are directed to American infrastructure. DNS-layer enforcement thus becomes a complementary safety net alongside application-level controls.

However, geolocation routing depends on the accuracy of IP mapping. Large ISPs often centralize DNS resolution in other countries, and enterprise VPNs can tunnel queries through remote gateways. This means a user in Switzerland might appear to originate from Germany or even the United States if their resolver is remote. AWS mitigates these effects by frequently refreshing its geolocation databases and by supporting ECS when available. Still, architects should design for imperfection—defining broad catchments (e.g., continent-level) or a robust default record that always provides a reachable endpoint.

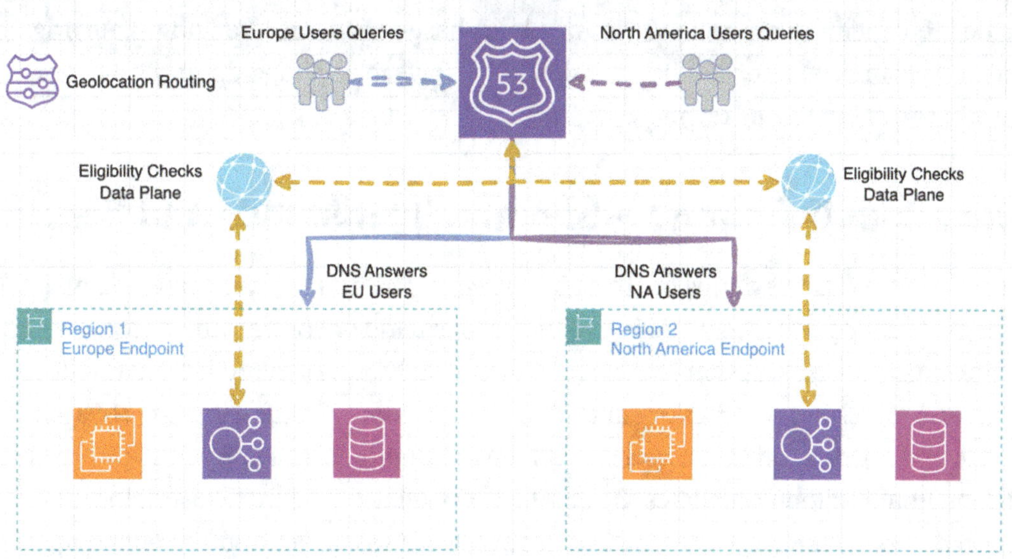

Figure 4-5. *Geolocation Routing*

In Figure 4-5, Amazon Route 53 selects DNS responses based on the geographic origin of each query. In this example, European users are directed to the Europe endpoint, while North American users resolve to the US endpoint. Each endpoint is validated through independent data-plane health checks. Geolocation routing enables localization, compliance with data-residency requirements, and regional fault isolation by steering users to endpoints that correspond to their physical location.

Azure Traffic Manager implements a comparable geographic routing policy, while Google Cloud DNS provides geolocation and geofencing rules for more granular control. All share the same resilience philosophy: use geography to enforce compliance, isolate failures, and preserve user experience across diverse regulatory and latency domains.

When combined with latency-based routing, geolocation routing forms a **layered strategy**: users first land in the correct geographic zone, and within that zone, latency policies fine-tune endpoint selection. Together, they balance compliance, proximity, and performance, ensuring users connect to the right place for the right reason—even during network stress or regional disruption.

Example:

A media-streaming service operates endpoints in North America, Europe, and Asia. Using geolocation routing, European resolvers receive answers resolving to *eu.example.com*, while Asian resolvers receive *apac.example.com*. This keeps content delivery local and enforces region-specific licensing.

The key to resilience here is the **default record**. Not every resolver's IP maps neatly to a defined region—corporate VPNs and cloud-based resolvers often obfuscate origin. A default ensures that unclassified queries still resolve to a valid endpoint instead of returning an *NXDOMAIN* response.

Geoproximity Routing—Steering by Distance and Bias

Geoproximity routing extends the traditional geographic model by introducing **bias**—a manual weighting factor that allows architects to expand or contract the effective reach of a region. While geolocation routing responds strictly based on predefined political boundaries (such as countries or continents), geoproximity routing operates in a **spatial model**, treating each endpoint as a coordinate pair (latitude and longitude) on the globe. Amazon Route 53 then calculates the **geodesic distance** between the user's location (inferred from the resolver or EDNS0 Client Subnet) and each endpoint, returning the one that lies closest in mathematical terms.

The unique power of this model lies in the **bias adjustment**. By default, Route 53 divides the world into *catchment areas*—zones of influence—around each resource. Each bias value, expressed as a positive or negative percentage, expands or contracts those catchments relative to one another. In **Route 53 Traffic Flow**, bias is specified in the range ±1 to ±99, enlarging (positive) or shrinking (negative) a region's catchment accordingly.

A positive bias increases the proportion of queries directed to that region, effectively *pulling* its boundary outward and capturing a larger audience.

A negative bias does the opposite, *pushing* users toward neighboring regions even if those are slightly farther away in physical distance.

This feature is available exclusively through **Route 53 Traffic Flow**, an advanced policy engine that enables architects to design complex routing trees visually or through JSON-based configuration. Traffic Flow compiles those policies into a single global routing rule set and applies them consistently across all AWS edge locations. This approach makes bias adjustments both instantaneous and reversible—a crucial property for resilience operations.

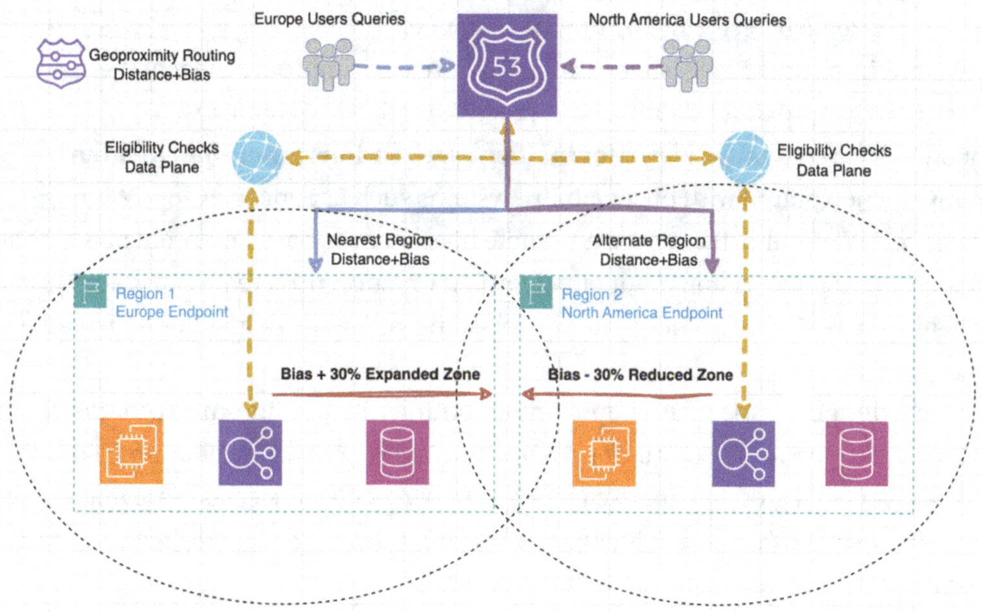

Figure 4-6. *Geoproximity Routing*

In Figure 4-6, Amazon Route 53's Geoproximity Routing steers users to the nearest region based on geographic distance and configurable bias. Each region defines a catchment area—shown as overlapping zones—representing its influence range. Positive bias expands a region's coverage (here, +30% for Region 1), while negative bias reduces it (–30% for Region 2). Adjusting bias allows operators to proactively shape global traffic distribution, offload overloaded regions, or preempt failures without waiting for health checks to trigger.

Example:

Imagine a streaming media platform operating two active regions: *us-east-1 (Virginia)* and *us-west-2 (Oregon)*.

Under normal conditions, Route 53 distributes queries evenly based on distance: users in Chicago are routed to Virginia, and those in San Francisco to Oregon. Suddenly, the Oregon region experiences rising CPU load or limited network throughput.

Instead of waiting for a health check to fail, operators apply a bias of –30% (within the supported ±1 to ±99 range) to us-west-2. Within minutes, the boundary between catchments shifts eastward, diverting part of the western U.S. traffic toward Virginia. The Oregon region stabilizes without triggering a full failover. Once demand normalizes, the bias can be reset to 0, restoring the original balance.

This ability to proactively shape traffic—before thresholds are breached— differentiates geoproximity routing from reactive failover mechanisms.

It provides a soft-control lever for **incident prevention rather than incident response**. When paired with observability systems such as Amazon CloudWatch, Grafana, or AWS Health, teams can automate bias changes based on predictive signals like rising latency, saturation, or queue depth. In practice, this creates an adaptive layer of **preemptive resilience**, where routing decisions anticipate degradation instead of merely reacting to it.

From a design perspective, geoproximity routing can also fine-tune user distribution across multi-region architectures for cost optimization or capacity planning. For instance, if a new region has spare capacity and lower compute costs, applying a small positive bias, say +10%, can gradually attract more traffic to it, allowing teams to test performance before committing to a full migration.

Neither Azure Traffic Manager nor Google Cloud DNS provides a direct equivalent of geoproximity biasing. Azure's Performance routing approximates the intent using latency measurements, and Google's geofencing policies can achieve similar outcomes, but neither supports real-time, manual control of distance-based influence zones.

This makes Amazon Route 53's Geoproximity Routing a uniquely flexible mechanism—bridging the gap between deterministic geographic boundaries and fully dynamic latency-based routing.

When implemented thoughtfully, geoproximity routing becomes a tool for **traffic choreography across continents**—not a binary on-off switch, but a gradient control for graceful scaling, load balancing, and failure avoidance. It reflects the essence of operational resilience: not just recovering from failure, but continuously steering the system away from it.

IP-Based Routing—Deterministic Control

IP-based routing reintroduces **determinism** into what is otherwise a probabilistic, policy-driven DNS world. Introduced by AWS in 2022, this feature extended Amazon Route 53 with CIDR-aware policies for precise, rule-driven responses. It allows architects to define explicit **CIDR (Classless Inter-Domain Routing)** ranges—specific blocks of source IP addresses—and associate each with a unique DNS answer. When a resolver's query originates from an IP that falls within one of those ranges, Route 53 serves the corresponding record, bypassing latency measurements, health checks, and geolocation heuristics entirely.

This mechanism functions as the **DNS-layer equivalent of network ACLs (Access Control Lists)** or routing tables. It enables DNS decisions to follow clear, rule-based boundaries rather than dynamic evaluation. The design intent is **control**—to guarantee that traffic from specific networks always resolves to predefined endpoints. This level of determinism is critical when compliance, regulatory segmentation, or customer isolation must be enforced at the name-resolution layer.

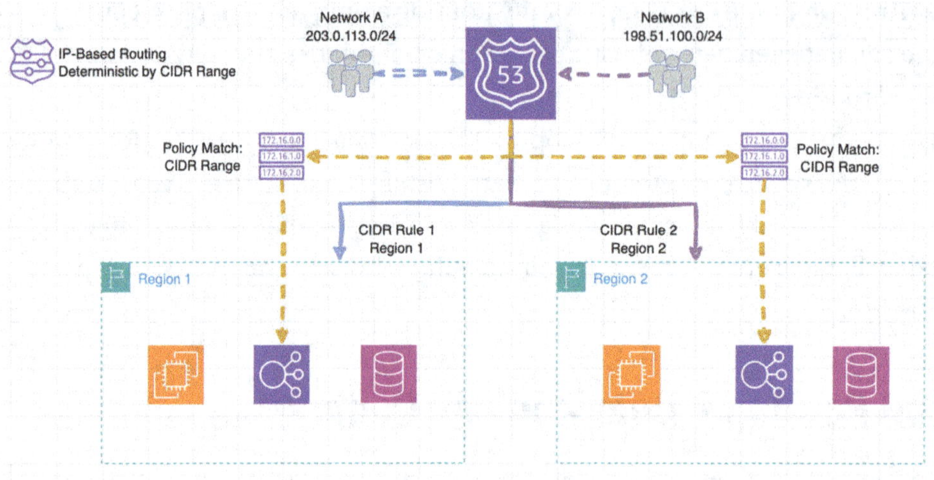

Figure 4-7. *IP-Based Routing*

In Figure 4-7, Amazon Route 53 evaluates each incoming DNS query against predefined **CIDR ranges**. Each range deterministically maps to a specific endpoint or region. In this example, queries originating from **Network A (203.0.113.0/24)** are directed to **Region 1**, while queries from **Network B (198.51.100.0/24)** resolve to **Region 2**. This policy-driven routing model enforces compliance, governance, and customer segmentation at the DNS layer, ensuring predictable and isolated traffic flows.

Example 1—Data Sovereignty Enforcement

A multinational financial institution operates separate AWS environments for European and North American clients to comply with data sovereignty requirements under the **General Data Protection Regulation (GDPR)**.

Using IP-based routing, the company maps all IP ranges belonging to European ISPs to the **Frankfurt region (eu-central-1)** and all North American ranges to **Ohio (us-east-2)**. Regardless of network latency or performance, queries originating from European networks always resolve to Frankfurt. This guarantees that European user data never traverses or is processed outside the EU, even under transient routing or failover conditions.

Example 2—Tenant Isolation in SaaS

A multi-tenant SaaS (Software-as-a-Service) provider serves enterprise customers across distinct verticals—healthcare, finance, and government—each operating under unique compliance obligations.

By defining IP-based routing policies, the provider maps corporate IP spaces to their dedicated back-end stacks. Healthcare clients resolve to one environment, financial institutions to another, and government tenants to a third. This deterministic DNS mapping eliminates the risk of accidental cross-tenant routing or data leakage and reinforces contractual isolation at the network boundary.

From a **resilience standpoint**, IP-based routing can also play a defensive role. During large-scale incidents or DDoS (Distributed Denial-of-Service) mitigation events, administrators can temporarily remap specific IP ranges to alternate endpoints—such as scrubbing centers or limited-capacity "safe" environments—without modifying application code or reconfiguring load balancers. In this way, DNS becomes part of the **incident response toolkit**, capable of re-segmenting traffic flows with surgical precision.

At an architectural level, IP-based routing operates atop the same **Route 53 Traffic Flow** engine that powers weighted and geoproximity policies. Records are evaluated in a deterministic order: first by CIDR match, then by default if no match applies. Because this logic executes within the AWS global DNS fleet, the performance overhead is negligible.

Azure Traffic Manager offers a comparable feature through its **Subnet routing policy**, which similarly maps source IP address ranges to specific endpoints. **Google Cloud DNS**, as of this writing, does not provide a native equivalent; architects must emulate the effect using geofencing or external ACL-based controls.

Azure Traffic Manager offers a comparable feature through its **Subnet routing policy**, which similarly maps source IP address ranges to specific endpoints. **Google Cloud DNS**, as of this writing, does not provide a native equivalent; architects must emulate the effect using geofencing or external ACL-based controls.

In practice, IP-based routing is a powerful blend of **security, compliance, and operational precision**. It transforms DNS from a performance-oriented control plane into a **policy enforcement layer**, ensuring that governance rules are applied at the very first step of a connection, before any packet even leaves the client's resolver.

When combined with other policies such as latency or geolocation routing, IP-based routing provides the ultimate degree of control—allowing global architectures to remain fast, compliant, and predictable even as traffic patterns evolve.

Multi-value Answer Routing—Lightweight Redundancy

After exploring how routing policies can control *where* traffic goes—through weighted, latency-based, or geolocation mechanisms—it's time to look at a policy that focuses on *how many* targets are available at once.

Multi-value Answer Routing (MVAR) offers one of the simplest yet most effective forms of DNS-level redundancy. When a client or resolver issues a DNS query, Amazon Route 53 can return multiple healthy records, typically several A (IPv4) or AAAA (IPv6) addresses, instead of a single one. Each record points to an independent, healthy endpoint, and the resolver or client chooses one to use, often at random or in round-robin order. In practice, Route 53 returns up to eight healthy records per response, giving resolvers multiple viable targets in a single lookup.

Unlike **weighted routing**, which deliberately skews proportions toward or away from specific endpoints, MVAR treats all records equally. And unlike **failover routing**, it does not maintain a strict primary-secondary hierarchy. Every endpoint is a peer; as long as it passes its health check, it is eligible to appear in the answer set. **This peer model reflects resilience through symmetry**—no endpoint is privileged, and the system can lose any subset of nodes without requiring reconfiguration. When one fails, Route 53 simply stops including it, allowing DNS responses to self-adjust without explicit failover logic.

At its core, MVAR delivers **resilience through diversity**. By presenting multiple valid paths, it increases the probability that at least one endpoint is reachable when parts of the infrastructure degrade. Clients or their local resolvers effectively perform a natural load distribution, choosing whichever target succeeds first. If a chosen endpoint fails mid-connection, most modern clients automatically retry the next available IP from the DNS list, creating a seamless, protocol-level failover without any orchestration at the application layer. Each DNS answer therefore represents a *snapshot of health*, not a fixed topology. As instances recover or fail, the answer set evolves naturally, allowing DNS to function as a self-updating catalogue of reachable capacity.

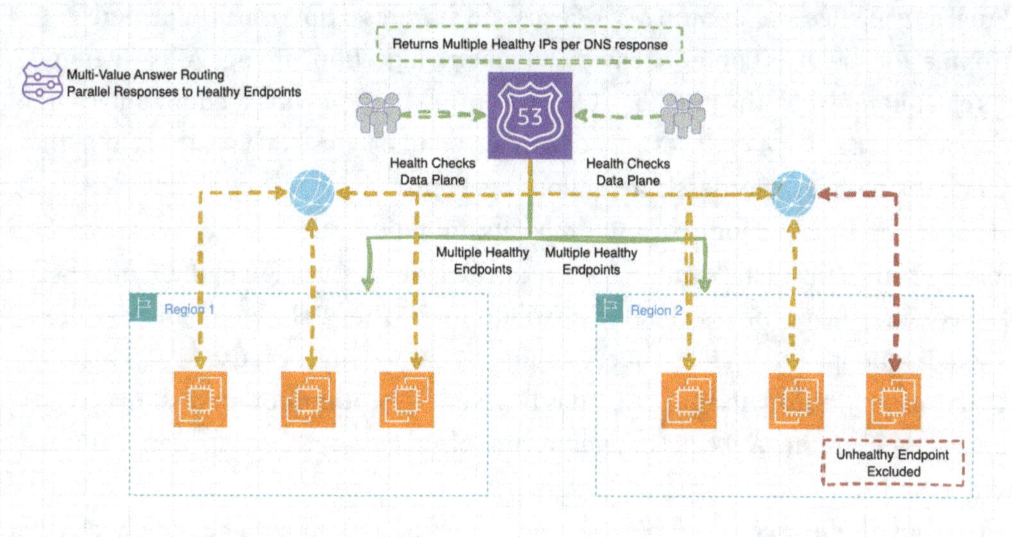

Figure 4-8. *Multi-value Answer Routing*

In Figure 4-8, Amazon Route 53's Multi-Value Answer Routing (MVAR) policy increases resilience by returning multiple healthy IP addresses for a single DNS name. Each endpoint is independently monitored through data-plane health checks, and only healthy targets are included in DNS responses. Clients or resolvers select one endpoint— typically at random—and automatically retry another if the connection fails. In this example, Route 53 excludes an unhealthy endpoint from its response set, allowing the service to self-heal without explicit failover logic. This approach provides lightweight redundancy and natural load distribution for stateless, horizontally scaled workloads such as API gateways, IoT ingestion endpoints, or content delivery tiers.

Example:

An IoT telemetry platform operates dozens of ingestion nodes across North America. Each node runs the same lightweight API for collecting device data. The platform configures a single DNS name, *ingest.example.com*, with a multi-value routing policy that includes eight IPs. Health checks continuously verify reachability and response codes. If three nodes fail due to maintenance or network issues, Route 53 automatically removes their addresses from DNS answers. Millions of devices continue sending telemetry to the remaining healthy nodes with no configuration changes or downtime. As nodes recover, Route 53 re-adds them automatically—illustrating self-healing at the DNS layer.

From a resilience standpoint, MVAR excels in **stateless, horizontally scaled environments**—such as content delivery, telemetry ingestion, or edge APIs—where clients can tolerate reconnecting to a different endpoint. It provides redundancy without the overhead of a Layer 4 or Layer 7 load balancer, and because decisions occur at the resolver level, it scales effortlessly to millions of clients.

However, architects should be mindful of its limitations. DNS responses are cached, and resolvers may reuse the same subset of records for the duration of the **Time-to-Live (TTL)**, reducing the evenness of traffic distribution. Shorter TTLs help refresh address sets more frequently but increase query volume. Additionally, because MVAR relies on clients retrying alternate addresses, it is best suited for **idempotent or short-lived requests**—for example, API calls or telemetry submissions—rather than long-running or stateful sessions.

To maximize effectiveness, MVAR should always be **paired with health checks** that evaluate the complete application path. Testing only TCP port availability may produce false positives; a node that responds to a socket but fails at the application layer will still appear "healthy" to DNS. Using **HTTP(S) health checks** that verify expected responses (such as a 200 OK) ensures DNS only returns endpoints that are genuinely ready to serve traffic.

Multi-value answer routing therefore embodies the idea of **resilience through probability**—not by eliminating failure, but by making individual failures statistically irrelevant. Each DNS response becomes a snapshot of the system's current health, and as that health evolves, Route 53 adapts automatically. It's a simple yet powerful model for globally distributed services where agility, low cost, and graceful degradation matter more than perfect load symmetry.

Having explored routing policies that depend on topology and health, the next step is to understand how Route 53 determines *where a query originates*—the foundation of proximity and latency decisions. This is where **EDNS0 Client Subnet (ECS)** enters the picture, refining DNS responses with network-level context.

Understanding EDNS0 Client Subnet (ECS)—Precision in DNS Decision-Making

So far, we've seen how DNS routing policies decide *where* to send users. But all proximity-based mechanisms share a common challenge: accurately determining where a query originates.

The Domain Name System (DNS), by design, was never built to know who is asking—it only sees the recursive resolver that performs lookups on behalf of clients. While this indirection is essential for scalability, it introduces ambiguity: if millions of users share the same public resolver—such as Google Public DNS (8.8.8.8), Cloudflare (1.1.1.1), or a corporate forwarder—all their queries appear to originate from that single IP, even when they are geographically scattered across continents.

To the authoritative name server, every user behind that resolver seems to live in one place. This misalignment can cause, for example, users in Singapore to be routed to U.S. endpoints simply because their resolver is located there—resulting in higher latency, suboptimal routing, and degraded user experience.

The Origin of EDNS0 and ECS

To overcome this limitation, the Internet Engineering Task Force (IETF) introduced **Extension Mechanisms for DNS (EDNS0)**, defined in *RFC 6891*, as a way to extend DNS messages with optional metadata. Later, *RFC 7871* formally specified the **Client Subnet option (ECS)**—a mechanism that allows recursive resolvers to include a small portion of the original client's IP address in the DNS query.

When a resolver supports ECS, it embeds a truncated prefix of the client's IP network—typically a /24 prefix for IPv4 or a /56 prefix for IPv6—into the query sent to the authoritative server. This prefix doesn't reveal the full client address, only the approximate network from which the query originates, maintaining a balance between precision and privacy.

Armed with this additional context, authoritative servers such as **Amazon Route 53** can make more accurate routing decisions. Instead of assuming that all users of a shared public resolver are in the same place, Route 53 can distinguish between regional network segments, mapping users to the nearest or most appropriate AWS Region.

In essence, EDNS0 with ECS adds a missing layer of context-awareness to DNS—turning a system that once operated blind to user geography into one that can make routing decisions based on the user's true network proximity.

How Route 53 Uses ECS

When a DNS query containing ECS information reaches **Amazon Route 53**, the service inspects the *client subnet field* and cross-references it with internal **latency maps**,

geolocation databases, and any configured **CIDR-based routing policies**. The response that Route 53 returns is therefore specific to that subnet, rather than the generic location of the recursive resolver.

To ensure accuracy and cache integrity, Route 53 includes a **scope prefix** in each DNS response. This field tells the resolver how broadly the cached answer should apply. For example, if the authoritative response specifies a /24 scope, the resolver knows the answer is valid for all clients within that /24 network, but not beyond. This prevents resolvers from reusing the same cached response for users outside that range—avoiding stale or incorrect geographic mappings.

This mechanism turns Route 53 into a highly adaptive, context-aware routing engine. By combining ECS data with its continuous global performance telemetry, Route 53 can make fine-grained, near-real-time decisions that match user traffic to the most suitable AWS Region. In large-scale environments, this precision improves not only latency but also the *stability of routing under stress*—as clients are automatically steered to closer, healthier endpoints without manual intervention. Let's go through an example now to better understand in practice what happens during the resolution.

Consider a user in São Paulo whose Internet Service Provider (ISP) forwards all DNS queries to Google Public DNS, with the resolver servers physically located in California. Without ECS, the authoritative name server only sees the California IP address and assumes the user is nearby. As a result, Route 53 selects the **us-east-1 (N. Virginia)** endpoint, believing it to be the closest. The user's traffic must then traverse thousands of kilometers across multiple network domains, adding latency and potential packet loss.

When ECS is enabled, the recursive resolver appends a prefix from the user's actual Brazilian network—such as 200.150.0.0/24—to the DNS query. Route 53 recognizes that prefix as belonging to South America, cross-references it against its internal latency and geolocation data, and responds with the **sa-east-1 (São Paulo)** endpoint instead. The user now connects to a local region, reducing latency by hundreds of milliseconds and improving application reliability even during periods of global network congestion.

This simple change transforms the user experience. Without any alteration to client software or application logic, ECS ensures that DNS responses are regionally appropriate, aligning routing accuracy with physical reality. The result is a DNS layer that not only knows *where* the service is but also *where the user truly is*.

Privacy and Adoption Landscape

Despite its operational advantages, ECS introduces an inherent privacy trade-off. The client subnet information reveals a portion of the user's network identity to every authoritative server that receives the query. While this prefix is truncated and anonymized, it still exposes regional metadata that some operators and regulators regard as sensitive.

For this reason, ECS adoption varies across the industry. **Google Public DNS** and **Cloudflare's 1.1.1.1** support ECS by default, while **OpenDNS** implements it selectively. In contrast, privacy-focused resolvers such as **Quad9** and **NextDNS** disable ECS entirely to avoid transmitting user location data. Some enterprise DNS resolvers also strip ECS headers from queries as part of their internal compliance policies, ensuring that employee or customer locations remain undisclosed to external systems.

This uneven adoption means that ECS should be viewed as an *opportunistic enhancement* rather than a guaranteed feature. Architectures that rely on DNS-based routing must account for partial visibility—some queries will include client subnet data, others will not. To maintain resilience under these conditions, always define robust fallback paths such as global default records or continent-level mappings. That way, even when ECS data is missing, users still resolve to a safe and reachable endpoint.

Implications for Resilience

From a resilience standpoint, ECS strengthens both performance stability and fault isolation. By improving the accuracy of client-to-region mapping, it prevents distant regions from being overloaded by misrouted traffic and maintains balanced distribution even when parts of the global network degrade. This precision helps systems absorb failures gracefully: when each user connects to the closest healthy region by default, fewer routing changes are required during an incident, reducing both response time and operational noise.

ECS also decreases dependency on aggressive **Time-to-Live (TTL)** adjustments. Because users already reach their optimal endpoints under normal conditions, fewer need to be rerouted during failovers or planned maintenance. This stabilizes global query patterns and makes DNS behavior more predictable during stress events—a critical property of any resilient control plane.

However, ECS introduces a trade-off in operational complexity. Since authoritative servers now vary responses based on client subnets, recursive resolvers must store multiple cached entries for the same domain—one per ECS prefix. This *cache fragmentation* increases memory consumption and slightly elevates DNS query traffic, a deliberate compromise in favor of routing precision. For large-scale public resolvers, this trade-off is measurable but manageable, and for enterprise or cloud workloads, the performance gains often far outweigh the overhead.

In short, ECS enhances the system's ability to deliver consistent, latency-aware routing even in turbulent conditions. By aligning routing decisions with real network geography, it transforms DNS from a reactive lookup service into a proactive participant in resilience—one that keeps users close to healthy endpoints without requiring manual recovery actions.

Cloud Provider Perspectives

Across the major cloud platforms, ECS support varies in depth but follows the same guiding principle—enhancing routing precision through client context. **Amazon Route 53** implements ECS-aware routing natively across its global authoritative network. When a resolver includes ECS data, Route 53 automatically applies it to latency-based, geolocation, and IP-based routing policies, refining each decision according to the user's actual subnet rather than the resolver's location.

Microsoft Azure Traffic Manager and **Google Cloud DNS** also benefit from ECS indirectly, provided that the querying resolvers preserve and forward ECS fields. In these cases, the authoritative systems don't generate ECS data themselves but consume it when available, using the information to fine-tune their geographic and latency decisions.

Ultimately, an authoritative server's ability to act on ECS data depends on one critical variable: whether the upstream resolver includes it. For example, a corporate VPN that tunnels DNS traffic through a central gateway effectively removes any client context—ECS or not. To the authoritative name server, every query then appears to originate from the VPN's exit node, nullifying proximity awareness entirely.

For this reason, architects must align ECS expectations with *real-world client behavior*. Mobile workforces, global ISPs, and enterprise networks often centralize DNS forwarding in ways that mask user geography. In such environments, ECS should be viewed as an opportunistic optimization rather than a deterministic mechanism. When it's present, it dramatically improves routing accuracy and resilience; when it's not, fallback defaults ensure continuity without degradation.

Design Recommendations

To leverage ECS effectively while preserving resilience, architects should treat it as a precision enhancement, not a dependency. ECS can dramatically improve routing accuracy when available, but designs must assume that some resolvers will omit it. The following practices ensure that DNS-based architectures remain both accurate and fault-tolerant:

Assume partial visibility. Always define a default record for queries that arrive without ECS data. This prevents NXDOMAIN responses and ensures continuity when location inference fails.

Use broad geographic groupings. Map records at the continent or subcontinent level rather than at the city or ISP level. Narrow mappings are prone to drift as Internet routing changes.

Pair ECS with latency or IP-based routing. ECS amplifies the effectiveness of these policies by improving location precision while maintaining health-aware decision logic.

Monitor resolver diversity. Use synthetic probes from multiple providers—such as Amazon CloudWatch Synthetics, ThousandEyes, or RIPE Atlas—to confirm that major public resolvers interpret DNS answers as intended.

If we look at the AWS ecosystem, several best practices amplify the benefits of ECS and ensure predictable behavior under load. Keep **Route 53 health checks** close to your endpoints—ideally within the same region—to reflect true data-plane health. Use **short TTLs (30–120 seconds)** for failover-sensitive records, balancing agility with query efficiency. For latency or geolocation routing, verify **EDNS0 support** from your users' common resolvers; Cloudflare and Google Public DNS typically preserve ECS, while corporate DNS appliances may not. Finally, integrate **Route 53 Resolver Query Logs** and **CloudWatch metrics** to monitor how ECS-influenced queries are resolved in production. This visibility ensures that proximity-based routing remains aligned with real-world network paths.

In essence, EDNS0 Client Subnet transforms DNS from a best-effort lookup into a context-aware decision system. It bridges the gap between global Anycast reachability and user-specific experience, refining resilience from the control plane down to the user edge. While it cannot guarantee perfect precision, ECS elevates DNS routing from coarse-grained steering to a dynamic, adaptive mechanism—one that embodies the principles of proximity, performance, and resilience.

Best Practices and Operational Considerations

Routing policies are among the most powerful tools in the DNS architect's arsenal—but without disciplined governance, they can silently introduce new failure modes. DNS itself is deceptively simple: it will faithfully serve whatever records it is given, even if those records direct users to unhealthy or unreachable endpoints. True resilience emerges only when routing logic, health validation, and caching strategies are managed with deliberate intent.

One of the most critical parameters is the **Time-to-Live (TTL)**. TTL defines how long a resolver caches a DNS record before requesting it again, effectively determining how fast routing decisions propagate. During canary deployments, failovers, or maintenance events, shorten TTLs—typically to **30–120 seconds**—so that resolvers discard outdated answers quickly. Once stability returns, extend TTLs to reduce query load and operational noise. As discussed earlier, TTL values must align with the system's **Recovery Time Objective (RTO)**: if the DNS cache persists as long as your intended recovery window, the failover mechanism will not meet its target.

Resilience also depends on **visibility across resolvers**. DNS operates through thousands of intermediaries, each with its own caching and forwarding behavior, and not all respect EDNS0 Client Subnet (ECS) data. Continuous synthetic monitoring from multiple vantage points—using tools such as **Amazon CloudWatch Synthetics**, **ThousandEyes**, or **RIPE Atlas**—verifies that queries from different networks receive the intended answers. This global perspective ensures that latency-based, geo-aware, or failover policies behave as expected in the real world.

Another foundational rule is to **always define a default record**. Geo-based and IP-based policies can leave gaps where queries do not match any defined region or subnet. Without a default, those queries return NXDOMAIN responses, effectively breaking connectivity. A global fallback record guarantees that every request, even from unmapped or privacy-filtered resolvers, resolves to at least one healthy endpoint— eliminating one of the most common configuration oversights in multi-region architectures.

Complex architectures often achieve the best outcomes by **combining multiple routing policies**. Weighted routing layered atop failover provides graceful degradation under load; geolocation combined with latency-based routing balances compliance with performance; and IP-based routing enforced with health checks preserves deterministic control even as network conditions fluctuate. The art of resilient DNS design lies in pairing these mechanisms so that each compensates for the others' limitations—latency for speed, geography for governance, and health for assurance.

Finally, the integrity of **health checks** determines whether DNS failover can be trusted. Probes that merely confirm port 443 availability often yield false positives while the application itself is failing silently. Robust designs validate full transaction paths—checking HTTP 200 OK responses, API authentication flows, or business-logic endpoints—so that DNS transitions reflect genuine service health rather than basic reachability. Many operators integrate these health signals with observability pipelines, using aggregated telemetry to decide when to initiate or reverse failover events.

When these principles are applied consistently, DNS routing policies transcend static configuration. They evolve into a **resilience control plane**—an intelligent, self-correcting layer capable of orchestrating global traffic, adapting to change, and preserving continuity even under systemic stress.

What's Next?

Routing policies define *where* users should connect under normal conditions—balancing performance, compliance, and geographic proximity. But resilience is not only about choosing destinations; it is also about knowing *when* to move away from them. The next challenge lies in timing: detecting when a primary region is no longer trustworthy, validating that a standby is ready to serve, and executing that transition seamlessly before users notice any disruption.

In the next section, we will shift from spatial decision-making to temporal resilience. We will explore how health checks, readiness validation, and automation determine *when* DNS should change its answers, not just *what* those answers should be. My primary focus will be on **Amazon Route 53** and the **Application Recovery Controller (ARC)**, since AWS is the platform I work with most closely and the one through which I can provide the deepest technical insight. The same principles apply to other cloud providers, but in this discussion, we will examine them through AWS's lens—understanding how its failover mechanisms transform routing intent into continuous availability.

Section 4.3: DNS Failover Strategies with Amazon Route 53 and Application Recovery Controller (ARC)

From reactive recovery to orchestrated resilience

DNS routing policies define *where* clients should connect under normal conditions. But resilience is not just about optimized distribution—it's about what happens when things go wrong, how our application reacts, and how we absorb the service impairment without our users being aware. In this book we look at the networking lens concerning our application, so we need to answer some questions: how does DNS know *when* to abandon a failing region, *when* to promote a standby, and how to ensure the destination is actually ready before users are redirected?

This section explores how Amazon Route 53 transforms DNS into a proactive component of high availability and disaster recovery. We'll begin by revisiting the foundational concepts of the **data plane** and **control plane**, showing how their separation underpins AWS's entire resilience strategy. From there, we'll examine DNS failover patterns, health checks, readiness validation, and the orchestration capabilities introduced by the **Application Recovery Controller (ARC)**—including its **Region Switch** feature, which enables seamless cross-region recovery and orchestration.

The goal is to move from reactive failover—where DNS responds only after an outage—to *orchestrated recovery*, where detection, validation, and redirection work together as a coordinated system.

The Two Planes, Revisited: From Reachability to Orchestration

In the previous section, we explored how routing policies determine *where* users are directed during normal operation—weighted for controlled releases, geolocation for compliance, latency for performance, and failover for continuity.

But routing intent alone does not make an architecture resilient. True resilience depends on how *fast* and *safely* traffic can shift when a fault occurs—and that brings us back to a foundational concept first introduced in Chapter 2: the **data plane** and the **control plane**.

The **data plane** is where packets actually flow and where user experience lives.

For DNS, this corresponds to the layer where **Amazon Route 53 health checks** continuously probe endpoints using HTTP(S) requests, TCP socket tests, or CloudWatch metrics.

These probes run from multiple AWS Regions, independent of any central coordination system. Their purpose is simple but critical: to determine, in real time, whether the destinations advertised by DNS are reachable from a user's perspective.

When a quorum of health checkers reports a failure, Route 53 marks the affected record as unhealthy and automatically stops including it in responses.

This instant reflex—driven by the data plane—keeps users connected to healthy endpoints even while parts of the system degrade. It's the network's autonomic response: sense, react, and reroute.

The **control plane**, in contrast, governs orchestration and validation. Within AWS's resilience architecture, this responsibility is shared by the **Application Recovery Controller (ARC)**—a service that bridges both planes.

ARC's **control plane** manages **Readiness Checks**, **Safety Rules**, and **Recovery Plans**.

It continuously validates that target environments have sufficient capacity, correct configuration, and no blocking dependencies before authorizing a failover.

These validations prevent "false recoveries," where DNS might otherwise route users to an environment that appears reachable but cannot yet serve production load.

ARC's **data plane**, however, executes the *actions* themselves. Through its **Routing Controls** and the newer **Region Switch** feature, ARC exposes highly available **regional endpoints** that remain operational even when one or more AWS Regions are impaired.

These endpoints allow you—or your automation systems—to shift traffic deterministically between regions without relying on the very infrastructure you're trying to evacuate.

This design ensures that orchestration commands themselves are resilient; the mechanism of recovery cannot be taken down by the failure it is responding to.

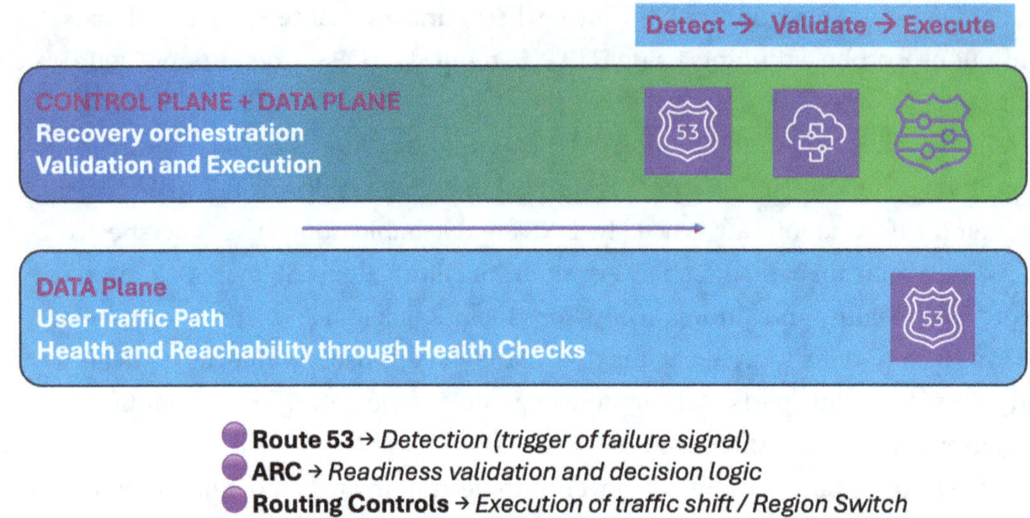

Figure 4-9. The Two Planes of Resilience (Applied to DNS)

In Figure 4-9, the data plane (bottom) represents Route 53 health checks that continuously monitor endpoint reachability. The control + data plane (top) orchestrates recovery across AWS resilience layers: Route 53 detects failure, ARC validates readiness through routing controls, and executes region-level recovery via the Region Switch feature.

Together, they form AWS's failover principle—**Detect ➤ Validate ➤ Execute**—turning health signals into coordinated recovery.

Working Together

Think of the two planes as complementary reflexes in a living system.

The **data plane** reacts instantly to loss of heartbeat, preserving reachability by removing unhealthy endpoints from DNS answers.

The **control plane** reasons about *why* and *when* a shift should occur—verifying readiness, dependencies, and quotas—while ARC's **data plane** executes that shift safely and independently of the failing region.

When these layers operate in concert, failover becomes a *governed* and *auditable* process:

Route 53 continues serving only healthy endpoints.

ARC's control plane ensures that any new target is viable.

ARC's data plane performs the switchover through its globally available endpoints.

Together, they transform reactive failover into **coordinated resilience**, a system that is both fast and correct. This architectural separation addresses one of the most common resilience pitfalls: **conflating detection with recovery**.

DNS health checks can detect degradation, but not every signal warrants an immediate switch.

By coupling Route 53's real-time data-plane awareness with ARC's governed control-plane validation—and executing changes through ARC's data-plane APIs—AWS architectures achieve **measured automation**: recovery that is rapid yet deliberate.

Let me be dramatic; I like that! Automation without validation is chaos; validation without execution is paralysis. ARC unifies both through distinct planes that communicate, not compete.

Here are some lessons I learned throughout my journeys I want to share with you:

1. Treat the data plane and control plane as **independent failure domains**.

2. Always perform orchestration—Region Switch or Routing Control updates—through **ARC's regional data-plane endpoints**, never through a single region's management API.

3. Validate readiness before you shift traffic, and rehearse failover periodically using **ARC practice runs** to verify propagation time, TTL behavior, and safety-rule enforcement.

Now, let's explore how these planes manifest across common deployment models—**Active–Passive**, **Active–Active**, and **Cell-Based topologies**—and how Route 53 and ARC combine features such as **Routing Controls**, **Safety Rules**, and **Region Switch** to deliver recovery patterns that scale from regional to continental levels of resilience.

Patterns of Regional Resilience

With the data and control planes now clearly defined, we can examine how AWS services combine them to achieve regional continuity.

The objective of DNS-driven resilience is not merely to *react* when a region fails; it is to design systems that know *how* to react, *where* to recover, and *when* to act.

Amazon Route 53 and the Application Recovery Controller (ARC) together form the backbone of this orchestration.

Route 53 provides the **data-plane heartbeat** through health checks and routing decisions, while ARC delivers the **governed control and data-plane execution**, ensuring that those routing actions occur only when safe, validated, and compliant.

Across industries, three primary patterns have emerged for implementing regional resilience on AWS: **Active–Passive**, **Active–Active**, and **Cell-Based** architectures.

Each pattern represents a step up in automation, complexity, and fault isolation.

Active–Passive—Predictable and Controlled

The **Active–Passive** pattern is the most straightforward: a single active region handles production traffic while a secondary region stands by, kept warm or cold depending on business tolerance and recovery objectives.

This model aligns closely with traditional disaster-recovery thinking, where cost control and procedural clarity take precedence over instantaneous recovery.

Within AWS, this pattern typically integrates

> **Route 53 failover routing**—to promote standby records when primary data-plane health checks fail

> **ARC readiness checks**—to continuously verify that the standby region has up-to-date configuration, quotas, and dependencies

> **ARC routing controls and region switch**—to execute the transition through regional data-plane endpoints that remain functional even when the primary region is degraded

Because ARC's data-plane APIs operate independently of the region being evacuated, recovery can be triggered from any healthy region or even from on-premises automation.

This decoupling ensures that orchestration commands themselves are resilient and available during the very incident they are intended to mitigate.

The result is deterministic recovery. Traffic shifts only after ARC's control plane confirms readiness, and the switchover executes through ARC's data plane, which is measured, safe, and repeatable.

The trade-off, of course, is efficiency and cost optimization: the passive region consumes cost but remains underutilized until failover.

Nevertheless, industries such as financial services and healthcare favor this approach because **Safety Rules** can enforce manual authorization before DNS promotion, maintaining compliance and auditability.

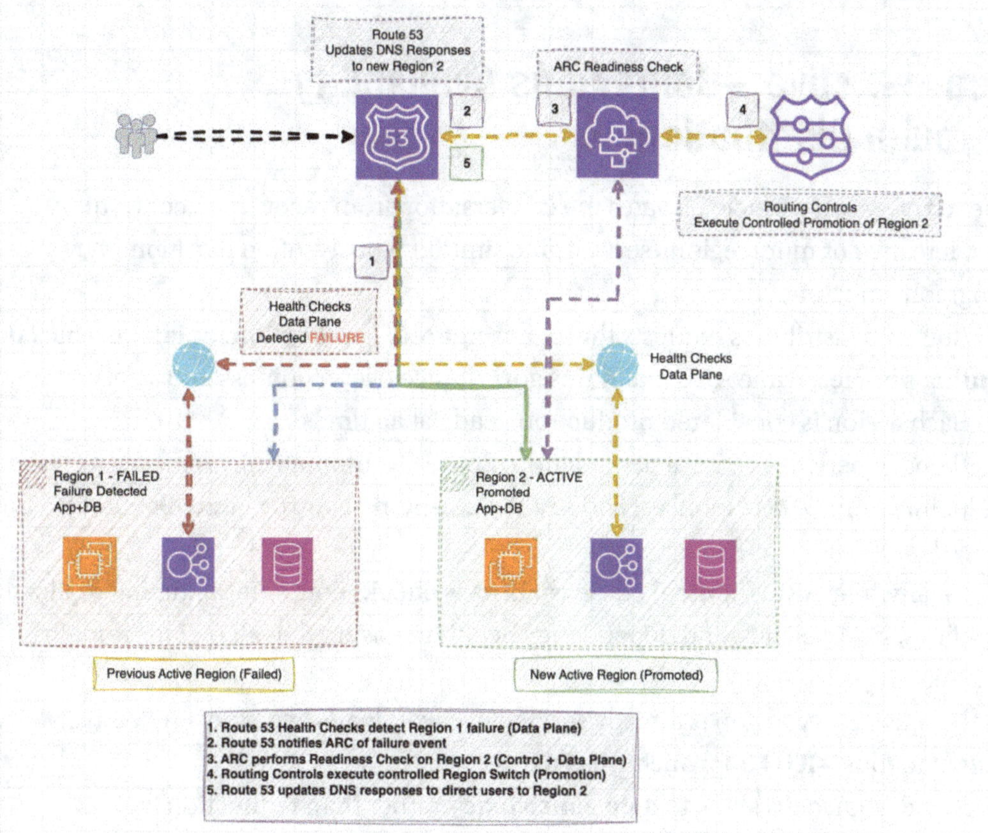

Figure 4-10. *Controller Promotion After Failure (ARC Region Switch)*

In Figure 4-10, we can observe the complete failover sequence executed through the **ARC Region Switch** process, where Route 53 and the Application Recovery Controller work together to ensure a deterministic, controlled transition between regions. When Region 1 (the active site) experiences a failure detected by Route 53 health checks at the **data plane**, the event triggers ARC's **readiness validation** phase. ARC confirms that Region 2, the standby environment, has sufficient capacity, configuration integrity, and dependency health to safely assume production workloads. Once validated, **Routing Controls** perform a controlled promotion of Region 2 using the data plane execution path introduced in August 2025. Finally, Route 53 updates its DNS responses to direct users toward the newly promoted region, completing the **Detect ➤ Validate ➤ Execute** workflow. This process ensures that traffic redirection occurs only after the standby region is fully prepared, avoiding premature or unsafe failover and maintaining operational continuity without manual coordination.

Active–Active—Continuous Availability Through Distribution

The **Active–Active** model elevates the conversation from recovery to continuity.

Here, two or more regions serve traffic simultaneously, often partitioned by geography or latency.

Route 53 distributes requests through **weighted, geolocation,** or **latency-based routing policies**, while **ARC** maintains governance over readiness and safety.

Each region is considered production-ready at all times.

If one experiences partial degradation, Route 53 automatically removes its unhealthy endpoints from DNS responses, and ARC's **data-plane routing controls** can bias traffic away dynamically.

Meanwhile, ARC's **control plane readiness checks** continue validating replication pipelines, IAM policies, and dependency health to ensure that all regions remain equivalent.

Because every region is already serving live workloads, recovery is effectively instantaneous—**RTO approaches zero.**

The design focus shifts to **data consistency** rather than redirection latency.

AWS provides services that make this model viable, including Amazon Aurora Global Database, DynamoDB Global Tables, Amazon S3 Cross-Region Replication, and AWS Global Accelerator for low-latency ingress.

The key benefit of Active–Active architectures is their ability to tolerate partial failure without perceivable downtime.

From a resilience perspective, the user never "fails over"—they simply continue to reach a healthy endpoint.

However, this comes at the cost of complexity: maintaining state synchronization, conflict resolution, and operational parity across regions requires mature processes and testing discipline.

Please note: ARC's Regional Switch is not limited to Active–Passive recovery.

In Active–Active setups, it can selectively drain or isolate regions as a **preemptive containment tool**, executing the change through its regional data plane even during ongoing traffic flow.

Cell-Based Resilience—Isolate, Don't Collapse

Cell-based architectures push resilience to its natural end state: instead of protecting one global monolith, they divide workloads into **independent, fault-isolated cells**, each capable of autonomous operation.

A single AWS Region may host multiple cells, each owning its own micro-stack of compute, data, and DNS resources.

If one cell experiences issues, Route 53 and ARC can isolate it without affecting others.

ARC's **Routing Controls** act as fine-grained switches—enabling or disabling specific cells based on health signals.

Route 53 associates DNS records with those controls, dynamically hiding unhealthy cells from client resolution.

ARC's **Regional Switch** can then reassign affected cells to alternate regions, performing a **cell-level recovery** rather than a full-region cutover.

This pattern minimizes blast radius and accelerates recovery. Rather than a single global failover event, each cell self-heals independently, maintaining service continuity for unaffected customers.

We will revisit this concept in greater technical depth in Chapter 6, where cell isolation, scoped routing tables, and Transit Gateway segmentation form the foundation of blast-radius reduction.

Choosing the Right Pattern

Table 4-1 summarizes these patterns and their trade-offs:

Table 4-1. *Pattern Summary and Trade-Offs*

Pattern	Typical RTO	Typical RPO	ARC Control Plane Role	ARC Data Plane Role	Route 53 Role	Complexity
Active/Passive	**3–10 min** (TTL, health-check quorum, readiness verification, promotion)	**Seconds → minutes** (async replication) **Minutes → hours** if pilot-light/cold-standby	Validates readiness, aplies safety rules	Execute Region Switch/Routing updates via data-plane endpoints	DNS Failover on health-check loss	Medium
Active/Active	**< 60 s** (often **seconds**) — instant from user perspective once one Region is withdrawn	**0–seconds** depending on data tech: 0 with true multi-writer semantics; **sub-second to a few seconds** with Aurora Global Database/DynamoDB Global Tables	Continuous validation and scaling	Dynamic routing bias, regional containment	Latency/Weighted routing	High
Cell-Based	**Seconds** (per-cell isolation/redirect)	**Near-zero per cell** (state scoped; async lag limited to the impacted cell)	Coordinates cell health and dependencies	Isolates/Redirects specific cells	Cell-level DNS visibility	Verry High

Table 4-1 illustrates how recovery objectives evolve as architectures mature from Active–Passive to Active–Active and finally to Cell-Based models.

In **Active–Passive** designs, recovery time is governed primarily by DNS caching (TTL), health-check thresholds, and automation speed. Even in well-tuned systems, end-to-end **RTO typically ranges from three to ten minutes** once you include propagation and validation delays.

The **RPO**—the acceptable amount of data loss—is usually in the **seconds-to-minutes range** when asynchronous replication is used, as is common for databases or file systems.

Only highly specialized deployments using synchronous cross-region writes can achieve near-zero RPO, and they do so at the expense of latency and cost.

In these models, the control plane's role is to confirm that the standby region is genuinely ready before the data plane executes a **Region Switch** or promotes secondary records, avoiding premature failover.

Active–Active architectures narrow both objectives dramatically; because every region already serves live traffic, the **RTO is effectively instantaneous** from the user's point of view—DNS merely removes the failing region's records.

The **RPO** depends almost entirely on the data technology in use: multi-writer databases or DynamoDB Global Tables can sustain near-zero data loss, while systems with replication lag (Aurora Global Database, S3 CRR) operate within sub-second windows.

Here, Route 53's routing policies manage distribution, ARC's control plane enforces readiness and scaling consistency, and its data plane adjusts traffic bias or isolation through routing controls in real time.

Cell-based resilience changes the recovery metric itself. Instead of measuring global downtime, each cell owns its own state and recovery boundary, meaning **RTO and RPO are calculated per cell** rather than per region.

If one cell fails, only that isolated slice of traffic shifts—often in a few seconds—while others remain untouched.

ARC's Routing Controls and Safety Rules enable this fine-grained governance, and Route 53's DNS mappings expose each cell independently, preventing localized incidents from scaling into systemic outages.

Across all three models, the lesson is clear: reducing RTO and RPO is not a matter of one mechanism but of layering disciplines.

Route 53 provides rapid, data-plane-driven detection; ARC adds control-plane validation and data-plane execution; and architectural patterns determine how much of the system must move before users see recovery.

As organizations evolve along this spectrum, resilience shifts from **reactive recovery** to **continuous availability**—the hallmark of modern cloud design. We will go deep in each of these patterns in Chapter 6.

Design Takeaways

ARC is dual-plane by design.

The control plane validates and governs readiness; the data plane executes routing control and Region Switch actions via independent regional endpoints.

Choose the pattern that fits your maturity.

Start with Active–Passive for clarity, evolve to Active–Active for continuity, and adopt Cell-Based for isolation once operational automation is mature.

Rehearse the process, not just the plan.

Use ARC Practice Runs to measure propagation, validate TTL alignment, and confirm that orchestration APIs remain callable from non-affected regions.

Integrate observability.

Combine ARC Readiness Checks with CloudWatch alarms and Route 53 health-check metrics to maintain a closed feedback loop between detection, validation, and action.

Route 53 Health Checks—The Heartbeat of DNS Failover

At the core of every DNS-based recovery strategy lies a simple but powerful idea: **you can only route intelligently if you know what is healthy**.

Amazon Route 53's health checks form the data plane's sensory system—the distributed network of probes that continuously measure service reachability from multiple vantage points across the globe.

Together, they serve as the heartbeat of DNS failover, translating raw availability into routing decisions that keep users connected even when infrastructure suffers service impairments. So, let's try to understand together how they do work.

Each **Route 53 health check** is an independent probe that evaluates a target endpoint's availability.

Checks can target a public hostname, an IP address, a CloudWatch metric, or even the health of another health check (known as a **calculated health check**).

They run at regular intervals—typically every 30 seconds—from multiple AWS health-checker regions spread across North America, Europe, and Asia-Pacific.

When a health check is created, Route 53 automatically deploys it to **a global fleet of health checkers**, each performing requests over separate network paths.

These distributed agents simulate real user traffic, using either HTTP(S) requests, TCP socket opens, or HTTPS with optional string matching to verify content.

Each checker independently records success or failure, and a **majority quorum** determines the global health status. This approach filters out localized Internet noise: a single region's transient packet loss will not mark an endpoint as unhealthy.

Aggregating and Acting on Results

Once results are aggregated, Route 53 updates the endpoint's health status within seconds.

If a quorum of checkers report failure, the record is marked unhealthy, and DNS answers referencing it are removed from subsequent responses. This transition is purely data-plane-driven—it requires no control-plane interaction, making it resilient even when AWS management APIs are degraded.

Health check results can also feed higher-order decisions through **calculated health checks**, which combine multiple child checks using Boolean logic.

For example, you can define a parent check that evaluates as "healthy" only if *two of three* application endpoints succeed, or one that requires both an application server and its database dependency to respond.

This allows architects to express complex dependency trees directly in Route 53's data plane, enabling DNS to act only when true service health—not just network reachability—is confirmed.

In failover routing policies, health checks are the trigger that demotes the primary endpoint and promotes the secondary one.

In weighted or multi-value policies, they determine which records remain eligible for inclusion in DNS answers.

The principle is consistent: **Route 53 never serves an endpoint marked unhealthy**, regardless of routing policy.

Advanced Configurations and Integration

Beyond direct probing, Route 53 supports integration with **Amazon CloudWatch** for service-level health.

You can configure health checks to evaluate a CloudWatch metric instead of making network calls—for example, triggering "unhealthy" if latency exceeds a threshold or if error rates spike.

This approach extends DNS awareness into higher layers of the stack, aligning it with application telemetry rather than simple TCP success. We are moving away from networking here, but it's important to understand that we should be "aware" of the upper layers also to better deploy resilience mechanisms.

Health checks can also monitor **private resources** inside VPCs through **Private Health Checks**, evaluated via VPC endpoints. These checks are critical for hybrid and internal systems, where external probing cannot reach internal IPs but failover or routing decisions are still required.

Private health checks follow the same quorum model but operate from within the AWS network boundary, ensuring consistent logic with global checks.

To centralize visibility, all health check data can be streamed into **Amazon CloudWatch Metrics**, allowing teams to build dashboards, alarms, and automation workflows.

Common practices include setting alarms to notify operators when checks approach unhealthy thresholds or using AWS Lambda to trigger custom recovery actions. This is very important, as its part of operational resilience, which includes monitoring and observability, and it's foundational. Without testing and observability, any type of resilience we structure is almost ineffective. As I mentioned already previously, without testing, we don't know if the application will be able to sustain service impairments as we would have expected.

Ultimately, when combined with ARC, these same signals can trigger **Routing Controls** or **Region Switch operations**—bridging detection with orchestration through both planes.

Best Practices for Reliable Health Monitoring

And just because we talked about observability and testing, here are some best practices:

Test the full path, not just the port.

Avoid health checks that only verify TCP port 443 availability. Instead, perform an HTTP(S) check that expects a specific status code or string match. This confirms application-level readiness, not just network connectivity.

Balance frequency and cost.

Default 30-second intervals provide fast reaction time with minimal cost. For mission-critical systems, 10-second checks can be justified but should be reserved for endpoints with low latency variance and clear thresholds.

Leverage calculated health checks.

Combine multiple signals—application API, backend database, and dependency health—into one logical indicator of service readiness.

Monitor from multiple perspectives.

Use both Route 53's internal health checkers and external tools like **ThousandEyes**, **RIPE Atlas**, or **CloudWatch Synthetics** to verify that results align with real user experience.

Tune TTL values for propagation.

Shorter TTLs (30–60 seconds) reduce recovery lag but increase resolver load. Adjust TTLs according to your RTO goals, as discussed in Section 4.2.

Integrate with observability.

Export health check metrics to CloudWatch, Grafana, or third-party dashboards, ensuring visibility across DevOps and SRE workflows.

Pair detection with governance.

Health checks detect loss; ARC decides *when* and *how* to respond. Integrate both to avoid overreaction to transient faults.

Example: Layered Detection and Action

Consider a financial-trading platform hosted across eu-central-1 and eu-west-1.

Each region's web tier, application tier, and order API are individually monitored through HTTP health checks.

A calculated parent check evaluates the entire region as healthy only if all three succeed.

When the Frankfurt web tier begins returning 500 errors, its check fails, but the parent remains healthy until the dependent checks also fail—preventing premature regional failover.

Once a quorum of checkers reports full service degradation, Route 53 removes the Frankfurt records from DNS answers, ARC validates the readiness of Dublin, and the **Region Switch** executes the transition, all automatically.

From the user's perspective, the shift occurs within a minute, with no manual intervention.

Health checks provide the *detection layer*; they know what's unhealthy.

ARC adds the *decision and execution layer*—it knows when and how to act.

In the next subsection, we'll connect these signals to the mechanisms that govern global traffic movement, exploring how automation transforms failover from a reactive event into a continuous, auditable process.

Orchestrating Failover with ARC: Routing Controls, Safety Rules, and Region Switch

Health checks tell us *what* is unhealthy.

Orchestration decides *what happens next*.

Within AWS, this responsibility lies with the **Application Recovery Controller (ARC)**—a service designed to make failover both **automatic** and **auditable**.

ARC connects Route 53's data-plane signals to a distributed orchestration system that spans both planes: the **control plane**, which governs readiness and authorization, and the **data plane**, which executes the actual traffic shift through **Routing Controls** and **Regional Switch** operations.

Together, these capabilities turn reactive failover into **coordinated resilience**, ensuring that recovery occurs quickly, safely, and with full situational awareness.

Routing Controls—The Data Plane Switchboard

At the heart of ARC's data plane are **Routing Controls**—binary switches that represent whether a specific traffic path should be active or inactive.

Each Routing Control belongs to a **Routing Control Group**, which defines the logical boundaries of traffic management—commonly one per region, AZ, or application cell.

These controls are exposed through highly available **regional data-plane endpoints**.

Even if the control plane or the affected region is impaired, the Routing Control APIs remain callable from any healthy region.

This separation ensures that the mechanism of recovery is itself resilient—operators and automation systems can perform failover actions even when part of the AWS management stack is unavailable.

Routing Controls are typically integrated with **Route 53 ARC-managed health checks** or with **traffic management systems** like Global Accelerator.

When a Routing Control is toggled from "off" to "on," the change propagates immediately across AWS's distributed DNS data plane, enabling or disabling corresponding endpoints.

In practice, this provides near-instant traffic redirection without touching DNS configuration or redeploying infrastructure.

Example:

A media-streaming company maintains two active regions, each with its own Routing Control.

When latency in the Frankfurt region spikes, ARC automatically toggles its Routing Control to "off" based on predefined metrics.

Within seconds, Route 53 and Global Accelerator stop advertising Frankfurt endpoints.

When latency normalizes, the control is toggled back to "on," restoring balance.

All of this occurs via ARC's regional data plane—independent of the impaired region.

Safety Rules—Guardrails for Automation

While automation accelerates recovery, it also magnifies the consequences of error.

ARC mitigates this through **Safety Rules**—policies that enforce operational sanity before a Routing Control or Region Switch can execute.

Safety Rules are evaluated in the **control plane**, but their enforcement gates actions in the **data plane**.

They can require manual approval, ensure quorum among multiple operators, or restrict the number of simultaneous failovers within a given scope.

For example, a rule might state that no more than one region per application may be disabled at once, or that a manual authorization token is needed before promoting a standby region to production.

By codifying these safeguards, ARC turns recovery from an ad-hoc event into a **policy-driven operation**.

It also provides **auditability**: every action—automated or manual—is logged in AWS CloudTrail, satisfying governance requirements for regulated industries.

Example:

A financial trading platform defines a Safety Rule requiring two separate approvals for Regional Switch operations.

When health checks fail in eu-central-1, the automation workflow proposes a switch to eu-west-1.

ARC evaluates the rule, detects that approval is pending, and blocks execution until both authorizations are received.

Once approved, the data-plane switch executes instantly.

The result: automation with accountability.

Region Switch—Coordinated Recovery Across Regions

On **1 August 2025**, AWS introduced one of the most significant advancements in multi-region resilience: **ARC Region Switch**.

Until now, orchestrating a region-wide failover required custom scripts or fragmented runbooks. Region Switch consolidates these tasks into a managed, globally available system that can promote, demote, or rebalance entire regions through a single workflow.

A **Region Switch plan** defines an ordered set of *execution blocks*—each representing a recovery action. These can include enabling or disabling routing controls, updating Route 53 records, scaling compute capacity in the standby region, promoting database replicas (e.g., Amazon Aurora Global Database failover), or invoking custom AWS Lambda functions for bespoke steps such as cache warm-ups or IAM policy adjustments. The entire plan is executed atomically: either all steps succeed, or none do, preserving operational consistency even in complex topologies.

Crucially, Region Switch relies on **regional data-plane endpoints**, so failover can be initiated from a healthy region even if the affected region's control plane is unavailable. Each region can trigger its own switch, ensuring that recovery paths remain viable during partial outages. This design aligns perfectly with AWS's *static stability* principle—systems must be operable even when control infrastructure is impaired.

Before any Region Switch executes, ARC performs **Readiness Checks** that validate the standby region's capacity, dependencies, and service quotas. Only when every prerequisite passes does the data-plane operation proceed. This measured approach transforms failover from a race against time into a predictable, governed transition.

Example

Consider a global SaaS provider operating its primary control plane in us-east-1 and a secondary replica in eu-central-1. ARC Readiness Checks continuously validate that Frankfurt maintains synchronized databases, sufficient EC2 capacity, and all dependencies online. When us-east-1 begins to degrade, ARC triggers a Region Switch plan that deactivates routing controls in the United States, scales Frankfurt to full capacity, updates Route 53 health checks and DNS records, and finally reclassifies us-east-1 as standby. Because execution occurs via regional data-plane endpoints outside both regions, the switch completes seamlessly—without waiting for management-plane recovery.

This new model also allows nested or *child* switch plans, enabling selective recovery of specific applications or cells without promoting an entire region. Large enterprises can therefore orchestrate tiered failovers—switching only high-priority workloads first—while maintaining governance through safety rules and audit logs.

Operating Region Switch Effectively

Region Switch introduces new operational patterns that blend automation with preparedness. Plans can be triggered manually by operators, scheduled through AWS EventBridge, or automatically invoked when CloudWatch alarms breach defined thresholds. Each plan is continuously validated by ARC's internal 30-minute readiness evaluation, ensuring that latent misconfigurations are surfaced before a real incident occurs.

Architects should treat Region Switch plans as living runbooks, versioned, rehearsed, and tested regularly in non-production scenarios.

The ability to include Route 53 updates within these workflows is particularly transformative. DNS no longer operates in isolation; it becomes one of many coordinated actions, executed alongside compute scaling, database promotion, and routing control updates. This alignment brings consistency to multi-region recovery, replacing human coordination with deterministic automation.

From AWS's operational guidance, several principles have emerged since the launch of Region Switch.

First, always design **Region Switch plans to execute from outside the regions they affect**, ensuring survivability under worst-case isolation.

Second, codify Safety Rules and Readiness Checks under version control and review them during Game Days just as rigorously as application code.

Third, integrate telemetry from ARC and Route 53 into unified dashboards to visualize both planes of resilience—detection and orchestration—in one view.

Finally, conduct frequent *practice runs* to validate that propagation delays, TTL expirations, and workflow latencies align with business RTO targets.

Like I mentioned already, true resilience is not the absence of failure; you will fail, just embrace it... Resilience is the ability to perform recovery, adapt, and recover with confidence and efficiency.

In summary, Region Switch elevates DNS failover from reactive redirection to **governed orchestration**. It closes the loop between Route 53's detection and ARC's decision-making, uniting health awareness, readiness validation, and controlled execution under a single framework.

With these mechanisms in place, resilience ceases to be a manual procedure—it becomes part of the network's living fabric.

In the next section, we will take this concept one layer higher, exploring how organizations combine Route 53 with secondary authoritative systems to ensure that even DNS itself never becomes a single point of failure.

Section 4.4: Using Multiple DNS Providers for Redundancy

Up to this point, we've focused on building resilience within a single DNS system—designing architectures that stay available even when regions, endpoints, or networks fail. However, no matter how globally distributed a provider is, it remains a **single administrative and operational domain**. True fault isolation requires diversity not just across regions but across providers.

This section explores how organizations extend their resilience strategy beyond one platform by adopting **multi-DNS architectures**—a design where two or more authoritative DNS providers serve identical zones in parallel. We will examine how this approach protects against provider-level outages, what synchronization and governance challenges it introduces, and how to implement it effectively when **Amazon Route 53** is the primary authoritative source.

While AWS Route 53 delivers exceptional global availability through its Anycast edge network, health-checked routing, and Application Recovery Controller (ARC) integration, the modern resilience landscape may demand an additional layer of assurance. As digital systems underpin financial services, healthcare, regulated entities, and critical infrastructure, even the rarest DNS-provider event can have a disproportionate business impact. Multi-DNS designs exist to make such events survivable.

Why Multi-DNS Architectures Exist

In earlier sections, we explored how resilient DNS design within a single provider—using failover, weighted, latency, or geolocation routing—can achieve high availability through distributed infrastructure and intelligent health-based decision-making. Yet even the most distributed DNS platform is bound to the limits of its own ecosystem. When the provider itself experiences a control-plane or data-plane impairment, that resilience boundary collapses.

This is the problem that **multi-DNS architectures** were built to solve.

The turning point came after several large-scale DNS disruptions that exposed the fragility of relying on a single provider. The most notable was the **Dyn DNS DDoS attack of 2016**, where the Mirai botnet overwhelmed Dyn's infrastructure, interrupting name resolution for major global brands despite Dyn's own geographic redundancy. Other less visible—but equally instructive—events include propagation slowdowns, stale zone updates, or API-layer outages across multiple cloud DNS services. Each demonstrated that *redundancy inside a provider* is not the same as *redundancy across providers*.

For enterprises operating under tight SLAs or regulatory frameworks—such as banks, insurers, and digital-commerce platforms—this realization reframed DNS from a performance feature into a **risk domain**. Outages, even brief ones, erode customer trust and can breach contractual availability commitments.

The multi-DNS approach distributes that risk by maintaining two or more **independent authoritative zones** hosted on different networks. In AWS-centric architectures, **Amazon Route 53** often serves as the primary provider, paired with a secondary such as **Cloudflare**, **NS1**, or **Akamai**. Both hold synchronized records, allowing resolvers to query either provider interchangeably. If one suffers a control-plane or propagation failure, global resolution continues seamlessly via the other.

Beyond disaster mitigation, multi-DNS also delivers operational advantages. It allows teams to test new configurations on a secondary provider before propagating globally, benchmark resolver reachability between networks, or compare Anycast edge performance by geography. In effect, it turns DNS from a static dependency into a **measurable, testable layer of resilience**.

However, this design also introduces new complexities: managing serial alignment, propagation consistency, and health-check parity between independent systems. These will be discussed in the following subsections.

At its core, multi-DNS is an **evolutionary step**—from relying on a single global network to orchestrating multiple authoritative planes of control. It is not simply a backup; it is the foundation of true **cross-vendor resilience**, where no single provider can silence a name.

However, it is important to understand that **multi-DNS is not a universal requirement**. This level of redundancy introduces operational overhead, financial cost, and architectural complexity. Not every organization—or every workload—needs it. For many modern cloud-native applications, the inherent resilience of a single provider such as Route 53, backed by Anycast routing and distributed health checks, already meets or exceeds their recovery objectives.

Multi-DNS architectures should therefore be adopted **deliberately**, not reflexively—driven by business requirements such as regulatory uptime mandates, risk diversification policies, or mission-critical latency and availability targets. In the absence of these drivers, the added complexity may outweigh the resilience benefits. As with all aspects of resilient architecture, the goal is not maximal redundancy but **appropriate redundancy**—right-sized for the risk, cost, and recovery expectations of the system.

Operating Modes at a Glance

Multi-DNS deployments are typically operated in two modes: **active–active**, where multiple authoritative providers serve the same zone concurrently, and **active–passive**, where a secondary provider remains idle until needed. Active–active maximizes availability and reduces failover delay by leveraging resolver diversity, but it demands strict synchronization. Active–passive is simpler and reduces the risk of drift, at the cost of slower authority switching. We'll compare these models in detail later in this section.

Meanwhile, the following section quickly illustrates how an active–active configuration operates in real-world AWS environments and how Route 53 coordinates with secondary providers to maintain parity and responsiveness. We'll then return to a deeper comparison later in this section after we walk through an active–active example and its supporting automation.

How It Works in Practice

For AWS environments, **Amazon Route 53** typically acts as the primary provider, serving authoritative responses through its global Anycast edge network and integrating health-based routing decisions via the data plane. A secondary DNS provider—such as **Cloudflare**, **Akamai Edge DNS**, or **NS1**—is configured with an identical zone. Both publish their name servers in the parent domain's delegation records, meaning resolvers can query either provider interchangeably.

When properly configured, recursive resolvers treat the two DNS providers as peers. If Route 53 becomes temporarily unreachable, queries are automatically resolved through the secondary provider's network. This passive failover happens at Internet scale, without requiring API calls, ARC orchestration, or DNS record edits—making it one of the simplest and most powerful forms of vendor-level redundancy.

Zone Synchronization and Automation

Running multiple authoritative sources requires **strict synchronization discipline**. Both providers must maintain identical zone contents, record types, and TTL values. Even minor drift—such as one zone having an outdated CNAME or stale SOA serial—can lead to inconsistent responses across resolvers.

There are several ways to achieve this consistency in AWS environments:

> **API-Based Synchronization:** Use AWS Lambda or AWS Step Functions to pull Route 53 zone data via the list-resource-record-sets API and push updates to the secondary provider through its REST API (e.g., NS1 or Cloudflare's Zone Update endpoints).

> **EventBridge Automation:** Configure EventBridge to detect ChangeResourceRecordSets API events in Route 53 and automatically replicate those changes to the secondary provider, ensuring near real-time synchronization.

> **DNS Zone Transfers (AXFR/IXFR):** Although less common in managed cloud DNS, some providers support secure zone transfers, allowing one to act as a master and others as secondaries. This model, however, is not supported natively by Route 53 and typically requires a synchronization function or partner integration layer.

To verify alignment, operators can implement **zone-diff checks**, comparing SOA serials and record hashes across providers. Cloud-native monitoring tools such as **CloudWatch Synthetics**, **Catchpoint**, or **DNSCheck** can continuously probe both providers and flag deviations before they propagate globally.

TTL Alignment and Convergence

Time-to-Live (TTL) consistency is critical in Active–Active DNS because it defines how long recursive resolvers cache responses before querying again. If one provider uses a TTL of 60 seconds and the other 300 seconds, resolvers may favor cached records from the slower-expiring provider, resulting in asymmetric failover behavior.

To maintain predictable resolution behavior, always align TTLs across all providers, using **short values (30–120 seconds)** for failover-sensitive records. Longer TTLs can be used for static data such as TXT or MX records, where freshness is less critical. TTLs should also reflect the architecture's **Recovery Time Objective (RTO)**, as established earlier in this chapter, and align TTLs with RTO so DNS convergence doesn't consume your entire recovery window.

Health Checks Across Providers

While both DNS networks answer the same queries, only **Amazon Route 53** integrates **data-plane health checks** and automated failover logic natively. Secondary DNS providers typically rely on **static record states** or **external health signals** to determine endpoint availability. To synchronize health status across providers, architects can export Route 53's real-time health information through **Amazon CloudWatch** and **EventBridge**, enabling other systems to consume those signals.

In practice, this is achieved by configuring **CloudWatch alarms** on Route 53 health checks. When a monitored endpoint transitions to an *unhealthy* state, the alarm triggers an **EventBridge rule**, which invokes an automation function—often an **AWS Lambda** or external webhook—to notify the secondary DNS provider's API. The automation disables or modifies the corresponding record on that provider's network, mirroring Route 53's state. When the health check later recovers, the process reverses, restoring the record to "active" status.

This event-driven model keeps both DNS providers synchronized without relying on periodic polling or manual intervention. It also aligns with the **networking discipline** underpinning this book: maintaining data-plane parity across control boundaries. The architecture ensures that when Route 53 withdraws an endpoint from service, the secondary provider reflects the same change within seconds—preventing divergence where one DNS network continues to advertise an unhealthy destination. Because these health signals and automations are provider-agnostic, the same pattern extends directly to steering between clouds—a topic we cover next.

Multi-cloud with DNS: Steering Across Clouds

Multi-cloud DNS is not only about surviving a single provider's outage; it's also a way to steer users between clouds (e.g., AWS ↔ Azure ↔ Google Cloud) while preserving the same resilience principles you've applied within AWS. At the name layer, the pattern is straightforward: publish a single, stable hostname (e.g., api.example.com) whose answers can point to independently operable front doors in each cloud—an Amazon ALB/NLB or Global Accelerator in AWS, an Azure Front Door profile, or a Google Cloud external HTTP(S) Load Balancer. Route 53 remains your "source of truth," but your secondary DNS provider is kept in sync so either network can resolve the hostname during control-plane incidents.

Two technical details make this work in practice. First, **health detection** must reflect each cloud's *data plane.* Route 53 health checks can monitor Internet-reachable endpoints anywhere (not just in AWS) and can be driven by direct probes (HTTP/TCP), by aggregating other checks, or by following a CloudWatch alarm—useful when you want failover decisions to hinge on application SLOs or synthetic tests rather than raw port up/down. Second, **event propagation** must carry those health signals across DNS providers. CloudWatch alarm state changes appear on Amazon EventBridge, where rules can invoke automation (e.g., AWS Lambda) to toggle records in your secondary DNS via its API. That keeps both authoritative networks consistent within minute-scale TTL windows, instead of drifting during an incident.

Because Route 53 doesn't act as an AXFR/IXFR master, zone parity is achieved via APIs: detect Route 53 ChangeResourceRecordSets events (or poll), then replicate the exact change set to the secondary provider. NS1 Connect exposes a comprehensive REST API and SDKs to update records deterministically, which makes it a common pairing in the field. For cryptographic integrity in multi-cloud, prefer **multi-signer DNSSEC** (RFC 8901): each provider signs the same zone with its own keys, while the registrar publishes a coherent DS set (we will talk about DNSSEC later in the next section of this chapter). Cloudflare and other networks document this model, and it's become the de facto way to keep DNSSEC enabled across multiple authoritative platforms without pausing signing during migrations.

Operationally, success looks like this: endpoints in each cloud are independently healthy and observable; Route 53 health checks (and/or CloudWatch alarms) reflect user-visible behavior; EventBridge + Lambda replicate state to the secondary DNS; short, aligned TTLs govern convergence; and DNSSEC (multi-signer) preserves authenticity across providers. The net result is cross-cloud failover that is *data-plane aware, event-driven,* and *cryptographically verifiable*—not just "two places answering."

The following example shows this pattern in a mixed AWS–Azure deployment, with Route 53 driving health and a secondary provider mirroring state.

Operational Example

Let's see how **multi-cloud DNS** works in practice. Consider a **global financial-services platform** operating in a **multi-cloud architecture**: its primary workloads run on **AWS**, while regulatory data-processing services reside in **Azure**, both fronted by independent load balancers. To provide unified resolution and cross-cloud resilience, the company uses **Amazon Route 53** as its primary authoritative DNS and **NS1** as a secondary provider.

Both zones—examplebank.com—contain identical A and CNAME records with a TTL of 60 seconds, pointing to endpoints in each cloud. Route 53 health checks continuously monitor both AWS and Azure front-end URLs from multiple regions. When a health check fails—for instance, if the AWS Region experiences a localized outage—the Route 53 failover policy automatically withdraws the unhealthy record from its DNS responses.

At that moment, a **CloudWatch alarm** triggers an **EventBridge rule**, invoking an **AWS Lambda** function that calls the **NS1 API**. The function disables or updates the corresponding record on the NS1 side, ensuring that both DNS networks reflect the same failover state. Within about one TTL interval, resolvers worldwide converge on the healthy Azure endpoint.

As the AWS Region recovers, the same workflow reverses: Route 53 health checks mark the endpoint healthy, the EventBridge rule re-enables it in NS1, and both DNS providers resume normal dual operation.

This architecture demonstrates how **event-driven coordination between Route 53 and a secondary DNS provider** forms the backbone of **multi-cloud resilience**. Health signals flow from AWS's data plane through CloudWatch and EventBridge, while NS1 (or any other compliant network) mirrors those signals via API. The result is consistent, near-real-time synchronization across clouds, where a failure in one provider or platform never translates into downtime for users.

Ultimately, this pattern exemplifies the highest level of DNS maturity: **a federated control plane** spanning multiple clouds, synchronizing through automation rather than manual updates. It's not simply "two clouds answering," but a **unified DNS fabric** that reacts instantly, preserves trust, and keeps the global namespace continuous—even when individual clouds falter.

When Active–Active Becomes Overkill

As mentioned above, despite its advantages, Active–Active DNS should be implemented only when justified by strict resilience or regulatory mandates. For most workloads, Route 53's inherent availability—backed by its Anycast edge distribution, multi-region health checks, and Application Recovery Controller (ARC) integration—already satisfies business continuity objectives.

Active–Active architectures introduce operational complexity: maintaining parity, monitoring drift, and reconciling audit trails across multiple administrative systems. Unless your business model explicitly demands **cross-provider fault isolation**, the added overhead may provide diminishing returns.

Consistency, Propagation, and Control Trade-Offs

Operating multiple authoritative DNS providers introduces a new category of resilience challenge—**consistency drift**. While redundancy across providers protects against control-plane or network-wide failures, it also multiplies the number of places where record data, serial numbers, and propagation behaviors must stay synchronized. Achieving resilience across vendors requires maintaining a **deterministic state** between systems that were never designed to coordinate natively.

Propagation Asymmetry

Each DNS provider maintains its own Anycast edge network, resolver caches, and propagation cycle. Even when two zones are identical, queries may yield different responses for short periods after an update. For example, Route 53 may publish a record change globally within seconds, while another provider's propagation takes several minutes to reach its full Anycast footprint. During this interval, resolvers querying one provider may receive new data, while those hitting the other still serve stale records.

This asymmetry is not a sign of misconfiguration—it is a natural artifact of **distributed DNS convergence**. However, when left unmanaged, it can create user-visible inconsistencies such as mixed-version service endpoints or asymmetric routing paths.

The simplest mitigation is **TTL discipline**. By keeping record TTLs consistently short—typically 30 to 120 seconds for dynamic entries—you reduce the window in which resolvers cache divergent answers. Longer TTLs can still be used for static data (MX, TXT, SPF), but operational records should expire quickly to maintain convergence between providers.

SOA Serial Tracking and Version Control

Each DNS zone includes a Start-of-Authority (SOA) record containing a **serial number** that increments whenever the zone changes. In single-provider environments, this field is mostly administrative; in multi-DNS systems, it becomes the synchronization checksum of truth.

To prevent silent drift, automation pipelines should periodically compare SOA serials between Route 53 and the secondary provider. A mismatch indicates an update has not propagated or an API call failed. Some operators extend this check further by computing **record-level hashes** (e.g., SHA-256 of the zone file) to detect differences invisible to the SOA, such as metadata or TTL discrepancies.

In AWS environments, serial comparison can be automated through a **Lambda function** scheduled by **EventBridge**, which queries both providers' APIs, compares results, and emits an alert if divergence exceeds a defined threshold. While this does not eliminate propagation delay, it surfaces misalignment early enough to correct it before customers notice inconsistent routing.

Resolver Behavior and Cache Divergence

Not all recursive resolvers behave uniformly. Some respect TTLs precisely; others impose floor and ceiling values (for instance, capping very low TTLs at 60 seconds). Large ISPs and enterprise resolvers may also consolidate DNS queries through central forwarders, obscuring the original client's geography and introducing caching bias.

In multi-DNS deployments, this means users behind different resolver ecosystems may experience inconsistent failover timing or record freshness. A record withdrawn from Route 53 due to a health-check failure might still be served by a secondary provider if that resolver cached an earlier response.

This phenomenon cannot be eliminated, but it can be bounded. Continuous **synthetic monitoring**—from multiple global vantage points—helps quantify propagation lag and cache behavior. Tools such as **Amazon CloudWatch Synthetics**, **ThousandEyes**, and **RIPE Atlas** can probe specific hostnames and validate that both providers return identical answers within acceptable latency thresholds.

Control-Plane Complexity

Every additional DNS provider introduces its own API semantics, authentication model, and rate limits. Updating a record in Route 53 may involve a single ChangeResourceRecordSets call, while the same update in another network may require multiple REST calls or JSON payload transformations. These differences complicate automation and testing, especially under time pressure during failover events.

Best practice is to implement an **abstraction layer**—for example, a lightweight internal service or IaC module—that normalizes record operations across all providers. This reduces human error and ensures that when automation replicates Route 53 changes, the payloads conform to each provider's API expectations.

From a governance standpoint, it is also essential to control who can write to each zone. A single misissued update on one provider can cause global inconsistency faster than any outage. Use **IAM roles** and fine-grained API keys to restrict update rights, mirroring your least-privilege policy across providers.

Active–Active vs. Active–Passive Multi-DNS Deployments

When introducing multiple authoritative DNS providers—such as Amazon Route 53 and a secondary like NS1 or Cloudflare—the next architectural decision is how these networks should operate together. Should both serve live traffic simultaneously, or should one remain dormant until the other fails? The distinction between active–active and active–passive topologies, while conceptually similar to those explored in Section 4.3, carries unique operational implications in a multi-provider environment.

In an **active–active configuration**, both DNS providers answer live queries at all times. Each hosts an identical copy of the same zone, synchronized continuously through APIs or infrastructure-as-code workflows. Queries may land on either network depending on resolver behavior, latency, or cached name server preferences. This approach maximizes availability and often improves performance, as it allows resolvers to choose from multiple globally distributed authoritative sources. Yet it demands exceptional operational discipline.

Even minor discrepancies in TTLs, record weights, or health-check status can lead to conflicting responses. Health synchronization is particularly challenging: Route 53 natively integrates data-plane health checks, while secondary providers may rely on external signals or API-driven updates to replicate record status. Without precise automation and continuous monitoring, such systems risk serving inconsistent answers across networks.

In contrast, an **active–passive model** keeps Route 53 as the live authoritative source while maintaining a synchronized but idle copy of the zone in a secondary provider. The passive network remains invisible under normal circumstances and activates only when Route 53 or its data plane becomes unreachable. This pattern is simpler and safer because only one system serves traffic at any given time. It eliminates drift and reduces the risk of conflicting updates, but it trades speed for predictability. Switching to the secondary DNS—either through automated registrar updates or a predelegated dual-NS arrangement—may take several minutes to propagate globally as resolvers refresh cached authority information. For most enterprises, this delay is acceptable given the reduced complexity; for highly regulated or mission-critical workloads, it may not be.

Choosing between these models depends on organizational maturity and tolerance for operational complexity. Active–passive deployments provide a straightforward safety net and are often the first step toward eliminating single-provider dependency. As automation, observability, and event-driven pipelines mature, teams can evolve toward active–active designs that deliver near-instant continuity—where both providers collaborate in real time to ensure global resolution even during partial outages.

In essence, active–passive offers **control and simplicity**, while active–active delivers **speed and seamless continuity** at the cost of precision and governance effort. The transition between the two represents not just a technical upgrade but a maturity milestone in an organization's operational resilience journey.

This brings us to an often-overlooked dimension of multi-DNS architecture—the **operational balance between speed and safety**. The faster a system propagates change, the higher the risk of inconsistency; the safer it becomes through validation, the slower its convergence. Managing this balance requires not only technology but intent: knowing when automation should react instantly and when human or policy-based gates should intervene.

While both DNS networks answer the same queries, only Amazon Route 53 integrates data-plane health checks and failover logic natively. Secondary providers usually depend on static state or external APIs to replicate this behavior. Achieving real-time parity between them requires event-driven coordination, where health data from Route 53 flows into external systems that can act on it.

As we saw in the previous example of Route 53 and NS1 integration, automation can reconcile speed with safety. Route 53 acts as the real-time source of truth for endpoint health, while the secondary provider enforces redundancy at the network level. The result is a resilient DNS control plane capable of surviving provider outages without introducing inconsistency—a system that remains both fast and correct, even under failure conditions.

Balancing Speed and Safety

Ultimately, multi-DNS consistency is a balance between update velocity and confidence in propagation. Aggressive TTLs and rapid automation yield faster convergence but higher query volume and operational noise; conservative settings reduce churn but risk serving stale data during dynamic events. The optimal configuration depends on business tolerance for transient inconsistency—an architectural decision that should be explicit, measurable, and reviewed periodically.

In AWS's resilience framework, Amazon Route 53 serves as the **data-plane anchor**, providing real-time health visibility and deterministic failover logic. External DNS providers extend that resilience horizontally but at the cost of synchronization complexity. As we'll explore in the next subsection, maintaining parity between providers requires **continuous verification, not just redundancy**—because redundant data without consistency is simply another failure mode.

Security, Integrity, and Trust Between DNS Providers

When multiple authoritative DNS providers are in play, your resilience is only as strong as the weakest link in the trust chain. Each network that serves your domain effectively becomes an extension of your perimeter. A single configuration error, drifted record, or compromised API key can ripple across the Internet in seconds, erasing the benefit of redundancy.

In other words, resilience without integrity is just chaos moving faster.

Building trust in multi-DNS architectures rests on two foundations: **data integrity** and **operational trust**.

- **Data integrity** ensures that what users receive is genuine and unaltered.

- **Operational trust** ensures that any change—manual or automated— is deliberate, verified, and traceable.

On the integrity side, Amazon Route 53 has a distinct advantage: it inherits AWS's identity, audit, and encryption ecosystem. Permissions are governed by **AWS Identity and Access Management (IAM)**, every change is logged in **AWS CloudTrail**, and sensitive credentials can be rotated and encrypted in **AWS Secrets Manager**.

Other providers—like **NS1**, **Cloudflare**, or **Neustar UltraDNS**—typically rely on API tokens and access keys. That flexibility is powerful but comes with responsibility. Automation pipelines that push updates across these providers should be treated as part of your trusted boundary, secured with the same rigor as production systems. When automation spreads configuration, its authority must be provable—through signatures, audit logs, or, at minimum, version-controlled manifests.

A further safeguard is **delegation isolation**. Instead of granting every provider control of your entire domain, delegate specific sub-zones—such as secondary.example. com—to additional DNS networks. This limits the blast radius of human or system failure. In highly regulated sectors, it also satisfies governance requirements by keeping the root of authority inside AWS, where IAM policies and CloudTrail logging maintain accountability.

But once multiple networks begin answering for your brand, trust must evolve from policy to **proof**. That is where **DNSSEC (Domain Name System Security Extensions)** enters the story.

DNSSEC adds cryptographic signatures to DNS data, allowing resolvers to verify that every response truly originates from your zone and has not been modified in transit.

In **Amazon Route 53**, DNSSEC signing uses customer-managed **AWS Key Management Service (KMS)** keys—tying cryptographic assurance directly to your AWS security perimeter.

Under the hood, each signed zone uses two key types: a **Zone-Signing Key (ZSK)**, which signs resource record sets, and a **Key-Signing Key (KSK)**, which signs the DNSKEY set itself. The **Delegation Signer (DS)** record stored at your registrar links that signature chain all the way to the Internet root, completing a globally verifiable trust path.

Route 53 enforces specific operational constraints—such as a **maximum TTL of 1 week** for signed zones—and requires a waiting period equal to the previous TTL before unsigned data expires when enabling signing. These small but vital details prevent signature mismatches during rollout or rotation.

Coordinating DNSSEC across multiple providers introduces an additional layer of complexity. Each network must either share the same signing keys or use the **multi-signer DNSSEC model** defined in **RFC 8901**, where multiple providers can sign the same zone concurrently with their own keys.

Providers like Cloudflare and NS1 now support this approach, but it requires precise orchestration: synchronized key rollovers, aligned signature validity windows, and consistent DS record management at the registrar. DNSSEC, in this context, becomes less about cryptography and more about discipline—the precision choreography of trust.

Ultimately, maintaining trust between DNS providers is not just about encryption or access policies; it's about **verifiable intent**. Every update, health check, and synchronization event should leave a cryptographic or audit trail proving that it came from an authorized system and was applied correctly.

By combining CloudTrail's immutable change logging, KMS-managed key custody, and continuous cross-provider record reconciliation, teams can move beyond simple availability toward verifiable integrity—where every DNS change, signature, and propagation event is both intentional and provable, marking a true maturity milestone in resilience engineering.

While this chapter focused largely on multi-DNS within and across providers, these same principles extend naturally into **multi-cloud architectures**. In a world where enterprises distribute workloads between AWS, Azure, Google Cloud, other cloud providers, or on-prem environments, DNS becomes the universal control plane that unifies them. Route 53's event-driven automation and health awareness allow AWS to act as the authoritative source of truth, while synchronized external DNS providers bridge resolution across clouds. When combined with well-governed APIs, cryptographic signing, and disciplined TTL management, DNS evolves from a simple naming layer into a **cross-cloud orchestration fabric**—capable of steering users seamlessly between clouds based on health, geography, or compliance context.

Trust ensures that what's published is authentic, but guaranteeing that authenticity endures through every resolver, cache, and recursive layer requires something deeper than process; it requires mathematics.

That's where we turn next, in Section 4.5, to explore how cryptographic signing anchors DNS trust in the same way certificates anchor the web and how AWS Route 53 implements DNSSEC at a global scale to make that trust verifiable by every resolver on Earth.

Section 4.5: DNSSEC for Security and Integrity

In previous sections, we explored DNS resilience through distribution, intelligence, and automation—ensuring that DNS remains reachable (Anycast), responsive (routing policies), and continuous (failover and multi-provider redundancy). Yet all these mechanisms share a hidden assumption: that the data being served is authentic. Availability without integrity is an illusion of safety. This is where **DNS Security Extensions (DNSSEC)** complete the resilience model, transforming DNS from a trust-based directory into a verifiable, cryptographic system.

DNSSEC adds digital signatures to DNS data, allowing resolvers to confirm that each response was produced by the legitimate zone owner and not tampered with in transit. It achieves this through a chain of trust that starts at the DNS root and extends downward through each zone via **Delegation Signer (DS)** records. Each zone holds two key pairs: a **Zone-Signing Key (ZSK)**, which signs individual records, and a **Key-Signing Key (KSK)**, which signs the ZSK's public key set. Together, they form the cryptographic link between domain and delegation, turning DNS into an auditable, tamper-evident control plane.

For resilience engineers, DNSSEC doesn't just prevent spoofing—it guarantees correctness under failure. Even if an attacker compromises a network path or cache, signed DNS ensures that clients can detect invalid data instantly. Correctness becomes verifiable, not assumed.

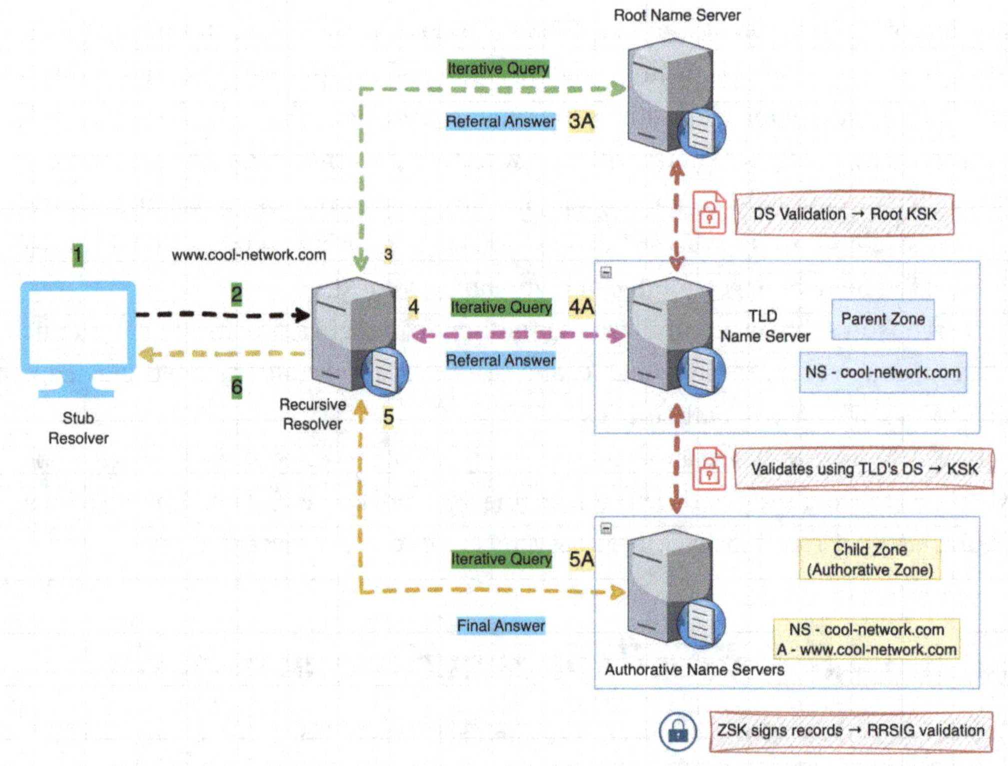

Figure 4-11. *DNSSec Chain of Trust*

In Figure 4-11, the full DNSSEC validation sequence is illustrated from the perspective of a client resolver, revealing how cryptographic trust propagates downward through the DNS hierarchy. The process begins when the **stub resolver**—typically an application or operating system component—submits a query for `www.cool-network.com` to its configured recursive resolver. The recursive resolver, acting as the intelligence behind DNS resolution, performs an **iterative lookup** beginning at the **root name servers**, which return a referral to the top-level domain (TLD) name servers responsible for *.com*. At this point, the resolver verifies that the TLD's **Delegation Signer (DS)** record matches the **Key-Signing Key (KSK)** at the root, establishing the first cryptographic link in the chain of trust.

The resolver then queries the **TLD name server**, which provides a referral to the authoritative name servers for *cool-network.com*. Before proceeding, the resolver performs another validation step, confirming that the TLD's DS record correctly signs the child zone's **KSK**. This ensures that the delegation from the parent (.com) to the child zone is authentic and unaltered. The process continues as the resolver sends a query to the **authoritative name server** for the final record—such as an **A** or **AAAA** record—belonging to `www.cool-network.com`. Each record in the authoritative zone is signed using a **Zone-Signing Key (ZSK)**, producing a **Resource Record Signature (RRSIG)**. The resolver retrieves both the RRSIG and the public **DNSKEY**, verifies that the ZSK is itself signed by the KSK, and confirms the integrity of the record's signature.

Once these verifications succeed, the resolver has effectively walked the entire chain of trust—from the DNS root, through the TLD, to the final authoritative zone—validating that every delegation and record signature is cryptographically authentic. The recursive resolver then returns the **authenticated final answer** to the stub resolver, completing a fully trusted DNSSEC resolution. What the reader observes in this diagram is not just name resolution but a step-by-step enforcement of integrity across distributed authorities. Each validation stage ensures that no forged, altered, or spoofed data can be accepted, transforming a traditionally trust-based protocol into a verifiable security system.

How Route 53 Implements DNSSEC

When DNSSEC is enabled in **Amazon Route 53**, the hosted zone transitions from a trust-based model to one backed by cryptographic proof. Route 53 automatically signs the zone data using two coordinated key pairs—the **Key-Signing Key (KSK)** and the **Zone-Signing Key (ZSK)**—each with a distinct role in the DNSSEC chain of trust.

The **KSK**, stored securely in your AWS account, is managed through **AWS Key Management Service (KMS)** hardware security modules (HSMs) that comply with **FIPS 140-2 Level 3** standards. It signs the DNSKEY record set, effectively attesting to the validity of the ZSKs that sign the zone's operational records. The **ZSK**, managed within Route 53's own signing infrastructure, handles day-to-day record signing—A, AAAA, CNAME, MX, and others. This separation allows frequent ZSK rotations without requiring updates to the domain's delegation records, reducing operational risk while maintaining strong key hygiene.

Each record set is accompanied by an **RRSIG (Resource Record Signature)**, generated by the ZSK, and published alongside its corresponding **DNSKEY**. To defend against zone enumeration, Route 53 commonly uses **NSEC3** (with the opt-out option) to provide authenticated denial of existence without exposing the internal structure of the zone.

All DNSSEC data—RRSIG, DNSKEY, and NSEC3 records—is distributed across AWS's **global Anycast authoritative network**, ensuring that validation metadata remains consistent and performant worldwide. Because signing and propagation occur within the same distributed system that serves DNS queries, signature freshness and latency remain uniform regardless of region.

Route 53 supports modern elliptic-curve algorithms such as **ECDSAP256SHA256 (Algorithm 13)**, offering robust cryptographic integrity with smaller signatures suitable for high-throughput DNS operations. Key rotation follows industry best practice: the ZSK is rotated automatically on a regular cadence (typically every 90 days) using the **double-signature rollover pattern**, in which both old and new signatures coexist temporarily to ensure continuous validation. The KSK, being more sensitive, is rotated manually when required—often during compliance-driven key lifecycle operations. Route 53 allows up to two concurrent KSKs per hosted zone, simplifying safe transitions during rollover.

The validation sequence for DNSSEC-enabled zones adheres to the standard Internet hierarchy of trust:

1. A validating resolver retrieves the DNSKEY record and checks the RRSIG signature for each resource record set.

2. It confirms that the ZSK was itself signed by the KSK.

3. It verifies that the parent zone's **Delegation Signer (DS)** record matches the digest of the KSK.

4. Validation concludes at the DNS root trust anchor, ensuring the authenticity and integrity of the data.

If any part of this chain fails—whether due to an expired signature, a missing DS record, or a mismatched key—the resolver rejects the response and attempts resolution through fallback paths. This guarantees that forged or modified data cannot be accepted, provided that resolvers validate and the DS delegation is intact.

AWS indicates that its infrastructure continuously monitors key propagation, signature freshness, and latency to ensure consistent validation across the Route 53 fleet. These internal controls, combined with global Anycast replication, minimize the likelihood of drift between signed zones and their cryptographic metadata.

In practice, Route 53's DNSSEC model blends **cryptographic rigor** with **cloud-scale automation**. KMS-backed key custody, automated signing workflows, and distributed Anycast propagation together deliver verifiable integrity without operational friction. What once required manual key ceremonies and complex rollover scripts now occurs transparently within a managed, fault-tolerant system—providing global consistency, authenticity, and resilience at the foundation of DNS itself.

Operating DNSSEC at Scale

Deploying DNSSEC in a production environment is not a simple toggle—it's a process that requires deliberate sequencing, operational discipline, and an understanding of how DNS resolvers, caches, and registrars behave in the wild.

Where earlier sections focused on how Route 53 implements DNSSEC internally, this one explains how to operate it safely at enterprise scale, especially when key management, automation, and multi-provider integration come into play.

Enabling DNSSEC begins by creating or selecting a **KMS key** that will serve as your **Key-Signing Key (KSK)**. Once signing is enabled in Route 53, the service automatically generates and manages the **Zone-Signing Key (ZSK)** used for record signing. Route 53 then signs all existing resource record sets with the ZSK using **ECDSAP256SHA256**, adds the corresponding **DNSKEY** and **RRSIG** records, and returns a **Delegation Signer (DS)** record.

That DS record must be published at the domain registrar to link your hosted zone's trust chain to its parent zone. Only once that DS record is accepted and prior unsigned data has expired from resolver caches will DNSSEC validation become fully active—a subtle but critical stage that determines whether rollout completes smoothly or creates transient validation failures.

All private key operations occur within **AWS-managed hardware security modules (HSMs)** that never export key material. The ZSK rotates automatically on a regular cadence (typically every 90 days), while the KSK rotation remains a controlled, manual process that must be coordinated with registrar updates. To minimize validation risk, AWS supports two concurrent KSKs per hosted zone, allowing "double-sign" rollover without downtime. Route 53 also enforces bounded TTLs—typically no more than seven days—for signed data, ensuring rapid signature refresh and mitigating cache staleness.

Resilience Considerations

Operating DNSSEC at scale extends resilience from "Is it available?" to "Can I prove it's authentic?" Every signature Route 53 publishes is ephemeral: signatures expire automatically, forcing continual renewal.

If signing were to stall due to mis-scoped IAM permissions or throttled API access, new records would eventually become unsigned—so monitoring is essential. AWS exposes **CloudWatch metrics** that track signing latency, key freshness, and propagation status, while **CloudTrail** logs every configuration and key-management action. Integrating these signals into existing observability dashboards gives operators the same real-time assurance over authenticity that they already maintain for uptime.

Performance-wise, signed responses are larger—typically 30 to 50% bigger—and may trigger fragmentation on networks with strict MTU or firewall limits. Testing DNSSEC responses across VPNs, MPLS links, and legacy appliances helps identify where EDNS0 buffer sizes need adjustment. Within AWS environments, enabling EDNS0 and validating that Route 53 health checks traverse signed zones without truncation ensures that DNSSEC remains both secure and performant.

Multi-DNS and Multi-signer Operations

Large enterprises increasingly distribute authoritative responsibility across multiple DNS providers for resilience or latency optimization. DNSSEC does not preclude this approach but introduces an extra layer of coordination.

The most scalable model is the **multi-signer DNSSEC** architecture, defined by the IETF, where each provider (e.g., Route 53, Cloudflare, or NS1) signs the same zone using its own key set. All participating providers then share coordinated DS records at the registrar so that validating resolvers can verify signatures from any source.

This eliminates single-provider dependency while preserving cryptographic trust, but it requires careful orchestration: synchronized key rollovers, matching signature validity windows, and strict registrar governance. Some providers, including Cloudflare and NS1, publish APIs for automated multi-signer coordination, while AWS focuses on integration through external automation using **Lambda**, **EventBridge**, and **Route 53 APIs**.

Security and Governance Practices

While DNSSEC enhances authenticity, it also changes the operator's security model.

Once you enable signing, you are no longer just managing records—you are managing *trust itself*.

Your AWS KMS key becomes the cryptographic authority for your domain; if that key is ever compromised, rotated incorrectly, or deleted, the entire trust chain collapses. In practice, that's equivalent to losing control of the domain name.

This is why operational discipline must evolve alongside technical implementation.

Access to KMS keys and Route 53 APIs should follow a **least-privilege principle**, limited only to the automation or personnel responsible for signing operations. Service Control Policies (SCPs) in AWS Organizations can enforce this at scale, preventing accidental key deletion, disabling DNSSEC, or rotating a KSK before its successor is ready. Even a well-intentioned rotation can break validation if performed without proper overlap.

Beyond AWS, governance extends to your registrar—the root of your delegation chain. Multi-factor authentication (MFA) should be mandatory for any registrar changes, and DS (Delegation Signer) record updates should follow auditable, change-controlled workflows. Every edit to a DS record affects the global trust anchor for your domain; those actions belong in the same class of scrutiny as production credential rotations or root certificate renewals.

When combined, these practices transform DNSSEC from a static checkbox into an active component of your organization's **governance, risk, and compliance (GRC)** framework.

It doesn't just prove authenticity to external resolvers—it ensures that the authenticity itself cannot be tampered with from within.

In this way, DNSSEC becomes both a **technical safeguard** and a **governance mechanism**, binding operational integrity to cryptographic assurance.

Completing the Chain of Trust

When viewed in the broader context of this chapter, DNSSEC is more than an optional feature—it is the final piece in the resilience puzzle.

Each of the mechanisms explored so far reinforces a different layer of continuity:

> **Anycast (Section 4.1)** ensures the DNS service itself remains reachable even during network-level disruptions.

> **Routing policies (Section 4.2)** make responses intelligent, steering users dynamically to the healthiest or closest endpoints.

> **Failover strategies (Section 4.3)** maintain operational continuity when entire regions or Availability Zones fail.

> **Multi-provider architectures (Section 4.4)** remove single-provider dependency, guaranteeing availability even if one global DNS network becomes unreachable.

> **DNSSEC (Section 4.5)** then overlays the entire system with *verifiable trust*—mathematical proof that every answer received is genuine, untampered, and traceable back to an immutable root of authority.

In practical terms, this elevates DNS from a best-effort naming service into a **globally distributed control plane**—a system where both *availability* and *authenticity* are continuously verifiable.

Network engineers often focus on keeping packets flowing; DNSSEC ensures those packets are flowing to the right destination.

In a world of increasingly complex cloud and hybrid architectures, this distinction is crucial.

A resilient DNS without authenticity can still mislead users during an attack or misconfiguration; DNSSEC ensures that every failover, every routing change, and every redundant path still leads to the truth.

The convergence of these capabilities creates what could be called the **Resilient DNS Stack**—a layered model where:

- the *network layer* (Anycast) guarantees physical reachability

- the *service layer* (routing and failover) manages logical continuity

- the *trust layer* (DNSSEC) certifies integrity end-to-end

Together they deliver not only fault tolerance but also *confidence under failure*: the assurance that when everything else is unstable, your resolution path still tells the truth.

However, modern enterprise networks don't live entirely in public DNS.

Private namespaces, on-premises workloads, and hybrid environments introduce internal resolution paths that never touch the public root zone.

These private domains—often powered by Active Directory, Route 53 Resolver, or on-premises BIND servers—pose a new resilience question:

> **How do you extend the same principles of authenticity, continuity, and isolation into the internal fabric of an enterprise network?**
>
> In the next section, *Private DNS and Hybrid Cloud Considerations*, we'll explore exactly that.

We'll examine how Amazon Route 53 Resolver integrates with on-premises DNS systems through forwarding rules, conditional queries, and hybrid architectures—ensuring that resilience isn't confined to the edge of the cloud but extends all the way to the data center.

We'll also discuss how concepts like split-horizon DNS, recursive resilience, and conditional forwarding loops must be handled carefully to avoid new single points of failure inside private namespaces.

Ultimately, DNSSEC may secure the truth of your public presence, but hybrid DNS resilience secures the continuity of your entire ecosystem—the part of the network where real transactions, authentication flows, and service discovery actually live.

Section 4.6: Private DNS and Hybrid Cloud Considerations

In the previous sections, we treated DNS as the public face of resilience: Anycast reachability (Section 4.1), policy-driven steering with latency and geolocation routing (Section 4.2), failover with Route 53 and Application Recovery Controller (Section 4.3), multi-provider and multi-cloud redundancy (Section 4.4), and authenticity with DNSSEC (Section 4.5).

Yet for most enterprises, the bulk of name resolution doesn't happen on the open Internet at all—it happens behind the firewall: inside VPCs, across regions, through AWS Direct Connect (DX) and Site-to-Site VPN links, and between cloud and on-premises data centers.

Here, the resilience challenge shifts from Internet-scale survivability to **continuity and consistency across trust boundaries**.

This is where **Private DNS** becomes decisive. It determines whether an application in AWS can still reach an internal service when a tunnel flaps, a resolver cluster fails, or a VPC endpoint becomes isolated.

The same principles you've seen so far—redundancy, health awareness, and blast-radius control—still apply, but their implementation looks different on the inside.

The Role of Private DNS in Hybrid Architectures

In hybrid networks, private DNS provides name resolution for internal resources—VPC endpoints, databases, legacy systems, and on-prem applications that never expose public records.

AWS implements this through **Amazon Route 53 Resolver**, a fully managed recursive service with inbound and outbound endpoints:

- **Inbound endpoints** allow on-premises servers to resolve private AWS names (e.g., db.internal.example.com).

- **Outbound endpoints** enable AWS-based workloads to query on-premises DNS servers, such as Active Directory or BIND.

These endpoints bridge the resolution process across environments without traversing the public Internet. When paired with AWS Direct Connect or Site-to-Site VPN, they form the backbone of hybrid DNS continuity.

Yet connectivity alone doesn't guarantee resilience. A private DNS failure—whether an on-premises name-server crash, a VPC endpoint misconfiguration, or a lost DX link—can disrupt service discovery just as much as a public outage.

Modern enterprises increasingly recognize this risk: in industry forums and customer briefings, architects often ask, *"Do I really need DNS resilience inside my private network?"* The answer is unequivocally **yes**, because private resolution underpins authentication, API communication, and cross-region replication. If it breaks, everything above it stalls—even when workloads themselves remain healthy.

Resilience Patterns for Private DNS

Distributed Resolver Endpoints: Just as Route 53's public DNS uses Anycast to distribute traffic globally, resilience in private DNS begins with zonal distribution.

Deploy at least two Route 53 Resolver endpoints—both inbound and outbound—by specifying **multiple subnets in different Availability Zones** for each endpoint. **Each selected subnet contributes one IP address (one ENI per IP)**, so two subnets yield two IPs, and so on. This gives every endpoint zonal redundancy without any client changes and eliminates the "single-resolver bottleneck" that appears when all forwarding lands in one subnet.

If one AZ experiences degradation or a networking fault, the other endpoint continues to serve requests transparently, without client reconfiguration.

This approach eliminates the "single-resolver bottleneck" that often exists when organizations place all DNS forwarding in a single VPC subnet.

Enterprises running hybrid connectivity (Direct Connect or VPN) should ensure that each on-premises DNS forwarder has IP reachability to **all** inbound endpoint ENIs, not just one.

In practice, configure multiple target IPs on the conditional forwarder (e.g., ForwarderIPs: 10.10.0.5, 10.11.0.5) so that queries fail over gracefully if one endpoint AZ becomes unavailable.

The benefit mirrors what we achieved with Anycast in earlier chapters—**redundancy through path diversity rather than complex logic**.

Redundant Hybrid Links: Resilient name resolution depends on resilient network transport.

Even if Resolver endpoints remain healthy, queries can fail if the underlying Direct Connect (DX) or VPN path breaks.

For production environments, AWS recommends either:

- **Two independent DX connections** terminating on separate routers and facilities (high-resiliency or maximum-resiliency models, discussed previously and expanded in Chapter 7).

- **A DX + VPN combination**, where the VPN serves as an encrypted fallback channel through the Internet.

In practice, hybrid customers often attach both links to a Transit Gateway (TGW), using **TGW route-table associations/propagation** and **BGP policy on the enterprise edge (local-preference or AS-path length)** to prefer Direct Connect while keeping the

VPN hot standby. When a DX circuit fails, traffic shifts to the VPN **if** both attachments (DX and VPN) are present and the TGW route tables and BGP/route priorities are configured to prefer DX with VPN as hot standby. Resolution continues at slightly higher latency. This keeps internal DNS zones (e.g., corp.local) reachable from AWS workloads and avoids resolver reconfiguration. Transport resilience is therefore a prerequisite for name-layer resilience.

Forwarding Rules for Isolation: A resilient DNS design also minimizes blast radius. Within AWS, Resolver forwarding rules allow architects to segment query flows by domain—for instance:

- Forward ad.corp.local to on-prem Active Directory servers.

- Forward research.internal to a private zone hosted in a dedicated AWS account.

- Let all other queries resolve through public DNS.

This separation prevents a misbehaving on-prem DNS server from impacting lookups for AWS-hosted services.

If the Active Directory resolver slows down or returns malformed responses, only queries for its delegated domain are affected.

From a governance standpoint, this also helps meet regulatory isolation requirements—particularly in financial and healthcare contexts—by keeping resolution for certain domains confined to specific trust boundaries.

The design principle echoes the segmentation concept introduced in Chapter 6: **contain failure within its own namespace.**

Conditional Forwarding with Failover: Out of the box, Route 53 Resolver's conditional forwarding supports static target lists, not dynamic health-based routing.

However, with a small amount of automation, you can build resilient conditional forwarding using the same event-driven techniques discussed earlier in this chapter.

How It Works:

1. Deploy multiple on-prem DNS servers (e.g., two BIND instances or domain controllers).

2. Configure your forwarding rule with both IPs as targets.

3. Enable a lightweight Lambda-based health check that periodically tests resolution latency and availability for each server.

4. When a target fails, the function **reorders or prunes** target IPs in the forwarding rule so that healthy resolvers are tried first. Avoid fully de-associating the rule unless an alternate resolution path is verified—this prevents accidental SERVFAIL conditions or namespace blackouts during transient faults.

5. Add a guardrail test: periodically validate that conditional rules don't create **forwarding loops** (A → B → A). A simple canary query chain test in CI/CD can detect and block circular resolution before deployment.

This pattern mimics DNS failover within the private namespace, ensuring that AWS workloads can still resolve names even if a corporate DNS server is offline.

It's especially valuable for environments that rely on **Active Directory**, where domain controller discovery depends on **SRV record lookups** (e.g., ldap.tcp.dc._msdcs), and Kerberos authentication requires timely resolution of **KDC hostnames**.

Please Note: Native Route 53 health checks can't probe private IP targets. For private targets, use **CloudWatch-alarm–based health checks** (calculated checks) that reflect Lambda/VPC probes or application metrics; then let automation update Resolver rules accordingly.

While Route 53 Resolver has no native "weighted" forwarding like public Route 53 policies, this hybrid model achieves a similar outcome—automatic continuity without manual intervention.

Monitoring and Visibility: DNS failures are often silent—they appear as latency, not outages. One way to detect these early is to integrate **Route 53 Resolver Query Logs** with Amazon CloudWatch Logs, Amazon S3, or Kinesis Data Firehose and layer analytics on top—using CloudWatch metric filters or Athena queries to surface anomalies such as:

- Sudden spikes in NXDOMAIN responses (indicating misrouted forwarding).

- Increases in average query latency from specific VPCs.

- Repeated timeouts to the same on-prem resolver.

Query logs delivered to **S3** (directly or via Firehose) can be explored with **Athena**, whereas logs in **CloudWatch Logs** are best surfaced with metric filters and dashboards.

For a more active posture, use **CloudWatch Synthetics** or **AWS Systems Manager Automation documents** to perform scheduled DNS-resolution tests between AWS and on-prem endpoints.

These simulations emulate application behavior and validate hybrid name-resolution paths before users notice issues.

The operational rule is simple: observe DNS as you would observe an application.

A resilient DNS design is measurable—latency, success rate, and failover time are metrics, not assumptions.

TTL matters—sometimes more than anything else. Long or inconsistent TTLs are the silent killers of failover. A tunnel may recover or a resolver endpoint may heal, but if clients continue caching stale answers, recovery remains invisible. Keep TTLs for **dynamic or failover-sensitive records** (such as service aliases or cell pointers) short—typically **30–120 seconds**—so recovery aligns with your RTO. Use longer TTLs for **static or identity-critical records** (e.g., Active Directory SRV entries) to reduce load and churn. The goal isn't uniformly short TTLs but **TTL discipline**: match freshness to volatility. In resilient DNS design, TTL isn't merely a cache timer—it's a recovery timer.

These five patterns together form a holistic blueprint for hybrid DNS resilience.

They transform Route 53 Resolver from a mere connectivity component into a reliable control plane that sustains identity, discovery, and service reachability across on-premises and cloud environments.

Multi-region Private DNS

In the last subsection, we instrumented private DNS—turning query logs, latency, and synthetic checks into early-warning signals. Monitoring, though, only buys you time; it doesn't keep names resolvable when a region blips, a link flaps, or a resolver dies. The next step is structural: carry the resilience guarantees you built for public DNS into the private namespaces your systems actually depend on—identity domains, database endpoints, internal APIs—without conflating the goals. Public DNS steers users from the Internet. Private DNS keeps your own estate able to find itself.

That distinction matters. The multi-region patterns from Sections 4.2–4.4 optimized reachability from the edge—Anycast, health-aware answers, and (optionally) multi-provider delegation. Here, "multi-region" means something different: a **private** resolution fabric that survives regional control-plane issues, transport failures, or on-prem hiccups while remaining invisible to the public Internet.

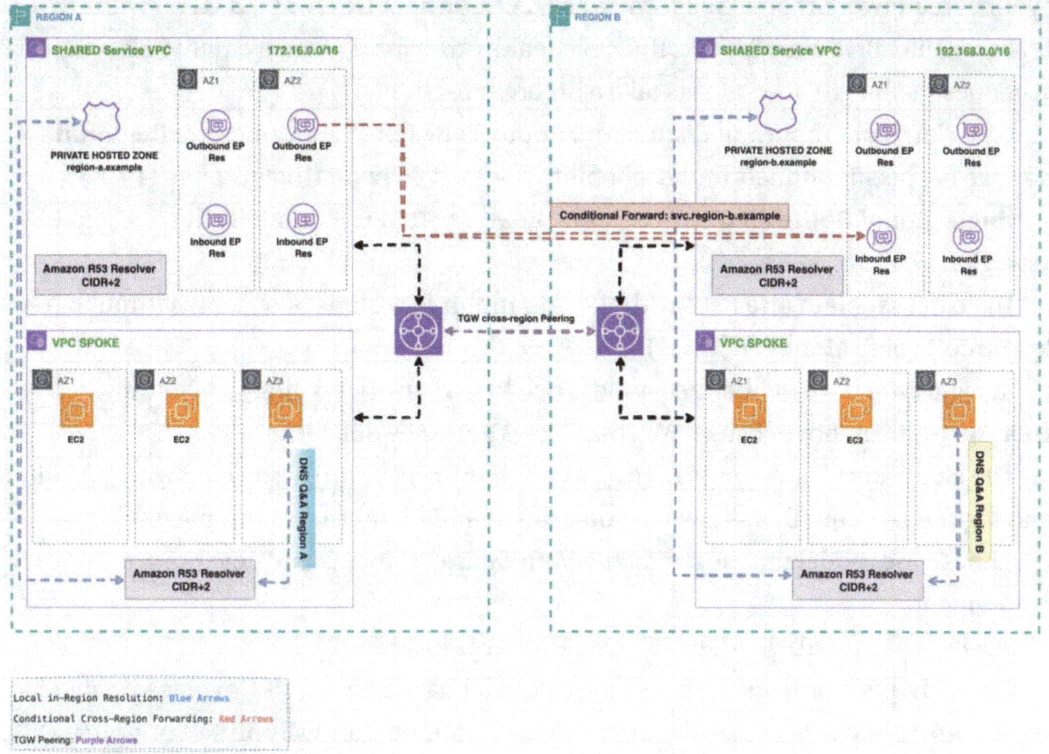

Figure 4-12. *Private DNS Resolution*

At the center of Figure 4-12 are **Amazon Route 53 Resolver** (the managed recursive layer) and **Route 53 Private Hosted Zones (PHZs)** (your authoritative data for internal names). In this pattern, the namespace is **deliberately split by region** to minimize blast radius:

- **Region A** hosts a PHZ for region-a.example.

- **Region B** hosts a PHZ for region-b.example.

Each region runs both **inbound** and **outbound** resolver endpoints in a shared-services VPC (two IPs in different AZs per endpoint is the recommended baseline). Spoke VPCs in the same region use their VPC-local Route 53 Resolver to query their **local** PHZ (blue arrows in the figure)—no cross-region lookups for day-to-day traffic.

To connect the two halves, a **conditional forwarding rule** in Region A sends queries for a B-scoped suffix (e.g., svc.region-b.example) to Region B's **inbound** endpoint; Region B does the symmetric thing for svc.region-a.example. Those cross-region forwards ride **Transit Gateway (TGW) peering** on the AWS backbone (purple arrows).

If your core network is attached through **Direct Connect Gateway (DXGW)** with **DX + VPN** available, BGP simply picks the next healthy transport when a circuit fails—the DNS layer doesn't change; the packets take a different road.

Let's clarify an important distinction. Route 53 Resolver endpoints are **Regional**—they live in specific subnets and Availability Zones. A **Private Hosted Zone (PHZ)** is a **single global Route 53 resource**, not something that is automatically replicated per region.

You can **associate one PHZ** with VPCs in multiple regions or accounts through **AWS Resource Access Manager (RAM)**.

In Figure 4-12, we deliberately model two PHZs (one per region) to show an **isolation pattern**, not because AWS duplicates zones by default.

The alternative—a single PHZ (e.g., *internal.example.com*) associated with VPCs in both regions—is equally valid when you want a unified internal namespace.

Choose the model that best matches your failure domains and governance requirements.

Design choice rubric—One PHZ vs. Per-Region PHZ

One PHZ per namespace → Associate it to all participating VPCs when you need a **single source of truth**, consistent answers across regions, and **simplified operations**.

Separate PHZs per region or cell (e.g., region-a.example, region-b.example) → Choose this when you require **blast-radius isolation**, **sovereignty segregation**, or **independent change control**.

If you adopt isolation, **encode it in the name itself** rather than creating duplicate PHZs for the same root (internal.example.com)—this prevents split-brain behavior and keeps record ownership explicit.

How the Pieces Cooperate Under Failure

Authoritative truth (by region). Because region-a.example and region-b.example live in separate PHZs, a bad change—or an availability issue—in one zone doesn't immediately contaminate the other. Record updates are made in the local region's PHZ and served locally to that region's workloads.

Recursive reachability (zonal and regional). Each region's inbound/outbound endpoints sit in at least two subnets across AZs and advertise multiple IPs. OS stub resolvers and enterprise forwarders naturally retry the next IP/next server when an ENI or AZ dies, which gives you first-hop failover without touching clients.

Forwarding intent (and containment). Resolver rules keep traffic scoped:

- *.region-a.example → **authoritative in Region A** (local PHZ).

- svc.region-b.example → **forward to Region B inbound** (red arrows).

- Everything else → **public DNS** (normal recursion).

This keeps an issue with, say, Active Directory in Region A from poisoning unrelated lookups, and it prevents circular forwarding because the rules are strictly suffix-scoped.

Transport resilience. Transit Gateways (TGWs) are peered across regions, and the core network connects through a Direct Connect Gateway (DXGW). With two independent Direct Connect circuits—and a Site-to-Site VPN as fallback—routing policies such as **BGP local-preference** or **AS-path length** determine the active path. In steady state, DNS traffic flows over Direct Connect; during failure, it automatically shifts to the VPN without resolver reconfiguration. When Region A experiences a data-plane issue, Region B continues serving its local namespace and, through conditional forwarding, also resolves Region A queries. The DNS layer remains unaffected; only the transport path changes.

Health as a switch, not a guess. Lightweight canaries (CloudWatch Synthetics or a VPC-resident Lambda) in both regions continuously resolve representative private names and time responses. Alarms on latency, SERVFAIL, or timeout raise EventBridge events that trigger automation to

- Remove a failed on-prem or cross-region **target** from a forwarding rule.

Temporarily disable a conditional rule **or re-associate it to the peer region's inbound endpoint** if it starts black-holing queries.

- **Reorder** resolver target lists so the healthy region is tried first.

For higher-consequence actions (e.g., drifting application endpoints between regions), **AWS Application Recovery Controller (ARC)** can enforce readiness checks and safety rules so you don't swing traffic to an unprepared region.

All of this stays **inside** your private boundary. You're not publishing NS records or exposing internal names publicly; you're preserving the internal map so authentication, replication, and service-to-service calls continue while the network heals.

The question now is, why does this differ from the public patterns earlier? It does for the following reasons:

- **Audience.** Public DNS serves end users and their resolvers; private DNS serves your workloads and identity systems.

- **Surface.** Public answers ride Anycast edges; private answers traverse **TGW/DX/VPN** you control.

- **Consistency model.** Public needed short TTLs and health-weighted answers; private favors **stable TTLs**, **authoritative locality** (PHZ per region here), and **transport redundancy**.

- **Failure semantics.** Public failure shouts "website down." Private failure shows up as **auth timeouts** and **stuck queues**, and it **can't find the host**—even when the application fleet is otherwise healthy.

Implementation Best Practices

After instrumenting private DNS, the next step is to harden the mechanics that keep it alive under stress. Think of this as moving from "see the problem" to "design it out." The patterns below don't change what names resolve; they change **how** your resolution fabric behaves when links flap, AZs hiccup, or an upstream resolver stalls—turning transient faults into non-events for your workloads.

PHZ topology. Keep one PHZ per namespace and associate it with all participating VPCs across regions. Use AWS RAM for cross-account association. Avoid duplicate PHZs for the same name (split-brain). When you must diverge by cell or environment, encode that in the name (e.g., orders.cell-a.internal.example.com), not with multiple PHZs for internal.example.com. Operationally, a single PHZ can be associated with multiple VPCs—even across regions and accounts—through AWS's control plane replication. This eliminates the need for zone-copy scripts and ensures consistent answers globally.

Endpoint placement. For each inbound/outbound endpoint, **select at least two subnets in different Availability Zones**. Resolver assigns **one IP per selected subnet (one ENI per IP)**; spreading subnets across AZs keeps the endpoint available through a zonal event. Place subnets behind distinct NAT/egress paths if you use inspection or firewalls, so a single appliance failure doesn't black-hole both IPs.

Ensure that **UDP and TCP port 53** are explicitly allowed in **security groups, network ACLs, and any inspection or firewall paths** between on-premises resolvers and Route 53 Resolver endpoints. DNS failures often appear as timeouts, not explicit denials, when asymmetric or stateful filtering drops one side of the exchange.

Remember that Route 53 Resolver endpoints are **not transitive**: a workload in one VPC can query an endpoint it can reach via routing or TGW attachments, but those endpoints don't forward queries for other VPCs. If multiple VPCs require resolution, each must have network reachability—directly or through TGW—to the Resolver endpoint ENIs in its region.

On-prem forwarders should list all inbound IPs across regions—let the retry logic work for you.

Forwarding rules. Model rules narrowly (by suffix) to contain failure, and apply priority in the client: most enterprise resolvers allow ordered target lists; put the local region first, then the peer region, then on-prem (or vice-versa depending on where the authoritative lives). Avoid circular forwarding (A→B→A) by testing rule graphs as you'd test routing tables.

Hybrid transport. Prefer DXGW + TGW attachment for steady state, with VPN as hot standby. Validate MSS/PMTU on the VPN path; DNS is small, but fragmentation/ICMP filtering will still turn recoveries into timeouts. If you do per-region egress filtering, ensure resolver endpoint IPs are explicitly allowed.

Split-horizon. If example.com is public and private, keep the record of intent aligned: internal names should not accidentally shadow public ones. A good pattern is to keep business-critical internal names on a dedicated private suffix (internal. example.com) and use Route 53 Resolver DNS Firewall to **block outbound DNS queries from your VPC to disallowed or sensitive domains**, preventing accidental leakage of internal names.

Observability you can act on. Turn Resolver query logs into SLOs: median and p95 DNS latency per VPC/region; NXDOMAIN rate by suffix; timeout rate per forwarding target. Alarms should point to automation, not just dashboards—DNS issues degrade gracefully, so humans show up after the blast radius has grown.

Practical considerations. Resolver endpoints are billed **per IP per hour**, so plan capacity deliberately—two IPs per endpoint across two AZs is the normal baseline. Query logging to CloudWatch Logs or S3 also incurs data-volume charges; enable full fidelity only where you need detailed forensics, and use sampling or aggregation elsewhere. Check current **service quotas**—for example, the number of resolver rules, rule associations, and endpoints per account—and request increases in advance to avoid deployment delays.

Taken together, these design principles turn a static configuration into a living network fabric, one that anticipates disruption instead of merely reacting to it. Every element, from PHZ association to endpoint topology, plays a specific role in removing single points of dependency: cross-region zones keep the namespace consistent, redundant endpoints absorb zonal faults, and conditional forwarding rules limit the blast radius of on-prem failures. When stitched together through resilient transport and continuous health telemetry, they form a DNS system that behaves less like a set of records and more like an adaptive service.

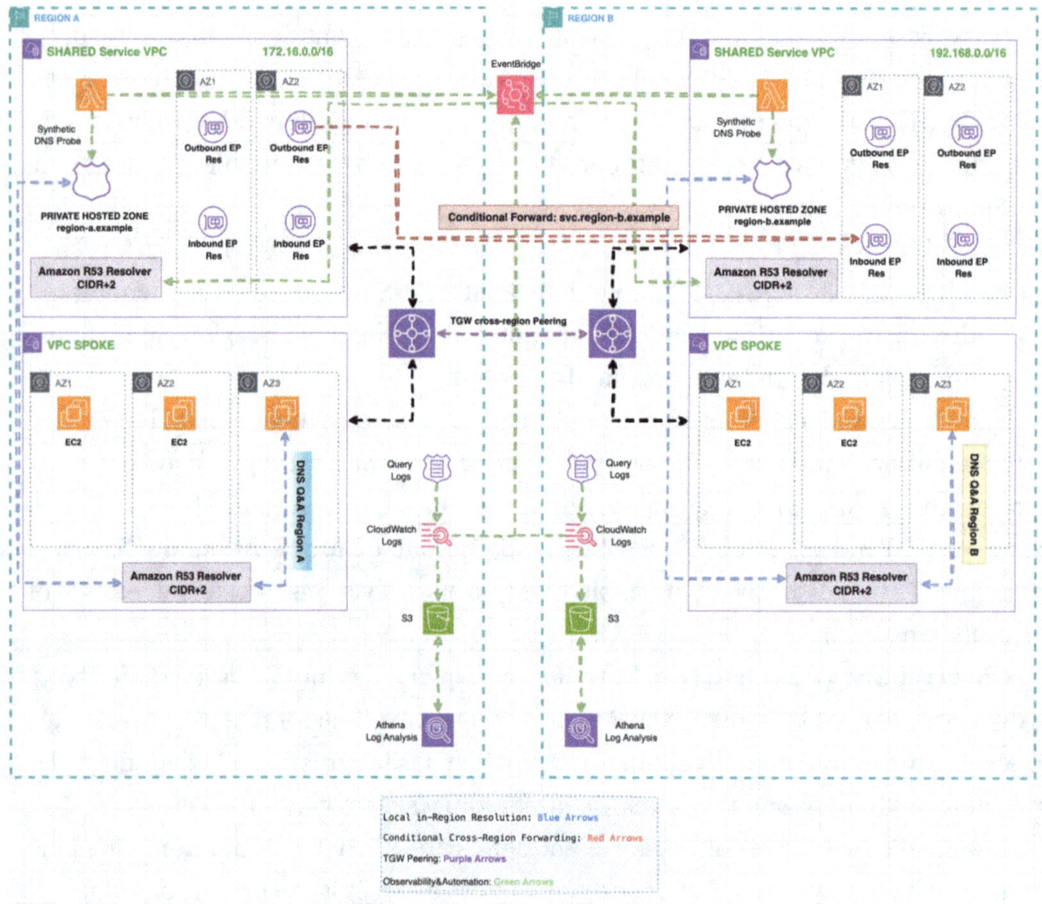

Figure 4-13. *End-to-End Multi-region Private DNS with Observability and Automation*

Figure 4-13 extends Figure 4-12 by overlaying operational components. Route 53 Resolver query logs flow into CloudWatch Logs and, via a Logs subscription to Kinesis Data Firehose, into S3 for analysis in Athena. CloudWatch Synthetics canaries continuously probe DNS health across regions. CloudWatch alarms emit events to EventBridge, which triggers Lambda automation to adjust Resolver rules or forwarding paths—closing the loop that transforms a resilient topology into an adaptive, self-healing service.

To see what that looks like under stress, let's trace a failure scenario from start to recovery.

A Quick Walk-Through (How a Failure Plays Out)

Imagine a global enterprise with workloads distributed across **two AWS Regions (Frankfurt and Ireland)** and an on-premises data center in Zurich. Both regions host workloads that depend on the private namespace internal.example.com.

The zone is defined once as a **Private Hosted Zone (PHZ)** and associated with VPCs in both regions. Each region runs dual **Route 53 Resolver inbound and outbound endpoints** across two Availability Zones, creating four independent interfaces per region. The on-premises resolvers forward hybrid queries to these inbound endpoints through **AWS Direct Connect (DX)**, with a **VPN link** standing by as an encrypted backup.

Normal steady state

Under normal conditions, on-premises applications resolve db.orders.internal.example.com via their corporate DNS. The conditional forwarder sends the query to the Frankfurt inbound endpoint. The resolver routes it to the local PHZ association in Frankfurt, retrieves the record, and replies within milliseconds. Queries from workloads in Ireland follow the same process through their local endpoints—no cross-region dependency, same answer everywhere.

The fault

One morning, a network maintenance event causes a DX transport interruption on the Frankfurt circuit. At that instant, Route 53 Resolver endpoints in Frankfurt remain healthy, but packets from on-premises DNS forwarders can no longer reach them. Ordinarily, this could cause partial name resolution failure for internal hosts pointing to Frankfurt.

Automatic rerouting

BGP on the enterprise edge detects the DX loss and shifts traffic to the VPN tunnel via the **Direct Connect Gateway (DXGW)** and **Transit Gateway (TGW)**.

The on-premises forwarder is configured with ordered target IPs—Frankfurt first, then Ireland—so when the primary path times out, the resolver automatically retries the next target in sequence. Because stub resolvers retry automatically, queries seamlessly pivot to Ireland. DNS latency rises slightly—from ~3 ms over DX to ~35 ms over VPN—but resolution continues without human intervention.

Detection and insight

Within seconds, CloudWatch metrics register the change: Resolver query counts in Frankfurt drop; VPN traffic increases; and synthetic canaries measuring internal resolution show elevated latency but no failures. Query logs and canary metrics feed CloudWatch alarms, which publish state changes to EventBridge. EventBridge then records the failover event and can invoke Lambda automation to adjust forwarding rules or resolver associations if required. A CloudWatch alarm triggers an EventBridge event that logs the path change and notifies the operations team—not as an incident, but as an **observed failover event**.

Recovery and rollback

When DX connectivity is restored, BGP preference returns to the primary path. Traffic automatically resumes its low-latency route to Frankfurt. Because the PHZ was continuously replicated and the resolver endpoints never lost state, there's **no cache corruption, no record drift, and no service restart required**.

The monitoring system logs the fail-back, updates dashboards, and clears the alarm. From an application perspective, the outage never existed—the DNS layer absorbed it completely.

This scenario demonstrates why DNS is not merely a convenience layer but the **invisible connective tissue** of a resilient hybrid environment. Properly engineered, it allows internal systems to continue authenticating, replicating, and communicating even as parts of the transport fabric fail and recover behind the scenes.

By applying the same principles that made public DNS robust—redundancy, observability, and deterministic failover—to the private namespace, organizations create a **continuity domain** of their own: one that never depends on luck or manual intervention. In later chapters, we'll look beneath this DNS layer—examining how the underlying routing and transport mechanisms, such as Direct Connect and Transit Gateway, deliver high- and maximum-resiliency models that make this seamless behavior possible.

Multi-region and Cross-Account Private DNS Resilience

In the previous sections, we explored how hybrid DNS can stay operational when a tunnel flaps, a link fails, or a resolver endpoint goes dark.

Yet few modern enterprises operate within the boundaries of a single region or account.

Networks today are mosaics of regulatory zones, business units, and regional clusters—each owning its own resources, VPCs, and connectivity, yet all relying on one another's names to function.

At that scale, **DNS becomes the connective fabric of trust**, and its resilience depends on how well that fabric is woven across administrative and geographic lines.

Unifying Names Without Losing Control

At the core of AWS private DNS lies the **Private Hosted Zone (PHZ)**—the authoritative database for a private namespace such as *internal.example.com.*

A PHZ is a Route 53 (global) resource **owned by a single account** and **associated with one or more VPCs**; those VPCs can be in any region or account via AWS Resource Access Manager (RAM).

To make it multi-region or multi-account, you extend that scope through **AWS Resource Access Manager (RAM)** associations.

The owning account—often a "shared services" or "network-core" account—creates the PHZ, then shares it with consumer accounts.

Each participating account accepts the share and associates its VPCs to the PHZ, giving workloads in every region identical resolution behavior without duplicating the zone.

This model keeps a **single authoritative source of truth**, ensuring that updates— say, a new A record for *db.internal.example.com*—propagate consistently everywhere.

It also centralizes governance: IAM policies in the owning account define who can modify records, while consuming accounts can only query them.

In production, many organizations back the PHZ repository with infrastructure-as-code (CloudFormation, Terraform, or CDK) so every change is version-controlled and peer-reviewed before deployment.

When you need isolation, such as for sovereign regions or cell-based deployments, you shouldn't clone the entire PHZ.

Instead, encode the separation in the namespace itself—*api.eu.internal.example. com* and *api.us.internal.example.com*—each mapped to its own PHZ.

This keeps resolution deterministic and prevents the split-brain behavior that occurs when multiple PHZs claim the same domain name.

Deploying Regional Resolver Endpoints

A shared PHZ gives you a single authority, but resolution still happens locally. Every region that hosts workloads must have its own **Route 53 Resolver inbound and outbound endpoints.**

These endpoints are regional constructs, each spanning multiple Availability Zones for high availability.

When an on-premises DNS server sends a query to AWS, it targets the IP addresses of the inbound endpoints; when an AWS workload looks up an on-prem name, its outbound endpoint forwards that query down the hybrid link.

To implement this effectively, create a dedicated *network-services VPC* in each region.

Inside it, deploy at least two inbound and two outbound endpoints, placing each in a different AZ.

Associate these endpoints with the local Transit Gateway (TGW) so that any attached VPC—application, data, or shared services—can reach them via VPC attachments rather than per-VPC peering.

This model is common in multi-account Landing Zone Accelerator (LZA) deployments because it scales cleanly: new accounts automatically inherit DNS resolution through TGW routing.

On the on-premises side, configure conditional forwarders (in BIND or Active Directory) with multiple target IPs—one for each inbound endpoint across regions.

DNS queries then fail over automatically using standard resolver retry logic.

If one region or link becomes unreachable, resolvers continue through the next IP without manual intervention. This is how multi-region continuity emerges from simple retry behavior.

Building the Transport That Keeps It Alive

No DNS architecture can outlive its transport.

Even with redundant endpoints, queries die if packets can't traverse the network.

For hybrid environments, the best practice is to use **two independent Direct Connect (DX) circuits** terminating on separate routers and facilities.

Attach both to a **Direct Connect Gateway (DXGW)**, and connect that gateway to a **Transit Gateway (TGW)** that spans all regions via inter-region peering.

Then, provision at least one **site-to-site VPN** as an encrypted Internet fallback.

By adjusting TGW route priorities or BGP local-preference, you can ensure that DNS traffic always prefers DX but immediately fails over to VPN if a circuit fails.

Because Route 53 Resolver uses standard UDP/TCP on port 53, failover is instantaneous: there is no stateful session to rebuild.

During maintenance or fiber outages, private DNS remains functional—the latency rises, but the system stays alive.

Governing Change Across Accounts

As DNS domains cross accounts and regions, their resilience increasingly depends on governance discipline rather than pure redundancy.

The account that owns the PHZ becomes the **root of administrative trust**, so its security posture must be uncompromising.

Restrict ChangeResourceRecordSets API access to automation roles, not humans.

Every update should trigger an AWS CloudTrail event, ingested by AWS Config or a SIEM pipeline to flag unauthorized changes.

Many regulated enterprises even wrap DNS change workflows in AWS Service Catalog or Control Tower Customizations so that modifications require approval and can be rolled back predictably. Equally critical is **monitoring what happens downstream**.

Resolver Query Logs, when streamed to Amazon S3 or CloudWatch Logs, reveal drift patterns long before they become incidents—look for rising NXDOMAIN rates or persistent lookup delays tied to a particular region or account.

In multi-account setups, these logs feed centralized dashboards that visualize the health of the entire DNS ecosystem: which regions respond fastest, which links are failing silently, and which zones show stale cache behavior.

Regional Isolation and Recovery

Resilience planning also means preparing for the unthinkable—a full regional isolation event.

If a region hosting the primary PHZ or its owning account becomes unreachable, workloads elsewhere must continue resolving names.

The first line of defense is **local caching**: each region's resolver endpoints cache successful answers, keeping services running for the TTL duration even without access to the authority.

For extended disruptions, infrastructure-as-code pipelines can deploy **secondary PHZs—independent zones kept in sync by scheduled automation and protected by strict IAM so they behave as "read-only" operationally.** These replicas are associated only with the local region's VPCs and can be promoted manually or through automation by updating delegation records once the primary zone is restored.

While this pattern introduces complexity, it's widely used in financial services and public-sector workloads where regulatory uptime requirements mandate DNS autonomy under isolation.

Bringing It All Together

Multi-region and cross-account private DNS resilience isn't about making DNS faster; it's about making it *dependable everywhere.*

A single PHZ, governed centrally but shared deliberately, acts as the canonical truth.

Regional Route 53 Resolver endpoints give that truth multiple access points.

Direct Connect, VPN, and Transit Gateway keep those access points reachable.

And strict governance ensures no human or automation error can silently break the fabric that connects it all.

When these layers come together, private DNS evolves from an invisible utility into an intentional resilience mechanism—one that preserves identity, service discovery, and operational coherence even when the network beneath it trembles. It is, quite literally, the language that keeps hybrid systems talking when everything else goes quiet.

Lesson Learned from Chapter 4

Throughout this chapter, we've watched DNS evolve from a static naming system into a distributed control plane for resilience—an intelligent, verifiable layer that keeps cloud and on-premises architectures coherent, even when their underlying components fail.

We began by exploring **Anycast routing**, where distributed edge networks deliver reachability through path diversity, ensuring that users continue to resolve names even amid regional disruptions.

We then examined **intelligent routing policies**—weighted, latency-based, and geolocation-driven—that make DNS not only available but also adaptive, steering users toward the healthiest and fastest endpoints in real time.

From there, we turned to **failover strategies** and **Application Recovery Controller (ARC)**, which transformed recovery from a static, manual process into a continuous, testable operation.

We then expanded outward to **multi-region, multi-provider DNS architectures**, showing how true fault isolation demands diversity of authority across independent networks.

With **DNSSEC**, we anchored that authority in cryptography—ensuring that every resilient answer is not only fast but also *authentic.*

Finally, we ventured into the enterprise interior, where **private DNS and hybrid name resolution** determine whether cloud workloads and on-prem systems can still talk to each other when tunnels flap, links drop, or resolvers fail.

Across every one of these techniques, the same truth emerged:

Resilience is not just about redundancy—it's about coordination.

Multiple regions, endpoints, or providers mean little without synchronized state. Failover logic achieves nothing if the data being served can't be trusted.

DNSSEC, logging, and automation matter because integrity and observability are the only currencies that retain value when networks fracture.

By now, you can see that DNS is more than a service—it's a **nervous system for distributed resilience.**

It senses degradation, makes autonomous decisions, and ensures that identity, routing, and discovery remain intact across domains, providers, and trust boundaries.

The tools we explored—Anycast, ARC, PHZ topology, resolver endpoints, event-driven failover, and multi-signer DNSSEC—are not isolated tactics.

They are *design reflexes*: principles that, once mastered, apply far beyond DNS. The key takeaways from this chapter are clear and deeply practical:

- **Design for diversity, not duplication.** True fault tolerance comes from independent failure domains—across providers, regions, and network paths.

- **Govern through automation.** Every record, health check, and zone change should be auditable, reversible, and event-driven.

- **Authenticate every answer.** DNSSEC transforms reachability into provable integrity—making DNS not only redundant but also verifiably trustworthy.

- **Segment trust deliberately.** Use private zones, forwarding rules, and IAM boundaries to contain fault domains and regulatory scope.

- **Measure DNS as you would measure uptime.** Latency, NXDOMAIN rates, and propagation lag are early indicators of operational drift.

Taken together, these practices define the blueprint for resilient naming—one that shifts DNS from being *an afterthought* to being *the foundation* of multi-cloud and hybrid continuity.

When implemented intentionally, DNS becomes a self-healing nervous system that can lose pieces of its network without losing its purpose.

And yet, DNS is only the beginning.

Behind every resilient name lies a deeper stack: the physical circuits, virtual links, and logical protocols that carry, protect, and recover the data itself.

Resilience doesn't stop at who you connect to—it extends to *how* that connection survives stress, latency, and partial loss.

Resilience is only real once it is practiced, so we'll close this chapter with short, repeatable exercises that turn DNS design into measurable operational behavior.

Practice: Turning DNS Resilience into Operational Behavior

The concepts in this chapter are intentionally architectural: they describe how resilient DNS should behave under stress. To make that behavior real, you need repetition—small drills that validate assumptions, expose weak links, and create measurable confidence in how DNS will respond during disruption. The goal of the exercises below is not to teach one cloud console but to operationalize the design principles in any platform.

Exercise 1—Build your DNS dependency map (control plane vs. data plane)

Write down the exact chain required for one critical hostname to resolve and connect (e.g., api.example.com): recursive resolver ➤ authoritative provider(s) ➤ routing policy decision ➤ endpoint health signal ➤ application front door. Mark which components are data plane and which are control plane. Then answer: which single failure would make the name resolve but send users to a dead destination?

Exercise 2—TTL as a recovery budget

Pick your most failover-sensitive name and record its TTL. Then define a target RTO (e.g., 2 minutes). If your TTL is longer than your RTO, the DNS layer alone can consume the entire recovery window. Adjust TTL to match your intended recovery behavior, and document the trade-off (query volume vs. agility).

Exercise 3—Observe real resolver behavior (not theory)

From at least three vantage points (e.g., a public resolver, an enterprise resolver, and a cloud-hosted probe), query the same hostname repeatedly and record: answer stability, latency, and whether responses vary by geography. If you rely on geolocation/latency policies, validate whether EDNS0 Client Subnet (ECS) is present in practice for your user population.

Exercise 4—Simulate a "bad answer" incident

Without changing the application, simulate a DNS failure mode: point a low-impact hostname to an intentionally unhealthy endpoint or disable health eligibility for one target. Measure: time-to-withdrawal, time-to-convergence across resolvers, and any clients that continue to use stale answers. This exposes where caching and resolver floors/ceilings defeat your expectations. Remember, resilience testing is imperative; we will discuss this in detail in Chapter 8 in the book.

Exercise 5—Private and hybrid: test the inside path

For one private name used by workloads (authentication, service discovery, database endpoints), test resolution during a controlled impairment: one resolver endpoint AZ unavailable, one hybrid link down, and one forwarder unreachable. Validate that retry behavior and alternative paths keep resolution alive and that observability (query logs, canaries) detects the event early. Again, we will dive deep into observability in Chapter 8 in the book.

Game Day scenario—"DNS survives, but the service is down"

Run a tabletop: DNS continues answering, but answers route to a degraded region/cell. Define the decision logic: what health signal triggers withdrawal, what safety rule prevents a premature switch, and what "ready" means before you redirect. Success is not "we failed over," but "we failed over safely, predictably, and measurably."

Table 4-2. *DNS Resilience Practice Exercises*

DNS Resilience Concept	Practice/Exercise	What to Validate	Success Criteria
DNS as a distributed control plane	Trace the full resolution path for a critical hostname (recursive resolver → authoritative zone → routing policy → endpoint). Classify each element as control plane or data plane.	Whether DNS resolution and traffic steering depend on distinct systems and signals.	Resolution continues even when one control-plane component is impaired, and routing decisions remain intentional.
TTL as a recovery budget	Compare TTL values for failover-sensitive records with documented RTO targets. Temporarily lower TTLs in a non-production environment and observe resolver behaviour.	Whether DNS caching aligns with recovery objectives rather than default values.	DNS propagation time does not exceed the defined RTO, and cache behaviour is predictable.
Health-based routing and safety	Simulate an unhealthy endpoint by disabling health eligibility or injecting a failing health check. Observe DNS answer changes over time.	Time to withdraw unhealthy endpoints and consistency across resolvers.	Unhealthy destinations are removed within the expected window, without oscillation or premature failback.
Anycast and resolver behaviour	Query the same hostname from multiple geographic vantage points (public resolvers, enterprise resolvers, cloud-based probes). Compare latency and answers.	Whether routing policies behave as expected given resolver location and, where applicable, EDNS0 Client Subnet (ECS) support.	Resolver answers align with intended geography or latency policies, and deviations are understood and documented.
Private and hybrid DNS continuity	Simulate a failure of one private resolver endpoint or one hybrid connectivity path (DX/VPN). Test name resolution from dependent workloads.	Redundancy of resolver endpoints and fallback behaviour across network paths.	Name resolution remains available through alternate endpoints or paths without manual intervention.
Governance and blast-radius control	Review who can modify DNS zones, routing policies, and health checks. Run a tabletop scenario of an accidental change.	Whether guardrails prevent unintentional global impact.	Changes are scoped, auditable, and reversible; unauthorized or risky changes are blocked.
Observability and detection	Enable DNS query logging and metrics for critical zones. Introduce a controlled anomaly (e.g., NXDOMAIN spike or latency increase).	Visibility into resolver behaviour and early detection of anomalies.	DNS anomalies are detectable early enough to support incident response, with clear signals and alerts.
Failure without silence	Run a scenario where DNS remains healthy, but endpoints are degraded (partial service failure). Evaluate decision-making for routing changes.	Whether DNS routing decisions are based on meaningful health signals, not just availability.	Traffic is redirected only when safe, and continuity is preserved without amplifying the failure.

The exercises introduced in this section are intentionally concise and repeatable, designed to expose how DNS behaves under operational stress rather than idealized conditions. Table 4-2 summarizes these exercises, mapping each core DNS resilience concept to a concrete validation step and practical success criteria, including how routing decisions are influenced by resolver location and, where applicable, EDNS0 Client Subnet (ECS) support. HERE When practiced regularly, they transform name resolution from an assumed utility into an observable and governable system—one whose failure modes are understood before they are encountered in production.

If Chapter 4 focused on how to locate and verify what is alive during disruption, Chapter 5 builds on that foundation by examining how resilience is sustained across the stack—layer by layer, fault by fault—until continuity becomes an inherent property of architecture rather than an outcome of last-minute intervention.

CHAPTER 5

Implementing Resilience Throughout the OSI Model with AWS Examples

In Chapter 4, we explored the Domain Name System as the nervous system of distributed resilience.

We saw how Anycast routing, health-aware policies, DNSSEC integrity, and Route 53's private resolution fabric let workloads find what's still alive even when the network shakes.

DNS turned out to be more than naming—it was the coordination plane that kept identities coherent while regions, tunnels, or endpoints failed.

But DNS alone doesn't keep packets moving.

Beneath that elegant control layer lies a mesh of circuits, links, routers, and protocols that must survive faults before any name can even be resolved.

This is where our focus now shifts: from resilient *discovery* to resilient *delivery*.

Building from the Foundations

Resilience in the cloud is not a single feature—it's a posture built layer by layer.

Each chapter so far has revealed a different face of that posture, and together they've shaped the mindset we'll need for the journey ahead.

In Chapter 1, we defined what resilience truly means in a digital world obsessed with availability. We distinguished it from mere uptime, exploring the spectrum between protection, preparation, and recovery. We also introduced the mental model that underpins every design choice in this book: resilience is about continuity under failure, not the absence of failure.

© Cristian Critelli 2026
C. Critelli, *Cloud Networking and Resilience*, https://doi.org/10.1007/979-8-8688-2436-4_5

Before going further, it's worth revisiting the framework that underlies how we discuss these layers: the **OSI (Open Systems Interconnection) Model.**

Originally formalized by the ISO in the 1980s, the OSI model divides communication systems into seven conceptual layers—Physical, Data Link, Network, Transport, Session, Presentation, and Application.

Each layer provides specific services to the one above it and depends on the integrity of the one below.

In practice, modern Internet protocols blur some of these distinctions—the session and presentation layers are often absorbed into the application—but the OSI model remains invaluable as an architectural lens.

It lets us reason about *where* a failure occurs and *how* recovery should propagate upward.

In this chapter, we'll use that model not as an academic taxonomy but as a blueprint for understanding how AWS implements resilience from fiber to application logic.

Chapter 2 then gave that definition a networked body. We looked at cloud networking fundamentals—the shift from static infrastructure to programmable fabrics built on software-defined networking and elastic topologies. There, we learned that Availability Zones, Virtual Private Clouds, and routing domains are more than conveniences—they are deliberate fault boundaries.

In Chapter 3, we went deeper into the virtual layer, examining how abstraction changes the way we think about reliability. We discussed network function virtualization and the way AWS decouples logical constructs from the underlying hardware. Virtual routers, gateways, and firewalls became elastic building blocks rather than physical choke points. That abstraction, we saw, was both the promise and the challenge of cloud resilience.

Chapter 4 moved one level higher—to the control plane that holds everything together.

We learned how DNS, through Anycast, routing policies, failover logic, and authentication with DNSSEC, became the nervous system of distributed continuity.

It kept identities consistent and traffic steerable even when the network itself was changing beneath it.

Now, in Chapter 5, we travel downward—into the mechanics that keep those control planes alive.

If DNS is how systems *find* what's healthy, this chapter explains how the network *stays* healthy long enough for DNS to matter.

We will explore what resilience looks like across the OSI model, not as a classroom exercise but as an architectural lens for AWS and hybrid environments.

The Physical Reality of the Cloud

Before we peel back each layer of the OSI stack, it's worth remembering that the "cloud" rests on something very real: a sprawling physical network built, owned, and operated by AWS.

Today, the AWS global network spans **38 Geographic Regions** and over **120 Availability Zones**, tied together by more than **9 million kilometers of terrestrial and submarine fiber**—enough to circle the Earth more than 200 times.

At the core lies a **400 GbE-capable backbone** delivering **multi-terabit-per-second** capacity between regions and edge locations.

The network carries *billions of packets per second* through a globally distributed fleet of routers, with continuous telemetry and path validation ensuring that any fiber cut or link degradation triggers automated rerouting within milliseconds.

On the enterprise side, over **100 AWS Direct Connect locations** act as private on-ramps to this backbone—physical routers and cross-connects, not just logical tunnels.

Resilience in this network is engineered through **path diversity, automated failover, and continuous self-healing**. Multiple redundant optical rings connect every region, while control-plane systems automatically withdraw affected paths and redistribute load when transport faults occur. AWS network operations teams continuously expand capacity—often by double-digit percentages each year—to absorb both failures and traffic surges without human intervention. These capabilities aren't just abstractions; they are the reason cloud workloads rarely notice when parts of the physical world underneath them fail.

This global physical infrastructure is not incidental: it is the foundation on which every VPC, transit gateway, load balancer, and DNS system rides. The resilience of your application begins here—with how fiber is landed, how many paths converge, which conduits carry your packets, and how isolated those paths are. In the sections that follow, we move downward into the stack—not because connectivity is glamorous, but because without it, nothing above works.

At the **physical layer**, we'll examine redundant circuits and diverse **Direct Connect** paths that protect against fiber or facility loss.

At the **data-link layer**, we'll see how **Link Aggregation Groups (LAGs)** and multi-NIC designs provide fault tolerance without sacrificing performance.

At the **network layer**, we'll introduce the foundations of **Border Gateway Protocol (BGP)**—the signaling language of the Internet—and explain how AWS uses it across **Direct Connect Gateways** and **Transit Gateways** to maintain predictable failover between Direct Connect and VPN paths. We won't go deep into traffic engineering here; that discussion awaits in Chapter 7, but we'll build the conceptual grounding needed to understand it.

At the **transport layer**, we'll observe how load balancers, health checks, and protocol behaviors like **TCP retransmission** and **QUIC** contribute to session continuity.

And at the **application layer**, we'll revisit familiar components—**Application Load Balancer**, **CloudFront**, caching, and rate-limiting—to see how software logic completes the chain that begins in hardware.

Each of these layers has its own vocabulary for failure: a broken circuit, a dropped frame, a withdrawn route, a reset session, and a timeout.

Resilience lies in translating those signals from one layer to the next so that what looks like failure at the bottom becomes a momentary detour at the top.

That translation is the art of layered design—the art of ensuring that no single fault can claim more than its own layer's worth of damage.

By the end of this chapter, we'll have a full vertical picture of resilience—from the cables that carry packets to the logic that decides what happens when those packets don't arrive.

You'll see how AWS constructs—**Direct Connect**, **Transit Gateway**, **Network Load Balancer**, **Application Load Balancer**, and **Route 53**—map naturally onto the OSI model, turning theory into architecture.

Together, they form the foundation on which higher layers like automation, recovery orchestration, and observability—our topics in later chapters—can stand without trembling.

Section 5.1: Layer 1 (Physical): Redundant Circuits and Direct Connect Models

Resilience begins where photons move. Before any policy can steer traffic or any protocol can retry a session, light has to reach the other side. The physical layer (OSI Layer 1) is the level at which we decide whether higher layers will have a chance to recover at all. It deals with media and presence: fiber strands and patch panels; racks, cages, and meet-me rooms; optics, power, and the geography that ties all of it together. When this layer fails without an alternative, no amount of cleverness above it can help. That is why, in cloud networking, **AWS Direct Connect** belongs here first—not because it is glamorous, but because it is gravity.

Why Direct Connect Belongs in Layer 1

Direct Connect is often introduced as "a dedicated private link to AWS," which tempts people to think in logical terms—BGP sessions, route advertisements, and traffic preference. But at its core, **Direct Connect is a physical circuit**: a fiber-optic cross-connect between your router and an AWS router inside a Direct Connect location. You order a Letter of Authorization and Connecting Facility Assignment (LOA/CFA), a technician pulls and labels the patch, and light begins flowing between two specific devices. VLANs and BGP belong to Layers 2 and 3.

The resilience decisions that matter first are physical: Which buildings are involved? Which conduits? Which carriers? Which power feeds? Do your "independent" circuits secretly share a riser or a splice tray? Those are Layer-1 questions.

Thinking this way also clarifies responsibility. At Layer 1 there is a clean demarcation: the AWS side (their routers, optics, and power) and your side (your routers and cross-connects). Between you sits the colocation operator and often one or more carriers providing metro or long-haul transport. When we speak of "Direct Connect resiliency models," we are really talking about how many of those **physical dependencies you duplicate or eliminate**—and how far apart you push them.

Failure Modes Are Physical First

Most outages that defeat clever routing policies start with basic, tangible events. A backhoe finds the wrong duct. A meet-me room loses a power distribution unit. A line card or DWDM mux fails. An optic overheats under a poorly ventilated lid. A building's HVAC stalls on a hot afternoon. A fire-suppression drill disables a room.

These are not theoretical; they happen, and they are correlated. Two circuits in the same duct enjoy the same risk profile. Two cross-connects in the same meet-me room share the same power panel and technician pool. **Layer-1 resilience is the discipline of breaking those correlations**: diversity of *place*, *path*, and *plant*.

- **Place** is geography—two different facilities or metros, each with its own cage, MMR, and power.

- **Path** is how the fiber gets there—distinct conduits, risers, and metro rings that don't converge into a single sheath.

- **Plant** is the provider's hardware—different carrier networks, shelves, line cards, and AWS router pairs.

If the two ends of your "redundancy" meet inside one room—or the two long-haul routes join the same aerial span across a river—you have cost, not resilience. Routing can only choose between paths that still exist.

The Direct Connect Resiliency Patterns—Read As Physical, Not Logical

AWS defines its **Resiliency Toolkit models** in physical terms:

- A **single connection** is intentionally fragile—a lab or test configuration, not a production story.

- The **high-resiliency model** uses **two independent connections** terminating on **separate AWS devices within one location**, countering device or cross-connect failures but not a site-wide event. (Target SLA ≈ 99.9%.)

- The **maximum-resiliency model** extends diversity across **two Direct Connect locations**, ideally via different carriers and entry paths, to survive device, carrier, and facility loss. (Target SLA ≈ 99.99%.)

Read these models with your as-built drawings in hand. Ask the colo for entrance-facility and riser maps; ask carriers for path-diversity letters; verify that your "redundant" fibers are not merely different lambdas on the same DWDM shelf. If both contracts trace back to the same splice enclosure halfway to the DX site, you do not own your risk.

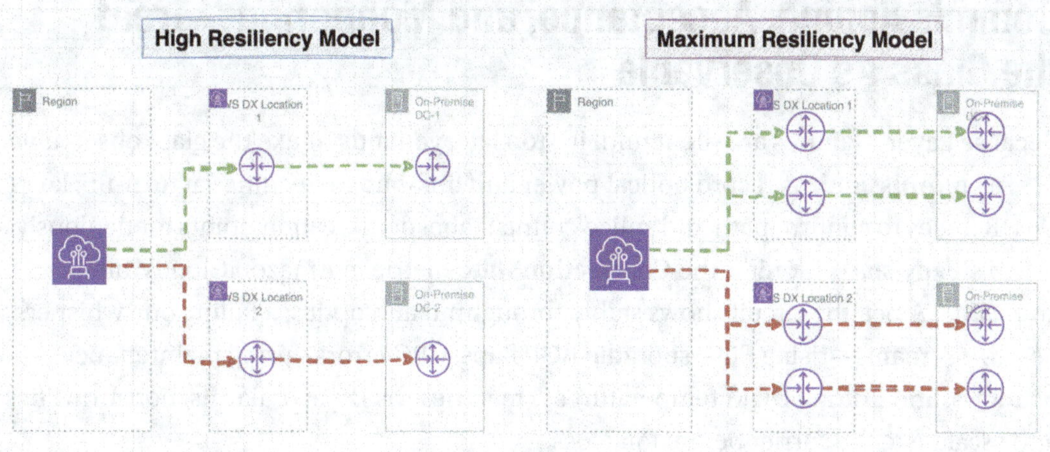

Figure 5-1. *High Resilience Model vs. Maximum Resilience Model for Direct Connect*

The **High-Resiliency Model** (left) mitigates device or cross-connect failures within a single DX location by using dual physical connections to separate AWS routers.

The **Maximum-Resiliency Model** (right) extends diversity across independent DX locations, each with its own routers, carriers, and entry paths, protecting against device, carrier, or facility loss.

In both cases, the **Direct Connect Gateway (DXGW)** decouples physical landings from regional topology, enabling continued reachability even when one site is impaired.

DXGW As Blast-Radius Containment, Physically Expressed

The **Direct Connect Gateway (DXGW)** is often described as a way to share connectivity across regions and VPCs. At Layer 1 its virtue is **blast-radius containment**. DXGW is a **globally available attachment construct that operates outside the data path,** allowing you to land physically diverse circuits in different locations without pinning your architecture to a single regional edge. A facility or metro incident can be absorbed at the perimeter while traffic continues through the gateway's global control plane.

Commissioning, Acceptance, and Monitoring—Treat the Glass As Observable

Because Layer 1 failures are silent until it's too late, you must make the glass observable.

At **commissioning**, record optical power and link-budget readings at turn-up; keep OTDR traces to confirm path and splice counts; label demarcation points meticulously.

In **steady state**, monitor the **ConnectionState** metric in Amazon CloudWatch and your NMS. A healthy circuit shows stable throughput and optics; a failing one whispers before it screams—rising FEC, sporadic BGP flaps, CRC errors during maintenance windows, and drifting DOM temperatures. Treat these as Layer-1 alarms, not curiosities, and escalate to the carrier before total loss.

Maintenance is also physical. Carriers schedule invasive work on rings or shelves—coordinate those windows. If both "diverse" providers close the same tunnel the same night, you lose redundancy for those hours. Resilience includes calendar discipline and the nerve to say no until windows are staggered.

Hosted vs. Dedicated—What Changes Physically

You can obtain Direct Connect via a **dedicated port** ordered directly from AWS or through a **hosted connection** provided by a partner at the DX site. Both ultimately become light between your router and an AWS router, but the operational envelope differs. With hosted connections, you inherit the partner's fabric; verify that your "redundant" paths truly land on different provider equipment and optical shelves. With dedicated ports, you own the port, LOA/CFA, and visibility into the exact AWS device and cage. Neither model guarantees resilience; both depend on true independence of place, path, and plant.

The Internet Is Not the Enemy—Use It As Physical Insurance

A site-to-site VPN over the public Internet often traverses an entirely different **set of conduits, carriers, and power domains** than your leased optical circuits. That physical independence makes it a useful hedge at Layer 1. The latency may differ, but when glass breaks in the metro, the encrypted tunnel across another ecosystem can keep the business breathing long enough for field teams to splice the world back together.

What Not to Do at Layer 1

If there is a single truth about Layer 1, it is this: what you cannot see, you cannot trust.

Many designs that claim "redundancy" look solid on paper but collapse the moment a splicer opens a cabinet or a carrier optimizes its metro ring. The following pitfalls are not theoretical—they are the ghosts of failed audits and sleepless nights in dark data centers.

First, never mistake VLANs for diversity.

Tagging traffic into separate VLANs may isolate it logically, but it still rides the same glass. VLANs are constructs of Layer 2; they share the same conduit, the same fiber strand, and the same splice tray. When that fiber breaks, every VLAN goes dark together. VLAN separation is valuable for segmentation, not survival.

Second, two LOAs on the same meet-me panel are not independent—they are a shared-fate risk.

A meet-me panel is a single physical object, powered by the same PDU, managed by the same technician, and typically located in the same rack. If that panel fails, or if someone mislabels a port during maintenance, both connections vanish in one move. True resilience demands that each connection live in a separate rack, cage, or at least a separate distribution path within the facility.

Third, never accept the phrase "diverse paths" without proof.

Ask for the carrier's physical route maps, fiber entrance diagrams, and splice documentation. Request signed *path diversity statements*—not marketing promises. If both circuits exit the same manhole, share the same bridge crossing, or merge into a single metro ring ten kilometers away, their independence is an illusion. Physical diversity must be verifiable, not aspirational.

Fourth, beware of optimization disguised as efficiency.

Carriers love to consolidate services to save on fiber strands, DWDM shelves, or transponders. It makes their operations cleaner—and your redundancy meaningless. Two "separate" circuits riding the same optical shelf or backplane will fail together when that hardware resets. Always verify the *plant diversity*—different line cards, different chassis, and different optical paths.

Finally, don't skip failure drills because they make you nervous.

Every redundant architecture looks resilient until someone dares to pull a plug. The only way to prove independence is to break it on purpose. Schedule controlled tests. Take one leg dark, observe failover behavior, and validate recovery time. Agree on rollback plans and maintenance windows, but do it.

You cannot claim resilience you have never witnessed.

True Layer-1 engineering is not about adding more cables; it is about *knowing exactly what those cables depend on*. Resilience is not an adjective—it is an audit trail. The more you question, the more resilient your network becomes.

The Layer-1 Contract with the Layers Above

Every layer in a network depends on the one beneath it.

If the foundation fails, the rest can only react. Layer 1 defines whether higher layers even have a chance to recover. When the light keeps flowing, routing protocols can reconverge, BGP can make new decisions, and sessions can re-establish. When the light stops, everything above it simply stops too.

Physical resilience isn't about perfection; it's about isolation. A well-built foundation doesn't prevent faults, but it ensures they stay local—a single circuit down, not a whole region. That's the real meaning of redundancy at the physical layer: making sure every failure has somewhere else to go.

This is the contract Layer 1 holds with everything above it. A router's convergence logic, a transit gateway's path propagation, or an application's retry loop can only work if there's another live path to use. Without that physical diversity, resilience becomes theory rather than reality.

And it's worth remembering that even in the cloud, everything ultimately runs on physical infrastructure—on fibers, optics, and power feeds in real buildings managed by real people. "The cloud" is only as resilient as the physical networks it rides on.

As we move up to Layer 2, we'll build on that principle. Now that the light is flowing, the next challenge is how to keep it organized—how links, frames, and aggregation mechanisms like LAGs and VLANs turn raw connectivity into predictable behavior when a fault occurs.

Section 5.2: Layer 2 (Data Link): LAGs and Active/Standby Failover in Hybrid Links

If the physical layer is the world of light and copper—the fiber strands, optics, and power keeping bits alive—then Layer 2, the Data Link Layer, is where those bits first gain structure and intent. It is the layer that organizes electrical or optical signals into recognizable frames, identifies the devices exchanging them, and recovers from the small imperfections that physical reality introduces. At this layer, the network stops being just a bundle of cables and starts behaving like a cooperative system that can detect faults and adapt in real time.

Layer 2's purpose is to provide reliable communication over a single physical segment. It defines how data is packaged into frames, how devices address each other through MAC addresses, and how errors are detected, retransmitted, or filtered before data ever reaches the routing layer above. It sits between the raw medium and the logical world of IP, translating link failures, congestion, or noise into recoverable behaviors rather than outages.

In cloud and hybrid environments, Layer 2 transforms physical diversity into logical resilience through **link aggregation (LAG/LACP)**, which turns multiple circuits into a single fault-tolerant channel; **segmentation with VLANs (802.1Q)**, which isolates workloads on shared links; **hop-by-hop protection using MACsec (802.1AE)**, which secures frames between endpoints; and **frame-size consistency via MTU alignment**, which prevents fragmentation and hidden loss during failovers. Together, these mechanisms ensure that a single cable fault, configuration drift, or frame mismatch remains invisible to upper layers.

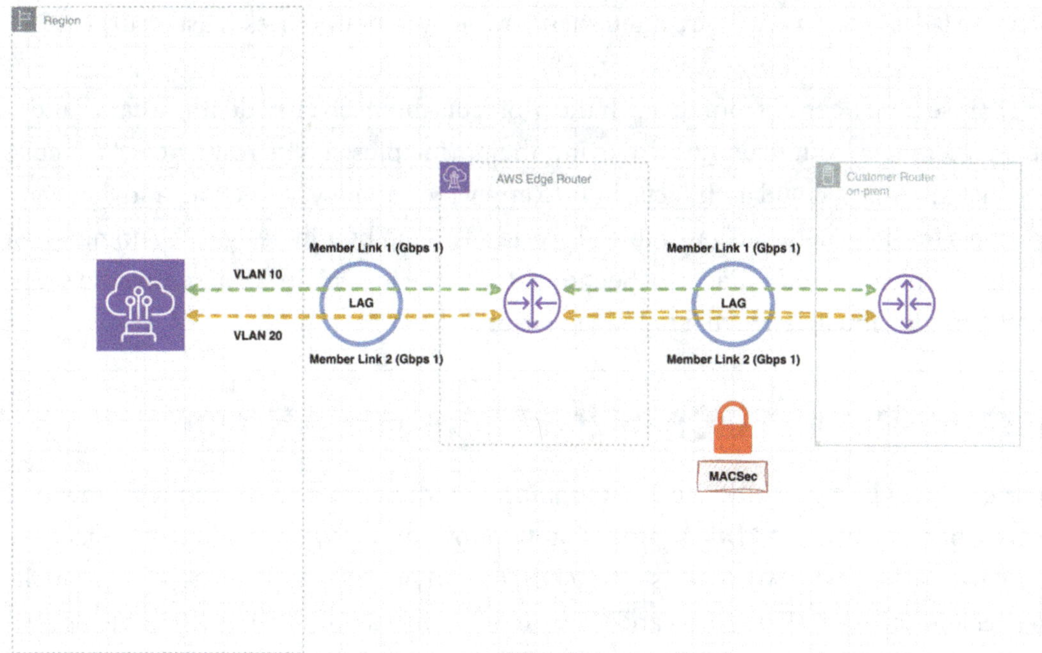

Figure 5-2. *LAG, VLAN, MACSec with Direct Connect*

In Figure 5-2, VLANs (IEEE 802.1Q) segment traffic across shared circuits, isolating workloads while preserving link utilization. Multiple 1 Gbps member links are bundled into a single logical interface using a Link Aggregation Group (LACP, IEEE 802.3ad) to provide both increased throughput and fast intra-device failover. MACsec (IEEE 802.1AE) adds frame-level encryption and integrity protection between routers, securing the data link against tampering and interception. Together, these mechanisms convert physical diversity into logical stability, ensuring that upper layers perceive continuous connectivity even when individual links fail.

Each of these technologies operates below the routing layer, invisible to BGP or OSPF, yet together they form the first line of operational defense. They ensure that when a physical circuit fails, higher layers still perceive a functioning connection and continue operating normally. In other words, Layer 2 doesn't decide where traffic goes—it guarantees that there is always a stable and consistent way to get there.

At the data-link layer, resilience is a shared responsibility. Cloud providers supply the physical port, facility power, and service-side termination, but the correctness of Layer-2 behavior is determined by customer configuration. LACP timers and thresholds, VLAN tagging and isolation, MTU consistency across every hop, and—where enabled—MACsec policy and key management all sit firmly in the customer's operational domain. Because failures at this layer are often silent, ownership boundaries must be explicit before production traffic depends on the link.

This section does not aim to teach the protocols themselves in depth—that would fill another book—but to demonstrate how their principles enable resilience. We focus on what matters to cloud architects: how to apply redundancy, detection, and failover concepts from the data-link layer to real-world AWS and hybrid designs. By doing so, we extend the physical redundancy of Section 5.1 into the logical domain, setting the stage for the routing intelligence that follows in Layer 3.

Turning Many into One: Link Aggregation Groups

At the heart of Layer 2 resilience lies a simple idea: when one link isn't enough, make several behave as one. A **Link Aggregation Group (LAG)** bundles multiple physical connections between two devices—switches, routers, or edge appliances—into a single logical interface that shares load and tolerates loss. Instead of viewing each fiber as an independent point of failure, the system treats them collectively, distributing frames across all members while continuously monitoring their health. If one member link fails, traffic is rebalanced across the remaining ones within milliseconds, keeping sessions alive and bandwidth proportional to what's left.

A small callout I would like to mention: a Direct Connect LAG improves throughput and intra-device member-link failover, but it does not create device or site independence because all member ports must terminate on the same AWS Direct Connect device (AWS does not support multi-chassis LAG). Treat LAG as "many links behaving as one," not as a substitute for high-resiliency or maximum-resiliency multi-site designs.

This behavior is standardized in **IEEE 802.3ad**, with **LACP (Link Aggregation Control Protocol)** providing the heartbeat of coordination. LACP exchanges small control frames—LACPDUs—between peers to detect mismatches and confirm link state. When a member goes silent, it's withdrawn from the bundle automatically, without affecting upper-layer sessions. To Layer 3 and above, the bundle appears as a single, stable link, even when one of its underlying fibers has vanished.

In the context of **AWS Direct Connect**, LAGs bring the same concept into the cloud era. You can group multiple dedicated Direct Connect connections—typically 1, 10, or 100 Gbps—into a single logical interface to simplify management and increase aggregate bandwidth. However, AWS documentation makes an important clarification:

> "AWS doesn't support multi-chassis LAG ... A LAG is not
> recommended for a high-availability strategy." (source: `https://`
> `docs.aws.amazon.com/wellarchitected/latest/hybrid-`
> `networking-lens/dedicated-networking-setup.html?utm_`
> `source=chatgpt.com`)

All member ports terminate on the *same physical device* within the same Direct Connect location. As such, a LAG improves *throughput* and *intra-device failover*, but it does **not eliminate the location or device as a single point of failure**. A power event, maintenance window, or hardware issue on that device can still take down the entire LAG.

In Figure 5-3, a Link Aggregation Group (LAG) combines multiple physical circuits into one logical interface, improving throughput and offering intra-device failover within a single Direct Connect location. Each 10 Gbps member link participates in the same LACP session (IEEE 802.3ad), distributing frames and automatically removing failed members from service.

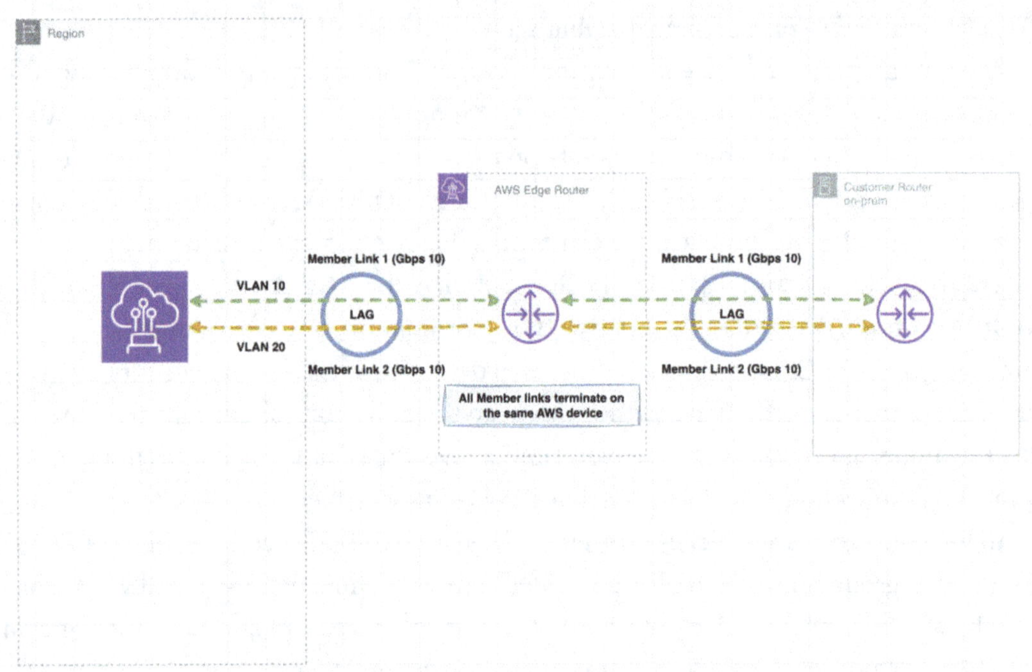

Figure 5-3. *Direct Connect LAG Focus*

However, as shown here, all member links terminate on the same AWS Edge Router—meaning that the device and facility remain a single point of failure. For high-availability designs, AWS recommends multiple LAGs across independent routers or Direct Connect locations, following the High-Resiliency and Maximum-Resiliency models as we mentioned in Section 5.1.

Taking the risk to repeat myself here, but I really would like to stress that to achieve true physical resilience, we should and can use the two higher-order models in its **Direct Connect Resiliency Toolkit**—the **High-Resiliency Model** and the **Maximum-Resiliency Model**. The high-resiliency model uses two independent connections across separate AWS routers within one facility; the maximum-resiliency model extends that further by deploying redundant connections across **two distinct Direct Connect locations**, ideally through different carriers and entry paths. We first introduced these patterns in Chapter 4 when discussing hybrid DNS transport resilience, where redundant circuits preserved private resolution paths during outages. The same logic applies here: redundancy across devices and sites turns link-level aggregation into true *service-level continuity.*

In practice, many enterprises combine both concepts: a LAG at each Direct Connect location to maximize bandwidth and internal link fault tolerance, and **paired LAGs** across geographically separated sites to deliver high or maximum resiliency as AWS defines it. In this configuration, LACP manages intra-location link health, while BGP at Layer 3 (covered in the next section and explored in depth in Chapter 7) provides inter-location route diversity. Together, they bridge the gap between physical and logical continuity—ensuring that even if an entire site fails, the connection fabric as a whole remains intact.

Failures at the data-link layer rarely announce themselves loudly. A link can remain administratively up while silently dropping frames, misrouting traffic across LAG members, or fragmenting packets due to MTU mismatches. Effective Layer-2 resilience therefore depends on observability signals such as LACP state transitions and member counters, indicators of MTU black-holing (e.g., selective timeouts on larger responses), and—where MACsec is enabled—encryption and security-association status. These signals often surface degradation long before routing protocols detect a problem, reinforcing the idea that resilience is preserved—or quietly sabotaged—well below Layer 3—and before flow behavior and member-link dynamics come into play.

Flow Distribution and Member Failure Behavior

While a LAG appears as a single logical pipe, traffic within it is never randomly sprayed across links. Frames are distributed according to a **hashing algorithm**—usually derived from fields like source and destination MAC or IP address, or even Layer 4 ports. The purpose is to ensure that all packets belonging to the same flow traverse the same physical member, preserving order and minimizing reassembly jitter. The side effect is that not all member links carry the same load: a handful of heavy flows can saturate one path while others remain underused. In high-throughput environments, this uneven distribution can translate into unpredictable performance during failure or recovery events.

When a link inside a LAG fails, **LACP** immediately removes it from the active bundle, redistributing affected flows among the surviving members.

This transition is typically sub-second, but the user experience hinges on two often-overlooked parameters: the **hash seed** and the **minimum-links threshold**.

- The *hash seed* determines which flows are mapped to which members; changing it during failover can cause widespread packet reordering, while keeping it consistent allows existing flows to persist seamlessly.

- The *minimum-links threshold* defines how many members must remain active for the LAG to stay up. If you configure this threshold too high—say, 4 of 4—the entire bundle drops even if three links are still healthy. Set it too low, and you may degrade performance without visibility, as 10 Gbps of traffic now squeezes through 5 Gbps of available bandwidth. Finding that balance is key to graceful degradation: the system should **slow down, not break**.

These nuances are especially relevant for **AWS Direct Connect LAGs**, where each member represents a full physical circuit. A mis-tuned threshold or hashing imbalance can turn a partial failure into a major incident even though the architecture "looks redundant." Because AWS LAGs distribute traffic at Layer 2 and rely on upper layers for multipath routing, operations teams must design for both scopes: LACP keeps the bundle consistent *within* a location, while BGP maintains reachability *between* locations. We'll expand on that interaction in the next section, where Layer 3 logic—BGP timers, route convergence, and path preference—takes over as the guardian of resilience.

Segmentation, Frame Integrity, and Link-Layer Protection

Once aggregation ensures that multiple paths can act as one, the next task is to make sure those paths remain ordered, isolated, and trustworthy.

Resilience at the data link layer depends not only on redundancy but also on **discipline**—on maintaining boundaries, consistency, and integrity beneath the routing layer. In practical terms, this comes down to three pillars: **segmentation with VLANs, frame hygiene through MTU alignment**, and **hop-by-hop protection via MACsec**. Together, these transform a collection of fibers into a predictable, controlled medium—one that can tolerate disruption without propagating confusion upward.

In Figure 5-4, VLANs (IEEE 802.1Q) segment shared circuits to confine failure domains; MTU is **aligned end-to-end** (1500/8500/9001 as applicable) to avoid fragmentation during failover; and MACsec (IEEE 802.1AE) provides hop-by-hop confidentiality and integrity on dedicated DX ports at supported sites. Together, these controls make the link fabric predictable and trustworthy under partial failure.

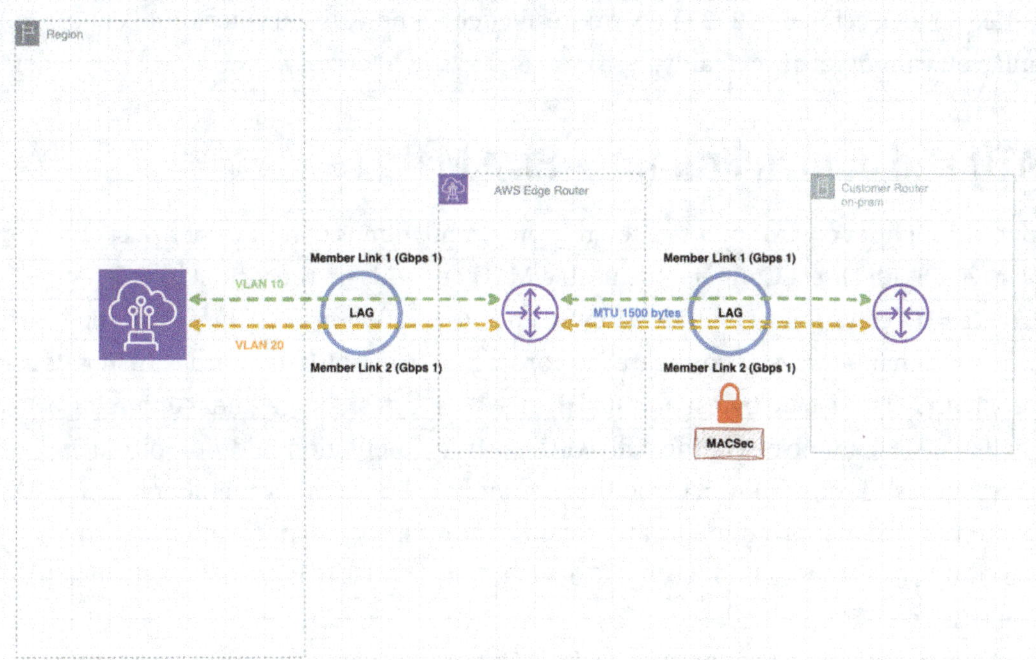

Figure 5-4. *Resilience Beyond Redundancy at Data-Link Layer*

VLANs (IEEE 802.1Q)—Isolation on Shared Wires

Modern hybrid and colocated environments often share infrastructure between different workloads or tenants. VLANs provide the first line of logical defense. By tagging frames with a VLAN ID, you partition a physical link into multiple virtual lanes, ensuring that a broadcast storm, configuration error, or maintenance event in one service domain doesn't leak into another.

In **AWS Direct Connect**, every Virtual Interface (VIF) is assigned a VLAN ID that isolates its traffic: private VIFs connect VPCs, transit VIFs attach to Transit Gateways, and public VIFs reach AWS services through the same physical circuit. This separation allows one interface to degrade or be reconfigured without affecting others. It's resilience by containment—the same principle we saw in Chapter 4 with DNS forwarding rules, now expressed one layer lower.

In today's industry, VLAN segmentation is more than a convenience. As networks become denser and multi-tenant, the risk of **cross-service coupling** grows. Analysts increasingly describe VLAN discipline as a "control of failure blast radius at the data plane," an idea echoed in 2025 network-resilience frameworks: if you cannot contain a fault, you cannot recover cleanly.

MTU and Jumbo Frames—Size Matters

High-throughput environments often rely on jumbo frames to reduce per-packet overhead. With Direct Connect, the usable MTU depends on the virtual interface type: **Private VIFs** can support up to **9001** bytes end-to-end (when every hop, including ENIs and on-prem interfaces, is configured accordingly); **transit VIFs** toward **transit gateway** use a path MTU of **8500** bytes; **public VIFs** are **1500** bytes. Any segment enforcing a smaller MTU than the rest of the path will trigger fragmentation or drops, producing "gray failures" during failover. Operationally, audit MTU on **every** member link in a LAG, monitor fragmentation counters, and set **minimumLinks** so bandwidth reduction is linear and visible rather than abrupt. Consider how an MTU mismatch would look like in a real case scenario.

A hybrid environment operates a Direct Connect private VIF with jumbo frames enabled to support steady-state throughput, while a backup path enforces a smaller effective MTU once encapsulation overhead is considered. During routine maintenance, one member of a Direct Connect LAG fails, and traffic is redistributed across the remaining LAG members. At the same time, a subset of flows begins traversing the lower-MTU path. The outcome is not a clean outage but intermittent application failures: small requests succeed, larger responses stall, retries increase, and timeouts appear sporadically. Routing remains stable, and interfaces stay up, masking the root cause. This is a classic MTU "gray failure"—where partial link loss and inconsistent frame sizing silently degrade delivery. Validating MTU end-to-end across primary and backup paths, and testing behavior under partial member failure, is essential to avoid these conditions surfacing only during real incidents.

MACsec—Protecting the Hop at Layer 2

Finally, resilience is not only about surviving failure—it's also about **ensuring integrity under stress**. When links span colocation facilities, exchanges, or carrier domains, the segment between your router and AWS's device may be exposed to interception or mispatching. **MACsec** secures this hop by encrypting every Ethernet frame independently of IP or higher-level protocols, preserving confidentiality and authenticity without changing routing behavior.

AWS offers MACsec-capable ports for dedicated connections in supported locations. In regulated industries—finance, healthcare, and defense—this feature is rapidly becoming a best practice. It protects the data plane itself, ensuring that the redundancy engineered through LAGs and diverse circuits isn't undermined by a compromised intermediate segment.

Operationally, MACsec introduces its own resilience considerations: key management (CAK/CKN rotation), re-authentication timers, and fail-open versus fail-closed policies. When misconfigured, these can silently block traffic even while link lights stay green. Observability here matters as much as encryption itself.

Bringing It All Together

Layer 2's contribution to resilience is quiet but fundamental. It enforces order where physical chaos meets logical intent. VLANs confine failure domains, MTU alignment preserves consistency during transitions, and MACsec ensures that trust doesn't end at the router port.

In a 2025 network landscape increasingly shaped by **hybrid workloads**, **edge interconnects**, and **compliance-driven connectivity**, the data-link layer remains the unsung guardian of continuity. It's where the difference between a graceful degradation and a cascading outage is decided—one frame at a time.

The following checklist summarizes the key considerations for validating Layer-2 resilience before relying on routing for recovery.

- LAG intent

  Use Link Aggregation Groups to increase throughput and tolerate member-link failures only. Do not treat a LAG as device or site redundancy; all members terminate on the same Direct Connect device.

- Minimum-links threshold

  Configure minimum links to allow graceful degradation. The bundle should slow down under partial failure, not collapse abruptly.

- Hashing awareness

  Validate flow-distribution behavior under load and during member loss. Expect uneven utilization and plan capacity accordingly.

- MTU consistency

  Audit MTU end-to-end across every hop for each path (primary and backup). Test partial-failure scenarios to detect MTU "gray failures" before production traffic is impacted.

- VLAN containment

  Scope VLANs intentionally and document their purpose. Treat VLANs as fault-containment boundaries, not survivability mechanisms.

- MACsec readiness (where used)

  Enable MACsec only where supported and operationally understood. Treat keying, policy alignment, and status monitoring as production-critical configuration.

- Observability

  Monitor LACP state and member health, watch for MTU-related symptoms, and track MACsec status. Assume Layer-2 failures will degrade silently before they break loudly.

One last word of caution: layer 2 preserves frame delivery, maintains link integrity, and absorbs individual circuit failures within a physical domain. What it cannot do is select alternate paths when an entire device, facility, or location becomes unavailable. Once the failure boundary exceeds a single site, resilience depends on Layer 3 decisions—routing intent, path diversity, and controlled convergence. This is where BGP becomes essential, transforming link-level continuity into end-to-end survivability across independent failure domains.

Section 5.3: Layer 3 (Network): BGP Path Selection, AWS TGW, DX + VPN Backup

If Layer 2 gives structure to the physical world, Layer 3 gives it direction.

It's here that networks stop being a set of cables and switches and start behaving like an ecosystem with intent. Routing at this layer decides not only where packets go, but also how quickly an environment can recover when something along the path disappears. Resilience at Layer 3 means ensuring that a broken link, router, or region changes the route, not the outcome.

In cloud architectures, this logic is expressed through the Border Gateway Protocol (BGP)—the same protocol that glues together the global Internet and underpins private hybrid connectivity between on-premises networks and AWS. Every decision at Layer 3 is made in terms of reachability: which paths exist, which are preferred, and which are withdrawn when a failure occurs. The purpose of resilient routing is to ensure that, no matter which cables or circuits break underneath, a reachable path remains visible above.

AWS's routing fabric implements this idea across multiple domains. Inside a single region, VPC route tables and Transit Gateway attachments act as micro-routing domains, controlling traffic between subnets, accounts, and workloads. At the hybrid edge, Direct Connect and Site-to-Site VPN use BGP to exchange prefixes between customer routers and AWS edge devices. Beyond a single region, Direct Connect Gateway and inter-region Transit Gateway peering extend routing intent globally while still preserving the blast-radius boundaries introduced in earlier chapters. Together, these constructs allow AWS to propagate reachability without requiring global broadcast or centralized control—a distributed system for distributed resilience.

From a design perspective, Layer 3 resilience has two goals: **redundant paths and predictable convergence**.

Redundant paths ensure that there's always an alternate way to reach a destination, ideally through independent facilities, carriers, or Availability Zones. Predictable convergence ensures that the transition between paths happens quickly and deterministically—fast enough that upper layers (like TCP or application retries) can absorb the transient loss without user impact. In AWS hybrid designs, this is achieved through a combination of BGP attributes and automation: prefixes advertised over multiple links, local-preference policies steering primary versus backup routes, and health-based withdrawal when a connection fails.

Table 5-1 distills these goals into concrete design choices. It summarizes how primary and backup paths are expressed through BGP, how preference and failure detection are encoded as policy rather than scripts, and how convergence targets can be defined and measured. The table is not a checklist of features but a reminder that resilience at Layer 3 emerges from a small set of deliberate decisions—made explicit, validated under failure, and repeated consistently across environments.

Table 5-1. *Layer 3 Resilience Design Summary*

Design Aspect	Recommended Practice	Operational Outcome
Primary Path	Direct Connect (single or dual, per resiliency model).	Deterministic latency and bandwidth.
Backup Path	Secondary Direct Connect or Site-to-Site VPN.	Transport diversity across failure domains.
Path Preference	Higher LOCAL_PREF on primary, AS-path prepend on backup. Use LOCAL_PREF across multiple locations/Use AS-path prepend within the same location.	Predictable steady-state routing.
Failure Detection	BFD enabled as a fast failure-detection companion to BGP sessions.	Sub-second detection of link failure.
Convergence Target	< 1s detect, < 5s withdraw + re-advertise.	Failover absorbed by transport/application layers.
Validation	Controlled failover testing and route verification.	Deterministic recovery under stress.

Every cloud network that aspires to high availability eventually reaches this same realization: **resilience at the routing layer is where physical diversity becomes logical survivability**.

Multiple circuits and LAGs mean little until routing policies understand when and how to use them.

When designed well, a BGP-driven edge can lose a router, a link, or even an entire colocation site and still continue forwarding traffic through a secondary path without manual intervention.

The following sections build on this foundation.

We'll start with a focused look at how BGP achieves path control in AWS and hybrid environments—examining local preference, AS-path length, and community tagging as the dials that steer resilience. Then, we'll explore how these mechanisms integrate with

Direct Connect Gateway and Transit Gateway to maintain stable connectivity across regions and providers, setting the stage for the deeper traffic-engineering discussion in Chapter 7.

Introduction to BGP in AWS and Hybrid Architectures

Routing resilience in the cloud depends on intelligent path selection, and no protocol embodies that logic better than the **Border Gateway Protocol (BGP)**.

BGP is often described as the *language of the Internet*—the system by which routers exchange information about which networks they can reach and how to get there. It's worth noting, however, that **BGP itself is not a network-layer protocol**. It operates at the **application layer**, running over **TCP port 179**, but its *purpose* is to influence and control the **network layer (Layer 3)** by distributing **Network Layer Reachability Information (NLRI)**.

This distinction is important. BGP doesn't forward packets; it *tells routers how to forward packets*. It sits one layer higher to provide intelligence, stability, and policy over the dynamic behavior of Layer 3. In the OSI model, this makes BGP a kind of "control-plane application"—one that enables distributed systems to agree on which paths exist, which are preferred, and which should be withdrawn when failures occur.

In cloud architectures, BGP is the foundation of routing resilience.

It links physical and data-link redundancy from the lower layers with logical continuity at the network layer.

In AWS, BGP governs how customer networks connect to AWS through **Direct Connect**, **Site-to-Site VPN**, and **Transit Gateway attachments**, ensuring that routing decisions automatically adapt when links or facilities fail.

How BGP Thinks: Attributes That Shape Resilience

BGP's core function is to choose the *best* route among many possible ones.

It evaluates routes using a deterministic series of attributes, or "hints," that express routing policy.

Although the full decision tree is long, a handful of attributes dominate AWS and hybrid designs—and understanding them is enough to build resilient behavior.

Local Preference (LOCAL_PREF)—Determines *outbound* traffic flow within your own autonomous system (AS).

The higher the value, the more preferred the path. In AWS hybrid networks, this is the main lever for defining primary versus backup circuits. For example, you can advertise the same prefixes via two Direct Connect links, assigning a higher local preference to the primary link. When it fails, the secondary path automatically takes over.

AS-Path Length—Influences *inbound* path selection.

The shorter the AS-path, the more attractive the route. You can artificially lengthen (prepend) the backup route by adding repetitions of your own ASN, discouraging its use until it's needed—an elegant standby mechanism without manual intervention.

Multi-Exit Discriminator (MED)—Suggests a preferred entry point into an AS when multiple exist.

While often ignored on the public Internet, MED is useful in controlled environments like multi-region AWS Direct Connect deployments, where you want to guide inbound paths between your own edge routers and AWS.

BGP Communities—Metadata tags that carry policy.

AWS supports community values such as 7224:9100 and 7224:9200 to signal preference for specific regions or Availability Zones, controlling how AWS propagates your routes. Communities are also essential for traffic-engineering policies, selective advertisement, or black-hole signaling during security events.

Together, these attributes let you define intent at the routing layer: which paths are active, which are hot standby, and which are suppressed.

They transform link state into policy. When a circuit fails, BGP withdraws its routes, and traffic is automatically steered to the next best option. No operator intervention is required. Let's see how BGP Path Selection works in practice.

When multiple paths exist, BGP selects a route by evaluating attributes in a deterministic order. In AWS hybrid environments, the effective decision flow can be summarized as follows:

1. Is the path reachable?

    If the BGP session is down or a route is withdrawn, the path is immediately excluded.

2. Which path has the highest LOCAL_PREF?

    This determines the preferred outbound path within the customer's autonomous system and is the primary control for steady-state routing.

3. Which path has the shortest AS path?

    Among otherwise equal routes, shorter AS-paths are preferred,
    making AS-path prepending an effective standby mechanism.

4. Is an MED value present and honored?

    When used in controlled environments, MED can influence which
    entry point is preferred into an autonomous system.

5. Do AWS-specific BGP communities apply?

    Community tags control how AWS propagates routes across
    regions, Availability Zones, or edge locations.

6. Install the selected path and forward traffic.

    Once installed, traffic flows until a failure or policy change restarts
    the evaluation.

This simplified flow illustrates how link failure becomes route withdrawal and how policy—not topology—determines which path carries traffic next.

BGP in the AWS Hybrid Edge

At the AWS edge, BGP sessions form the backbone of hybrid connectivity.

Each AWS Direct Connect Virtual Interface (VIF) or Site-to-Site VPN tunnel establishes one or more BGP peerings between the customer's on-premises router and AWS edge devices.

In a Direct Connect configuration, every VIF is assigned a unique VLAN ID at Layer 2, providing link-level isolation for the connection.

A small Layer 3 subnet is then configured across that VLAN, and the BGP session runs over TCP port 179 between those IP endpoints. This design means BGP does not operate on the VLAN itself; it runs over the IP subnet that the VLAN encapsulates, exchanging Network Layer Reachability Information (NLRI) for the prefixes each side advertises.

Over VPN, the same principle applies: BGP peers exchange routes across an encrypted IPsec tunnel, providing identical control-plane logic atop a different physical transport.

In a Direct Connect Gateway (DXGW) model, BGP enables multiple AWS Regions to learn the same on-premises prefixes.

The DXGW maintains separate BGP sessions for each regional attachment, and when a region becomes unreachable, the associated routes are automatically withdrawn—allowing traffic to flow through healthy attachments without manual reconfiguration.

In a Transit Gateway (TGW) topology, BGP operates on the external attachments—between the TGW and its connected DXGW or VPN—while internal VPC routing remains static for stability and predictability. This combination of dynamic routing at the hybrid edge and deterministic routing within AWS enables environments to scale globally while preserving control and isolation.

Because routing decisions emerge from this interaction between managed infrastructure and customer-defined policy, resilience at Layer 3 is a shared responsibility. AWS manages the availability of its edge routers, the stability of the Direct Connect Gateway and Transit Gateway control planes, and the propagation of routes across the AWS backbone. Customers, however, are responsible for BGP session design, attribute selection, BFD configuration, and convergence tuning. AWS guarantees reachability when routes are advertised and accepted; engineers determine when routes are preferred, withdrawn, or reintroduced. Making these ownership boundaries explicit is essential, because most routing failures arise not from infrastructure loss, but from policy that behaves differently than intended under stress.

Multi-region TGW peering extends this model further: even if one region experiences a disruption, BGP-based hybrid connections in another region can maintain reachability across the AWS global backbone. Route-table segmentation ensures that these events remain contained, echoing the blast-radius isolation principles introduced in earlier chapters.

Operational Simplicity As a Resilience Strategy

Complexity is one of the most persistent enemies of resilience.

In theory, a network rich with route maps, conditional advertisements, and granular policies sounds like control. In practice, it's fragility disguised as sophistication. The more levers an engineer must touch to make the network behave, the more likely one of them will fail silently when it matters most.

In enterprise and hybrid cloud networks, **BGP policies** are particularly prone to this trap. Engineers often build elaborate route maps, community-based filters, and conditional advertisements to sculpt traffic flow across regions or data centers. But during an outage, no one remembers which condition matched or why one prefix carried a different local preference than another. In those moments, clarity becomes the difference between a clean failover and an extended incident.

Table 5-2 captures the most common Layer-3 misconfigurations observed in real hybrid AWS environments and pairs each with a concrete mitigation. These issues rarely surface during steady-state operation, but they consistently emerge during disruption— when routing policy is forced to react rather than merely exist. Addressing them explicitly reinforces the principle that simplicity and predictability are the foundations of resilient routing.

Table 5-2. *Common Layer 3 Misconfigurations and How to Prevent Them*

Misconfiguration	Why it Causes Failure	How to Mitigate (Operational Guidance)
Slow failure detection on routing sessions	Default BGP timers delay failure detection by tens of seconds, causing prolonged blackholes during link loss.	**For Direct Connect:** Enable BFD on all BGP sessions and tune detection timers to meet recovery objectives. **For VPN:** Ensure Dead Peer Detection (DPD) is enabled and align IKE/IPsec and BGP timers so tunnel failure triggers timely route withdrawal.
Asymmetric routing between primary and backup paths	Traffic exiting over one path and returning over another breaks stateful firewalls, NAT, and load balancers, resulting in intermittent or partial failures.	Design symmetric path preference using consistent local-preference, AS-path prepending, and AWS BGP communities. Validate symmetry using traceroute and flow logs during failover tests.
Inconsistent MTU across Direct Connect and VPN paths	Jumbo-frame private links combined with lower-MTU encrypted paths cause fragmentation or silent drops during failover.	Normalize MTU and MSS values across all primary and backup paths. Explicitly test large-packet behaviour during simulated link failures.
Overly complex routing policies	Layered route maps and conditional logic behave unpredictably under failure, obscuring root cause and delaying recovery.	Favor minimal, deterministic policy: local preference for primary/backup, AS-path prepending for inbound influence, and limited, well-documented use of communities.
Unvalidated convergence behavior	Failover may technically occur but exceed acceptable recovery time, causing application-level disruption.	Measure and rehearse convergence: track time to detect, withdraw, and converge. Test under controlled failure scenarios and validate repeatability.

In **AWS hybrid architectures**, the strongest designs are usually the simplest.

Resilience here is not achieved through layers of configuration—it's achieved through consistency and predictability.

Each Direct Connect or VPN attachment already inherits the fault isolation and path diversity of AWS's edge. Your job is to express *intent* clearly enough that BGP can act on it automatically when something fails.

That means using only the attributes that matter:

- **Local Preference** for outbound control—define which path should be primary.

- **AS Path Prepending** for inbound influence—make backups less attractive until needed.

- **BGP Communities** for AWS-specific regional behavior—use them to signal scope, not to micromanage routing.

Each of these is explicit, observable, and reversible. They can be validated in both directions: what you send and what you receive. This transparency shortens recovery time because operators can verify BGP's state with a single command, such as:

```
show ip bgp summary
show ip bgp <prefix>
```

These simple checks answer the only question that matters under pressure: *Did the right path become active?*

Operational simplicity also supports automation.

Infrastructure-as-Code tools like AWS CloudFormation or Terraform can safely replicate clear, bounded BGP policies. When configurations are minimal and declarative, automated systems can enforce them consistently across environments. This reduces configuration drift—the silent erosion of resilience that happens when two routers start "almost matching" instead of being identical.

Equally important is **observability**. BGP exposes its own operational truth: prefixes advertised, prefixes received, and the state of each session. *These should be continuously monitored via a combination of CloudWatch metrics, Transit Gateway route-table events, control-plane health signals,* or **custom health checks** that verify expected routes are present. If a key route disappears or a session drops, automation can trigger alerts or failover scripts before users notice any effect.

Finally, simplicity is a mindset, not a limitation.

It's the discipline of building only what you can explain under stress.

A network that requires multiple engineers to interpret is not resilient—it's fragile.

In contrast, a simple BGP architecture, with a clear attribute hierarchy and consistent naming, can be operated, audited, and repaired by anyone on the team.

The paradox is that simplicity often takes more engineering effort than complexity. It forces you to understand exactly what you want the network to do—and to remove everything that doesn't contribute to that goal. But when the next failure arrives, and it will, that clarity is what keeps systems online while others are still reading route maps.

The Convergence Imperative

Every resilient network eventually faces its moment of truth: when a path goes dark and packets start disappearing. What happens next defines whether users notice the event— or whether the system simply heals itself before anyone has time to open an incident ticket. This is the world of **convergence**, the silent choreography of detection and redirection that determines how fast a network recovers from failure.

Convergence can be evaluated objectively. In resilient hybrid networks, recovery is measured not in sentiment but in timestamps: Time to Detect, Time to Withdraw, and Time to Converge. These metrics define whether a routing event is absorbed silently or escalates into an outage. Mature architectures are designed and tested against these values deliberately, ensuring that detection, policy reaction, and route installation are all completed within bounds that upper layers can tolerate.

When a link between an on-premises router and AWS suddenly fails, it's not the fiber that matters anymore; it's how quickly the control plane realizes it, recalculates the map, and restores connectivity through another path. The difference between a one-second and a one-minute reaction is the difference between a user's experience of "it just slowed down for a moment" and "the service went offline."

Traditional BGP wasn't built for speed. It was engineered for the open Internet, where patience was a form of stability. Default BGP timers—30-second keepalives and 90-second hold times—were designed to prevent flapping, not to deliver failover. In the modern cloud, those defaults are an eternity. A web application losing connectivity for a minute might as well be down entirely. AWS hybrid architectures therefore rely on **Bidirectional Forwarding Detection (BFD)** as a companion to BGP. BFD doesn't replace routing—it accelerates awareness. It's a tiny heartbeat protocol that runs beneath BGP, sending rapid keepalives across the link every few hundred milliseconds. If a handful of those go missing, the system declares the session dead, and BGP immediately withdraws the affected routes.

In practice, this means that instead of waiting a full minute for a link to time out, failover can happen in **under a second**. Direct Connect supports BFD to accelerate failure detection; VPN failover depends on tunnel liveness detection (DPD) and BGP session teardown, so timer alignment matters.

In well-tuned configurations, convergence time becomes fast enough to preserve sessions even in interactive applications—voice calls, trading systems, or live video feeds. BFD is the stethoscope pressed to the line, catching the first skipped heartbeat of a failing link before the patient collapses.

Detection, however, is only the beginning. Once a failure is known, the routing fabric has to make a decision: where does the traffic go now? That process—the recalculation and reinstallation of routes—is what engineers mean when they talk about "convergence." In simple topologies, this happens cleanly: one path disappears, and the other takes over. But in distributed systems with multiple Direct Connects, Transit Gateways, or VPNs, convergence is as much about discipline as it is about algorithms. The network must not only recover—it must recover *predictably*.

AWS's control plane enforces this hierarchy through its architecture. The **Direct Connect Gateway (DXGW)** handles route withdrawals region by region; when a session drops in one location, the associated routes are retracted, allowing another location to advertise the same prefixes without conflict. The **Transit Gateway (TGW)**, by contrast, converges internally at its own speed—faster than traditional routers, but still bounded by control-plane processing time. This is where realism matters: BFD can detect a failure in 500 milliseconds, but TGW route propagation may take a few seconds to ripple through. The goal is not absolute speed; it's predictability.

Real-world resilience means designing for *deterministic recovery*. A well-architected AWS hybrid edge behaves the same way every time a link fails: Direct Connect routes withdraw, VPN routes become active, prefixes reappear, and traffic resumes on the backup path. You can measure that process—how long each step takes, from detection to steady-state reachability—and express it as metrics that matter:

Time to Detect, Time to Withdraw, and Time to Converge.

These are not abstract ideas; they're operational truths. The most mature organizations track them like uptime. They simulate fiber cuts, record the timestamps, and refine their configurations until the numbers fall within their recovery objectives.

But convergence is not just about speed—it's about *grace*. A network that reacts too quickly can thrash itself into instability. BGP's dampening mechanisms exist for a reason: to prevent a single flapping link from poisoning the entire routing table. Fast detection without restraint leads to route churn, CPU spikes, and cascading withdrawals that look like instability instead of resilience. The art lies in knowing which links deserve millisecond responsiveness and which ones can afford a few seconds of patience.

Symmetry plays an equally important role. When a primary path fails, the new route may introduce differences in latency, MTU, or even directionality. In hybrid networks where traffic traverses both Direct Connect and VPN, this can create asymmetric flows—packets heading out through one link and returning through another. Stateful firewalls and NAT gateways rarely tolerate such asymmetry well. The result is often a "gray failure": half the flow survives, the other half disappears, and users report intermittent connectivity that defies simple diagnosis. Testing for symmetry before an incident—through traceroutes, VPC Flow Logs, and Traffic Mirroring—prevents those mysteries from becoming production issues.

Ultimately, convergence is not just about recovering from failure; it's about being able to prove that you did. After every failover, the network should validate its own state. AWS tools such as **Network Manager Connectivity Insights**, **Route Analyzer APIs**, and custom health-probe Lambdas make this verification continuous. They confirm that the right prefixes are advertised, that redundant paths are active, and that no unexpected leaks or oscillations occurred. A converged network that self-checks its correctness doesn't just survive failure—it learns from it.

This is the quiet rhythm of a resilient system: detect, withdraw, converge, verify, repeat.

It's what turns raw infrastructure into living architecture. And it's what allows the layers above—transport, application, and business logic—to keep operating as if nothing happened, even as the paths beneath them shift and heal in real time.

DX + VPN Hybrid Failover Patterns

Every hybrid architecture eventually meets its storm. A fiber is cut, a provider's maintenance window overruns, or a meet-me room loses power—and suddenly your carefully engineered Direct Connect circuit goes silent. What happens next defines the true maturity of your design. This is where resilience ceases to be a design principle and becomes a lived experience: when the private link fails, the system either hesitates or exhales through another path. The best networks are built for the latter—quiet, automatic, and graceful.

In AWS, the backup path is *not always* a VPN, but it often starts there.

A Site-to-Site VPN offers the simplest form of transport diversity: it rides the public Internet, across independent carriers, fibers, and power domains that share nothing with your Direct Connect provider. That independence is its greatest virtue. When a metro ring collapses or a colocation switch fails, the VPN continues to flow through a completely different physical universe.

But VPN is only one tool in the kit. Some enterprises prefer dual Direct Connects from separate locations, each with unique carriers and entry points, achieving deterministic performance without relying on Internet transport. Others blend the two—Direct Connect for primary connectivity and VPN for continuity—forming a layered defense where one failure domain can never silence the system completely.

These combinations map directly to the official AWS **resiliency models**.

The **High-Resiliency model** delivers roughly 99.9% availability through two independent Direct Connect connections, ideally in distinct locations or at least on different AWS devices within the same facility. The **Maximum-Resiliency model** extends that design to multiple colocation sites, each with its own devices, carriers, and paths, reaching roughly 99.99% availability. When these private circuits are complemented by a VPN fallback, the result is a multi-domain architecture where no single building, provider, or conduit holds the keys to availability.

The choice between these models is ultimately a business decision: cost versus risk, complexity versus continuity.

Hybrid failover itself is not magic—it is discipline expressed through the **control plane**.

At its heart lies BGP, once again deciding which road to take. Both Direct Connect and VPN sessions advertise the same AWS and on-premises prefixes, but with different attributes that express intent. The private circuit should always be preferred in a steady state; the VPN should remain a warm standby, ready but not dominant. That preference is communicated not by scripts or orchestration but by **numbers**: *Local Preference* for outbound direction, *AS Path Length* for inbound, and—where needed—*MED* or *BGP community tags* to influence AWS routing behavior.

We will explore those mechanisms in detail in **Chapter 7**, where traffic engineering becomes its own discipline of resilience.

On the customer edge, routes learned from Direct Connect are assigned a higher local preference so that outbound packets always favor the private link. On the AWS side, community tags such as 7224:7100 (Direct Connect) and 7224:7300 (VPN) can signal how return traffic should flow. When the Direct Connect session drops, BGP withdraws those routes, allowing the backup path to take over—no manual action, just convergence in motion.

This is resilience through clarity: deterministic behavior arising from explicit policy. Physical and logical alignment remains essential.

A Direct Connect link may support jumbo frames—up to **9001 bytes**—while IPsec tunnels typically reduce effective MTU to about **1436 bytes** after encryption overhead. If this mismatch goes unchecked, packets that glide through the private link fragment or drop across the VPN just when resilience is needed most. Harmonizing MTU, validating MSS settings, and testing both paths under load ensures that failover is not only functional but also performant.

Monitoring turns design into assurance.

A resilient edge does not simply fail over—it knows that it failed over, and it proves it.

Metrics such as **VpnTunnelState**, **BGPNotificationSent**, or **TransitGatewayPacketsDropCount** reveal whether sessions dropped, prefixes changed, or packets were discarded. Combined with **CloudWatch alarms**, **Transit Gateway route-table logs**, and synthetic health probes from **AWS Lambda** or **Systems Manager**, these metrics create a feedback loop of awareness. When the private link fails, alerts confirm that the backup is active, throughput remains stable, and latency stays within expected bounds. A network that cannot observe its own recovery is not resilient—it is guessing.

When the private circuit returns, **graceful failback** matters as much as failover.

Let BGP settle naturally; resist the urge to rush convergence. Impatient failback can cause "ping-ponging," as transient conditions make the system oscillate between Direct Connect and VPN. Stability, not immediacy, is the hallmark of an engineered recovery.

The same philosophy scales globally. In multi-region designs, each region can maintain its own Direct Connect pair for primary traffic, with **Transit Gateway peerings** or **inter-region VPNs** acting as alternate paths. When one region loses its physical edge, another continues to advertise healthy routes through the **Direct Connect Gateway (DXGW)**, keeping workloads reachable across the AWS backbone. It is resilience expressed through geography.

The true measure of hybrid resilience is not the presence of backup links but the **predictability of their behavior**.

The most effective teams rehearse failure like pilots rehearse engine loss: deliberately, methodically, and without drama. They take circuits down during controlled windows, observe BGP timers tick, and confirm that failover and failback occur exactly as planned. Every rehearsal transforms theory into confidence.

This is the quiet strength of the Direct Connect + VPN design pattern.

It does not depend on external orchestration or heroics. It accepts that failures are inevitable and ensures that, when they arrive, users never notice. Packets continue their journey—through light or through air, through private fiber or public backbone—guided by the same calm, resilient control plane that unites the hybrid cloud into a single, self-healing system.

Closing Thoughts for Section 5.3

Layer 3 gives the network its compass. Through BGP, routing intent is expressed across Direct Connect, VPN, Direct Connect Gateway, and Transit Gateway, allowing failures to become changes of path rather than losses of reachability. With redundant paths in place and convergence tuned to behave predictably, routing restores connectivity when links, devices, or locations disappear.

But routing alone does not preserve connections. Layer 3 determines where traffic can go; it does not decide whether active flows survive the transition. Once a new path is selected, responsibility shifts upward. It is the transport layer that governs session continuity—how connections are retried, drained, reused, or reset as the network converges beneath them.

In Section 5.4, we move to Layer 4 and examine how transport protocols and AWS load balancers absorb routing change. This is where TCP, UDP, and QUIC mechanics, health checks, keepalives, and fail-drain timing determine whether fast convergence is invisible to users or manifests as disruption.

And because not every failure can be contained at the transport layer, Section 5.5 completes the picture at the application edge. Rate limiting, caching, circuit breakers, and DNS policy constrain blast radius and traffic amplification, ensuring that failures remain within boundaries the system can actually defend. Together, these layers transform routing discipline into end-to-end resilience—quiet, automatic, and unnoticed by the users it protects.

Section 5.4: Layer 4 (Transport): Load Balancing Strategies in AWS (NLB) and Session Continuity

Layer 4 does not decide where traffic goes—that was Layer 3's job—but it determines whether active connections survive when those paths change. If routing is how networks *find* a path, transport is how they *keep* it.

Layer 4 is the bridge between reachability and experience—the moment where packets become conversations. A router may know fifty ways to reach a destination, but only the transport layer decides how those routes translate into living sessions that users actually perceive as continuous. When a link drops or a region fails, it's not the change in routes that customers notice—it's the broken download, the frozen video, or the API timeout. Layer 4 resilience is what stands between "we failed over" and "no one noticed."

At this layer, data stops being anonymous traffic and becomes part of a relationship.

A TCP handshake isn't just a technical ritual; it's an agreement to maintain order and reliability despite chaos underneath. Every byte is acknowledged, every gap retransmitted, and every delay interpreted as feedback about network health. **UDP**, its younger and lighter cousin, assumes nothing and recovers nothing; it's the language of voice calls, multiplayer games, and streaming telemetry—domains where losing a packet is cheaper than waiting for it. Then comes **QUIC**, a modern hybrid born from Internet-scale necessity, taking TCP's guarantees and reimagining them over UDP for mobility, encryption, and low-latency failover. Together, they form the behavioral DNA of modern transport resilience.

Resilience here is not about alternate routes—that was Layer 3's job.

It's about what happens *while* those routes are changing. When BGP withdraws a prefix and reconverges, when a Direct Connect link drops and traffic spills over to VPN, it's Layer 4's duty to hide that turbulence from the application above. Retransmission, reordering, and congestion control—these are the muscles that keep the digital heartbeat steady. If routing is the circulatory system, transport is the pulse.

In the cloud, this layer becomes even more consequential.

A microservice may talk to hundreds of peers through load balancers, NAT gateways, and firewalls. A hybrid edge may rely on TCP sessions spanning thousands of kilometers between on-premises data centers and AWS. Across all that distance and abstraction, Layer 4 protocols must still deliver a coherent experience. They are the glue between AWS's global network fabric and the application logic that rides it. Every Network Load

Balancer (NLB), Gateway Load Balancer (GWLB), and Elastic Load Balancer (ELB) exists to preserve that illusion of stability—to make scaling, failover, or rebalancing invisible to the users in flight.

This section explores how transport resilience is implemented in practice: how AWS distributes sessions, absorbs node or zone failures without interrupting flows, and uses timing discipline to drain, redirect, and recover gracefully. We'll see that Layer 4 is not a passive courier—it's an active stabilizer. It ensures that every route Layer 3 finds remains *usable*, every load-balancer decision remains *predictable*, and every transient network event remains *forgettable*.

By understanding transport-layer behavior, architects can predict how resilience actually feels to an end user—not just how it's diagrammed on a whiteboard.

From Reachability to Reliability: How Transport Protocols Create Resilience

Every packet that leaves a network interface is just a pulse of energy until it reaches the transport layer, where communication acquires intent. This is where the Internet stops being a loose collection of routers and links and becomes a system capable of maintaining a conversation. The transport layer adds discipline to motion—it decides not only how data travels, but also how it survives disruption, reorders itself after confusion, and keeps communication coherent when the underlying path falters.

The most widely used guardian of that discipline is **TCP**, the Transmission Control Protocol. TCP is *connection-oriented*, which means it begins by formally establishing a relationship before exchanging data. That establishment happens through the **three-way handshake**—the client sends a SYN, the server responds with a SYN-ACK, and the client finishes with an ACK. Only then does real communication begin. This process is more than a ritual; it confirms that both directions of communication work and that both sides agree on initial sequence numbers and expectations. Once connected, TCP continuously tracks what has been sent and acknowledged. If a segment is lost, it retransmits. If congestion slows the network, TCP automatically adjusts its sending rate. The protocol's built-in intelligence—through algorithms like CUBIC or BBR—interprets delay as feedback and rebalances its flow, maintaining stability even as the network changes underneath.

In cloud environments, this behavior defines resilience. When a Direct Connect circuit drops or a Network Load Balancer drains a target, TCP's session state allows communication to continue without collapse. It is cautious by nature, conservative in timing, but relentlessly persistent. A single lost packet is not a failure—it's just a signal to try again.

Where TCP establishes relationships, **UDP**, the User Datagram Protocol, dispenses with them. UDP is *connectionless*—there is no handshake, no tracking, and no confirmation that anything was received. Each datagram stands alone, sent and forgotten. It's a protocol designed for immediacy rather than certainty, trading reliability for speed. In real-time applications—voice calls, video streams, online games, DNS queries—the cost of delay outweighs the cost of loss. There is no need to rebuild every missing frame in a video conference or every dropped packet in a heartbeat message. When a route changes or a link resets, UDP doesn't notice, because there was never a "connection" to break. It simply keeps sending, and the next packet finds its own way.

The newest player in this story, **QUIC**, was designed for a different era of computing—an era where clients roam between networks, where encryption is default, and where milliseconds matter. QUIC runs on top of UDP but behaves like a modern, encrypted, connection-oriented transport. It merges the TLS handshake and transport setup into a single round trip, reducing startup delay by half. But its most profound contribution to resilience is *connection migration*. A QUIC session is not bound to IP addresses or ports; it is identified by a random connection ID. This allows a device to change networks—say, from Wi-Fi to 5G—without breaking its connection. The network path can change completely, yet the session remains intact. QUIC also supports multiple independent streams within one encrypted tunnel, so if one stream experiences loss or delay, the others continue unaffected. This design eliminates the head-of-line blocking problem that has long haunted TCP-based HTTP/2.

AWS has embraced QUIC where it matters most: at the edge. Amazon CloudFront and API Gateway both support HTTP/3, which is powered by QUIC. These services deliver web content and APIs over a transport that can handle changing routes, wireless variability, and transient congestion with grace. It's a transport designed for the realities of global, mobile, cloud-native applications.

Each of these protocols—TCP, UDP, and QUIC—embodies a different philosophy of resilience. TCP's is *persistence*: maintain order, retransmit what's lost, and adapt to change. UDP's is *freedom*: avoid the burden of the state, keep moving, and let the application decide what matters. QUIC's is *adaptation*: preserve continuity even when the ground shifts.

In AWS, these philosophies coexist in practice. Network Load Balancers preserve TCP and UDP flows faithfully, ensuring that their native recovery behaviors remain effective even as targets scale or fail over. Route 53 resolvers and DNS rely on UDP's speed and simplicity. CloudFront and other edge services leverage QUIC's mobility and encrypted reliability to ensure users stay connected as their conditions change.

The transport layer is not just another step in the OSI model; it's the heartbeat that keeps distributed systems alive. It doesn't prevent failure—it makes failure tolerable. By establishing, maintaining, or adapting connections as conditions evolve, it allows applications to keep their promises even when the network beneath them bends.

Network Load Balancer: Keeping Flows Consistent Through Disruption

If the transport protocols define how communication endures, the Network Load Balancer (NLB) is the mechanism that keeps those conversations uninterrupted when parts of the network fail. It sits squarely at **Layer 4 of the OSI model**, operating at the transport layer where connections are established and maintained—not interpreted. Unlike an Application Load Balancer (ALB), which makes decisions based on HTTP headers and content, the NLB concerns itself only with TCP and UDP flows—ports, IPs, and sessions. Its mission is not to understand traffic but to ensure it never stops.

The NLB is built for **massive concurrency and minimal latency**. It can process millions of connections per second and sustain terabit-scale throughput while maintaining sub-millisecond forwarding delay. This makes it ideal for workloads that demand deterministic performance: financial trading platforms, IoT brokers, DNS resolvers, or custom TCP applications that depend on consistent latency.

Yet its real contribution to resilience is not raw speed—it's continuity.

An NLB distributes connections across multiple **Availability Zones (AZs)**, each with independent load-balancing nodes. With cross-zone load balancing **disabled**, clients are served only by targets in their local zone—**containing the blast radius** and isolating faults. When it's **enabled**, the NLB routes traffic across all healthy targets in the region, ensuring that a zonal failure does not interrupt service.

The choice between the two modes is strategic: isolation provides containment, while cross-zone distribution provides continuity.

Mature architectures often blend both—front-end NLBs use cross-zone balancing for availability, while back-end tiers remain zonally isolated to prevent cascading faults.

Internally, the NLB relies on **deterministic flow hashing** based on a five-tuple (protocol, source IP, source port, destination IP, destination port). Once a client connection is established, that flow remains mapped to the same target until it closes. If AWS adds or removes nodes during scaling or maintenance, existing connections persist—the control plane updates silently while the data plane keeps forwarding packets without interruption.

To ensure availability, the NLB performs **active health checks** using TCP, HTTP, or HTTPS probes against registered targets. When a target fails, it's immediately withdrawn from routing for new connections, but existing sessions are allowed to complete naturally—a behavior similar in spirit to connection draining. This design prevents abrupt termination of in-flight transactions during failover events.

To see how this plays out in practice, consider a regional Network Load Balancer fronting a TCP-based API, with targets distributed across three Availability Zones. A client establishes a long-lived connection to a target in AZ-A. Mid-request, that target fails—due to a crash, deployment error, or zonal disruption—and immediately stops responding to health checks.

Within seconds, the Network Load Balancer redirects new connections to healthy targets in AZ-B and AZ-C. Crucially, the existing TCP session is not reset. Packets already in flight are delivered, retransmissions occur if needed, and the client receives a complete response without awareness of the underlying failure.

From the user's perspective, nothing failed. From the system's perspective, a node disappeared, and traffic adapted around it. This is Layer-4 resilience in practice: preserving active conversations while the infrastructure heals itself underneath.

In Figure 5-5, users connect via **Route 53 DNS** to a **regional NLB endpoint** spanning multiple Availability Zones. The NLB forwards traffic to healthy targets within each AZ, continuously monitoring them through active health checks. Unhealthy targets are withdrawn without interrupting existing flows.

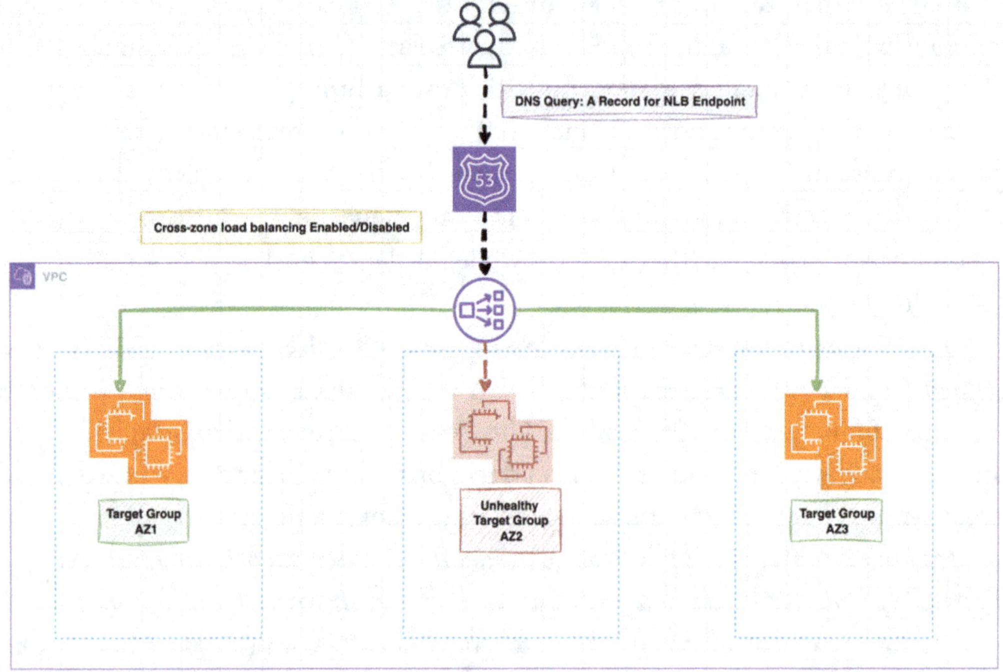

Figure 5-5. *Network Load Balancer Architecture*

When **cross-zone load balancing** is enabled, the NLB distributes connections across all healthy targets in the region; when disabled, each zone serves its own traffic to contain faults.

The VPC spans all AZs, allowing the NLB to maintain **regional reach and consistent flow mapping**.

Because the NLB operates purely at the **transport layer**, it doesn't parse payloads or terminate TLS unless explicitly configured. When TLS termination is enabled, **session resumption and cross-zone certificate caching** prevent spikes in handshake latency during failover. AWS also isolates NLB nodes per AZ, so even during maintenance, traffic within an AZ remains served by local capacity; if a node fails, the service automatically redirects to a healthy peer in the region.

Resilience at this layer depends on **failover granularity**. When a target fails, the NLB reacts within milliseconds—steering new flows elsewhere while allowing active connections to persist until natural timeout. For stateful TCP applications—from payment APIs to streaming services—this behavior preserves continuity where it matters most.

The transition feels invisible: sessions stay alive even as topology changes underneath.

Many production architectures pair NLBs with complementary AWS constructs to extend resilience across boundaries.

AWS Global Accelerator provides static Anycast IPs that route client traffic over the AWS backbone to the nearest healthy NLB endpoint. If an entire region becomes unavailable, Global Accelerator reroutes users automatically—maintaining global availability without DNS changes.

AWS PrivateLink builds on the same foundation to expose private services across accounts or VPCs without traversing the public Internet, inheriting the same fault tolerance and flow stability.

It's worth clarifying that the NLB itself doesn't perform dynamic path routing within the AWS backbone. *Instead, it relies on AWS's redundant global network fabric—high-capacity links and geographically diverse paths—*to maintain connectivity between load-balancing nodes and targets. The resilience of this underlying network ensures that even if one path degrades, another carries the traffic seamlessly, without affecting the load balancer's behavior.

Ultimately, the NLB represents **architectural composure**.

It translates the reliability of transport protocols into infrastructure-level guarantees: stable flow mapping, graceful recovery, and isolation between faults. It neither overreaches nor oversimplifies.

It simply ensures that when packets arrive, they find a healthy destination—even as the world around them changes.

Table 5-3 distills the most common transport-layer failure patterns observed in production AWS environments—issues that rarely appear in diagrams but frequently surface during real failover events. Unlike Layer 3 failures, which are often visible as lost reachability, Layer 4 failures tend to manifest as intermittent resets, stalled sessions, or partial outages that are difficult to diagnose under pressure. By mapping each pitfall to a concrete mitigation, the table translates transport-layer theory into operational guardrails, ensuring that the continuity promised by the Network Load Balancer is preserved not just in steady state, but during disruption and recovery.

Table 5-3. *Common Layer 4 Pitfalls and How to Prevent Them*

Layer-4 Pitfall	Why it Breaks Resilience	Recommended Mitigation
Idle timeouts too aggressive	"Healthy" connections can still be dropped if they sit idle longer than the load balancer's timeout, creating resets that look like random failures during failover or scale events.	For **NLB TCP listeners**, set an idle timeout appropriate for your application (default **350s**, configurable **60–6000s**). For **NLB TLS listeners**, the idle timeout remains **350s** (not configurable), so rely on application/TCP keepalives and proper client behavior where needed.
MTU / MSS mismatch across paths	Failover from jumbo-frame private paths to lower-MTU encrypted paths can trigger fragmentation or silent drops, causing stalls and "gray failures."	Normalize MTU/MSS across primary and backup paths. For Site-to-Site VPN, AWS configuration examples commonly set tunnel MTU to **1436**, which makes MSS tuning/validation especially important when mixing with jumbo-frame paths.
Asymmetric return paths through stateful devices	Even if Layer 3 reconverges, asymmetric return paths can break stateful firewalls/NAT/inspection chains, causing intermittent resets or one-way traffic.	Design for symmetry across failover (especially when inserting inspection/NAT). Validate with failover tests and flow logs; ensure policies don't cause "out one path, back another" through stateful middleboxes.
Health checks misaligned with real service readiness	Targets can pass simple transport checks while still failing real workloads; conversely, incorrect HTTP(S) health checks can mark good targets unhealthy (e.g., host header mismatches), amplifying an event.	Use appropriate NLB target group health checks (**TCP/HTTP/HTTPS**) and tune them to reflect real readiness. For UDP/QUIC services, use non-UDP health checks as AWS recommends.
Cross-zone load balancing enabled without understanding blast radius and costs	Cross-zone increases continuity during zonal impairment but can shift load and increase cross-AZ traffic patterns; in some architectures, this can surprise capacity planning and costs.	Use cross-zone deliberately: enable when continuity matters more than zonal containment; validate backend capacity and understand cross-AZ data transfer implications in your topology.
Draining/deregistration delay too short (or not planned)	During scale-in, replacement, or deregistration, abrupt removal can terminate in-flight sessions, making failover visible to users.	Use target group **deregistration delay** (default **300s**, configurable **0–3600s**) to allow in-flight traffic to complete; consider connection termination behavior at the end of the delay via target group attributes where relevant.

Before relying on Layer 4 to absorb routing changes and infrastructure failures, validate the following controls to ensure session continuity under stress.

- **Health checks**

  Configure NLB health checks that reflect real service readiness (TCP for pure transport, HTTP/HTTPS only when application response is meaningful). Verify detection time aligns with recovery objectives and does not flap under load.

- **Cross-zone load balancing**

  Decide explicitly whether cross-zone balancing is enabled. Enable it when continuity across AZ failures is required; disable it when strict fault isolation and zonal blast-radius containment are the priority.

- **Connection-draining behavior**

  Ensure targets are deregistered gracefully during deployments or failures. Validate that existing TCP sessions are allowed to complete naturally and that idle timeout settings match application expectations.

- **Idle timeouts and keepalives**

  Align client, load balancer, and target idle timeouts to prevent
  silent connection resets during failover or low-traffic periods.

- **Path symmetry and MTU/MSS consistency**

  Confirm that primary and backup paths (Direct Connect, VPN,
  intra-AZ) preserve symmetry and compatible MTU/MSS values
  so that session continuity is maintained during transport-layer
  failover.

*Taken together, these behaviors show why the Network Load Balancer is the
cornerstone of transport-layer resilience in AWS: it preserves flow continuity while
infrastructure changes underneath. But continuity alone is not enough. In many
environments, traffic must also be inspected, filtered, or enforced consistently without
reintroducing fragility. This is where the Gateway Load Balancer extends Layer-4 resilience
beyond reachability into trust.*

Gateway Load Balancer in an Inspection VPC

In the previous section, we explored the **Network Load Balancer (NLB)**—a service built
for speed, scalability, and transport-layer resilience. NLB ensures that traffic reaches
healthy endpoints quickly and predictably, even under failure or surge. But resilience
isn't only about reachability—it's also about **trust**. Before packets reach your workloads,
they often need to be inspected, filtered, or shaped for compliance and security. This is
where the **Gateway Load Balancer (GWLB)** comes in.

While NLB manages the *distribution* of connections, GWLB manages the *insertion*
of inspection—placing firewalls, intrusion detection systems, or data loss prevention
appliances transparently between sources and destinations.

In other words, NLB delivers packets efficiently; GWLB ensures those packets
are safe.

Both live at Layer 4, but their missions differ: NLB routes based on connection health
and endpoint availability, whereas GWLB routes through inspection chains, preserving
symmetry and state for every flow. Together, they close the loop between transport
reliability and traffic integrity—two sides of the same resilient fabric.

The Inspection VPC Pattern

Deep packet inspection shouldn't be a single point of failure. In AWS, the cleanest and most resilient way to insert stateful security into network paths is by centralizing inspection into a **dedicated Inspection VPC**, fronted by **Gateway Load Balancer (GWLB)**.

Spoke VPCs keep their applications and route tables simple: traffic destined for inspection is forwarded to a **GWLB endpoint (GWLBe)** deployed in each Availability Zone. These endpoints use **AWS PrivateLink** to forward traffic privately to the GWLB service in the Inspection VPC, which then distributes flows across a fleet of virtual appliances such as firewalls, IDS/IPS, or custom packet processors.

GWLB operates at Layer 4 and uses **GENEVE encapsulation (UDP port 6081)** to forward the *original* packet, unmodified, to its target appliances. Once processed, the packet is returned to GWLB for decapsulation and sent on to its final destination. Importantly, **five-tuple flow hashing** (source/destination IP and port, plus protocol) ensures that both directions of each session are handled by the same appliance—preserving stateful inspection even when the appliance fleet scales or rebalances.

If an appliance fails health checks, GWLB stops sending *new* flows to it while continuing to serve others. Deployed across multiple Availability Zones, this pattern ensures that an outage in one zone doesn't disrupt global inspection capacity.

The **Inspection VPC** separates concerns cleanly:

> **Spoke VPCs** forward traffic to the local GWLBe and keep routing minimal.
>
> Return traffic follows the same path, maintaining flow symmetry for stateful inspection.
>
> **The Inspection VPC** owns all appliance management—scaling, patching, replacement, and vendor diversity—behind the GWLB target groups.
>
> Because this interaction happens through PrivateLink, the inspection service can be shared across AWS accounts or entire organizations while keeping traffic private on the AWS backbone.

This decoupling of routing from security enforcement is the cornerstone of operational resilience. It allows network and security teams to evolve their respective layers independently without coordination bottlenecks—the Inspection VPC can scale, rotate, or even change firewall vendors without a single route update in application VPCs.

In Figure 5-6, spoke VPCs route traffic requiring inspection to **zonal Gateway Load Balancer Endpoints (GWLBe)**. **PrivateLink (GENEVE UDP 6081)** carries encapsulated packets directly to the **Gateway Load Balancer** in the Inspection VPC, which distributes flows across a fleet of security appliances using **five-tuple flow hashing** to maintain stateful symmetry.

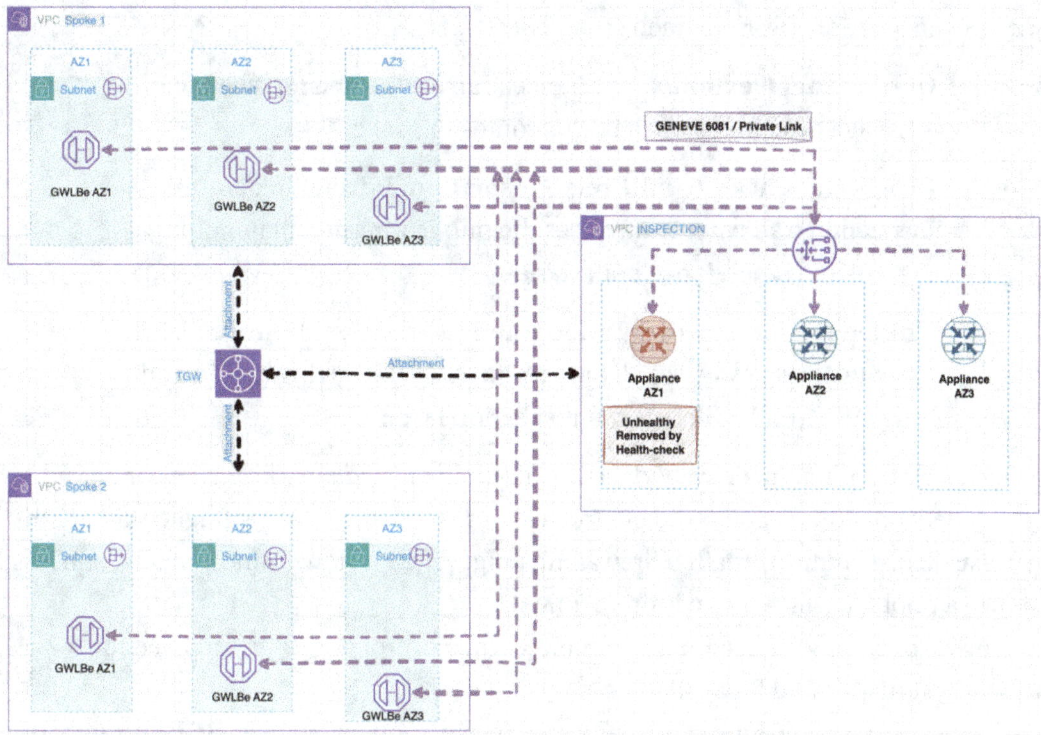

Figure 5-6. *Inspection VPC with Gateway Load Balancer and GWLB Endpoints*

Unhealthy targets are automatically withdrawn by health checks, while **multi-AZ deployment** ensures that failures remain contained within a single Availability Zone.

To prevent asymmetric routing during scale-out or zonal recovery events, **Gateway Load Balancer supports appliance mode**, which preserves flow directionality and guarantees that both directions of a connection traverse the same appliance instance. This behavior is essential for stateful firewalls and intrusion-prevention systems that rely on consistent bidirectional inspection.

We will explore appliance mode, flow symmetry, and advanced routing control—including BGP communities, AS-path prepending, and weighted route policies—in detail in **Chapter 7**.

So, why this pattern increases resilience?

- **Zonal Fault Tolerance:** Endpoints and appliances are deployed per-AZ, containing failure impact.

- **Stateful Flow Integrity:** Five-tuple hashing ensures consistent inspection paths for each connection.

- **Operational Flexibility:** Appliances can scale or be replaced one zone at a time, without changing routes in spoke VPCs.

- **Cross-Account and Multi-region Isolation:** PrivateLink ensures inspection traffic never traverses the public Internet, maintaining control and compliance boundaries.

- **Unified Hybrid Posture:** Traffic entering via **Direct Connect**, **VPN**, or **Transit Gateway** can all pass through GWLB, giving hybrid and intra-AWS traffic a consistent inspection layer.

Gateway Load Balancer embodies the principle of *resilience through abstraction.*

It hides individual appliances behind a logical service, replacing fragile static paths with elastic distribution. A failed firewall no longer means downtime; it means one less node in a pool that self-heals within seconds.

The Inspection VPC becomes an architectural control point—centralized for security, yet distributed for availability.

As we'll explore in **Chapter 7**, traffic engineering policies such as **BGP communities**, **AS-path prepending**, and **route weighting** can extend this model across regions and hybrid edges, ensuring that even as routes shift, the inspection layer remains consistent and transparent.

At this level of design maturity, resilience and security are no longer competing goals—they are the same system seen from two different directions. ***Inspection must be elastic: if security appliances cannot scale, fail, and recover with the same transparency as the traffic they inspect, they become a new single point of failure rather than a control plane for trust.***

From Transport Integrity to Application Awareness

With the Gateway Load Balancer and the Inspection VPC, we've extended resilience from the transport layer into the security plane—ensuring that even the inspection of traffic is elastic, redundant, and transparent.

At this point in the stack, the network can detect, forward, and protect flows without interruption. Failures of cables, links, or appliances are no longer existential events—they're just changes in topology that the system absorbs automatically.

But resilience doesn't stop at secure packet delivery. Once traffic reaches the upper layers, reliability becomes a matter of **how applications react**—how they balance incoming requests, manage surges, and recover from partial failures.

This is where the architecture transitions from *network resilience* to *application resilience*: from moving packets efficiently to ensuring that every user transaction completes, even when dependencies falter.

In the next section, we'll explore **Layer 7**, where control shifts from routers to software logic.

Here, services such as the **Application Load Balancer (ALB)** and **Amazon CloudFront** take center stage, implementing **rate limiting**, **caching**, and **failover logic** that preserve the customer experience during stress or failure.

If GWLB represents resilience through invisible protection, Layer 7 represents resilience through visible stability—keeping applications responsive and trustworthy when everything beneath them is adapting in real time.

Section 5.5: Layer 7 (Application): Rate Limiting, Caching, and Failover Logic (ALB)

Layer 7 is where resilience becomes user-visible: even when paths change, targets fail, or regions degrade, it decides whether users see an error—or never notice a failure occurred at all.

By the time traffic reaches Layer 7, the lower layers have already done the heavy lifting: fibers stayed lit (L1), links stayed coherent (L2), and routes converged predictably (L3). The transport negotiated sessions and retransmissions (L4). Here, at the application edge, resilience becomes visible to users. It's where we shape request volume, absorb surges with cache, and decide—request by request—what happens when a backend falters. In AWS, the primary instruments are **Application**

Load Balancer (ALB) for HTTP/HTTPS routing, **AWS WAF** (often attached to ALB or CloudFront) for rate-based controls, and **Amazon CloudFront** for a protective cache layer at the edge.

Connection Semantics at the Edge

ALB operates as a Layer-7 proxy: it terminates client TCP/TLS and speaks HTTP/1.1 or HTTP/2 to targets (and supports gRPC over HTTP/2). It does **not** support HTTP/3/ QUIC as of today, so when your clients use HTTP/3 at the CDN (CloudFront), the hop to ALB remains HTTP/1.1 or HTTP/2 after CloudFront re-originates the request. That distinction matters for performance tuning: QUIC's gains (fast handshakes, better loss recovery) apply on the client↔edge leg; the edge↔origin leg still follows classic TCP/TLS semantics. CloudFront explicitly supports HTTP/3/QUIC for viewers, so it can harvest those benefits at the edge while protecting your origin from connection churn.

Shaping Load Before It Hurts: Rate Limiting and Back-Pressure

Because ALB does not implement per-client rate limiting, this control is typically enforced at the edge using AWS WAF (attached to CloudFront or ALB) or via API Gateway for API-centric workloads. WAF's rate-based rules apply a sliding-window counter (five-minute window) per IP (or per label if you use advanced rules) and can block or count once a threshold is exceeded. In practice, this behaves like a coarse token bucket at the edge: allow brief bursts, then shed excess load before it reaches the origin. For API backends, API Gateway's throttling/quotas complement this with method-level precision; for web apps, WAF on ALB/CloudFront is the simplest "pressure valve."

A resilient stance at Layer 7 is to **reject early, cheaply, and consistently** when the system is under stress. Returning standardized 429 responses from the edge with clear retry hints preserves origin capacity and reduces tail latencies. It also keeps the system predictable: user experience degrades gracefully, not randomly.

Buying Time with Distance: Caching As a Resilience Primitive

Caching isn't just a performance trick; it's a resilience tool. Placing Amazon CloudFront in front of an ALB fundamentally changes the failure mathematics of an application. Hot objects are served from the edge, request coalescing flattens stampedes, and the origin sees fewer simultaneous connections. Most importantly, CloudFront supports *stale-while-revalidate* and *stale-if-error* cache directives, allowing it to serve slightly stale content when the origin is slow or unreachable—a powerful circuit breaker for read-heavy surfaces such as product pages, documentation, or dashboards with tolerant freshness.

Two practical disciplines keep this effective:

- **Cache key discipline**

  Keep keys stable and minimal (path plus only essential headers). Avoid volatile headers that explode the cache and turn edge storage into a pass-through.

- **TTLs tuned to risk**

  Use short TTLs for highly dynamic JSON and longer TTLs for static assets. For semi-dynamic HTML, pair modest TTLs with *stale-while-revalidate* so the edge can mask brief origin hiccups while refreshing in the background.

A real outage illustrates why this matters. Consider an e-commerce site fronted by CloudFront with ALB origins in a single region. During a regional control-plane incident, the origin ALB becomes intermittently unreachable. Without edge caching, users experience cascading 5xx errors as retries amplify the load against an already impaired backend.

With CloudFront in place and *stale-if-error* enabled, the failure mode changes entirely. Product pages and catalog responses already cached at the edge continue to be served—even as the origin times out or returns errors. Revalidations are deferred, background refresh attempts fail quietly, and users continue browsing uninterrupted. From the outside, the site appears slow to update—but not broken.

This is Layer-7 resilience in its most practical form: not preventing failure, but buying time. By decoupling user experience from origin availability, CloudFront converts a backend outage into controlled degradation rather than a public incident.

Common Layer-7 Pitfalls That Undermine Resilience

Even well-designed edge architectures can fail to deliver user-visible resilience if a few common mistakes slip in. These issues rarely surface during steady state, but they consistently amplify outages when the origin is under stress.

- **Over-broad cache keys**

  Including volatile headers (authorization tokens, cookies, or user-specific metadata) in the cache key collapses cache efficiency. When every request becomes a miss, CloudFront loses its ability to shield the origin during failure.

- **Missing or inconsistent 429 handling**

  Rate limiting only works if clients are taught how to respond. When 429 (Too Many Requests) responses lack retry hints—or are applied inconsistently across paths—clients retry aggressively, worsening load instead of relieving it.

- **Mis-tuned health checks**

  Health checks that are too sensitive eject healthy targets during transient latency; overly lax checks delay failover when backends are genuinely impaired. Both convert short disturbances into prolonged incidents.

- **Cache TTLs that ignore failure modes**

  Extremely short TTLs maximize freshness but eliminate the safety window caching provides. Without *stale-if-error* or *stale-while-revalidate*, the edge has nothing to serve when the origin falters.

Layer-7 resilience depends as much on restraint as capability. Edge services are powerful—but only when configured to fail *gracefully* instead of *precisely*.

Failover Where Users Notice: ALB Routing, Health, and Steady Handovers

ALB's job is to keep sending traffic only to healthy targets—and to do so predictably. Health checks are per target group; ALB removes unhealthy targets from rotation and only routes to healthy ones. You control detection speed with health-check interval and thresholds (down to seconds-level cadence), balancing fast reaction with false-positive risk.

For staged rollouts and controlled failovers, ALB can forward to multiple target groups with weights—for example, 90% to v1 and 10% to v2. If a group's targets all fail health checks, ALB simply stops sending to that group, producing a clean de facto failover without orchestration. This is the right place to implement blue/green ramps or canaries or to keep a "pilot light" pool warm in a second AZ or region behind a smaller weight.

For transport-layer neutrality—with fixed anycast IPs, protocol-agnostic routing (TCP/UDP), and edge-to-origin isolation—**AWS Global Accelerator** sits in front of the ALB or NLB. It's not a cache or a WAF; it's a traffic steering layer that uses the AWS edge network to reach the healthiest, closest endpoint and preserves static anycast IPs for clients. Supporting both TCP and UDP, it provides a clean, protocol-agnostic entry point that keeps client IPs stable and minimizes Internet path variance—especially in multi-region designs.

In Figure 5-7 a user request reaches **Amazon CloudFront**, where **AWS WAF** enforces edge-level rate-based rules. CloudFront forwards conforming traffic to the **Application Load Balancer (ALB)**, which distributes requests across weighted target groups (e.g., 90/10). Continuous health checks monitor each target; if v2's targets fail, the ALB automatically routes 100% of traffic to v1, achieving seamless failover. Meanwhile, CloudFront's **stale-while-revalidate** mechanism serves cached responses during origin latency or transient errors, concealing short-lived disruptions.

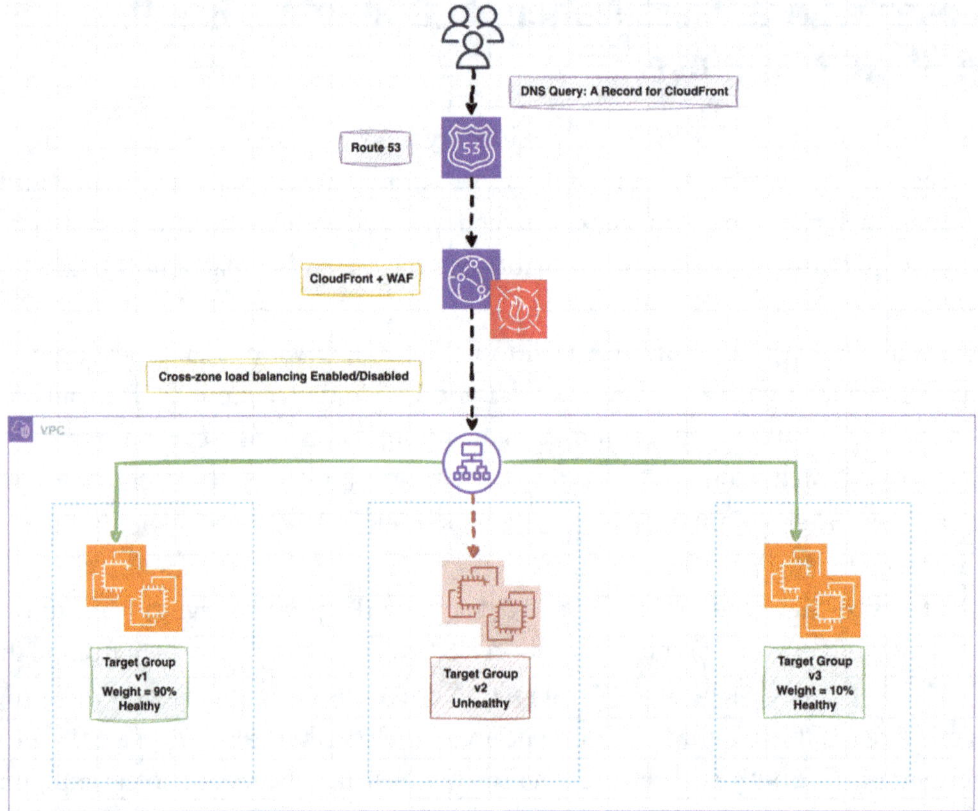

Figure 5-7. *Edge-In Resilience Chain: CloudFront+WAF+ALB (Weighted Target Groups)*

(Client ↔ Edge may use HTTP/3 / QUIC; Edge ↔ ALB typically uses HTTP/1.1 or HTTP/2.)

Putting the Pieces Together

Resilience at Layer 7 is not about adding endless tools—it's about applying a few principles with precision. The strongest application architectures absorb pressure at the edge, route intelligently in the middle, and remain stable at the front door no matter what happens behind it.

At the outermost edge, Amazon CloudFront and AWS WAF absorb pressure before it reaches the application. CloudFront reduces origin dependency through caching, request coalescing, and controlled staleness during failure, while AWS WAF

**enforces predictable rate-based limits that shed excess load early. Together, they
ensure that traffic entering the system is both regulated and survivable.**

Behind them, the **Application Load Balancer (ALB)** provides order and continuity.
It routes requests based on content and context, forwarding traffic only to healthy targets
as determined by its configurable health checks. When paired with weighted target
groups, ALB enables smooth blue/green deployments and automatic failover—diverting
traffic away from troubled back-ends without manual intervention or complex scripts. In
practice, this transforms the ALB into an intelligent control plane for application health,
one that reacts to change faster than any human operator could.

Finally, for applications that demand a consistent and performant entry point,
AWS Global Accelerator brings stability through static **anycast IPs**. By routing user
traffic over the AWS global backbone instead of the unpredictable public Internet,
Global Accelerator detects impaired endpoints and quietly shifts flows to the healthiest
available target. It supports both TCP and UDP traffic, providing the same steady entry
point regardless of protocol or geography.

All of this builds upon the foundation laid in previous sections: physically diverse
circuits, clean and isolated links, deterministic routing at Layer 3, and the transport-
layer tuning introduced in Section 5.4. Each layer contributes its own form of resilience,
and together they create a system that not only survives disruption but also conceals it
entirely.

With the edge components and their interactions established, Table 5-4 provides
a concise decision guide for selecting the appropriate Layer-7 entry point based on
workload characteristics, resilience objectives, and operational constraints.

Table 5-4. *Choosing the Right Layer-7 Entry Point*

Requirement / Scenario	CloudFront	Application Load Balancer (ALB)	Global Accelerator
Primary purpose	Edge caching, request shielding, global distribution	HTTP/HTTPS request routing and app-aware failover	Global traffic steering with static anycast IPs
Protocols supported (client side)	HTTP/1.1, HTTP/2, HTTP/3 (QUIC)	HTTP/1.1, HTTP/2, gRPC	TCP, UDP
TLS Termination	Yes (at edge)	Yes (at load balancer)	No (TCP termination at edge; TLS terminates at the endpoint)
Caching Capability	Yes (TTLs; stale-while-revalidate / stale-if-error)	No	No
Native WAF Integration	Yes (WAF with CloudFront)	Yes (WAF can be associated with ALB)	No
Rate Limiting	Via AWS WAF rate-based rules (commonly attached to CloudFront)	Via AWS WAF rate-based rules (regional)	No
Health-based Origin Failover	Yes, via origin failover (origin groups) (primary/secondary)	Yes, via target group health checks	Yes, via endpoint health checks + routing logic (edge steering)
Weighted Traffic Shifting	Yes, for continuous deployment (staging distributions), with quotas	Yes (weighted target groups)	Yes (endpoint weights, Region traffic dials)
Static Client IPs	No	No	Yes (Anycast IPs)
Multi-Region Entry Point	Indirect: origin failover / multi-origin patterns (not a native anycast "front door")	Regional scope (multi-Region requires an upstream mechanism)	Native multi-Region front door (edge routes to healthiest endpoint group)
Typical Best Fit	Web, APIs, static & semi-dynamic content, origin shielding	L7 routing, blue/green & canary at the application tier	Latency-sensitive, multi-Region entry, protocol-agnostic front door
Key Resilience Strength	Can mask origin errors with stale content, reduce origin load	Routes only to healthy targets; L7 routing logic	Fast global failover without DNS dependency; stable IPs

This decision guide highlights a critical Layer-7 principle: resilience is achieved not by choosing a single service, but by placing each control at the layer where it is most effective. CloudFront absorbs volatility and distance, ALB enforces application health and intent, and Global Accelerator stabilizes the entry point itself. When combined deliberately, these services transform lower-layer recovery—link failover, routing convergence, and transport continuity—into behavior users never notice. With these roles clarified, we can now step back and examine how they operate together as a coherent resilience system.

Operational Checklist: Making Layer-7 Resilience Real

Before relying on application-layer controls to mask failures beneath them, validate the following:

- **WAF rate limits and responses**

  Set rate-based rules with thresholds aligned to backend capacity, not peak traffic. Ensure blocked requests return consistent 429 responses with clear retry behavior to prevent client retry storms.

- **Cache TTLs and staleness behavior**

  Define TTLs by failure tolerance, not just freshness. Enable *stale-while-revalidate* and *stale-if-error* where acceptable so the edge can continue serving content during origin impairment.

- **Cache key discipline**

  Keep cache keys minimal and stable. Avoid volatile headers, cookies, or query parameters unless they are strictly required for correctness—otherwise cache effectiveness collapses exactly when it's most needed.

- **Health-check thresholds**

  Tune ALB health-check intervals and failure thresholds to balance fast detection with stability. Checks that are too aggressive cause flapping; checks that are too lax delay failover and prolong user impact.

- **Weighted routing and failover intent**

  Use weighted target groups deliberately. Maintain small but healthy standby pools ("pilot lights") and verify that weights converge to zero automatically when health checks fail.

Taken together, these controls ensure that Layer-7 logic does not merely *route* traffic but actively **shapes failure into a predictable, user-tolerable experience**.

In **Chapter 7**, we'll take this a step further. There, we'll explore how **BGP communities, weighted routing policies, and cross-regional traffic-engineering strategies** transform these same mechanisms into a global resilience fabric—one that doesn't just recover from failure but anticipates it.

From Layers to Boundaries

Resilience in the cloud is not a single mechanism or checklist; it is a dialogue that happens across layers—between light and logic, between hardware and software, and between what we can control and what we must design to survive.

In this chapter, we followed that dialogue through the OSI model, watching how each layer contributes to the continuity of systems we often take for granted.

We began at the **physical layer**, where everything depends on photons, fibers, and power. There, redundancy is tangible: two buildings, two carriers, and two independent conduits. It's where resilience starts, because no amount of clever routing or automation can compensate for a single severed path. From there, we rose to the **data link layer**, where structure emerges from raw transmission—link aggregation, VLAN segmentation, and per-frame integrity converting simple cabling into a stable channel for higher layers to depend on.

At **Layer 3**, we saw the shift from structure to intelligence. The Border Gateway Protocol (BGP) became the nervous system of hybrid connectivity—running at the application layer (TCP/179), yet governing the logic of the network layer. Here, physical diversity transformed into logical survivability: redundant circuits became alternate routes, and failover became policy. We also learned that simplicity—not complexity— is the foundation of routing resilience. Predictability is the most reliable form of intelligence a network can have.

Moving upward, **transport resilience** showed us that reliability isn't only about finding another path but also about preserving conversations. TCP's three-way handshake—SYN, SYN-ACK, and ACK—defines connection-oriented trust, while UDP offers connectionless speed. Newer protocols like **QUIC**, adopted by services such as CloudFront and HTTP/3, bring both together—combining UDP's agility with TCP's order and encryption—showing how transport resilience continues to evolve toward lower latency and faster recovery from loss.

Finally, at **Layer 7**, we reached the application edge, where logic meets experience.

Here, resilience became not just about continuity but about perception. Health checks, rate limiting, caching, and multi-region routing ensure that even when failures occur below, users still see continuity above. The Application Load Balancer, CloudFront, Global Accelerator, and Route 53 work in concert to transform infrastructure turbulence into a seamless user experience—the true goal of resilience.

Layer 7 completes the resilience chain by translating lower-layer recovery into user confidence, ensuring that link failover, routing convergence, and transport continuity manifest not as disruption, but as stability.

Across these layers, one principle emerged consistently: **resilience is built in depth but proven in interaction.**

Each layer can only protect the one above it if its own boundaries are clear and its behavior is predictable. When the layers align—when physical diversity supports logical policy, when routing reinforces application stability, when detection meets graceful recovery—the system becomes more than the sum of its safeguards. It becomes alive: able to sense, adapt, and heal without panic.

Lessons Learned from Chapter 5

We began this chapter by peeling back the layers of the OSI model—not as a theoretical stack, but as a living anatomy of how cloud networks survive failure.

Each layer, from the physical to the application, carries its own responsibility for continuity and its own mechanisms for repair.

Together, they form a hierarchy of defense where no single point of weakness is allowed to break the system entirely.

Every layer speaks a different language of failure and recovery: a broken fiber, a dropped Ethernet frame, a withdrawn BGP route, or a reset TCP session all describe the same event: loss of continuity.

Understanding how one layer's "failure" becomes another layer's "signal to recover" is the foundation of fault-tolerant design.

Resilience isn't about eliminating errors; it's about ensuring that when one layer stumbles, the next knows exactly how to catch it.

Physical diversity is the seed of logical resilience: you can't route around a severed cable if every link runs through the same duct.

The smartest BGP policy or load balancer means little without independent fibers, power domains, and facilities.

Every redundant path must begin with physical separation—only then can logic turn diversity into survivability.

Simplicity is the highest form of stability: networks don't collapse because they lack features; they collapse because they contain too many.

Minimal, well-understood BGP policies, clean route maps, and predictable health checks recover faster than ornate control planes filled with conditional logic.

When failure strikes at 2 a.m., clarity is your only SLA.

Convergence is the moment where design meets reality: detection, withdrawal, and reconvergence are not theoretical steps—they define how long a user waits before a page loads again.

A 500 ms failover feels invisible; a 30 s reconvergence feels like downtime.

Measure these intervals. Tune them. Make them part of your resilience vocabulary.

True resilience is systemic, not additive: adding more features doesn't make a system more reliable—aligning its layers does.

A resilient design turns one layer's degradation into another's correction.

Each tier—physical, logical, transport, and application—becomes both guardian and backup for the others.

That's the difference between redundancy and resilience: one duplicates; the other cooperates.

Looking Ahead—From Layers to Boundaries

The architecture we've built in this chapter is a vertical one—a spine of resilience running from photons to packets to policies.

But vertical strength alone cannot contain horizontal collapse.

In the real world, entire Availability Zones, regions, or service domains can fail, and when they do, the question shifts from *how quickly can we recover* to *how far will the impact spread.*

That shift marks the next evolution of resilience: **from layering to isolation**. Resilience through isolation accepts that no system is too redundant to fail—only too entangled to recover cleanly.

The answer lies in **boundaries**: deliberate divisions of control and responsibility that stop failures where they begin.

This philosophy, in cloud networking, takes form as **cell-based architectures**.

In a cell-based design, each unit—a VPC, an application stack, or even an entire regional footprint—operates as a self-contained system. It has its own routing domain, its own control plane, and its own recovery path. When one cell suffers a service impairment, the others continue without pause. This and other mechanisms are described as fault isolation.

AWS applies this principle at a massive scale: Availability Zones, service partitions, and independent fault domains are all variants of the same principle of isolation.

Customers can extend the same principle through segmented VPCs, dedicated Transit Gateways, and scoped DNS zones; they can create the same copies of their applications and replicate across cells—boundaries that ensure local problems remain local.

The objective is simple but profound: when failure occurs, it must not become contagious, meaning, if you remember Chapter 1, shared fate, we must be able to avoid failing because of some other component failing.

In **Chapter 6**, we move from the vertical logic of the OSI model to the horizontal logic of containment. We will study how network isolation, routing intent, and cell-based topologies create systems that do not merely recover but remain dependable in the face of failure.

In modern cloud design, continuity is also measured by how gracefully you stay standing when part of your applications/services falls.

CHAPTER 6

Building Network Isolation with Cell-Based Architectures, Availability Zones, and Regions

Before we dive into this topic, I would like to point out that cell-based architecture is not a good choice for every workload, because it increases architectural and operational complexity by duplicating infrastructure and components across independent units. It is most warranted for the most critical services—especially those vulnerable to correlated failures such as misconfigurations, faulty deployments, or overloads that can take down all "redundant" copies simultaneously. For many applications, a well-architected multi-AZ design already meets resilience objectives; cells become appropriate when the primary requirement is to bound blast radius so that a single software or operational failure cannot become a service-wide outage.

In the previous chapter, we explored how resilience permeates the **Open Systems Interconnection (OSI)** model—from physical links and routing at Layer 3 to load balancers and application recovery mechanisms at Layer 7. Each layer brought its own tools for survival: redundant paths, health checks, circuit breakers, and failover logic. Yet even the most disciplined, multilayered design eventually collides with a boundary it cannot defend—the **shared fate** of the system itself.

Consider a scenario familiar to many cloud operators: a routine configuration rollout introduces a malformed parameter to every instance of a service. The network remains stable; Domain Name System (DNS) records resolve correctly; the Application Load Balancer (ALB) continues routing traffic exactly as designed. Still, every target group

begins failing simultaneously. No link has broken. No zone has gone dark. The fault
lies not in the infrastructure, but in *architecture-wide coupling*—a single, synchronized
dependency that ties all instances to the same destiny.

This is the point where the OSI model reaches its limits. Below the application layer,
we can engineer redundancy. Above it, we must engineer **independence**. The next
logical step in the resilience hierarchy is not another failover mechanism but a change in
how the service itself is divided. That change leads us to **cell-based architecture**.

Before defining what a cell is, it helps to place cell-based architecture in context
alongside the resilience patterns most architects already use. The following comparison
highlights how different architectural models address failure—and, critically, what kinds
of failures they cannot contain. We will explore these architectures throughout this
chapter, but it is important to set the stage.

Table 6-1 shows why cell-based architecture is not a replacement for Availability
Zones or Regions but a response to a different class of failure—those created by shared
logic, shared control, and shared decision-making.

Table 6-1. *Evolution of Resilience Architectures and Failure Containment*

Architectural Model	Primary Purpose	Protect Against	Does not Protect Against	Blast Radius	Typical AWS Pattern
Monolithic Deployment	Simplicity	None	All failures (infra, config, code, ops)	Global	Single VPC, single AZ, single Region, single deployment, single control plane
Multi-AZ Architecture	Infrastructure availability	Instance, host, AZ failures	Correlated software, config, or control-plane errors	Region-wide	ALB + Auto Scaling across AZs, single deployment pipeline
Multi-Region Architecture	Geographic resilience	Regional outages, disasters	Global misconfigurations, shared automation, shared IAM	Global	Route 53 failover, replicated stacks, shared CI/CD
Cell-Based Architecture	Blast-radius containment	Correlated software, config, operational failures	Cell-local failures only	Bounded to one cell	Per-cell VPCs, load balancers, pipelines, data ownership

Section 6.1: What Is Cell-Based Architecture?

A *cell* is a **self-contained, independently operable instance of a service**, complete with its own compute, data, and control plane. It's not a mere scaling group or a regional deployment; it's a complete replica of the service's capabilities for a defined portion of its users or data set. Each cell functions as a miniature version of the entire platform, able to serve its users without relying on other cells.

Inside a well-architected cell, you'll find all the familiar components of a modern cloud service: application endpoints fronted by load balancers, business logic implemented through microservices, storage systems and databases tailored for that cell's data domain, and its own observability and operational pipelines. Crucially, these elements are **isolated** from their counterparts in other cells—so that configuration, failures, or overloads within one cell never propagate outward.

A useful mental model is to picture a service as a honeycomb: each hexagonal compartment has the same structural pattern, but none leaks into another. When one compartment is punctured, the honey remains inside its boundary. That containment defines the **blast radius** of failure—a measurable, predictable unit of risk that the organization consciously accepts.

A concrete example of this pattern appears in AWS guidance around shuffle sharding and zonal isolation for large-scale services. In these designs, traffic is deterministically mapped—often via DNS or edge routing—to a bounded subset of infrastructure rather than to a global pool. If one shard or slice becomes unhealthy, only the users mapped to that slice are affected, while the rest of the service continues uninterrupted. The architecture is not defined by where it runs but by what it can fail without affecting others—a principle that mirrors the cell boundary shown later in this chapter.

Unlike an **Availability Zone (AZ)**, which represents a *physical* fault domain managed by AWS, a cell defines a *logical* fault domain managed by you. An AZ prevents hardware failures from cascading across a region; a cell prevents *software or operational failures* from cascading across your service. In many ways, a cell is to the application what an AZ is to the data center: a compartment designed to fail independently.

Technically, a cell consists of two inseparable layers of autonomy:

- The **data plane**, which handles user traffic, state, and processing.

- The **control plane**, which manages configuration, deployment, scaling, and monitoring.

321

For a cell to be truly independent, both planes must live within the same boundary. If the control plane that governs all deployments is global, then a single bad release can still disable every cell simultaneously—defeating the purpose of the design.

This principle mirrors the evolution of core AWS services such as Amazon S3, Amazon DynamoDBAmazon DynamoDB, and Amazon Route 53Amazon Route 53. As these systems scaled, it became clear that multi-AZ and multi-region redundancy alone could not prevent failures caused by globally shared control actions. The architectural response was compartmentalization—breaking services into independently governed units so that configuration and deployment decisions could not propagate failures system-wide.

When engineers talk about the autonomy of a cell, they're not just describing topology—they're describing **governance**. Each cell must be operable, observable, and deployable without coordination with others. The test is simple: if you can deploy, roll back, monitor, and recover a cell in isolation, then you've achieved true cellular independence. If not, you still have hidden coupling.

In practice, this design approach transforms how we think about resilience. It moves away from a reactive stance—recovering after failure—to a proactive stance: architecting so that a single failure *cannot* grow into an outage of consequence.

In Figure 6-1, each cell contains its own load balancing, compute, data, and control planes and is deployed within one or more Availability Zones (each AZ made up of one or more data centers). Amazon Route 53 directs users to the appropriate cell's ingress endpoints, ensuring isolation and predictable blast-radius containment.

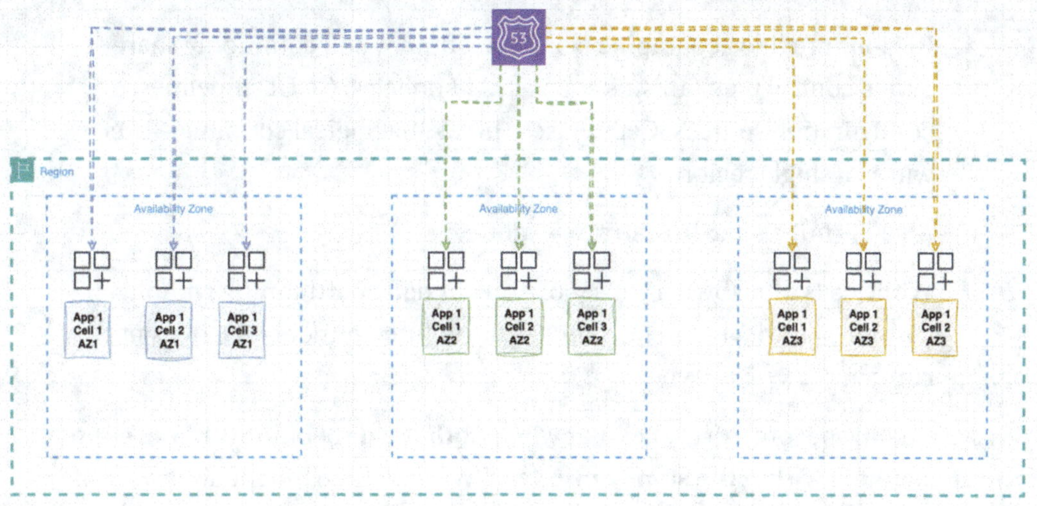

Figure 6-1. *Logical View of a Cell-Based Architecture Across Multiple AZs*

What a Cell Is Not

A cell-based architecture is often misunderstood because it borrows familiar building blocks while changing how they are composed. To avoid confusion, it's important to clarify what a cell is *not*:

- **A cell is not an Availability Zone (AZ).**

  AZs are physical fault domains managed by AWS. A cell is a *logical* fault domain managed by you. A cell may span one or multiple AZs, but its boundaries are architectural, not geographic.

- **A cell is not a cluster or auto-scaling group.**

  Scaling groups replicate capacity; cells replicate *capability*. If all instances share the same control plane, configuration, and deployment lifecycle, they still fail together.

- **A cell is not a region.**

  Regions provide geographic isolation, but they still commonly share global control mechanisms such as IAM policies, CI/CD pipelines, or configuration sources. Cells exist to break that logical coupling—even within a single region.

- **A cell is not a sharding strategy alone.**

  While cells often own a subset of users or data, partitioning without control-plane isolation only moves the failure boundary—it does not contain it.

A system only becomes truly cellular when **both the data plane and the control plane are isolated within the same boundary**. Without that, independence is an illusion.

The Problem Cells Solve

In **Chapter 1**, we defined *resilience* as the *ability of a system to sustain its intended outcome despite adverse events.* That framing was deliberately broad—because adversity in distributed systems is multidimensional. Some failures are *physical* (a power loss or fiber cut), some *logical* (a configuration or software bug), and some *emergent* (a cascade of interacting side effects). In **Chapter 2**, we began categorizing these failures by their **scope of impact**, distinguishing between *local, zonal,* and *systemic* events. The further a failure propagates from its point of origin, the more it mutates from a technical issue into a governance problem.

Cell-based architecture was born to contain precisely that escalation. It answers the question left unresolved by the network-centric view of resilience developed in **Chapter 5**: *What happens when the network is fine, but everything riding on it fails at once?*

Traditional high-availability design leans heavily on **redundancy**. Deploy across multiple **Availability Zones (AZs)**, replicate storage across regions, and add failover policies in **Amazon Route 53 (R53)**—and the system appears indestructible. Indeed, redundancy guards effectively against *infrastructure-level faults*: AZ outages, hardware degradation, and link saturation. But it does nothing against *logical simultaneity*—the class of failures where all redundant components break in exactly the same way because they share identical configuration, code, or state.

Consider three examples drawn from years of cloud operations:

- A microservice deployed simultaneously to six AZs with an automation script that contained a malformed environment variable. The rollout succeeded everywhere, and the service crashed everywhere—instant global outage.

- A schema migration executed on a globally replicated database that locked metadata across shards. The system was multi-region but logically single-pointed.

- A control-plane misconfiguration that throttled internal APIs used by auto-scaling groups. Instances remained healthy, but nothing could scale or heal.

Each of these incidents demonstrates the same pattern: *shared control equals shared failure or shared fate.*

As systems grew in complexity, this became the dominant failure mode—the kind of event that no amount of packet-level redundancy could mitigate.

Correlated Failures and the Limits of Layer 7

In **Chapter 5**, we examined how resilience manifests across the OSI model. We learned that Layers 3 and 4 deal with connectivity, and Layers 5–7 with sessions and applications. Yet every layer shares a single point of exposure: **configuration coupling**. When identical logic or parameters propagate globally, the OSI stack becomes irrelevant; each layer executes the same flawed instruction in perfect synchrony.

This is the **correlated-failure problem**, and it explains why large-scale services began to evolve from "redundant clusters" into "isolated cells."

At Amazon, this recognition emerged in the early evolution of S3 and DynamoDB. Both services were already multi-AZ and multi-region, yet still susceptible to incidents triggered by global control actions—such as simultaneous configuration pushes or back-pressure miscalculations. The solution was architectural compartmentalization: break the control plane itself into self-governing segments, each with its own change rhythm and telemetry loop.

Cells thus became the antidote to correlated failure. They replace the notion of *global uniformity*—once considered elegant—with a new axiom: *variation is safety.* If each cell can be in a slightly different version, deployment state, or failure mode, the probability of simultaneous catastrophe approaches zero.

Control-Plane Fragility

In **Chapter 4**, when discussing DNS and control of name resolution, we noted how *the system that orchestrates resilience can itself become the weakest link.* The same is true at the architectural level. A centralized deployment pipeline or shared configuration service aggregates operational risk. When that system slows, fails, or misbehaves, it paralyzes the fleet.

Cellular decomposition resolves this by making the **control plane per cell**. Each cell owns its own deployment pipeline—whether through isolated AWS CodePipeline stacks, per-cell AWS CloudFormation templates, or independent CI/CD stages. Configuration changes are versioned and applied within the cell boundary; automation has no authority beyond its domain. This makes it possible to pause global rollouts, recover one cell while observing others, or quarantine a failing environment without halting the service worldwide.

This approach reflects one of the **properties of resilient applications** described in **Chapter 2**. An application is not resilient merely because it can restart quickly; it is resilient when the act of recovery in one part does not endanger the rest. In cellular design, that independence is literal and enforced.

When Multi-region Isn't Enough

It's tempting to assume that multi-region replication already provides this protection. After all, regions are geographically isolated, each containing multiple AZs with distinct power, cooling, and connectivity. However, regions still share the same global control mechanisms: account-level Identity and Access Management (IAM) policies, cross-region deployments, shared S3 buckets, or global automation scripts. Logical coupling ignores geography.

A region-wide outage can therefore still originate from a non-geographic source—a misapplied IAM policy, an expired certificate, or an automation script run from a single developer laptop. These failures are *logical monocultures* rather than physical events. Cells are designed to break that monoculture. They decouple regions not only physically but also operationally, ensuring that even if one cell's governance fails, the others remain unaffected. Having said that, we will go into details later in this chapter in relation to when and if you need to implement multi-region deployments, so stay tuned.

From Redundancy to Independence

The transition from redundancy to independence marks the evolution of mature cloud services. Redundancy assumes that all copies behave the same and survive together. Independence assumes that copies are *allowed to differ*—in code version, configuration, or deployment timing—so that one can fail alone. The difference seems philosophical, but its operational implications are profound.

Cells institutionalize independence. Each one forms a miniature universe with its own *resilience lifecycle*: monitoring, deployment, failure, recovery, and steady state. The system as a whole no longer depends on a single global rhythm of change. It becomes asynchronous by design, absorbing shocks the way a biological organism uses compartmentalization to limit infection.

In this sense, cell-based architecture is the architectural realization of the core principle we established in **Chapter 1**—that *resilience is continuity of intent under bounded uncertainty*. The cell defines that bound, gives it shape, and turns it into something engineers can measure, reason about, and limit.

Operational Checklist: Validating a Cell-Based Design

Before labeling an architecture as cell-based, validate the following conditions. If any item fails, the design still contains hidden coupling that can amplify failure.

Data Ownership

- Each cell owns its data stores end-to-end (databases, object storage, caches).

- No synchronous reads or writes cross cell boundaries.

- Cross-cell data movement is asynchronous and replayable (replication streams, events, or logs).

Control Plane Isolation

- Deployment, configuration, and rollback operate per cell, not globally.

- A failed deployment in one cell cannot automatically propagate to others.

- Scaling decisions, alarms, and recovery actions are driven by telemetry generated inside the same cell.

Routing Boundaries

- Users or tenants are deterministically mapped to a specific cell under normal operation.

- Load balancers (ALB/NLB), target groups, and auto-scaling groups never span multiple cells.

- Global routing layers (e.g., Amazon Route 53) select *which* cell receives traffic but do not balance dynamically *between* cells in steady state.

Failure Containment

- A control-plane error, configuration mistake, or overload inside one cell affects only that cell's users.

- Removing a cell from service does not require reconfiguring other cells.

- Recovery actions (rollback, scale-out, isolation) can be executed independently per cell.

If these conditions hold, failure is no longer a system-wide event—it is a bounded incident by design. That is the defining property of a true cell-based architecture.

Core Design Principles of Cellular Architecture

Like we just discussed in the operational checklist, a system earns the title of "cell-based" only when each of its compartments behaves like a miniature, self-governing service. In practice that comes down to a handful of recurring design properties seen across large distributed systems: **autonomy, uniformity, isolation, asynchrony, and observability.** Together they define how failure is contained rather than merely survived.

Autonomy is the first and most important. Each cell must be able to operate, deploy, and recover without coordination from a global authority. Its scaling logic, alarms, and recovery workflows all exist within its borders. In AWS terms, for example, that means separate stacks, IAM roles, and CloudWatch metrics, so that one malfunctioning control process cannot paralyze the fleet. When autonomy is real, a team can roll back a faulty release in one cell while the rest continue uninterrupted.

Uniformity follows naturally. All cells share the same shape and build process—a template that can be reproduced at will. Uniformity isn't about central control; it's about predictable behavior. Identical topology and configuration mean that when an issue appears in one cell, engineers understand its environment instantly. Services such as CloudFormation StackSets or the AWS CDK make this repeatability trivial to codify. Consistency of form combined with independence of control is what allows hundreds of cells to evolve safely.

Isolation is the real boundary. Every synchronous dependency inside a cell must terminate at its edge. Anything that crosses between cells does so asynchronously— through queues, replication logs, or event buses. That simple rule prevents cascading failures. Each cell owns its data and its APIs; no transaction straddles two domains. The effect is geometric containment: an error's impact can expand only to the perimeter that allows synchronous coupling.

Asynchrony is the tolerance that makes isolation viable. Information can lag; the system can heal while messages catch up. Durable storage such as S3, SQS, or streaming logs carries state between cells without imposing real-time coupling. It feels like a concession—accepting eventual consistency—but it converts fragility into resilience. When time is decoupled, fate is decoupled.

Finally, **observability** closes the loop. Every cell must be visible to itself. Metrics, logs, and traces should reveal its health without relying on a central analytics system. A global dashboard may aggregate these signals, but it never serves as a dependency. Observability turns isolation from blindness into control: engineers can detect, reason, and repair locally, keeping recovery times small and predictable.

These principles are not slogans—they are part of the resilience concept at scale. When autonomy and uniformity provide order, isolation and asynchrony define safe boundaries, and observability ensures awareness, the result is a topology that can absorb failure without coordination or panic. A well-designed cell doesn't prevent incidents; it confines them. The larger system becomes a federation of small, predictable experiments, each bounded by design rather than by luck.

Routing and Tenant Placement

If isolation defines the boundaries of a cell, routing defines how the traffic reaches it. The routing layer is the thinnest part of the design—deliberately simple, deterministic, and stateless. Its job is not to make decisions in real time but to map each request or user to a pre-assigned cell and then get out of the way.

In a cloud environment, this usually begins at the Domain Name System (DNS) layer. **Amazon Route 53 (R53)** is often used as the first line of indirection, where weighted, geolocation, or latency-based routing policies decide which entry point a client hits. Each endpoint in turn corresponds to a single cell. Behind the scenes, these endpoints might front **Application Load Balancers (ALBs)** or **Network Load Balancers (NLBs)**, but from the user's point of view, they are simply "the service." What matters is that the routing logic stays shallow: if it becomes aware of live cell states or tries to balance dynamically across cells, it re-creates coupling at the very layer meant to prevent it.

Routing design introduces a trade-off between **determinism** and **flexibility.** Deterministic assignment—"this user always maps to cell A"—simplifies data locality and debugging, since every transaction lives and dies inside one domain. Flexible assignment—where a router can redirect users to any healthy cell—maximizes availability but risks breaking locality and cache affinity. Mature architectures often use a hybrid approach: deterministic placement under normal conditions and controlled re-routing only during failover events.

Tenant placement follows the same logic. In large multi-tenant systems, each customer or account is bound to a specific cell through metadata stored in a **cell registry**. That registry acts as a static map, not an orchestrator: it records which cell owns which tenants but does not arbitrate at runtime. Changes to it are deliberate, auditable operations, not automated reactions. The key is to treat mapping as *data*, not as *control logic.*

To prevent concentration of risk, many organizations employ a statistical strategy known as **shuffle sharding**. Each tenant or user is assigned to a small, pseudo-random subset of cells. If one cell fails, only that tenant's slice of users is affected, while the rest remain untouched. Mathematically, the probability of two tenants sharing the same failure domain drops exponentially as the number of cells increases. Shuffle sharding turns isolation from a static design into a probabilistic shield.

Data locality completes the loop. Routing and placement mean little if the data they reference sits elsewhere. Each cell must own the storage that corresponds to its tenants—its own **Amazon DynamoDB** tables, **S3** buckets, or **Amazon Relational Database Service (RDS)** instances. Cross-cell reads are performed asynchronously through replication or event streaming. In practice, this localizes both data gravity and operational ownership: when a cell is dark, its data is already quarantined with it.

At scale, routing and placement logic are the only globally shared components of a cellular system. Their simplicity is therefore sacred. They should be infrastructure, not intelligence. When routing becomes clever, it becomes dangerous.

Routing in Practice

Conceptually, routing maps users to cells; physically, it maps *packets* to *endpoints.*

In an AWS environment, that means orchestrating three routing tiers: **DNS-level routing, edge or global entry points**, and **in-cell load balancing.**

At the outermost layer sits **Amazon Route 53 (R53)**. It's the public interface of the system—the brain that decides *which* cell a user should reach.

Each cell exposes one or more public endpoints, typically the DNS names of **Application Load Balancers (ALBs)** or **Network Load Balancers (NLBs)** deployed inside that cell.

R53's policies—weighted, latency-based, or health-checked—point to those endpoints.

When a cell becomes unhealthy, R53 simply stops returning its record.

This decision is stateless and declarative: DNS doesn't query internal state; it trusts health checks, and that simplicity keeps it reliable under pressure.

Inside the AWS network boundary, traffic handed to the correct endpoint arrives at the **in-cell load balancer.**

Each cell owns its own ALB or NLB, deployed in *that cell's VPC subnets*, usually spanning multiple AZs for zonal resilience within the cell.

Because every cell has its own load balancer, there is no shared transport layer that can mix sessions or leak faults across boundaries.

Each ALB fans traffic only to its own target groups—the application servers, containers, or functions belonging exclusively to that cell.

To visualize this, imagine a service spanning three Availability Zones—**us-east-1a, 1b**, and **1c.**

You choose to create one cell per AZ for maximum blast-radius reduction.

Each cell hosts its own VPC segments, compute fleet, and an internal ALB.

At the DNS layer, Route 53 presents three aliases: *cell-a.example.com, cell-b.example.com*, and *cell-c.example.com.*

Users mapped to cell A always resolves to its ALB endpoints in 1a; users mapped to cell B hit 1b, and so on.

If cell B's health checks fail, Route 53 withdraws its record, effectively isolating the impairment without any need for cross-cell coordination.

When an application prefers a single global hostname—*service.example.com*—Route 53 still acts as the multiplexer beneath that name.

It can direct a user to their assigned cell by returning the corresponding ALB alias based on tenant metadata, geography, or shuffle-shard token.

The key is that **the load balancer never spans cells.**

It lives *inside* them, terminating connections only for the workloads it fronts.

Route 53 sits *above* them, mediating access without becoming a shared control plane.

This two-tier arrangement—global DNS routing plus per-cell load balancing—is what makes cellular designs workable in AWS.

DNS defines *which* cell, and the load balancer defines *how* requests enter it.

Both layers are redundant, both are independently health-checked, and neither introduces cross-cell dependency.

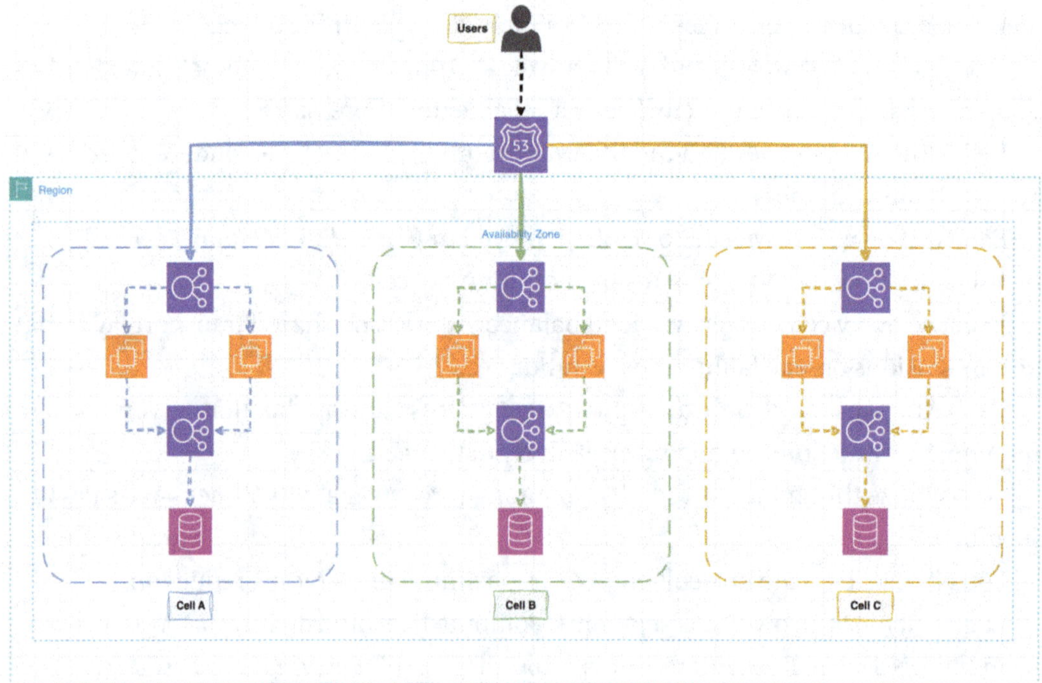

Figure 6-2. Practical Routing Topology for Cellular Services

Building on Figure 6-1, which introduced the logical structure of a service cell. In Figure 6-2, we zoom in to show how routing operates in practice. Amazon Route 53 performs DNS-level routing, directing users to the appropriate cell's Load Balancer (e.g., ALB or NLB) within its Availability Zone. Each cell owns its own compute tier and data store, ensuring that no load balancer or control path crosses cell boundaries. Isolation is maintained end-to-end—from DNS resolution through the target group and down to the data plane.

In a **multi-region deployment**, this topology simply extends one level higher. Each region hosts its own set of isolated cells—each with its own Route 53 health checks, load balancers, and back-end data stores—and a global Route 53 layer or latency-based routing policy determines which region's cell a user should reach. From the client's perspective, there is still a single global entry point (e.g., service.example.com), but behind the scenes, Route 53 resolves that request to the most appropriate region based on geography, latency, or explicit routing rules. Within the chosen region, the request then follows the same pattern shown in this figure: it lands on the region's designated cell load balancer and flows to local compute and storage resources.

This preserves the same principle of *cellular independence*, only now extended across continents—each region functions as a self-contained universe of cells, capable of serving, recovering, and evolving without affecting others.

Control-Plane Design Inside Cells

If the data plane is what a service *does*, the control plane is what tells it *how* to do it. It's the nervous system of the architecture—the part that decides when to scale, where to deploy, and what "healthy" looks like. In most systems, this plane is shared across all environments because that feels efficient: one deployment pipeline, one configuration service, and one monitoring setup. But convenience is often the first crack in resilience. When that shared control layer misbehaves, it doesn't just degrade performance; it can paralyze the entire service.

A cell-based design breaks this dependence by giving every cell its own command center. Each cell owns the authority to deploy, scale, and observe itself. That doesn't mean running a dozen different CI/CD systems—it means structuring automation so that it can stop safely at cell boundaries. A rollout that fails in Cell A should not even be visible to Cell B, let alone contagious. In practice this looks like independent **AWS**

CodePipeline stages, separate **AWS CloudFormation** stacks, and cell-specific health alarms and dashboards. If one cell needs to pause, roll back, or rebuild, it can do so in isolation while the rest of the service keeps running.

This way of operating turns deployment from an event into a rhythm. Updates move through the system one cell at a time—start with a pilot, watch its metrics, then continue. You gain feedback before you gain exposure. It's a principle that echoes what we discussed back in **Chapter 4** when exploring **DNS routing policies**: Route 53 evaluates health and makes discrete, independent routing choices, never allowing a single unhealthy endpoint to contaminate the entire namespace. The control plane follows the same philosophy. It treats each cell as a self-contained destination and avoids global decisions that could propagate mistakes system-wide.

Independence also extends to permissions and secrets. Every cell carries its own **Identity and Access Management (IAM)** roles, encryption keys, and runtime parameters. This isn't only about security; it's about reducing blast radius. A misconfigured policy or leaked credential in one cell has nowhere to spread. Even failure becomes a local affair.

Scaling logic must follow the same rule. Auto Scaling Groups and lifecycle hooks operate from telemetry generated inside their own cell—never from global averages. When load surges in one geography, that cell reacts on its own terms without starving resources elsewhere. Aggregation still happens at the organizational level, but aggregation is for *observation*, not *control*.

For rare moments when coordination really is needed—say, shifting traffic away from a degraded region or verifying readiness during a disaster exercise—**Amazon Route 53 Application Recovery Controller (ARC)** steps in. ARC provides the connective tissue that allows cells to collaborate without hierarchy. Its *routing controls* and *readiness checks* act as circuit breakers between cells, offering a safe way to redirect traffic or quarantine an impaired area. During a failover, ARC doesn't improvise; it executes a known choreography. It disables routing to failing cells, enables healthy ones, and logs every change for audit and rollback.

ARC's **Zonal Shift** feature adds even finer control, temporarily draining traffic from a single Availability Zone when health checks falter. Combined with the cellular model, these tools let operators act surgically instead of globally—rerouting a trickle of traffic rather than flipping the entire system upside down.

When you reach this level of maturity, the control plane stops being a single, fragile brain and becomes a federation of steady hands. Each cell can change at its own pace, recover in its own way, and still play in tune with the rest. In a sense, operations turn from orchestration to choreography—independent dancers following the same rhythm rather than a conductor waving a single baton.

That's the promise of cell-based control: to make resilience not just a property of infrastructure but a property of *decision-making itself*.

Interaction with AWS Fault Domains

So far, we've treated cells as logical constructs—independent worlds of compute, data, and control. But every logical boundary still sits on something physical. In AWS, those physical boundaries are called **fault domains**: the **Availability Zones (AZs)** and **Regions** that make up the global infrastructure. How your cells align with—or deliberately diverge from—these domains determines the true shape of resilience in your system.

An **Availability Zone** is AWS's fundamental unit of physical isolation. Each region is composed of multiple AZs, and each AZ contains *one or more separate data centers*, each with its own power, cooling, and connectivity. These data centers are spaced far enough apart to prevent local disasters from cascading, yet close enough—typically within tens of kilometers—to allow synchronous replication and single-digit-millisecond latency.

Most architectures already spread resources across AZs: load balancers route traffic evenly, databases replicate synchronously, and Auto Scaling groups distribute instances. This multi-AZ approach protects against hardware or facility failures. What it doesn't protect against are *logical failures*—a misconfigured deployment, a shared credential, or an automation bug that strikes every instance simultaneously. That's where cell-based architecture steps in.

In a **cell-per-AZ** model, each Availability Zone hosts a complete, self-contained instance of the service. The AZ becomes both the physical and logical boundary. A failure inside one data center, or even across the whole AZ, affects only that cell's users. This delivers near-perfect containment at the cost of duplication—each cell must own its own data tier, monitoring, and control pipelines—but it's the cleanest form of isolation.

A more common pattern is the **multi-AZ cell**, where each cell spans two or three AZs within a region. Internally, the cell uses cross-AZ replication for durability, but it remains logically fenced off from its peers. If one AZ goes dark, the cell continues serving traffic from the surviving zones. This strikes a balance: physical redundancy within the cell and logical isolation between cells.

Choosing between one-AZ and multi-AZ cells is an architectural trade-off. The former maximizes isolation and simplicity of fault boundaries; the latter increases availability and cost-efficiency. There's no universal right answer—each design reflects how much downtime, complexity, and expense you're willing to tolerate.

At a higher level, **regions** introduce geographical and regulatory separation. Each region consists of multiple AZs and acts as a self-contained fault domain. Cells can exist entirely within a region or be distributed across them: a European region might host an "EU cell," while a North American region runs a "US cell." This satisfies both latency and compliance goals while maintaining the same architectural blueprint.

Routing across regions typically relies on **Amazon Route 53 (R53)** using latency-based or geolocation routing policies—the same mechanisms we explored in **Chapter 4** when discussing DNS routing strategies. Back then, we used DNS to direct users to the closest infrastructure; here we use it to direct them to their *assigned fault domain*. In doing so, DNS becomes not just a network convenience but a resilience boundary.

When logical cells align cleanly with physical domains, resilience gains depth. A power outage or fiber cut stays confined to a data center. A software or configuration error stays confined to a cell. And even if an entire region suffers an outage, other regions—and their cells—remain untouched. It's layered defense in the truest sense: geography below, architecture above, each reinforcing the other.

Operational Advantages and Engineering Economics

When engineers first encounter cell-based architecture, the reaction is often a mix of admiration and apprehension. It feels elegant, but it also feels heavy. And that's fair—it's a pattern designed for systems that simply cannot afford surprise. Building in cells takes more planning, more pipelines, and more operational rigor. Yet the trade is rarely regretted: once you've contained failure, it's hard to go back.

Operationally, the first benefit is **containment**. A misconfiguration, a faulty release, or a local overload remains confined to its own cell. Incidents become smaller, quieter, and easier to reason about. Recovery happens within minutes, not hours, because you're fixing one environment, not a global platform. The mean time to repair drops because the scope of repair shrinks.

The second is **confidence in change**. In a monolithic deployment, each release is a gamble; in a cellular deployment, it's a controlled experiment. You push to one cell, observe, and expand gradually. This rhythm turns fear of change into confidence through observation. Engineers stop hesitating to improve things because the worst-case outcome has been engineered down to something survivable.

Then comes **clarity of ownership**. Each team knows its boundaries, its data, and its responsibilities. The cultural benefits mirror those of microservices—autonomy with accountability, standardization without bureaucracy. Each team can move fast without putting the entire service at risk.

Of course, this model is **not mandatory**. Just as multi-region design is reserved for workloads that justify its cost and complexity, cell-based architecture is an *option*, not an obligation. Many applications achieve their resilience goals with simpler patterns: multi-AZ deployments, asynchronous backups, or blue-green pipelines. But for **mission-critical systems**—where downtime translates directly into revenue loss or safety risk—the calculus changes dramatically.

International Data Corporation (IDC) estimates that downtime for Fortune 1000 companies costs between **$500,000 and $1 million per hour** for mission-critical applications.[1] At that scale, even a single large-scope outage can outweigh years of additional infrastructure expense.

Source: IDC, *DevOps and the Cost of Downtime: Fortune 1000 Best Practice Metrics Quantified*, 2014. `https://kapost-files-prod.s3.amazonaws.com/published/54ef73 ef2592468e25000438/idc-devops-and-the-cost-of-downtime-fortune-1000-best-practice-metrics-quantified.pdf`

The economics reflect that same pragmatism. Yes, running multiple cells increases duplication—extra pipelines, data stores, and monitoring dashboards—but it flattens risk. Instead of rare, global crises that paralyze the business, you get routine, local incidents that teams can handle quietly. It replaces catastrophic volatility with predictable, bounded cost. In resilience terms, that's a winning exchange.

It also enables **progressive scaling**. Because cells can scale independently, capacity can follow demand instead of being centralized and over-provisioned. Regional traffic spikes, seasonal patterns, or tenant-specific workloads can be served locally without inflating global infrastructure bills. Over time, what once looked like "duplication" often proves to be optimization—capacity aligned precisely to need.

And perhaps the most underappreciated benefit is human. Cellular design changes the psychology of operations. Engineers sleep better knowing that one bad deployment won't make headlines. Experimentation becomes safe again. In the long run, that sense of control and predictability is worth as much as the technical resilience itself.

In short, the cell model is a tool, not a rule. It's a high-end option in the architect's toolkit—complex, yes, but powerful when the stakes justify it.

In the next section, we'll learn how to design fault domains that achieve exactly that—structures small enough to isolate damage, yet large enough to deliver meaningful value to users.

Section 6.2: Designing for Fault Domains and Blast Radius Reduction

In the previous section, we explored how *cell-based architecture* turns resilience from an abstract goal into a structural property. Each cell operated as a self-contained world—with its own compute, data, and control planes—while **Amazon Route 53 (R53)** handled routing and health-based isolation from above. That gave us a blueprint for *logical containment*.

Now we step back to ask a deeper question: *how do these logical fault domains interact with the physical ones*—the **Availability Zones (AZs)** and **Regions** that form the backbone of AWS? We touched on these constructs earlier in **Chapter 3**, when discussing cloud topologies and the global AWS network, and in **Chapter 5**, where we linked network-layer resilience to fault isolation at the OSI level. Here, we connect those ideas: the relationship between physical boundaries managed by AWS and logical ones defined by you.

Designing fault domains is about shaping the geometry of failure. AZs and regions already provide physical separation; cells let you define *logical separation* that overlays it. The art lies in choosing how large each boundary should be—how many users, tenants, or transactions live inside one fault domain—and ensuring that a single disturbance can't become a systemic event.

This section sets the foundation. Later in **Chapter 6**, we'll expand these concepts into detailed design patterns for **multi-AZ** and **multi-region** architectures, exploring how they interact with network routing, replication, and control-plane orchestration. But first, we need to understand what a fault domain truly represents and how to reason about its size, shape, and impact.

At a practical level, the goal is twofold:

- **Control the scope of impact**—how far a fault can propagate (its *blast radius*).

- **Optimize speed of correction**—how quickly the affected domain can recover on its own.

When those two dimensions are deliberate, resilience stops being reactive and becomes a measurable property of design.

The takeaway is that fault-domain size should be chosen by working backward from impact tolerance, not infrastructure convenience. A domain must be small enough that its complete loss remains within your service's error budget, yet large enough to be operated and recovered reliably. AWS describes cell-based (bulkhead) architectures as a way to reduce the scope of correlated failures—misconfigurations, faulty deployments, or overloads that defeat redundancy. In practice, cells are warranted when the primary resilience risk is shared fate rather than hardware loss, and when bounding blast radius matters more than minimizing infrastructure duplication. For workloads whose failure modes are dominated by physical faults, a well-architected multi-AZ design is often sufficient; cells become appropriate when logical failures must be contained by design.

Table 6-2 compares the three common cell-granularity choices—one-AZ, multi-AZ, and multi-region—highlighting how each shapes blast radius, recovery behavior, and operational trade-offs in practice.

Table 6-2. *Cell Granularity and Fault-Domain Trade-Offs*

Cell Granularity	Fault Domain Boundary	Typical Blast Radius	Failure Types Contained	Recovery Characteristics	Cost & Operational Overhead
One-AZ Cell	Single Availability Zone	Smallest	Software bugs, misconfigurations, zonal infrastructure failures	Fast local recovery; continuity requires routing to another cell	High duplication; highest operational complexity
Multi-AZ Cell	Multiple AZs within one Region	Medium	Zonal infrastructure failures; limited physical outages	Automatic zonal failover; degraded but continuous service	Moderate cost; standard production pattern
Multi-Region Cell	Entire Region	Largest logical unit; smallest geographic risk	Regional outages, regulatory isolation, large-scale control-plane events	Slower failover; dependent on routing and replication lag	Highest cost; heavy operational and data-management burden

These boundaries are not theoretical—they define how much failure the system can absorb before users notice, which is why fault-domain size must be reasoned about explicitly rather than inherited by default.

Reasoning About Fault Domains and Blast Radius

A **fault domain** is the largest collection of resources that can fail together by design. Physically, that could be a single AZ—a cluster of one or more data centers with independent power, cooling, and connectivity. Logically, it could be a cell, a tenant, or a shard of your application. The purpose of defining it isn't to eliminate failure; it's to make failure predictable, bounded, and recoverable.

Start by anchoring your design around the **unit of value**—what your users actually experience as "the service." For a streaming platform, it might be a catalog region; for a financial system, it might be an account domain; for SaaS, it's often a tenant. The right fault-domain size is the one where an outage remains visible but acceptable within your **Service Level Objectives (SLOs)** and **error budget**.

A simple sanity check links **blast radius** to **SLO math**. Suppose your system targets 99.9% monthly availability (roughly 43 minutes of total allowable downtime). If one cell serves 20% of traffic and goes dark for 20 minutes, the effective global impact is 0.2 × 20 = 4 minutes—tolerable. If that same cell served 60% of traffic, it would consume 12 minutes, almost one-third of the monthly budget. The fault hasn't changed; the geometry has.

The same reasoning applies at a regional scale. Suppose a global service is deployed across three regions, each serving roughly one-third of traffic, and targets the same 99.9% monthly availability. If one region becomes unreachable for 30 minutes, the effective global impact is one-third of that outage—about 10 minutes consumed from the error budget. If, instead, that region carried 70% of user traffic, the same incident would burn over 20 minutes, pushing the service close to an SLO breach. Once again, the failure mode is identical; only the distribution of responsibility has changed.

Latency and data locality complicate the picture. A **one-cell-per-AZ** design maximizes isolation but can fragment low-latency datasets or create cross-cell chatter if not engineered carefully. A **multi-AZ cell** sacrifices some isolation for intra-cell redundancy, reducing exposure to hardware or network events but expanding the logical blast radius. The right balance depends on the workload's sensitivity: identity and payments favor smaller cells; read-heavy catalogs or streaming services tolerate broader ones.

Compliance and sovereignty rules can also draw fault-domain boundaries for you. If EU data must remain in-region, your "EU cell set" already exists by regulation and should carry its own IAM boundaries, encryption keys, and change cadence. Design doesn't fight these constraints—it formalizes them.

Finally, make **observability** the first criterion, not the last. A fault domain you can't see is one you can't contain. Local dashboards, alarms, and traces—such as per-cell **Amazon CloudWatch** metrics and **AWS X-Ray** segments—turn theoretical boundaries into provable isolation. When an incident occurs, you'll know exactly *where* it lives and *why* it stops there.

At this point, it's worth calling out a few recurring design errors that quietly undermine fault-domain intent:

- **Hidden Shared Control Planes**: single CI/CD pipelines, global configuration stores, or centralized IAM roles that can change or fail across all domains simultaneously

- **Globally Scoped Configuration Changes**: parameters or feature flags applied synchronously across cells, reintroducing correlated failure during rollout

- **Synchronous Cross-cell Dependencies**: direct calls between cells that bypass routing and health boundaries, allowing latency or failure to propagate instead of being contained

Each of these patterns reintroduces shared fate—turning logical isolation into an illusion. Fault-domain design only works when independence is enforced not just in topology, but also in change, control, and communication; these trade-offs become clearer when visualized across different cell placements.

Lastly, before comparing fault-domain layouts, it helps to validate whether a proposed boundary will actually hold under real operating conditions. A fault domain is only as strong as the invariants enforced around it in routing, control, and visibility:

- **Routing Isolation:** Traffic must enter and terminate within the intended domain; load balancers, target groups, and network paths should not span multiple cells by default.

- **Control-plane Independence:** Deployments, configuration changes, and scaling actions must be executable per domain, without a single global pipeline or parameter store pushing change everywhere at once.

- **Observability Scoping:** Metrics, logs, and traces should carry an explicit fault-domain identifier (cell, AZ slice, or region slice), so operators can verify where an incident is contained and measure its blast radius.

If any of these invariants are violated, the architecture may appear compartmentalized on diagrams, but it will behave as a shared-fate system under stress.

Figure 6-3 contrasts two common cell-placement strategies within a single AWS Region.

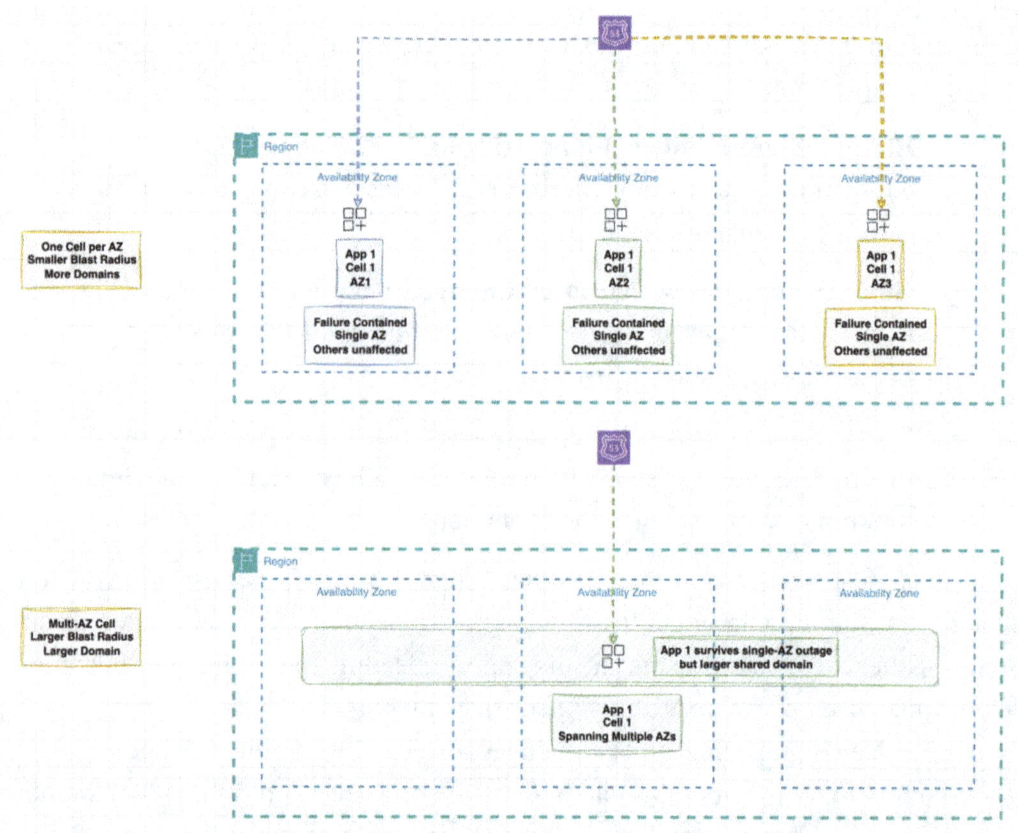

Figure 6-3. *Fault Domain Hierarchy and Blast-Radius Trade-Offs*

The upper design shows one cell per Availability Zone, maximizing blast-radius containment.

The lower design shows a single multi-AZ cell, trading tighter isolation for higher zonal durability through synchronous replication.

Choosing Cell Granularity (One-AZ vs. Multi-AZ vs. Multi-region Cells)

With fault domains defined, measured, and validated, the remaining decision is no longer theoretical—it is architectural: how large should each cell be in practice?

Cell granularity determines how much failure you are willing to absorb locally versus how much complexity you are prepared to operate globally. Too fine-grained, and operational overhead grows faster than resilience gains; too coarse, and a single incident consumes disproportionate error budget and attention.

In the previous section, we saw how **blast radius** connects to service level objectives (SLOs). Now we'll translate that theory into topology. The cell boundary can align with an **Availability Zone (AZ)**, span **multiple AZs** within a region, or even extend across **regions** for global workloads. Each step upward changes what kind of failure you're protecting against, how much latency and cost you can tolerate, and how far you're willing to replicate.

One-AZ Cells: Maximum Isolation, Minimum Safety Net

A **one-AZ cell** is the most isolated expression of the pattern.

Each cell is confined to a single Availability Zone, inheriting the AZ's physical isolation as its outer failure boundary.

The upside is purity: a complete failure of that AZ or a logical misconfiguration inside it cannot spill elsewhere.

This is the model used by high-risk control planes and by internal Amazon teams during early decomposition of services such as **Amazon Route 53** and **Amazon DynamoDB**, where correlated change posed greater danger than infrastructure loss.

The trade-off is availability. Because all compute and data for that cell live in one AZ, the cell itself is subject to the AZ's uptime characteristics.

If your system targets four or five nines of regional availability, you'll need at least two independent cells so users can fail over between them.

This pattern excels when you value containment above raw uptime—for example, in financial or safety-critical systems where it's better to fail small than to fail large.

Of course, a single-AZ cell by itself is *not* resilient in the availability sense—it's resilient in the *containment* sense. The point isn't that one-AZ cells survive a zonal outage; it's that their failures don't cascade. True service-level resilience comes from deploying *multiple* one-AZ cells, each in its own Availability Zone or even region, and using **Amazon Route 53** or **Application Recovery Controller (ARC)** to steer users between them. In that model, the loss of one AZ equals the loss of one cell, not the entire service. The cell design makes that trade explicit: you isolate to protect the rest, and you replicate to restore continuity.

Multi-AZ Cells: Balancing Independence and Durability

Most production workloads adopt **multi-Availability Zone (multi-AZ)** cells as the pragmatic midpoint.

Here, each cell spans two or more Availability Zones within the same AWS Region.

A multi-AZ cell leverages that infrastructure diversity to achieve zonal fault tolerance: it runs redundant compute, storage, and load-balancing capacity in more than one AZ so that the loss of any single zone doesn't take the service offline.

If **AZ 2** fails, the cell continues to operate using resources in **AZ 1**, because the cell's load balancer—regional by design—routes traffic only to healthy targets.

The cell may degrade in throughput or latency, but it remains *available*.

This distinction is subtle but essential: a **multi-AZ cell** isn't spreading risk; it's *absorbing* risk within a bounded domain.

The cell still remains logically isolated from its peers—it has its own routing layer, data stores, and deployment pipeline—but internally it synchronizes data across zones.

This shields the cell from physical outages while still confining software or configuration faults to that cell's perimeter.

Several AWS services embody this pattern:

- **Amazon RDS Multi-AZ** is a *regional* deployment that maintains synchronous database replicas across at least two AZs within a region, automatically failing over if the primary zone fails.

- **AWS Elastic Kubernetes Service (EKS)** clusters are *regional*; worker nodes are distributed across AZs so that if one zone disappears, pods reschedule automatically in another.

- **Elastic Load Balancing (ALB/NLB)** is also *regional*, with nodes placed in multiple AZs to distribute incoming traffic and mask a zonal loss.

From an application's point of view, the multi-AZ cell behaves as one coherent entity: traffic enters through a per-cell load balancer, fans out across AZs, and continues even if one zone falters.

This is the topology shown conceptually in Figure 6-1, only now a single cell encloses multiple AZs instead of mapping one-to-one.

However, many architects—especially those building mission-critical control planes—choose a stricter pattern: instead of a single cell stretched across AZs, they deploy **replicated one-AZ cells**, each confined to one zone but cloned across several.

In that model, **AZ 1** hosts *Cell A, B, C*; **AZ 2** hosts *Cell A, B, C*; and **AZ 3** hosts *Cell A, B, C* again.

Each cell is entirely self-contained, and inter-cell routing—handled by **Amazon Route 53** or **AWS Global Accelerator**—directs users to a healthy copy in another zone if one fails.

The benefit is perfect blast-radius containment and clear failure semantics: if *Cell A in AZ 2* is lost, the other copies of *Cell A* in AZ 1 and AZ 3 remain unaffected.

The trade-off is operational overhead: stateful data must be replicated between cells, automation must scale horizontally, and costs rise because every AZ carries a full replica of each cell.

AWS internal services such as **Route 53**, **S3**, and **DynamoDB** eventually evolved toward this approach—many one-AZ cells per region—once automation and scale made it practical.

The **design choice** therefore depends on what kind of failure you're trying to survive.

A **multi-AZ cell** offers *durability* by absorbing a zonal fault inside a single domain; a **replicated one-AZ cell** offers *isolation* by routing around a fault entirely.

One keeps running inside the box; the other avoids the box altogether.

Both patterns can coexist: multi-AZ cells often serve as the foundation for early-stage resilience, while replicated one-AZ cells define the architecture of hyperscale, mission-critical systems.

In the next subsection, we extend this concept beyond a single region to understand how these cellular boundaries interact at a planetary scale.

At this stage, most architectures fail not because they chose the wrong granularity, but because they unknowingly reintroduce shared fate across otherwise well-defined boundaries.

Common Design Mistakes That Collapse Fault-Domain Isolation

Even when cells and fault domains are clearly defined on paper, a few recurring design mistakes can silently undo their isolation. These issues often remain invisible during normal operation and only surface during large-scale incidents—when it is already too late.

- **Hidden shared control planes**

  Centralized deployment pipelines, configuration services, or feature-flag systems can reintroduce global coupling. A single faulty rollout or configuration push can still disable every cell simultaneously, despite clean data-plane separation.

- **Global configuration or credentials**

  Account-wide IAM policies, shared secrets, or globally scoped parameters create monocultures. When a permission change, certificate expiry, or secret rotation fails, it propagates instantly across all fault domains.

- **Synchronous cross-cell dependencies**

  Direct API calls or synchronous database queries between cells defeat isolation. When one cell slows or fails, backpressure spreads transitively, turning a local issue into a cascading outage.

- **Smart routing layers**

  Routing systems that attempt to make real-time decisions based on live cell health often become a hidden control plane. Declarative routing (DNS, static endpoint mapping) is resilient; dynamic orchestration under stress is not.

Isolation only holds when boundaries are enforced, not just in topology but also in **change authority, dependency direction, and time**.

Multi-region Cells: Continuity at Planetary Scale

At some point, availability within a single region stops being the constraint.

You can survive zonal failures—even regional-scale hardware events—but what happens when an entire region becomes unreachable because of a control-plane bug, a fiber cut, or a compliance lockdown?

That's where **multi-region cells** come in. Each region hosts a complete, autonomous replica of the service—built to continue serving users even if every other region disappears from the map.

Conceptually, this is the same idea introduced in Figure 6-1: cells nested within Availability Zones inside regions.

Now, the entire region becomes the cell's outer boundary. Each region functions as an autonomous fault domain, with no live operational coupling to its peers.

From a user's perspective there is still a single global entry point (e.g., *service. example.com*), but under the hood **Amazon Route 53** or **AWS Global Accelerator** evaluates latency, geography, and health to decide which region's cell should handle the request.

Inside each region, traffic then follows the same intra-region routing patterns described earlier. Route 53 resolves to that region's per-cell load balancer, which directs flows into local compute and storage.

If a region fails its health checks or is withdrawn for maintenance, the global routing layer stops returning its records, automatically shifting traffic to healthy regions.

No inter-region coordination is required—the logic is declarative, driven by DNS and health policy rather than shared state.

Data replication across regions remains intentionally asynchronous to preserve isolation.

AWS mechanisms such as *S3 Cross-Region Replication*, *DynamoDB Global Tables*, *Aurora Global Database*, and *Database Migration Service* propagate data eventually, not instantly.

That delay is a deliberate safety buffer—it prevents faults or corruption in one region from spreading globally.

Where latency or financial precision makes even that lag unacceptable, architects often layer **application-level reconciliation** or append-only replication to maintain consistency.

Operationally, this model is heavy. Each region therefore becomes an autonomous disaster-recovery boundary and must host its own observability stack—CloudWatch metrics, alarms, and tracing—because cross-region telemetry may be delayed or unreachable during the very events it is meant to diagnose.

Yet the payoff is profound: even a complete regional outage becomes just another routing event rather than a catastrophe.

In regulated industries, multi-region cells help meet **data sovereignty and compliance** goals.

European customers can be served entirely from Frankfurt and Dublin, while U.S. users stay within Northern Virginia and Oregon.

Each region's cell set remains autonomous, satisfying residency requirements while maintaining global continuity through intelligent routing.

Ultimately, multi-region cells are the top tier of cloud resilience: they transform "disaster recovery" into **continuous availability**.

This is the same philosophy underpinning AWS global services such as Route 53, CloudFront, and IAM—constellations of independent regional cells stitched together by deterministic routing.

The pattern scales indefinitely, but so does its complexity; few workloads require it, and fewer still operate it correctly without strong automation.

Designing at this level means treating geography as just another fault domain.

You're not asking whether a region can fail—you're assuming it will and proving your architecture survives it.

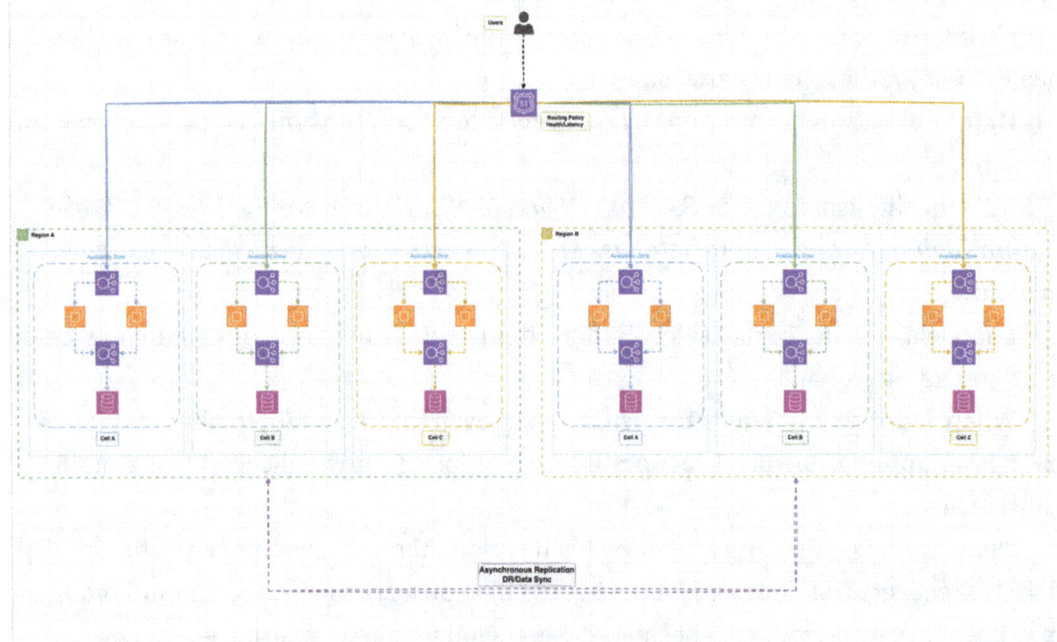

Figure 6-4. *Multi-region Cellular Architecture*

In Figure 6-4, each AWS Region hosts an autonomous set of cells—each with its own load balancers, compute, data, and control planes. Amazon Route 53 (or AWS Global Accelerator) serves as the global routing layer, directing users to the healthiest region based on latency or health checks. Inter-region replication remains asynchronous to contain faults and maintain independence. A regional impairment triggers controlled rerouting at the global layer without cross-impact on the other region.

No matter which topology you choose—one-AZ, multi-AZ, or multi-region—the principle is the same: every boundary is a deliberate trade between isolation, availability, and operability.

A narrow boundary reduces blast radius but multiplies moving parts; a broad one simplifies management but risks correlated failure.

The art lies in drawing the line so that the loss of any single cell stays within your error budget, while your team can still manage the total number of cells you deploy.

Isolation without manageability is fragility in disguise.

In practice, one-AZ cells deliver the strongest containment for high-risk or control-plane systems.

Multi-AZ cells strike the pragmatic balance and remain the default for most AWS workloads.

Multi-region cells are reserved for the rarest tier—those where downtime is existential or compliance demands geographic separation.

Each pattern is a different zoom level of the same idea: repeatable, self-contained units of service whose boundaries mirror both physics and business needs.

Also consider, if the failure of a single cell can impact more users or consume more error budget than you are prepared to spend on one incident, the cell is too large. Fault domains are not chosen to prevent failure, but to ensure that when failure occurs, its consequences remain intentional, explainable, and survivable.

In the next section, we'll move from designing these boundaries to **proving** them—testing, measuring, and enforcing blast-radius containment so that architectural intent becomes operational reality.

Designing Blast-Radius Containment Strategies

We've drawn the lines: cells, Availability Zones (AZs), and regions. But lines on a diagram are aspirations. Containment becomes real only when the running system behaves as if those lines were made of steel—change stops where it should; traffic stays where it belongs; failures refuse to spread. In networking terms, blast-radius control is the operational equivalent of a route filter: what's not explicitly permitted to cross a boundary must be silently dropped by design.

AWS provides the physical perimeter. Each AZ consists of one or more discrete data centers with independent power, cooling, and networking, while regions are composed of multiple AZs connected through the AWS global backbone. Inside that substrate, we create the logical perimeter: the **cell**. From that point forward, resilience is no longer a topology—it's a practice. It's the way we route, deploy, and observe so that local turbulence never becomes global weather.

Containment begins at the network layer. Each cell must terminate its own traffic and its own control signals. Connections should land on that cell's load balancer—**Application Load Balancer (ALB)** or **Network Load Balancer (NLB)**—and fan inward to targets that exist only within that cell's VPC subnets. Cross-cell traffic, when absolutely required, should traverse explicit, named attachments—**AWS Transit Gateway (TGW)** routes you can inspect and audit—rather than implicit defaults or shared subnets. Think of cells as neighboring autonomous systems: they may peer, but they never merge their routing tables. That separation prevents transport-layer instability or feedback loops in one domain from rippling into another.

Change is where most outages are born, so change is where containment must be most visible. A cell that can only be updated by a central pipeline is not a cell—it's a shard with a shared fate. The safer pattern is quieter and slower on purpose: one cell at a time. Deploy to a single domain, observe its health through that domain's telemetry, and only then promote. The build artifact may be identical everywhere—immutability buys you consistency—but the decision to introduce it is local. In practice, this becomes a **cell-level canary deployment**: a controlled rollout that treats each fault domain as an independent experiment. One cell absorbs the risk first; if it passes, others follow. If it fails, the blast radius is exactly the size of that one domain. This is how large AWS services operate in practice—autonomy in rollout, independence in rollback, and patience in promotion.

Control planes deserve the same insulation. Monitoring, configuration, and operational tooling should be scoped so that the loss—or misuse—of one set of credentials, one parameter namespace, or one dashboard affects only the intended cell. Global systems exist to **observe**, not to **command**. During an incident, you should be able to freeze a single domain—halt its deployments, rotate its secrets, and silence its alarms—without depriving others of their ability to heal or serve. If your tools can't do that, your boundaries are still theoretical.

Visibility is the proof that containment holds. Metrics, logs, and traces must carry the identity of the domain that produced them. When an alarm fires, you should know not only what broke but also where the blast stopped. In practice, that means per-cell **Amazon CloudWatch** dashboards and alarms, traces annotated in **AWS X-Ray** with the cell identifier, and logs partitioned into groups or indices that mirror the fault domains introduced back in Section 6.1. The monitoring fabric should resemble the network itself: local views for local truths, aggregated ones for global posture, and never a single undifferentiated stream that hides the boundaries you worked to build.

None of this is trustworthy until it survives deliberate harm. Boundaries are hypotheses until you attempt to break them. The mature path is to inject failure within one domain—degrade targets behind a single load balancer, add latency to one dependency, or terminate instances in one AZ—and watch the rest of the system remain unmoved. **AWS Fault Injection Service (FIS)** exists for exactly this purpose. Amazon engineers practice this constantly through internal *GameDays* and *Cell Drills*. We'll revisit this discipline in **Chapter 8**, when we examine resilience testing and chaos engineering in depth. For now, the principle is enough: a boundary you haven't broken on purpose is a boundary you can't trust.

Over time, containment becomes a loop rather than a milestone. You draw the domain; you instrument it; you stress it; you refine it. As your footprint grows, invisible couplings reappear—an innocuous global metric, a shared configuration key, a convenience script that touches every cell at once. The work is to expose and retire them, to turn shortcuts into explicit, scoped dependencies. It's unglamorous engineering, and it pays off every time something fails.

When all of this is in place, a failure changes category. It ceases to be a platform-wide event and becomes a local story with a predictable ending. Traffic meant for the impaired cell never crosses its boundary; **Amazon Route 53 (R53)** or **AWS Global Accelerator (AGA)** steers users elsewhere; operators fix the problem at a human scale. That is the quiet triumph of blast-radius design: not heroics, but routine.

Figure 6-5 illustrates a controlled fault-injection scenario validating network and operational boundaries.

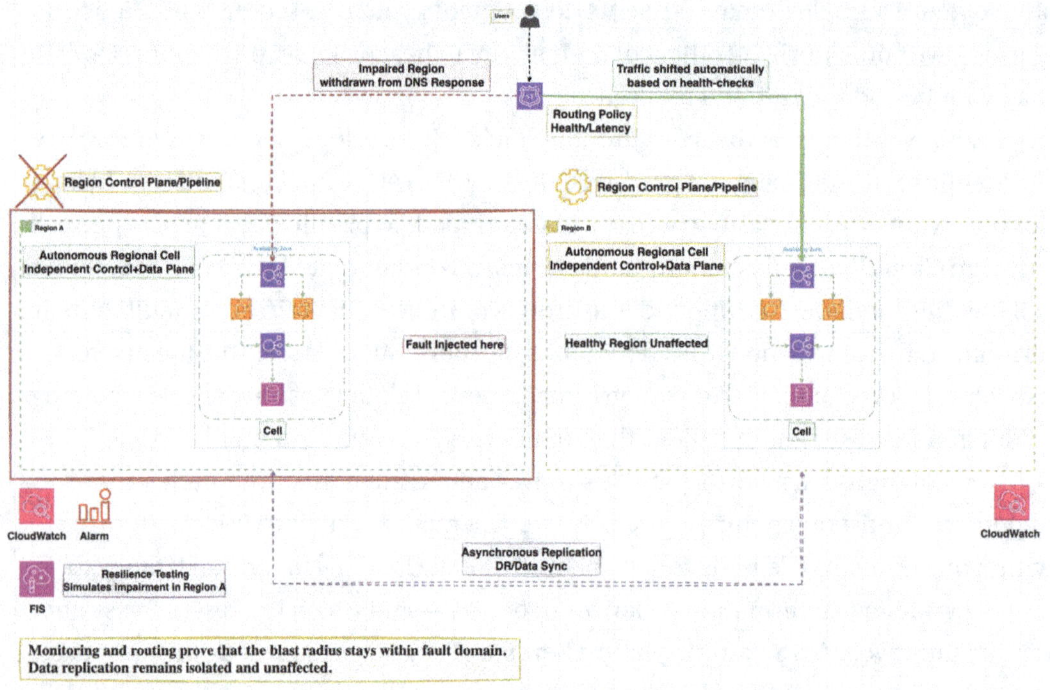

Figure 6-5. *Validating Blast Radius Containment*

A simulated failure is introduced in **Region A**, causing its local alarms to trigger
and the regional control plane to pause operations. **Route 53** detects the loss of health
and automatically withdraws the impaired region from DNS responses, rerouting all
user traffic to **Region B**. Because each region maintains **independent control and
data planes**, the impairment is fully contained; monitoring in Region B confirms no
cross-impact.

AWS Fault Injection Service (FIS) and **CloudWatch** provide observability and proof
that boundaries hold, while **asynchronous replication** ensures data integrity without
propagating corruption or lag.

Together, these mechanisms validate that the **blast radius remains confined** to its
fault domain—transforming failure into a controlled, measurable event. Note: In this
scenario, each region functions as an autonomous cell, containing its own control and
data planes; internal cells further limit fault scope within the region but are not the
source of cross-region containment.

With structural containment established, we can shift from walls to roads. Section 6.3 explores *traffic isolation and fault-domain separation*—how names resolve, how paths converge, and how packets find a different destination when one domain falters, often before anyone notices.

Section 6.3: Traffic Isolation and Fault Domain Separation

In the previous section, we built walls—fault domains and containment strategies that keep failures where they belong.

But resilience is not just about drawing boundaries; it's about what happens when those boundaries are tested—how traffic moves when walls hold and how users stay connected when one of them falls.

Traffic isolation across fault domains is enforced by a simple routing stack with three time constants. **DNS** provides the declarative, second-scale control loop that maps a service name to a healthy boundary. **Anycast edge routing** (e.g., AWS Global Accelerator or a CDN) adds a faster, connection-friendly reflex that can steer new flows to healthy regions without waiting for DNS TTL. **In-region ingress** (ALB/NLB) then distributes traffic only to local targets inside the chosen domain. The rule is consistent: routing decisions stay *above* the fault domain they protect; load balancing stays *inside* it.

In cloud networking, **motion is meaning**.

Every routing decision—every DNS answer, edge handoff, and load-balancer choice—is a micro-act of resilience. Together, those decisions form the **resilient path**: the flow of packets, sessions, and users through a distributed system without ever violating its fault domains.

Where Section 6.2 focused on containment—ensuring that a cell's failure doesn't spread—this section explores how routing ensures that users rarely even notice a failure.

Conceptually, three layers cooperate to make this possible: DNS routing, edge routing, and regional ingress. Selecting one or more of these layers is less about "which service" and more about **where the failover decision is made**—at DNS time, at the edge, or inside the domain.

Table 6-3 shows "when to use what" by working backwards from your requirements.

Table 6-3. *Routing Layer Decision Matrix*

If you need...	Use DNS routing (Route 53) as the decision layer	Add Anycast Edge Routing (GA)	Use in-domain ingress (ALB/NLB)
Fail over new users/sessions when an endpoint is unhealthy (you can tolerate DNS caching effects)	✅ Yes — Route 53 routing policies + health checks decide which endpoint is returned	Optional	✅ Yes — traffic still needs an in-domain entry point
Static entry IPs for allow-lists, partners, or fixed "front door" addressing	❌ No — DNS answers can change and clients may cache	✅ Yes — GA provides static IPs and routes to healthy endpoints	✅ Yes — GA forwards to ALB/NLB/EC2/EIP endpoints
Faster steering for new connections without waiting for DNS TTL expiry	❌ TTL/caching can delay client switching	✅ Yes — GA health-based steering happens at the edge; traffic dials affect new connections	N/A
HTTP-aware routing (paths/headers), auth-related health semantics	N/A	N/A	✅ ALB (Layer 7)
TCP/UDP (non-HTTP) workloads with very high throughput/low latency	N/A	N/A	✅ NLB (Layer 4)
Keep isolation boundaries clean (routing above the domain, LB inside it)	✅ DNS chooses the domain	✅ Edge chooses among healthy regions/endpoints	✅ LB stays inside the chosen domain (cell/AZ/Region slice)

With that selection in mind, the three layers below operate as a nested routing system: DNS selects the boundary, the edge accelerates and steers, and in-domain ingress distributes traffic locally.

DNS routing translates a global service name into the entry point of a healthy fault domain—a cell, Availability Zone slice, or region.

This layer operates in the control plane: declarative, policy-driven, and tolerant of short delays. We already studied its fundamentals and routing policies in Chapter 4; here, DNS acts as the routing brain, enforcing isolation intent consistently across the network.

Edge routing, provided by services such as AWS Global Accelerator or content delivery networks (CDNs), establishes stable anycast entry points.

These edge layers monitor regional health and latency continuously, steering new connections toward the nearest healthy region within seconds—without waiting for DNS TTL expiry.

Regional ingress, handled by Application Load Balancer or Network Load Balancer, receives traffic inside the selected cell or Availability Zone and fans it out to local targets.

This layer enforces the final boundary: traffic may adapt within the domain, but it never crosses into another one implicitly.

Each load balancer enforces the principle from Section 6.1: it lives *inside* the fault domain it serves—never across it.

Together, these three layers form the **traffic-isolation stack**.

They work like nested routing tables:

Route 53 directs clients to a healthy region or cell, the edge routes packets to the nearest boundary, and the in-region load balancer steers them to the right subnet and instance.

Each layer absorbs its own class of failure—logical, network, or physical—and hides it from the layer above.

This hierarchy mirrors the logic of fault domains themselves.

Availability Zones protect the physical layer from hardware collapse.

Cells protect the logical layer from software faults.

Routing unites them, deciding which boundaries to cross—and which to avoid—to preserve continuity even when the ground shifts.

In Figure 6-6, Route 53 enforces routing policy at the control plane, returning regional aliases or Global Accelerator hostnames based on latency or health. Global Accelerator anchors anycast edges that monitor endpoint status and reroute new connections within seconds when regions fail. Within each region, ALB and NLB terminate traffic locally and distribute only to in-cell targets, maintaining zonal fault boundaries. Together, these three layers—DNS policy, edge routing, and regional ingress—keep users aligned with healthy domains while preventing failures from propagating beyond their fault domain.

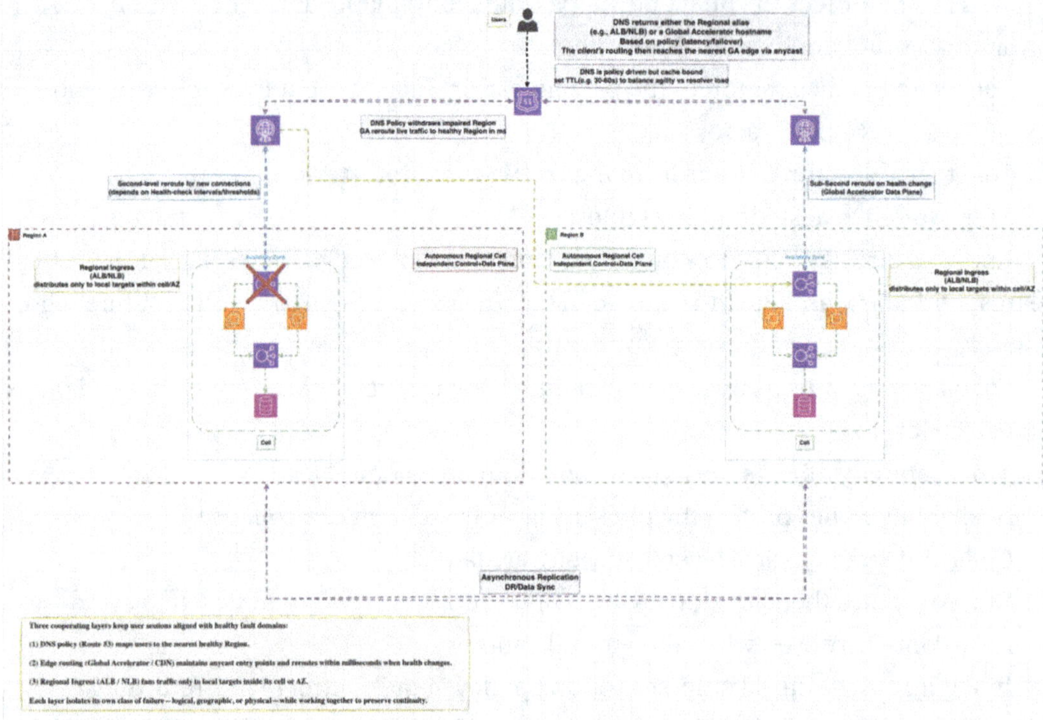

Figure 6-6. *The Traffic Isolation Stack*

Next, we'll see how DNS—the same mechanism we explored earlier for resilience and policy—acts as the **routing brain** of fault-domain separation, translating architectural intent into the live map that keeps users consistently aligned with healthy cells.

DNS as the Routing Brain, Not the Teacher

Resilience begins to move the moment a name resolves. DNS is the first control surface where our static fault domains—cells, Availability Zones (AZs), and regions—become an operational choice. In Chapter 4, we separated naming from addressing and made the point that DNS is a control plane in its own right: declarative, deliberately slow, and globally authoritative. Here we use that control plane to encode fault-domain intent. Where Section 6.2 drew the walls, DNS decides which wall is open to traffic now.

With Amazon Route 53, the distinction you introduced earlier—**control plane** versus **data plane**—matters more than anywhere else. Route 53 is a global service: you configure hosted zones, records, and health checks via AWS APIs, while DNS answers are served from a globally distributed fleet of authoritative name servers and health checkers.

The data plane is a global fleet: anycast authoritative resolvers and health-checking nodes distributed at AWS edge locations. *Configuration is managed centrally, while queries and health decisions are enforced directly at the global edge.*

This separation mirrors the pattern we've been building throughout the book: configure centrally, decide locally. *Even if the control plane is constrained, the global DNS data plane continues answering with the last known healthy state and routing around impaired regions.*

That is fault-domain awareness baked into the naming layer.

Once you see Route 53 this way, records stop being static entries and start looking like small programs. Each record set describes a boundary—"this cell endpoint," "this AZ ingress," "this region's front door"—together with the conditions under which that boundary is considered safe. Health checks are the inputs; DNS answers are the outputs. Crucially, those health checks originate from the Route 53 data plane, not from inside your workload. They probe from outside your regions, from networks that are not subject to the very outage you're trying to detect. In Chapter 2, we called this orthogonal observation: a liveness signal that is independent of the failure domain it evaluates. When a probe fails for long enough to trip the policy, the edge resolvers simply stop returning that record. There is no failover script to run, no API to race, and no shared controller to rely on; the decision is made where queries are answered, and it propagates at DNS timescales.

Time, in DNS, is part of the contract. We said earlier that a time-to-live (TTL) is the half-life of a past decision; here it is the half-life of risk. Short TTLs bound evacuation time when a domain becomes unhealthy; longer TTLs reduce global churn when the world is stable. The right value is not folklore; it is arithmetic: health-check interval plus TTL is your practical upper bound for convergence, and that bound should be chosen to fit the user experience you promised. Equally important is *how* a boundary is withdrawn. Removing a record invites negative caching and inconsistent clients; withdrawing it by failing a health check preserves policy, preserves semantics, and keeps your telemetry intact. Names retain their meaning; only their eligibility changes.

You do not need cells to benefit from this. Everything we have just described applies as naturally to AZ and regional isolation as it does to cellular topologies. Many teams publish one endpoint per AZ and let DNS de-prefer an impaired zone while per-AZ load balancers drain in place. Others publish one endpoint per region and let DNS either prefer the closest healthy region or fall back to a designated secondary when a primary fails its checks. The mechanics are identical; only the granularity of the boundary changes. That was the thesis of Chapter 5 when we discussed routing intent through the OSI layers: the same control surface can steer very different topologies as long as the boundaries are explicit.

Partitioning is where DNS becomes more than a switchboard. When we introduced shuffle-sharding, the point was to keep tenants from sharing the same fate. DNS is the cleanest enforcement mechanism for that idea. If tenant-to-boundary assignment is deterministic—by token, account, or geography—then the authoritative layer need only answer with the slice that tenant is allowed to see. Even a misconfigured client cannot "discover" its way into another fault domain because the resolver never reveals those endpoints. In the language we've used throughout, the routing brain is now encoding *who is allowed to cross which wall*, not merely *which wall is open*.

Private resolution follows the same rules. Inside a region, private hosted zones should mirror the external structure, not undermine it. Service names within a cell resolve to endpoints within that cell; cross-cell lookups require an explicit, audited resolver path. Split-horizon is a tool for scoping trust, not a backdoor. If changing a resolver lets an internal client escape its domain, the boundary is a diagram, not a property.

All of this reduces to a simple shape that matches the book's recurring model. Route 53's regional **control plane** holds configuration and policy; its global **data plane** answers the world with health-filtered truth. Your records delineate AZs, regions, or cells; your health checks define what "alive" means at that scope—port liveness for per-cell ingress, application SLIs from CloudWatch for regional failover. *Convergence time is bounded by the health-check interval plus TTL; safety comes from decisions made outside the evaluated domain.*

It is the smallest reliable brain you can put in front of a distributed system.

In Figure 6-7, Route 53 separates a regional control plane (configuration and policy management in us-east-1) from a global data plane distributed across AWS edge locations. The global data plane performs independent health checks and serves DNS answers based on health and policy, continuing to operate even if the control plane is impaired. Records represent isolation boundaries—cell, AZ, or region—and are withdrawn by health policy rather than deletion. DNS translates architectural intent into routing behavior that remains trustworthy even when a domain fails.

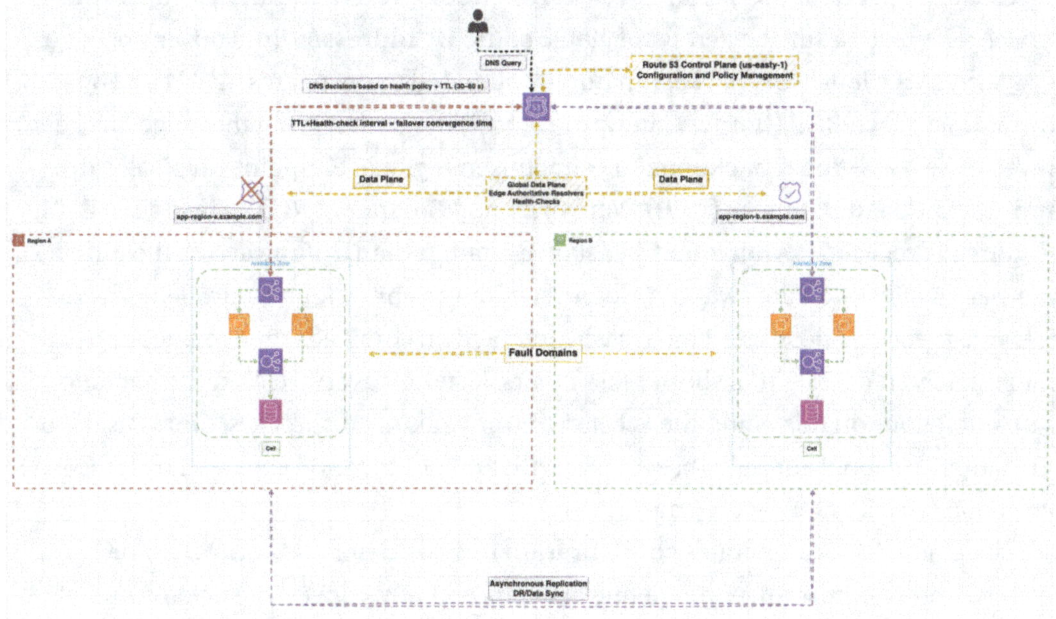

Figure 6-7. *DNS as the Routing Brain*

Next, we leave seconds-scale control and step down to the edge, where **anycast entry points** keep connections stable while regions or cells move beneath them. That is what we will be discussing next, and it will let us join the DNS brain to a faster reflex without violating the boundaries we've just enforced.

Edge Entry with Anycast: When to Use AWS Global Accelerator

We have leaned on DNS for many pages now: first to describe its control/data planes, then to show how it encodes fault-domain intent across cells, Availability Zones (AZs), and regions. That was deliberate. DNS is the slow, dependable brain of the internet; it tells clients where to begin. But once a connection has formed—TCP established, TLS negotiated, QUIC in flight—DNS is no longer in the room. At that moment resilience belongs to networking and transport, the layers we grounded in Chapter 5. If DNS is the map, the network carries the feet. This is precisely the gap **AWS Global Accelerator** is built to fill.

Global Accelerator (GA) is an **anycast front door** backed by the AWS edge. The service advertises a small, fixed set of global **static IP addresses** from dozens of edge locations, so a client's first packet is naturally attracted to the nearest AWS edge by the internet's own BGP (Border Gateway Protocol) dynamics. From that edge, packets traverse the **AWS global backbone** to your chosen regional endpoint—typically an **Application Load Balancer (ALB)**, **Network Load Balancer (NLB)**, **Elastic IP (EIP)**, or a directly registered **Amazon EC2** instance—rather than drifting across the public internet. In effect, you are swapping internet path variability for a controlled private network as early as possible, which is why interactive workloads tend to benefit immediately (reduced jitter, shorter loss bursts, faster recovery). GA's documentation is unambiguous on this point: the accelerator provides fixed entry IPs, routes users to the optimal regional endpoint based on health and policy, and keeps traffic on the AWS backbone once it enters at the edge.

Like Route 53, GA separates **configuration** from **decision**. Its **control plane** is regional and administrative: you define listeners and port ranges, create **endpoint groups** per region, attach endpoints to those groups, and set **traffic dials** (the proportion of flow a region should receive when healthy). Those settings are pushed out to the **global data plane** at the edge, which continuously **probes endpoint health** and makes per-flow forwarding decisions locally. When an endpoint—or an entire region—fails health, the nearest edge simply stops selecting it; new flows are directed to a healthy regional group **without waiting for DNS time-to-live (TTL) to elapse; new flows are steered to healthy endpoint groups immediately, and existing sessions recover according to application and client retry behavior.**

In practice, that turns a seconds-scale control loop (DNS convergence) into a **milliseconds-scale reflex** at the edge, which is exactly what you want when users are mid-transaction and the geography under them shifts.

This is also where GA's **static anycast IPs** matter more than marketing suggests. DNS returns names; firewalls remember addresses. Many enterprises and payment rails insist on allow-listing source IPs for egress or callback flows; webhooks and partner integrations do the same. With GA, your public entry never changes: two global IPv4 addresses (and, when dual-stacked, an additional pair for IPv6) represent the service worldwide, while you can still move or rebalance regional capacity beneath. That property—stable addressing above dynamic topology—is often the deciding factor for regulated systems.

Notice how this pairs with the cell/AZ/region story you've been telling. GA does **not** replace DNS or your fault domains. DNS remains the outer brain: it maps the service name to the accelerator's anycast IPs and can still implement tenant partitioning or geo policy at the name layer. GA becomes the **transport guardian** inside that mapping: it holds the client near an edge, watches regional health in real time, and forwards only to healthy regional ingress—where your own per-cell ALB/NLB boundaries continue to enforce isolation. We maintain the same separation of planes we emphasized earlier: a regional **control plane** you configure deliberately and a global **data plane** that reacts continuously without calling home. Think of it as Route 53's philosophy carried down a layer and run faster.

Two operational details make the difference between a neat diagram and a durable design. First, **health**. Route 53's health checks already taught us to measure liveness from outside the fault domain. GA follows suit: its edge fleet probes your endpoints from the network vantage points where decisions are made and withdraws them only after a configurable threshold of failures. That means regional failover is driven by the same edge that receives the client packets; there is no central orchestrator to stall. Second, **traffic dials**. During deployments, brownouts, or regional cost events, you can shift the dial for a region to 0% without touching DNS. The accelerator keeps the IPs stable and nudges new flows to the remaining regions until you restore the dial—an extremely effective way to practice **cell-level or region-level canaries** at the transport layer. Both capabilities are natively supported by Global Accelerator's control plane and can be configured directly through the API or console—reflecting how AWS designed the service for operational control rather than ad-hoc workarounds.

Protocol semantics matter here. GA is **Layer-4 (L4)** transport: it accelerates **TCP and UDP** workloads generically, and it does **not** cache or rewrite application payloads the way **Amazon CloudFront** (Layer-7) might. That distinction is why GA is the better fit for raw APIs, gaming protocols, financial FIX gateways, live media control channels, or anything else that isn't best served by HTTP caching semantics. Conversely, for static or cacheable web content, CloudFront remains the natural front end; GA's own guidance positions the two as complementary rather than competitive. In mixed stacks, it's common to terminate browser traffic at CloudFront while placing latency-sensitive API or session-heavy traffic behind GA—both still referenced by DNS policies at the top.

None of this demands a cellular architecture. Everything above works for **multi-AZ** and **multi-region** topologies exactly as it does for cells. You might point GA directly at per-region ALBs that themselves front multi-AZ target groups; or, in stricter designs, you might dedicate one ALB per cell and register those as GA endpoints with region-scoped endpoint groups. In both cases the invariants from the first part of this chapter still hold: load balancers belong **inside** the domain, never across it; GA operates **above** the domain as a routing surface, never as a shared control plane across cells.

One final alignment with Chapter 5's OSI discussion is worth making explicit. With Route 53 you accepted **seconds-scale** control in exchange for global determinism and independence; with GA you add a **milliseconds-scale** reflex that preserves session continuity and path stability when geography changes. Together they form a layered control system that respects isolation boundaries at every stage: DNS selects a healthy domain; GA selects a healthy region within that domain; your ALB/NLB selects healthy targets within the cell. Each layer has its own health signals, its own time constants, and its own failure domain. When tuned together, users feel continuity even as the system reroutes beneath them.

When Not to Use AWS Global Accelerator

Global Accelerator is not a prerequisite for resilience. If your architecture meets its objectives with DNS-based routing and regional load balancing alone, adding GA may increase cost and operational complexity without measurable benefit.

Do not default to Global Accelerator when

- The workload is HTTP-based and already fronted by CloudFront

- Latency sensitivity is low, and DNS TTL–based failover is acceptable

- Static anycast IP addresses are not required (for allowlists or partner integrations)

- The service operates in a single region or has no active multi-region posture

- Simplicity and minimal operational surface area are higher priorities than sub-second convergence

Use Global Accelerator deliberately—when you need fast transport-layer failover, stable entry IPs, or consistent performance for long-lived or latency-sensitive connections.

In Figure 6-8, a single accelerator advertises static anycast IPs from AWS edge locations worldwide. Clients connect to the nearest edge, where Global Accelerator's data plane performs continuous health checks and forwards traffic across the AWS backbone to the healthiest regional endpoint (e.g., a per-cell ALB). The control plane, managed regionally, defines endpoint groups and traffic dials, while the edge enforces health and policy in milliseconds—complementing the slower, declarative control of DNS at the name layer.

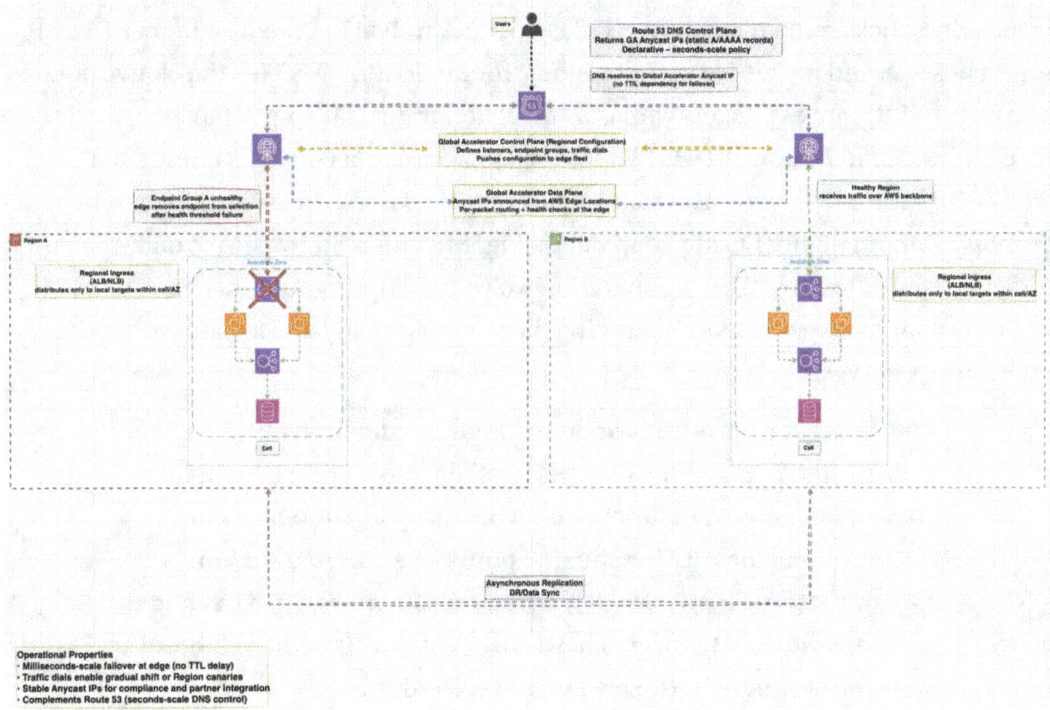

Figure 6-8. *Anycast Edge to Regional Cells*

With the edge handled, the stack is nearly complete. We began at the top—DNS as the routing brain—dropped to the edge for fast reflexes, and now we descend into the region, where **ingress lives inside the fault domain** and **network segmentation** keeps east-west traffic from wandering. The next subsection ties that together: **per-cell ALB/ NLB design and VPC/TGW routing** that enforces the same boundaries inside the region that we established at the edge.

In-Region Traffic Isolation and Ingress Boundaries

By the time traffic reaches a region, the problem shifts from *steering between* fault domains to *keeping faults local* as packets traverse subnets and services. DNS and the edge have already done their part. Now the regional fabric—load balancers, VPC routing, and service networks—must prove that boundaries are real, not just lines on a diagram.

The front door is the load balancer, and ownership matters. A cell (or a simpler per-service slice) should expose **its own** load balancer so that misconfigurations, brownouts, or capacity shocks remain local. For HTTP(S), the **Application Load Balancer (ALB)** terminates TLS and makes Layer-7 decisions; for raw TCP/UDP/TLS, the **Network Load Balancer (NLB)** moves packets with minimal latency; for transparent inspection fleets, the **Gateway Load Balancer (GWLB)** inserts appliances via GENEVE encapsulation (UDP/6081) without becoming a routing shortcut. ALB and NLB are configured by a *regional* control plane (Elastic Load Balancing) but enforced by per-AZ data-plane nodes—exactly the control/data separation we've used throughout this book.

A word on **cross-zone load balancing**, because it directly affects fault containment and recovery curves:

- **ALB**: cross-zone is **always on at the load balancer level**; an ALB node in any AZ may select targets in **all** enabled AZs. **You can turn off cross-zone load balancing on a per-target-group basis to enforce zonal locality for specific pools (e.g., one-AZ-in/one-AZ-out patterns inside a cell). When cross-zone is off, each node sends traffic only to targets in its own Availability Zone, tightening fault containment at the cost of less smoothing.**

- **NLB**: by default, each NLB node selects **only targets in its own AZ**. If you **enable cross-zone**, any NLB node may select targets in all enabled AZs; you can also toggle this at the **target-group** layer. Trade-offs are explicit: enabling cross-zone improves within cell availability during a zonal loss but increases coupling across zones and may introduce data-transfer charges for cross-AZ traffic on NLBs.

Read that again through a resilience lens. With **ALB**, the default posture is "heal within the cell by using all AZs," and you opt out per target group if you want stricter locality. With **NLB**, the default posture is "keep traffic zonal," and you opt in to cross-zone when continuity is more important than strict independence. Neither is universally "right"; the right choice is the failure you're willing to have: a slightly wider blast radius with better continuity or stricter isolation with faster evacuation by the upper layers (Route 53/Global Accelerator).

ALB vs. NLB Cross-Zone: A Practical Rule of Thumb

- **Prefer ALB (cross-zone on by default)** when application continuity matters more than strict zonal isolation and when brief capacity loss should be absorbed inside the cell.

- **Disable ALB cross-zone per target group** when you want one-AZ-in/one-AZ-out behavior to tighten blast-radius containment and let upper layers (DNS or edge routing) evacuate traffic instead.

- **Prefer NLB (cross-zone off by default)** when zonal locality and deterministic traffic paths are more important than smoothing capacity during a zonal failure.

- **Enable NLB cross-zone** only when maintaining availability within the cell during an AZ loss outweighs the increased coupling and cross-AZ data-transfer cost.

The choice is not about correctness, but about which failure you are willing to accept:

a sharper, well-bounded loss that evacuates quickly, or a softer degradation that stays local. Those choices govern how traffic enters a fault domain. The next set of failures tends to appear after ingress—when traffic moves laterally inside the region and begins traversing shared routing and inspection layers.

Common Failure Patterns That Break Fault-Domain Isolation

Once traffic is inside the region, even architectures that look sound on diagrams can lose isolation guarantees due to a few recurring implementation mistakes:

- **Asymmetric routing through inspection layers**, where forward and return traffic do not traverse the same Availability Zone or appliance, causing stateful flows to reset or fail under load.

- **Overly shared or permissive Transit Gateway route tables**, which introduce unintended transitivity and allow traffic to leak laterally between domains that were meant to remain isolated.

- **Loss of Availability Zone affinity when steering traffic through shared services**, turning localized faults into multi-domain incidents.

These failures are not rare edge cases—they are the most common ways well-designed architectures lose their isolation guarantees. The remainder of this section shows how AWS load balancing, Transit Gateway routing, and Gateway Load Balancer patterns either prevent or amplify these failure modes, depending on how they are configured.

To prevent these failure modes, the design must enforce explicit routing boundaries and symmetry for any path that crosses shared services.

Ingress is only half of containment. Inside the region, **east–west** paths determine whether incidents stay private. The **AWS Transit Gateway (TGW)** is the managed router that connects VPCs and on-premises, and its **route tables** are your isolation lever. Associate each cell (or service VPC) with its **own** TGW route table and propagate routes **only** where you intend visibility. That one choice prevents "unintended transitivity," the silent default route that lets one domain wander into another. Best practices reinforce this: use TGW route-table design to isolate subsets of attachments; enable propagation and association deliberately rather than globally.

Sometimes the boundaries must span geographies. **TGW inter-region peering** lets you connect transit gateways in different regions over the AWS backbone and route IPv4/IPv6 between them. The peering is **non-transitive** and **static** by design: you explicitly create the peering attachment and add routes to reach the remote prefixes. That preserves the same predictability we want inside a region—traffic flows only where the routing tables say it can. In multi-region topologies, this becomes the network substrate beneath the DNS/edge steering logic you built earlier.

Security and inspection often need to be "shared," but shared must not mean *shared fate*. **Gateway Load Balancer (GWLB)** lets you centralize virtual appliances (firewalls/IDS/brokers) in a separate VPC and connect application VPCs through **GWLB endpoints (GWLBe)**. GWLB encapsulates packets with **GENEVE (UDP/6081)** to the appliance fleet and then returns them to the original path; from the workload's point of view, source/destination and routing semantics are preserved.

Resilience hinges on **symmetry**. Stateful appliances expect the **request and response** of a flow to traverse the **same appliance**; if the return path hits a different node or a different AZ, the session state won't match and the firewall will drop the packet. Out of the box, GWLB keeps data-plane processing **AZ-local**: a **GWLBe in AZ-A** forwards to **appliance targets in AZ-A** and will fail over to *other targets in the same AZ* if one fails. This minimizes cross-AZ coupling and avoids asymmetric flows by default. If you **enable cross-zone load balancing** on GWLB, a node in one AZ can select targets in other AZs—useful to maintain inspection capacity during a zonal loss, but it introduces inter-AZ dependency and data-transfer costs. Choose it only when the availability of the inspection plane outweighs strict AZ isolation.

In multi-VPC designs, **AWS Transit Gateway (TGW)** is often the "router" that steers traffic to and from the inspection VPC. Here, **appliance mode support** on the TGW **attachment** is the key to symmetry: it pins the *return* traffic to the **same AZ** where the *forward* traffic entered, ensuring response packets traverse the **same GWLBe and the same firewall node**. Without it, TGW may hairpin the return path through a different AZ, creating classic asymmetric routing and dropped flows on stateful devices. (TGW appliance mode is deliberate: it's a per-attachment setting that maintains AZ affinity for both directions of a flow.)

There are valid exceptions. For **internet ingress/egress hub** patterns, some teams prefer **disabling** TGW appliance mode and instead **force symmetry with routing**—for example, by sending both forward and return traffic through the **same AZ-local GWLBe** via explicit route-table entries. The principle remains identical: guarantee that forward and return packets hit the **same** AZ endpoint and appliance. Pick the mechanism— appliance mode or precise routes—that best matches your topology.

Finally, keep "shared services" isolated in fate. Give **each application domain** its **own GWLBe** (per AZ), its own routing and security boundaries, and register **multiple appliances per AZ** so GWLB can stay local while surviving single-node failures. If you must span AZs for capacity, do it knowingly (cross-zone on) and measure the blast-radius implications. GWLB does **not** rescue asymmetric flows it never saw; if the first packet didn't traverse GWLB, sending the reply through it later is unsupported and will degrade performance or fail.

Where identities matter more than IPs, **Amazon VPC Lattice** adds a Layer-7 service network on top of routing: producers and consumers authenticate, authorize, and communicate under policy, not proximity. It's the same philosophy as TGW—explicit intent or nothing—but expressed at the request layer rather than subnets. In practice, teams use TGW for IP reachability and Lattice to ensure only permitted service calls can ever occur, even when IP reachability exists.

Look at the failure story now. Lose an AZ: ALB withdraws the lost zone's nodes automatically; NLB either contains impact to that zone (cross-zone off) or continues by pulling from healthy targets elsewhere (cross-zone on). Lose a cell's compute tier:

target-group health fails; that ingress stops selecting targets; upper layers (Route 53 and/ or Global Accelerator) stop returning that endpoint. Misconfigure east–west routing: the TGW route table scopes the blast to one attachment; nothing "leaks" laterally. Degrade an inspection fleet: only domains using that fleet's GWLB endpoints are affected. In every case, **the control plane declares intent, the data plane enforces it, and the failure ends where the boundary begins**.

This is why we introduced the services briefly here and stopped short of deep product tutorials. The book is not a catalogue; it's a guide to *design intent*. The specifics of a listener rule or a TGW CLI flag will change. The shape does not include per-domain ingress, explicit routing, inspection as a service, and identities above addresses where appropriate. If you can sketch those four ideas for your region, you can operate under stress.

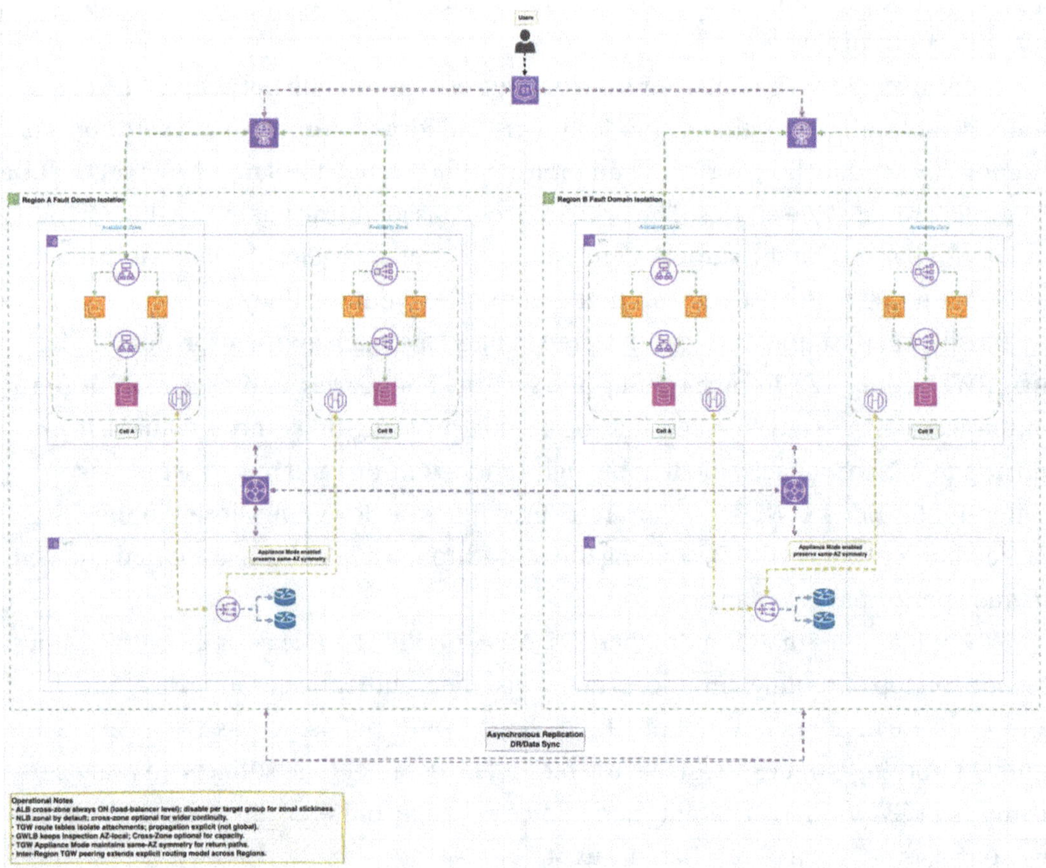

Figure 6-9. *Regional Ingress and Fault-Domain Isolation*

In Figure 6-9, each region hosts isolated fault domains, with per-cell ALBs/NLBs handling ingress inside their VPCs. **ALB cross-zone routing is enabled by default (and can be disabled per target group for zonal locality)**, while NLBs are zonal unless explicitly enabled for cross-AZ routing. East-west paths traverse AWS Transit Gateway with appliance mode for symmetric return flows and Gateway Load Balancer providing per-AZ inspection through local endpoints. Inter-region TGW peering extends the same explicit, non-transitive routing across regions, preserving isolation and predictable recovery boundaries.

In-Cell Load Balancing and Resilient Path Selection

Resilience inside a cell is not about grand gestures; it is about what happens in the first seconds after something goes wrong. By the time a request reaches this boundary, the global steering work is finished—names have resolved, the edge has chosen a region, and ingress has placed the packet inside the right Virtual Private Cloud (VPC). From here on, the user's experience depends on a few small decisions made quickly and made well: which target receives the next connection, how quickly a sick target is taken out of rotation, and whether change—deployments, scaling, failovers—looks like turbulence or like nothing at all. This section is about those decisions, because they are the difference between an incident that stays private and an outage that becomes public.

Inside the cell, the **Application Load Balancer (ALB)** and **Network Load Balancer (NLB)** are the conductors. Both follow the same structural pattern you've seen throughout this chapter: a **regional control plane** determines the desired state, and **Availability Zone (AZ)** data-plane nodes enforce it locally. That separation matters. It allows a node set in one AZ to falter without dragging its neighbors down, and it means health, routing, and target membership can change near the problem rather than somewhere far away. Failures stay where they start because the decision makers closest to them are allowed to act first.

Detection sets the tempo. Each target group emits a steady rhythm of health signals. Probes are simple—HTTP(S) responses, TCP handshakes—but their cadence and thresholds define your **Mean Time to Detect (MTTD)**. Short intervals surface faults faster but flirt with false alarms; longer intervals avoid flapping but widen the window in which users might notice trouble. The goal is not simply to detect; it is to detect fast enough that mitigation can begin before perception catches up. That brings us to a metric we introduce here, alongside the MTTD/MTTR/MTBF trio used earlier in the book: **Mean Time to Mitigate (MTTM)**. If MTTD measures awareness and **Mean Time to Recover (MTTR)** measures repair, MTTM measures composure—how long it takes to make the problem invisible to users by routing around it. When a load balancer stops sending traffic to a failing target, when a per-cell endpoint is withdrawn from DNS, or when Global Accelerator selects a different regional group at the edge, you haven't fixed the fault yet; you've made it irrelevant. Good cells live on low MTTM.

Mitigation is not only about speed; it is about grace. Two features do more for grace than any others. **Connection draining** lets an instance or pod leave quietly: the load balancer stops assigning new work, in-flight sessions finish, and clients never see a reset they would have retried in unison. A **slow start** lets a newcomer arrive politely: the load balancer offers a small share of traffic, observes how it behaves, and increases the share as confidence grows. Draining prevents exit thrash; a slow start prevents entrance shock. Together, they turn the constant churn of deployments and auto-scaling from sharp edges into rounded corners, and in doing so, they compress MTTM without forcing anyone to sprint.

Routing inside the cell is where the two load balancers show their character. ALB, operating at the application layer, prefers the target with the fewest outstanding requests; it spreads the load to protect tail latency and to keep noisy neighbors from dominating. NLB, closer to the wire, uses a five-tuple flow hash to keep transport-layer flows predictable for TCP and UDP workloads. In both cases, the nodes that accept connections are zonal, and **zonal locality** is the default safety rail: a node in one AZ serves the targets in that AZ first earlier in this section, we discussed **cross-zone load balancing** and the trade-off it encodes; here is the practical restatement. For ALB, cross-zone routing is available by default, and you selectively disable it per target group when you want a strict one-AZ-in, one-AZ-out pattern to harden blast-radius boundaries. For NLB, cross-zone is off by default; you enable it when continuity within the cell during a zonal loss matters more than keeping zones completely independent (and you accept the coupling and data-transfer implications that come with that choice). Resilience is rarely about the "right" switch position; it is about choosing consciously which failure you prefer: a small, crisp loss you evacuate around, or a broader, softer dip you ride through.

Not every error deserves a human or a global reaction. Transient loss, microbursts, and short pauses are part of distributed life. The way clients retry determines whether those small events remain small. Retries that are bounded, spaced with exponential backoff, and randomized with jitter cooperate with your load balancer: they reduce synchronized thundering herds, leave room for draining to work, and let slow start finish its job. Retries that are immediate, aggressive, and aligned turn the load balancer into a drum that amplifies the problem you were trying to mask. The difference is not configuration trivia; it is the way application behavior and network behavior acknowledge each other.

When all of this works together, the cell acquires a kind of internal physics. Health checks keep **MTTD** low without flapping; draining and slow starts keep **MTTM** low by smoothing exits and entrances; capacity headroom and automation pull **MTTR** down by restoring healthy targets before queues run long; and the absence of stormy retries protects **MTBF** from avoidable self-inflicted incidents. None of these mechanisms are dramatic. That is precisely their value. Resilience at this level is the slow, predictable change of state—small, local decisions made quickly enough that the rest of the system does not need to know.

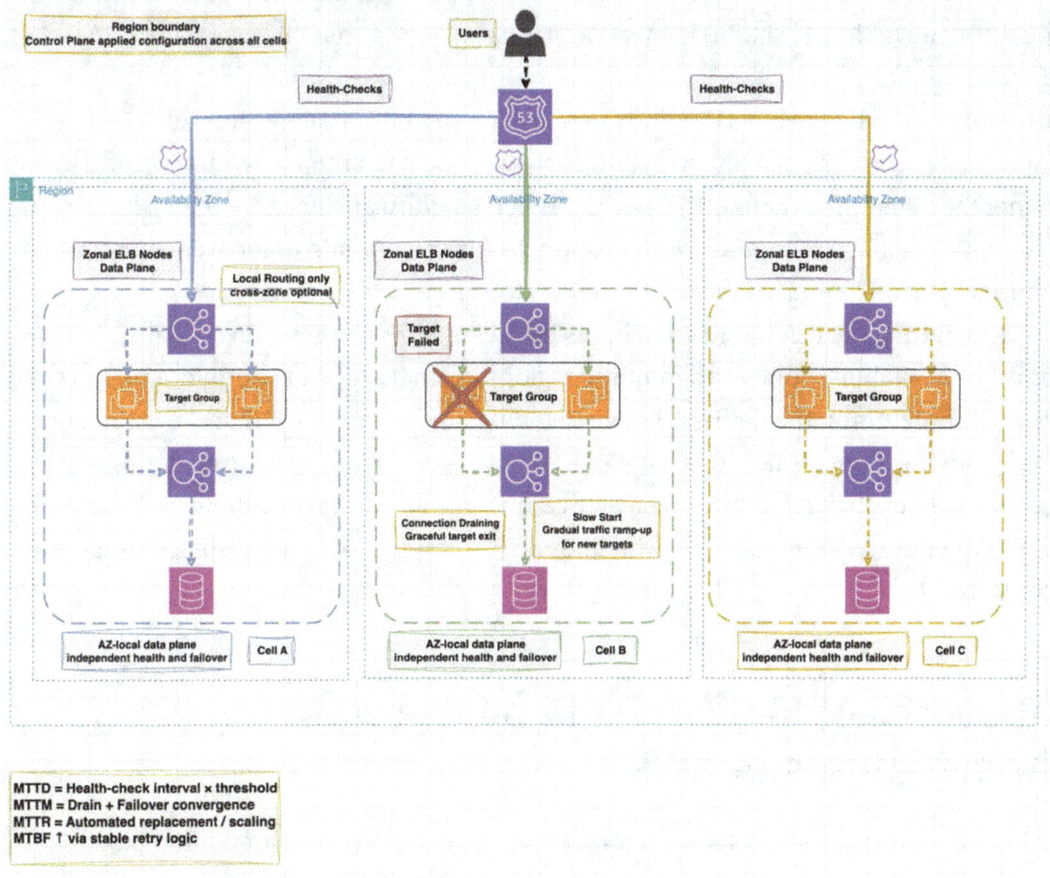

Figure 6-10. *Resilient Path Selection Within a Cell*

In Figure 6-10, each Availability Zone hosts its own cell with zonal load-balancer nodes (ALB/NLB data planes) that route only to healthy, cell-owned targets. Health checks detect failures locally, while connection draining and slow start ensure graceful target exits and controlled traffic ramp-up for new instances. The regional control plane applies configuration across all cells, but health and failover remain AZ-local and autonomous. Aggregated health signals flow upward to Route 53 or Global Accelerator, keeping global routing informed while isolating faults at the source. Together, these mechanisms—fast local detection, smooth mitigation, and bounded propagation— preserve user continuity and make most failures invisible.

Design Heuristic: Routing Must Sit Above the Fault Domain It Protects

A simple rule emerges from the patterns in this section: *routing decisions must always be made outside the fault domain they are meant to protect.* If a routing layer shares fate with the resources it governs—whether through shared load balancers, shared route tables, or shared inspection paths—it cannot reliably evacuate traffic when that domain fails.

Practically, this means DNS and edge routing sit above regions and cells; regional ingress sits inside the cell it serves; and east–west routing enforces symmetry and locality rather than spanning domains implicitly. When a failure affects more than a bounded fraction of traffic—or requires coordination *within* the domain to recover—the routing boundary is too low, and the fault domain is too large.

The natural next step is to stretch this behavior across larger fault domains, such as multiple availability zones and multiple regions. A single AZ can stumble; a region can momentarily strain; the network between them can shape what "failure" even means. In the next section, we take the same ingredients—independent control planes, zonal data planes, explicit routing, and measured mitigation—and apply them to designs that span zones and continents. The principles do not change; only the distances and time constants do.

Section 6.4: Multi-AZ and Multi-region Architectures in AWS

When we first discussed cells, we learned how resilience can be carved from logic— boundaries drawn by configuration, not concrete. But logical isolation can only go so far; sooner or later, the physical world reasserts itself. Power fails. Fiber breaks. A cooling unit trips.

That is why cloud resilience always rests, in the end, on geography.

This section moves the conversation from logical independence to physical separation—from a single self-contained domain to architectures that span data centers, Availability Zones (AZs), and entire regions.

Our goal is to understand how AWS networking stitches those spaces together while still keeping failures from bleeding across them.

To do so, we will use four recurring fundamentals—requirements, data, dependencies, and operational readiness—as a compass. Each fundamental shape not only affects how you replicate and route but also how you decide what not to connect.

Table 6-4 maps common resilience requirements to the minimum architecture that satisfies them—so you can start with intent before you add complexity.

Table 6-4. *Decision Summary Mapping. Single Region/Multi-AZ, Multi-region, Networking Implications*

Primary Driver	Multi-AZ (Single Region)	Multi-Region	Networking implications (AWS examples)
Survive **single AZ** impairment	✅ Typically sufficient	❌ Not required	Regional ALB/NLB + multi-AZ targets; health checks withdraw impaired zonal capacity.
Very low RTO for **AZ impairment** (seconds–tens of seconds)	✅ Often achievable	❌ Not required	Depends on health-check cadence and client/session behaviour; NLB/ALB health + draining/slow start help.
Survive **Region-level disaster**	❌ Not covered	✅ Required	Requires multi-Region capacity + global steering (Route 53 failover / ARC / Global Accelerator). Multi-AZ does not protect against Region outages.
Very low RTO for **Region disaster** (seconds–minutes)	❌ Not possible	✅ Usually required	DNS-based failover is bounded by TTL + health checks; GA/ARC can reduce dependence on DNS TTL by shifting traffic at the edge / via routing controls.
RPO near zero	✅ Possible within Region for some services	⚠ Rare across Regions	Cross-Region synchronous writes are usually impractical at scale; AWS DR guidance generally frames cross-Region strategies around async or managed global patterns.
Data residency / sovereignty	⚠ Sometimes	✅ Often	Region choice may be dictated; replication and telemetry must respect boundaries.
Lowest latency for global users	❌ Limited	✅ Often	Multi-Region active/active reads, geo/latency routing; avoid cross-ocean dependencies.

With that baseline decision made, we can now examine how Availability Zones provide the first physical fault boundary—and how AWS networking uses them as the perimeter of regional resilience.

Availability Zones as the Physical Perimeter of Resilience

An Availability Zone is the smallest physical boundary AWS exposes to you and the first that can truly fail on its own.

Each AZ contains one or more discrete data-center clusters with separate power, cooling, and physical networking; all AZs in a region are joined by redundant, high-bandwidth, **low-latency** fiber (sub-millisecond is typical for intra-region links). You can think of them as neighborhoods linked by expressways—close enough to commute, far enough that a local fire does not spread.

For most workloads, multi-AZ design is the first step beyond the single-fault domain.

Within one region, an **Application Load Balancer (ALB)** or **Network Load Balancer (NLB)** distributes connections across AZs. **ALB cross-zone load balancing is on by default** (zonal nodes still fail independently), and **NLB cross-zone load balancing is off by default but can be enabled** when you prefer smoother utilization across zones over strict zonal independence. Both are regional control planes driving zonal data-plane nodes, so when one zone is impaired, the others quietly continue.

This mirrors the behavior we observed inside a cell: autonomy enforced by distance and duplicated infrastructure. Unlike the logical boundary of a cell, however, an AZ is guaranteed to fail independently because it lives on different circuits, routers, and roofs.

Multi-AZ provides fast recovery from zonal impairment. Regional disasters require multi-region architectures (or an external DR site), as Multi-AZ does not protect against region-level outages.

Designing across AZs is therefore not optional—it is the baseline expression of production-grade resilience.

AWS itself builds critical regional services—**Amazon S3, Amazon DynamoDB, Amazon EKS**, and **Amazon RDS Multi-AZ**—to withstand a single-AZ impairment. For example, **RDS Multi-AZ** maintains a **synchronous** standby in another AZ; **Aurora** synchronously replicates each write to six storage nodes across three AZs (quorum write). **Amazon EFS Standard** stores data redundantly across multiple AZs by design (and offers **asynchronous** cross-region EFS Replication when you need DR).

For networking, this pattern translates into zonal subnets, redundant route targets, and health-driven withdrawal of impaired zonal nodes by the load balancer. The goal is not to hide zonal loss but to make it boring: a brief dip in metrics, not a headline event.

At this level, the network becomes the arbiter of truth. **Routes decide which
AZ serves which flow; health checks decide when a route or node is withdrawn.**
Availability Zones are where physical engineering meets logical intent, turning isolation
from an architectural ideal into a physical fact.

Service Scope in Practice: Global, Regional, and Zonal

To design across regions and zones, you must first understand where AWS services live.
Every AWS component has a **scope of control**, and that scope defines the size of its
potential blast radius.

Service Scope Legend

- **Global** → Internet-facing routing and acceleration

  (DNS resolution, anycast ingress, edge-based steering)

- **Regional** → Control-plane isolation with intra-region redundancy

  (Region-scoped configuration; AZ-redundant data planes)

- **Zonal** → AZ-local packet handling and fault containment

  (Subnets, ENIs, gateways, and inspection endpoints bound to one AZ)

Global services—such as **Amazon Route 53 (R53)**, **AWS Global Accelerator (AGA)**,
and **Amazon CloudFront**—operate from worldwide edge locations. Their **data planes**
are **anycasted** (the same address is announced from many edges), so users are steered
to the nearest healthy point of presence; their control planes, which decide policy
and interpret health, are centralized but built for high durability. These layers are the
Internet's front door: they make routing decisions in milliseconds, withdrawing a failing
region quickly. In networking terms, global scope equals immediate reach but a larger
control-plane blast radius if misused, which AWS mitigates with strong separation of
control and data (e.g., R53 health checkers and GA edge POPs continue serving health-
based decisions even if their management APIs are rate-limited).

Regional services—such as **Elastic Load Balancing (ALB/NLB/GWLB)**, **AWS
Transit Gateway (TGW)**, and **VPC Lattice**—are the backbone of day-to-day networking.
Each region owns its own control plane, so a capacity or configuration issue in
one region does not spill into another. Data planes span AZs in that region, giving
redundancy without geographic coupling. Here you build the fabric: TGW route tables
and attachments, GWLB for inspection, and Lattice for service-to-service trust.

Finally, **zonal constructs**—subnets, ENIs, NAT Gateways, and GWLB endpoints—
are the true packet handlers. They sit at fault-domain edges, enforcing which flows stay
local and which cross boundaries. A subnet lives entirely inside one AZ; a route table
associated with it determines egress. That simplicity is deliberate: it's what turns "one
AZ down" from a crisis into a localized condition your routing logic already knows how
to handle.

These scopes define not only blast radius but also cost boundaries because every
time traffic crosses one, it is metered.

Cost Awareness Callout: Hidden Network Costs in Resilient Designs

Cost awareness matters as much as topology.

Many resilient architectures fail not technically, but financially, because network
costs appear *only after traffic shifts under failure.*

Common surprises include:

- **Cross-AZ Data Transfer**: Traffic between Availability Zones is billed,
  even within the same region. Designs that rely heavily on cross-zone
  load balancing, shared inspection, or east–west chatty services can
  accumulate significant cost during steady state *and* failover.

- **Cross-Region Traffic**: Replication, health probing, and user failover
  across regions incur inter-region data transfer charges. These costs
  spike precisely when resilience mechanisms activate.

- **Centralized Inspection and Egress**: Routing all traffic through
  shared gateways or inspection fleets increases both blast radius *and*
  metered traffic, especially when paths cross AZ or region boundaries.

Resilient networking must therefore be **cost-aware by design**: keep traffic local
by default, cross boundaries deliberately, and size budgets for failure—not just for the
happy path.

Let's start from the most complex deployment—**multi-region**—then move to **multi-
AZ** inside a single region. There are **four fundamentals** we need to understand before
we even think of architecting multi-region; let's explore them so that with the scopes
defined, we can choose with intent. The next four fundamentals provide the decision
framework we'll use before drawing any lines between regions or zones.

Fundamental #1—Understanding the Requirements

Every multi-region journey begins with an uncomfortable question: **What are you
willing to pay to never be surprised again?**

That payment isn't just in currency—it's in latency, complexity, and operational
overhead. Before connecting a second region, define your **availability targets, Recovery
Time Objective (RTO)**, and **Recovery Point Objective (RPO)**. These numbers are
not paperwork; they are the contracts between your architecture and your business.
Additionally, decide whether your objectives can be met with **multi-AZ within one
region** (we'll return to this shortly) or whether you truly need multi-region.

From a networking standpoint, these objectives become physical parameters. **RTO**
defines how quickly you must redirect users to a new region—therefore, how fast your
Route 53 health checks or **Global Accelerator** traffic dials must detect and act. **RPO**
defines how much data divergence you can tolerate—therefore how you replicate over
the network: **synchronously, asynchronously, or not at all**. Latency SLOs determine
whether users can be served equally well from both regions or whether routing must
respect geography. Jurisdictional requirements—data residency, regulatory zones, and
compliance boundaries—often dictate region choice outright.

Every one of these decisions surfaces in the network. If your RTO is measured in
seconds, **Route 53 health-check intervals** or **AGA traffic-dial adjustments** become
your mitigation instruments. If your RPO approaches zero, replication demands
low-latency, consistent links—potentially **Direct Connect** (for hybrid) and carefully
engineered private backbone paths between regions. If your goal is both compliance and
speed, you may need **multi-region ingress** where each region serves local users through
its own ALB/NLB fleet, while **ARC (Application Recovery Controller)** and Route 53
coordinate safe promotion and withdrawal. Resilience isn't achieved by redundancy
alone; it's achieved by redundancy that matches requirements precisely—no more,
no less.

By articulating requirements first, you avoid designing by accident. Only after
you know what you must survive and how quickly you must recover can you decide
which network boundaries to reinforce and which to bridge. Everything else—data,
dependencies, operations—flows from that clarity.

*Next we will explore the second fundamental, understanding the data: why replication
is primarily a data challenge with a network consequence, and why synchronous dreams
often meet the speed of light. This will lead us into cross-region links, Transit Gateway
peering, and how data topology sets the stage for active-active versus standby models.*

Fundamental #2—Understanding the Data

Resilience is never stronger than the data that underpins it. When an outage happens, packets can be rerouted in milliseconds—but if the destination doesn't have the right data, the service is alive in name only. That's why, in multi-AZ and multi-region architectures, the network isn't merely a transport layer; it's the bloodstream that carries state. Designing how data moves, synchronizes, and ages across regions is the most critical—and the most technically demanding—part of building for resilience.

Synchronous replication is the gold standard of data integrity—and the most unforgiving constraint. In a synchronous system, every write must be acknowledged by multiple storage nodes (sometimes in different AZs) before commit; the **slowest acknowledgment sets your write latency**. Inside a region, with short, predictable fiber between AZs, this underpins patterns like **RDS Multi-AZ** and **Aurora's quorum writes across three AZs**. Across regions, the speed of light and WAN variance dominate; even on AWS's backbone, latency and jitter make cross-region synchronous writes impractical for most write-heavy systems.

That is why most global architectures lean on **asynchronous replication**. Writes are acknowledged locally and propagated later; the cost is **RPO > 0**. For many workloads, seconds or minutes of potential data loss are acceptable; for financial ledgers, they are not. Networking's job is to make replication **predictable and isolated**: separate sync/async traffic from user flows, size bandwidth for worst-case write surges, and, when needed, carry replication over **TGW inter-region peering** or private links so it never competes with customer traffic.

Not all "databases" behave the same. **Aurora Global Database** designates a **single primary write region** with read-only secondaries (fast failover, but asynchronous—non-zero RPO); **Amazon DynamoDB Global Tables** are **multi-region, multi-active**, allowing **writes in any region** with built-in conflict resolution (last-writer-wins) and eventual convergence. Your network and routing must reflect that: **active-active writes across regions require multi-writer-capable stores** or **application-level partitioning** to keep writes local.

This is the quiet appearance of the **CAP trade-off**: under network partitions or high latency, you choose availability (serve now, reconcile later) or strong consistency (wait for confirmation). In practice, most teams do **write-local/read-local** for latency and availability and replicate asynchronously for DR; where strong consistency is required,

378

they **contain writes to a primary region** and use global reads with controlled promotion on failover. The network enforces these choices by keeping replication paths explicit, measured, and separate from user paths.

Finally, remember that replication isn't just databases. **S3 Cross-Region Replication** and **EFS Replication** are asynchronous DR features; **Kinesis** or other log pipelines also ride the network. Treat replication networks as first-class citizens: private, metered, and monitored for throughput and **lag**. Only then does data resilience become operational resilience.

Fundamental #3—Understanding the Dependencies

No system operates alone. If data is the lifeblood of resilience, **dependencies** are its nervous system—they decide what moves with you when a region fails and what stays behind. Mapping these dependencies early prevents the discovery that your "redundant" stack still relies on a single region for identity, logging, or policy enforcement.

Let's begin with what you control. Most applications lean on three fabrics: a **service network** (or **VPC Lattice**) for workload-to-workload calls, a **routing backbone** (AWS **Transit Gateway**) to interconnect VPCs, and shared **inspection/egress** (often **GWLB** or NAT). Each has its own blast radius. **TGW and Lattice are regional**; with **TGW inter-region peering**, you get **explicit, non-transitive** paths between regions (packets cannot wander into places they don't belong). That explicitness—attachments and route tables you can point at—is why TGW is the backbone of multi-region safety.

Now extend the view upward to **global dependencies. IAM, AWS Organizations,** and **Route 53** operate at a global scope with extremely high availability, but their reach is universal. Mitigation is not duplication but **decoupling run-time from real-time control**: cache IAM tokens locally; keep DNS zones health-checked but relatively static; avoid orchestration that needs live global writes during failover. In other words, apply **static stability**: keep **data planes** serving even if a **control plane** stalls.

Interdependencies often hide in shared services: central logging stacks, security tooling, CI/CD runners, and monitoring collectors in one "utility" region. From a networking perspective, that's a silent single point of failure. Treat these like production: per-region replicas behind ALBs with Route 53 health checks and inter-region replication over controlled TGW peering or private endpoints. Don't let convenience become coupling.

At the perimeter, inspection deserves special attention. **GWLB** lets you "share" inspection safely: one fleet per region, one policy domain per region. If a region fails, traffic re-enters through that region's own inspection stack; it must not hairpin across regions to reuse another fleet (that simply relocates the bottleneck).

Dependencies also include telemetry. For resilience, **visibility must be regionally redundant**. Collect logs/metrics per region, replicate asynchronously to a global analytics account or third-party SIEM, and **observe Region A from Region B** so you don't ask a failed region for its own heartbeat.

Finally, remember that dependencies are as much about **control planes** as **data planes**. Every interconnect, endpoint, and load balancer has both. If your routing logic, inspection policies, or service registry rely on a single control plane, your fault domain is already larger than you think. In practice, **regionalize control, localize data, and use global routing only when it's stateless and trustworthy.**

Anti-Patterns That Undermine Multi-Region Resilience

Before moving into operational readiness, it is worth pausing at the dependency layer to surface a small set of architectural anti-patterns that repeatedly undermine otherwise sound multi-region designs. These failures are structural, not procedural: if regions are unintentionally coupled through shared services, data paths, or change mechanisms, no amount of operational discipline can restore true isolation.

- **Shared inspection or egress across regions**

  Routing traffic from one region through inspection, NAT, or security services hosted in another region creates hidden coupling. During a regional failure, traffic may hairpin across geographies or stall entirely, turning a localized outage into a cascading one. Inspection and egress must be region-local, even when policy is globally consistent.

- **Synchronous cross-region writes**

  Attempting to synchronously replicate application or database writes across regions couples availability to WAN latency and backbone stability. Even on private cloud backbones, speed-of-light delays and jitter make this pattern fragile and expensive. Cross-region replication should be asynchronous, with RPO explicitly accepted and managed.

- **Global CI/CD and configuration pipelines**

  Single pipelines, global parameter stores, or globally scoped feature flags that push changes to all regions simultaneously reintroduce shared fate at the worst possible moment—during change. Safe multi-region systems deploy and configure one region at a time, with explicit promotion and rollback boundaries.

These are not edge cases; they are the most common ways otherwise well-designed architectures lose their fault-domain isolation. Multi-region resilience only holds when inspection, data flow, and change control are explicitly bounded per region.

*Next, we'll turn to Fundamental #4—Operational Readiness—and examine how teams prepare, test, and safely operate these multi-region topologies in real life, using tools such as **AWS Application Recovery Controller (ARC)** to coordinate network failovers without turning resilience into chaos.*

Fundamental #4—Operational Readiness

I always say, **"architecture can only promise what operations can prove."** You can design the cleanest multi-region topology in the world, but if no one has practiced failing it over, it's still theory. Operational readiness is where diagrams meet muscle memory—where teams, automation, and monitoring learn how to behave when the unexpected becomes routine.

Readiness begins with the philosophy of change. Every release, every configuration update, and every network rule is a potential resilience event. Mature organizations deploy as they would fail over: **one region at a time**, with guardrails that prevent uncoordinated global rollout. A deployment that can take down both regions at once isn't a deployment—it's a disaster waiting for calendar time.

AWS provides scaffolding for safe change. **Route 53** health checks and **Global Accelerator** traffic dials let you shift users gradually instead of flipping a binary switch. A traffic dial at 10 percent is a rehearsal; at 50 percent, confidence under load; at 100 percent, a failover executed without panic. These are control-plane primitives that encode your ability to **mitigate** at a human pace.

Above them sits **AWS Application Recovery Controller (ARC)**. ARC doesn't run your workloads; it governs how and when you change their routing. It maintains **readiness checks** that confirm secondary-region capacity, health, and configuration before failover; it exposes **routing controls** integrated with R53/AGA; and it enforces

safety rules ("only promote B if A is impaired," "never send >60% traffic to a region under recovery"). This turns operational resilience from runbook instruction into policy, ensuring no single keystroke can cause global harm.

Testing is the other half of readiness. **If you don't test, you don't know.** Use controlled experiments—scheduled failovers, **Fault Injection Service (FIS)** drills, or zonal black-hole tests—to verify not only that traffic moves, but that it moves for the right reasons and **stops at the right boundaries**. These exercises validate **MTTD** and **MTTM** in the real world, turning theoretical metrics into lived experience. We will double-click on this in **Chapter 8**.

Finally, observability must match your architecture's shape. Collect metrics/logs **per region and per AZ**, replicate asynchronously, and monitor from **independent vantage points**. If Region A fails, Region B continues observing and alerting without relying on Region A's telemetry plane. CloudWatch, X-Ray, and third-party APMs are only as resilient as the network paths they depend on—treat monitoring as a production workload with its own RTO/RPO.

Operational readiness, then, isn't an end state—it's a habit. It's the confidence that every change, every drill, and every alarm already assumes failure and knows how to behave when it happens. Only when operations are predictable does the architecture become trustworthy.

With requirements, data, dependencies, and operations in hand, we can finally trace packet paths. Before proceeding, I want to leave you with a single sentence to reinforce the core lesson of this section.

Do not connect regions or AZs until requirements are defined, data replication limits are understood, dependencies are isolated, and operational failover can be executed independently per region.

We now move from decision-making to behavior on the wire, starting with the smallest physical fault domain (multi-AZ) and expanding outward to multi-region architectures.

Patterns on the Wire: From Multi-region to Multi-AZ

If the previous fundamental describes how people and processes uphold resilience, this one describes how packets obey it. On the wire, resilience expresses itself through patterns—architectural rhythms that determine how traffic enters, flows, and evacuates under stress. At this scale, the network is the boundary of both fault and recovery. We have discussed the fundamentals of multi-region architectures; now let's see **multi-AZ** and how they stack together.

Multi-AZ Within a Region

The same fundamentals compress neatly inside a single region: the distances shrink, but the logic does not. Multi-AZ design is the base layer of physical resilience. Every production VPC should span at least two AZs, with **independent subnets, route tables, and load-balancer nodes**. Ingress occurs through regional **ALBs or NLBs**, which distribute across AZ-local targets. Cross-zone load balancing, which we explored earlier, remains your tuning knob for coupling: enabling it trades perfect isolation for smoother utilization (**ALB is on by default; NLB is off by default**). The network's responsibility is to make a zonal failure uneventful—connections drain, health checks withdraw unhealthy nodes, and surviving AZs continue seamlessly. Services such as **RDS Multi-AZ**, **Aurora clusters**, and **EKS node groups** embody this pattern with **synchronous cross-AZ durability** or replica placement.

A resilient multi-AZ network is defined by three behaviors:

- **Subnets never straddle zones.**

- **Route tables never imply transitivity between zones except through controlled load balancers.**

- **Each zone has enough headroom to absorb the other's load.**

This last point—capacity planning—is the one most often neglected. If both zones run at **70%** utilization, losing one means the survivor must carry **140%** of steady-state demand; no amount of clever routing will save you.

Multi-region Resilience

We begin at the continental scale, where latency, sovereignty, and backbone behavior decide what resilience can mean in practice. Here distances are no longer microseconds but tens of milliseconds; risks include jurisdictional boundaries, backbone events, and sovereign compliance zones. Here, **routing becomes the language of resilience. Route 53** provides policy-driven DNS—weighted, latency-based, or health-checked—and can remove a region's record within seconds when health fails. **Global Accelerator** pushes that logic to the edge with **anycast IPs** and **per-region traffic dials**, allowing gradual shifts of real-time flow without DNS propagation delay. Underneath, **Transit Gateway inter-region peering** offers **private, non-transitive** connectivity for replication or control traffic that must traverse regions but stay off the public internet.

This is where we see the spectrum of **Disaster Recovery (DR) models** through a networking lens.

- **Backup-and-Restore**: The network is dark until invoked: simple but slow; RTO in hours.

- **Pilot Light**: Critical data replicated and networking pre-provisioned but dormant; failover ignites compute and opens ingress.

- **Warm Standby**: Partial capacity already running; network live at low load; **ARC/R53** promotion makes it primary.

- **Hot Standby:** Near-full capacity active, user traffic normally routed elsewhere.

- **Active-Active:** Both regions serve continuously; the network must provide **symmetric ingress**, **consistent health models**, and **explicit isolation for replication**. Active-active is not a toggle; it's a way of living, and unless your data layer supports multi-writer (e.g., **DynamoDB Global Tables**), you'll need **write partitioning** or a designated write region (e.g., **Aurora Global Database** with promotion on failover).

Networking is the through-line across all of these models. It decides whether replication can keep up, whether DNS/GA failover actually reaches the healthy region, and whether an inspection fleet in one region becomes the bottleneck for all. Each step up the DR ladder increases cost and complexity but shortens the pain curve when things go wrong. Your architecture's position on that ladder should be set by requirement, not ego.

Each posture, from backup-and-restore to active-active, ultimately depends on the same orchestration loop beneath: health detection, control-plane coordination, and data-plane redirection.

Figure 6-11 shows the continuous feedback system of resilient routing. Regional health probes feed the Global Accelerator at the edge, which aggregates signals and reports to the Application Recovery Controller (ARC). ARC evaluates readiness and safety rules before Route 53 updates routing policy. Together, Route 53 and GA coordinate control-plane decisions while the regional data planes enforce them. The loop—detect, mitigate, recover—runs continuously, ensuring user traffic always flows toward healthy regions without manual intervention.

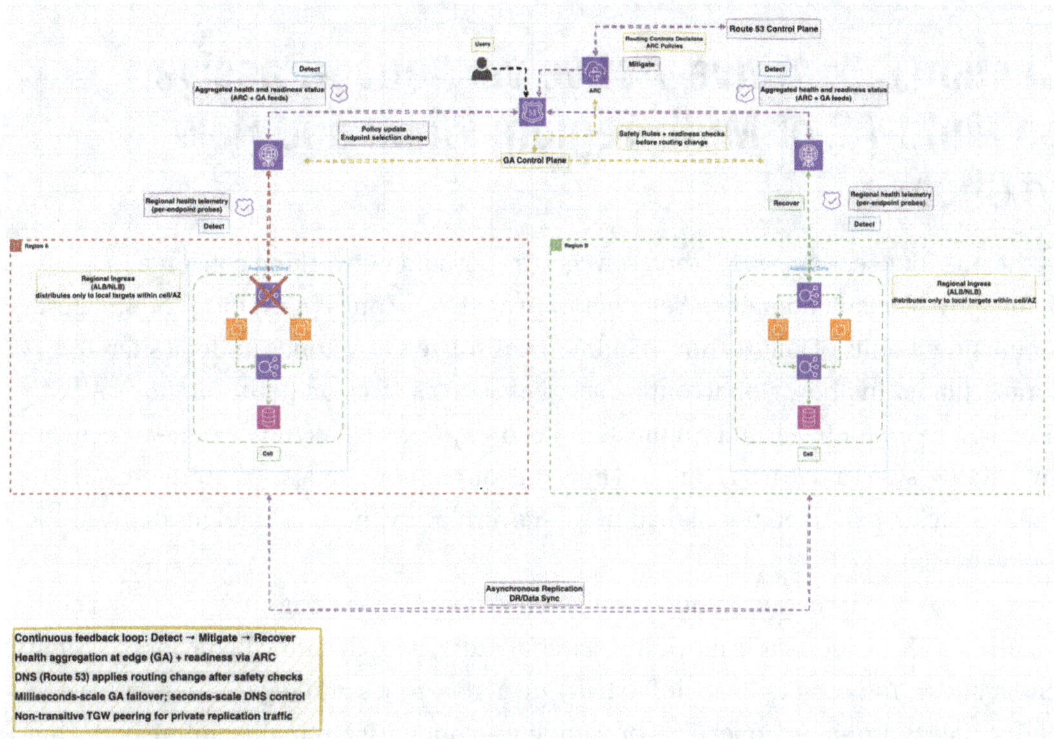

Figure 6-11. *Multi-region Control Loop*

The line between zones and regions is one of scale, not philosophy. The principles remain the same: isolate, replicate, detect, and mitigate. At the zonal scale, you fight hardware; at the regional scale, you fight geography. In both, networking is the fabric that either contains the blast or amplifies it.

To reinforce the core idea of this section, I'll leave you with a single rule of thumb:

Move to multi-region only when the requirements truly demand it—such as region-level continuity, regulatory or data-sovereignty constraints, or latency objectives combined with strict RTO/RPO—and only after the fundamentals are proven: requirements are explicit, the data replication model and its latency/consistency limits are understood and accepted, dependencies are bounded so regions do not share fate, and operational readiness demonstrates that failover can be executed safely and repeatedly.

In the next section, we'll synthesize these ideas into the practical question every architect must answer: When should an environment operate in active-active versus active-passive mode? We will explore that decision through the lens of networking topology, routing intent, and the trade-offs between cost, complexity, and true resilience.

Section 6.5: Active-Active vs. Active-Passive on Multi-AZ or Multi-region: When and How to Choose

In the previous section, we learned how geography and networking converge to define physical fault domains. We saw how Availability Zones (AZs) form the smallest independent units of failure, how regions encapsulate those zones under a shared control plane, and how global routing services such as Amazon Route 53 (R53), AWS Global Accelerator (GA), and Application Recovery Controller (ARC) connect them into an adaptive system. We also explored how the four fundamentals—requirements, data, dependencies, and operational readiness—govern every multi-AZ and multi-region design.

Now we turn from *how to build* resilience to *how to operate it.*

Resilience is not a static property of architecture; it's a dynamic behavior of systems under stress. You can duplicate infrastructure across zones and regions, but until you define how those sites cooperate—or compete—your design remains unfinished. That cooperation model is the real topic of this section.

Active-active and active-passive are not marketing labels; they're operational philosophies that determine how your network behaves minute by minute. They decide whether traffic is balanced or failover, whether replication is continuous or staged, and whether human intervention is required when trouble appears. In other words, they define whether your system treats failure as an event or as a routine condition.

But before we choose between them, we must first decide *where* our boundaries lie. The question every architect faces isn't only "active or passive?"—it's also "multi-AZ or multi-region?" These two axes together determine the true scope of fault isolation and recovery.

Choosing the Right Scale: Multi-AZ or Multi-region

The question is never "Do we want more availability?"—it's **where** you buy it and **how** your network will uphold it when physics and failure arrive at the same time. Multi-Availability Zone (Multi-AZ) architectures harden you inside one region; multi-region architectures defend you from the region itself. The craft is knowing which tier your *actual* risks and *actual* data flows demand.

Before we explore each option in detail, it helps to make the decision space explicit. **Table 6-5 summarizes a practical decision path: workload tier ➤ required failure scope ➤ recommended scale and operating stance, with the minimum network and data assumptions that must hold.**

Table 6-5. *Resilience Decision Summary by Workload Tier*

Workload Tier	Credible Failure to Survive	Recommended Scale	Typical Stance
Non-critical / internal	Instance or small component failure	Single Region (Multi-AZ optional)	Active-passive
Customer-facing (standard)	Availability Zone impairment	Single Region, Multi-AZ	Active-active across AZs
Mission-critical	Regional outage or isolation	Multi-Region	Active-passive (pilot light / warm / hot)
Mission-critical / Global / latency- or sovereignty-driven	Regional outage plus latency or residency constraints	Multi-Region	Active-active (read-local / partitioned writes)

With this decision framing in place, we can now examine how multi-AZ and multi-region patterns behave on the wire and what they require from data, routing, and operations.

Multi-AZ as the default posture. Within a region, AWS gives you physically separate facilities—Availability Zones (AZs)—joined by low-latency, high-bandwidth fiber. This is where most production workloads should start and often finish: subnets scoped to individual AZs, independent capacity in each zone, and regional load balancers that fan traffic across zonal nodes. Application Load Balancer (ALB) enables cross-zone distribution by default; Network Load Balancer (NLB) is zonal by default and lets you enable cross-zone when you prefer smoother utilization over strict zonal independence. The control plane is regional; the data plane runs per-AZ nodes, so an impaired zone sheds capacity without dragging its neighbors down. This is not fashion; it's table-stakes resilience and a well-architected best practice to deploy across multiple AZs.

Multi-AZ shines when your **RTO (Recovery Time Objective)** is seconds to minutes and your **RPO (Recovery Point Objective)** is near-zero inside the region, because synchronous durability is realistic at sub-millisecond latencies. This is precisely how regional services achieve their SLAs: Amazon RDS Multi-AZ maintains a synchronous standby in another AZ; Amazon Aurora writes to multiple storage nodes across three AZs for quorum; Amazon EFS Standard stores data redundantly across AZs. In other words, if your failure model is "lose a data center, not a continent," Multi-AZ gives you availability with minimal replication pain and no cross-region choreography.

But **not all applications need the same tier**. Treat scale as a classification problem, not a blanket policy. Mission-critical customer-facing systems that drive revenue or safety justify broader perimeters; internal analytics or batch jobs often don't. Put another way: *tiers first, topology second*. Multi-AZ is the sensible default for most tiers; reserve broader perimeters for the few that truly require them. (We'll use this tiering again when we choose active-active versus active-passive later in the section.)

Where Multi-AZ stops paying the bills. On October 19–20, 2025, a significant service disruption in AWS's US-EAST-1 region originated from a latent defect in the **DynamoDB DNS management system**, which caused the regional DynamoDB endpoint to become unreachable and triggered cascading errors in dependent services across that region. Even well-architected Multi-AZ designs within a single region experienced impact because the failure affected a core regional service and related subsystems. Teams with true multi-region ingress and replicated state, on the other hand, were able to evacuate traffic and continue serving users by directing requests to healthy regions. (source: `https://aws.amazon.com/message/101925/`).

The lesson is not to fear rare events, but to match your resilience perimeter to the credible failure domain: Multi-AZ covers zonal faults; only multi-region can cover region-wide impairments.

A necessary counterpoint is that many systems were correctly designed to absorb the kinds of failures they planned for—zonally scoped disruptions—without needing multi-region architecture. For workloads whose primary failure model is Availability Zone faults, Multi-AZ deployments do exactly what they promise: survive isolated hardware, network, or power issues without cascading failures. The October 2025 incident was a *regional* control-plane and DNS-level event that overwhelmed even well-engineered Multi-AZ stacks because it touched services and orchestration logic shared across the region. That does not invalidate Multi-AZ resilience for zonal risk—it reinforces that multi-region designs are appropriate *only when the credible failure includes regional or provider-wide conditions*, and that you should match your perimeter to the failure domain you need to survive.

Multi-region when geography is part of the risk. If the outage you fear *is the region itself*—whether from provider incidents, jurisdictional isolation, or backbone events—you need two things your network must deliver: **a second place to land** and **the right data when you land**. At the edge, Amazon Route 53 (policy-based DNS) and AWS Global Accelerator (anycast IP ingress with traffic dials) give you steering that respects health and geography; in the middle, Transit Gateway (TGW) inter-region peering carries replication and control traffic privately and non-transitively; at the top, AWS Application Recovery Controller (ARC) wraps failover in readiness checks and safety rules so promotion is controlled and reversible. This is not "extra availability"; it's **business continuity** across distance.

Data is the fulcrum. Inside a region, synchronous replication is practical; across regions, **the speed of light** and **WAN variance** force you to pick your consistency model. Many teams adopt **write-local/read-local** with **asynchronous** cross-region replication and deliberate promotion on failover (Aurora Global Database: single-writer with fast regional promotion; DynamoDB Global Tables: multi-region writes with conflict resolution). Your network then enforces the discipline: edge routing keeps users near their write region; east–west paths are explicit and metered; replication traffic is separated from user flows and never hairpins through inspection or shared "utility" VPCs in another region. If your data is single-writer, your "active-active" is really active for reads and passive for writes; if your data layer supports multi-writer, your network must partition traffic so each write lands in its rightful shard, or you'll trade downtime for distributed chaos.

So how do you *decide* the scale, without platitudes? Start with the outage you are buying down and trace it **on the wire:**

- If your credible failures are **zonal** (power, cooling, local network), Multi-AZ gives you synchronous durability, automatic fail-in-place via the regional load balancers, and simple operations. You still operate one region and one control plane, and your replication looks like short, predictable ACK paths between AZs. (ALB is cross-zone on by default; NLB is zonal by default, opting in to cross-zone based on the coupling you want.)

- If your credible failures are **regional** (provider incident, sovereign boundaries, major backbone disruption), multi-region gives you a second ingress, independent control planes, and replication lanes that survive a regional partition. Your edge must steer away quickly (Route 53 or Global Accelerator), your data model must tolerate the distance (asynchronous most of the time), and your operations must *practice* the move with guardrails (ARC).

Notice what isn't said: there's no universal "always go multi-region." The October 2025 incident proved that **some** systems needed it to remain up; it did not prove that **every** system warrants the cost, latency, and complexity. The mature answer is a **tiered scale**: Multi-AZ everywhere that is customer-facing or stateful in steady state; multi-region for the subset where a regional dependency is a business risk you're unwilling to carry. And when you do go multi-region, choose your data stance with eyes open: asynchronous plus promotion for most transactional systems; multi-writer only when your conflict semantics and partitioned routing are truly ready for it.

With scale chosen, we can finally talk about **stance**. Given your perimeter—Multi-AZ or multi-region—do you operate *both sides* all the time (active-active), or keep one ready in reserve (active-passive)? In the next subsections we'll translate that choice into concrete networking behavior at the edge (Route 53 vs. Global Accelerator), in the region (ALB/NLB, TGW, GWLB, Lattice), and across regions (TGW inter-region peering), so the packets do the right thing automatically when the world does the wrong thing.

Understanding Operational Stances: From Active-Passive to Active-Active

By now we've chosen the **scale** of failure we're willing to tolerate—Multi-AZ for availability inside a region, multi-region when geography itself is part of the risk. What remains is the **stance**: how those fault domains behave while the system is healthy and how they react when one side falters. Stance is observable "on the wire." You can see it at the edge in how names resolve and IPs are announced; you can see it inside the region at the load balancer; you can see it between regions in the shape of replication lanes. The labels (active-passive, active-active) only matter insofar as they predict those packet paths.

Active-passive is the simplest to recognize. One site carries users; the other carries **readiness**. At the edge, the passive site is visible but not selected—DNS weights at zero or a Global Accelerator traffic dial set to idle. Inside each region, the network is "lit but quiet": per-region ingress exists, east–west routing is attached and tested, inspection is local to the region, and data replication flows continuously, but no user traffic is steered there yet. When impairment hits the active site, the edge changes its mind and the passive site becomes primary. The virtue of this stance is that writes stay local and consistent under normal conditions; the price is choreography at the moment of promotion. Operationally, it works best when promotion is governed by pre-agreed rules—readiness checks, capacity assertions, and a single, safe switch for traffic—rather than a collection of human steps.

Active-active (read-local / write-local) keeps both sites in play for users all the time, while protecting mutable state by pinning writes to their "home." At the edge, latency-based routing or anycast ingress keeps users near their nearest healthy region; inside each region, the load balancer terminates connections for that region's users; between regions, replication is deliberate and asynchronous so the system converges without stalling. This stance turns most incidents into partial events: losing a region withdraws its edge presence, and its users shift to the survivor, while the write owner either promotes (if single-writer) or the application partitions writes intentionally by tenant or geography. The discipline is to **prevent write leakage across regions**—no well-meaning client retries that hop the ocean; no background tasks that "help" by writing in both places. Reads can be global; writes must be local by design.

Active-active (multi-writer) is a different thing. Both sites accept writes, either because the data layer natively supports it or because the application is partitioned so each write lands in its rightful shard. On the network, this looks like symmetry: the edge can land any tenant in either region, but the routing logic (often at Layer 7) ensures tenant A's writes always reach the partition that owns tenant A. East-west links exist for replication and conflict resolution, not for live user flows. The benefit is obvious—no promotion needed, no single write home—but so is the cost: your blast radius now includes conflict semantics and partition boundaries. If you cannot test and observe those boundaries, you have distributed entropy, not resilience.

These stances are not marketing choices; they are traffic patterns with operational consequences. In active-passive, your confidence comes from **promotion discipline**. In read-local active-active, it comes from **routing locality** and **replication headroom**. In multi-writer active-active, it comes from **partition-aware routing** and **conflict control**. In every case, the control plane declares intent, and the data plane enforces it: edge steering decides *where* a user goes, regional ingress decides *how* they enter, and east–west routes decide *what* can cross and at what cost.

If all of that feels abstract, there is a simple way to sanity-check your choice before you reach for diagrams or tooling: start with how your data accepts writes.

A practical routing heuristic emerges:

Single-writer data model ➤ Active-passive or read-local active-active

Writes are pinned to one region; the network enforces locality, and promotion is explicit.

Multi-writer data model ➤ Partition-aware active-active only

Writes may occur in multiple regions, but routing must enforce ownership and conflict semantics.

If writes cannot be safely accepted in more than one place, the network must prevent them from ever going there. If writes can occur anywhere, the network must make ownership explicit.

With the shapes clear, we can make the choice repeatable. The next subsection distills the four fundamentals from Section 6.4 into a decision framework—requirements, data, network, and operations—that lets you pick a stance for each application tier and prove it with the traffic it produces.

Decision Framework: Requirements ➤ Data ➤ Network ➤ Operations

Choosing between active-passive and active-active is never a matter of taste; it's an engineering decision that starts with *requirements* and ends with *operations*. Every failure you defend against consumes budget, bandwidth, and human attention, so the right choice is the one that meets objectives precisely—no looser, no tighter. The path is fourfold: **requirements**, **data**, **network**, and **operations.**

Step 1—Start with Requirements

All resilience design starts with a contract. What promises must the system keep when things break? Recovery Time Objective (RTO), Recovery Point Objective (RPO), and Service Level Objectives (SLOs) for latency and availability define that contract.

If your RTO lives in seconds and your RPO is effectively zero *within a region*, multi-AZ active-passive (or evenly balanced active-active reads) may satisfy both—synchronous durability across zones supports this. When the promise shifts to "never dark anywhere," multi-region ingress and evacuation become essential.

Constraints turn abstractions into geography: residency, sovereignty, or contractual uptime tiers will often dictate region choices before you debate stance. You cannot pick a stance until you know which promises you are legally and commercially bound to keep—and for which *application tiers*. (Not every workload deserves the same perimeter; tier them first, design second.)

Step 2—Shape the Data Model

Resilience collapses when data disagrees with itself. Once objectives are clear, consider how state lives and moves.

- **Single-writer systems** (e.g., an Aurora primary with cross-region replicas) naturally favor active-passive or *read-local/write-local* active-active. The writer region is authoritative; secondaries lag by milliseconds to seconds. Promotion changes *who* writes—not *how* users connect.

- **Multi-writer systems** (e.g., DynamoDB Global Tables) accept concurrent writes in multiple regions but introduce conflict semantics (last-writer-wins or application reconciliation). The network must route each write deterministically to its owning partition or region; otherwise you trade downtime for distributed inconsistency.

- **Stateless layers**: Edge caches, idempotent APIs—comfortably run active-active, provided configuration and session state are externalized.

Distance sets the shape of truth. Inside a region, synchronous replication (Multi-AZ) is feasible and keeps RPO ~ 0. Across regions, the speed of light and WAN variance push you to asynchronous replication and deliberate promotion. Most real-world stacks land here: **write locally for correctness, replicate for continuity, and read wherever it's fast**.

Step 3—Design the Network to Match the Data

Once the data topology is chosen, networking becomes the enforcement layer that keeps it honest.

At the **edge**, decide how users enter:

- **Amazon Route 53** provides DNS steering (weighted, latency, or failover policies).

- **AWS Global Accelerator** provides anycast IPs with per-region traffic dials, useful when client DNS caching would slow your reaction or when fixed IPs are required.

Inside each region, **Elastic Load Balancing** terminates and spreads flows across AZs (Application Load Balancer (ALB) cross-zone is on by default; Network Load Balancer (NLB) is off by default and opt-in when you prefer utilization smoothing over strict zonal independence). **AWS Transit Gateway (TGW)** provides the routing backbone between VPCs; **Gateway Load Balancer (GWLB)** inserts per-region inspection without shared fate; **VPC Lattice** constrains service-to-service calls by identity and policy rather than IP alone.

Between regions, use **TGW inter-region peering** (non-transitive, private) or other private backbone paths for replication and control traffic. Keep these lanes explicit and narrow: enough to replicate and operate, never so broad that production requests can "leak" sideways during stress.

Two practical guardrails make designs behave:

1. If your data layer is single-writer, **enforce write locality**—by tenant token, geography, or partition key—so retries can't wander into the wrong region.

2. If your data layer is multi-writer, **make partition ownership visible in routing**—the path for a write must point to the shard that owns it. Either way, the network expresses your consistency rules as packet motion.

Step 4—Operationalize the Stance

Architecture without practiced operations is fantasy. Once requirements, data, and network align, operations close the loop.

- **Automation of Change:** Deploy one fault domain at a time (cell, AZ, or region). Pipelines should prevent simultaneous rollout across domains; a single bad push must remain a local story.

- **Readiness and Safety: AWS Application Recovery Controller (ARC)** codifies pre-checks (capacity, health, configuration) and enforces safety rules so failover and promotion are policy-driven instead of adrenaline-driven.

- **Observation That Mirrors Topology:** Build per-AZ and per-region dashboards and alarms; replicate logs and metrics asynchronously; watch replication lag, steering decisions, and health propagation— not just CPU and memory.

- **Exercises:** Light drills verify mean-time-to-detect (MTTD) and mean-time-to-recover (MTTR); deeper resilience testing and chaos engineering practices will follow in Chapter 8. The goal isn't drama; it's muscle memory.

Bringing It Together

Here's the mental model that makes the choice obvious: **your data defines the truth; the network enforces that truth; operations prove it holds under change.** Start with the promises (RTO/RPO/latency); choose how truth is stored (single-writer, multi-writer, or stateless); engineer ingress and east–west paths that *only* allow traffic consistent with that truth; then practice until fail-over looks like a routine. Follow that sequence, and the stance—multi-AZ or multi-region, active-passive or active-active—stops being a debate. It becomes the only design that matches the physics of your data and the promises of your business.

Active-Passive Done Right

The active-passive stance is the quiet workhorse of cloud resilience. It is simple in intent—one environment serves traffic, another waits in reserve—but surprisingly intricate in execution. Done well, it delivers predictable failover with minimal cost. Done poorly, it becomes a "disaster-recovery mirage": pretty diagrams, empty capacity, and a cut-over that fails when it's most needed.

An effective active-passive architecture behaves as though both regions or Availability Zones (AZs) are live all the time, even if only one is serving users. The secret lies in keeping *the network warm, the data current,* and *the control plane safe.*

Keeping the Network Warm

The passive site must be dark to users but bright to the infrastructure. That means all networking components—Virtual Private Clouds (VPCs), subnets, route tables, Transit Gateway (TGW) attachments, and Gateway Load Balancer (GWLB) endpoints—exist and are operational before a failover.

At the edge, two mechanisms express which region should serve traffic:

- Amazon Route 53 declares *routing intent* through DNS policies, selecting regions for new connections based on health and policy.

- AWS Global Accelerator enforces that intent *in real time* through traffic dials, shifting live flows within seconds without relying on DNS cache expiry.

Internally, each region keeps its own **regional Application Load Balancer (ALB)** or **Network Load Balancer (NLB)** nodes live, cross-zonal, and health-checked. **Cross-zone load balancing** remains on for ALB by default and off for NLB unless you opt in, so the zonal data planes fail independently even when the control plane is regional. This ensures that when the secondary region becomes active, its internal routing is already known to be good; only the edge needs to redirect users.

Isolation is equally critical: never share inspection fleets or egress appliances across regions. **GWLB** makes this easy—deploy one inspection VPC per region, attach both production and standby through region-local endpoints, and encapsulate traffic with GENEVE. If one inspection fleet falters, only that region's traffic feels it; the other region remains untouched.

Keeping the Data Current

Replication determines whether failover is real recovery or an illusion. Inside a region, synchronous replication across AZs (e.g., Amazon RDS Multi-AZ or Aurora storage quorum) guarantees no data loss. Across regions, asynchronous replication (Aurora Global Database, DynamoDB Global Tables, S3 Cross-Region Replication, or EFS Replication) keeps the passive site close to current.

The practical discipline is *segregation of lanes*: replication traffic must flow on its own paths—Transit Gateway inter-region peering or private backbone links—so it cannot congest user flows during crisis. Monitor replication lag as a first-class metric, not an afterthought. A passive region with stale data is not passive; it is poisoned.

Where your data layer supports *promotion*, practice it. In **Aurora Global Database**, the read-only cluster can promote in under a minute once the writer region is marked unhealthy. **ARC (Application Recovery Controller)** readiness checks can confirm the secondary's capacity, schema alignment, and endpoint health before that promotion flag is flipped. If readiness fails, ARC refuses the switch—a small act that prevents a small outage from turning into a global one.

Keeping the Control Plane Safe

A common mistake is to manage both regions through a single, globally scoped pipeline or deployment role. The instant you deploy simultaneously to both sides, you lose your redundancy.

Each region must have its own release guardrails, IAM roles, and operational credentials. **Static stability**—the ability of the data plane to serve traffic even when the control plane is unavailable—should be non-negotiable.

ARC's **routing controls** formalize this safety. You can codify policies such as *"only promote if Region A is impaired"* or *"never exceed 60% of total traffic to a region under recovery."* Those policies live outside the normal deployment flow, giving operations a trusted, low-risk path to make routing decisions without touching production infrastructure.

When Promotion Happens

During an event, the sequence should read like choreography, not improvisation:

Detection. Route 53 and GA health checks mark the primary as unhealthy.

1. **Validation:** ARC confirms secondary readiness; if checks pass, its routing controls activate.

2. **Promotion:** R53 begins returning the secondary's records; GA raises its traffic dial.

3. **Steady state:** Users reconnect; replication reverses direction so new writes travel back to the now-active region.

The goal is that this sequence runs the same way during a drill and a disaster.

When executed correctly, end-user sessions experience a brief reconnection; the business experiences continuity.

In AWS terminology, *active-passive* can take several shapes depending on how "warm" the standby is. A **pilot light** pattern keeps only the minimal critical resources—databases, configuration, and replication—continuously running, while application servers and routing components are launched only during failover. It minimizes cost but adds minutes to RTO because capacity must be started and scaled. A **warm standby** keeps a smaller-sized version of the full stack operating in the secondary region; replication and health checks stay live, but traffic is minimal until promotion. Failover is faster since the infrastructure already exists. A **hot standby** is almost a mirror of the primary: full capacity, current data, and pre-validated routing, but idle user flow until cutover. All three patterns are *active-passive* at heart—they serve one active region—but they trade cost for RTO and operational readiness. Networking best practices remain the same across them: pre-provisioned ingress (Route 53 or Global Accelerator), live replication paths (TGW or Direct Connect), and independent per-region control so the secondary can light up without orchestration bottlenecks.

Trade-Offs and Evolution

Active-passive offers simplicity and predictable cost—one live region, one standby—but its reliability is bounded by the fidelity of its drills. RTOs rarely reach zero because even automated promotions take minutes to validate and redirect. In return, you gain strong consistency and operational focus; all writes flow to a single source of truth.

Many organizations mature naturally toward read-local active-active: once replication is proven and monitored, they begin serving read traffic from both regions while keeping writes local. This evolution preserves the same design tenets—warm networks, current data, controlled routing—but turns standby capacity into live utility instead of idle insurance.

In Figure 6-12, the active region serves user traffic through its own Elastic Load Balancer and inspection path, while the passive region mirrors infrastructure and data but remains idle under normal conditions. Route 53 and Application Recovery Controller (ARC) govern failover: ARC verifies readiness before Route 53 promotes the standby region. Replication flows privately over non-transitive Transit Gateway peering, maintaining data consistency without shared fate. When failover is triggered, Route 53 redirects user traffic to the healthy region within minutes, preserving control-plane safety and data-plane independence.

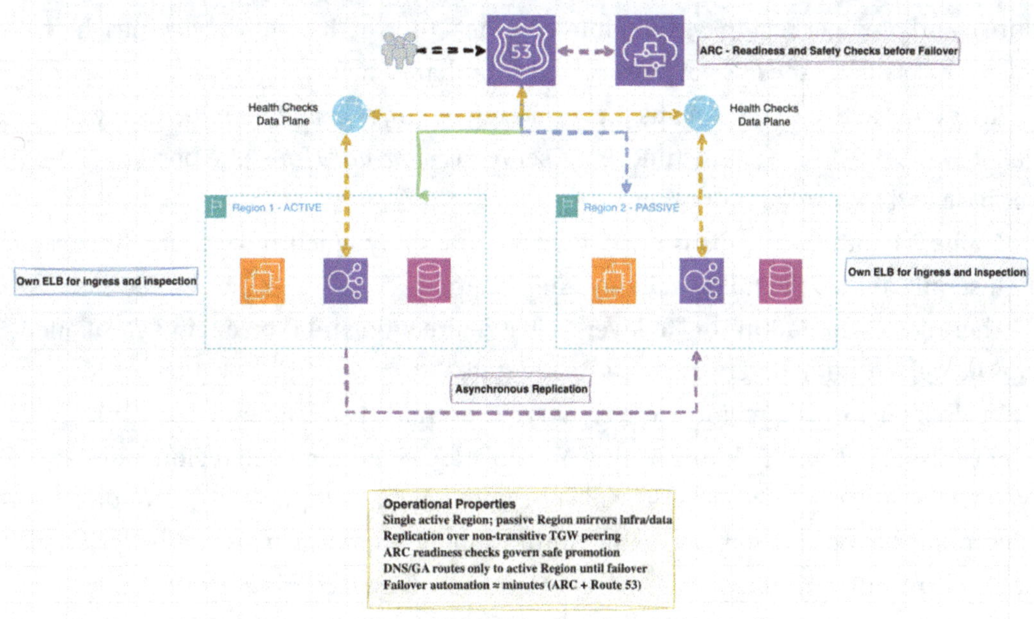

Figure 6-12. *Active-Passive Architecture on AWS*

Active-Active: Resilience in Motion

Active-active architectures are often portrayed as the holy grail of resilience—but in truth, they're a specialized tool, not a universal prescription.

They are the most complex, costly, and operationally demanding way to achieve fault tolerance, and for most workloads, they are unnecessary.

In my experience, I would recommend building multi-region active-active systems only when specific requirements make them unavoidable: **ultra-low latency for a globally distributed user base, strict data sovereignty or regulatory constraints, and mission-critical availability targets where even brief downtime is unacceptable.**

If none of these apply, a well-architected **multi-AZ or active-passive** setup delivers equivalent resilience at a fraction of the cost and complexity.

But when they do apply—when a system must serve millions of users across continents, maintain in-region data storage to meet privacy laws, or survive the loss of an entire cloud provider region without interruption—then active-active becomes the only pattern that satisfies the laws of physics and compliance alike.

At its core, active-active means that every region (or, at a smaller scale, every Availability Zone) is live all the time: each serves as a *primary* for some portion of the user base and a *secondary* for others.

Traffic is continuously distributed, data is continually synchronized, and both sides can instantly absorb the full load if the other falters.

There's no "promotion" or "failover"—just redirection and rebalancing. Resilience stops being a reaction and becomes a steady state.

In Figure 6-13, both regions actively serve user traffic using latency-based or weighted routing through Route 53 or AWS Global Accelerator. Each region maintains its own ingress and inspection layers, while bi-directional data replication keeps databases synchronized in near-real time—using Aurora Global Database or DynamoDB Global Tables as examples. Application Recovery Controller (ARC) continuously validates readiness and safety before any routing changes are applied. Because both regions are live, failover becomes merely traffic rebalancing; resilience operates as a steady state rather than a reaction.

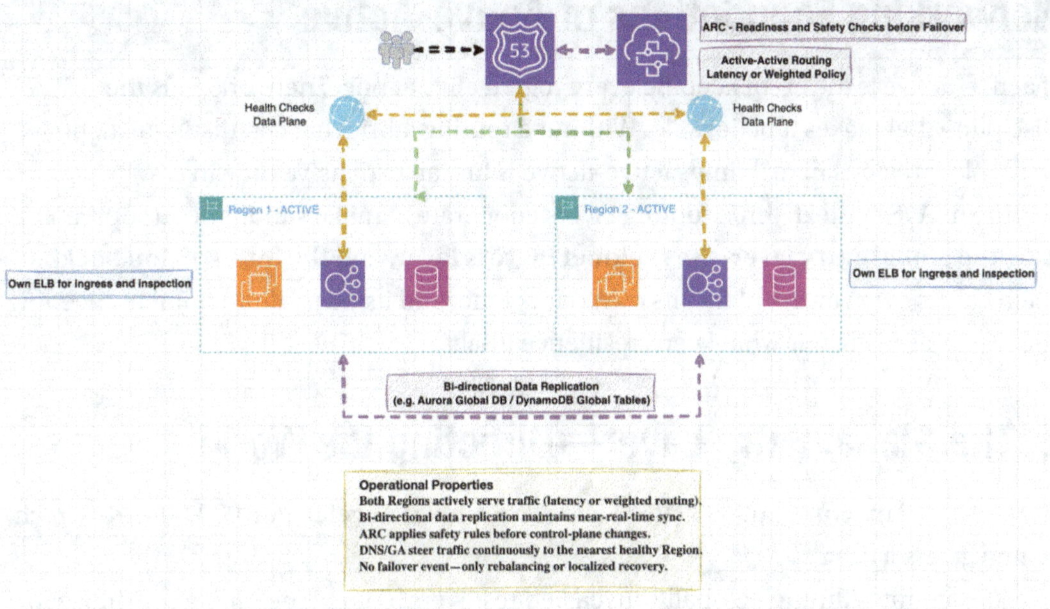

Figure 6-13. *Active-Active Architecture on AWS*

This pattern powers some of AWS's own global services—Amazon Route 53, CloudFront, and DynamoDB Global Tables all operate active-active across multiple regions—but adopting it for your workload means embracing operational maturity.

Each region must carry complete copies of compute, data, networking, and inspection stacks.

Each control plane must act autonomously but report its health truthfully through global services like AWS Global Accelerator (GA), Route 53, and Application Recovery Controller (ARC).

Each routing decision must be explicit, never implicit, so that user flows remain local until the network decides otherwise. Sounds complicated? It is—because it has to be

The payoff, when justified, is profound. Active-active architectures deliver the fastest user experience, eliminate the operational uncertainty of failover, and make large-scale recovery instantaneous.

But, like I mentioned, they come with sharp edges: data consistency challenges, coordination complexity, and relentless operational vigilance.

They are for the few systems where downtime has a measurable business or most importantly, human cost—trading simplicity for certainty and safety.

Networking Foundations of Active-Active

If active-active is the art of keeping every region alive at once, networking is the discipline that makes it believable. Without a routing fabric that can distinguish, prefer, and isolate regions in real time, active-active is just an expensive drawing.

In an AWS context, three routing layers cooperate to make simultaneous operation safe: **the global entry layer**, **the regional ingress layer**, and **the inter-region backbone**. Each has its own control plane, its own data plane, and its own failure domain. Keeping those planes distinct is what keeps resilience intact.

1. The Global Entry Layer—Directing the World

At the edge, **Amazon Route 53 (R53)** and **AWS Global Accelerator (GA)** decide which region greets a user.

R53 operates through globally anycasted resolvers (data plane) and a regionalized control plane, currently anchored in *us-east-1*. When you configure **latency-based routing**, users automatically resolve to the region with the lowest observed network latency. **Weighted routing** lets you tune global load distribution deliberately, using Route 53 health checks as the guardrails. Because health data is served from the resolvers themselves, DNS continues to function even if the management API or the primary control plane is unreachable. That property—data-plane autonomy—is the first requirement of safe global routing.

GA extends that autonomy further. Instead of relying on DNS caching and TTLs, GA advertises **anycast IPs** from AWS edge Points of Presence (POPs) worldwide. Traffic is steered dynamically over the AWS backbone to the closest healthy endpoint group— each mapped to a region and its load balancer. When one region degrades, GA's health checks detect it within seconds and redirect sessions, often before the user even retries a connection. Because GA's data plane is global but its control plane is regional and isolated, a control failure in one region cannot interrupt delivery elsewhere.

Together, R53 and GA provide global intent: "this user ➤ that region ➤ those endpoints." Their role is steering, not serving. They make geography and health part of the routing equation so that latency and resilience trade-offs can be expressed directly in network behavior.

2. The Regional Ingress Layer—Owning Traffic Locally

Once traffic reaches a region, **regional load balancers** take over.

Every active-active region runs its own **Application Load Balancer (ALB)** and/or **Network Load Balancer (NLB)** fleet. ALB's cross-zone load balancing is enabled by default, distributing evenly across Availability Zones while preserving independent zonal data planes; NLB's cross-zone feature is disabled by default and should be enabled only when you need smoother utilization at the expense of strict zone isolation. Both are regional constructs—each region's control plane deploys and manages its own balancers, so a configuration issue in eu-west-1 cannot disable ingress in us-east-1.

Behind the load balancers, VPC subnets, route tables, and **Gateway Load Balancers (GWLB)** enforce per-region fault containment. Inspection fleets sit in their own VPCs, reachable through GWLB endpoints. Traffic from application VPCs enters through these endpoints, is encapsulated in GENEVE, inspected, and returned on the same Availability Zone path—a behavior enforced when **appliance mode** is enabled. Appliance mode is critical for stateful devices: it guarantees symmetric routing on the return path so that packets traverse the same firewall instance in both directions, avoiding asymmetric-routing drops. Each region hosts its own inspection stack; there is no cross-region hairpin. If one region's appliances fail, only that region's flows see it.

Within the region, **AWS Transit Gateway (TGW)** provides the routing backbone that connects VPCs and shared services. TGW route tables and attachments are explicit and non-transitive by design, meaning packets cannot leak into another region or unrelated domain unless you've declared that path. That intentional friction is a resilience feature—it keeps blast radii confined to the networks that own them.

3. The Inter-Region Backbone—Synchronizing Without Sharing Fate

Active-active depends on data that stays coherent but not co-dependent. For that, AWS provides **Transit Gateway inter-region peering**: a static, non-transitive link between TGWs in two regions over the AWS private backbone. It's used for replication, control messaging, or back-office traffic that must remain private. Because the peering is one-to-one and explicitly attached, a route misconfiguration in Region A cannot automatically propagate to Region B. This is the network-level expression of the CAP trade-off: connectivity without coupling.

Replication traffic and user traffic should never share interfaces or bandwidth. The best practice—validated by the **AWS Well-Architected Reliability Lens**—is to allocate dedicated subnets and, when needed, **Direct Connect** or **Direct Connect Gateway** paths for cross-region data sync. Monitoring those links for throughput, jitter, and retransmission gives early visibility into replication lag, which is often the first signal of deteriorating health long before user impact.

The result is a three-tier network hierarchy that mirrors your fault-domain hierarchy: **Global routing steers. Regional ingress isolates. Inter-region links replicate.**

Each layer can fail, heal, or evolve independently, yet together they maintain a single continuous experience for users worldwide.

In the next part, we'll confront the hardest piece of that puzzle—the data itself—and examine how consistency models, latency, and partition tolerance define what "active" really means in a multi-region world.

Data Consistency and the CAP Reality

Networking gives us reach; data decides whether that reach can be trusted.

In a single region, the distance between replicas is measured in microseconds and the network rarely lies. Across regions, latency, jitter, and transient packet loss are unavoidable—and every bit of distance stretches the definition of "consistency." That is why multi-region active-active is not just a network problem; it's a data problem shaped by physics.

I often describe this tension through the **CAP theorem**, which states that in the presence of a network partition—and in distributed systems, there's always the potential for one—you can choose only two of three properties: **Consistency**, **Availability**, and **Partition tolerance**. We mentioned the CAP theorem before, let's understand better how this applies to our architectural choices.

Partition tolerance isn't optional; it's the cost of running across continents. What remains is a choice: serve every request (availability) or wait for all replicas to agree (consistency). Active-active systems live in that trade-off.

Write-Local, Read-Local: The Practical Default

Most globally distributed applications choose a **write-local, read-local** approach.

Each region serves its local users, writing to the closest data source and reading from replicas nearby. Replication happens asynchronously across regions to converge state over time. This design favors *availability* and *performance* at the cost of short-lived divergence—your data may be slightly out of date across regions for a few seconds or minutes, but your users stay productive.

Amazon DynamoDB Global Tables embody this model.

Each region maintains a fully writable table replica, and updates are propagated asynchronously across regions. DynamoDB resolves write conflicts using a deterministic *last-writer-wins* approach based on timestamp metadata. For most workloads—web apps, IoT telemetry, gaming, content personalization—this delivers the perfect balance: high local responsiveness and eventual global convergence.

But this same mechanism means you must design your application for **idempotency** and **conflict tolerance**. You can't assume that every read in every region represents the absolute latest write everywhere.

When Strong Consistency Matters

Not all workloads can tolerate divergence.

In systems where precision defines correctness—financial ledgers, identity stores, or real-time trading platforms—data must be consistent before it can be trusted. For those, AWS offers **Amazon Aurora Global Database**, where one region is the designated *writer*, and others are *read-only* replicas. Writes replicate asynchronously, but failover promotion can happen in under a minute, ensuring that only one region ever accepts writes at a time.

This approach favors *consistency* over *availability*—you never risk conflicting transactions, but if the writer region becomes unreachable, users must wait for promotion.

Synchronous replication across regions is technically possible, but almost never practical. Even on AWS's private backbone, round-trip latency between distant regions like Frankfurt (eu-central-1) and Singapore (ap-southeast-1) exceeds 150 ms. Waiting for acknowledgments from multiple regions would turn milliseconds of local latency into hundreds of milliseconds of global coordination.

That's why AWS services implement **synchronous replication only within a region** (e.g., Aurora Multi-AZ, RDS Multi-AZ) and **asynchronous replication between regions**—a deliberate balance between integrity and physics.

Designing for Predictable Divergence

In active-active, you don't eliminate divergence; you control it. The goal is to make differences small, observable, and correctable.

That means monitoring **replication lag** as a first-class metric, exposing **conflict resolution counts**, and ensuring your application logic is **idempotent**—meaning repeating the same operation yields the same result. If a user's update is replayed twice due to network retries, the state should remain consistent.

Isolation in the network helps here. By routing replication over **dedicated Transit Gateway peering links** or **Direct Connect** paths, you prevent data synchronization traffic from competing with user flows. Latency jitter on the replication channel directly maps to RPO (Recovery Point Objective), so keeping that channel predictable is resilience, not optimization.

Security and sovereignty also come into play. Some regions—particularly in regulated sectors—cannot export or import certain data types. That's where architectural partitioning matters: design your data model so that personal data, payment data, or regulated records are **owned and processed within their legal region**, and replicate only what's legally transferable. Networking boundaries become compliance boundaries.

Reading and Writing the Right Way

For global systems, **data access patterns are architectural decisions.**

You can either

- **Read Local, Write Local:** Maximize performance, accept temporary divergence.

- **Read Global, Write Local:** Use global tables or replicated caches to increase read reach.

- **Write Global, Read Global:** Rely on a single authoritative region with read replicas elsewhere; simplest consistency model, slowest recovery.

The best choice depends on user experience expectations and tolerance for stale data.

A collaborative document editor might tolerate a few seconds of lag; a banking ledger cannot. The network makes these trade-offs visible: latency budgets, throughput, and propagation delay define how much truth you can afford per millisecond.

In essence, the CAP theorem isn't a constraint—it's a design language.

Active-active systems don't defeat it; they declare where they stand on it.

Networking enforces that declaration through routing isolation, replication paths, and monitoring of latency and loss. Once those are explicit, you can turn consistency trade-offs into measurable engineering outcomes: replication lag, RPO, and RTO are no longer mysteries; they're dials you control.

Routing Patterns for Active-Active

Back in Chapter 4, we learned the vocabulary of DNS routing—latency-based, weighted, failover, and the geo family—and why **Amazon Route 53** (R53) works the way it does. Here, we put that vocabulary to work for **active-active**. Think of this as moving from grammar to composition: the same policies, now orchestrated to keep multiple regions live at once **and** ready to absorb each other without drama.

From "policy" to "behavior"

In active-active, **latency-based routing** usually sets the steady state: users resolve to the nearest *healthy* region because that's where their experience is best. **Weighted routing** becomes your steering wheel—progressive cutovers, traffic rebalancing, canarying a region after a patch, or deliberately biasing load for cost or capacity reasons. **Failover** isn't your daily driver here; it's the guard rail—if a region's health turns red, it's removed from answers regardless of your weights. That blend—latency for default, weight for intent, failover for safety—is the stable triad for active-active.

DNS Is Fast—But Not Instantaneous (and That's OK)

R53 resolvers answer from the edge and evaluate health with a globally distributed checker fleet, so new queries react within seconds. But **DNS caching** at recursive resolvers means **existing** clients won't switch until their TTLs expire. This is why, in Chapter 4, we stressed right-sizing TTLs for the apex and service records. In active-active you'll typically keep TTLs modest (tens of seconds) so rebalancing happens quickly without turning every resolver into a thundering herd. When you truly need **sub-second** diversion (market data, real-time APIs, gaming backends), you pair DNS with **AWS Global Accelerator** (GA): fixed anycast IPs at the edge, per-region endpoint groups behind them, and **traffic dials** that shift live flows without waiting for DNS.

Health Models Must Prove the Path You Care About

Chapter 4 introduced health checks; here we tighten them. In active-active, your global layer should validate **the same path users take**. If your ingress is ALB, don't health-check a raw EC2 IP at Layer 4—check an **HTTP(S) endpoint on ALB** that exercises auth, routing rules, and a shallow dependency (e.g., a lightweight read). This avoids "green DNS on a red app." For **Global Accelerator**, register the ALB/NLB as the endpoint; GA's health integrates with ELB target health so the global decision and the regional reality stay aligned.

Affinity and Stickiness: Who Holds the Session?

Two knobs decide whether users *stay put* when both regions are healthy:

- **Global Accelerator Client Affinity:** GA can keep a client's flows pinned to the same endpoint group (region) based on source IP. That reduces "session drift" while still giving you the ability to turn the dial if health changes.

- **Load Balancer Stickiness:** ALB can set cookie-based stickiness to keep HTTP sessions on the same target; NLB flows are inherently hashed by 5-tuple. Combine this with **cross-zone load balancing** semantics: ALB cross-zone is **on by default** (smoother utilization across AZs); NLB cross-zone is **off by default** (stricter zonal isolation unless you opt in). In active-active, that choice is about **blast radius vs. smoothing** inside each region, independent of the global decision.

The golden rule: use **affinity** to improve user experience when healthy, but never make affinity a *requirement* for correctness—health overrides must be allowed to break stickiness.

Private Clients and Split-Horizon

If part of your user base lives inside your networks (branch, partner, B2B), mirror the same intent privately. Split-horizon zones in **Private Hosted Zones** (or on-prem resolvers) should apply the same latency/weight logic to **regional endpoints exposed privately** (e.g., NLB with private IPs, or PrivateLink). Consistency across public and private name paths prevents "half the world failed over, half didn't."

Why Global Accelerator Plus DNS Is the Steady Combo

Route 53 sets where **new** clients should go; GA keeps **current** clients safe when milliseconds matter—especially with long-lived TCP/UDP sessions or when enterprise resolvers ignore short TTLs. GA's anycast edge and health model give you sub-second re-routing; R53 gives you the broad distribution and population-level shifts. Both layers read the same truth (ELB target health), so you don't get split-brain steering.

ARC for Guardrails, Not Guesses

Active-active still needs governance. **Application Recovery Controller (ARC)** turns your intentions into rules: "only route to a region if readiness checks pass," "cap region B at 60% while it is recovering," "require quorum approval for dial changes." ARC integrates with **Route 53** and **Global Accelerator** so the changes that matter (weights, traffic dials, routing controls) are executed atomically and safely. We'll go deeper on the operational playbooks in Chapter 8; for now, remember that **routing is code, and code needs policy**.

Putting It Together

A healthy request resolves through R53 (latency policy, weights applied), or hits GA's anycast IPs, lands in the nearest healthy region, traverses ALB/NLB across multiple AZs, and reaches scoped targets. If a region degrades, ELB health flips first; **GA withdraws it for new sessions quickly; existing sessions recover via client reconnect/retry**; R53 stops returning it for new resolutions; ARC confirms readiness before any dial/weight increase elsewhere. Each layer moves on its own clock, but all of them follow the same rule: **only healthy regions get traffic**.

Chapter 4 taught the *what* of DNS policy. In the last paragraphs we applied it to the *how* of active-active: TTL strategy, health that proves user reality, GA for sub-second steering, affinity without lock-in, split-horizon parity, and ARC as the safety net. It's the same tools, now wired to keep two (or more) regions truly live at once—fast when healthy, decisive when not.

Next, we'll look at what happens when that health is challenged, and how the network contains failure without letting it echo across the globe.

Failure Scenarios and Blast-Radius Behavior

Healthy systems are quiet; broken ones are instructive. In an active-active design, the difference between a blip and a headline is whether failure is **contained** by the boundaries you drew—zonal, regional, and global—and whether your routing and health models act in the right order.

How a Failure Unfolds—On Purpose

It rarely starts with a region. More often, a single Availability Zone (AZ) begins to misbehave: CPU saturation on a target fleet, a bad config, or an AZ-local event. **Application Load Balancer (ALB)** and **Network Load Balancer (NLB)** continuously probe their registered targets and withdraw the unhealthy ones. Because ALB/NLB nodes are **zonal data planes** coordinated by a **regional control plane**, healthy zones continue to serve; the first blast radius ends at the zonal edge.

If the impairment grows and **all AZ-local targets in the region** are compromised, your **regional boundary** engages. The endpoints that Route 53 (DNS) and Global Accelerator (transport) are watching—typically the regional ALB/NLB front doors—flip to unhealthy. At that moment:

- **Route 53 removes the impaired region from new resolutions, shaping where *new* clients connect.**

- **AWS Global Accelerator withdraws the region for new sessions almost immediately, redirecting traffic at the edge without waiting for DNS behavior.**

Users reconnect to the surviving region. You'll see a wave of new TCP handshakes and a short-lived spike in 4xx/unauthorized or re-authentication if the app relies on session cookies that aren't globally valid. That isn't a "network problem"—it's a **state propagation** decision showing itself. Systems that keep **edge state stateless** (tokens, idempotent APIs, externalized sessions) ride through without user-visible damage.

Why It Stays Contained

Three choices you made earlier keep this from cascading:

1. **Regional Ingress Symmetry:** Each Region has its own ALB/NLB fleets and **Region-local inspection** (GWLB + endpoints with appliance mode for symmetric return). No cross-region hairpin means one region's bottlenecks can't throttle the other.

2. **Explicit Backbone Paths: Transit Gateway (TGW) inter-region peering** is **non-transitive and explicit**. Replication rides private links you can meter and alarm. A busy failover **cannot** bleed into replication capacity unless you configured it to share pipes.

3. **Control/Data Separation:** Global steering (Route 53 resolvers, GA edges) keeps serving health-based decisions even if a management API is having a day. Region-scoped CI/CD, IAM roles, and dashboards ensure that an operator mistake in the failing region **cannot** reconfigure the healthy one.

If humans get nervous, **Application Recovery Controller (ARC)** is the brake pedal. Its readiness checks (capacity, replication catch-up, endpoint health) must pass before routing controls allow more traffic to shift. Policy like "never exceed 60% to a region under recovery" prevents over-eager promotion from turning one incident into two.

Addressing Hidden Couplings

Containment isn't a spell you cast once and forget.

Even the cleanest architecture can betray you if one piece of it quietly stayed central. Authentication, logging, observability—those are the usual culprits. When they're anchored in a single region, every other region inherits that region's fate. One choke point, many dependencies.

The cure is the same pattern we've practiced all chapter: **Regionalize, replicate, and observe crosswise.** Each region should authenticate on its own, emit logs locally, and export them asynchronously to a global analytics account or security lake.

Never ask a failed region to tell you why it failed. Look at Region A from Region B, not from inside the smoke.

Stateful applications need the same humility about distance. If you've chosen a **multi-writer model**—like DynamoDB Global Tables—you're betting on eventual convergence. Conflicts will happen, and your logic must handle them idempotently so replayed or duplicated writes land cleanly.

If you're running a **single-writer design**, such as Aurora Global Database, promotion isn't instantaneous; it's bounded by replication delay and policy. You traded a few seconds of recovery for the guarantee that your data will never fork.

The network enforces those choices faithfully—it won't lie for you. What it can do is carry the truth faster and make that delay predictable.

The rest is expectation management: your users will forgive latency; they won't forgive confusion.

The Return to Steady State

Recovery should feel boring.

When the impaired region starts breathing again, load balancer targets turn green one by one. Replication catches up, caches refill, alarms quiet, and then Application Recovery Controller (ARC) runs its readiness checks—capacity, sync state, endpoint health—and only when everything passes does traffic return.

Route 53 adds the region back to its answer set, and the system settles into symmetry again.

There's no dramatic switch flip, no "cut-back" moment. It's more like letting a new heartbeat fall back into rhythm with the old one. The network resumes balance, users stay connected, and the only people who notice are the ones watching dashboards. Ultimately, this is what resilience means: the ability to absorb failure without users noticing—continuing to serve, quietly and predictably.

In Figure 6-14, when a region becomes impaired, health checks detect the failure and Route 53 immediately stops returning that region in DNS responses. Application Recovery Controller (ARC) validates readiness and safety before promoting the remaining region to serve all user traffic. Bi-directional data replication continues privately over non-transitive Transit Gateway peering, maintaining data integrity throughout. Once ARC confirms recovery, the impaired region is safely restored to the routing set, and traffic rebalances automatically—resilience achieved through continuous control, not manual intervention.

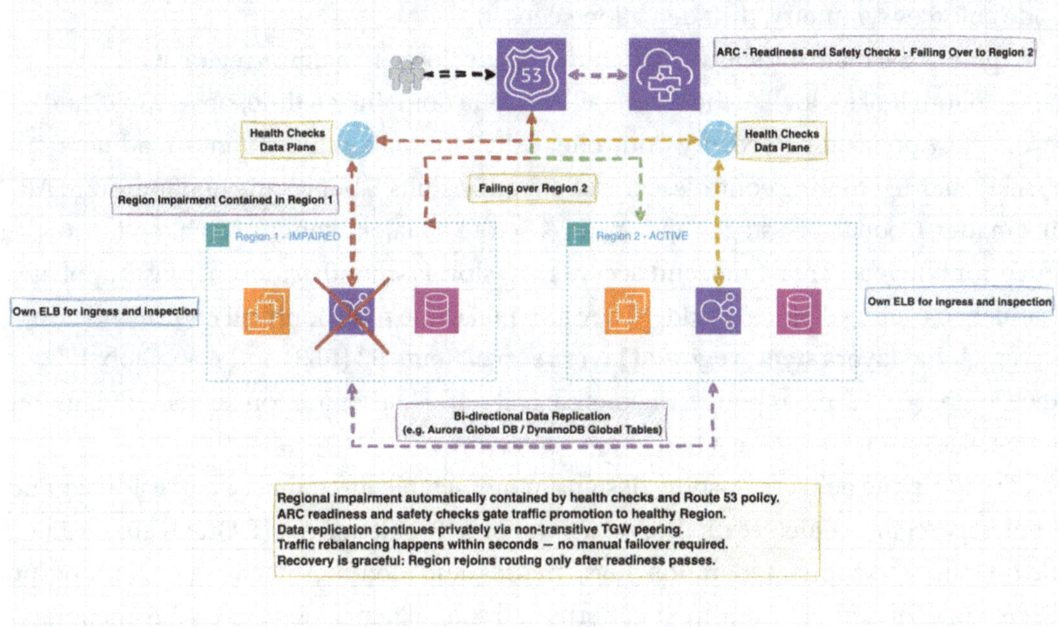

Figure 6-14. *Containment and Recovery in Active-Active Systems*

Operational Discipline and Cost Realities

Architecture gives you structure; operations give you truth. Multi-AZ and multi-region designs look tidy on a diagram, but they only become resilience when teams, tooling, and budgets can carry them day after day. The discipline is not in drawing two regions—it's in running two regions without turning every Tuesday into a release freeze.

The first reality is cost, and not just the obvious kind. Yes, redundancy multiplies infrastructure: more load balancers, more fleets, more storage, more inter-AZ and inter-region traffic. But the real expense is complexity. Two live regions mean two of everything that makes production safe—monitoring, on-call depth, incident tooling, change controls, compliance checks, and a way to keep configurations aligned without copy-pasting risk. Organizations that succeed here don't buy resilience one workload at a time; they **standardize** it: shared templates for VPCs and ingress, repeatable Transit Gateway (TGW) patterns, consistent Gateway Load Balancer (GWLB) insertion, and a single way to expose services (whether that's Application Load Balancer (ALB)/Network Load Balancer (NLB) or a service network like Amazon VPC Lattice). Infrastructure as Code enforces symmetry; drift detection keeps it.

Operational maturity shows up in how change flows. In a multi-region world, the safest rollout looks a lot like the safest failover: one domain at a time, observable, and reversible. Application Recovery Controller (ARC) formalizes that intent—readiness checks, guarded routing controls, controlled traffic shifts—but it's the habits around ARC that matter. Good teams stage capacity days before a major change, watch replication lag and error budgets in real time, and accept that "slow is smooth, smooth is fast" applies as much to routing dials as to code. They also make one philosophical choice and never waver: **global layers steer; regional layers serve.** Route 53 (R53) and AWS Global Accelerator (GA) express policy; regions carry it out. That separation keeps a bad minute in one place from becoming a bad afternoon everywhere.

Trends in the field are pushing designs in predictable directions. Data residency and regulatory regimes (such as the Digital Operational Resilience Act (DORA)) are raising the floor for operational separation: logs, metrics, and identities need regional shape, not just regional endpoints. Zero-trust patterns and shared inspection via GWLB encourage "shared, not shared fate": you can centralize controls without centralizing blast radius. At the same time, user bases are more global, and expectations are tighter; the rise of anycast entry points and edge-aware routing (GA plus latency-based DNS) makes it feasible to keep latency down while preserving fault isolation. FinOps practices are also maturing: rather than asking "How much does multi-region cost?" the question becomes "Which **tier** of application earns multi-region, and which is fine with multi-AZ?"— because not everything is mission-critical, and treating it as such is how programs stall.

Observability is the currency that pays for confidence. Each region must be able to see itself and be seen by its peers. Metrics, traces, and logs should land locally first and replicate out; during a regional impairment, you cannot ask a failed region to explain itself. Dashboards that are organized by fault domain (cell → AZ → region) turn incidents into bounded stories: you don't just know *what* broke—you see *where it stops*. That framing changes behavior. Operators move dials with less fear because they can measure the blast radius as they move.

Finally, a word on practice. We'll go deep on testing in Chapter 8, but the short version belongs here: **a boundary you have not intentionally crossed in rehearsal is a boundary you should not trust in production**. You don't need chaos for chaos's sake; you need drills that mirror what you've built—Route 53 record withdrawals, GA traffic-dial exercises, TGW peering cuts, controlled ALB/NLB target drains. The aim isn't drama; it's familiarity. Teams that practice failover treat a regional wobble as routine traffic engineering. Teams that don't treat it as breaking news.

Lessons Learned from Chapter 6

This chapter began with logical isolation through cells, expanded into physical separation across Availability Zones and regions, and ended by grounding those abstractions in operations, cost, and practice. The lessons are not just technical—they are behavioral, organizational, and architectural.

Resilience starts with boundaries: Fault domains—cells, AZs, and regions—define how far failure can travel, best practices call this *limiting the blast radius*: ensuring that a single misconfiguration, deployment, or fault cannot take down the entire system. Every networking construct, from subnet boundaries to Transit Gateway route tables, should trace back to these containment lines.

Isolation and autonomy are two halves of real resilience: Isolation means faults don't spread; autonomy means each part can heal independently. Independence at the control plane prevents shared-change failures (e.g., a misapplied automation run); independence at the data plane prevents shared-load failures (e.g., overrun targets). We can practices this through cell-based architectures—each region's systems can deploy, fail, and recover without coordination.

Geography is physics, not preference: Multi-AZ is the baseline for production-grade resilience; multi-region exists only when distance itself becomes a failure domain—through latency requirements, regulatory boundaries, or existential business risk.

You should always evaluate the business impact, data residency laws, and user distribution before choosing multi-region. Build globally only when your users, regulators, or RTO/RPO objectives demand it.

Routing is the nervous system of resilience: Route 53, Global Accelerator, and Transit Gateway translate health into motion. Network topology decides whether a failure is local or global. Designing explicit routing paths, separate health domains, and dedicated inspection layers (via GWLB or Lattice) ensures that traffic can move safely without shared fate.

Data defines recovery reality: Synchronous replication is achievable within regions and powers services like RDS Multi-AZ and Aurora quorum writes.

Cross-region replication is almost always asynchronous, trading consistency for reach.

Choose intentionally: write-local/read-local for performance and availability, or single-writer with controlled failover for strict consistency.

This is where CAP theorem becomes practical—your replication strategy is your resilience model..

Automation and observability close the loop: AWS recommends *automated recovery* and *observability by design*. Infrastructure as Code (IaC) keeps regions symmetrical and guardrails enforce configuration parity. Application Recovery Controller (ARC) and CloudWatch readiness checks turn resilience from documentation into policy.

What you can't observe, you can't trust—telemetry must mirror your fault domains.

Cost and complexity are tools, not punishments: Every layer of redundancy trades cost and operational load for smaller impact zones. AWS guidance is clear: align resilience investment with workload criticality.

Tier your applications—mission-critical systems justify multi-region; business-important workloads thrive in multi-AZ; everything else belongs in well-tested backup or pilot-light patterns. The goal isn't maximum availability—it's proportional availability.

Standardization makes resilience boring—and that's the point: Reusable networking blueprints, shared ingress standards, and repeatable deployment models (e.g., consistent TGW topologies and GWLB insertion) eliminate surprises.

Standardization reduces human error and operational fatigue—the two most common causes of outages in most of the cloud providers postmortems.

Practice turns architecture into instinct: No topology is resilient until it has failed safely at least once. Routine, low-drama testing—health check withdrawals, traffic dial rehearsals, or Transit Gateway fault drills—teaches teams what diagrams can't.

We'll go deep into resilience testing in **Chapter 8**, but the habit begins here: testing validates that your boundaries behave as designed.

Boundaries define containment, automation enforces consistency, data dictates truth, and people provide judgment.

Together, they transform networks from fragile constructs into living systems—ones that can fail gracefully, recover predictably, and evolve confidently.

Before you leave this chapter, here's a simple way to sanity-check any active-active design.

If you can't explain—clearly and in one sentence—what happens to your data when a region fails, then active-active is probably premature.

With Chapter 6, we've drawn the lines and learned to live inside them: from cells to AZs to regions; from logical isolation to physical distance; from policy at the edge to execution in the region. In **Chapter 7**, we'll turn those boundaries into instruments—shaping paths, smoothing load, and using the network itself to make systems faster when healthy and calmer when not.

Traffic Engineering for Cloud Resilience and Performance

In Chapter 6, we practiced the art of quiet recovery—containment that narrows the blast radius, promotions that happen only when the system is ready, and failbacks that feel boring by design. But choreography lives on a stage, and that stage is the network. If the underlay can't deliver predictable reachability when the winds pick up—if latency shivers, if BGP flaps, if the internet's edge forgets you exist—then even the most elegant recovery stumbles. This chapter begins at that seam: where resilient applications meet the messy, probabilistic world of packets.

Section 7.1: The Cloud–Hybrid Reality: Why Traffic Engineering Matters

Most estates aren't "all-in on one cloud, one region, one path." They are a mesh of data centers and branches, regulated workloads that won't move, SaaS dependencies, and two—or three—public clouds stitched together by APIs and identity. GenAI has only intensified this: inference fans out to GPU pools in specific regions; model updates and feature stores cross providers; data-sovereignty lines act like invisible guardrails. Resilience in that world isn't just failover; it's *deterministic failover*. We need traffic behavior we can explain under stress, performance that doesn't collapse when we shift load, and visibility that extends beyond our own ASN. That's the promise of traffic engineering: underlay and overlay, working together, so a global system keeps its rhythm even when something vital blinks.

419

© Cristian Critelli 2026

C. Critelli, *Cloud Networking and Resilience*, https://doi.org/10.1007/979-8-8688-2436-4_7

Why "Hybrid" Is the Center of Gravity (Now)

This isn't a transitional awkward phase; it's where the market has landed. Gartner projects that **90% of organizations will adopt a hybrid-cloud approach through 2027** and flags GenAI data synchronization across hybrid environments as a near-term operational challenge. In the same breath, it pegs worldwide public-cloud end-user spending at **$723 billion in 2025**—growth that expands the surface area between clouds and everything else. Flexera's 2025 survey tells the same story from the finance side: cloud budgets keep climbing, with **roughly a third of organizations now spending over $12 million annually** on public cloud alone. Spend rises, but on-prem and private footprints persist, ensuring that more traffic crosses hybrid seams and more resilience questions are answered by routing, not just code.

The connectivity strategy is catching up to this reality. IDC describes an inflection in **multicloud networking**, driven by the need to connect and secure AI models and inference across providers—exactly where path diversity, explicit BGP policy, and global steering stop being "telco concerns" and become core platform engineering. And its Cloud Pulse data shows **the vast majority of buyers either operating hybrid or actively moving there**, with most already using multiple clouds. Hybrid is no longer a side quest; it's the main quest.

The Stakes: Outages, Cost, and Customer Trust

Outages didn't disappear; they evolved. Uptime Institute's 2024 analysis underscores that high-impact failures continue to bite, with costs trending upward even as some incident frequencies ease—an uncomfortable reminder that correlated failures and third-party dependencies can turn a blip into a board-level event. At internet scale, ThousandEyes observed notable **shifts in outage patterns through 2024**, including a rising share attributed to cloud service providers and configuration changes—problems you *feel* even when your own stack is green. The lesson is old and new at once: your customer's experience depends on paths you don't own.

What Leading Organizations Are Actually Doing

The leaders we study don't bet on heroics; they bet on structure. They design **path diversity** across carriers, regions, and clouds to reduce correlated risk. They replace "best-effort internet luck" with **policy**—local-preference to shape egress, AS-path prepending, and MED to influence ingress, communities to stamp intent—and they verify those policies with **observability** that treats jitter, packet loss, and convergence time as first-class SLOs. This isn't just performance tuning; in financial services and other regulated industries, it's edging into compliance: you must demonstrate that critical services remain available when connectivity falters. The hybrid era has made traffic engineering part of operational resilience, not a footnote of WAN operations. (For a wider read on the skills platforms are prioritizing—platform networking, integrated security, and AI-assisted ops—Cisco's 2024 networking trends report mirrors these investments.)

Pain and Challenges You Must Design For

Hybrid routes are prone to **asymmetry** that breaks stateful inspection and surprises downstream systems. BGP **convergence** can be correct *and still late*, long enough to black-hole sessions during failover. **Sovereignty and data gravity** force you to route through specific regions whether you like it or not, turning "global" into a series of constrained corridors. And at the **internet edge**, resolver caching, DNS TTLs, and Anycast behavior can either smooth or amplify a failover—meaning your recovery timing is a product of *your* health-check semantics and *their* caching strategy. None of this is unsolvable. All of it is unsolved by default. Let's dive deep into some examples:

- **Asymmetric Routing and Unpredictable Convergence**: Without clear BGP policy and route hygiene, failovers can "work" but still backhaul or black-hole traffic during reconvergence.

- **Sovereignty and Data-gravity Constraints**: Regulatory and data-locality rules force **region-aware** and **provider-aware** path choices—global steering must respect where data may flow.

- **Internet Edge Variability**: DNS TTLs, resolver behavior, and Anycast dynamics can amplify or dampen failover timing; health-check design is as critical as the compute behind it.

- **Tool and Policy Sprawl**: Multiple networks, clouds, and vendors create policy drift. Without shared primitives (communities, tagging, standardized health semantics), "global" architecture behaves locally.

How This Chapter Addresses It

We'll start by establishing the **routing foundation for hybrid**—a concise BGP primer tuned to cloud and edge realities—then move to **traffic-engineering techniques** organized by *intent*: ingress control, egress control, and deterministic failover. We'll define **hybrid connectivity resilience models** (high vs. maximum) using AWS Direct Connect as a concrete canvas, and we'll layer on **global steering**—DNS, Anycast, and load-balancing—so the overlay complements, not contradicts, the underlay. Finally, we'll anchor operations in **metrics that matter**—latency, jitter, packet loss, and convergence—so you can prove the system behaves the way your architecture diagrams promise.

Traffic engineering is the connective tissue between a graceful recovery plan and the real networks that carry it. Make the underlay and overlay sing the same melody—policies you can explain and timings you can measure—and recovery stops being theater. It becomes rhythm.

Section 7.2: Building the Foundation: Hybrid Connectivity and Routing Basics

Hybrid connectivity in 2026 is far beyond "a VPN from a data center to a region." Modern enterprise networks are a mesh of private circuits, shared exchange fabrics, cloud on-ramps, branch overlays, edge sites, and sovereign zones—each with its own control plane and failure modes. Enterprises interconnect multiple on-premises data centers with multiple cloud regions; they front hundreds of branches over SD-WAN; they operate factory and retail edge sites that need real-time links; they depend on SaaS and partner networks; and they anchor it all in carrier-neutral colocation facilities that host several cloud on-ramps under one roof. This **edge–cloud continuum** is no longer aspirational—it's the physical map your packets traverse every minute.

The consequence is **complex failover paths**. When an application fails over, a single user session may move from a branch in Tokyo to a region in São Paulo and then back through a European on-premises core—without interruption. The network must make that seamless despite crossing multiple administrative domains. In hybrid networks, **path symmetry** (outbound and return traffic following the same route) is not guaranteed by default; it's something you **engineer on purpose**. Wherever multiple paths exist, **asymmetric routing** is the baseline risk, and preventing it is essential for consistent performance and security.

In Figure 7-1, user traffic from Tokyo enters AWS through the primary Direct Connect (DX1) and is deliberately steered via the Transit Gateway to a centralized inspection VPC before reaching the service VPC (green path). On the return leg, however, traffic follows a different—but still valid—route, exiting AWS through a secondary Direct Connect in São Paulo and traversing the WAN back to the users (red path), bypassing centralized inspection. This behavior highlights a fundamental property of hybrid networking: AWS routing is deterministic but stateless. Without explicit design controls, failover and routing preferences can introduce asymmetric paths that affect security posture, latency, and compliance.

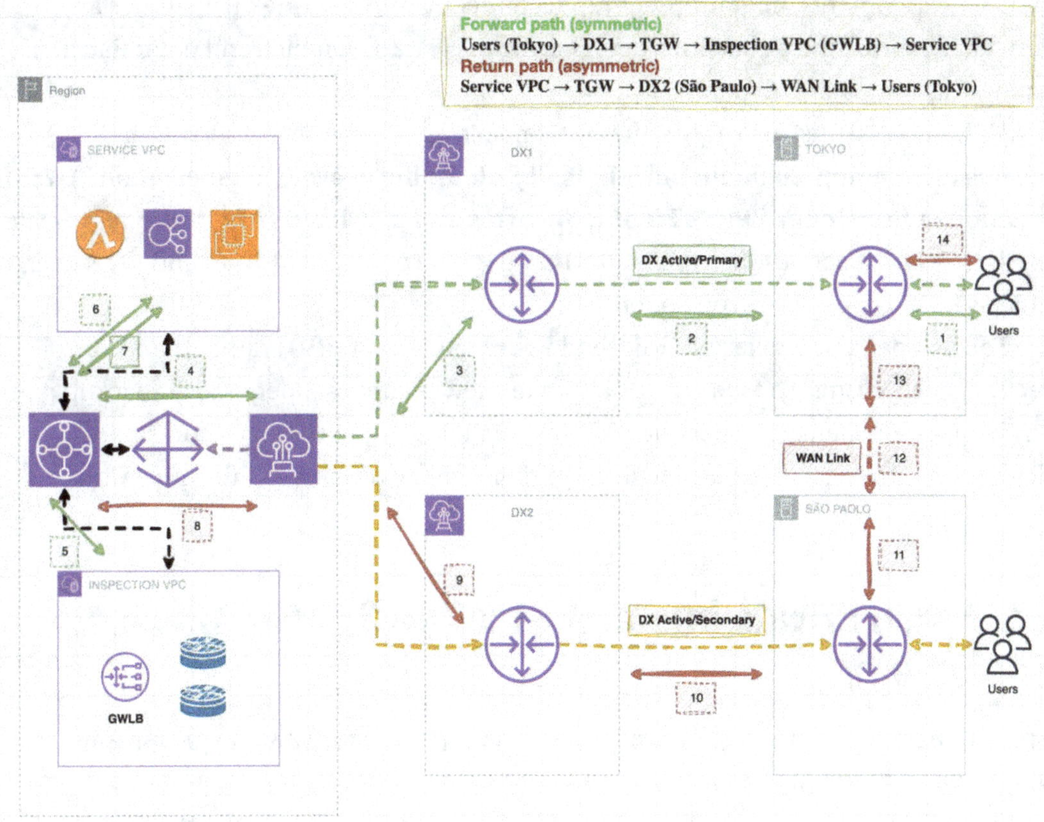

Figure 7-1. *Symmetric and Asymmetric Routing in a Hybrid Architecture*

Next, we'll survey the building blocks and the distinct latency, control, and failure characteristics each one brings.

Building Blocks: VPNs, Direct Connect, Exchanges, and Edge Links

Although the building blocks of hybrid connectivity repeat across designs, each category behaves differently in terms of latency, control, and failure modes.

Internet IPsec VPN Tunnels

These are the fast on-ramps—quick to deploy globally and inexpensive—making them ideal for experiments, migrations, or rapid connectivity. They ride on an underlay you don't control: the public Internet. This means variable latency and potential path changes as routes shift dynamically.

VPN tunnels must also accommodate smaller payloads due to encryption overhead, requiring techniques like **TCP MSS clamping** to avoid fragmentation. **AWS recommends an inner VPN MTU of 1,446 bytes and a TCP MSS of 1,406 bytes** for Site-to-Site VPN connections. Internet paths may degrade occasionally but tend to recover quickly through routing reconvergence.

Failover detection relies on IKE **Dead Peer Detection (DPD)** rather than sub-second mechanisms, so failovers usually take a few seconds—adequate for backup paths but not for low-latency applications. VPNs remain invaluable as an elastic, rapid-deployment option in hybrid designs, especially when combined with Direct Connect as a secondary path.

Dedicated Private Interconnects (AWS Direct Connect and Others)

These trade higher costs and provisioning lead time for **deterministic performance**. They deliver fixed bandwidth, lower jitter, and fewer surprises than Internet VPNs.

AWS Direct Connect (DX) is the archetype. DX links use **802.1Q VLAN tagging and BGP peering**. You can choose between

- A **Private Virtual Interface (VIF)** to connect one VPC or multiple VPCs through a **Direct Connect Gateway (DXGW)**, or

- A **Transit VIF**, which connects to a DXGW associated with one or more **Transit Gateways (TGWs)**, enabling multi-VPC, multi-region reachability

- A **Public VIF**, to connect via the Direct Connect link to public AWS services with public endpoints such as S3, DynamoDB, etc.

A single DX circuit can be associated with Transit Gateways in multiple regions via a Direct Connect Gateway, avoiding mandatory application-level hairpinning through a single hub region. However, architects should avoid advertising identical prefixes from multiple regions unless active-active behavior is intentional.

Bidirectional Forwarding Detection (BFD) is strongly recommended. AWS enables asynchronous BFD on all DX endpoints; when configured on your router with sub-second intervals (e.g., 300 ms interval, multiplier 3), failures are detected and BGP routes are withdrawn in under one second. Without BFD, standard BGP timers (90-second hold time) would make failover far too slow for production environments.

Dedicated interconnects provide the highest predictability but require careful design for physical diversity (separate facilities or metros) and quota awareness, which we'll explore later in this chapter.

Cloud Exchange Fabrics

Located in **carrier-neutral colocation facilities**, these fabrics—such as **Equinix Cloud Exchange**, **Megaport**, or **Digital Realty Interxion**—allow a single physical cross-connect to reach multiple cloud providers and carriers. This model simplifies **multicloud connectivity** by creating a central "meet-me" point, reducing provisioning time and cost for multi-provider links.

However, shared exchanges introduce a new operational domain—the **exchange itself**—that must be monitored and managed. While they accelerate connectivity and reduce physical complexity, they can complicate troubleshooting and incident correlation. If a shared switch or service chain in the exchange experiences an issue, multiple tenants may be affected simultaneously.

For regulated workloads, visibility into this domain—link state, SLA metrics, and maintenance transparency—becomes part of the resilience equation.

SD-WAN Overlays

Software-defined WAN appliances and cloud controllers can bond together multiple transport types—broadband Internet, MPLS, LTE/5G—under a unified policy framework. SD-WAN edges continuously monitor performance metrics such as **loss, jitter, and latency** on each underlay and dynamically steer traffic according to policy or real-time measurements.

For example, a branch edge might prefer broadband Internet for cost efficiency but instantly switch to MPLS if latency or packet loss on the Internet path exceeds thresholds. This **dynamic path selection** improves application experience and makes WAN behavior adaptive rather than static.

However, this flexibility introduces dependency: the overlay can only perform as well as its underlays. Internet segments can vary in performance, and path shifts can momentarily affect latency or jitter. SD-WAN therefore enhances availability through agility but does not eliminate underlay imperfections—it simply manages them more intelligently.

Edge Links (Including Private 5G)

New edge-access technologies, such as **private 5G networks**, extend hybrid connectivity to industrial plants, warehouses, and retail sites that demand low-latency local processing. These edge networks often integrate directly with the corporate WAN and cloud environments, adding new ingress and egress points.

Each edge node becomes a potential path entry or exit and often includes **local breakout** to cloud services for near-real-time analytics. This decentralization reduces round-trip time for critical workloads but also expands the **attack and failure surface**. Every new link adds another policy and telemetry requirement to maintain predictable routing and security posture.

Edge connectivity strengthens resilience at the local level but must adhere to the same design principles—redundancy, monitoring, and controlled failover—that govern the global network.

Understanding Failure Patterns

Each connectivity category fails differently—and at different speeds:

- **Private circuits** rarely fail but may take hours or days to repair when they do (fiber cuts, facility outages).

- **Internet paths** experience transient degradation more often but self-heal quickly through global routing convergence.

- **Shared exchange fabrics** introduce coordination risks: a single misconfiguration or maintenance window can affect multiple tenants simultaneously.

Understanding these trade-offs is critical for designing networks that balance **performance, cost, and resilience**. The art of hybrid architecture lies in combining these building blocks—each with distinct strengths and weaknesses—into a topology where no single failure compromises the system's rhythm.

Regulatory Constraints on Routing

Regulations can bend network routes as surely as physics does. **Data residency** and **data sovereignty** laws enforce zones where specific data flows must remain within defined geographic boundaries. This means you might need to **ingress and egress traffic in-region** and use only **approved interconnects** for certain classes of data. Compliance requirements effectively turn your network diagram into a **map of legal boundaries** as much as a map of cables.

In practice, architects deploy **local processing clusters**—either on-premises or within regional cloud footprints—to handle sensitive or latency-critical data and then use **carefully governed pathways** for any traffic that must leave the region.

For example, a European bank may require that **EU-resident personal data never traverse networks outside the EU**. This would necessitate **private links or EU-based transit** for that data and possibly filtering of routes to ensure that a backup path through a non-EU region isn't even advertised. Such policies translate into **concrete network configurations**: controlling **BGP route advertisements**, using **route maps and community tags** to limit propagation, and applying **ACLs or firewall policies** to enforce routing constraints.

AWS guidance for avoiding asymmetric routing—especially with **centralized firewalls**—echoes the same principle: if return traffic doesn't come back through the intended inspection point, the firewall cannot perform stateful inspection and policy enforcement. Therefore, **compliance and security requirements must be embedded in routing design**, ensuring **symmetrical paths** and **restricted egress** for sensitive data.

Additional factors in 2026 make this even more critical.

- Under the **EU Digital Operational Resilience Act (DORA)**, financial institutions must demonstrate that ICT and data dependencies remain controllable, including the geographic routing of critical information.

- **Data transfer frameworks** such as GDPR and the EU-U.S. Data Privacy Framework further restrict the movement of personal data outside approved jurisdictions.

- Many public-sector workloads now require **regional AWS partitions** (e.g., *AWS Europe Sovereign Cloud*) or **VPC endpoint controls** that guarantee data stays within a sovereignty boundary.

Ultimately, network topology and compliance architecture have become inseparable.

Designing for resilience now means designing for **jurisdictional resilience**—where the failure of a region, link, or provider still respects the laws governing where your data can flow.

Volume Demands Control: Policy and Telemetry over Guesswork

As the number of sites and connections grows, accidental misrouting becomes a real risk. With hundreds of sites, dozens of VPCs, multiple carriers, and multiple clouds, a lack of explicit policy and good telemetry can lead to unintended consequences such as traffic hairpinning through distant regions or hidden single points of failure that diagrams don't show. Every new edge node or link is another potential point of ingress/egress and another potential failure surface.

The only way to manage this complexity is through deliberate design and control.

Path Diversity on Purpose: Design for multiple paths by intent. Use at least two carriers or ISPs, diverse physical paths, multiple Direct Connect ports in separate locations, and redundant VPN tunnels. This way, if one path fails, traffic has a designed alternate path that is known to be good (not just whatever the Internet happens to choose). For example, enterprises achieve higher Direct Connect resilience by using AWS's recommended multi-location, multi-port models (the Direct Connect Resiliency Toolkit provides specific blueprints for achieving 99.9% ("High") or 99.99% ("Maximum") availability via redundant connections and locations). We will dive deep in the next sections of this chapter.

Policy-Driven Path Selection: Don't rely on default route preferences or random chance to decide how traffic flows. Implement routing policies that reflect business intent. For instance, use BGP local preference to prefer a low-latency Direct Connect over a VPN for primary traffic. Use AS path prepending on certain routes to make them less preferred for inbound traffic from AWS, guiding AWS to send return traffic over the desired path. Understand how AWS's routing constructs choose routes (e.g., Transit Gateway route table rules, described below) and design your route advertisements accordingly. The goal is to know which path traffic is using and why and to predict how it will reroute during failures—rather than being surprised by "Internet default" behavior.

Visibility and Telemetry: Deploy robust monitoring of all links and paths. This includes traditional network telemetry (SNMP, flow logs, CloudWatch metrics for Direct Connect, etc.) as well as synthetic probing from branches to apps. With many possible paths, it's critical to quickly detect if traffic is accidentally taking an inferior or non-compliant path (e.g., a misconfigured route causing a long-haul hairpin). Good telemetry allows operators to catch these issues and adjust policies before they impact users. Like I said multiple times by now, a good or even great resilience implementation is nothing if it hasn't been tested or if there's no monitoring and observability.

When growth in network complexity is matched with strong control mechanisms, failures can become predictable and "boring." That is, when something breaks, the pre-planned backup takes over in a controlled way, rather than an ad hoc failover that surprises everyone. In summary, volume breeds complexity, and complexity demands intentional control.

Route and Scale Guardrails (Key Limits and Considerations)

Before diving deeper, it's important to note a few practical limits and guardrails in hybrid network designs—these often influence the architecture.

BGP Route Limits on Direct Connect: AWS Direct Connect imposes limits on how many routes you can advertise over each BGP session. For private or transit virtual interfaces, the limit is 100 prefixes (routes) for IPv4 and 100 for IPv6 per BGP session from on-premises to AWS. If you exceed 100 advertised routes, AWS will shut down the BGP session (state goes to "Idle"). This means you should aggregate and summarize routes before advertising into AWS, rather than announcing every little subnet. For Direct Connect public VIFs (used to reach AWS public services over your own IP space), the limit is higher (1000 routes) but cannot be increased. These limits are not just theoretical—advertise too many routes and your connectivity will drop.

Transit Gateway Route Table Limits: An AWS Transit Gateway (TGW) by default supports up to 10,000 routes across all its route tables. This is adjustable via service quotas if needed, but 10k is the planning baseline. If you have hundreds of sites and many networks, you need to plan summarization so that you don't exceed 10k routes in the TGW. (AWS also limits each TGW to 20 route tables and 5,000 attachments by default.) On the VPC side, AWS recently (mid-2025) raised the default route table capacity from 50 to 500 routes per VPC subnet route table. This increase helps avoid running out of routes in larger VPCs, but it doesn't eliminate the need for route design discipline.

VPN Throughput and ECMP: A single AWS Site-to-Site VPN tunnel can drive around 1.25 Gbps of throughput under ideal conditions. If you need more aggregate bandwidth, Transit Gateway supports equal-cost multi-path (ECMP) routing across multiple VPN tunnels, effectively bundling tunnels in an active-active fashion. **ECMP for Site-to-Site VPN is supported only on Transit Gateway attachments; VPNs terminating on a Virtual Private Gateway remain active–passive for egress.** As a result, scalable VPN throughput and true active–active utilization require TGW-based designs. For scalable VPN throughput and active-active use of multiple tunnels, TGW is the preferred pattern.

Jumbo Frames (MTU) Usage: Jumbo frames can significantly improve throughput for heavy data transfers by reducing packet overhead. AWS Direct Connect supports jumbo MTUs: 9001 bytes on private VIFs and 8500 bytes on transit VIFs. Inside a VPC, most modern instance types support 9001 MTU on Elastic Network Interfaces (the default MTU in AWS is 9001 for EC2 instances), and AWS Transit Gateway supports 8500 bytes when forwarding between attachments (VPC, DX, etc.). However, any segment in the path that isn't "jumbo-clean" (set to standard 1500) will cause IP Path MTU Discovery to downshift the entire flow. One mismatched interface MTU drags the whole path back to 1500 bytes. For example, if an intermediate router or perhaps a peering exchange is limited to 1500, you lose the jumbo benefit end-to-end. Changing the MTU of a Direct Connect VIF after creation triggers a reconfiguration of the physical port and briefly disrupts connectivity (up to ~30 seconds), so plan changes carefully. In summary: use jumbo frames for large flows (database replication, backups, etc.), but verify MTU end-to-end and clamp MSS for any 1500-byte segments to avoid fragmentation.

BFD for Fast Failover: Enabling BFD on BGP sessions (where supported) is crucial for reducing the detection time of link failures. On Direct Connect, AWS supports asynchronous BFD with a minimum interval of 300 ms and a multiplier of 3. If you configure your router for 300 ms BFD heartbeats, a dead link can be detected and BGP torn down in under 1 second (as opposed to the default BGP hold timer of 90 seconds!). AWS automatically has BFD enabled on their side of DX connections—you just need to enable it on your side. This is not supported on standard VPN attachments (only on Direct Connect or Transit Gateway Connect GRE attachments), which rely on traditional keepalives (DPD in IPsec) with second-level timers.

By keeping these guardrails in mind, you avoid designs that look good on a diagram but fail in practice (e.g., advertising 200 routes to AWS and wondering why your DX BGP session is down). Summarize routes to fit limits, use multiple TGWs or Cloud WAN if you need to segment route scale, and plan capacity within known throughput limits.

These constraints are well documented—but in practice, hybrid outages rarely come from obscure edge cases. They come from a small set of recurring design mistakes.

Top 5 Hybrid Networking Anti-patterns (and Why They Break Resilience)

Anti-Pattern #1: Route Explosion and Prefix Sprawl

Symptom: BGP sessions flap, TGW route tables hit limits, or DX goes idle unexpectedly.

Root cause: Advertising hundreds of granular prefixes instead of summarized routes.

Why it breaks resilience:

Failover may technically "work," but control planes destabilize under stress. In AWS, exceeding Direct Connect or TGW route limits doesn't degrade gracefully—it disconnects.

Design rule: Summarize aggressively, design aggregation boundaries early, and treat route scale as a first-class constraint.

Anti-Pattern #2: MTU Mismatch Across the Path

Symptom: Random packet loss, slow replication, TCP stalls that disappear during testing but reappear in production.

Root cause: Mixing jumbo-enabled segments (DX, TGW, EC2) with 1500-byte bottlenecks (firewalls, exchanges, VPN).

Why it breaks resilience:

During failover, traffic often shifts paths. If the backup path is not MTU-clean, recovery amplifies performance degradation exactly when systems are already stressed.

Design rule: Verify MTU end-to-end and clamp MSS deliberately. Assume failover paths matter just as much as primaries.

Anti-Pattern #3: Shared Exchange As a Hidden Single Point of Failure

Symptom: Multiple clouds or regions fail "at the same time" for no obvious reason.

Root cause: Treating a shared cloud exchange fabric as independent redundancy.

Why it breaks resilience:

An exchange outage, maintenance event, or misconfiguration can impact all attached clouds and carriers simultaneously—turning perceived diversity into correlated failure.

Design rule: Treat exchanges as their own failure domain. Pair them with true physical and provider diversity.

Anti-Pattern #4: Write Traffic Leaking Across Regions

Symptom: Compliance findings, unexpected latency spikes, and data sovereignty violations.

Root cause: Failover policies that steer all traffic, including writes or stateful operations, without regional awareness.

Why it breaks resilience:

Failover that ignores data gravity or legal boundaries can create a "working system" that is operationally or legally unacceptable.

Design rule: Separate read vs. write paths, apply region-aware routing, and explicitly constrain propagation of sensitive prefixes.

Anti-Pattern #5: No Fast Failure Detection (Missing BFD)

Symptom: Long black holes (30–90 seconds) during link failures, despite redundant paths.

Root cause: Relying on default BGP timers or IPsec DPD for critical links.

Why it breaks resilience:

Failover speed is a control-plane problem. Without BFD, your architecture diagram promises instant recovery, but reality delivers visible outages.

Design rule: Use BFD wherever supported (especially Direct Connect). Sub-second detection is not an optimization—it's a requirement.

Traffic Engineering Considerations

With the foundation in place, what do these realities mean for traffic engineering in a hybrid environment?

> **Design for Diversity:** Ensure you have multiple, independent ways for traffic to reach critical destinations. This includes using multiple ISPs or carrier networks for Internet VPNs, multiple

Direct Connect circuits (preferably in different colocation facilities or metros), and multiple cloud on-ramps or points of entry. For example, if all your branches connect via a single SD-WAN provider's backbone, consider a backup path over the Internet or a secondary MPLS for diversity. If you have Direct Connect, provision at least two connections in different locations (e.g., one in Equinix Ashburn and another in Equinix Dallas for AWS us-east-1). Also diversify at the port level (multiple interface connections aggregated, or at least redundant routers). This way, a single failure domain doesn't take you completely offline—failover always has "somewhere good to land."

Policy-Governed Routing: Rely on your own routing policy, not on default behavior. In BGP terms, you set the local preference for egress and use AS PATH and MED for ingress influence, rather than hoping AWS (or the Internet at large) will "do the right thing." Know why each traffic flow takes the path it does. For example, if traffic from branch offices to AWS is supposed to prefer Direct Connect, make sure the BGP local preference on your branch routers is higher for routes learned via DX than for those learned via VPN. Conversely, for AWS to on-premises traffic, if you have two on-prem links, use AS path prepending on the backup link's routes so AWS sees the primary as shorter (AWS's DXGW will prefer the route with the shorter AS path or the one with the default lower MED if paths are equal length). When a failure occurs, the change in BGP (withdrawal or MED/Pref difference) should drive the new path selection according to your plan, not by accident.

Align Latency with Locality: Always try to serve users from the closest or most appropriate region and route traffic into that region as directly as possible. If a user in Asia needs to fail over to a backup server in Europe, consider how the network will carry that traffic—perhaps have an Asia-to-Europe private backbone or use an AWS Accelerator to minimize the long-haul latency. Steer traffic toward the "right" region for a given workflow. AWS offers services like Global Accelerator, which can Anycast user traffic to the nearest AWS edge, then carry it over AWS's backbone to the chosen region—this can improve both latency and consistency for public-facing applications. For internal traffic, design your routing so that, for instance, a branch in Tokyo reaches the Tokyo local region for primary services and only goes to another region when necessary (and even then, possibly through a private backbone or SD-WAN overlay that optimizes that path). If conditions change (latency spikes, a region fails), be ready to steer again—meaning your failover mechanisms and policies should account for latency and not just binary up/down.

Test Failovers and Monitor: A core lesson from previous chapters is that calm recoveries depend on clear intent. In networking, that means simulating failures and verifying the intended behavior. Test that if you drop a primary Direct Connect, BGP indeed fails over to the backup VPN within the expected time. Check that when a primary path is restored, you don't oscillate too rapidly (sometimes you may intentionally delay reversion to primary to avoid flapping). Use route monitoring (BGP route feeds, CloudWatch for DX BGP status, etc.) to ensure that when a link goes down, the routes are withdrawn or de-preferenced as expected.

Design intent alone is not sufficient for resilience—operators must continuously observe and validate that routing and failover behave as expected under real conditions.

Operator Checklist: What to Monitor in Hybrid Traffic Engineering

Once routing intent is defined, resilience depends on whether the network actually behaves that way during failures, maintenance, and load shifts. The following operational signals are critical for validating hybrid traffic-engineering designs in production.

BGP and BFD State

Monitor BGP session status across all hybrid links (Direct Connect, VPN, SD-WAN edges), including session uptime, flap frequency, and route withdrawals. Where BFD is enabled (notably on Direct Connect), monitor BFD session state and detection timers. Fast failover depends on the control plane reacting in milliseconds, not minutes.

Direct Connect Metrics

Use Amazon CloudWatch to monitor Direct Connect connection state, virtual interface status, and traffic levels. Watch for unexpected drops in throughput, sustained near-capacity utilization, or asymmetric traffic patterns—these often surface during failover or regional traffic shifts.

Transit Gateway Routing State

Continuously inspect effective routes in Transit Gateway route tables. Validate which prefixes are active, which attachments are selected as next hops, and whether backup routes are present but correctly de-preferenced. Misaligned propagation or association is a common cause of black holes during incidents.

Latency, Loss, and Synthetic Probes

Track latency, packet loss, and jitter across primary and secondary paths. Because AWS does not provide end-to-end latency metrics for hybrid links, synthetic probes from branches or edge locations are essential. Degradation often appears here before a hard failure occurs.

Replication and State Lag

For stateful workloads, monitor replication lag and write acknowledgment latency alongside network metrics. A routing failover that succeeds technically but increases latency can still violate recovery objectives (RPO/RTO), especially for databases and distributed systems.

Test Failovers Regularly

Periodically simulate failures—link down events, BGP withdrawals, or path de-preferencing—and confirm that traffic shifts according to design. Verify not just that failover occurs, but that it occurs within expected time bounds and preserves symmetry, inspection paths, and compliance constraints.

With these operational signals in place, we can now follow how traffic actually moves through a hybrid network and see how control-plane decisions translate into real forwarding behavior.

How Data Travels in a Hybrid Network: The Journey

Picture a user tapping an app on a phone in Geneva. That single gesture triggers a complex journey for the data. Let's walk through a plausible hybrid path step by step, from the branch to the cloud and back, highlighting points of interest:

Branch LAN and SD-WAN Edge.

The packet starts on the branch's local network (e.g., a Wi-Fi network, then onto Ethernet). It first hits a local gateway device, which could be an SD-WAN appliance or router that handles NAT, segmentation (like VRFs or VLANs for different departments), and security policy enforcement. This device then encapsulates the traffic into an SD-WAN overlay tunnel. The overlay might be using a proprietary protocol or standard GRE/IPsec, but essentially it's going to choose between multiple available underlays. Suppose the branch has both a broadband Internet link and an MPLS circuit: the SD-WAN monitors both and decides to send this packet over the path with less latency and packet loss at the moment. If it's an IPsec VPN toward AWS, note that encryption overhead will reduce the effective MTU—hence the need to clamp TCP MSS (e.g., to **1406 bytes**) with an inner VPN MTU of **1446 bytes** to avoid fragmentation inside the tunnel.

Underlay Transport (Internet/MPLS).

The packet (encrypted and encapsulated by SD-WAN) travels over the chosen underlay network. If it's the Internet, the packet might traverse several ISPs and exchange points. If it's MPLS, it goes through the carrier's private network. The key here is the underlay is outside your direct control (especially in the Internet case). Latency or routing changes can occur without your input. Your SD-WAN overlay might react to these by shifting tunnels, but at any given time, the underlay quality affects the overlay performance. *(Conceptual, accurate.)*

Carrier or Colocation Meet-Me Point.

Many enterprises bring traffic from branches into a regional colocation facility where they have a presence (routers) and where cloud on-ramps exist. In our Geneva example, perhaps the traffic goes to a meet-me room in Zurich. In that colo, your router connects to an AWS Direct Connect device via a VLAN. Let's say this branch's traffic is destined for AWS, so it enters the Direct Connect on a VLAN that is tied to a **transit virtual interface (VIF)**. Over this VIF, your on-prem router and AWS exchange BGP routes. Typically, you'll have BGP with fast keepalive settings **or BFD** to detect issues quickly. The Direct Connect link provides a deterministic path into AWS's network, with a known capacity (e.g., 1/10/100 Gbps, etc.) and **supports jumbo frames—8500 bytes on Transit VIFs and 9001 bytes on Private VIFs.**

AWS Edge—Direct Connect Gateway and Transit Gateway.

Once over the DX link, the packet reaches the **AWS Direct Connect Gateway (DXGW)**. The DXGW is a global resource that distributes routes between your on-prem BGP session and one or more **Transit Gateways (TGWs)** in AWS Regions. In our scenario, the DXGW is associated with a TGW in **eu-central-1** (Frankfurt), where our application lives. The DXGW passes your branch's route advertisements into the TGW, and vice versa. The TGW is a central routing hub: it has attachments—one for Direct Connect (via DXGW), others for VPCs, maybe some VPNs or peering—and it routes according to its TGW route tables.

Cloud Network—VPC and Subnet.

The packet lands on the Elastic Network Interface (ENI) of an EC2 instance inside the target VPC (or perhaps hits a load balancer ENI first if going to, say, an ALB). Within the VPC's subnet route table, there was a route for the branch's subnet pointing to the TGW attachment (enabling return traffic). The instance receives the packet, and the application processes the request. *(AWS VPC route tables are LPM-based; this description is correct.)*

Return Path and Symmetry.

Now the server needs to reply. Ideally, we want the return path to be symmetric—going back out via Direct Connect to the branch in Geneva. To achieve this, routing on the cloud side must prefer the private path. **When both DX and VPN propagate the same prefix into TGW, AWS prefers the DX path by default** (because DX routes carry a **lower default MED** than VPN routes). On the on-prem side, configure branch/core routers to prefer routes learned via DX (e.g., higher local-pref). In our example, the branch's prefix is advertised over both DX and a backup VPN, but the on-prem core assigns a higher local preference to the DX-learned prefix. Thus, return traffic from the app goes TGW ➤ DXGW ➤ Direct Connect to the Zurich colo and back to the branch via SD-WAN—the same path in reverse. **Symmetry is achieved by routing policy design.**

Handling Other Traffic (SaaS, Internet Egress).

If the application server in AWS needs to call an external service (say a SaaS API or an AWS public service like S3), special care is needed. A common pitfall is **asymmetric egress**: the client reached the server over DX, but the server's outbound call exits via a NAT Gateway to the Internet, bypassing on-prem inspection and confusing stateful firewalls. Mitigations include:

- **VPC endpoints** so traffic to S3/DynamoDB stays on the AWS network without an Internet Gateway or NAT;

- **Interface endpoints (AWS PrivateLink)** for private access to many AWS services and some partner/SaaS offerings;

- If public egress is required, make sure the on-prem firewall policies account for those flows.

For example, adding a **Gateway VPC Endpoint for S3** keeps instance→S3 traffic within AWS (no NAT/IGW), while vendor APIs without private options will still egress via **NAT Gateway**—which you should document and secure.

Mini failover scenario (performance and resilience).

We have two Direct Connect connections at the Zurich colo (in different port groups/devices for redundancy). **BFD** runs on both. Branch traffic normally uses the primary DX. We simulate a primary DX failure (interface shutdown). **BFD detects loss in ~300 ms**, and the BGP session on that VIF drops; the **DXGW/TGW** path via the primary withdraws. Immediately, the backup DX (or a VPN, if present) takes over; TGW selects the alternate propagated route (already present but less preferred). Because we engineered this with BGP (and BFD), failover is fast and automatic. The SD-WAN edge may only see a brief blip, and user traffic continues on the secondary path. When the primary returns, you can damp reversion to avoid flaps, then restore the primary if that's policy.

This end-to-end example underscores the importance of **routing intent**. Every segment—branch, SD-WAN, DX, TGW, VPC—must be configured so the packet goes where it should and returns via the intended path. You don't get symmetry or optimal latency by accident in hybrid networks; **you get it by design**.

Inside AWS: Transit Gateway and VPC Routing Details

Now that we've followed the data path, let's dig into how AWS's routing constructs make decisions (as this often confuses architects expecting traditional router behavior). Two main constructs in AWS govern hybrid routing: VPC subnet route tables and Transit Gateway route tables. Each has its own logic:

VPC Subnet Route Tables: Every subnet in a VPC has an associated route table. The rules here are simple: longest-prefix match wins, and there is no route priority beyond that. You can have both a propagated and a static route for the same prefix in a VPC route table; when that happens, the static route simply takes precedence and the propagated one is ignored. If one route is more specific (/24 vs. /16), the /24 wins, period. There's no BGP in the VPC, no path selection based on AS path or metrics—it's purely table lookup. Also, VPC route tables include implicit routes like "local" (for the VPC's own CIDR), which always have the highest priority (since they are effectively the most specific for the VPC's range). For example, if your VPC is 10.0.0.0/16, the route "10.0.0.0/16 local" ensures internal traffic never goes to TGW. If you had a broader route (0.0.0.0/0 IGW) and a more specific (10.0.0.0/16 TGW), the latter would never take effect because AWS reserves that prefix as local.

Transit Gateway Route Tables: A Transit Gateway has its own route tables that you create and associate attachments with. Transit Gateway's routing logic is a bit more complex due to multiple attachment types and propagation. Key rules based on AWS best practices:

1. Longest-prefix match is evaluated first on the TGW route table (just like a normal router).

2. If two routes have the same prefix length, static routes beat propagated routes. This means if you manually define a route in TGW (pointing to a certain attachment), it will override any dynamic routes to that prefix coming from BGP. This can be used as a form of route preference or to black hole routes deliberately.

3. If two propagated routes of equal specificity are learned from different attachment types, AWS has a fixed priority order for attachment types; this attachment-type priority applies when prefix length is equal and no overriding BGP attributes (such as a more specific AS path or explicit MED) alter the decision. The documented order is VPC > Direct Connect > Transit Gateway Connect (GRE) > VPN (including VPN-over-DX) > then TGW peering. In other words, if the same prefix is advertised from a VPC attachment and also from a Direct Connect, the VPC route "wins" (which typically would mean the packet stays in VPC rather than going out to on-prem, unless that static scenario is unusual). If it's between Direct Connect and VPN, Direct Connect wins by default. This is actually implemented by AWS using BGP attributes: when AWS receives routes from DX vs. VPN, if no MED is sent, AWS assigns a default MED of 0 to DX and 100 to VPN. Thus, DX is preferred (lower MED). AWS also prefers routes coming from external BGP (which DX and VPN are) over internal (which in TGW might not apply much except maybe to Connect peers).

4. If two propagated routes have the same prefix and the same attachment type (e.g., two VPNs both advertised 10.1.0.0/16), then AWS does consider BGP attributes: it looks at AS Path, MED, and so on. Shorter AS Path wins, then lower MED, etc., similar to standard BGP. But AWS warns that if everything is equal, they cannot guarantee consistent tie-breaking in that scenario. In practice, you shouldn't rely on two equal routes from the same attachment type—instead, try to design so that one is more specific or one has an AS path prepend to break the tie intentionally. If you want both to be used, consider enabling ECMP (which TGW does support across VPNs or Connect attachments, up to 4)—but that's only if the traffic is hashed across equal-cost routes.

5. Transit Gateway route table association vs. propagation: Each TGW attachment (VPC, DX, VPN, etc.) is associated with one TGW route table. That means when traffic arrives on that attachment, the TGW looks in that specific route table to decide where to send it. Separately, attachments can propagate routes into one or more TGW route tables. Propagation means the routes learned over that attachment's BGP will be inserted into those route tables (if they fit, etc.). One attachment can propagate to multiple tables, but it's only associated with one table for lookup. A common mistake is assuming that if an attachment propagates routes to a table, it will also use that table for egress—not true, unless it's also associated with that table. You must set the association properly. This design allows segmentation: you might have a "branch route table" and a separate "datacenter route table" on the TGW to isolate who can talk to whom. But it also means misconfiguring propagation/association leads to black holes. Always verify that for each attachment, the intended route table is associated, and all necessary routes from other attachments are propagated into it.

To illustrate AWS's route selection, imagine your on-prem network (10.50.0.0/16) is advertised via both a VPN and Direct Connect into TGW. TGW will see 10.50.0.0/16 from the DX attachment and from the VPN attachment. Both are propagated routes of equal prefix length. TGW will prefer the Direct Connect because DX attachments rank higher than VPN attachments (and/or the MED 0 vs. 100 difference). If that DX goes down and the route withdraws, the TGW will then automatically use the VPN route (which now is the only route for 10.50.0.0/16, so it wins). AWS's internal logic selects a single active route for forwarding at any given time. While backup routes may exist, only the active path is used for data forwarding, and the selected route is the one reflected in effective forwarding behavior. This is why your BGP design (using those attributes) and the AWS precedence rules together result in the failover behavior. If you wanted the opposite (prefer VPN unless DX is up, for some reason), you'd have to manipulate MED or prepend AS path on the DX side to make it less preferred despite the defaults.

Lastly, note that Direct Connect Gateway (DXGW) can associate with Transit Gateways in multiple regions. AWS does not document a deterministic tie-break if the same prefix is advertised from more than one region, so designs should avoid that scenario unless active-active operation is intentional. Keep regional route announcements distinct, or use BGP communities and filters to control propagation. AWS doesn't give a direct knob to change that—it's implicit. So generally avoid advertising identical prefixes from different regions unless you want an active-active scenario; otherwise, keep regional route announcements distinct or use BGP communities to control them.

In summary for AWS routing: Within a VPC, think static and specific; within a TGW, remember the fixed priority order and plan your routes to avoid ties. The cloud doesn't run full BGP inside, but it does interpret the outputs of your BGP (via propagated routes) according to these deterministic rules.

For completeness, AWS has another construct called AWS Cloud WAN, which uses core network edges and segments, but that's beyond our scope here. If you use Cloud WAN, similar ideas of route propagation and priority apply, but with a different model.

Control Planes: Who Tells the Packets Where to Go?

Earlier we talked about control plane vs. data plane in the context of failovers. In networking, this concept originated: the data plane forwards packets at line rate according to a forwarding table, and the control plane is responsible for computing and distributing that forwarding table. When a failover is "boring," it's usually because the control plane converged on a new correct route before users realized there was a problem.

In hybrid networking, the primary control-plane protocol between your network and AWS is BGP (Border Gateway Protocol). BGP exchanges reachability information (routes) between your on-premises Customer Gateway (CGW) device and AWS's endpoints (VGW or TGW via DX). Let's pinpoint where the control planes meet and how they operate:

> **Customer Gateway (CGW):** This is your device on the edge—it could be a physical router or an SD-WAN appliance—configured as a BGP peer to AWS. If you use Site-to-Site VPN, your CGW establishes IPsec tunnels to AWS (two tunnels per VPN connection for redundancy) and then runs BGP over those tunnels (inside the encryption). In this case, liveness is tracked by VPN keepalives (IKE Dead Peer Detection) rather than BGP's own timers, because if the tunnel drops, the BGP session will drop. If you use Direct Connect, your CGW peers via BGP on the dedicated circuit's virtual interface. Depending on whether you want to reach one VPC or many, you choose a private VIF (to a specific Virtual Private Gateway on a VPC) or a transit VIF (to a Direct Connect Gateway, which then links to one or more TGWs). In either case, the CGW and AWS exchange routes. You'll use either a private ASN or public ASN for your side, and AWS has its own ASN (e.g., 7224 on public VIFs; for private VIFs and TGW, the ASN is configurable and commonly defaults to 64512).

> **AWS Edge (VGW/TGW/DXGW):** If connecting to a single VPC via VPN, AWS has a Virtual Private Gateway (VGW) attached to that VPC; the BGP session terminates there. If connecting via TGW (the more modern approach), the VPN or DX terminates on a Transit Gateway (or technically on an AWS VPN endpoint, which is associated with a TGW). For Direct Connect, the BGP actually terminates on an AWS device at the colo, which is associated with a DX Gateway. The DX Gateway then reflects routes into the Transit Gateways you attached to it. In any case, once AWS receives your routes, it distributes them internally: the DXGW to TGW path is internal (not something you see, but AWS propagates

the prefix to the TGW route table if propagation is enabled). Similarly, routes from a TGW (like VPC routes or other sites) get advertised back to you via DXGW or VPN BGP.

BGP Timers and BFD: By default, BGP isn't superfast at detecting dead peers (**AWS commonly uses 30s keepalive/90s hold**). In a critical network, you'll want to reduce those. While you can set the hold timer as low as 3 seconds (keepalive 1 second), a better approach is often to use **BFD where available**. BFD gives sub-second detection without stressing the CPU as much as ultra-fast keepalives might. **On AWS Direct Connect, asynchronous BFD is enabled on the AWS side**—if you configure a ~300 ms interval and multiplier of 3 on your router, failures can be detected and BGP routes withdrawn in well under a second. **On VPN, AWS does not support BFD** (Accelerated VPN uses AWS Global Accelerator health checks under the hood, which is different). So VPN failover is typically a few seconds at best (DPD might detect a dead peer in, say, ~10 seconds by default, though vendors allow some tuning).

Now, what does BGP do with all these routes? BGP's job is to allow two autonomous systems (your network and AWS's network) to exchange reachability while each retains control. Unlike an interior gateway protocol (OSPF, EIGRP, etc.), BGP doesn't assume full trust or a single metric like cost. Instead, BGP is a policy-driven protocol—it's all about the attributes attached to routes, which convey preferences.

Recap of BGP Best-Path Selection (let's simplify things a bit): When a BGP router has multiple routes to the same prefix, it goes through a series of rules to pick the "best" one:

- **Highest local preference wins** (this is a numeric value you assign inside your own AS to prefer one path over another for outgoing traffic). This attribute does not leave your AS; it's purely internal. Typically, you might set local-pref high for a route coming in via Direct Connect (to prefer sending traffic out that way) and lower for the same route coming in via VPN.

- If local-pref is tied, the **shortest AS path wins**. This looks at how many AS hops the route has traversed. For incoming traffic to you, AWS will examine the AS path on routes you announce—e.g., if you prepend your ASN multiple times on one announcement, AWS will see that as a longer path and prefer a different one if available. On your side, you might see AWS advertisements, usually with a fixed AS path (they often originate from an ASN like 7224 or 9059, etc., with maybe an internal hop if TGW adds one).

- If AS path length ties, then BGP considers the **Origin type** (prefer routes that were originally from an IGP vs. "incomplete"), which in the AWS context is usually not relevant since everything is "incomplete" origin typically.

- Next, it looks at **MED (Multi-Exit Discriminator)** if the routes are from the same neighboring AS. MED is a hint from the neighbor about which path is preferred into that AS. **AWS applies default MEDs when none are set: 0 on Direct Connect and 100 on VPN/ Connect**, effectively preferring Direct Connect by default. You can override this by setting an explicit MED on your routes if you want AWS to choose differently (some advanced cases might, but rare).

- If still tied, it then prefers **eBGP over iBGP**, then the **lowest IGP cost to the next hop** (internal to your device), and finally the **oldest route** (to avoid flapping) or the **lowest router ID** as a last resort.

Two points often forgotten:

- A BGP route isn't considered at all if its **next hop is unreachable**. This is critical when you have route reflectors or iBGP—but in our context, if you receive a route from AWS, your router will only use it if the next hop (e.g., the AWS router's IP) is in the routing table via connected or static.

- BGP by default will choose **one best path**. It doesn't load balance over multiple unless you explicitly configure **maximum-paths** for BGP (and even then, the routes must be identical in most attributes). So even if two VPN tunnels have the same prefixes, you won't use both unless you enabled **ECMP** in the TGW (for egress from AWS) or configured your router for multipath (for egress from you). **TGW supports ECMP across up to 4 equal-cost VPN or Connect peers; VGW does not.**

Now, how does this apply to hybrid resilience? If you design BGP attributes correctly, you can achieve a situation where: The **primary path is preferred** (higher local-pref, shorter AS path); **backup path is ready but not used** (lower preference). When primary fails, BGP withdraws it; backup immediately kicks in. When primary comes back, you might hold off (using something like route flap damping or just relying on the fact that BGP won't instantly withdraw the backup until primary is stable)—thus avoiding oscillation. This is exactly analogous to the failover choreography we discussed at the application layer—detect ➤ decide ➤ promote—except here the "promotion" is of a backup route to the best route. If done well, users barely notice the failover or just see a minor blip.

Where AWS-specific BGP fits in: AWS does not run BGP inside VPCs, but it does at the edges (DXGW, TGW). AWS will honor standard BGP attributes at the border:

- It pays attention to **AS Path** on routes you advertise (for ingress into AWS).

- It supports **MED** on routes from you **(and applies the default MED 0 vs. 100 behavior noted above)** when evaluating multiple inbound attachments from the same AS.

- It does not propagate your **Local Preference**—that's your internal decision.

- AWS can send communities and accept some communities (e.g., AWS has specific BGP community tags you can use to control route propagation/scope, and they tag public routes appropriately, often with NO_EXPORT semantics).

- **Private ASN handling:** If you use a private ASN for your side on a **public VIF**, AWS removes the private ASN from the AS path before announcing it to the Internet. On **private VIFs/TGW**, your ASN (even if private) is preserved because it's only between you and AWS.

Accelerated VPN Note: Earlier we mentioned AWS Accelerated Site-to-Site VPN. From a control plane perspective, accelerated VPN doesn't change BGP itself— you still run BGP over the VPN tunnels. What changes is the **underlay path**: instead of your IPsec traffic traversing the open Internet all the way to the AWS VPN gateway in the region, it is forwarded to the nearest **AWS Global Accelerator** edge and then rides the AWS private backbone to the region. This can shorten the route and avoid unstable Internet segments. You **must create a new VPN with acceleration enabled** (you can't toggle an existing one). Once up, AWS manages two hidden Global Accelerator endpoints for your tunnels. The routing (BGP) over it remains the same, but the transport quality (latency/jitter) is typically more consistent. It's a useful interim when you don't yet have Direct Connect but need better than Internet paths or for backup paths that you want more reliability from.

Hybrid Connectivity Options: VPN and Direct Connect

Now that we have an understanding of how routing works in a hybrid environment, let's zoom in on the primary connectivity options enterprises use to link their on-premises networks to AWS: **AWS Site-to-Site VPN** (including **Accelerated VPN**) and **AWS Direct Connect**.

The choice between them is typically a trade-off between **speed of deployment**, **performance**, and **cost**. Site-to-Site VPNs can be established within minutes over the public Internet and are ideal for **rapid setups**, **proof-of-concept environments**, or as a **redundant backup path**. Direct Connect, by contrast, requires physical provisioning through an AWS-approved provider but delivers **consistent, private, low-latency connectivity** with **predictable bandwidth** for production workloads and steady data transfer.

In practice, many organizations use **both**—VPN for agility and redundancy and Direct Connect as the **primary transport** for critical or high-throughput workloads. This dual-path design enables resilience as well as performance optimization across hybrid networks.

Site-to-Site VPN: The Universal On-Ramp

AWS Site-to-Site VPN is often the starting point for hybrid connectivity. It uses IPsec tunnels over the public Internet to connect your router to AWS. Key characteristics:

> **Quick Deployment:** You can typically set up a VPN within hours—no need to wait for circuit provisioning. AWS VPN is a managed service; you allocate a VPN connection (which creates

two endpoints on the AWS side) and configure your router accordingly. This makes it great for rapid onboarding of new sites or as an immediate solution while waiting for Direct Connect circuits.

Two Tunnels for HA: Each VPN connection from AWS comes with two redundant tunnels, usually terminating on different AWS devices/AZs for resilience. Both are up, and AWS will prefer one as primary (you can influence that by BGP AS path or priorities if needed). If one tunnel or its path fails, the other is there. Note that with a VGW, AWS uses one tunnel at a time for egress; with TGW, AWS can do ECMP and use both simultaneously for egress up to 1.25+1.25 Gbps aggregate.

Throughput and Performance: As mentioned, a single VPN tunnel can do about 1.25 Gbps under ideal conditions (that's a soft cap due to single-tunnel throughput and crypto overhead). Latency is obviously dependent on the Internet path; jitter can be high if the route fluctuates. The encryption overhead means the maximum packet size for data (MTU) is around 1446 bytes, since the IPsec headers (ESP, new IP header, etc.) consume bytes out of the standard 1500. Path MTU Discovery (PMTUD) absolutely must be allowed (ICMP type 3 code 4 messages) for things to work smoothly. If PMTUD is blocked, large packets will get dropped or fragmented incorrectly. AWS recommends setting your tunnel interface MTU to 1436-1446 and clamping TCP MSS to 1406 (as noted before). They also note that certain encryption algorithms with bigger overhead (like longer authentication tags) can reduce that even further, so always consult AWS's VPN documentation for current guidance.

Failover Time: Standard VPN relies on IKE keepalives (Dead Peer Detection) to detect a lost tunnel. This usually operates on the order of several seconds. You can tune the DPD timeout on some devices. But you will not get sub-second failover on traditional VPN—typically it might be ~10 seconds or more before the BGP session drops if a tunnel goes dark (because the underlying IPsec is still up until DPD times out). There is no BFD for VPN, except in Accelerated VPN, where Global Accelerator's health checks might help a bit. So plan for a few seconds of potential interruption in a failover if using VPN as primary. If this is not acceptable, that's an argument for Direct Connect or Accelerated VPN.

Cost: AWS VPN is charged hourly per connection and per GB data. It's generally quite cost-effective for moderate traffic levels, but if you push terabytes, Direct Connect's flat port fees plus lower data transfer rates can be cheaper. VPN has an advantage that data transfer out from AWS over VPN is charged at the same rate as over the Internet (cheaper than over DX in many cases, unless you have a lot of volume where DX's port fee amortizes well). It's worth noting that as of 2024, AWS also introduced VPN tiered pricing where high data usage can get cheaper per GB.

Common use cases for Site-to-Site VPN: initial migrations (getting started quickly), remote or smaller sites that can't justify a DX, backup paths (having a VPN as a standby in case DX fails), and overflow capacity (if DX is at capacity, you might spill to VPN). Also, some customers use VPN for encryption compliance even if they have DX, since basic DX is not encrypted (unless you add MACsec on dedicated 10/100G, which many do for security).

Accelerated VPN: Squeezing Performance from the Internet

AWS Accelerated Site-to-Site VPN is an enhancement to standard VPN that leverages the **AWS Global Accelerator** infrastructure to improve performance and reliability. When acceleration is enabled on a VPN connection (**only available for Transit Gateway–based VPNs, not VGW**), AWS provisions **two Global Accelerator edge endpoints**, one per tunnel.

These endpoints are **Anycast IPs** hosted at AWS edge locations close to your customer gateway's geographic region. Your VPN tunnels terminate at those nearby edges, and AWS then carries the encrypted IPsec traffic over its **private backbone** to the VPN termination point in the target AWS Region. This can significantly reduce **latency and jitter**—especially when Internet last-mile performance is acceptable but the **long-haul Internet path** was previously unstable. It can also mitigate transient BGP routing changes and congestion events by shifting the long-haul segment to AWS's managed backbone.

Operational Behavior

Enabling Accelerated VPN is simply a matter of **selecting the acceleration option** (via console, CLI, or API) when creating a **new VPN attachment**.

It cannot be enabled for an existing VPN connection—you must **create a new VPN** and cut over traffic once verified.

A few key requirements:

- The **Customer Gateway (CGW)** device must initiate the **IKE negotiation**, as Global Accelerator edges operate in a responder mode. Most on-prem routers already support this behavior.

- **Not all AWS Regions** currently support Accelerated VPN; AWS continues expanding coverage, so always check the latest supported Regions list.

- **Accelerated VPN cannot terminate on VGW**, nor can it run over Direct Connect public VIFs—it is exclusively for **Internet-based TGW VPNs**.

Performance Characteristics

Accelerated VPN does **not change encryption, routing, or BGP behavior**; it simply replaces the long-haul public Internet path with the AWS backbone.

Encryption (IPsec) and route exchange (BGP) work exactly as in standard VPNs. In testing and field reports, customers have observed:

- Noticeably **lower latency variance** and **improved stability** compared to regular Internet VPNs.

- **Faster failover recovery**, since Global Accelerator edges detect tunnel health more consistently than typical Internet paths.

- **No change in throughput limits**—the same per-tunnel bandwidth (~1.25 Gbps) applies.

Think of Accelerated VPN as a **middle ground** between public-Internet VPN and private circuits like Direct Connect: a quick way to gain **backbone-grade reliability** without the lead time or cost of physical provisioning.

When to Use Which

- **Use a standard VPN** when rapid deployment is critical, bandwidth requirements are moderate, or it serves as a backup to private links.

- **Use Accelerated VPN** when Internet instability impacts latency or jitter, but you don't yet have Direct Connect—or as a **permanent solution** for partner or branch connections that need predictable performance without full DX investment.

Let's now move to dedicated, private connectivity, Direct Connect.

AWS Direct Connect: Determinism by Design

Rather than reintroducing Direct Connect as a service, this section focuses on how its routing behavior, failure detection, and scale characteristics influence hybrid resilience.

AWS Direct Connect provides a private, deterministic network path into AWS, trading deployment speed for predictable latency, bandwidth, and routing control. In resilience design, its primary value is not connectivity itself, but the ability to engineer traffic behavior precisely during failure.

> **Dedicated vs. Hosted:** Define the available capacity and operational control. A Dedicated Direct Connect is a port you order directly from AWS at a DX location (typically a colocation facility such as Equinix or Digital Realty). It comes in 1 Gbps, 10 Gbps, 100 Gbps, and now 400 Gbps capacities. You (or your colocation provider) physically cross-connect your router to the AWS device port. A Hosted connection is when an AWS Partner already has a big pipe to AWS and gives you a sub-port (anywhere from 50 Mbps up to 25 Gbps). Hosted saves you from having your own presence but relies on the partner's infra. Hosted have some

limits (e.g., only 1 virtual interface and such for some types). If possible, dedicated gives you full control.

Virtual Interfaces (VIFs): A single Direct Connect port can host multiple virtual interfaces, partitioned by VLAN tags. The VIF type determines how routes are distributed and which AWS constructs (VGW, DXGW, TGW) participate in forwarding decisions.

Private VIF: Used for private IP connectivity into VPCs, either directly via a Virtual Private Gateway (one VPC per VIF) or through a Direct Connect Gateway that fans out to multiple VPCs, potentially across regions. Private VIFs are typically chosen when connectivity scope is limited and tightly controlled.

Transit VIF: Terminates on a Direct Connect Gateway that is associated with one or more Transit Gateways, enabling scalable hub-and-spoke architectures across many VPCs and regions. Transit VIFs are the standard choice for large hybrid environments. A Direct Connect Gateway configured for Transit VIFs cannot simultaneously host Private VIF attachments to Virtual Private Gateways, which is an important design constraint.

Public VIF: This lets you reach AWS public endpoints (for services like S3, DynamoDB, SNS, etc., or even AWS public IPs of EC2 in any region) over the private link, instead of via the internet. You advertise your public IP prefixes (the ones you own) to AWS, and AWS advertises all AWS public IP ranges to you (with BGP communities to help you filter by region/service if you want). Public VIFs are less common if you have good internet, but some enterprises use them to get a consistent high-speed path to AWS services or to avoid exposure to the internet. Keep in mind, public VIF traffic still must originate from or be destined to your advertised IPs (you can't reach someone else's IP that's not AWS or yours).

Let's now explore what other benefits and capabilities come with DX.

MACsec Encryption: By default, Direct Connect is not encrypted—it's a layer 2 Ethernet link. If you require encryption, you either run an IPsec VPN on top of it (many do, basically treating DX as a big pipe for private VPN) or use MACsec. AWS supports MACsec (802.1AE) on dedicated 10 G, 100 G, and 400 G connections at select locations. MACsec is data-link-layer encryption that can operate near line rate. For example, financial institutions often require it. You need a supported device (many enterprise routers/switches support MACsec), and you have to request a MACsec-capable port from AWS. They periodically update which locations have MACsec; as of now, many major US/EU/Asia locations do. With MACsec, you can securely use DX even for sensitive data (the data is encrypted between your router and the AWS router).

Deterministic Performance: Direct Connect offers consistent bandwidth—if you have a 1 Gbps port, you get 1 Gbps (well, minus Ethernet overhead) always available. There's no competing traffic from other customers on that link (beyond AWS's internal handling if you oversubscribe a region's capacity, but AWS capacity is generally robust). Latency is often the propagation delay plus a small AWS network transit. It's usually lower than going over the Internet because you eliminate extra hops and routing indirection. Jitter is very low. For applications like voice, video, financial transactions, or large-scale data transfer (backups, migrations), this predictability is a big win.

Costs: Direct Connect has a port-hour cost and a data transfer cost (per GB) that is lower than Internet egress costs. For high volumes, it's much cheaper. However, you also have to factor in the colocation cross-connect and possibly the last mile if you're extending from your data center to the colo. DX is generally justified when you have either significant data transfer (>TBs per month) or need steady low latency. If you only send a few hundred GB, a VPN might be cheaper than paying for a 1 G port. AWS has no long-term contract for DX; you can shut it anytime (though providers might have terms for cross-connects). And you can aggregate multiple links in a LAG for more bandwidth or redundancy.

Best Practices for Direct Connect: Always provision redundant connections. AWS recommends at least two in different locations for production (for 99.9% uptime, two at one site in a LAG + two at second site; for 99.99%, four total across two sites)—see the Resiliency Toolkit guides. We will go into more detail about this, in Section 7.4 of this chapter. Use BGP (DX requires it anyway) and tune BGP timers or use BFD for fast failover. Enable jumbo frames end-to-end if you can—for example, set your VIF to 9001 for private if going to VGW, or 8500 for transit, and make sure your on-prem interface is MTU 9000+. Then ensure your instances in VPC use MTU 9001 and any switches in between allow it. This can significantly improve throughput for large flows such as replication, provided jumbo frames are configured consistently across the end-to-end path. Monitor the DX connection via CloudWatch and set alarms on connection state, BGP state, and TX/RX.

One More Feature: One more feature is Direct Connect SiteLink. SiteLink allows you to use the AWS global network to connect on-premises sites through Direct Connect locations without routing traffic through a VPC. In other words, if you have Direct Connect connections at different locations, SiteLink can carry traffic between those locations over the AWS global infrastructure instead of hairpinning through a regional router. This can be useful for building or augmenting a private backbone. SiteLink is enabled on supported VIFs, and the routers at the two locations can exchange routes over BGP. If you already have a private WAN, SiteLink may be unnecessary, but some organizations use it to augment or replace costly telco networks.

VPN vs. Direct Connect—When to Use Which?

To wrap up, here are general guidelines on when to use VPN or Direct Connect, or both:

Start with VPN for new cloud deployments due to its speed and ease. It's perfectly fine for light workloads, dev/test environments, or as interim connectivity.

Use Direct Connect when you require guaranteed bandwidth, lower and more stable latency, or have a large data transfer volume that makes VPN costs or performance untenable. Especially for production-critical workloads (database replication, VDI, etc.), DX provides that determinism.

Many enterprises deploy both: Direct Connect as the primary path and VPN as an encrypted backup. With BGP, you can have VPN carry routes with a higher AS path so they're only used if DX is down. This gives high reliability. (Alternatively, if security mandates always-encrypted traffic, some run IPsec over Direct Connect itself; though if MACsec is available, that's often cleaner.)

If compliance requires encryption for all paths and MACsec isn't available, you might still run VPN over Direct Connect. That way you get the routing benefits of DX and encryption of IPsec. It will, however, impose the MTU penalty (around 90 bytes overhead) and some CPU overhead on your routers.

Accelerated VPN can act as a stopgap for offices that aren't near a DX location or when you need improved latency but can't justify a circuit. It won't replace DX if you need consistent 1+ Gbps throughput (VPN is still limited), but for moderate traffic where latency variation was the issue, it's a viable enhancement.

Finally, always design with failure in mind; embrace failure, like I mentioned many times. Resilience is about being able to absorb failure and recover gracefully without having users noticing it. Any single DX connection can go down (fiber cut, router issue, even a power outage at the colo). VPNs can also drop (internet hiccup, device reboot). So a combination—e.g., two DX in hot standby, plus a VPN for extra backup—is not overkill for mission-critical or important workloads. AWS's well-architected principle of "anticipate failure" certainly applies to network links.

Best Practices Recap:

> **Design with Quota Headroom:** Check AWS quotas for routes, attachments, etc., during design. Don't create a design that uses 100% of a limit out of the gate—you might need to grow or adjust, so leave a margin or know how to increase.

> **Routing Precedence Is Deterministic:** The longest prefix match wins everywhere. On TGW, static beats propagated. On VPC, there's no tie-break beyond specificity (no BGP attributes). So if you want to prefer one path, use more specific routes or adjust at BGP input—don't assume the cloud will consider things like AS path unless the routes are equal-length in TGW.

Understand Performance Limits: VPN ~1.25 Gbps per tunnel; use TGW ECMP for scaling VPN if needed (VGW won't ECMP). If you need multi-Gbps continually, plan Direct Connect or multiple VPNs. Latency over VPN = Internet latency; over DX = fiber path (often better). If latency or packet loss on VPN is an issue, Accelerated VPN or an MPLS backup might be needed.

Jumbo Frames and BFD for Heavy Workloads: If you're doing large data transfers (backups, HPC, etc.), jumbo frames can improve throughput by sending ~6x more payload per packet (9001 vs. 1500 bytes)—less overhead. Ensure end-to-end jumbo: instance ENI (9001), TGW (8500), DX VIF (8500/9001), and your router NIC (9000+). And use BFD on DX to detect issues in sub-seconds; it's not really optional when failing over quickly matters—waiting 30+ seconds for BGP could mean a noticeable outage.

Before we move into intentional traffic shaping, it's useful to distill these connectivity options into a practical operator view—when to use each underlay and what behavior to expect under normal operation and during failure.

Cheat Sheet: When to Use VPN, Accelerated VPN, Direct Connect, Exchange, or SD-WAN

Standard Site-to-Site VPN (Internet IPsec)

- **Use When:** Rapid deployment, smaller or remote sites, migrations, temporary or backup connectivity

- **Latency and Jitter:** Variable, dependent on Internet routing conditions

- **Failover Behavior:** Typically seconds, driven by tunnel liveness (IKE Dead Peer Detection) and BGP reconvergence

- **Operational Notes:** IPsec overhead reduces payload size; AWS recommends an inner MTU of 1446 bytes and TCP MSS of 1406 bytes, with exact values dependent on encryption algorithms

Accelerated Site-to-Site VPN (Transit Gateway only)

- **Use When**: VPN is required, but Internet path instability causes unacceptable latency or jitter.

- **What Changes**: IPsec traffic is steered to the nearest AWS edge and carried over the AWS backbone.

- **What Does Not Change**: IPsec encryption, BGP behavior, and per-tunnel throughput limits.

- **Constraints**: supported only for Transit Gateway–attached VPNs; not available on VGW; cannot be used with Direct Connect public VIFs.

AWS Direct Connect (DX)

- **Use When**: Consistent latency, low jitter, predictable bandwidth, and fast, deterministic failover are required

- **Latency and Jitter**: Stable and predictable compared to Internet paths

- **Failover Behavior**: With BFD enabled, link failures can be detected and routes withdrawn in sub-second timeframes

- **Operational Notes**: Requires physical diversity (ports, locations) and careful route-scale planning

Cloud Exchange Fabrics (e.g., Equinix, Megaport, Interxion)

- **Use When**: Fast multi-cloud connectivity and flexible provisioning are needed without building many physical cross-connects

- **Latency and Jitter**: Generally good, but dependent on the exchange and attached providers

- **Failover Behavior**: Varies by provider; the exchange itself becomes an additional shared operational domain that must be monitored and made redundant

SD-WAN (Overlay)

- **Use When**: Large numbers of branches require policy-based steering across multiple transport types

- **Latency and Jitter**: Optimized dynamically by the overlay, but still bounded by underlay quality

- **Failover Behavior**: Often fast within the overlay, but end-to-end outcomes remain dependent on underlay events

- **Operational Notes**: Improves agility and visibility but does not eliminate underlay failures

Rule of thumb:

Resilient hybrid architectures commonly combine Direct Connect as the primary underlay, VPN or Accelerated VPN as a backup, and SD-WAN for branch-level policy and observability.

By building on these fundamentals—a solid underlay (VPN or DX), an expressive control plane (BGP with the right policies), and awareness of how AWS routes traffic—you set the stage for the next step: turning routing into an active tool for resilience and performance. In the next section, we will see how to use BGP attributes (Local Pref, AS Path, MED, Communities) to intentionally shape traffic and how to ensure that when a failure happens, the network behaves exactly as planned, keeping recoveries calm and users happy—no more "the Internet chose a weird path" excuses, because you will choose the paths.

Section 7.3: Engineering Traffic Paths with BGP

Section 7.2 established the foundations of hybrid connectivity: connecting on-premises networks to AWS via VPNs, Direct Connect links, Transit Gateways (TGWs), and BGP route exchange. In that phase, BGP functioned as a neutral conduit—it passed along routes and ensured basic reachability between environments. We could largely rely on default BGP behavior (like shortest-path selection) to get traffic from A to B. The result would be connectivity, but passive connectivity—the paths taken were whatever BGP's algorithm deemed "best" by default, not necessarily what we intended. Now, in Section 7.3, we shift from reachability to intent. This is the realm of traffic engineering: deliberately shaping and influencing routing decisions so that the hybrid network not only works but also works on our terms.

Traffic engineering in a hybrid AWS environment means using the tools of routing policy to coax traffic onto the paths we prefer. Rather than letting BGP blindly pick an arbitrary "best" route, we inject our architectural objectives into the process. These objectives can be varied—minimizing latency, maximizing bandwidth use, reducing cost, avoiding asymmetric paths, or all of the above. In an enterprise data center, engineers have long tweaked routing protocols to meet such goals, and the same is true in the cloud. BGP was designed to be highly flexible: by itself it's impartial (e.g., it doesn't inherently prefer a private Direct Connect over a VPN), but it offers many levers we can pull to enforce policy. The key levers are BGP attributes—properties like Local Preference, AS Path, Multi-Exit Discriminator (MED), and communities that influence path selection. Before diving into individual attributes, it helps to ground traffic engineering in a simple intent map. Table 7-1 summarizes which BGP mechanisms control egress, ingress, and failover behavior in AWS hybrid networks—and in what order they are evaluated.

***Table 7-1.** BGP Intent Map: Which Knob Controls What*

Design Goal	Traffic Direction	Primary Control	Secondary Control	Tie-Breaker / Last Resort	Notes (AWS Behaviour)
Prefer one exit site	On-prem → AWS (egress)	Local Preference (customer AS)	AS-Path (rarely needed)	MED (rare)	Local Pref never leaves your AS
Prefer one DX for return traffic	AWS → on-prem (ingress)	DX BGP Communities (7224:7100/7200/7300) / VPN As-Path	AS-Path prepending	MED	Communities map to AWS internal local-preference
Build active / standby paths	Both directions	Communities (ingress) + Local-Pref (egress)	AS-Path	MED	Deterministic and recommended
Force traffic regardless of attributes	Both directions	Longest Prefix Match	/	/	Always wins, even over communities
Fine-tune equal paths from same AS	AWS → on-prem	/	/	MED (Same Neighbour AS)	Only evaluated if Local-Pref & AS-Path equal (Non-transitive attribute)
Speed up failure detection	Control Plane	BFD (DX)	BGP Timers	/	VPN uses tunable BGP timers (min 1s/3s)

Table 7-1 serves as a mental shortcut: before tuning any attribute, decide whether you are controlling egress, ingress, or failover—and then select the highest-order knob available for that goal.

Note that MED is intentionally listed as a tie-breaker rather than a primary control: in AWS hybrid routing, Local Preference (via communities or customer policy), AS-Path length, and prefix specificity dominate path selection, with MED only evaluated when those signals are equal.

When AWS Ignores Your BGP Tuning

Not all BGP attributes are treated equally inside AWS. While AWS honors standard BGP mechanisms such as communities, AS-path length, and prefix specificity, some AWS-managed components apply **fixed routing preferences** that override customer-side tuning.

In particular, **AWS Transit Gateway and Virtual Private Gateway inherently prefer Direct Connect routes over VPN routes** when both are available for the same destination—regardless of AS-path length or MED values. This bias is intentional and reflects AWS's assumption that Direct Connect provides higher reliability and performance than Internet-based VPNs.

As a result, attempts to make VPN "win" over Direct Connect using AS-path prepending or MED alone may be ignored. When explicit control is required, use **clear, AWS-recognized signals**—such as **BGP communities, longest-prefix match, or distinct route advertisement scopes**—rather than relying on subtle attribute manipulation.

Understanding where AWS enforces opinionated behavior is essential to avoiding false assumptions during failover testing and incident response. With these constraints in mind, we can now look at how individual BGP attributes are used—where they work reliably and where AWS-specific behavior shapes the final outcome.

Using BGP Attributes to Express Routing Intent

Network operators tune these attributes to "bend" traffic flows to their will, a practice generally known as **BGP traffic engineering**. In effect, we take BGP's neutral decision process and imbue it with our strategy, making routing decisions align with business intent rather than raw reachability.

Crucially, BGP's attributes are the language of intent. By adjusting an attribute, we signal our preferences to routers in our network and even to our BGP neighbors. For example, Local Preference is a well-known attribute used inside an autonomous system to prefer one path over another for outgoing traffic. If our on-premises network learns about two paths to a given AWS VPC—perhaps one via a Direct Connect in New York and another via a Direct Connect in London—we can set a higher local preference on the New York route throughout our AS.

This one tweak would ensure that all our routers send traffic to AWS via New York by default, even if BGP would otherwise pick London. Local Preference is not advertised across BGP session boundaries; it's an internal flag exchanged among iBGP peers. That makes it a pure expression of our policy: we tell our own routers, "prefer this exit." As Cisco's documentation notes, the higher the local preference, the more an AS favors that path for egress.

By default, all paths might be equal at local-pref 100, but if we raise one to 200, it becomes the preferred outbound route everywhere in our domain. In short, outbound traffic engineering is typically achieved by manipulating local preference (or an analogous mechanism like weight on individual routers), since we have full control over how we send traffic out of our network.

Indeed, in a hybrid scenario with multiple data center egress points, one of the first steps to impose intent is often to agree on a common egress for certain destinations. This is done by configuring a policy on our routers to assign a higher local-pref to routes learned via the desired egress point. All else equal, that policy change causes traffic to funnel out through the chosen site, rather than each site following its own nearest exit. In the context of AWS, this could mean, for example, forcing all outbound requests to a particular VPC to go through a primary Direct Connect link (say, the one in the same region as the VPC) instead of a secondary link. BGP doesn't do that by itself—we're making it happen by design.

Inbound traffic engineering—influencing how AWS sends traffic back to us—is more challenging, because now we're trying to affect routing decisions made in AWS's network, outside our direct control. In traditional internet routing between ISPs, this is analogous to shaping incoming traffic by manipulating what routes you announce to your providers. Common techniques include AS path prepending (making one path look longer and thus less favorable) and BGP communities that ask the provider to prefer or de-prefer certain routes.

AWS, acting as the "provider" in our hybrid scenario, likewise gives us hooks to express our intent for incoming traffic. The primary mechanism is through BGP communities—essentially metadata tags on route announcements. By attaching specific community values to the routes we advertise from on-premises, we can signal to AWS how we want those routes treated inside the AWS cloud. In fact, AWS has defined a well-known set of community values for Direct Connect that map to different internal route preferences.

These are sometimes called local preference communities because that's exactly what they do: they cause AWS to assign different local preference values to your prefixes within the AWS routing domain. Concretely, AWS reserves **community**

values 7224:7100, 7224:7200, and 7224:7300 to mean **"low," "medium," and "high" preference, respectively**. If we tag our on-prem route to network X with 7224:7300 when advertising it over Direct Connect, AWS will prefer that path for reaching network X over any other possible path. Conversely, if we tag the route with 7224:7100, AWS will consider it lower priority. In practice, to make AWS favor one Direct Connect location (or one Customer Gateway) over another, we tag the primary path's routes with high preference and the secondary's with low preference. This simple step causes AWS's routers to choose the primary path for traffic destined to us, even though BGP's default would see the two paths as equivalent. We have moved from letting AWS decide arbitrarily to explicitly communicating our intent—all via a couple of numeric tags on BGP routes.

This use of communities is a controlled way of influencing AWS's internal local preference on our behalf. It's analogous to how enterprise customers influence ISP routing: many ISPs (and cloud providers) allow customers to send communities that map to policies like "prefer this link" or "do not export this route beyond region." In fact, communities are purely advisory—they don't do anything by themselves in the BGP decision process. Their power comes from the fact that the receiving network (AWS) has a policy that interprets them.

AWS in this case interprets 7224:7300 as "set a high local-pref for this route in the AWS network." The community is a flag, and AWS's routing policy takes action on it. It's worth noting that if you attach arbitrary or unsupported communities, AWS will simply ignore or strip them. Only the documented AWS communities have the special effect. By using these, we essentially reach into AWS's routing decision process and tweak the first knob (local preference) in our favor. Under the hood, a route marked with 7224:7300 might be given a higher local preference value than unmarked routes, causing AWS to pick that route even if an alternative exists. This technique is central to traffic engineering for AWS Direct Connect; it's how we implement active/passive or primary/backup path preferences for incoming traffic. From this point on, the pattern is consistent: AWS BGP communities are the primary mechanism for expressing inbound path preference, while AS-Path prepending serves as a secondary tool when communities alone are insufficient or finer differentiation is required.

Alongside communities, we have the more blunt instrument of **AS path manipulation** for influencing **inbound traffic**. BGP's best-path algorithm prefers the route with the shortest AS path by default. So if our on-premises network is advertising the same prefix to AWS via two different paths (e.g., two DX locations or a DX and a

VPN), making one path's AS sequence artificially longer will cause AWS to favor the other, shorter path. This is done by **AS path prepending**—we add extra copies of our ASN to the path we advertise on the route we don't want AWS to prefer.

From AWS's perspective, the longer AS-Path simply makes that route less attractive than the alternative. For example, suppose our ASN is **65000**, and we normally advertise a prefix with AS path "65000" to both **DX link A** and **DX link B**. If we prepend our ASN twice on advertisements over link B, **AWS will see path "65000 65000 65000" via B vs. "65000" via A,** and thus **favor link A** (shorter path) when sending traffic to us.

This method doesn't require any special agreement or community support—it's just how vanilla BGP works everywhere. The downside is that it's less granular than communities in some cases and can become clumsy if overused (long AS paths can complicate route visibility and debugging). Nevertheless, AS path prepending is a staple tool for inbound traffic engineering on the internet and remains useful in AWS hybrid designs, especially if communities alone can't achieve the desired outcome.

Following the established pattern, AWS communities define primary preference across locations, while AS-Path prepending is used only for secondary differentiation within a site. This enables clear hierarchies—such as preferring New York over London and a specific circuit within New York—without manual intervention during failover.

Another attribute, MED (Multi-Exit Discriminator), deserves mention, though it often plays a lesser role. MED is essentially a hint to an adjacent AS about which ingress point is preferred. If you advertise the same prefix to a neighbor from two different edge routers, you could set a lower MED value on one to indicate it is more preferred. AWS does allow MED on BGP routes, but by design, MED is considered only after local preference and AS path in the BGP decision process. That means if you've already manipulated local pref or AS path, those take precedence over MED. In fact, AWS documentation explicitly states that MED should not be relied on as a primary tool, given its lower priority in route selection; it's more of a tiebreaker.

For MED to even be considered, the competing routes must have equal local pref and AS path length and come from the same neighbor AS. In some hybrid scenarios (say, two connections from the same on-prem AS 65000 into AWS), MED could be used to nudge AWS to choose one link over the other if you hadn't set communities or prepends. But if you have used communities or adjusted the AS path, those signals render MED moot. Thus, while MED exists for completeness, most AWS-centric traffic engineering either happens at the local-pref level (communities) or the AS-path level, with MED only occasionally used as a final tie-breaker. It's generally safer to stick with the more deterministic controls unless MED fills a specific niche need.

It's worth emphasizing that one non-BGP method can "dissolve" all of the above: the longest prefix rule. BGP will always choose a more specific route over a less specific one, regardless of attributes. If one path is advertising a /24 and another path is advertising only a /16 that covers that /24, all traffic for that /24 will go via the path advertising the more specific /24 (since the other path's /16 is a less specific match). In practice, savvy network architects exploit this by splitting prefixes when they want to force traffic down particular links.

For instance, you might advertise 10.0.0.0/16 via both Direct Connect and VPN as a broad backup route, but also advertise 10.0.1.0/24 only via Direct Connect. AWS will route traffic for 10.0.1.0/24 exclusively over Direct Connect (because the VPN only has the /16). This can achieve traffic steering without relying on BGP attribute manipulation at all. AWS even recommends using more specific routes on different connections as a straightforward way to implement active/passive routing or load-sharing, especially when you have control over prefix allocations. However, this technique must be used carefully; managing numerous prefixes and their advertisements can become complex, and it assumes you're able to subnet your networks appropriately. In a large environment, purely attribute-based steering (with communities/local-pref or AS path) is often more scalable than juggling prefix granularities. Still, longest-prefix-match is the ultimate trump card in routing—no matter what your BGP attributes say, a more specific route will win. Thus, part of "moving to intent" is also designing your IP prefix announcements thoughtfully. Sometimes the simplest way to prefer one path is to only advertise a given prefix on that path and not elsewhere.

How AWS's Own Infrastructure Handles Routing Manipulations

Up to this point, we've discussed the general mechanisms of traffic engineering and how they apply to our hybrid AWS network. It's important to understand how AWS's own routing infrastructure handles these manipulations. AWS **is not a traditional ISP,** but it uses BGP internally for services like Direct Connect and Site-to-Site VPN, and it has its own logic on top of standard BGP.

One key component is the AWS Transit Gateway (TGW), which many hybrid architectures use as a central hub to connect VPCs and on-prem networks. A Transit Gateway does not simply behave like a normal router when it comes to route preference. In fact, AWS has a defined route evaluation order for TGWs that can override BGP preferences. Notably, a TGW will prefer routes learned via Direct Connect over routes learned via VPN if both exist for the same destination—even if the VPN route might have a shorter AS path or other "better" attributes. This is a built-in bias favoring Direct Connect. The logic makes sense (Direct Connect is usually a faster, more reliable link than internet VPN), but it means that some BGP tuning on the customer side could be ignored in practice.

For example, you might prepend the AS path on your Direct Connect routes to try to make the VPN path more attractive as a backup, but the TGW may still choose the Direct Connect route by default. In short, AWS components sometimes have fixed preferences. A Virtual Private Gateway (VGW, the predecessor to TGW for single-VPC attachments) similarly tends to prefer Direct Connect over VPN by default, treating the DX route as if it were a static superior path. As a customer, you should be aware of these inherent priorities so you're not scratching your head when a route with a longer AS-path (via DX) still "wins" over a seemingly shorter path (via VPN). The solution, if you need the opposite behavior, is usually to apply very clear distinctions—for instance, using the longest-prefix method or communities that AWS will honor—rather than relying on AS-path tweaks alone. Conversely, if the goal is to prefer Direct Connect (which it often is), AWS is effectively helping you by automatically favoring it in many cases.

Another element is the AWS Direct Connect Gateway (DXGW), which acts as a global routing intermediary when you use Direct Connect to reach multiple AWS regions. The DXGW is essentially a **route reflector** that shares routes between your on-prem BGP sessions and the AWS side (VPCs or TGWs). It generally passes BGP attributes along, but there is a subtle point about scope: when you use the AWS-provided community values to prefer one path, that preference applies within the DXGW's entire scope. In other words, **a DXGW defines a single routing domain for all its associated AWS regions and VIFs.**

Suppose you have two Direct Connects in two different cities, and you attach them to the same DXGW, advertising all your routes over both. If you tag certain routes as high preference, they'll be high preference for any AWS region attached to that DXGW. You cannot, for instance, tell DXGW, "for region A use DX1, for region B use DX2" using communities alone when both regions share the same DXGW—because the DXGW doesn't segment by region internally. All it sees is that one route came in with higher pref, so it distributes that preference globally.

To achieve per-region egress control, you would need separate DXGW instances or a more segmented approach. The takeaway here is that AWS's routing constructs interpret BGP attributes in specific ways and sometimes impose their own hierarchy of preferences. Our traffic engineering plans must align with those realities. AWS does give us the knobs (like communities), but within a framework that is somewhat abstracted compared to managing BGP on physical routers.

Finally, let's not forget the simpler AWS routing constructs. Many hybrid setups still use policy-based routing or static preferences at the VPC level; for instance, in a VPC route table you might have a static route pointing to a VGW over Direct Connect and use that as primary with a cloud-side failover to VPN via route priorities. However, when using dynamic routing with BGP, it's predominantly these attributes and communities doing the work. AWS also tags the routes it sends to us with communities in some cases—for example, all routes advertised over a public VIF via Direct Connect are tagged with the well-known NO_EXPORT community so that you don't accidentally leak AWS prefixes to the internet. In fact, **AWS tags all its customer-learned routes (whether public or private) with NO_EXPORT by default** as a safety measure. AWS also uses communities on public routes to indicate their region of origin (like **7224:8100 for same-region**, **7224:8200 for same-continent**). While these particular tags are more about route filtering and scope control than traffic engineering, they underline the broader theme: BGP communities are a major part of how intent is communicated in networks. They let a complex system like AWS's global network understand what we want it to do with our routes, beyond the basic announcement of "here's a prefix." With communities, we attach meaning: "Here's a prefix, and please treat it as low priority" or "Here's a prefix, only share it within Europe," etc. The neutral reachability information (prefix and ASN) is thus augmented with policy information (preferences and scope).

In summary, moving "from reachability to intent" means embracing BGP's policy mechanisms to shape traffic in a hybrid AWS environment. We establish connectivity with BGP, but then we refine how traffic flows using local preference, AS path tweaks, MED (sparingly), and especially BGP communities as provided by AWS. The result is that we can dictate primary and backup paths, balance loads across links, and ensure traffic takes the architecturally optimal route rather than a coincidental one.

Where Section 7.2 was about getting the routes in place, Section 7.3 is about sculpting those routes to suit our needs. With careful traffic engineering, a hybrid network can be tuned so that, for example, a critical application's users always reach it over the lowest-latency path, or data transfers always egress through a link with a favorable cost structure, all automatically governed by BGP policy. We've equipped ourselves with the BGP vocabulary to express intent; next, we will examine how to apply these techniques in practice and how they interplay with resilience. Indeed, a major use of traffic engineering is to build failover and load-sharing behaviors—ensuring that when a primary path is down, the secondary seamlessly takes over, or that multiple active paths share duty. We will delve into those design patterns in Section 7.4, tying together traffic engineering with high-availability strategies.

For now, it's enough to recognize that hybrid cloud routing is no longer just about connectivity—it's about control. We take BGP from a passive route distributor and turn it into an instrument of intent, using its rich palette of attributes to make the network follow the needs of the business.

Applying BGP Policy to Real-World Hybrid Designs

In the previous section, we learned how BGP provides a language of intent—attributes like *Local Preference*, *AS-Path*, *MED*, and *communities* that allow us to express which path we prefer and why. But attributes in isolation are just grammar; the real art lies in using that language to build something purposeful.

This section turns theory into practice. We'll apply those attributes in concrete AWS hybrid scenarios and see how routing intent becomes behavior.

From Concept to Configuration

Imagine you're the network architect for an enterprise running two data centers—one in Frankfurt and another in Paris. Each hosts a Direct Connect (DX) connection to AWS: DX-1 in Frankfurt and DX-2 in Paris.

Your goal is simple to state but non-trivial to achieve: all production traffic should use Frankfurt as the primary path into AWS, while Paris stands ready as a backup that can take over instantly if Frankfurt fails. You also want AWS to prefer returning traffic over the same Frankfurt link when both are available.

Left to itself, BGP wouldn't necessarily make that choice. It sees two viable paths and, unless you intervene, could pick either. We need to *teach* the control plane our intent.

The most direct way to do that on your routers is to use the **Local Preference** attribute. Local Preference controls *outbound* behavior—it tells every router in your autonomous system which exit to prefer when multiple paths exist. The higher the local preference, the more attractive the path. It's an internal signal; it never leaves your AS.

On your edge router at Frankfurt, you might write:

```
router bgp 65000
```

```
  neighbor 192.0.2.1 remote-as 7224
  neighbor 192.0.2.1 description AWS-DX-Frankfurt
  neighbor 192.0.2.1 route-map RM-AWS-FRA out
route-map RM-AWS-FRA permit 10
  match ip prefix-list AWS-ALL
  set local-preference 200
```

And on the Paris edge:

```
router bgp 65000
  neighbor 198.51.100.1 remote-as 7224
  neighbor 198.51.100.1 description AWS-DX-Paris
  neighbor 198.51.100.1 route-map RM-AWS-PAR out
route-map RM-AWS-PAR permit 10
  match ip prefix-list AWS-ALL
  set local-preference 100
```

These snippets (simplified and **not** production-ready) tell your routers to prefer AWS routes learned through Frankfurt. If Frankfurt fails, BGP automatically withdraws those routes, and traffic shifts to Paris—no scripts, no manual intervention. When Frankfurt recovers, its routes regain higher preference, and the network quietly returns to normal.

The key is simplicity: **failover becomes boring** because it's already encoded in the control plane.

Influencing Return Paths

So far, we've controlled how *we* send traffic to AWS. But hybrid networks are two-way systems. To complete the loop, we need AWS to prefer Frankfurt for *incoming* traffic as well.

AWS lets us express that through **BGP community tags**—metadata we attach to the prefixes we advertise. When AWS receives these routes, its edge routers interpret certain well-known communities as instructions for how to prioritize them.

Like we mentioned, AWS Direct Connect supports three community values that map to internal preference levels:

- 7224:7100—Low preference

- 7224:7200—Medium preference

- 7224:7300—High preference

If we advertise our prefixes from Frankfurt with 7224:7300 and from Paris with 7224:7100, AWS will prefer Frankfurt when both are available. The routes are still ours, but AWS now understands which one we want it to use.

An illustrative configuration might look like this:

```
route-map ADVERTISE-FRA permit 10
  match ip prefix-list ONPREM
  set community 7224:7300
route-map ADVERTISE-PAR permit 10
  match ip prefix-list ONPREM
  set community 7224:7100
  set as-path prepend 65000 65000 65000
```

What happens: Here, we reinforce intent by combining a high community preference on Frankfurt with a slightly longer AS-Path on Paris. When AWS evaluates both advertisements, it assigns higher internal preference to Frankfurt and, if that link fails, automatically shifts to Paris.

This approach mirrors the way Internet Service Providers let customers influence inbound traffic. The logic is identical—we're just applying it at the AWS edge instead of a carrier.

The Role of the Longest Prefix

As we mentioned before, even with perfect attributes, the **longest-prefix rule** remains the ultimate arbiter in routing.

If two paths advertise the same prefix length, attributes decide; but if one advertises a more specific subnet, it wins automatically.

Savvy architects often use this to their advantage. For example, you might advertise 10.0.0.0/16 over both DX links but advertise 10.0.10.0/24 only over Frankfurt. All traffic for that /24 will then flow exclusively through Frankfurt, regardless of other attributes. It's a powerful, simple way to control path selection without complex policy—though it requires careful address-management discipline.

When VPN Joins the Mix

Not every organization has dual Direct Connects. Many pair a single DX with a **Site-to-Site VPN** as backup. In that case, the design goal often shifts from "load balance" to "fail gracefully."

The mechanics are the same: advertise your on-prem prefixes to AWS via both connections, but make one less attractive. Over Direct Connect, you advertise normally; over VPN, you prepend your ASN multiple times or advertise a less-specific prefix.

```
router bgp 65000
  address-family ipv4
    network 10.0.0.0 mask 255.255.0.0
    neighbor 203.0.113.1 remote-as 7224
    neighbor 203.0.113.1 description AWS-VPN
    neighbor 203.0.113.1 route-map RM-VPN-OUT out
route-map RM-VPN-OUT permit 10
  match ip prefix-list ONPREM
  set as-path prepend 65000 65000 65000
```

What happens: This makes your VPN a ready standby. When the Direct Connect fails, AWS withdraws those preferred routes and immediately begins using the longer AS-Path VPN advertisement instead. Because both paths run BGP, the transition is smooth and self-healing.

Of course again, an important disclaimer here: these examples are simplified for illustration.

They omit filtering, authentication, and route-limiting, which are vital in production. Every organization's topology, security model, and routing domain differ. Always validate configurations in a controlled environment before deployment.

A View from Above

To understand how routing policies, attributes, and communities converge into an operationally resilient topology, imagine the hybrid architecture shown in Figure 7-1. Traffic from the corporate core flows through the primary Direct Connect location in Frankfurt, where routes are advertised with the high-preference BGP community **7224:7300** and no AS-Path prepending. AWS assigns these routes the highest local preference within its network, making the Frankfurt link the active path for inbound and outbound traffic.

At the secondary Direct Connect site in Paris, the same prefixes are advertised but tagged with the low-preference community **7224:7100** and padded with three additional AS-Path entries. This combination keeps the Paris route in a standby state—visible to AWS but less attractive. A Site-to-Site VPN, terminating on the Transit Gateway, announces only a summarized prefix with an even longer AS-path, serving as a last-resort backup when both Direct Connect circuits become unavailable.

The resulting hierarchy of preference is unambiguous:

Frankfurt ➤ Paris ➤ VPN.

No scripts, no manual intervention—just deterministic policy expressed through BGP.

In Figure 7-2, the primary Direct Connect in Frankfurt advertises high-preference routes (community 7224:7300, short AS-Path) and acts as the active data path.

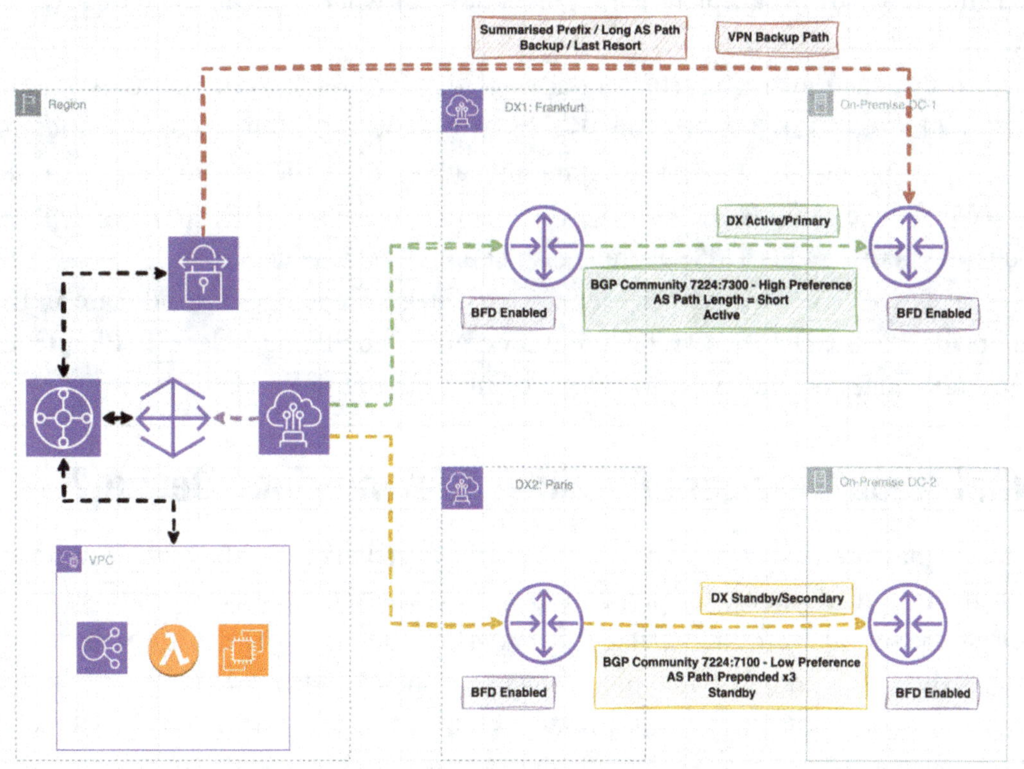

Figure 7-2. *Hierarchical Routing Intent in a Hybrid AWS Design*

The secondary Direct Connect in Paris advertises the same prefixes with lower preference (community 7224:7100, AS-Path ×3) and remains on standby.

A VPN connection provides a summarized prefix with the longest AS-Path, functioning as a backup path of last resort.

Bidirectional Forwarding Detection (BFD) is enabled on all DX virtual interfaces for sub-second loss detection.

Failover is automatic and deterministic: when Frankfurt's link goes dark, BFD on the DX virtual interface detects the loss within milliseconds, triggering an immediate route withdrawal. AWS's routers re-select the best available path—in this case, Paris—promoting it from standby to active with no manual change. From the user's perspective, the event is invisible: latency may shift slightly, but connectivity persists. Once Frankfurt recovers, its advertisements resume with the 7224:7300 tag, restoring normal traffic patterns.

This is **resilience made invisible**—the control plane negotiating quietly in the background while the data plane continues to flow. It's what we mean when we say, *"failover should be boring."*

As with all hybrid designs, continuous validation is essential. Monitor BGP session health with **CloudWatch metrics** on AWS and with show bgp summary on your routers. Track route-flap events, convergence time, and latency differentials across paths. Inspect **MTU consistency** end-to-end: a 9001-byte jumbo frame within a VPC may fragment to 1500 bytes across a VPN if MSS clamping isn't applied at the edge.

The network is a living system; even the most elegant topology demands care and calibration. We'll explore observability and continuous monitoring in depth in **Chapter 8**, where resilience becomes not only designed but continuously verified.

What About Resilient Public Virtual Interface Design?

Public virtual interfaces are less common than they used to be, but they still show up in real architectures: legacy workloads that can only reach AWS public endpoints, shared services that must talk to all AWS Regions, or designs that rely on Direct Connect to reach S3, CloudFront, or Route 53 without traversing the open Internet. For completeness—and because the traffic-engineering principles mirror what we did for private and transit VIFs—we'll briefly look at how to make public VIFs resilient and predictable.

Let's recap what they are. As mentioned at the beginning of the previous section, a public virtual interface (Public VIF) attaches your router to the AWS global network for public AWS services. Once the BGP session is established, your router advertises your own public prefixes, and AWS advertises all relevant public service prefixes (as listed in *ip-ranges.json* that you can download from the AWS website). This enables your on-premises workloads to reach AWS public endpoints—such as Amazon S3, DynamoDB, public ALBs, Global Accelerator, and other regional services—without traversing the open Internet. CloudFront traffic enters AWS through edge locations but still avoids ISP hairpinning and benefits from more predictable routing.

From a routing perspective, AWS applies clear policies to public VIFs:

- You must advertise only public IPv4/IPv6 prefixes that you own and that are registered with a Regional Internet Registry.

- For inbound routing (AWS ➤ on-premises), AWS follows standard BGP best practices: longest prefix match first, then AS_PATH. When the same CIDR block is announced both to the Internet and over Direct Connect, advertising a more specific prefix on the Public VIF allows you to bias inbound traffic toward Direct Connect.

- AWS advertises its public service prefixes to you with the 7224:9100 (NO_EXPORT) community, ensuring they are not propagated beyond your network. Customer prefixes learned on a Public VIF are also treated as NO_EXPORT internally; AWS does not re-advertise them to other DX customers, peers, or transit providers.

On top of that, AWS exposes a small but powerful set of scope BGP communities for Public Virtual Interfaces:

- **7224:9100**—advertise your prefixes only to the local AWS Region

- **7224:9200**—advertise to all regions within the same continent (NA, EMEA, APAC)

- **7224:9300**—advertise globally

If you do not apply a community, AWS behaves as if global scope (7224:9300) had been used.

For AWS-originated routes (AWS ➤ customer), AWS does not publish regional or continental scoping tags. Public service prefixes are advertised with the **NO_EXPORT (7224:9100)** community to prevent them from being propagated to external networks.

These communities give customers enough structure to build resilient, capacity-aware, and geographically scoped public VIF routing policies without leaking AWS prefixes or unintentionally redirecting global traffic.

A Note on Security Posture

At this point, many customers ask a very practical question: *"If AWS is advertising all these routes to me over a public VIF, or if I'm advertising my public ranges to AWS, does this change my security posture? Could another AWS customer suddenly reach my on-prem network just because of these advertisements?"*

The short answer is no—BGP reachability does not automatically translate into trust or access.

A few important clarifications I always share in design workshops:

Isolation inside AWS. Your public VIF session is established in a logically isolated context. Other customers do not "share" your BGP session, and AWS does not re-advertise your public prefixes to other Direct Connect customers as a transit path. Customer-learned routes over a public VIF are effectively treated as NO_EXPORT: they remain inside AWS's internal routing domain and are not offered to peers or other DX customers as a way to reach you.

From AWS's point of view, you look like an ISP. AWS simply learns that "for these prefixes, send traffic via this Direct Connect." It does not mean traffic from random tenants can bypass the Internet or your edge firewalls. Any packet that wants to reach your on-premises environment still has to traverse your CPE, firewalls, and security zones. If those devices have a default-deny posture (which they should), nothing new is exposed merely because an additional path exists.

Security is enforced where it always was. State, filtering, and segmentation still live on your edge: firewalls, ACLs, IPS, and so on. The public VIF only provides another way to reach that edge. Whether packets are allowed through remains entirely a function of your security policy.

Where you can hurt yourself is misconfiguration. If you accidentally treat the public VIF as "trusted" in your firewall policy, or if you advertise internal or private space over it and then allow it inbound, you can create exposure. That is not a property of Direct Connect itself, but of how you classify, zone, and filter that interface on your side.

The practical guidance I give customers is this: treat a public VIF like a high-quality, dedicated ISP path into the AWS backbone. Place it in the appropriate firewall zone, maintain a default-deny stance, and only open the ports and protocols you explicitly intend to expose. If you follow those principles, adding a public VIF for resilience or performance does not weaken your security posture; it simply gives you a more controlled alternative to the open Internet.

Let's explore some public VIF patterns now to better understand how traffic engineering is applied to this type of interface.

Pattern 1—Prefer Direct Connect over the Internet Using LPM

The first goal is usually: "when Direct Connect is healthy, send AWS-bound traffic over that private path; when it fails, fall back to the Internet." For public VIFs, you achieve this using the longest prefix match combined with traditional BGP attributes.

- Advertise **203.0.113.0/24** (or another relatively specific public prefix) to AWS over the public VIF.

- Advertise only a broader aggregate such as **203.0.112.0/23** through your Internet providers.

Because AWS follows LPM, it will send traffic to **203.0.113.0/24** via Direct Connect as long as the public VIF is up. If the public VIF or the BGP session goes down and the /24 is withdrawn, the only remaining route is the /23 learned through the Internet, and traffic automatically reverts to your ISP path.

If you also need redundancy within the Direct Connect path (e.g., two public VIFs in different DX locations), you announce identical prefixes on both VIFs and rely on **AS_ PATH prepending** or **local preference within your own network** to bias the preferred path. With a **public ASN**, prepends remain visible to AWS and influence AWS → on-prem routing. With a **private ASN**, AWS replaces your ASN with **7224**, so any prepends stay internal to AWS and your own network. In both cases, prepending affects only the Direct Connect path selection—not the global Internet—because AWS never re-advertises customer prefixes outside its network.

Pattern 2—Regional Primary, Global Backup Using Scope Communities

The second goal is to scope who is allowed to use a particular public VIF so that one circuit isn't unexpectedly swamped by traffic from every region.

Imagine you have two public VIFs:

- **Frankfurt DX location—primary for European workloads**

- **Virginia DX location—backup and global catch-all**

You can advertise your public prefixes with different scope tags:

- On the **Frankfurt** public VIF, tag your prefixes with **7224:9200** (EMEA-wide). AWS propagates those prefixes only to regions in Europe, the Middle East, and Africa.

- On the **Virginia** public VIF, tag the same prefixes with **7224:9300** (global) so that all public regions can reach you via that circuit.

The effect:

- European AWS Regions prefer the Frankfurt VIF because it is scoped to EMEA and typically topologically closer.

- Non-EMEA regions can still reach you, but they do so through Virginia, respecting both capacity and latency expectations.

If you want Frankfurt to be "primary for Europe, secondary for the rest of the world," you can advertise the same prefixes globally from both locations but expose a more specific prefix (or a higher-bandwidth aggregate) in Frankfurt and only a broader aggregate in Virginia. This lets you combine LPM, scope communities, and high/ maximum resiliency patterns for deterministic behavior.

On the outbound side (your routing toward AWS), you can prefer the closest DX location by applying local preference or AS_PATH conditioning on the two BGP sessions. AWS does not attach regional or continental scope communities to its own public service prefixes, so the outbound decision remains entirely under your control via your usual BGP policy mechanisms.

Pattern 3—High and Maximum Resiliency for Public VIFs

Physically, public VIFs follow the same high- and maximum-resiliency models as private and transit VIFs:

- **High Resiliency**: Two Direct Connect connections in one location (ideally in a LAG), terminated on separate devices on your side. Either link can host one or more public VIFs.

- **Maximum Resiliency:** Pairs of DX connections in two different locations, each on separate devices, with your public VIFs distributed across both sites.

Logically, you layer the BGP patterns described earlier:

- Advertise the same prefixes from both locations and use longest prefix match and AS_PATH conditioning to prefer the nearest DX location.

- Apply scope communities (7224:9100/9200/9300) to control which regions can use which circuit so that no single site absorbs global failover traffic beyond its capacity.

- Ensure your Internet providers continue advertising an aggregate covering your ranges so that, if an entire DX Region is lost, AWS still has a fallback path through the public Internet.

We include this pattern for completeness and because operational reality still requires it. Some industries continue to use public VIFs for global access to services such as Amazon S3 and DynamoDB or simply as a more controlled alternative to the open Internet. The same resilience principles apply: diversify physically, bias logically with BGP attributes, and make sure capacity, scoping, and fallbacks align so that the "backup" path is both reachable and sized to carry the extra load.

Before we move into the formal high-availability resilience models in Section 7.4, it's useful to summarize which traffic-engineering technique to reach for based on the outcome you are optimizing for.

With these goal-to-technique mappings in mind (Table 7-2), we can now apply them systematically in high and maximum resilience architectures discussed in the next section.

Table 7-2. *Traffic Engineering Goals* ➤ *Techniques*

Goal	Primary Technique	Secondary Technique	Why this works in AWS
Minimize Latency	DX local-preference communities (7224:7100/7200/7300) for AWS→on-prem + Local Preference for on-prem→AWS	Longest Prefix Match (more-specific prefixes)	AWS explicitly supports local-preference communities on Direct Connect to influence return traffic path preference. Local Preference is the standard way to steer egress within your AS.
Reduce cost (egress/WAN spend)	Local Preference (prefer lower-cost egress like VPN/SD-WAN vs DX, or vice-versa depending on billing model)	AS-Path prepending (only if you must influence AWS→on-prem)	Local Preference is the standard BGP attribute for outbound path selection inside your AS (what you pay for and where you exit).
Enforce symmetry / keep traffic through inspection	Communities + explicit route design (propagation/association + constrained advertisements)	Longest Prefix Match (hard pin specific flows)	In AWS hybrid designs, symmetric behavior is most reliable when you use AWS-recognized controls (DX communities for AWS→on-prem preference) and avoid relying on subtle tuning that TGW may override. TGW preference guidance highlights how DX vs VPN preference can matter. Longest Prefix Match is a proven steering mechanism for hybrid path control.
Deterministic backup / active-passive failover	DX local-preference communities (primary high, secondary low)	Longest Prefix Match for "hard" failover; AS-Path prepending for extra differentiation	AWS documents communities specifically for "route preference for incoming traffic to your network" over DX. AWS also documents/illustrates active-active/active-passive patterns using BGP attributes and LPM.

Bridging Toward Resilience

At this point, we've moved from reachability to intent. We've shown how Local Preference steers egress, how communities and AS-Path guide ingress, and how prefix control complements both—across private, transit, and **public** virtual interfaces. The mechanisms are the same; only the scope and the operational goals change.

In Section 7.4, we'll take these mechanisms and apply them at scale—combining them into the resilience models that AWS formalizes as **High Resilience** and **Maximum Resilience**. These architectures don't just steer traffic efficiently but survive faults gracefully, integrating VPN backup, redundant DX locations, and AWS backbone diversity. Public VIFs fit naturally into these models as well: physically they follow the same high/max patterns, and logically they use the same BGP tools we have been building throughout this section.

You won't see separate diagrams for public VIFs because the physical topology does not change; the same high/max-resiliency layouts apply regardless of VIF type. What varies is the **traffic-engineering intent** layered on top—scoping, prefix selection, and BGP attributes—not the underlying connectivity model.

Traffic engineering is therefore not a separate discipline from resilience; it's the mechanism that makes resilience predictable.

Section 7.4: Hybrid Connectivity Resilience Models—High vs. Maximum Resilience, VPN as Backup

Hybrid cloud architectures demand robust network connectivity between on-premises environments and AWS. In previous chapters, we established an **availability mindset** (Chapter 1) and explored general failover strategies (Chapters 4–6). Now we apply those principles to hybrid networking, examining AWS's **resilience models** for hybrid connectivity and how to integrate a VPN backup. We'll compare **High Resilience** versus **Maximum Resilience** topologies using AWS Direct Connect and discuss how a Site-to-Site VPN can serve as a cost-effective standby. Throughout, we highlight design trade-offs, failure domains, routing intent (as introduced in Section 7.3), and best practices aligned with AWS's latest recommendations, as my scope is within this cloud provider. Having said that, these principles easily apply to any other Cloud Service Provider (CSP).

High vs. Maximum Resilience with AWS Direct Connect

AWS Direct Connect resiliency recommendations define two standard connectivity patterns: High Resilience and Maximum Resilience.

High Resilience uses two Direct Connect connections deployed in two separate Direct Connect locations and is intended to *target* approximately 99.9% availability, provided all AWS resiliency requirements are met. Maximum Resilience extends this model by adding a second, independent connection at each location (four total connections), targeting 99.99% availability under the same conditions.

In practice, High Resilience represents a strong baseline when brief and rare connectivity interruptions are tolerable and cost is a constraint. Maximum Resilience is justified for mission-critical hybrid dependencies where the business cannot accept the combined failure of a location and an additional device or port at the surviving site. The distinction between the two models lies not in routing sophistication but in how many independent failure domains are eliminated by design.

Before diving into the detailed mechanics of each model, Table 7-3 provides a concise comparison of High and Maximum Resilience, highlighting their structural differences, failure tolerance, cost implications, and the types of workloads each pattern is designed to support.

Table 7-3. *High Resilience vs. Maximum Resilience Model Comparison*

Dimension	High Resilience	Maximum Resilience
Direct Connect Locations	2 geographically separate DX locations	2 geographically separate DX locations
Connections per Location	1 per location (2 total)	2 per location on independent devices (4 total)
AWS Device Redundancy	Per-location only	Full device redundancy per location
Failure Domains Tolerated	Any single link, device, or location failure	Loss of one entire location plus one additional link/device at the surviving site
Typical Topology Name (AWS)	Multi-site, non-redundant	Multi-site, redundant
Routing Model	BGP with automatic failover	BGP with deterministic or ECMP-based failover
Cost Profile	Moderate	High
Operational Complexity	Low–moderate	High
Target Availability (design goal)	~99.9% (when SLA conditions are met)	~99.99% (when SLA conditions are met)
Typical Workloads	Important production systems, enterprise apps	Mission-critical, regulated, always-on systems

With these high-level trade-offs in mind, we can now examine each resilience model in detail, starting with the High Resilience topology and its behavior under common failure scenarios.

High Resilience: Multi-site Non-redundant Topology

High resilience (sometimes called *multi-site non-redundant*) is achieved by deploying at least two DX connections in different locations, **one connection per location**. For example, an enterprise might have one 10 Gbps Direct Connect at a colocation facility in New York and a second 10 Gbps DX at a facility in Newark. Each DX connects the corporate network to AWS, often via a Direct Connect Gateway (DX Gateway), so that both links can reach the same target VPCs or Transit Gateways. This topology dramatically reduces risk compared to a single connection: even if an entire DX location goes offline (e.g., due to a power outage or fiber cut in New York), the other connection in the second location (Newark) continues to carry traffic. It also protects against *last-mile* telco issues—since each DX can be delivered by a different provider and path—and against AWS device failures (each location has distinct AWS routers). However, **within each location the connection is non-redundant**, meaning there's only one physical port/link. If that port or the associated AWS router fails, connectivity through that location is lost until the second site takes over. In essence, the design tolerates a single failure (of one link or location) but not multiple simultaneous failures.

In Figure 7-3, the on-premises network connects to AWS through two geographically independent Direct Connect locations—DX1 (Frankfurt) and DX2 (Paris). Each site hosts a single Direct Connect port and router pair, with BGP sessions and, where supported and explicitly configured, Bidirectional Forwarding Detection (BFD) enabled for sub-second failure detection and rapid convergence. Both DX links connect through a Direct Connect Gateway (DXGW) and a Transit Gateway (TGW) to reach workloads inside VPCs.

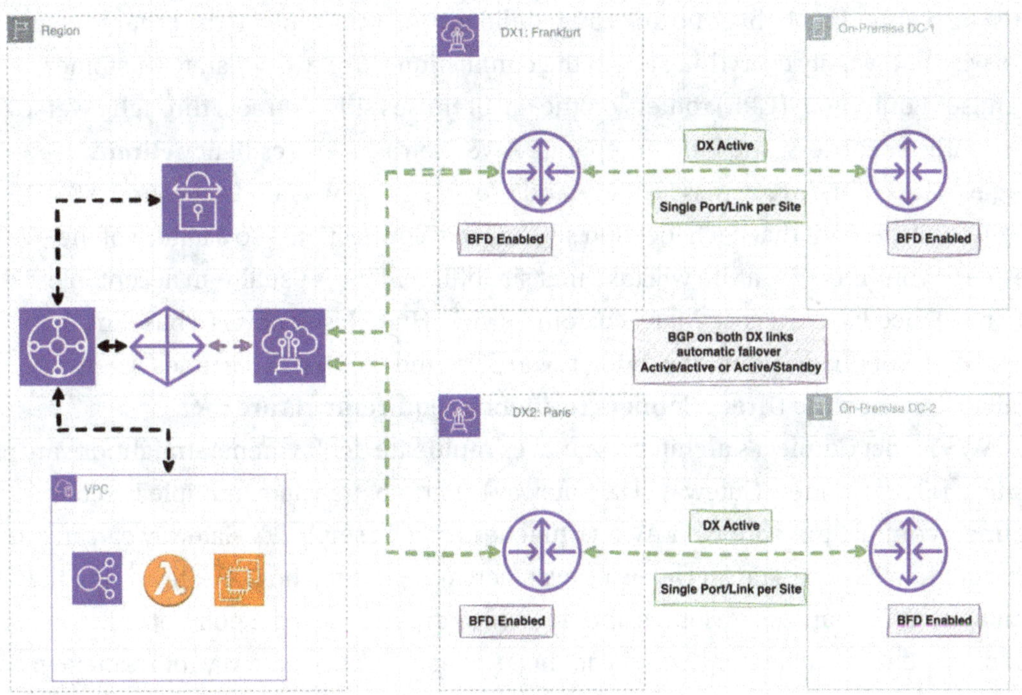

Figure 7-3. *High Resilience (Multi-site Non-redundant) Direct Connect Topology*

BGP runs across both links, enabling automatic failover in either active/active or active/standby mode.

If one DX link or facility fails, the surviving connection continues to carry traffic with no manual intervention.

This model eliminates single points of failure across sites and providers while remaining cost-efficient—often used as a planning target of approximately 99.9% network availability when all AWS Direct Connect resiliency requirements are met.

Let's dive deep. As we discussed previously in Section 7.3, a high-resiliency deployment should use **dynamic routing (BGP)** on both Direct Connect links to enable *automatic failover*. The principles of resilience related to the resilient properties of an application strongly advise using redundant, actively routed connections for any important workload to avoid introducing a single point of failure. Both DX connections can be active concurrently (carry traffic), or one can be designated as primary and the other as standby—the choice depends on traffic engineering preferences (I will dive deep later in *Routing and Failover*). Even if run active/active, the combined capacity must be planned such that one link can handle the full traffic load if the other fails. It's also wise to diversify everything about the connections: use two separate Customer Premises Equipment (CPE) routers on the on-premises side, connect through diverse fiber paths or carriers, and land in separate AWS metros. High resiliency **eliminates single points of failure** across facilities and providers that would affect your AWS connectivity, except that each location still has one connection—so a failure of the AWS device or your router at a site will take that site offline. This is usually an acceptable risk when balanced against cost. Many customers view High Resiliency as a baseline for important workloads, **often designing toward** around 99.9% ("three nines") network availability **when the Direct Connect resiliency requirements are met.**

AWS Direct Connect's architecture makes multi-site deployments straightforward. Using a Direct Connect Gateway (DX Gateway), you can associate multiple Direct Connect connections with your AWS virtual networks (a single DX Gateway can attach to multiple VPCs or a Transit Gateway, even across regions). The DX Gateway is a highly available, AWS-managed resource and does not introduce a single point of failure or additional data-path latency. You do not need a "backup" DX Gateway for resiliency; instead, resilience is achieved through multiple physical Direct Connect links.

A single DX Gateway automatically distributes traffic across all available Direct Connect connections and uses the shortest path on AWS's backbone to reach the target AWS Region, without requiring traffic to enter through a specific associated region. This means that if you have one connection at a location associated with *us-east-1* and another associated with *us-west-1*, either connection can still be used to reach resources in *us-east-1*, with AWS's global network carrying traffic internally.

That said, best practice is to have at least one Direct Connect connection in a location associated with the same Region as your primary workload. This avoids unnecessary dependency on long-haul network transit for critical traffic. In our example, if the workload is in the *us-east-1* Region, at least one DX location (e.g., Newark) should serve as an on-ramp for *us-east-1*. The second location may be in a different Region for geographic diversity, but using a faraway DX location can introduce additional latency and operational complexity. For this reason, many customers choose two DX sites within the same general geographic area as their AWS workload (e.g., two East Coast colocation facilities for an East Region), achieving location redundancy without materially different latency profiles.

Failure-Domain Summary (High Resilience)

This model tolerates any single failure affecting a Direct Connect link or an entire Direct Connect location. Connectivity is preserved as long as at least one Direct Connect connection remains available. However, it does not tolerate dual or correlated failures—for example, the simultaneous loss of both Direct Connect locations, or a failure of the remaining location combined with its single Direct Connect port or device. In practice, High Resilience protects against single-fault scenarios, but not against multiple concurrent failures.

Overall, the High Resiliency model offers strong protection against single failures at a moderate cost—essentially the cost of maintaining two Direct Connect ports in different facilities. If the business can tolerate a brief outage in the unlikely event that both links or sites fail simultaneously, this model strikes a solid balance. Later in this section, we'll discuss how to add a VPN backup to further reduce the likelihood of downtime. But first, let's examine the Maximum Resiliency design for workloads that truly cannot afford to fail.

Maximum Resilience: Multi-site Redundant Topology

Maximum resilience—sometimes called *multi-site redundant*—represents the highest level of fault tolerance for hybrid connectivity using AWS Direct Connect. In this model, at least **two Direct Connect (DX) circuits are deployed per location, across a minimum of two geographically distinct locations.**

For example, an enterprise might operate two 10 Gbps DX connections at the Frankfurt Direct Connect facility (each terminating on a different AWS router device) and two additional 10 Gbps connections at a second location in Paris (again, on separate

AWS routers). This results in four fully independent physical links—each backed by its own AWS hardware and its own customer router.

The rationale is simple yet critical: to remain connected to AWS under even the most extreme conditions. This design tolerates the simultaneous loss of an entire DX location and a single port or device failure at the surviving site. By doing so, it covers all common network failure domains—device failures, link cuts, and entire data center outages—without breaking connectivity to AWS. In practice, that means **no single event, and few dual events, can disconnect the hybrid network.**

This topology represents the gold standard for mission-critical workloads. AWS recommends it for financial, healthcare, and regulated enterprises requiring continuous availability. In AWS's Direct Connect resiliency guidance, the multi-site redundant model is commonly used to **design toward** up to 99.99% network availability **when the required redundancy conditions are met** (independent devices, locations, and diverse connectivity).

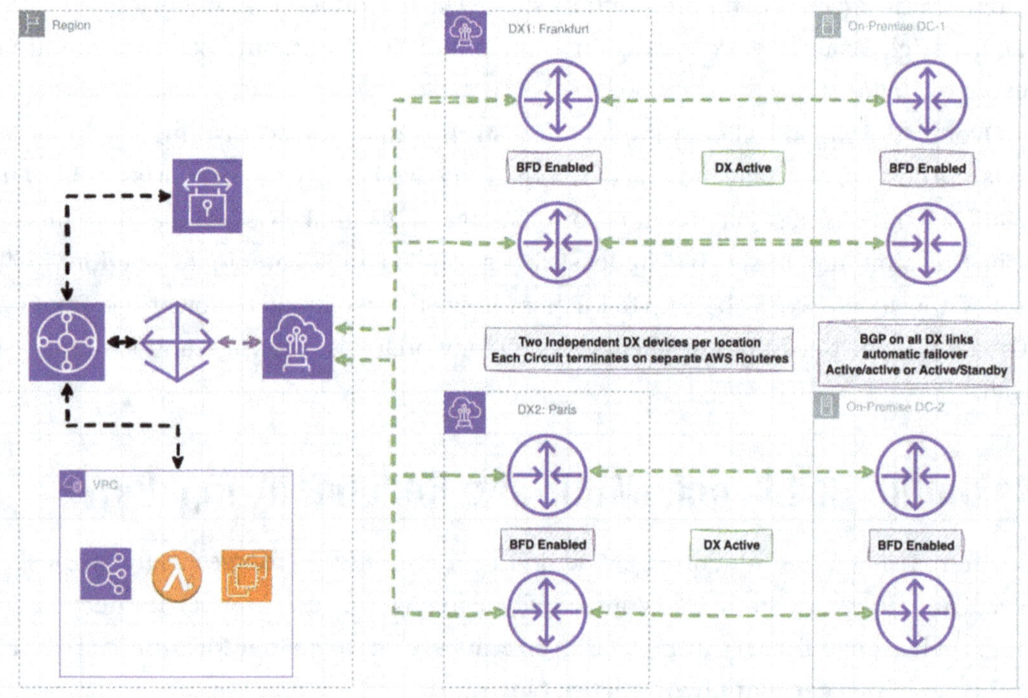

Figure 7-4. *Maximum Resilience (Multi-site Redundant) Direct Connect Topology*

In Figure 7-4, each on-premises data center connects to AWS through two independent Direct Connect circuits per site, across two geographically distinct DX locations—Frankfurt and Paris. Every circuit terminates on a separate AWS router, and all four links establish BGP sessions with asynchronous Bidirectional Forwarding Detection (BFD) for rapid detection and failover. A shared Direct Connect Gateway aggregates routing toward the AWS Transit Gateway and the attached VPCs, providing unified connectivity across Regions.

This topology withstands simultaneous failures of a full DX location and an individual port or router at the surviving site. With four diverse physical paths, dual devices per metro, and dynamic BGP routing, the design **targets** up to 99.99% network availability **when all resiliency requirements are met**—a recommended pattern for mission-critical hybrid dependencies.

Achieving **maximum resilience** requires careful attention to detail.

Each pair of DX connections within a single location must terminate on **separate AWS devices**. When ordering connections through the AWS Management Console, this can be guaranteed by selecting the **"Resiliency Toolkit"** option, which provisions the circuits on distinct hardware automatically.

On the customer side, the same principle applies: use two physically separate routers or Customer Premises Equipment (CPEs). For example, Router A terminates "Connection 1," and Router B terminates "Connection 2" at the same site. This ensures that a hardware failure in your network cannot negate AWS's redundancy. The result is a high-availability pair of DX circuits per site.

Geographic separation is equally important. Each DX location should reside in a distinct metro area—or, at minimum, in separate carrier facilities—to reduce the risk of correlated failure. Many organizations deploy this pattern by connecting one DX site in Frankfurt and another in Paris, or in North America, one in New York and another in Ashburn. This distance not only protects against localized disasters but also supports regulatory and latency objectives across regions.

From a routing perspective, BGP remains the control plane of resilience. Each connection advertises identical prefixes with carefully tuned attributes—typically equal Local Preference within a site and lower preference across sites—to achieve active-active forwarding within each metro and active-standby behavior between them. In the event of a site failure, AWS automatically withdraws the affected routes, allowing traffic to converge within seconds through the surviving DX pair.

In addition to active/active topologies, this design also supports a fully deterministic **active/passive** routing model using AWS Direct Connect BGP communities. For example, you can assign **7224:7300** (higher preference) to the Frankfurt circuits and **7224:7100** (lower preference) to the Paris circuits. This immediately establishes Frankfurt as the primary entry point and Paris as the secondary across locations. Within each location, path selection is refined using **AS-path prepending**, which is applied only between circuits in the *same* metro. As a reminder, AS-path prepending influences routing decisions inside a location, while Local Preference—controlled through DX communities—applies across *different* locations.

With this configuration, if the preferred primary Frankfurt circuit becomes impaired (the one with the shorter AS-path), the second Frankfurt link is automatically selected because it carries the same Local Preference and only differs by a longer AS-path. Should both Frankfurt links fail, AWS shifts traffic toward Paris, first choosing the Paris circuit with the shorter AS-path and then falling back to the second Paris link if necessary. Only when all four circuits across both metros are unavailable does connectivity fully degrade—at which point, as we like to say, *you have a much bigger problem*, but hey! VPN Site-to-Site can still help!

The outcome is **resilience without orchestration**: no manual routing change, no human intervention, just deterministic behavior encoded through policy.

In normal operation or when you want ECMP enabled, you can configure the multiple DX links to either all carry traffic (active-active across four links) or have some act as hot standby. AWS supports **BGP Equal-Cost Multi-Path (ECMP)** across multiple DX virtual interfaces, enabling active-active usage and even outbound load-balancing from AWS's side as long as the BGP announcements are of equal specificity and weight. Using all links can maximize throughput (e.g., aggregate 2×10 Gbps = 20 Gbps capacity), but it requires that your network and applications tolerate **asymmetric routing**. With four links, traffic from AWS may egress on any of them; for example, a flow could arrive via "New York Connection 1," but responses from on-prem might return via "New York Connection 2." Generally this is fine at the IP level, but any stateful firewalls in the path must accept that scenario (or you need to ensure flow affinity per link at your end). Alternatively, an **active/passive strategy** might be chosen as we discussed earlier: for instance, use one location (two links) as primary and only use the second location if the first fails. Section 7.3's discussion of routing intent comes into play here—by manipulating BGP attributes like local preference or AS path, you can prefer one site's routes so that it handles all traffic unless it goes down. Active/passive might simplify troubleshooting and avoid asymmetry, at the cost of leaving some bandwidth unused in normal times. Whichever approach is used, failover should be automatic. If a link or site fails, BGP will withdraw the routes, and traffic will shift to the remaining connections, typically within seconds.

It's worth highlighting that fast failure detection is critical in these designs. By default, BGP sessions can take up to 90 seconds to detect a lost peer (the standard BGP hold timer), which is far too long for most business-critical workloads.

To address this, AWS supports Bidirectional Forwarding Detection (BFD) on Direct Connect private virtual interfaces. When BFD is enabled and correctly configured on both the AWS side and the customer router, it provides sub-second failure detection using short keepalive intervals (e.g., a 300 ms liveness interval with a detection multiplier of 3).

With BFD successfully negotiated, a failed link can be detected in under one second, allowing BGP to rapidly converge and shift traffic to the remaining paths. This is strongly recommended for any multi–Direct Connect or Direct Connect plus VPN backup design. However, achieving sub-second convergence depends on customer device support and configuration—BFD must be explicitly enabled on the on-premises router to realize these benefits.

Failure domains in the maximum resilience model are reduced to a minimum. A single DX device failure at AWS won't interrupt service because a second device at that site still has your other connection. A complete fiber cut or provider outage affecting one link likely doesn't affect the other link (especially if you insisted on diverse carriers or fiber paths). Even losing a whole DX colocation (e.g., a building power loss) will not down your hybrid connectivity, because the other site's two links remain. Only very catastrophic events—such as losing both sites or multiple failures across both—would break connectivity, which is extremely unlikely if sites are independent. For companies needing **near-continuous connectivity**, this is the target architecture. It does come with a higher cost: at least four DX ports (which could be costly at high bandwidths) and more complex management. To make it cost-effective, some organizations start with the high resiliency (two sites, one link each) and then add a second link to each site over time as needs grow, evolving into maximum resiliency when justified.

Multi-Region Resiliency: As an extension of maximum resiliency, some designs also incorporate multiple regions in an active/passive arrangement. For example, a company might normally use Region A for production via two DX sites but have another set of DX links into Region B, ready to use if Region A has a major outage. AWS's DX Gateway allows you to share DX connections across regions (except China), and **Transit Gateway cross-region peering** can link VPC networks between regions. This way, if an entire AWS Region becomes unreachable or degraded, you could fail over your on-prem traffic to a secondary Region via the alternate DX. Such a plan adds complexity (including global routing considerations and data replication between regions), so it's usually reserved for only the most critical multi-region DR scenarios. Still, it underscores that "maximum resilience" can be considered at a global level—eliminating single points of failure even in AWS regional dependencies. For most readers, though, the focus will be on ensuring resilient connectivity to their primary AWS region, which is exactly what High and Maximum resiliency models achieve.

Failure-Domain Summary (Maximum Resilience)

This model tolerates multiple concurrent failures, including the loss of an entire Direct Connect location combined with a port, device, or circuit failure at the surviving location. Connectivity is preserved as long as at least one Direct Connect connection remains available in either location. By deploying two independent Direct Connect connections per location—each terminating on separate AWS routers and customer devices—this design eliminates single points of failure at both the site and device level. It does not, however, protect against extreme correlated events that simultaneously affect all Direct Connect locations (e.g., large-scale regional disasters or systemic provider-wide outages). In practice, Maximum Resilience is designed to withstand both single and compound failure scenarios and represents the highest level of resiliency achievable with Direct Connect alone.

Even with Maximum Resilience, some customers ask what to do next when the requirement is "reduce the chance of total disconnection even further." The answer is not to "improve" Direct Connect itself but to add an independent third path that does not share the same physical dependencies as the Direct Connect locations—most commonly an Internet-based Site-to-Site VPN (optionally Accelerated). This adds a separate escape route for the rare case where both Direct Connect locations are unavailable, which is exactly what we'll cover next.

VPN as a Backup for Direct Connect

So far we have assumed the primary connectivity is Direct Connect. But what if your Direct Connect underlay becomes unavailable—or you need a fast-deploy backup while DX capacity is still being built out? In these scenarios, AWS Site-to-Site VPN is commonly used as a backup connectivity mechanism. VPN connections run over the public Internet (or any IP network) and use IPsec encryption to securely link your on-premises router (Customer Gateway) to AWS. While VPN tunnels don't offer the consistent high throughput or constant low latency of Direct Connect, they are relatively quick to set up and inexpensive. Many organizations choose to deploy a VPN connection as a **backup path**—a kind of insurance policy—for their Direct Connect. In day-to-day use, all traffic goes over the DX, but if the DX fails, the VPN can automatically take over to keep critical connectivity alive.

Using a VPN for failover is a **cost-driven choice**. It's useful when budget or lead times prevent having a fully redundant DX right away, or to add another layer of resiliency beyond your DX setup. However, it's important to recognize that VPN over the internet provides a *lower level of reliability* and performance. There is no SLA on internet traffic, bandwidth can be inconsistent, and latency/jitter may be higher. I'd only consider this model when cost is a top priority or as a temporary solution until a secondary Direct Connect is in place. In other words, VPN backup can **keep you connected during an outage**, but likely with reduced quality (throughput limited to what the internet can deliver). As long as your workloads can tolerate that degradation for a short period, VPN backup is an excellent resilience tactic.

When traffic fails over to a Site-to-Site VPN, organizations should expect materially lower throughput, higher latency and jitter, and a degraded user experience compared to Direct Connect; the VPN path is intended to preserve connectivity for critical services, not to sustain full production performance.

There are two primary ways to integrate a VPN backup with Direct Connect: via a **Virtual Private Gateway (VGW)** on a single VPC or via a **Transit Gateway (TGW)** for multiple VPCs. In both cases, the VPN and Direct Connect will terminate on the same AWS gateway so that routes from on-prem can fail over between them. Let's first discuss the commonalities and then any differences.

Designing the VPN Backup: AWS Site-to-Site VPN connections come with *two* redundant tunnels by default (to two separate AWS endpoints). Always configure and **use both tunnels** for resilience, of course—if one tunnel goes down, the other can still carry traffic. Ideally, run them in active-active mode with BGP dynamic routing on each so that traffic can load-share and fail over seamlessly. AWS supports ECMP over multiple VPN tunnels when attached to a Transit Gateway, allowing you to use both tunnels simultaneously for higher aggregate throughput. On a VGW, by contrast, multiple VPN tunnels to the same VGW do *not* load-share for outgoing traffic—the VGW will prefer one tunnel and only use the second if the first fails, which results in active-passive behavior. Either way, ensure your on-premises router is configured to permit asymmetric routing if you use ECMP, since return traffic might come back over a different tunnel than it went out. Most modern routers handle this fine, but if there are stateful firewalls, they must allow the secondary tunnel's traffic as well.

Like I said, just like Direct Connect, the VPN should be set up with **BGP routing** whenever possible. Dynamic routing will let AWS and your router exchange routes and rapidly detect failovers.

It is important to clarify that, in Transit Gateway–based designs, route selection between Direct Connect and Site-to-Site VPN is not governed solely by the standard BGP best-path algorithm. Instead, the Transit Gateway applies AWS-defined route evaluation rules that prioritize attachment type before considering BGP attributes. For identical prefixes, routes learned via Direct Connect attachments are preferred over routes learned via Site-to-Site VPN attachments, regardless of AS-path length or MED. BGP attributes such as AS-path prepending or MED are evaluated only after attachment type precedence is resolved.

If using BGP, advertise the same prefixes over both Direct Connect and the VPN paths so that AWS evaluates truly equivalent routes. If you remember from the previous section, AWS's route priority rules ensure that the Direct Connect path is preferred over the VPN when both are available. This is true both for Transit Gateway (which explicitly prefers DX routes over VPN for the same prefix) and for VGW-based scenarios. Because of this, you typically don't need to do any fancy BGP tuning to make the DX primary. It will be primary by default as long as the advertised routes are the same. That said, you should also ensure from *your* side that you prefer the DX for outbound traffic when it's up—for example, by using a higher local preference for routes learned via DX or by static route preferences—so that you don't accidentally send traffic into the VPN when the DX is healthy (which could cause asymmetric routing). The key is alignment: both sides should prefer Direct Connect when it's available and fall back to VPN if not. When the DX goes down (or the BGP session over it drops), routes through DX are withdrawn, and the VPN's routes will automatically take over in AWS routing tables. **Even with these attachment-level preferences in place, one routing rule still sits above all others.**

Regardless of BGP attributes, attachment type, or routing intent, AWS routing always follows the longest prefix match (LPM) first. A more specific prefix (e.g., a /24) will always be preferred over a less specific prefix (such as a /16), even if the less specific route is learned via Direct Connect and the more specific route is learned via a Site-to-Site VPN.

This behavior can unintentionally override carefully designed failover and preference policies. Any resilience design that mixes Direct Connect and VPN must therefore ensure consistent prefix lengths across all paths or explicitly account for LPM behavior.

In practice, the most common manifestation of this rule is route specificity. If the VPN advertises more specific routes than the Direct Connect, it could inadvertently attract traffic even when the DX is up (because the longest-prefix-match wins in routing). For example, say your on-prem network is 172.16.0.0/16. If over Direct Connect you advertise only 172.16.0.0/16, but over the VPN you advertise both 172.16.0.0/16 *and* more specific segments like 172.16.10.0/24, then AWS will prefer to send traffic for 172.16.10.x over the /24 via the VPN (since /24 is a longer match than /16). This is clearly not what we want—VPN should not carry traffic when DX is up, in a typical design.

To prevent this, ensure the route advertisements are consistent and **filter routes** appropriately. A good practice is to **accept only summary routes from the VPN** or otherwise constrain the prefixes so that they match what the DX is advertising. By doing so, you guarantee that AWS sees the same prefix via both paths (e.g., just the /16), and then the built-in preference rules will choose the DX path. If you need more granular routing control (for instance, maybe you actually want to send some low-priority traffic over VPN even normally), that can be done with route filtering or BGP communities— but that's an advanced scenario outside our scope, maybe the next book!

Generally, keep it simple: advertise identical route sets and let the *Direct Connect be the active route*.

When using a **Transit Gateway (TGW)** for connectivity, the AWS side handles route priority automatically as described. The TGW route table will show the on-premises prefixes received via DX (through a DX Gateway attachment to the TGW) and via the VPN attachment. By rule, for identical prefix lengths, the Transit Gateway evaluates attachment type before BGP attributes, preferring Direct Connect attachments over Site-to-Site VPN attachments for the same destination. Since both DX and VPN here are dynamic, the TGW uses the type precedence: DX beats VPN for the same prefix. This means your failover order is set: DX is primary, and VPN is secondary. (If you wanted it the other way around for some reason, you'd have to influence it by making the prefixes or route types different—uncommon for backup use cases.) With a **VGW (Virtual Private Gateway)**, if both a VPN and a DX virtual interface attach to the same VGW, the VGW also typically will prefer the Direct Connect path for identical routes, as AWS's guidance indicates. One caveat with VGW is that it doesn't support ECMP across VPN tunnels or across VPN+DX together—it will pick one path for each prefix. But as long as priorities are set correctly, it will choose DX until that path fails, then switch to VPN. Once routing behavior is fully understood and controlled, the next limiting factor during a DX outage is raw capacity.

Bandwidth and Throughput Considerations: A major limitation of VPN backup is throughput. Each AWS Site-to-Site VPN tunnel currently supports a maximum of **1.25 Gbps** of throughput (due to AWS's implementation limits). If your Direct Connect is, say, 10 Gbps, a single VPN tunnel cannot handle that much traffic if all of it were to fail over. Even if you use both VPN tunnels (e.g., on TGW with ECMP, you might get up to ~2.5 Gbps by using two tunnels), it's still far below 10 Gbps. Therefore, it is not **recommended** to use a VPN as a backup for high-capacity DX circuits (>1 Gbps) unless your traffic volume during failover can be throttled down or is naturally lower. For DX bandwidths of 1 Gbps or less, a VPN can roughly match that capacity (with two tunnels on TGW achieving ~2x1.25 Gbps = 2.5 Gbps, which is sufficient to cover a 1 Gbps link with some headroom). If you have extremely high bandwidth needs (tens of Gbps), a single VPN backup is likely not viable. In such cases, multiple VPN connections can be used in parallel—for example, some customers set up multiple VPNs to multiple TGWs or multiple CGW devices, and with ECMP across many tunnels have achieved up to 10 or 20 Gbps over the Internet—but managing that gets complex, and often it's better to invest in a secondary Direct Connect. By using Transit Gateway with many VPN tunnels, you could scale VPN throughput up to ~50 Gbps aggregate, but that involves on-premises infrastructure capable of handling 40+ IPsec tunnels and is not trivial. For most, VPN backup is about keeping the lights on for critical traffic, not handling *all* production traffic at full bore.

Another option to improve VPN performance is to use an **Accelerated Site-to-Site VPN**. AWS allows you to enable acceleration for a VPN connection, integrating **AWS Global Accelerator** directly with your VPN endpoints.

With acceleration enabled, VPN traffic no longer traverses the public internet end-to-end. Instead, it enters the AWS network at the **nearest AWS edge location**, rides the **AWS global backbone** to the target region, and exits to the VPN endpoint.

This path dramatically reduces latency variability and improves throughput stability—especially when your offices are geographically distant from the AWS Region or when your internet path is suboptimal. It's important to be clear, though: this improves *stability and latency*, not raw bandwidth—the 1.25 Gbps per tunnel limit still applies. The feature introduces additional costs (Global Accelerator data-transfer charges), but for a **backup link**, the trade-off is often worth it. When failover occurs, an accelerated VPN ensures that the backup experience remains as smooth as possible. For organizations running interactive or low-latency applications during a DX outage, this can make the difference between degraded and tolerable performance.

In Figure 7-5, a corporate data center connects to AWS through a primary Direct Connect link (green path) and a secondary Site-to-Site VPN tunnel (red path) terminating on the same Transit Gateway. Both paths advertise identical prefixes to AWS. The Transit Gateway prefers the Direct Connect route under normal conditions and automatically reroutes traffic through the VPN if the Direct Connect BGP session drops. When acceleration is enabled, VPN traffic first enters AWS at the nearest Global Accelerator edge location and traverses the AWS global backbone to the region, reducing latency variation and improving performance during failover events.

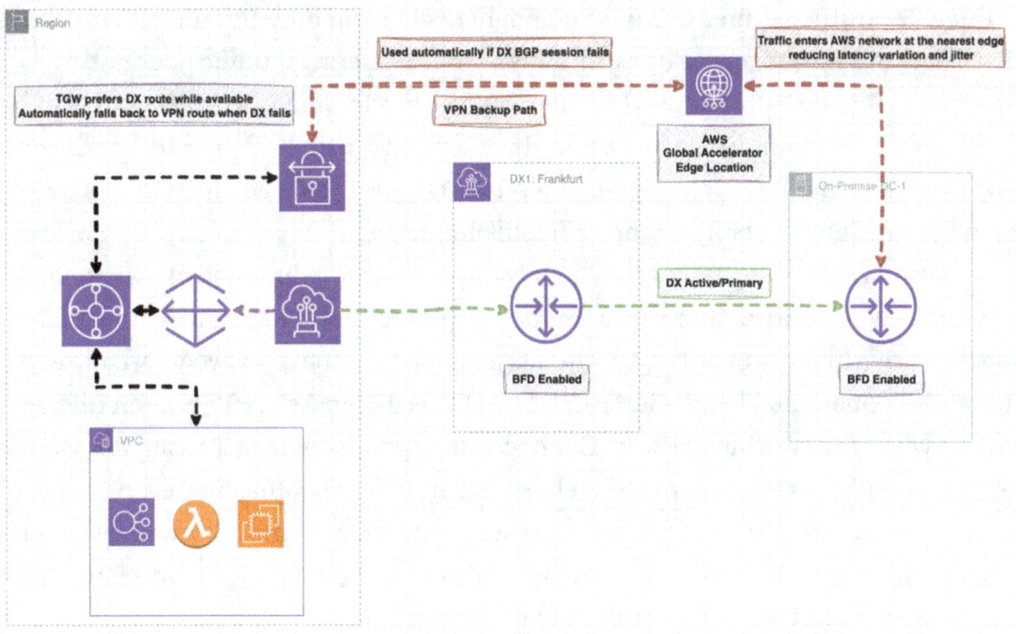

Figure 7-5. *Accelerated Site-to-Site VPN Backup for Direct Connect*

A VPN backup adds resilience to your hybrid architecture, but it requires discipline to be effective:

Test the failover periodically. It's easy to "set and forget" the VPN backup, but you don't want the first failover during a real incident to reveal a misconfiguration. Perform a scheduled simulation by temporarily shutting down your DX BGP sessions and ensure traffic truly switches to VPN and back with minimal disruption. Monitor how long the failover takes and whether any sessions reset. Fine-tune BGP timers or BFD if needed. Remember, any implementation of resilience practice that hasn't been tested is equal to zero. I repeated this many times because testing is imperative; actually, continuous testing is imperative!

Tune Dead Peer Detection (DPD) on the VPN. AWS VPN endpoints use DPD to detect if the on-prem peer is alive. Ensure your device also has appropriate keepalive/DPD intervals—most defaults are reasonable, but for faster detection you might lower them. However, be cautious to not set them so aggressively that they cause false detections on transient internet blips.

Use robust CPE devices for VPN termination. During a DX outage, potentially a lot of traffic could suddenly hit your VPN device. Make sure it has the CPU and capacity to handle the encrypted throughput and BGP routes.

Consider traffic segmentation—you might decide that only certain critical subnets will fail over to VPN (advertise those on VPN), while less critical traffic does not, to conserve the limited VPN bandwidth. This way, during an outage, you at least keep priority services running and avoid saturating the tunnel with background workloads. This ties back to the "routing intent" concept: design your route advertisements such that in a failure, the most important traffic still flows.

To summarize, a VPN backup can greatly improve your hybrid network's resiliency, but it comes with performance caveats. When deployed thoughtfully, it's a powerful tool: if the expensive high-throughput DX circuits go offline, an inexpensive VPN can keep your network operational in the interim. Many AWS customers use VPN as an **interim solution** when first moving to Direct Connect (since provisioning a DX can take weeks or months, the VPN fills the gap) and then keep it around as a contingency even after DX is up. Just remember that it's not magic—the user experience during failover may degrade, and therefore the business should understand the limitations (perhaps by referencing an SLA or expectations for the VPN path vs. the DX path).

Design Considerations and Best Practices

Bringing together the above topics, let's highlight key design considerations for hybrid connectivity resilience and best practices that I'd suggest you adopt

> **Eliminate Single Points of Failure:** This is the guiding principle. For mission-critical applications, use multiple DX connections and multiple locations (at least two of each for maximum

resiliency). Likewise, use multiple on-premises routers. Ensure power redundancy, diverse fiber paths, and, if possible, even diverse telecommunications carriers for each connection. Don't overlook "small" single points of failure—for example, if both your DX circuits leave your building through the same fiber conduit, that conduit is a single point of failure (a backhoe could take out both). Work with your providers to pursue path diversity wherever feasible.

Plan for Sufficient Capacity on Failover: As discussed, whichever topology you choose, make sure that the remaining connections can handle the traffic when one connection fails. In High Resiliency (two links total), each should ideally be sized to carry 100% of the peak load if the other fails. In Maximum Resiliency (four links), each pair at a site might be able to carry a full load if the other site goes down, etc. If using active-active load sharing, consider that loss of one link will put its traffic onto the survivors—do they have headroom? Oversubscribe links only if you have non-critical traffic that can be dropped during an outage.

Leverage Dynamic Routing and Health Detection: Static routing is possible but not desirable for resilience. BGP should be used on Direct Connect and on VPN. It provides automatic route failover and the ability to influence path selection with attributes. Use features like **BFD on Direct Connect** to speed up failure detection to sub-second levels. On VPN, ensure Dead Peer Detection is enabled. The goal is to minimize the time between a link going down and traffic switching to the alternate path. Chapter 6's discussion of failover emphasized detection and convergence time—apply those lessons here with BGP timers, BFD, and keepalives tuned for your needs.

Understand AWS Routing Priorities: AWS has deterministic rules for route preference when using multiple connectivity types. For example, **Transit Gateway** prioritizes Direct Connect over Site-to-Site VPN for the same prefix. A Virtual Private Gateway prefers static routes over BGP and generally will prefer Direct Connect routes over VPN if both exist. Knowing these rules helps avoid surprises. If you do need to override defaults (say, make VPN active in some scenario), you must adjust metrics or use route filtering to break the tie. In most cases, following the AWS defaults is simplest—they are configured to choose the highest bandwidth, lowest-cost path (DX) first, which aligns with most intents.

Use BGP Attributes for Intent-Based Routing: In more complex topologies (like multiple on-prem sites or multiple AWS regions), you may need to engineer which path is used for what traffic. AWS supports BGP communities on DX Gateway that influence route preferences. For instance, you can tag routes with a community that AWS interprets to set a lower local preference, making them secondary. Similarly, on your side, you can use Local Preference or AS path prepending to choose one DX location as primary for certain routes. These techniques (covered in Section 7.3 on routing intent) allow fine-grained control. A common pattern: set both DX links as active (equal preference) for load balancing, but prepend AS path on the VPN routes so that they are only used when DX is down. Another pattern: in a dual-site on-prem scenario, each site might normally carry its local traffic to AWS but act as a backup for the other site via an internal WAN— communities and localpref can enforce that "site A uses DX-A as primary, site B's DX-B as primary, and they back each other up." Always test these policies to ensure traffic actually flows as intended in failure scenarios (simulate link downs and observe BGP route changes).

Direct Connect Gateway Best Practices: Use a single Direct Connect Gateway to aggregate your connections and virtual interfaces, rather than multiple separate DX Gateways. The DX Gateway is highly available by design and not a throughput bottleneck. Having one central DX Gateway simplifies multi-region and multi-location routing. AWS will automatically carry traffic via the shortest path in its global network, so you don't need region-specific DX Gateways for resiliency. Also, there is *no need to deploy a "backup" DX Gateway*—it adds no value since it's not in the data path or failure path of the connectivity. Focus instead on adding more DX locations or links that actually improve resiliency.

Monitor and Baseline Performance: With multiple connections and failovers, visibility is key. Use CloudWatch metrics for Direct Connect (such as connection state and aggregate throughput) and CloudWatch logs for VPN tunnel status to alert on outages. Monitor VPC Flow Logs or other network monitoring to know what "normal" traffic distributions are across links. This helps in detecting anomalies (e.g., if the backup link is unintentionally carrying traffic when it shouldn't, or if failover did not occur when it should have). Tracking latency and throughput on the VPN vs. DX can also guide you if you need acceleration or more bandwidth.

Regularly Exercise Failover: It's a best practice to periodically test your resiliency mechanisms in a controlled way. For Direct Connect, AWS now provides the **Resiliency Toolkit** that even allows simulation of a connection failure to test your setup. You can also manually shut down BGP sessions during maintenance windows to verify that alarms trigger and traffic shifts to alternate paths. Incorporate these tests into your disaster recovery drills. This process not only validates the technical failover but also familiarizes your operations team with procedures and expected impacts (for instance, knowing that a 30-second BGP reconvergence might cause a brief application hiccup, so maybe sessions need retry logic). As noted in Chapter 6 and others before, *untested failover is merely hope*, not a strategy.

Plan for Growth and Scale: Over time, your network traffic patterns may change. Re-evaluate your hybrid connectivity annually (or more often) to see if the model still fits. Perhaps what started as "High Resilience + VPN backup" for cost reasons should become "Maximum Resilience + VPN" as the business grows more dependent on AWS. Or if workloads shift to a different region, you might need to add a DX location there. AWS's evolving services (like AWS Cloud WAN or Transit Gateway Network Manager) are making it easier to manage complex networks—consider using these tools to get a holistic view of your hybrid network health and to manage routing policies in one place.

Know the Limits and Responsibilities: While AWS ensures high availability within its network, you as the customer are responsible for your side of the resilience. Redundancy in AWS (multiple AZs, DX Gateway, etc.) won't help if your on-prem router room floods or if a misconfigured BGP on your router stops announcing routes. Build out redundancy in your data center (power, cooling, cabling) commensurate with the cloud side. Likewise, cultivate relationships with your DX providers/partners—in an outage, you may need to quickly coordinate with them.

Let's apply what we learned so far and visualize it with the following diagram.

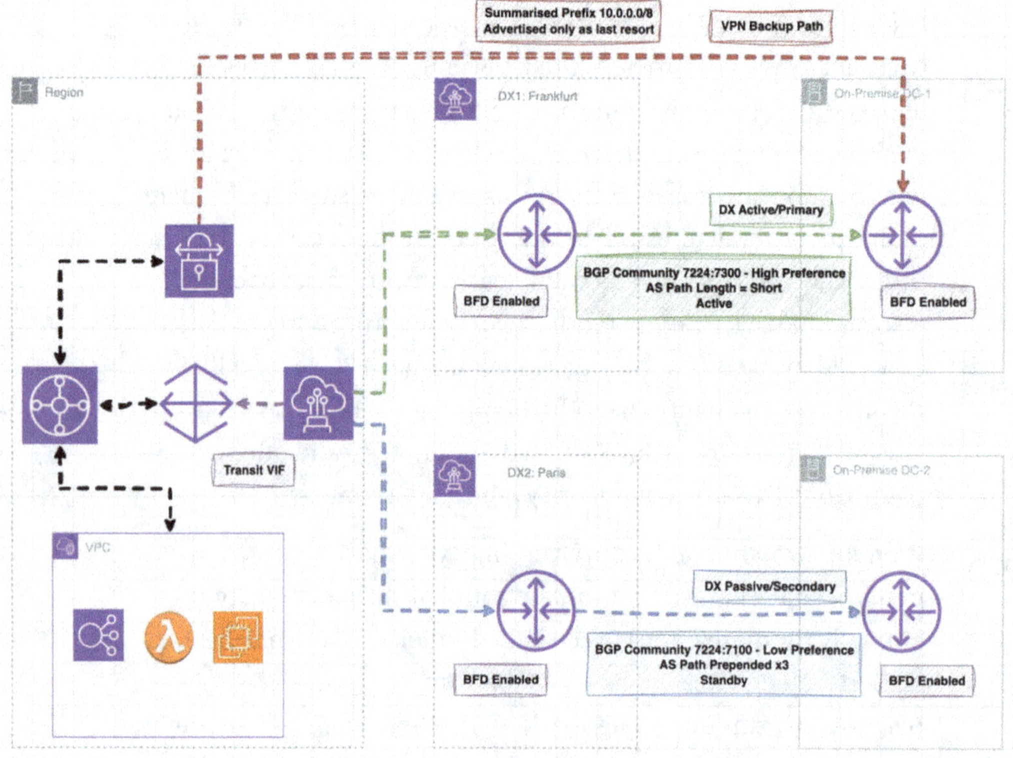

Figure 7-6. *Active/Passive Hybrid Connectivity with Transit VIF*

In Figure 7-6, each corporate data center connects to AWS through two distinct Direct Connect locations.

The primary location (Frankfurt) advertises its prefixes with the higher-preference BGP community 7224:7300 and a short AS Path, while the secondary location (Paris) advertises the same prefixes with the lower-preference community 7224:7100 and a three-hop AS Path prepend. Both sites use **Bidirectional Forwarding Detection (BFD)** for sub-second failure detection.

A **Transit Virtual Interface (VIF)** connects the Direct Connect Gateway to a **Transit Gateway**, providing scalable access to multiple VPCs within the region. A **VPN backup tunnel** advertises only a summarized prefix (10.0.0.0/8) as a last resort, ensuring connectivity if both Direct Connect locations become unavailable. This topology achieves deterministic failover using BGP attributes and community values, maintaining resilient hybrid connectivity without manual intervention.

The secondary DX site (Paris) advertises the same prefixes but marks them with the low-preference community 7224:7100 and optionally prepends its AS number two or three times (e.g., AS 64513 AS 64513 AS 64513). These signals make the path less attractive to AWS routers, keeping it in standby mode until required.

Outbound traffic from the corporate network mirrors this behavior. Routers in each data center use **Local Preference** to determine which egress to AWS to prioritize. The primary DX site's prefixes are assigned a higher local-pref value (e.g., 200 vs. 100), ensuring **egress symmetry**—packets exit and return through the same preferred region.

When a failure occurs at the primary DX site—whether due to a link, port, or BFD session loss—the corresponding BGP session drops. AWS immediately withdraws the routes tagged with 7224:7300, leaving the standby advertisements from the secondary site as the only available paths. Those lower-preference, longer AS-Path routes automatically become the best option, allowing traffic to reroute through the standby location within seconds. Because both paths are already established and exchanging keepalives, the transition is seamless and requires no operator intervention or manual route manipulation.

This deterministic behavior delivers what we called in Chapter 6 a **"boring" recovery**—precisely the goal of mature resilience engineering. The policies encoded in BGP attributes translate architectural intent into automatic action, achieving consistent reachability and predictable convergence.

In doing so, they align the control plane's design with the operational resilience philosophy developed throughout this book: a network that heals quietly, predictably, and continuously.

Achieving resilient hybrid connectivity is not about over-engineering; it's about deliberate design. By combining AWS's High and Maximum Resiliency models with intelligent route policy—communities, local preference, and AS-path control—you can dictate how traffic behaves under failure rather than leaving it to chance. For many organizations, this means dual Direct Connect locations with active/passive routing and a Site-to-Site VPN safety net. Others may operate dual active sites with symmetric policies to balance load and minimize latency. There is no universal recipe; there are only trade-offs between cost, complexity, and recovery time. What matters is that your hybrid connectivity reflects both the engineering discipline described here and the broader resilience mindset developed throughout this book. When every route, prefix, and attribute carries intent, the network becomes self-healing—able to absorb disruption and keep serving users quietly, predictably, and continuously. Resilience by design is only half of the story.

The other half is proving that the design behaves as intended once the packets start flowing. A network that looks resilient on paper can still hide fragility in its timing—slow convergence, uneven latency, silent packet loss. To close that gap between architecture and reality, we must measure.

In the next section, we move from topology to telemetry, from configuration to observation.

We'll learn how to quantify success: how to track performance, validate failover behavior, and tune hybrid connectivity until "resilient" becomes not just a design principle but a measurable property of the network itself.

Section 7.5: Measuring Success: Performance and Resilience Tuning Automation

In Chapter 1, we defined resilience as the ability to **absorb failure without breaking user experience**—a property earned through intent, evidence, and iteration rather than granted by diagrams. Chapters 3 and 4 showed how the DNS layer participates in that promise, keeping the control plane reachable and making sane, policy-driven choices even while a region coughs. Chapter 6 translated the same idea into recovery choreography: cell-based architecture, multi-AZ, multi-region. Sections 7.2–7.4 then brought the conversation down to the wire level—hybrid underlays, Direct Connect and VPN traits, TGW semantics, and the BGP vocabulary we use to make traffic do what we mean, not what the Internet happens to prefer on a Tuesday. This section turns the corner from *design intent* to *operational truth*. We ask, with a straight face: does the network you built actually behave like the network you drew?

What this section measures—and what it will not automate

Section 7.5 focuses on measuring and tuning network behavior, not redesigning architecture. We measure latency (including percentiles), packet loss, throughput, and convergence across Direct Connect, Site-to-Site VPN, and Transit Gateway paths, and we tune routing preference and failover posture based on those signals. Automation in this section is deliberately bounded: it adjusts routing intent (BGP attributes, communities, and preference), but it does not modify IP addressing, security policy, segmentation, or application-level failover. All tuning actions are threshold-driven, rate-limited, and designed to auto-revert when conditions normalize.

Within that scope, the answer lives in the relationship between **performance** and **resilience**. A fast path that collapses under a routine link flap is a liability; an indestructible path that adds 120 ms of latency to every round trip is a tax your users will not pay. In practice, the two are inseparable. When a primary Direct Connect fails, sub-second BFD detection is only half the story; the other half is whether latency, jitter, and loss on the surviving path stay within the envelope your SLOs permit. When you steer ingress with AWS communities and egress with local preference, correctness is not proven by a green BGP session but by packets taking the route you intended, at the quality you promised, while application metrics remain boring. Resilience is not "did we fail over"; it is "did users notice."

To measure that honestly, it helps to think in planes. Each plane answers a distinct question: what users experience, how routing decisions are made, and whether recovery stays within the promised service envelope.

For clarity, the metrics discussed throughout this section map cleanly to three operational planes:

- **Data Plane:** what traffic experiences

  Round-trip time (RTT), jitter, packet loss, throughput, and effective MTU/MSS. These metrics describe performance as felt by applications and users.

- **Control Plane:** how the network decides

  BGP and BFD state, route withdrawal and propagation, Direct Connect and Transit Gateway convergence behavior. These metrics describe how quickly and correctly routing intent adapts to change.

- **Resilience Plane:** what the business perceives.

  User-facing SLO impact, Recovery Time Objective (RTO) adherence, Mean Time to Detect (MTTD), Mean Time to Recover (MTTR), and the acceptable recovery envelope during failure.

Resilience emerges only when these three planes remain aligned.

The **data plane** is what customers feel: round-trip times across DX and VPN, retransmits during a flap, and throughput on a jumbo path that quietly fell back to 1500 because one interface lied about MTU. The **control plane** is how the network makes up its mind: the time between a keepalive expiring and a new best path being installed, the propagation delay from your CGW to DXGW to TGW, and the moment a more specific route suppresses your carefully crafted attributes. And there is a third layer that has been running through this book since Chapter 6—the **resilience plane**—where detection, decision, and redirection turn into a user-visible outcome. Healthy systems keep these three planes in step. When they drift, you see it: BGP converges on schedule, but sessions still reset because your TCP MSS clamp wasn't applied at the right edge; Route 53 fails over on time, but TTL choices consume your whole RTO; a TGW route table is perfectly populated, while NAT egress drags return traffic onto the public Internet and through the wrong firewall.

This is why measurement here is not a vanity dashboard; it is the continuation of design by other means. The policies you set in Section 7.3 (local-pref, AS-path, MED) and the models you chose in Section 7.4 (High vs. Maximum resiliency, VPN as safety net) are *hypotheses* until the system is exercised under stress and its behavior is recorded. "DX prefers Frankfurt" is a sentence; *ingress actually arrives in Frankfurt during a simulated loss of Paris while median p95 latency to the EU user cohort stays under 80 ms* is evidence. The difference between the two is the entire point of this section.

The craft is to make those outcomes observable at the right granularity. You already know from Chapter 4 that TTL is a recovery boundary; here it becomes a contract you can verify. You already know from Chapter 6 that calm failovers start with fast, trustworthy liveness; here you watch BFD, DPD, and BGP timers in the wild and relate them to application heartbeat and session durability. You already know from

Section 7.2 that hybrid paths carry different failure patterns; here you correlate them: a carrier maintenance on one DX location should show up identically in BGP state, DX port metrics, TGW propagation, ALB success rates, and user latency—*or something is lying to you.*

None of this is hand-waving toward Chapter 8's automation; it is the standard you will automate *to*. If design expresses intent, and automation enforces it at speed, then **measurement is what keeps the two honest**. We will tune route maps because a percentile moved in the wrong direction, not because a playbook said so. We will bias DNS geoproximity because a region is warming up, not because an incident declared itself. We will shorten a TTL because our RTO demands it, not because "60 seconds feels modern." The loop is tight by design: observe, orient, decide, and act—then observe again. When the three planes line up and stay lined up through failure, you have moved from *resilient architecture* to a **resilient system**.

What follows in this section is deliberately pragmatic. We will define what "good" looks like for traffic engineering when resilience is the goal; show how to instrument the paths you actually use (DX, SiteLink, TGW, VPN, Global Accelerator, and the edges that glue them together); and explain how to read the network's vital signs in production so your tuning decisions are boring and your recoveries are quieter still. The principles started high in Chapter 1, took shape in Chapters 3–4, and learned to move in Chapters 6–7. Here, they learn to **prove**.

Key Metrics for Network Resilience and Performance

Resilience in networking is proven through behavior, not diagrams. The metrics in this section exist to answer three operational questions: how quickly the network detects disruption, how predictably it reacts, and how gracefully it recovers. Together, they expose whether failure is absorbed smoothly—or merely survived.

Rather than treating performance and resilience as separate concerns, these metrics deliberately measure their interaction during the moments architectures fail quietly: convergence events, capacity reduction, and failover path transitions that change latency, packet size, or loss characteristics.

Success Criteria: Interpreting Network Resilience Metrics

A hybrid network can be considered resilient when the following measurable conditions hold true during normal operation and controlled failure events:

- **Latency stability across percentiles**

  Median latency remains stable, and the gap between p50, p95, and p99 stays bounded during failover or reconvergence events.

- **Controlled jitter under stress**

  Latency variation increases briefly during disruption but does not persist once routing stabilizes.

- **Fast and correct convergence**

  Control-plane failures are detected and reconverged quickly, and traffic is restored to the *intended* paths rather than merely any available path.

- **Graceful throughput degradation**

  Available bandwidth on surviving paths decreases in a predictable and limited way, without collapse or prolonged congestion.

- **Bounded packet loss**

  Packet loss may spike transiently at failure onset but subsides rapidly as convergence completes, without sustained retransmission storms.

- **MTU and MSS compliance across paths**

  End-to-end MTU and TCP MSS remain consistent across Direct Connect, VPN, and failover paths, preventing fragmentation, black-holing, or silent throughput degradation.

- **Timely detection and recovery**

  Failures are detected automatically (low MTTD), and connectivity is restored within the Recovery Time Objective (MTTR) defined by the business.

These criteria describe resilience as a measurable system behavior, not a static design claim. The metrics discussed in this section exist to verify that these conditions hold in production. With that contract defined, we now break the metrics down and show how each one behaves during normal operation, controlled failovers, and real-world degradation.

The remainder of this subsection examines each of these criteria in turn, starting with the metric users feel first: latency.

The first lens is **latency**—the time it takes for a packet to leave one end of the network and return from the other. It is deceptively simple yet profoundly revealing. Low latency is not enough; what matters is consistent latency. Two paths may both average 50 milliseconds, but if one varies between 20 and 100, the user will perceive instability. That variation is **jitter**—the invisible noise in the rhythm of your network. Jitter is what causes dropped frames in video calls, broken audio in conferences, and unpredictable transaction times in financial systems. It is the mark of a network that survives, but not gracefully.

To express this nuance, we rely on **percentiles rather than averages**. Percentile measurements—p50, p95, p99—describe not what the "typical" user experiences, but what most users endure when the network is under strain. The p50 (50th percentile) represents the median latency: half of your requests are faster, half slower. The p95 and p99 percentiles capture the outliers—the tail-end performance where resilience is truly tested. A small gap between p50 and p99 means your network is stable, predictable, and resilient. A large gap exposes hidden fragility: an architecture that performs beautifully on a good day but unravels under load. Measuring those tails, rather than the average, is what separates reliable systems from optimistic ones. **AWS CloudWatch** embraces this principle natively; many of its service dashboards report latency in percentiles because AWS engineers understand that resilience lives in the tails of distributions, not in their centers.

Latency, however, is just the surface. Beneath it lies the **tempo of change**—how fast the network stabilizes after disruption. This is what we call **convergence**. In BGP-based environments, convergence describes how long it takes for the control plane to detect a loss, withdraw invalid routes, and install new paths. A network that converges in seconds feels robust; one that takes minutes feels broken. As we learned previously, **AWS Direct Connect** supports **Bidirectional Forwarding Detection (BFD)** for exactly this reason. BFD acts as a heartbeat between peers, detecting unreachability in sub-second intervals. In practical terms, that means the network can reroute traffic before users even notice. Measuring convergence time gives us the most honest view of resilience—not the promise written in a design document, but the performance that actually unfolds in the field.

Still, speed alone is not enough. A network can converge fast and yet converge wrong. A misconfigured route map or unintended prefix advertisement can steer traffic into the wrong region or even out of compliance boundaries. True resilience includes **correctness**—the assurance that the network recovers not only quickly but safely. For this reason, convergence time should always be evaluated alongside **path integrity**. Tools such as **Transit Gateway Network Manager** or third-party systems like **ThousandEyes** can validate both metrics simultaneously, showing whether the routes that appear after convergence are the ones you intended to be active.

Throughput, the third pillar of performance, measures how much data can flow without friction. It is the ultimate expression of capacity and headroom. Hybrid networks often face a paradox here: during failover, available bandwidth drops just when demand peaks. Measuring throughput under normal and impaired conditions reveals whether your redundant links are truly resilient or merely redundant in theory. In AWS environments, **CloudWatch** provides granular visibility into throughput for each virtual interface, while active measurements—**iperf sessions**, synthetic probes, or controlled load tests—show how well the network holds under stress. A resilient system is not one that maintains perfect performance, but one that **degrades gracefully**, where throughput dips gently rather than collapsing.

MTU and MSS correctness form a quieter but equally critical dimension of network resilience. In hybrid environments, Direct Connect paths often support jumbo frames, while VPN tunnels and internet paths typically do not. During failover, traffic may suddenly traverse a path with a smaller effective MTU, triggering fragmentation or— worse—silent packet drops when intermediate devices block ICMP "fragmentation needed" messages. The result is a failure mode that is deceptively subtle: sessions establish successfully, BGP converges as expected, latency appears reasonable, yet throughput collapses and applications stall.

TCP Maximum Segment Size (MSS) clamping is the primary control used to mitigate this risk. By ensuring that TCP segments fit within the smallest MTU of any potential path, MSS clamping prevents fragmentation and preserves predictable performance during failover. From a resilience perspective, MTU and MSS should be treated as measurable invariants, not static assumptions. Operators should validate that effective MSS values remain consistent across Direct Connect, Site-to-Site VPN, and Transit Gateway paths, and that no change in forwarding path introduces a sudden reduction in usable packet size. A resilient network is not merely one that reroutes traffic, but one that preserves packet integrity and throughput when it does.

When MTU or MSS mismatches go undetected, their impact often surfaces indirectly—through retransmissions and packet loss rather than obvious forwarding failures. For this reason, packet loss must be interpreted not only as a capacity signal but also as a potential indicator of hidden path inconsistencies.

If latency is the heartbeat and convergence the reflex, **packet loss** is the pain threshold. It shows when the network starts dropping what it cannot carry. Even a loss rate as small as 0.1% can cripple TCP performance, reducing throughput dramatically due to retransmissions. Measuring packet loss across Direct Connect, Transit Gateway, and VPN paths gives early warning of saturation or congestion before it becomes visible to applications. Plotting loss alongside latency produces a **degradation curve**—a visual profile of how the network behaves under pressure. A shallow curve means resilience: the network absorbs increasing load without sudden failure. A steep curve, where performance plummets with minimal stress, signals fragility and the need for redesign.

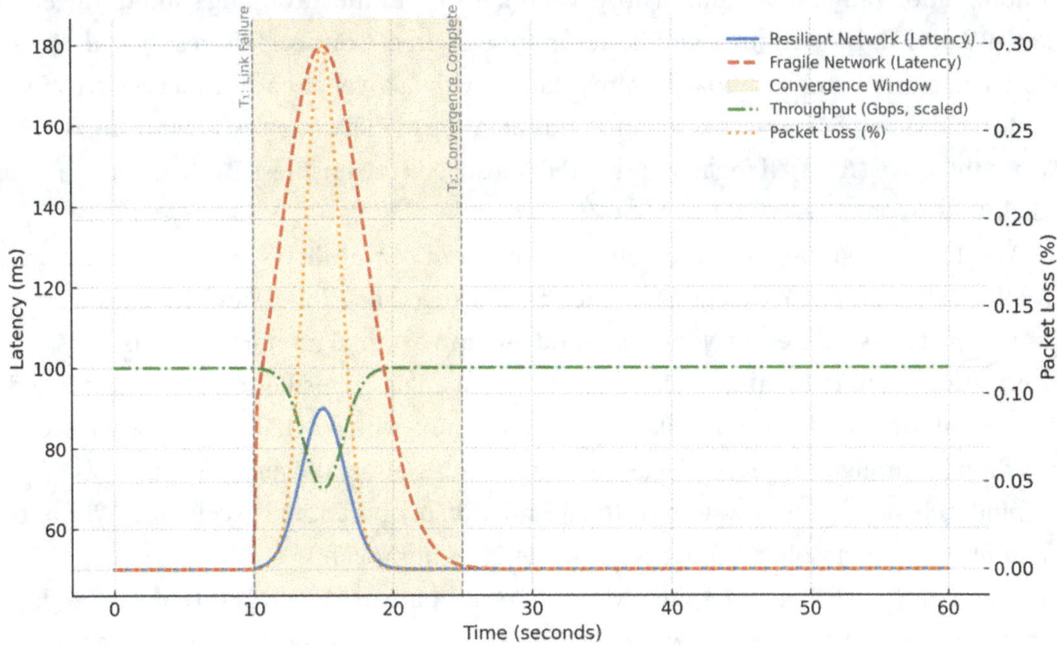

Figure 7-7. *Latency, Packet Loss, and Throughput During a Simulated Link Failure*

Figure 7-7 illustrates how a resilient network behaves before, during, and after a link disruption. The blue curve shows stable latency with a brief rise and fast recovery, representing rapid BGP convergence and sufficient capacity on the standby path. The red dashed line represents a fragile network where delayed convergence causes prolonged instability. The orange dotted line tracks packet loss, which spikes at failure onset and quickly subsides as routing stabilizes. The green line represents throughput, which dips modestly during the event and then returns smoothly, indicating graceful degradation rather than collapse. Together, these metrics visualize the essential properties of resilient networking—quick detection, deterministic convergence, and graceful recovery.

Beyond the network's data plane, resilience also depends on the **control plane's operational readiness**—how quickly issues are detected and resolved. Two metrics capture this human-mechanical interplay: **Mean Time to Detect (MTTD)** and **Mean Time to Recover (MTTR)**. MTTD measures how fast monitoring systems (or operators) recognize that something is wrong; MTTR measures how long it takes to restore normal service. In a well-instrumented hybrid architecture, both should be driven primarily by automation rather than human observation. A VPN tunnel dropping should trigger **CloudWatch alarms** within seconds, not minutes. Direct Connect failures should surface in operational dashboards immediately, with failover already underway. AWS's **Well-Architected Framework** recommends aligning MTTR targets with your **Recovery Time Objective (RTO)**. If the network's MTTR exceeds the business RTO, resilience exists only on paper.

What binds all these measurements together is **observability**—the ability to see, in real time, how the control and data planes behave together. CloudWatch metrics, VPC Flow Logs, **Transit Gateway Network Manager**, and external monitoring tools like **ThousandEyes** or **RIPE Atlas** each offer a different angle on resilience. When correlated, they reveal cause and effect: a spike in latency aligning with a BGP reconvergence event or a drop in throughput caused by asymmetric routing after failover. This synthesis of visibility across layers and systems is the foundation of operational excellence. Without it, numbers remain isolated, and resilience remains unproven.

Ultimately, metrics are not merely numbers; they are **evidence of intent realized**. When we measure p99 latency, we are not just timing packets—we are validating trust. When we observe convergence times, we are verifying discipline. When we calculate MTTR, we are testing readiness. Every measurement is a story about how the system behaves when pushed. Together, they form the vocabulary of resilient networking—one that is empirical, precise, and accountable.

In practice, these metrics become the inputs for **automated health models**—feeding resilience dashboards, triggering adaptive routing changes, and quantifying the "steady-state readiness" of your hybrid network. In the following section, we will turn these insights into practice, translating observation into optimization and transforming measurement into resilience you can prove.

Let's summarize:

- When analyzing network telemetry, focus on relationships, not absolutes.

- A p99 latency increase without packet loss may suggest congestion, not failure.

- A low MTTR is meaningless if MTTD is slow—detection always precedes recovery.

- And a network that converges in milliseconds but to the wrong route is not resilient; it's dangerous.

True resilience is measured not only by how *fast* systems recover but also by how *correctly* they do so.

Resilience Tuning and Continuous Optimization

Resilience only becomes real when the network can sense itself and change its mind without drama. In traffic engineering terms, that means closing the loop between what the **data plane** feels (latency, loss, jitter, congestion) and what the **control plane** does (prefer this path, demote that one, widen or narrow catchments). We've already built multiple viable paths (DX, VPN, SD-WAN), and we've encoded intent (Section 7.3). Now we teach the system to adapt—quietly, predictably, and for the right reasons.

A good tuning regime respects cadence. Fail fast on hard faults; adjust gently on soft impairments. We use **BFD** to collapse true failures to hundreds of milliseconds; we use **IP SLA** (or controller telemetry) to notice rising latency or loss; and we stitch those signals into BGP policy so egress and ingress shift before users feel pain. Tuning is not an endless chase of "lower number = better." It's the art of guarding stability while steering away from degradation.

We've already learned how to steer traffic intentionally—how to use BGP attributes, communities, and AS-path manipulations to dictate which Direct Connect or VPN path becomes primary or standby. That gave us deterministic control: when a link fails, routing adjusts exactly as designed. But resilience is not only about reacting to failure; it's about recognizing degradation before it becomes an outage. The next step, therefore, is preemptive tuning—using the metrics we introduced above in real time and also gathering performance metrics observed directly from routers to detect early signs of trouble and adapt routing behavior dynamically. In other words, we move from "failover when broken" to "reroute when breaking."

Measuring What Matters: Resilience Tuning Automation On-Premises Routers

Routers don't "know" latency by default; we must measure it. On classic Cisco IOS/IOS-XE, **IP SLA** probes (e.g., icmp-echo) give us round-trip time and reachability to a target that reflects the path users take—often the AWS TGW appliance IP or a health-checked endpoint behind the ALB. These probes run on a schedule, and their outcomes are exposed to the config via **object tracking** and the **event manager**. That's the bridge: probes produce facts; policies react.

Two classes of triggers are useful:

Hard Failure (Reachability): If the probe can't get a reply within a timeout, the track object goes **down**. We treat this like a mini-outage and move traffic decisively (BFD and BGP timers still provide the fastest cutover for link/device failure, but IP SLA can complement them for path-specific reachability).

Soft Impairment (Performance): If latency or loss crosses a threshold for a period, we **de-prefer** the path (e.g., lower local-pref outbound; add prepends and lower-preference communities inbound). Because classic track objects don't natively "go down when RTT > X," we use **IP SLA reaction messages + EEM** to toggle the policy when the router reports "over threshold" or "back under."

This is not "silver bullet automation." It's careful feedback: act when patterns persist, cool down before switching back, and never oscillate.

Pattern 1—Outbound (Egress) Steering by Measured Performance

Outbound is ours to control. We prefer the lower-latency Direct Connect when healthy; we fall back (or de-prefer) when latency inflates persistently. The example below shows the essential wiring: (1) measure; (2) react; (3) alter BGP attributes.

Config disclaimer: The following snippets are **illustrative only** (non-production). Exact commands, syslog IDs, timers, and neighbor policy hooks vary by platform/ version. Validate in a lab and follow your change process.

```
! 1) Measure RTT to an AWS-side IP that reflects the DX path
ip sla 10
 icmp-echo 52.95.255.1 source-interface GigabitEthernet0/0
 frequency 5
 timeout 1000
! Define an "excess RTT" threshold at 100 ms and generate events
ip sla reaction-configuration 10 react rtt threshold-type consecutive
   threshold-value 100 3   ! >100ms for 3 consecutive probes
   action-type syslog

ip sla schedule 10 life forever start-time now

! 2) Track hard reachability (up/down)
track 10 ip sla 10 reachability

! 3) BGP policy: two route-maps we will toggle between
ip prefix-list AWS-PFX seq 5 permit 10.0.0.0/8 le 24

route-map DX_PRIMARY_EGRESS permit 10
 match ip address prefix-list AWS-PFX
 set local-preference 200

route-map DX_DEGRADED_EGRESS permit 10
 match ip address prefix-list AWS-PFX
 set local-preference 100
! (Optionally) also mark to discourage equal-cost forwarding on this box
! set weight 0

router bgp 65000
 neighbor 169.254.100.1 remote-as 64512
 neighbor 169.254.100.1 description DX Transit VIF - AWS
 !
 ! Start in "primary" mode
 neighbor 169.254.100.1 route-map DX_PRIMARY_EGRESS in
 !
```

```
! 4) React to RTT threshold crossings with EEM (syslog-driven)
event manager applet RTT_HIGH
 event syslog pattern "RTTMON.*ThresholdExceeded.*rtt" maxrun 60
 action 1.0 cli command "enable"
 action 1.1 cli command "configure terminal"
 action 1.2 cli command "router bgp 65000"
 action 1.3 cli command "neighbor 169.254.100.1 route-map DX_DEGRADED_
EGRESS in"
 action 1.4 cli command "end"
 action 1.5 syslog msg "EEM: Switched to DEGRADEDegr egress due to
high RTT"

event manager applet RTT_RECOVERED
 event syslog pattern "RTTMON.*ThresholdFalling.*rtt" maxrun 60
 action 1.0 cli command "enable"
 action 1.1 cli command "configure terminal"
 action 1.2 cli command "router bgp 65000"
 action 1.3 cli command "neighbor 169.254.100.1 route-map DX_PRIMARY_
EGRESS in"
 action 1.4 cli command "end"
 action 1.5 syslog msg "EEM: Restored PRIMARY egress after RTT recovery"

! 5) Hard failure? Let BFD/BGP handle fast withdrawal; track can
still warn.
router bgp 65000
 neighbor 169.254.100.1 bfd
!
```

In practice probes run every 5s; if RTT > 100 ms for three consecutive samples, the router emits an IP-SLA "threshold exceeded" syslog; EEM catches it and flips the inbound route-map to a **de-preferred** local-pref. Outbound traffic moves to the alternate (e.g., second DX or Accelerated VPN) according to your policy. When RTT falls back under the threshold for consecutive probes, EEM restores the **primary** local-pref. BFD remains the first responder for hard faults.

The process forms a closed feedback loop between measurement, policy, and outcome. IP SLA continuously measures round-trip latency along the Direct Connect path, treating RTT as a living signal rather than a static statistic. When latency exceeds the configured threshold for multiple consecutive probes, the router generates a syslog event. Embedded Event Manager (EEM) intercepts that signal and dynamically adjusts the inbound route-map applied to the Direct Connect neighbor, lowering its local-preference value. The result is deterministic egress steering: outbound traffic shifts automatically toward the healthier path—perhaps a secondary DX circuit or an accelerated VPN—without human intervention. When latency returns to normal, the same feedback mechanism restores the primary policy.

BFD remains the first responder for hard faults, detecting physical or protocol loss within milliseconds, while IP SLA extends that reflex to soft degradation—congestion, jitter, or rising delay that often precedes failure. Together they create an adaptive control system where the network senses its own performance and adjusts before users experience impact. This is resilience in motion: a network that not only heals when broken but also rebalances itself when strained.

Why this works: Local Preference is the first decisive attribute within your autonomous system—it dictates which exit wins when multiple paths exist. By adjusting it dynamically, we turn policy into a living signal that reflects measured network health rather than static configuration. Unlike reactive failover, this approach introduces intelligence at the edge: routing decisions follow observed experience, not assumptions.

In effect, we've given the router a sense of judgment. It doesn't panic at every packet loss, nor does it wait for total failure. Instead, it reads the pulse of latency, reacts only when thresholds persist, and reverts calmly when the condition clears. This balance—fast on faults, gentle on impairments—is the essence of engineered resilience. It prevents oscillation, preserves user experience, and ensures that every shift in traffic is intentional, justified, and reversible.

Through this design, egress routing becomes more than just a BGP configuration; it becomes a feedback mechanism, a system that continuously aligns control-plane intent with data-plane reality.

Pattern 2—Inbound (Ingress) Steering by Measured Performance

Inbound routing is always the more delicate art, because those decisions happen in someone else's domain. We can control how we send traffic out, but how our cloud peers send it back depends on the signals we advertise. In AWS, that means influencing ingress through BGP communities and AS-Path prepending—two levers that shape how attractive our routes appear to the AWS routing plane. The principle remains the same as in egress control: measurement triggers a policy change, but now the action modifies what we announce rather than what we prefer.

We begin by measuring the network's health from the inside out. Using IP SLA probes, the router monitors latency or packet loss along the return path—typically between on-premises and an AWS endpoint (e.g., a TGW attachment or ALB VIP). When these probes detect persistent delay, they emit syslog events, which Embedded Event Manager (EEM) scripts use as triggers to change route-advertisement behavior dynamically.

```
! 1) Measure RTT/loss to a representative on-prem <-> AWS return-
path target
ip sla 20
 icmp-echo 52.95.255.1 source-interface GigabitEthernet0/1
 frequency 5
 timeout 1000
ip sla reaction-configuration 20 react rtt threshold-type consecutive
  threshold-value 120 3
  action-type syslog
ip sla schedule 20 life forever start-time now

! 2) Prefixes we advertise from on-prem to AWS
ip prefix-list ONPREM-EXPORT seq 5 permit 192.168.0.0/16
ip prefix-list ONPREM-EXPORT seq 10 permit 172.16.0.0/12

! 3) Two outbound advertisement policies:
!     PRIMARY: high-pref community, no prepend
!     DEGRADED: low-pref community, AS-path prepends
route-map DX_PRIMARY_ADVERTISE permit 10
 match ip address prefix-list ONPREM-EXPORT
 set community 7224:7300 additive
! (7224:7300 is AWS "high" preference; verify current docs before use)

route-map DX_DEGRADED_ADVERTISE permit 10
 match ip address prefix-list ONPREM-EXPORT
 set community 7224:7100 additive
 set as-path prepend 65000 65000 65000
```

```
router bgp 65000
 neighbor 169.254.100.1 remote-as 64512
 neighbor 169.254.100.1 description DX Transit VIF - AWS
 !
 ! Start by advertising with HIGH preference
 neighbor 169.254.100.1 route-map DX_PRIMARY_ADVERTISE out

! 4) EEM flips advertisements on impairment/recovery
event manager applet INGRESS_DEGRADE
 event syslog pattern "RTTMON.*ThresholdExceeded.*rtt" maxrun 60
 action 1.0 cli command "enable"
 action 1.1 cli command "configure terminal"
 action 1.2 cli command "router bgp 65000"
 action 1.3 cli command "neighbor 169.254.100.1 route-map DX_DEGRADED_
ADVERTISE out"
 action 1.4 cli command "end"
 action 1.5 syslog msg "EEM: Ingress de-preferred (low community +
prepends)"

event manager applet INGRESS_RECOVER
 event syslog pattern "RTTMON.*ThresholdFalling.*rtt" maxrun 60
 action 1.0 cli command "enable"
 action 1.1 cli command "configure terminal"
 action 1.2 cli command "router bgp 65000"
 action 1.3 cli command "neighbor 169.254.100.1 route-map DX_PRIMARY_
ADVERTISE out"
 action 1.4 cli command "end"
 action 1.5 syslog msg "EEM: Ingress restored (high community, no
prepends)"
```

In practice, the logic is simple but powerful. When the router detects sustained degradation on the inbound path—say, RTT exceeding 120 ms for three consecutive samples—it changes its advertisement from *high* to *low* AWS preference, while also adding multiple AS-Path prepends. These signals make the route appear less attractive to AWS's routers, prompting AWS to prefer another Direct Connect or VPN path for inbound traffic. When performance recovers, the advertisement switches back to its original state: high-preference community and clean AS-Path.

This dynamic adjustment gives you deterministic ingress engineering tied directly to measured user experience. No manual intervention, no guesswork—just routing intent expressed through live telemetry.

If you were to visualize it, you would see the router advertising the same on-premises prefixes with different "intent tags." Under normal conditions, the routes carry the **7224:7300** (high-preference) community. When degraded, the router advertises them with **7224:7100** (low preference) and three AS-Path preprends, causing AWS to reroute inbound traffic to a healthier location.

A note of caution: AWS's Direct Connect communities—**7224:7100, 7224:7200,** and **7224:7300** (low, medium, high)—are stable but may vary slightly by region or gateway type. Always confirm the latest values and behaviors in the AWS Direct Connect documentation before implementing this pattern in production.

Why this works: Ingress steering is ultimately about persuasion, not command. By altering how our routes look to AWS—raising or lowering their attractiveness—we influence decisions that aren't technically ours to make. This is resilience through subtlety: we guide AWS's control plane with facts gathered from our own measurements, not assumptions.

When latency or loss crosses our threshold, we don't wait for a ticket or a user complaint—we whisper to AWS's routers that another path is better suited. When conditions normalize, we quietly withdraw that suggestion. The exchange feels organic because it is: two autonomous systems cooperating through the shared language of BGP.

Together, the outbound and inbound patterns complete the loop. One ensures that what leaves our network follows the best exit; the other ensures that what returns finds the best entrance. It is a choreography of intent, built entirely on telemetry. And once these policies are in place, resilience stops being reactive—it becomes fluent.

Guardrails That Keep Tuning Stable

Adaptive networks can hurt themselves if they move too quickly or too often. We add **cool-down** logic (e.g., require N consecutive over-threshold samples before switching; require M consecutive "good" samples before restoring). We bind performance tuning to **time windows** (e.g., don't allow more than one flip per 10 minutes). And we let **BFD and BGP** handle hard faults—latency-based tuning is for degradation, not down events.

On the wire, we keep the path honest: **jumbo MTUs** end-to-end for DX/TGW where intended; **MSS clamping** on VPN fallbacks; consistent **QoS** on hand-off interfaces; and periodic **Path MTU** validation to avoid the silent "fragmentation tax" that masquerades as loss. Many "mystery" failovers are simply bad MTU stories wearing latency masks.

Where SD-WAN Fits

If your wide-area network is controller-driven—whether through **Cisco SD-WAN (vManage)**, **Palo Alto Prisma SD-WAN**, or another overlay—you already possess the foundation of an adaptive system. These platforms continuously measure latency, jitter, and packet loss, steering application traffic dynamically according to policy. The goal is not to replace that intelligence but to integrate it with the **BGP-based resilience controls** we introduced earlier in this chapter.

Think of the **SD-WAN controller** as the network's sense of perception and **AWS's routing layer** as its expression of intent. When the controller detects persistent degradation—rising RTT, sustained loss, or excessive jitter—it signals the edge routers to adjust BGP attributes accordingly. Telemetry becomes policy: local preference and community values evolve dynamically to match the current health of the network.

Figure 7-8 illustrates a hybrid feedback loop combining AWS telemetry and SD-WAN control. When AWS telemetry detects rising latency on the primary Direct Connect (Frankfurt), the SD-WAN controller lowers local preference and advertises a lower-preference community to AWS, shifting traffic to the secondary DX in Paris. When performance recovers, the controller restores the primary route map, re-establishing high-preference routing. BFD provides sub-second failover for hard faults, while telemetry enables proactive rerouting based on soft degradation. Together, these layers form a self-correcting network that balances automation with determinism.

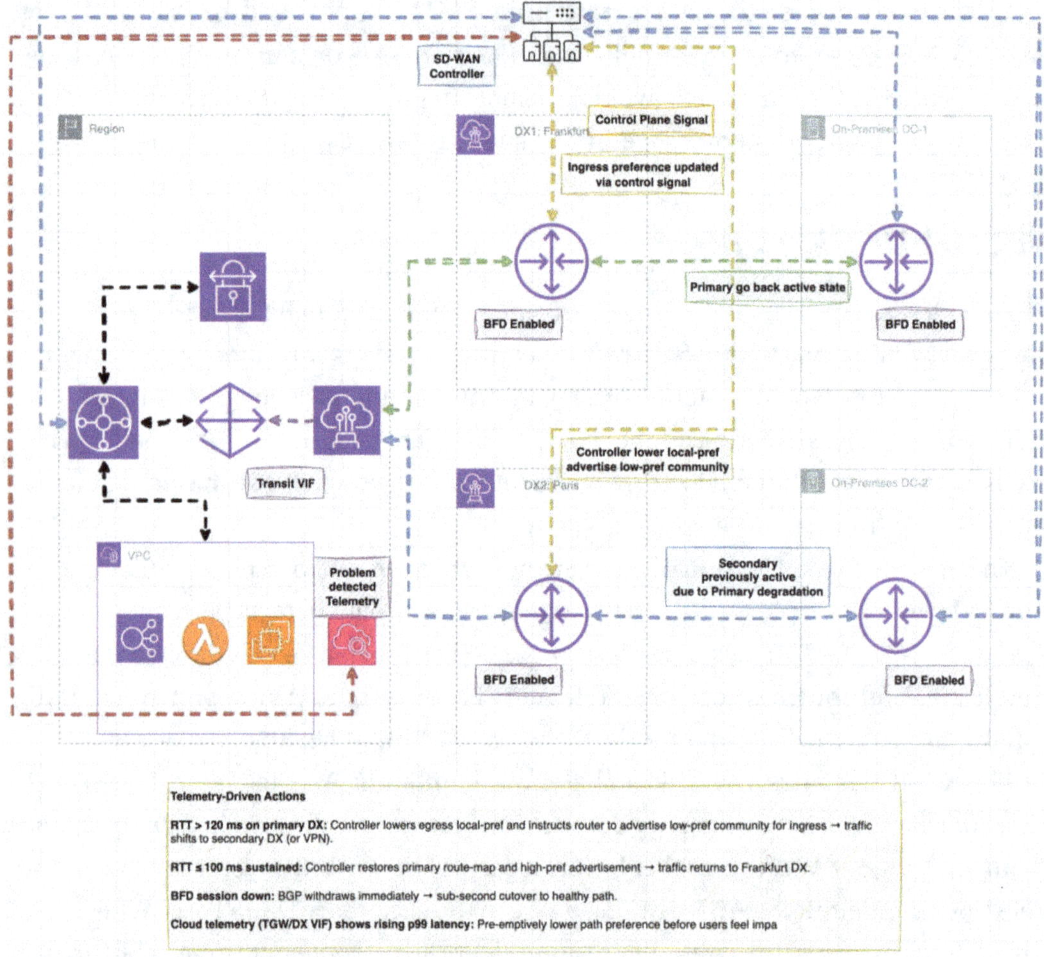

Figure 7-8. *Controller-Assisted Resilience Loop Using AWS Telemetry and SD-WAN*

For example, the **SD-WAN controller** might **lower local preference** on the egress path or trigger a **route map that advertises a low-preference community** (such as *7224:7100*) on the inbound side. In this way, the automation that governs your overlays can directly inform the policy that governs your **Direct Connect** and **VPN underlays**.

AWS Transit Gateway Network Manager and **CloudWatch** provide the complementary half of the loop. They supply telemetry from the cloud side: interface throughput, route-propagation state, attachment health, and BGP session stability. When those data points feed into the SD-WAN controller, the hybrid network behaves as an **adaptive mesh**—one where both the cloud and the edge agree on what "healthy" means and respond in sync.

This cooperative model defines **controller-assisted resilience**. Instead of managing dozens of localized policies independently, the orchestrator coordinates path selection across branch, core, and cloud using a single intent model. The result is a system that behaves as one living fabric, shifting gracefully between **Direct Connect**, **VPN**, and **Internet tunnels** as conditions evolve.

Validation: Show, Don't Assume

A tuning change that isn't validated is a superstition. Every policy flip should be followed by a quick runbook: did the preferred neighbor's **Adj-RIB-In** reflect our new attributes? Did AWS change the return path (check flow logs, traceroutes from EC2, and Route 53 health telemetry)? Did median and tail latencies drop? We keep **before/after** snapshots, and we graph them. Over time, those graphs become the confidence we lean on when real incidents arrive.

What This Gives Us

We move from reactive failover to **preemptive steering**. Hard failures still converge fast—BFD and BGP do that. But soft failures no longer linger; the network senses the drift and trims its sails. Most importantly, changes are not heroic one-offs. Their policies are tied to measurements, so the same wisdom applies at 2 a.m. on a Sunday as it does at noon on a Tuesday. That's what makes resilience feel boring to users and satisfying to us.

One more thing I'd like to remind you: the configurations above are **teaching scaffolds**, not production templates. Exact syslog patterns for IP SLA reactions, EEM permissions, BGP policy hooks, and community semantics vary by platform and by time. Always validate message IDs on your image (show logging | include RTTMON), add cool-downs in EEM, and test under load in a lab or a dark-launch environment before deployment.

Capacity Planning and Headroom As a Resilience Practice

Resilience begins long before a failover; it begins with foresight. The quiet discipline of capacity planning—often invisible beside design diagrams or routing policies—is what decides whether a network bends or breaks under stress. Resilient systems are built not only through redundancy but also through **margin**: the deliberate space between present load and structural limit. In cloud networking, that margin is called **headroom**.

When we spoke earlier about the principle of "remaining boring under duress," this was the deeper meaning: when a link fails, a router flaps, or an entire region experiences impairment, nothing dramatic should happen. Traffic shifts, convergence occurs, and the network continues to breathe. If every circuit, tunnel, and attachment already runs at its ceiling, a single fault becomes a cascade. In that moment, no amount of automation or clever BGP tuning can help. A network without headroom has already spent its resilience in advance.

AWS's **Well-Architected Framework** states it plainly in the Reliability pillar: *"Plan capacity to meet demand during component failures."* In hybrid connectivity, that becomes a design rule—**N–1 survivability**. Each path must sustain the full load of the others if they fail. Two Direct Connect links mean each can carry 100% of peak traffic; four links mean each pair must do the same. This is not theoretical neatness—it is engineering necessity. During real incidents, it separates graceful degradation from total collapse.

Capacity, however, is never static. Workloads evolve, replication patterns shift, and what was safe in 2026 may be saturated by 2027. AWS offers the instrumentation to prevent silent erosion: **CloudWatch** for Direct Connect throughput, **Transit Gateway Network Manager** for attachment visibility, and **VPC Flow Logs** for per-interface bandwidth and flow composition. Together they close the loop that turns headroom from assumption into measurable fact. When a CloudWatch graph shows sustained 70% utilization, you are not watching traffic—you are reading a countdown to the next redesign.

Headroom is not waste. It is the engineered gap between comfort and collapse. The art lies in keeping utilization high enough to stay efficient yet low enough to stay elastic. Industry practice settles around **60–70% steady-state load** on hybrid circuits— economical, but able to absorb double load without congestion. Beyond that, queues lengthen, retransmissions multiply, and resilience erodes invisibly long before links "fail." Capacity and reliability are two sides of the same discipline; ignoring one is betting against the other.

Balancing this equation requires **tools and tests, not optimism**. AWS's **Direct Connect Resiliency Toolkit** simulates link loss and verifies that secondary paths sustain expected throughput. Enterprises often complement it with **synthetic load tests** during maintenance windows to confirm that latency, jitter, and packet loss remain within their Service Level Objectives (SLOs). These SLOs should use **percentiles**, not averages: *p95* for user experience and *p99* for resilience. The tail matters most because it captures the edge—the 1% of samples where systems strain and users notice. Resilient architectures are built for that tail, not the mean.

Architecturally, headroom arises from **diversity and segmentation**. Multipath connectivity—combining **Link Aggregation Groups (LAGs)** with geographically distinct **Direct Connect locations**—provides both capacity scaling and fault isolation. A LAG protects against port failure; multiple sites protect against facility outages. Together they define AWS's **Maximum Resiliency Model**, where no single fiber cut or building loss isolates the enterprise.

Equally vital is **traffic segmentation**. Not every bit deserves the same path: latency-sensitive applications belong on primary circuits, while asynchronous replication or backup flows use secondary or VPN links. This separation prevents background processes from starving interactive workloads during recovery. Applying **Quality of Service (QoS)** at the WAN edge enforces that hierarchy—critical packets ride priority queues, and bulk transfers yield gracefully when the system contracts.

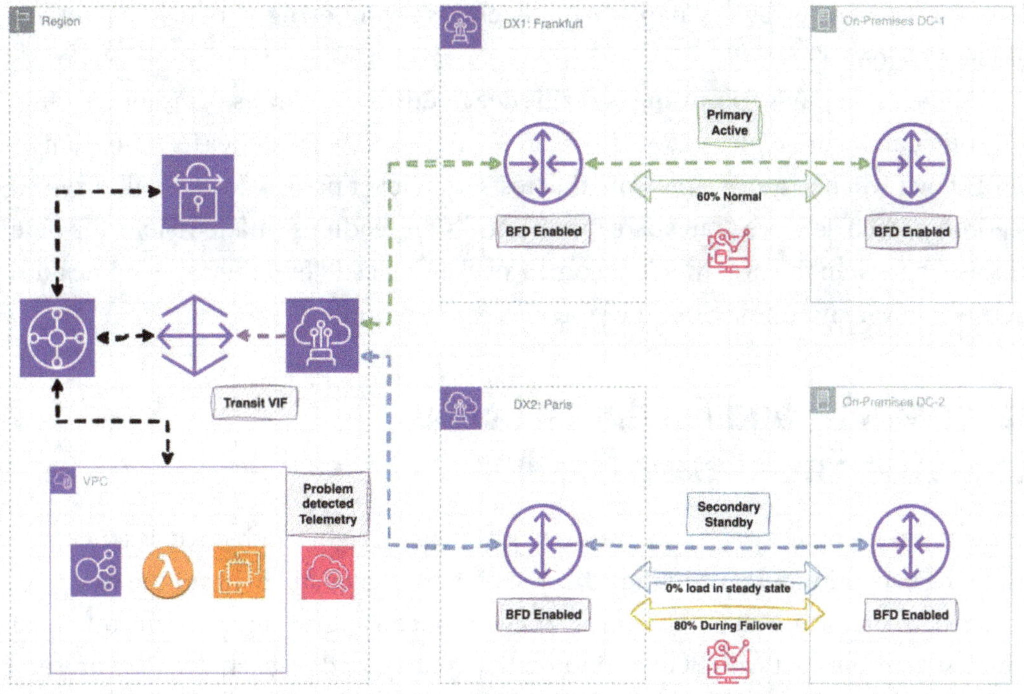

Figure 7-9. Headroom and Failover Load Distribution

Figure 7-9 illustrates an active/passive Direct Connect topology. Under normal operation, the Frankfurt DX link runs at 60% utilization, leaving sufficient headroom. When telemetry detects rising latency or link degradation, traffic shifts to the standby DX in Paris, which carries 80% of the load during failover. BFD provides sub-second detection, ensuring that aggregate utilization remains below capacity limits and preventing congestion-driven loss. Maintaining 30–40% headroom enables graceful degradation and N–1 resilience.

Forecasting growth is as crucial as designing for failure. Resilient networks project their future load as rigorously as they monitor today's. **CloudWatch** and **Transit Gateway metrics** provide the historical baseline; from there, traffic can be modeled seasonally or linearly. When projections show utilization breaching 80%, scaling is not a future improvement—it is current maintenance. Upgrading port speeds, adding Direct Connects, or redistributing prefixes across new Transit Gateways are acts of prevention, not expansion.

Forecasts, however, must be verified. **Stress tests**—temporary link shutdowns, **BFD failover drills**, or **packet-loss injections**—confirm that theory matches behavior. These exercises, revisited in Chapter 8 under **chaos engineering**, turn fear of failure into evidence of control.

Ultimately, **capacity planning is resilience in advance**. It transforms monitoring into anticipation and anticipation into action. A network that watches its saturation trend knows when to grow; a network that tests its failover paths knows it will survive. Headroom, then, is more than spare bandwidth—it is readiness made visible, the quiet promise that when the next incident comes, packets will still find their way home and users will never know how close the system came to its limits.

Observability and Feedback Loops for Traffic-Engineering Resilience

Resilient traffic engineering is not the art of picking the "right" path once; it's the discipline of continuously validating that the path we prefer still behaves the way we intended. In practice, that means observability is not an afterthought but the other half of policy. We set intent with BGP attributes, DNS policy, and edge choices; we preserve that intent with measurement, correlation, and carefully bounded automation. Without that loop, even elegant policies will drift quietly until the next incident forces them into the spotlight.

We start by observing the network from two planes that behave differently under stress. The control plane tells us about truth: which prefixes are reachable, which sessions are up, and which next-hops are viable. The data plane tells us about experience: latency, loss, jitter, and saturation along the path users actually traverse. A stable BGP session does not guarantee a healthy flow, and an available endpoint does not guarantee an acceptable p95. So we treat the signals as complementary. On the AWS side, Direct Connect exposes connection state and throughput in CloudWatch; Transit Gateway records attachment health and route propagation; Route 53 surfaces resolver behavior via query logs; VPC Flow Logs and ENA counters show per-interface reality; and Global Accelerator (where used) offers edge-to-origin telemetry. On the enterprise side, we combine router counters, NetFlow/IPFIX, and SD-WAN path metrics with third-party vantage points—ThousandEyes, RIPE Atlas, and CloudWatch Synthetics—because the Internet will not describe itself from a single seat.

Signals need meaning before they can guide action, so we set service level objectives in the language of probability rather than averages. When we say p95 latency, we mean 95% of requests complete at or below that value; p99 describes the tail where rare but expensive events live; p99.9 is our early-warning system for systemic stress. In healthy systems, the gap between p50 and p99 is modest; when queues build or loss spikes, the tail stretches first. That is why we watch percentiles for each critical hop (branch➤edge, edge➤colo, colo➤DX, DX➤region) and aggregate them to an end-to-end SLO. If p99 creeps above target on a single segment, we move traffic away from that segment; if p99 rises uniformly, we raise capacity, not policy. In other words, measurement is not a scoreboard—it is a decision engine.

With telemetry in place, we close the loop in three stages. The first is human-in-the-loop: dashboards that overlay BGP events with latency/loss, annotations for deploys and circuit maintenance, and runbooks that prescribe specific actions ("reduce geoproximity bias by 20% in ap-southeast-2 if p99>120 ms for 5 minutes while BGP remains stable"). The second is supervised automation: detectors that file a change with a guardrail ("propose AS-path prepends on the Paris DX for /22 only; require two approvals or auto-revert in 10 minutes"). The third is bounded autonomy: automation that acts within a narrow envelope and carries its own brake ("Route 53 Traffic Flow bias may change by at most ±10 in any 15-minute window; Global Accelerator weight shifts by ≤5% per step; revert automatically if the SLO improves by < x% after y minutes"). We are not trying to build a self-driving network; we are building a network that can change its mind safely.

A brief example makes this concrete. Late afternoon, p99 latency into ap-southeast-2 rises from 85 ms to 135 ms while BGP and BFD remain green. Flow logs show retransmissions growing on eastbound circuits; DX throughput is steady, but jitter doubles, and queue drops appear on the peer handoff. This is not a failure; it is saturation at the edge. We reduce Route 53 geoproximity bias for the region by 20, shifting ten to 15% of queries to a neighboring region already within our latency budget. p99 falls below 100 ms; the change auto-locks after a 30-minute stabilization window. At midnight local time, the system restores bias to zero. Nothing dramatic happened because the loop was already in place.

Finally, we keep the loop honest with evidence. Every automatic change includes a hypothesis ("reducing bias will cut p99 by $\geq$20 ms without violating data-sovereignty routing"), a measured outcome, and a built-in rollback. We also version policy, just as we version infrastructure, so that a problematic community map or Traffic Flow tree can be reverted cleanly. Observability without actuation is commentary; actuation without observability is gambling. Resilience lives in the discipline that binds the two.

Bridging to Multi-cloud Traffic Management

Once we can observe and steer a single hybrid network with confidence, the next logical step is to extend that discipline across clouds. Observability gave us the reflexes to adapt within AWS; multi-cloud teaches us to think beyond it. In a world where critical workloads span AWS, Azure, and sometimes Google Cloud, resilience is no longer just about shifting traffic between regions—it's about shifting intent between providers. The same control loops that detect a rising p99 on a Direct Connect path must now decide whether another cloud's backbone can deliver better stability or compliance. BGP, DNS, and SD-WAN remain our instruments, but the stage widens: exchanges like Equinix and Megaport become our inter-cloud synapses, and policy coherence becomes the new frontier of resilience. The next section explores how to design that federated nervous system—how to extend routing intent, failover logic, and measurement loops across multiple clouds so the network can route not only around fiber cuts but also around cloud outages themselves. We won't delve into the full depth of this topic here—it merits a dedicated volume of its own (perhaps a future project)—but it's important to touch on it for the sake of completeness and context.

Section 7.6: Multi-cloud Traffic Management

Industry surveys consistently show that multi-cloud is now the dominant operating model. The Flexera 2025 State of the Cloud Report, based on responses from 759 organizations worldwide, shows enterprises using an average of 2.4 public cloud providers, with AWS and Azure each adopted by roughly 80% of enterprises—clear evidence that the vast majority of organizations already operate across multiple clouds.

Network architects are now expected to weave AWS, Azure, and other platforms into a single resilient fabric—one capable of maintaining performance and compliance while absorbing failures at the provider level.

In this section, multi-cloud traffic management refers to the design and operation of connectivity between different cloud providers—combining private interconnects, routing intent expressed through BGP, DNS, and edge-based steering, and unified observability to control how traffic enters, traverses, and fails over between clouds.

We extend the hybrid-cloud routing concepts introduced earlier in this chapter and apply them across providers rather than across regions within a single provider. Both AWS and Microsoft offer private connectivity primitives—AWS Direct Connect and Azure ExpressRoute—that can be interconnected through neutral exchange fabrics. Services such as Equinix Fabric and Megaport Cloud Router provide Layer-3 connectivity between AWS, Azure, and other major clouds, while many Direct Connect locations are physically co-located with ExpressRoute edge points in global colocation hubs.

These interconnects significantly reduce exposure to public Internet variability, but they do not eliminate shared infrastructure entirely. Inter-cloud traffic still converges at specific metros, exchange points, or carrier handoff locations where provider networks interconnect. As a result, performance and resilience depend on *where* traffic enters each cloud, the design and capacity of the exchange fabric, and the physical proximity of Direct Connect and ExpressRoute edge locations. Multi-cloud traffic management therefore relies on deliberate entry-point selection and metro diversity—not on assumptions of a single, global private backbone.

The implementation of multi-cloud architectures is not driven by technology alone; it is driven by regulation.

Modern resilience frameworks such as the EU Digital Operational Resilience Act (DORA), the EBA Guidelines on ICT and Security Risk Management, and the UK's SS2/21 all converge on the same concern: *concentration risk.* Regulators are explicitly focused on systemic third-party dependency—the risk that an outage at a single cloud provider, network backbone, or control plane can simultaneously disrupt a large portion of the financial system or other critical services.

In architectural terms, this concern translates into concrete control objectives rather than abstract compliance: **provider diversity** to avoid single-vendor failure domains, **credible exit and substitution strategies** that can be executed under stress, and **testable failover mechanisms** that prove workloads can shift between providers within defined recovery objectives. Multi-cloud traffic management exists precisely at this intersection. It is the mechanism that turns regulatory expectations—diversity, substitutability, and operational proof—into observable, repeatable network behavior.

We will not explore every possible topology—doing so would require a book of its own (perhaps a future one)—but it is essential to touch on this domain for completeness. In the pages that follow, we will examine how to design and operate resilient inter-cloud connectivity using private interconnects, intent-based routing, and unified observability, ensuring that resilience extends not only *within* each cloud but also *between* them. Throughout this section, we will focus primarily on AWS and Azure, reflecting the environments I have worked with most extensively and the scope of my professional experience.

Private Interconnect and Exchange Fabric Solutions

The foundation of a resilient multi-cloud fabric is **private, backbone-based connectivity**. One classic pattern is a **colocation hub router**: deploy a physical router (or NVA) in a neutral exchange and uplink it to **AWS Direct Connect** and **Azure ExpressRoute**. You form **separate BGP peerings** to each cloud edge, and the router exchanges your enterprise prefixes between them. This is simple and fully under your control, but it introduces a **hairpin**—traffic detours through your device—adding an extra hop and avoidable latency compared with keeping flows on the exchange fabric.

In Figure 7-10, a physical router (or NVA) in a neutral colocation exchange establishes BGP sessions with both AWS Direct Connect and Azure ExpressRoute.

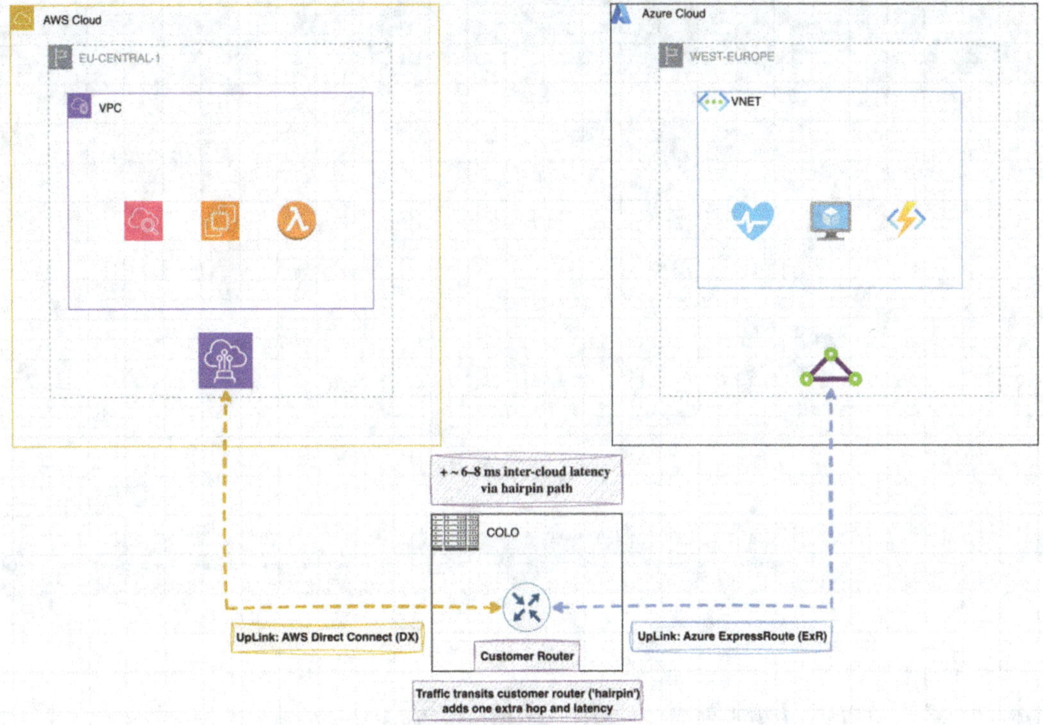

Figure 7-10. *Multi-cloud Transit Architecture with Colocation Hub*

Traffic between clouds transits the customer-managed router, introducing a "hairpin" path that adds an extra hop and latency compared with fabric-based interconnects.

To eliminate that detour, many teams use **fabric-resident virtual routers**. **Equinix Fabric Cloud Router (FCR)** and **Megaport Cloud Router (MCR)** terminate **BGP** to both clouds **on the exchange fabric itself**. Your AWS and Azure virtual circuits land on the fabric, the virtual router swaps routes, and traffic remains on private connectivity segments within each provider's backbone until it reaches the shared metro or exchange point. The result is **lower, more consistent latency** and **no on-prem backhaul**, plus **on-demand bandwidth** and rapid turn-up in new metros. (Provisioning and feature sets are documented by Equinix and Megaport; they describe FCR as an **Equinix-managed virtual router on Equinix Fabric**, not an AWS Marketplace appliance.)

In Figure 7-11, a virtual router running on the exchange fabric (e.g., Equinix Fabric Cloud Router or Megaport Cloud Router) terminates BGP sessions directly to AWS Direct Connect and Azure ExpressRoute.

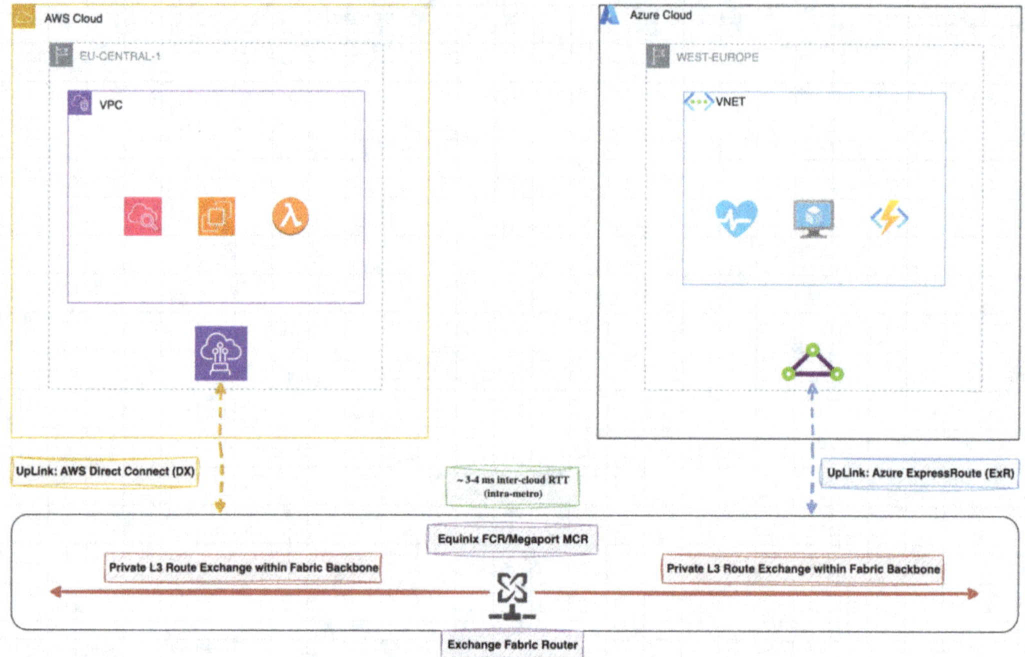

Figure 7-11. *Multi-cloud Transit via Virtual Router*

Routes are exchanged within the colocation backbone, minimizing latency and eliminating on-premises backhaul.

A third option is a **carrier-managed L3 interconnect**. Here, a telco/MSP stitches your DX and ExR into their **MPLS/IP backbone** and handles the BGP exchange on their PEs. You trade capex and operational overhead for a managed SLA and global reach—useful if you want turnkey operations or need to span regions where you don't have colo presence.

In Figure 7-12, a telecommunications or managed service provider integrates AWS Direct Connect and Azure ExpressRoute into its MPLS/IP backbone. Provider edge routers exchange routes between clouds using BGP/MPLS L3VPNs, offering SLA-backed global reach and operational simplicity at the cost of reduced customer control and flexibility.

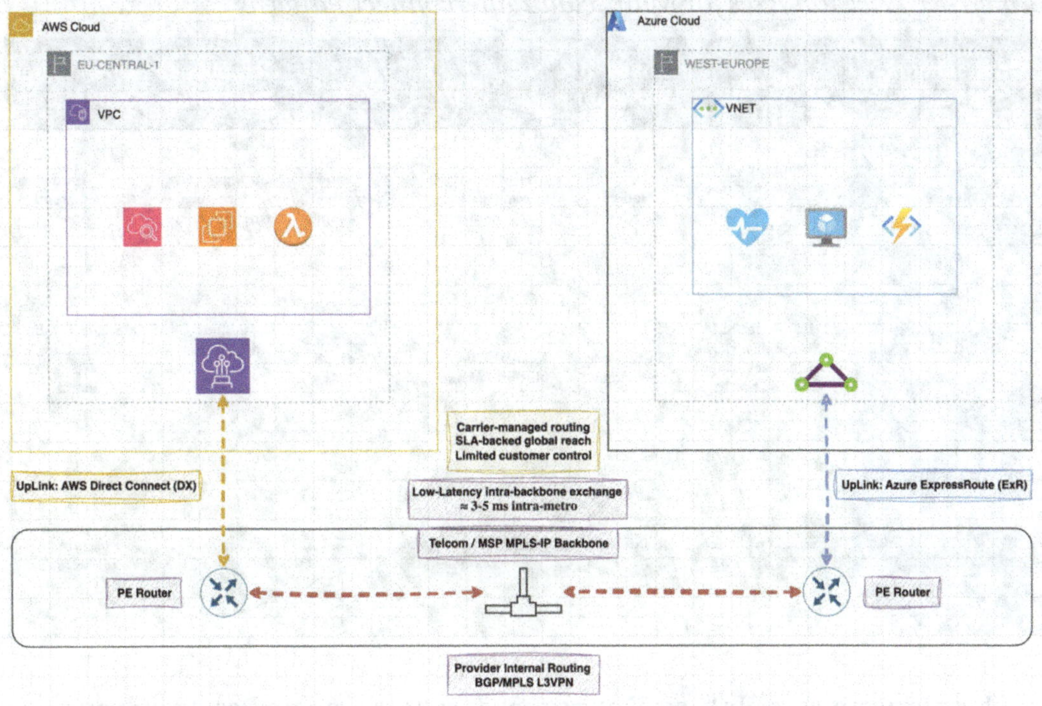

Figure 7-12. *Carrier-Managed Multi-cloud Interconnect*

Before we dive into the mechanics, it helps to choose the right interconnect pattern based on a few practical decision axes—latency, speed to provision, control, SLA expectations, compliance boundaries, and operational burden.

Table 7-4 shows a comparison of customer-managed colocation routers, exchange-fabric virtual routers (e.g., Equinix Fabric Cloud Router, Megaport Cloud Router), and carrier-managed Layer-3 interconnects across key architectural decision dimensions: latency, speed to provision, operational control, SLA ownership, compliance boundaries, and operational burden.

Table 7-4. *Decision Axes for Multi-cloud Interconnect Patterns*

Interconnect pattern	Latency	Speed of Provision	Control	SLAs	Compliance Boundaries	Operational Burden
Colocation Hub Router (Fig. 7.10)	Medium — additional hop due to customer router hairpin	Medium	High — full BGP, filtering, and security control	Cloud provider SLAs only	Strong — clear customer-owned trust boundary	High — hardware, lifecycle, routing ops
Fabric Virtual Router (Equinix FCR / Megaport MCR) (Fig. 7.11)	High — traffic remains on provider backbones to shared metro	High — rapid, on-demand provisioning	Medium — BGP intent, limited platform abstraction	Fabric SLA + cloud SLAs	Medium — depends on fabric POP placement	Medium — fabric operations, reduced device mgmt
Carrier-Managed L3 Interconnect (Fig. 7.12)	Medium–High — depends on carrier backbone design	Medium–High	Low–Medium — routing abstracted by provider	End-to-end carrier SLA	Medium — bounded by carrier footprint	Low — outsourced operations

There is no universally "best" interconnect pattern—only a best fit for your failure model.

The right choice is the simplest design that meets your latency and availability targets, satisfies regulatory expectations for provider diversity, and that your teams can operate, test, and recover under stress. If you cannot confidently simulate its failure modes and explain its recovery behavior, it is not resilient—no matter how elegant it looks on a diagram. To make those failure models explicit, we now examine what fails together in each interconnect pattern—and how to prevent correlated failure across clouds.

Failure domains by interconnect pattern

Colocation hub router (Figure 7-10)

In a colocation hub design, the primary failure domain is the metro and the customer-managed router itself. Power loss, fiber cuts, maintenance events, or misconfiguration at the colocation site can simultaneously impact connectivity to both AWS Direct Connect and Azure ExpressRoute. Because traffic hairpins through a single device, the router becomes both a data-plane and control-plane choke point. This mirrors AWS Direct Connect resiliency guidance: multiple connections only improve availability when they terminate on independent devices in independent locations. A single router in one metro, even with multiple circuits, remains a shared failure domain.

To reduce correlated failure, this pattern must be deployed at least twice: across two independent metros, with separate colocation providers where possible, distinct routers, and diverse carrier cross-connects into each cloud. BGP policies should treat each hub as an independent failure domain rather than equal-cost peers, ensuring that loss of one site does not trigger instability or oscillation.

Exchange-fabric virtual router (Figure 7-11)

Fabric-resident virtual routers remove on-premises hairpinning but shift the primary failure domain to the exchange fabric itself—specifically the metro POP and the fabric's routing and orchestration control plane.

While traffic stays on private backbones, a single fabric instance still represents a shared data-plane and control-plane dependency across all connected clouds.

Mitigation requires explicit separation of failure domains. Deploy independent fabric virtual routers in at least two distinct metros, avoid single-instance designs, and ensure that each fabric router terminates into separate Direct Connect and ExpressRoute locations. Each fabric instance should be treated as an independent routing domain with its own BGP sessions and health signals, rather than relying on implicit platform redundancy.

Carrier-managed Layer-3 interconnect (Figure 7-12)

Carrier-managed interconnects shift much of the operational burden to the provider, but they consolidate failure domains into the carrier's backbone and routing control plane. A single provider core can span multiple metros, regions, and cloud on-ramps, creating a broad correlated failure surface.

To limit correlated failure, enterprises should use at least two independent carriers for inter-cloud connectivity, avoid relying on a single provider's global backbone where systemic risk is unacceptable, and ensure that carrier diversity aligns with cloud-side diversity—separate Direct Connect and ExpressRoute locations, not just separate logical circuits. SLAs should explicitly cover inter-cloud routing behavior and convergence expectations, not only link availability.

Key principle: diversity must be explicit

Across all three patterns, resilience does not come from "having redundancy," but from ensuring that redundant components do not fail together. Two links in one metro, two circuits on one fabric instance, or two clouds reached through one carrier core do not constitute independent failure domains. Multi-cloud resilience emerges only when metros, fabrics, carriers, and control planes are deliberately separated and tested as such.

Whichever design you choose, keep the control-plane truth straight: there is no native AWS↔Azure peering. In every case, you are exchanging your prefixes through a neutral intermediary—whether a customer-managed router, a fabric-resident virtual router, or a carrier's backbone. Be explicit about resiliency boundaries: deploy redundant routers or fabric instances across at least two metros, use diverse Direct Connect and ExpressRoute circuits, and align the underlay with AWS Direct Connect High or Maximum Resiliency patterns rather than relying on logical routing alone.

Cost realism in multi-cloud interconnects

Multi-cloud resilience introduces cost vectors that do not exist in single-cloud or single-region designs. These costs are rarely obvious at design time and often surface only once traffic patterns change under failover. The most common cost drivers include:

- **Direct Connect and ExpressRoute port charges**

  Both AWS Direct Connect and Azure ExpressRoute incur fixed port costs per circuit and per location, independent of utilization. High-availability designs (multiple circuits, multiple metros) multiply these charges by design.

- **Exchange fabric or carrier bandwidth fees**

  Services such as Equinix Fabric Cloud Router, Megaport Cloud Router, or carrier-managed L3 services charge for provisioned bandwidth and, in some cases, for interconnection between virtual circuits. These costs scale with peak throughput, not average usage, and therefore grow quickly in failover scenarios.

- **Cloud egress charges across providers**

  Traffic leaving AWS toward Azure (or vice versa) is subject to standard cloud egress pricing. During failover, traffic volumes can spike precisely when alternative paths are active, making egress one of the most significant—and least anticipated—cost components in multi-cloud designs.

- **Cross-region backhaul and inspection hairpins**

  Poorly aligned entry points can force traffic to traverse inter-region backbones or centralized NAT, firewalls, or inspection appliances before reaching the destination cloud. These hairpins add both latency and cost, often doubling egress and fabric charges without improving resilience.

The practical implication is simple but frequently overlooked: **multi-cloud cost is traffic-shaped, not topology-shaped**. Architects should measure inter-cloud flows early—using flow logs, synthetic probes, and billing analytics—and re-measure them during failure simulations. Unexpected traffic paths are the most common source of surprise bills in multi-cloud environments, and they often reveal architectural issues long before they appear as outages.

Cost and failure, however, are still consequences of design choices. To operate multi-cloud traffic reliably under stress, it is equally important to understand which control layer is responsible for each decision during normal operation and during failure. Before moving into traffic engineering mechanics, it is essential to clarify which layer is responsible for which decision—so resilience is not over-attributed to any single mechanism.

Underlay vs. overlay: Who decides what

Multi-cloud resilience emerges from the coordination of multiple layers, each with a clearly defined role. Confusing these roles is a common source of brittle designs.

- **BGP (underlay) decides the network path**

  BGP controls how packets traverse private connectivity—Direct Connect, ExpressRoute, exchange fabrics, or carrier backbones. It governs path selection, convergence speed, and reaction to link or device failure. BGP does *not* decide which cloud a user enters; it decides how traffic flows once that choice has been made.

- **DNS and edge services decide the entry point**

  DNS systems such as Route 53 and Azure Traffic Manager determine which provider, region, or front door clients reach. This is where provider-level failover, geo-steering, and latency-based entry decisions occur. DNS operates at a slower timescale than BGP and is bounded by caching and TTLs.

- **SD-WAN or application-aware overlays decide service steering**

  Where present, SD-WAN or service-mesh overlays steer traffic based on application identity, policy, or performance signals. These overlays complement—rather than replace—BGP and DNS by expressing higher-level intent.

Resilient multi-cloud design requires all three layers to remain aligned. Expecting BGP to move users between clouds, or DNS alone to compensate for underlay failures, leads to unpredictable behavior under stress.

With failure domains explicit and the trade-offs between colocation hub routers, exchange-fabric virtual routers, and carrier-managed interconnects understood, we can now move from architectural choice to execution—examining how BGP attributes, backbone entry points, and controlled failover are applied in practice to steer traffic across cloud provider networks.

Traffic Engineering Across Cloud Backbones

Once connectivity is in place, the next task is to steer traffic intelligently across each provider's private backbone. Both AWS and Microsoft operate large global networks; your goal is to inject traffic into the "shortest/cleanest" backbone and keep it there until it reaches the destination metro. You do this with BGP attributes on the underlay and, when appropriate, DNS/edge steering on the overlay.

AWS (Direct Connect). AWS publishes BGP communities that map to inbound *local preference* on the AWS side (e.g., low/medium/high). On private VIFs, communities such as **7224:7100/7224:7200/7224:7300** influence which DX path AWS prefers for return traffic. Tag the primary circuit's prefixes with the **high** community and the secondary with **low** so AWS deterministically selects the primary under normal conditions. If a connection fails, AWS can ECMP across remaining equal-cost paths; communities let you bias that behavior toward active/passive if desired.

Microsoft Azure (ExR). Azure supports *BGP communities* on ExpressRoute private peering and lets you configure **custom BGP communities** on VNets. Those tags propagate toward on-prem over ExR and can be matched by your route maps/policies, which avoids brittle, ever-growing prefix lists. In practice, architects align tagging schemes across clouds (e.g., "prod-east", "sandbox-eu") so on-prem or exchange routers can apply consistent policies regardless of origin cloud. See Microsoft's guidance on configuring custom BGP communities for ExR.

DNS and edge entry. As we have learned so far, BGP shapes how packets traverse backbones; DNS (Route 53, Azure Traffic Manager, etc.) decides *which cloud endpoint* clients hit. Many teams combine the two: DNS shifts traffic between AWS and Azure front doors based on health/latency, while BGP attributes preserve deterministic underlay paths. Plan name resolution early—cross-cloud resolution typically requires forwarders or resolvers at the boundary (e.g., **Azure DNS Private Resolver** with outbound endpoints and rulesets for conditional forwarding), and the operational model differs from single-cloud designs.

Practical pattern:

- Primary DX circuit: tag exports with **7224:7300** (high) on AWS; on the enterprise router, set **local-pref** higher toward that DX for egress symmetry.

- Standby DX circuit (or second metro): tag with **7224:7100** (low) and optionally **AS-path prepend x2/x3** to de-prefer ingress.

- On Azure, assign **custom BGP communities** to the VNets attached to the preferred ExR circuit and write on-prem policy to prefer those tags; keep a lower-preference tag for the standby ExR.

- Use health-checked DNS to toggle front doors only when necessary; let BGP handle sub-second path changes.

Notes and caveats:

- AWS's documented BGP community scheme (including high/medium/low local-pref influence and *scope* communities) is the authoritative reference for DX behavior.

- AWS confirms that redundant DX connections can **ECMP** when equal cost; communities/attributes are how you bias away from symmetric load-sharing if you want active/passive.

- Azure ExR supports **custom BGP communities** for private peering policies; use them to simplify route filtering and intent expression on your edge.

- Cross-cloud DNS usually needs explicit forwarders/resolvers (e.g., **Azure DNS Private Resolver** with outbound rulesets) rather than "just working," so expect additional configuration and a small operational overhead.

Control-Plane Federation and Policy Challenges

One of the most persistent challenges in multi-cloud networking is the absence of a unified control plane. Each cloud operates within its own routing and policy universe—AWS with its **VPC route tables**, **Transit Gateway attachments**, and **Security Groups**, and Azure with its **User-Defined Routes (UDRs)**, **Virtual WAN hubs**, and **Network Security Groups (NSGs)**. These systems do not share a native protocol or API that synchronizes routing intent end-to-end. As a result, there is no single console that can simultaneously configure route propagation, firewall rules, and BGP advertisements across both AWS and Azure. Policy consistency must therefore be designed, not assumed.

In practice, architects approach this in one of two ways. Some choose to federate control through an **overlay controller**—for example, platforms such as **Aviatrix**, **Cisco SD-WAN**, or **VMware NSX+**—which provide a central policy engine and then translate those abstracted intents into the specific constructs of each provider. This creates what many architects call *centralized design with distributed enforcement*: a single blueprint for prefixes, ASNs, and connectivity, pushed outward into each cloud's native objects. The outcome is operational symmetry—route filters, segmentation policies, and security postures behave the same way whether applied to AWS Transit Gateway attachments or Azure Virtual WAN spokes.

Without such abstraction, configuration drift becomes inevitable. AWS and Azure differ fundamentally in how they propagate reachability. AWS **Transit Gateway** can automatically propagate routes from VPC attachments, but propagation must be manually associated with route tables, while Azure's **Virtual WAN** automatically distributes routes between hubs and spokes when enabled—but applies NSGs independently. Security enforcement models diverge as well: AWS Security Groups are stateful and applied per-ENI, while Azure NSGs are stateless at the subnet or NIC level. Translating between those paradigms is not a one-to-one operation and often requires custom tooling, templates, or human review.

For organizations pursuing a "DIY" approach, disciplined automation is the only sustainable countermeasure. Infrastructure as Code (IaC) frameworks such as **Terraform**, **Pulumi**, or **AWS CloudFormation** (combined with Azure Bicep) become the lingua franca for defining routing and policy intent declaratively. Coupled with CI/CD pipelines and automated validation, they turn configuration from a manual art into a repeatable, testable process. Some teams even integrate **policy-as-code** tools—like **Open Policy Agent (OPA)** or **HashiCorp Sentinel**—to enforce governance across clouds before deployment.

Ultimately, federation in multi-cloud networking is not about collapsing everything into one pane of glass; it's about creating a coherent *operating model* that spans heterogeneous control planes. Whether through an overlay controller or strict automation discipline, the goal remains the same: a **single source of truth and multiple planes of enforcement.** That principle ensures that routing intent, segmentation, and security posture remain consistent even as each cloud evolves independently.

Failover Routing and Resilience Patterns

The purpose of multi-cloud networking is not simply to connect clouds—it is to ensure *continuity of service when one of them fails.* A resilient architecture anticipates those failures and routes around them before users even notice. In multi-cloud networks, this continuity is achieved through a layered choreography between **BGP**, **DNS**, and **automation**, all tuned to express the same intent: if one provider goes dark, the other continues serving traffic.

At the foundation lies the **control plane** built on **BGP**. Both AWS Direct Connect and Azure ExpressRoute use dynamic routing to advertise enterprise prefixes to the cloud, and each can be configured to detect link failure and withdraw routes automatically. You can advertise the same set of prefixes—say 10.0.0.0/8—through both AWS and Azure and express your preference using BGP attributes. In AWS, this is typically done through **BGP community tags** such as 7224:7300 (high preference), 7224:7200 (medium), and 7224:7100 (low). By tagging your AWS routes with 7224:7300 and optionally prepending your AS path in Azure, you make AWS the preferred path. When the Direct Connect BGP session fails—whether due to link, device, or site loss—AWS automatically withdraws those routes, and traffic naturally converges toward Azure's ExpressRoute path.

Azure provides a similar level of control, though through slightly different mechanisms. ExpressRoute private peering supports **BGP communities** that identify the Azure region associated with each route (e.g., 12076:51010 for West Europe). You can use these tags to apply routing policies on-premises, filtering or prioritizing routes by region. When ExpressRoute drops, Azure withdraws those prefixes, and traffic reverts to AWS. Using both together creates a deterministic, self-correcting control plane where each cloud can assume the other's traffic in seconds.

Yet the control plane only covers transport. Real resilience extends higher—into DNS and application entry points—where most user traffic begins. Here, we combine **AWS Route 53** and **Azure Traffic Manager** to achieve dual-cloud, application-level failover.

Coordinating Route 53 and Traffic Manager

In a typical configuration, Route 53 acts as the **authoritative global zone** for your public domain, while Azure Traffic Manager manages DNS routing for your Azure endpoints underneath it. This approach leverages Route 53's global health checks and Azure's native load-balancing intelligence simultaneously. Let's see an example, step by step:

1. **Create a parent zone in Route 53.**

    Suppose your application is hosted in both AWS and Azure under the domain app.example.com. In Route 53, define two records:

    -   aws.app.example.com → pointing to an AWS Global Accelerator or ALB endpoint.

    -   azure.app.example.com → pointing to an Azure Traffic Manager profile.

    Route 53 health checks continuously probe both endpoints from multiple AWS Regions. You configure Route 53 with a **failover routing policy**—the AWS endpoint as **primary**, the Azure endpoint as **secondary**.

2. **Delegate fine-grained control to Traffic Manager.**

    The azure.app.example.com record maps to a **Traffic Manager profile** inside Azure that contains multiple Azure endpoints (for instance, one in westeurope and another in northeurope). Traffic Manager uses its own probes to balance traffic between those Azure regions based on performance or geographic proximity.

    If the AWS layer fails (e.g., an outage in the AWS Region or Global Accelerator endpoint), Route 53 marks the primary record as unhealthy and shifts traffic to the Azure Traffic Manager FQDN. Once traffic reaches Azure, Traffic Manager continues to perform region-level health checks and load-balancing within Azure, ensuring users are directed to the healthiest endpoint there.

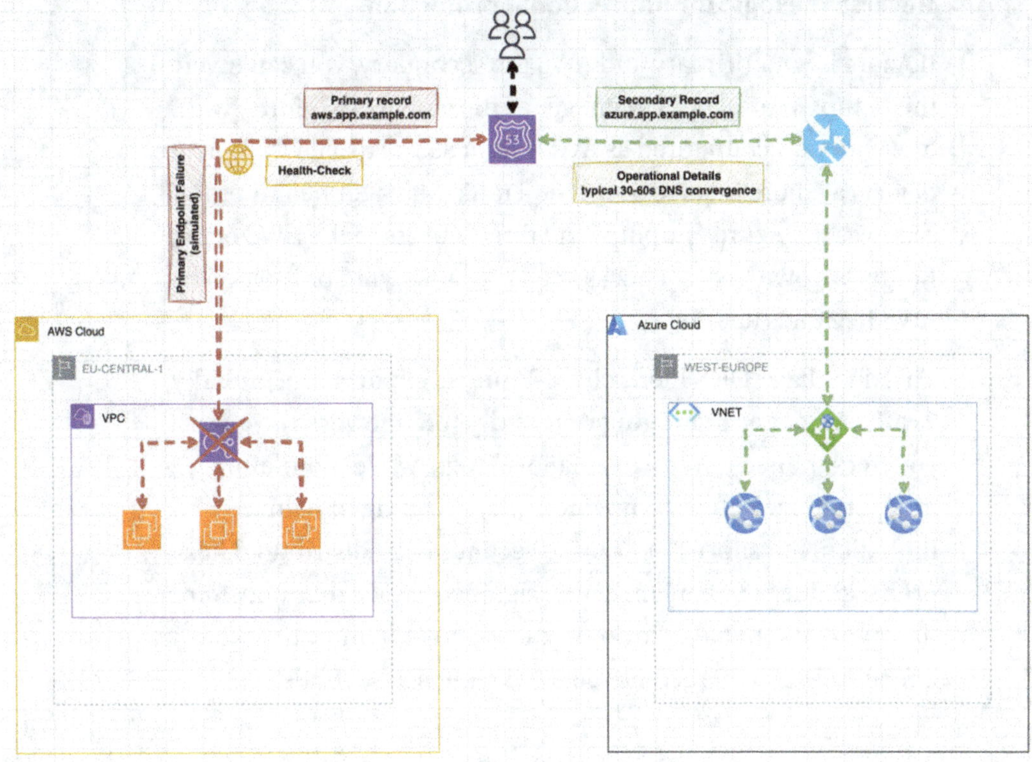

Figure 7-13. *Coordinated Failover Between Route 53 and Azure Traffic Manager*

Figure 7-13 illustrates a dual-layer DNS failover architecture between AWS and Azure. Route 53 serves as the global authoritative DNS zone, performing continuous health checks against the AWS Application Load Balancer. When the AWS endpoint becomes unavailable, Route 53 redirects user queries to the secondary record—an Azure Traffic Manager profile. The traffic manager then distributes requests across healthy regional Application Gateways, such as those in West Europe and North Europe, each performing its own backend health probes. When AWS recovers, Route 53 restores the primary DNS mapping automatically. This combination of global DNS supervision and regional performance-based routing ensures seamless continuity across providers, reducing user-visible downtime to well under a minute during failover events.

3. **Reverse the logic for bidirectional protection.**

If Azure is your primary and AWS the secondary, you can invert this setup: Azure Traffic Manager as the global DNS entry, with one endpoint configured as AWS's Route 53-alias FQDN. If Azure detects a failure in its regions, the Traffic Manager health probe removes the Azure endpoint and directs users to the AWS entry. Route 53's own health checks keep that alias valid only when the AWS Region is healthy.

This dual-layer DNS hierarchy—**Route 53 supervising globally, Traffic Manager managing regionally (or vice versa)**—gives you fine-grained control over failover logic while maintaining independence between providers. DNS caching remains a limitation, but short TTLs (30–60 seconds) and distributed health probes reduce convergence time significantly. In many customer deployments, global failover occurs in under a minute, while network-level BGP reconvergence happens in seconds.

Automating and Testing Multi-Cloud Failover

As we've repeated throughout this book: *untested resilience is not resilience at all.* Multi-cloud routing must be exercised regularly. Simulate a Direct Connect outage, watch your Azure route tables fill the gap, and confirm that DNS answers change accordingly. Then restore AWS and verify that normal operation resumes.

Automation tools can further integrate this logic. For example, you can use AWS **Lambda** functions or Azure **Automation Runbooks** triggered by BGP session events or CloudWatch alarms to perform DNS record updates or bias adjustments dynamically. Modern orchestration frameworks (such as Terraform Cloud or AWS Systems Manager Automation) can synchronize Route 53 and Traffic Manager policies programmatically, ensuring that DNS records reflect real network state.

At the same time, you must preserve **plane independence**. Failover logic must not depend solely on centralized management systems or APIs, as those may be unavailable during a cloud outage. Keep health checks and routing decisions close to the data plane—routers detecting link loss with **BFD**, DNS resolvers probing endpoints independently, and local automation running from unaffected regions.

Lessons from the Edge

As **Fastly** engineers emphasize in their own "resilience by design" approach, a network should be able to route around unhealthy regions automatically. The same applies to multi-cloud. When BGP, DNS, and automation collaborate, traffic simply finds the next best route without drama.

The truly resilient pattern is multi-layered:

- **BGP** provides fast, deterministic path failover between clouds.

- **DNS** ensures global client resolution to healthy providers.

- **Automation and observability** close the loop, confirming that decisions reflect reality.

And when we combine **Route 53's global intelligence** with **Traffic Manager's regional awareness**, we bridge the gap between clouds, creating what is effectively one federated control system across two distinct providers. This is resilience made visible only through its absence of disruption—the ultimate test of engineering success.

MTU, Route Propagation, and Asymmetric Flows

When building multi-cloud networks, the devil hides in the details—and the smallest of them can silently erode the resilience you so carefully designed. Three areas in particular deserve meticulous attention: **MTU alignment**, **route propagation**, and **path symmetry**. These are not glamorous topics, but they are the difference between a multi-cloud that "just works" and one that fails in subtle, expensive ways.

The first is **MTU (Maximum Transmission Unit).**

AWS Direct Connect supports **Jumbo Frames** up to **8500 bytes** on private and transit virtual interfaces, and even **9001 bytes** within VPCs when the path supports it. Azure ExpressRoute, by contrast, enforces a **standard Ethernet MTU of 1500 bytes** across its private peering domains. When packets larger than that traverse an AWS↔Azure interconnect without proper fragmentation or clamping, they are dropped silently at the border. The result is maddening: pings succeed, small packets flow, but application traffic stalls or resets under load.

The remedy is simple but essential: configure all cross-connect interfaces—whether physical ports in a colocation router or virtual NICs on a cloud-exchange fabric—to the **lowest common MTU**, typically 1500 bytes.

Alternatively, enable **TCP MSS clamping** at the edge routers or VNFs, so that TCP sessions negotiate a segment size that fits the smaller path. The rule of thumb: in a heterogeneous multi-cloud, smaller MTU means fewer surprises. Performance differences from dropping jumbo frames are negligible compared to the cost of fragmentation and retransmission during failover.

Next comes **route propagation**, which governs what each cloud "knows" about the other. AWS's Transit Gateway, by default, automatically propagates routes from attached networks (VPCs, VPNs, Direct Connect gateways) into its route tables, unless propagation is explicitly disabled. Azure's model is different. Each Virtual Network (VNet) relies on **User-Defined Routes (UDRs)** to control propagation; administrators can choose to **suppress ExpressRoute propagation** for specific subnets. This flexibility is powerful, but dangerous: a missing propagation flag in Azure can prevent your workloads from ever learning the backup path that AWS is advertising.

For resilience, document which prefixes are **learned**, **advertised**, and **filtered** on each hop—especially when connecting through exchange routers or cloud fabrics like Megaport Cloud Router. During testing, always verify that the intended routes appear in both BGP tables and that failover prefixes propagate correctly between clouds. Nothing undermines "automatic failover" faster than a prefix that never propagated where it should have.

Finally, and perhaps most deceptively, comes **asymmetric routing**. This occurs when traffic takes one path into the cloud and another path back out—a pattern that stateless routers handle fine but that **stateful firewalls, NATs, or inspection gateways** cannot. Microsoft's own documentation explicitly cautions:

> *"If traffic sent from your network to Microsoft uses ExpressRoute but the return traffic uses the internet path, a firewall that didn't see the original flow will drop those packets."*

In a multi-cloud topology, asymmetry can easily emerge. Imagine outbound traffic to an Azure service leaves your data center via ExpressRoute, but replies return through AWS Direct Connect or a VPN tunnel. To the firewall on either end, that return traffic appears unsolicited and is promptly dropped.

The fix is conceptual as much as technical: *keep paths symmetric*. For every destination prefix, ensure that ingress and egress use the same cloud link. This can be achieved in several ways.

- **Advertise consistent NAT pools** or public IP ranges on both clouds, ensuring that responses find the same return gateway.

- **Partition traffic by domain or service**—route all Microsoft-bound traffic (e.g., Office 365, Azure APIs) via ExpressRoute, and all AWS-specific or internet-bound traffic via Direct Connect.

- **Use deterministic routing policies** on your on-premises routers (e.g., route-maps that match destination ASNs or prefixes and prefer specific next-hops).

During testing, use **traceroute, flow logs, and firewall connection tables** to confirm that flows remain symmetric under failover conditions. When in doubt, prioritize predictability over efficiency: a slightly longer but symmetric path is always preferable to an unpredictable asymmetric one.

These mechanics may sound like plumbing—and they are—but they are the plumbing of resilience. Align MTUs, audit propagation, enforce symmetry. Together they ensure that when your multi-cloud architecture is tested under stress, the packets still find their way home.

Operational Best Practices: Observability and Testing

Even the most mathematically perfect architecture is only as resilient as the team's ability to *see* it and *trust* it under stress. Resilience is not static; it is the continuous feedback loop between design, observation, and adaptation. The network you draw on a whiteboard will not be the network you operate six months later—traffic patterns shift, providers change underlay routes, and configurations drift. That is why observability and testing are not the last steps of a project, but the heartbeat that keeps the system alive.

In a multi-cloud environment, visibility begins with the **control plane**. Each provider exposes its own telemetry: AWS CloudWatch for Direct Connect metrics (BGP session state, link utilization, error counters) and Azure Monitor for ExpressRoute circuit health and route propagation. Both can alert on session flaps, excessive route changes, or throughput degradation. Aggregating these metrics in a single observability platform—whether Datadog, Grafana, or native CloudWatch dashboards—creates your first layer of assurance.

But control-plane visibility is not enough. The **data plane** tells the true story: packet loss, latency, jitter, and throughput across your hybrid and multi-cloud paths. Tools such as **ThousandEyes**, **AWS CloudWatch Synthetics**, and **Azure Network Watcher** can simulate transactions between AWS and Azure endpoints, running continuous ICMP, HTTP, or TCP checks to measure real user experience. Configure synthetic tests between representative nodes in each cloud (e.g., from an EC2 instance in eu-west-1 to a VM in westeurope). These tests reveal whether the paths you intended to use are actually in service, and whether failover behaves as expected when a path degrades. In practice, a small battery of synthetic probes can prevent hours of blind troubleshooting later.

A second layer of observability lies in **network flow data**. Enable **VPC Flow Logs** in AWS and **NSG Flow Logs** in Azure to capture packet-level telemetry for key subnets. Combined with route table inspection (Transit Gateway or Virtual WAN hub routes), this allows you to confirm symmetric flows and detect anomalies such as asymmetric routing or unexpected hairpins. These flows also feed performance baselines—normal latency between AWS Frankfurt and Azure North Europe might be 12 ms; if it jumps to 30 ms, you know something in the underlay has shifted. Observability is not just about alarms; it is about building intuition for what "healthy" looks like.

Once the metrics exist, resilience depends on **how quickly you can interpret and act on them**. Fastly's internal engineering philosophy—*resilience by design and feedback by default*—underscores this point. Their Autopilot and PrecisionPath systems continuously re-balance traffic based on live telemetry, detecting congestion and re-routing before users are impacted. While we may not operate at Fastly's scale, the principle is the same: pair observability with automation. Cloud-native primitives like AWS Lambda or Azure Automation Runbooks can trigger predefined remediations—for example, recomputing health checks or adjusting routing bias in Route 53 or Traffic Manager when BGP sessions flap. Over time, this evolves into self-healing: the system repairs itself faster than an operator could respond.

Yet no amount of automation replaces the need for **testing**. Networks must fail regularly—safely, deliberately, and under observation. Both AWS and Azure support controlled testing through APIs: Direct Connect's **Resiliency Toolkit** can simulate port outages, and Azure ExpressRoute supports circuit disablement for validation. Schedule drills that mimic real disasters: bring down one Direct Connect link, disable a peering session, or fail a DNS health check, and observe whether traffic shifts exactly as designed. Measure convergence times—did BGP switch over in seconds, or did DNS TTLs delay resolution by minutes? Capture those outcomes and feed them back into your configuration baselines.

This is the mindset of **chaos engineering** applied to networking. Fail often, fail safely, learn continuously. Over time, you will develop operational reflexes that diagrams can never teach—how to recognize flapping sessions from the rhythm of alarms, how to distinguish a BFD-triggered event from an upstream carrier issue, how to tell when a path has silently degraded even though all sessions remain "up."

To close, resilience is not the sum of redundant links or perfect failover logic; it is the confidence that the system behaves predictably under pressure. Observability gives you that confidence; testing preserves it. A multi-cloud network without these disciplines is a single event away from chaos. One with them is alive, aware, and capable of self-correction.

It's also worth grounding our enthusiasm in pragmatism. Multi-cloud resilience is powerful, but it isn't free. It multiplies complexity, governance, and cost, and therefore should be pursued only where the **business criticality justifies it**—the same reasoning we applied to multi-Region design earlier in this book. Not every workload requires multiple clouds; only those whose interruption would materially impact the organization vital functions, for example, healthcare, finance, and/or breach regulatory obligations. For others, a well-architected single-cloud, multi-AZ design may be the more resilient choice, because simplicity is its own form of reliability.

Lessons Learned from Chapter 7

Chapter 7 transformed resilience from a static topology into a distributed, living network—one that senses, reacts, and self-balances. In earlier chapters we focused on containing faults within zones and Regions; here, we gave the network a nervous system and taught it to respond to stress. By the end of this chapter, resilience is no longer about recovering after failure—it is about routing around it before users even notice.

The journey through this chapter carried six recurring lessons.

> **Routing Manipulation Is Foundational to Resilience:** Traffic engineering across Private and Public VIFs ultimately comes down to understanding where control resides and how AWS interprets your intent. On the private side, Local Preference governs outbound flows, while AS-Path prepending and community-based preference shape inbound routing. On the public side, the tools are the same but the scope differs: scoping communities (9100/9200/9300) determine **which** Regions may

use a circuit, and longest-prefix-match determines **how** they use it. Across both models, BGP attributes are not abstractions—they are levers of resilience. Prefix granularity, consistent advertisements, and predictable failover behavior ensure that capacity is honored, fallback paths remain available, and no single link becomes an accidental global choke point. These patterns are therefore not optimizations but safeguards, turning connectivity into a controlled, intentional, and failure-tolerant system.

Hybrid Reality Has Become Multi-Cloud Reality: Hybrid was once a bridge; now it is the baseline. Enterprises no longer connect "data center to cloud"—they connect cloud to cloud as naturally as they once linked racks across a campus. Traffic shifts between AWS and Azure, or AWS and GCP, as part of normal operations. Connectivity fabrics like Equinix, Megaport, and cloud-adjacent SD-WAN have become the substrate for digital continuity. We learned that hybrid networking is only the midpoint of maturity—multi-cloud traffic engineering is the next step, where resilience depends not only on redundancy within one provider but on how seamlessly one cloud hands traffic to another.

Path Diversity Is Policy, Not Luck: Whether connecting a data center to AWS or AWS to another cloud, every path is the result of intent. Direct Connect, VPN, ExpressRoute, and SD-WAN are not isolated circuits—they are knobs within a single control system. BGP is the language of that system: Local Preference chooses the winning egress; AS-Path prepending and BGP communities determine inbound preference; MED and prefix specificity resolve tie-breaks. Resilience emerges not from having "many links" but from deterministic behavior—networks that know exactly how to respond when one of those links disappears.

Physical Diversity Still Anchors Logical Policy: AWS's High and Maximum Resilience models reminded us that logical routing only matters if the fiber underneath survives. Two links in one site protect against local failure; dual sites with dual links protect against complex ones. The principle holds across clouds as well: two providers, each with multiple circuits, connected through independent fabrics or exchanges. VPN overlays, redundant cloud-exchange circuits, and independent DX locations form the scaffolding; BFD, BGP timers, and consistent routing policy turn that scaffolding into motion, collapsing failover to sub-second reaction.

Measurement Turns Topology into Truth: Every resilient system must prove its own claims. We learned to measure latency, jitter, loss, and convergence time not as vanity metrics but as indicators of structural health. Pre-emptive tuning—IP SLA, BFD, event-driven automation—lets the network shift traffic before users feel the degradation. Percentiles like p95 and p99 quantify user experience more accurately than averages. In multi-cloud and hybrid designs, measurement also means watching the seams— the exchanges where AWS meets other clouds, where MTUs diverge, or where asymmetric paths may silently drop traffic.

Continuous Verification Is the Final Layer: No routing policy is resilient until it has failed safely at least once. Resilience testing—simulated link loss, BGP withdrawals, DX and cloud-exchange maintenance events—is the final validation of intent. The principle repeats: untested resilience is wishful thinking. Chaos experiments must include cross-provider and cross-path scenarios—Direct Connect outages, VPN failover, health-check failures, even edge-location impairments—each one an opportunity to prove that policy, automation, and routing intent hold under stress.

Looking Ahead—From Federation to Operation and Disaster Recovery

As we step toward **Chapter 8**, we now shift from design to discipline—from architectures that can fail gracefully to operations that prove it. The observability, telemetry, and testing practices introduced here become the raw material for automation. What we built in Chapter 7 is the nervous system of a resilient cloud network; in Chapter 8, we will teach it to act on its own signals. Chapter 8 takes this philosophy forward. We will operationalize the concepts we've learned here to test and validate the systems we've now interconnected. By the end of that chapter, resilience will no longer be something you design once—it will be something your infrastructure practices every day.

CHAPTER 8

Operational Resilience and Disaster Recovery

Monitoring answers, **"Is something wrong?"** by watching a small, predefined set of signals and alerting when thresholds or SLOs are breached. Observability answers, **"Why is it wrong (and who/where is affected)?"** by correlating **logs, metrics, and traces** with the right dimensions (Region/AZ, customer segment, deployment version, path). Resilient operations require both monitoring to minimize mean time to detect (**MTTD**) and observability to minimize mean time to recover (**MTTR**), and together they provide measurable evidence that the system stays within **RTO/RPO** under stress.

Traffic engineering, which we explored in Chapter 7, is about shaping how traffic flows when things go right *and* when things go wrong. We learned how to bias routes, fail over between regions, and keep users close to healthy capacity.

But there is an uncomfortable truth behind any beautiful routing diagram:

> **None of it matters if you cannot see what is happening; and**
> **seeing is not enough if you cannot trust what you see.**

Operational resilience is where design meets reality. It is where packets travel through imperfect networks, deployments introduce bugs, external dependencies misbehave, quotas are hit, and users do surprising things. The job of this chapter is to take the architectures you built so far and make them **observable, testable**, and **recoverable** under those conditions.

We will approach this in three steps:

- In Section 8.1, we define **monitoring and observability from a resilience standpoint** and apply them concretely to cloud networking. We will see how logs, metrics, traces, alarms, and dashboards combine into a feedback system that improves your ability to detect, diagnose, and fix problems before they violate RTO and RPO.

- In Section 8.2, we move from passive observation to active experimentation: **chaos engineering/resilience testing**. We will learn how to inject faults in a controlled manner and watch how the system responds, using the observability foundation from 8.1 as our measuring instrument.

- In Section 8.3, we look at **disaster recovery**, tying everything together into plans, playbooks, and architecture choices that can withstand major failures without losing critical data or business capability.

In other words, Chapter 7 showed you how to **steer** traffic. Chapter 8 shows you how to **know** when to steer, whether your steering works, and how to prove it repeatedly.

Section 8.1: Monitoring and Observability for Cloud Networking and Resilience

When people say "observability," they often mean "we have dashboards." From a resilience standpoint, that definition is too small.

From a resilience standpoint, observability is proven when you can answer questions like

1. Why did requests in one region suddenly slow down while others stayed fast?

2. Why did a specific customer segment start seeing errors when the global error rate stayed flat?

3. Why did our automatic rollback trigger, and did it actually fix the problem?

4. Why did a failover decision happen when none of the obvious health checks were failing?

Notice the pattern: each question starts with *why*. Observability is not just about knowing that something is broken; it is about being able to infer the *internal state* of a distributed system from the signals it emits.

From a resilience point of view, observability exists to support three outcomes:

1. **Diagnose issues**

   When resilience is at risk, you need to quickly understand whether you are dealing with a dependency failure, a capacity limit, a bad deployment, a traffic spike, or a subtle combination of all of them. The richer your signals—logs with structure, metrics with dimensions, traces that carry context—the easier it becomes to separate cause from noise.

2. **Find hidden problems**

   Many of the most damaging resilience issues do not show up in global numbers. A single Availability Zone that occasionally slows down, one misconfigured customer, a specific API that only fails under certain query patterns—all of these can remain invisible if you only watch averages. Observability lets you slice reality by dimensions: per-API, per-customer, per-AZ, per-instance, and per-deployment. That is how you uncover the weak points that would otherwise only surface during a real incident.

3. **Continuously improve**

   Observability is not just incident tooling; it is a learning system. Over time, you evolve from "did we stay up?" to "how often did we flirt with the edge of failure?" and "which changes made resilience better or worse?" By collecting the right metrics and traces and by questioning them, you can tighten error budgets, refine alarms, and design safer deployments.

In practical terms, observability brings together **three pillars**:

- **Logs:** Detailed, structured records of events and decisions: which customer, which API, which code revision, which error type

- **Metrics:** Numeric signals over time: latencies, error rates, cache hit ratios, queue depths, and quota usage

- **Traces:** End-to-end stories of a single request or transaction as it traverses services, networks, queues, and databases

On their own, each pillar is useful. Together, they let you answer resilience questions with confidence: "this particular order failed for this reason, in this availability zone, under this code revision, while this dependency was slow."

The key is **intentional instrumentation**. Code and infrastructure must emit signals that are aligned with your resilience concerns. That might mean adopting a common embedded metrics format, using a tracing SDK everywhere, and ensuring that important dimensions—Region, AZ, customer, API, deployment ID—are present in your logs and metrics. Without that intentionality, you will still have logs and metrics, but you will not have observability.

From this perspective, observability is less about tools and more about **curiosity encoded into telemetry**: you bake into your signals the questions you know you will want to ask when something breaks.

Monitoring: Watching for Symptoms

Monitoring, in the cloud and in traditional environments, is the practice of **watching a defined set of signals and raising alarms when they cross thresholds**. It is deliberately narrower than observability: it focuses on **symptoms** that indicate something might be wrong.

From a resilience standpoint, monitoring covers questions like:

- Are our key APIs succeeding at an acceptable rate?

- Is the error percentage for this service above its SLO?

- Is latency for this operation within the normal band?

- Are we approaching capacity limits—CPU, connections, threads, quotas?

- Are our background jobs draining queues fast enough?

Monitoring tends to be built around **units of work**: HTTP requests, messages in a queue, jobs in a worker pool. For each unit, we track whether it succeeded, how long it took, and whether the result was acceptable. We aggregate these into time buckets—typically one or five minutes—and compare them to expectations.

From there, we derive **availability metrics**. You can think of them at two levels:

- **Granular Availability**: Per-API or per-operation success rates computed over short intervals. These are useful for localizing problems: "add-to-cart is failing, checkout is fine."

- **Aggregate Availability**: A higher-level KPI such as "percentage of successful orders per day" or "percentage of healthy authentication attempts per hour." These align more closely with business outcomes.

To connect monitoring to resilience, we need to relate these signals to **MTBF, MTTR, and MTTD.** Let's recap briefly what they mean, as we discussed these previously already:

- **Mean Time Between Failures (MTBF)**: How often things go wrong

- **Mean Time To Detect (MTTD)**: How long it takes your monitoring to notice

- **Mean Time To Recover (MTTR)**: How long it takes to restore healthy behavior

Availability over a longer window (say, a year) is then a function of how often you fail and how quickly you recover. Monitoring affects both: good signals shorten MTTD by raising alarms early, and good alarm design can shorten MTTR by triggering automatic rollbacks or failovers.

Monitoring also forces you to define **what "downtime" means for your system.** Is it any five-minute interval where a critical API drops below 95% success? Is it when the order rate falls more than 10% below forecast? Is it when a subset of customers are impacted, or only when the majority are? Without such definitions, you cannot honestly say whether you met your resilience goals.

However, monitoring has natural limits. It reliably signals that something has changed—error rates rise, latency increases—but it does not explain the underlying cause. A per-API alarm cannot reveal whether the issue stems from a slow dependency, a saturated connection pool, a misconfigured cache, a faulty deployment, or traffic from a single noisy customer. Observability provides the context needed to make that distinction.

Why the Difference Matters for Resilience

Monitoring without observability gives you fast, loud alerts but no insight.

You know something is broken, but you do not know which dependency is failing, which deployment introduced the problem, or which customers are affected. During an incident, you end up guessing: rolling back multiple components, toggling feature flags, and failing over regions—sometimes fixing the problem, sometimes making it worse. Your MTTR becomes a function of luck and heroics, not engineering.

Observability without monitoring gives you beautiful dashboards and trace visualizations that nobody looks at until a customer complains. The data is there, but no one is watching the right metrics with the right alarms. Problems go undetected for too long, and your MTTD explodes. In resilience terms, this is the silent killer: the system *could* have warned you, but it never did.

Resilient systems need **both**:

- Monitoring to **raise the flag**: "this API is failing, this quota is being hit, this region is misbehaving, this network path has increased latency, users are experiencing timeouts."

- Observability to **explain the flag**: "the failures started right after deployment X, only affect one Availability Zone, and correlate with increased latency from a specific downstream database."

Imagine a single customer workflow: placing an order. That one action may pass through a front-end, a product catalog service, a cart service, a payment processor, a queue, a worker, and one or more databases.

Monitoring tells you, "order placement is failing more often than usual." Observability lets you trace a specific order attempt across that chain:

- Did the front-end return a 5xx, or did it return a 4xx due to an input validation bug?

- Did the catalog lookup hit local cache, remote cache, or fall through to the database?

- Was the database slow, out of connections, or rejecting requests due to a quota?

- Did the message reach the queue? Did the worker process it?

- Did these failures begin right after a new code revision rolled out to one AZ?

We can only answer these questions if our logs carry the right context (customer, API, trace ID, deployment ID), if our metrics are broken down by useful dimensions (instance, AZ, customer segment, revision), and if traces are propagated across service boundaries.

This is the **dimensionality story**: the ability to say "show me errors per API," "per webpage," "per instance," "per customer," and "per deployment," and then set alarms on the parts that matter most. Monitoring becomes smarter when it is built on top of observability-friendly metrics.

The same is true for **hidden and external issues**:

- A single bad customer or integration can suddenly send malformed requests and create a localised spike in 4xx errors that are "their fault" by definition—but in reality, the system may be failing to protect itself properly. Observability lets you compute metrics like "percentage of customers affected" rather than just "percentage of requests failing," so you can tell the difference between one misbehaving client and a systemic problem.

- A dependency outside your control—an external payment gateway, a third-party API, or an internet path—may degrade. Synthetic canaries and client-side telemetry give you a view of reality "from the outside," catching issues that your internal metrics miss. Monitoring can then use these synthetic metrics as first-class signals.

Finally, observability is what allows you to **evaluate and improve your monitoring itself**. Alarms have quality: they can be too sensitive (noisy) or too insensitive (blind). You can think of this in terms of precision and recall: how often do alarms fire correctly vs. incorrectly? Are there incidents where users were impacted but no alarm was triggered? Observability data—especially traces and detailed logs—helps you diagnose your diagnostics and tune thresholds, dimensions, and composite alarms so that they align with real resilience risk.

From a practical standpoint, the steps are:

1. **Define resilience objectives first.**

   Decide what "downtime" and "impact" mean for your workloads.
   Establish target availability, RTO, and RPO.

2. **Design monitoring for detection.**

   Choose a small set of critical metrics—success rates, latency,
   queue depth, and quota usage—and attach alarms with clear
   thresholds and actions. These are your early-warning signals.

3. **Design observability for explanation.**

   Instrument your code and infrastructure with structured logs, rich
   metrics (with dimensions that match your fault boundaries), and
   traces that propagate context. This is your diagnostic toolkit.

4. **Use observability to improve monitoring.**

   When an incident occurs, look back through logs, metrics, and
   traces to understand how early it could have been detected, where
   noise came from, and how your alarms behaved, then refine.

5. **Use both as the baseline for resilience testing.**

   In the next sections, when we introduce chaos experiments and
   disaster recovery drills, the same monitoring and observability
   stack will become your scoring system: it will tell you whether
   your system reacted quickly enough and whether users were
   protected.

With this foundation in place—monitoring for **when** resilience is at risk and
observability for **why**—we can now apply the concepts specifically to **networking**: the
signals, tools, and patterns that let you see not only whether packets move, but whether
they move in a way that keeps your resilience promises. That will be the focus of the next
part of this section.

Observability Applied to Networking

Networks are often treated as a silent substrate, an invisible platform on which applications run. Their success is measured by their absence from conversation: when nothing breaks, the network is presumed healthy; when something does, the network is the first to be blamed. But in resilient cloud architectures, the network is not a background character. It is a dynamic, adaptive system whose behavior shapes every millisecond of the user experience. Observing such a system requires a different mindset—one that sees the network not as a set of pipes, but as a living topology constantly negotiating thousands of micro-decisions per second.

Visibility into this behavior is never straightforward. Unlike applications, networks rarely announce their intentions. They do not log what they meant to do; they only reveal what actually occurred. A packet finds its path based on a shifting combination of routing tables, DNS choices, tunnel states, health signals, and global traffic policies that react autonomously to conditions around them. To understand the network, you must reconstruct its state from these clues. Observability in networking is therefore an act of inference, not introspection—a discipline of reading the system's footprints rather than hearing its voice.

From a resilience standpoint, the question is not "is the network working?" but "is the network behaving as designed under stress?" This includes all the subtleties that matter during incidents: did traffic shift when it should have, but also not shift when it shouldn't? Did latency rise evenly across Availability Zones, or did only one cell begin to drift? Did a DNS failover activate cleanly, or did only a subset of resolvers choose the secondary region while others remained stuck on stale records? Did a hybrid link fail gracefully, moving traffic to a backup path without amplifying the failure—or did it oscillate, repeatedly flapping in a destructive loop?

These behaviors define resilience at the network layer, and they are visible only to systems built with the sensitivity to detect them. The signals are rarely loud. A degraded ISP path between a metropolitan area and a cloud edge does not declare itself; it manifests as a slow, subtle rise in retransmissions that occur only for certain prefixes. A problematic Availability Zone does not go down entirely; it becomes hesitant, adding five or ten milliseconds of jitter to connections under load. A misbalanced load balancer does not raise an alarm; it simply begins routing too much traffic to a single target group in a single AZ, creating heat where there should be equilibrium. In complex distributed systems, these are the early signs of a future incident.

To see these patterns, network observability builds on a combination of signals that, on their own, are ambiguous but together form a meaningful whole. Flow records show the actual movement of traffic—the five-tuple truth of who talked to whom, how often, and with what outcome. Routing information, whether in the form of control-plane updates or inferred path changes, explains why traffic shifted at a particular moment. DNS logs reveal the decision-making of resolvers: which endpoints they selected, how clients reacted to TTL expiry, and how consistent failover behavior was across geographies. Synthetic checks represent the external viewpoint, the real experience of a hypothetical user approaching the system from multiple vantage points. And metrics about backbone latency, jitter, packet loss, or health check distributions fill in the physical properties of the path the packets travelled.

Individually, none of these signals is authoritative. Together, they allow us to interpret the network's behavior in the same way a doctor reads vital signs: no single reading tells the whole story, but a combination reveals the underlying condition with clarity.

Consider a simple example. A team notices that error rates in one region have started to rise, but CPU, memory, and healthy target counts remain normal. In a traditional monitoring setup, this discrepancy would be confusing. But with proper network observability, the story becomes readable. Flow records show an increase in retransmissions for traffic originating from a specific Availability Zone. DNS logs show a shift in resolver choices—some clients are still hitting the primary region, while others have drifted to the secondary. Latency metrics reveal that inter-AZ communication in that region has entered an unstable band, with spikes occurring intermittently during peak load. Taken together, these clues point not to an application bug but to a partial network degradation in a single cell—a brownout rather than an outage. This type of failure is invisible to simple health checks but deeply relevant for resilience, because brownouts cause unpredictable failover behavior and uneven user impact.

Network observability must be able to catch such partial failures early, long before they manifest as global incidents. The engineering reality is that networks fail far more often through hesitation than collapse. When a link is fully down, routing converges quickly and systems adapt. When a link is merely degraded, the network is indecisive: routing may not converge, traffic may oscillate between paths, and load balancers may continue sending traffic to targets that are technically reachable but effectively unusable. These transitional behaviors are the hardest to detect, and they account for a large portion of user-visible impact in distributed systems. A resilient network is one whose observability can see these transitions as they begin, not after they peak.

Another quality that sets networking apart is its sensitivity to external conditions. The majority of user-impacting network issues occur outside your infrastructure: on customer ISPs, on backbone segments between metropolitan areas, inside mobile networks, or at the edges of the internet. Application metrics inside the cloud may remain pristine while a user population in Southern Europe or Southeast Asia experiences outages or degraded performance. When your telemetry only reflects internal health, you are blind to this entire domain of resilience risk. Synthetic probes, edge health signals, and global path telemetry complete this missing dimension by showing what users actually experience at the boundary between your network and the world.

Yet observability is not purely external either. One of the most undervalued components of network resilience is understanding how the control planes behave. Cloud networking is configured by APIs—not by humans—and changes ripple through routing layers, load balancers, DNS, and service meshes over time. Every change has a propagation delay. Every failover has a ramp. Every routing update has a convergence pattern. Observability must capture these movements with enough fidelity to differentiate expected propagation from unexpected drift. The control plane is the nervous system of your architecture; observing it is as important as observing the data plane it influences.

What emerges from all these layers—data plane, control plane, edge behavior, client-side experience—is a picture of the network that is both precise and dynamic. This picture is the basis for resilient operations. When the network behaves exactly as expected, observability reinforces confidence. When the network deviates, observability provides the clues needed to diagnose the deviation, determine its significance, and act before users are impacted.

This conceptual foundation is essential before we explore the specific tools that make it possible. Flow logs, DNS logs, latency measurements, synthetics, routing signals, tracing, and backbone telemetry each offer a different lens, and each lens reveals a different truth about how the network behaves under real conditions. None is sufficient alone, but together they form the sensory system of a resilient cloud network.

When these tools are used in isolation, they produce noise. When used together— with intention, with understanding, with a clear view of the resilience objectives—they produce insight. And insight is what resilience depends on: the ability to interpret the system's behavior in time to preserve its capability.

In the next section, we will examine these instruments one by one—not as isolated utilities, but as components of a coherent observability fabric that allows cloud networks to be seen, understood, and trusted. Before doing so, it is worth understanding how even the right tools can fail when observability is designed poorly.

Common anti-patterns in network observability that undermine res0ilience

Before looking at specific tools, it is worth highlighting a few common anti-patterns that repeatedly undermine network resilience—not because the tools are insufficient, but because they are applied without the right intent.

- **Dashboards Without Dimensions**: Metrics exist, but cannot be broken down by Availability Zone, region, customer segment, deployment, or network path. When something degrades, everything appears "mostly fine," masking localized failure.

- **Global Averages Only**: Overall latency and error rates stay green while brownouts, single-AZ degradation, or partial customer impact remain invisible inside aggregated views.

- **Uncorrelated Telemetry**: Logs, metrics, and traces exist but share no common identifiers (such as trace ID, deployment ID, or customer ID), turning incident response into guesswork rather than diagnosis.

- **Alerting Without Intent**: Alarms fire on raw thresholds instead of resilience boundaries, creating noise during normal variation and silence during subtle but dangerous failure modes.

These patterns create a false sense of confidence: the network appears observable until the moment it actually matters.

Network Observability Instruments in AWS

To turn this conceptual view into something operational, we need instruments. In on-premises networks, these instruments were usually SNMP counters on routers and switches, syslog feeds, and trap-driven alerting wired into a ticketing system. In AWS, the same needs are met by a different set of building blocks: Amazon CloudWatch metrics, CloudWatch Logs, AWS CloudTrail, AWS CloudWatch Internet Monitor, AWS Network Manager, and event-driven automation through Amazon EventBridge and AWS Lambda. The principles are the same—measure, record, alert, act—but the way these capabilities are exposed is fundamentally different.

At the most basic level, CloudWatch metrics play the role once held by SNMP counters: time-series statistics describing throughput, connection counts, packet rates, health state, and control-plane behavior for AWS networking services. CloudWatch Logs becomes the structured, queryable equivalent of syslog, collecting VPC Flow Logs, Transit Gateway Flow Logs, and other textual telemetry. CloudTrail records configuration and API changes, closing the loop between observed network behavior and the administrative actions that may have caused it. EventBridge acts as the modern evolution of trap-based alerting—an event layer that reacts to alarms, state changes, and log patterns to trigger notifications, tickets, or automated remediation workflows. A cloud-native observability system only becomes effective when these signals are woven together intentionally; otherwise, valuable insight remains isolated inside dashboards.

In Figure 8-1, on-premises monitoring tools such as SNMP counters, syslog, and trap-based alerting have clear cloud-native equivalents in CloudWatch Metrics, CloudWatch Logs, CloudTrail, and EventBridge. While the interfaces differ, the underlying principles—measure, record, detect, and react—remain unchanged. This conceptual mapping helps teams transitioning from classical NMS tooling recognize that observability in AWS builds on familiar foundations expressed through modern, event-driven services.

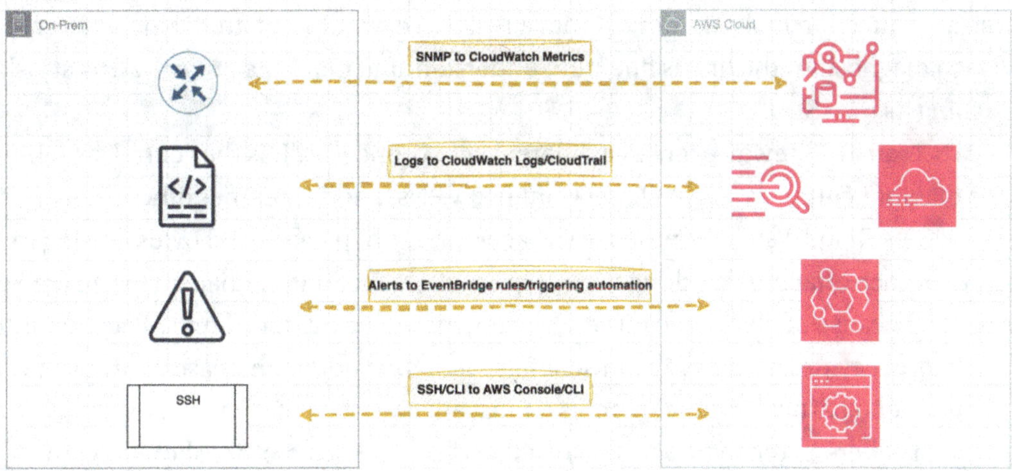

Figure 8-1. *Mapping Traditional Network Monitoring Concepts to AWS-Native Observability*

From this foundation, the next step is to understand how each major networking service surfaces its own health. **For AWS Direct Connect,** the primary signals live in the **AWS/DX** CloudWatch namespace. The most essential one from a resilience standpoint is the connection state: a sustained transition to *Down* on a primary DX link should trigger an immediate alarm, because it indicates loss of deterministic bandwidth and likely forces traffic onto a higher-latency or less predictable alternative—typically an IPsec VPN over the internet.

Beyond simple link state, Direct Connect publishes throughput metrics in bits and packets per second, as well as counters for errors and, on some circuits, optical light levels. Monitoring these values as a *fraction of provisioned capacity* is critical. Sustained utilization approaching eighty to ninety percent is an early indicator that buffers will begin filling, queuing delays will rise, and retransmissions will increase. Alerting on high utilization provides the operational headroom needed to rebalance traffic, adjust BGP preferences, or schedule capacity upgrades before congestion becomes user-visible.

Direct Connect also surfaces metrics per virtual interface. That granularity is important in multi-tenant hybrid designs where multiple VIFs share a physical link. A single, noisy VIF can starve others without pushing the aggregate link metrics into an obvious danger zone. When you consume DX telemetry per VIF, you can detect that one virtual interface is consistently close to capacity or suffering loss, even while the physical connection looks nominal. From a resilience standpoint, this is the difference between diagnosing "the link is fine" and understanding that "one critical VIF is at risk of breaching its own SLO."

AWS Transit Gateway exposes a different set of concerns. It is the central switching fabric that interconnects VPCs, Direct Connect, VPNs, and sometimes other Transit Gateways. Its CloudWatch namespace surfaces counts of packets and bytes flowing in and out of each attachment, along with drop counters that differentiate between packets discarded because of black hole routes, missing routes, or capacity limits. These counters provide direct evidence of routing misconfigurations: a sudden increase in drops due to "no route" for a particular attachment is almost always a sign of a missing or withdrawn prefix somewhere in the topology. In a resilient design, those metrics should not merely be observed after the fact; they should be used to trigger automated investigations or even automated rollback of recent route-table changes.

Transit Gateway Flow Logs add another layer: they record sampled flow information at the TGW boundary, giving you visibility into which attachments are exchanging traffic, which prefixes are involved, and where rejects occur. When combined with CloudWatch metrics and Network Manager's view of route tables, these logs make it possible to correlate specific traffic anomalies with control-plane events such as new route propagations, attachment states, or changes pushed through infrastructure-as-code. This is where observability moves beyond simple monitoring: you are no longer just watching counters; you are reconstructing the sequence of decisions that led to a resilience risk.

Beyond individual services, AWS now offers higher-level telemetry focused on path health.

AWS Network Flow Monitor provides active probing between sources and destinations across the network, measuring round-trip time, packet loss, and path health independent of application traffic. Within Network Flow Monitor, you define probes that target specific combinations of protocol, IP family, and packet size along particular paths—for example, from a monitoring subnet in one Availability Zone to an on-premises endpoint over Direct Connect. The resulting metrics reveal whether a path is healthy, degraded, or broken, and do so in a way that is independent of application traffic. This matters for resilience because it allows you to detect path-level issues before they accumulate enough application impact to show up as errors.

One of the more subtle but powerful concepts in Network Monitor is the notion of a health indicator for the AWS-managed segment of the path. When the destination is reached over Direct Connect, the system can tell you whether the backbone segment between the probe and the DX location is currently impaired. That distinction— between a fault in your own on-premises or partner network and a problem inside AWS connectivity itself—is critical during incident triage. It allows teams to focus their efforts on the segment they control and to escalate appropriately when the impairment lies outside their administrative domain.

Where Network Monitor focuses on specific paths you define, **AWS Network Manager—Infrastructure Performance** offers a systematic view of latency and health across Availability Zones and regions. It measures round-trip time between AZ pairs, within a region and across regions, and can export those metrics to CloudWatch. This provides a baseline of backbone performance against which you can compare application latencies and routing decisions. When inter-AZ latency in a region begins to drift outside its normal band, you gain an early signal that something in the underlying physical or logical topology has changed. Used well, these metrics inform decisions about evacuating an Availability Zone, rebalancing traffic, or delaying planned maintenance that would add further pressure to the system.

All of these instruments—Direct Connect metrics, Transit Gateway and PrivateLink telemetry, Network Monitor, and Infrastructure Performance—tell you about the behavior of network elements and paths. To understand what is actually flowing over them, you still need packet-level context at scale, and this is where **VPC Flow Logs** and **Transit Gateway Flow Logs** become central.

Flow Logs can be enabled on individual Elastic Network Interfaces (ENIs), at the VPC level, or at the Transit Gateway attachment level. They record metadata about accepted and rejected traffic, including source and destination addresses, ports, protocols, and the decision taken by the network (accept or reject). For serious observability work, it is worth moving beyond the default log format and enabling the richer later versions that include fields such as VPC ID, subnet ID, Availability Zone, flow direction, and traffic path. These additional dimensions are not cosmetic; they are what allow you to distinguish cross-AZ traffic from local flows, to attribute traffic to specific subnets or constructs, and to see which flows are traversing NAT gateways, Transit Gateways, or other middleboxes.

Once Flow Logs are delivered to Amazon S3, services such as Amazon Athena can query them directly using SQL. This is where they become operationally powerful for resilience. You can run "top talker" analyses to see which prefixes, instances, or AZs are responsible for most of the traffic at the time of an incident, correlate spikes in rejects with recent security group or network ACL changes, and identify flows that cross unexpected boundaries. When a particular Availability Zone begins to misbehave, aggregating flow records by AZ ID and traffic path can reveal whether cross-Zone chatter has increased, whether retries are exploding for one downstream dependency, or whether a new deployment has caused traffic patterns to take a less resilient route.

Flow Logs can also be sent directly to CloudWatch Logs, where engineers use CloudWatch Logs Insights for ad-hoc, incident-driven querying. This is often the fastest way to investigate anomalies, especially during an evolving event: identifying sudden spikes in rejected flows, isolating traffic patterns affecting a particular subnet or AZ, or verifying how routing changes influenced traffic distribution. S3 and Athena underpin dashboards and historical analysis, while CloudWatch Logs Insights provides the interactive, real-time investigative tooling needed during active triage. Figure 8-2 shows how these parallel analysis paths work together to create a complete operational view of traffic behavior.

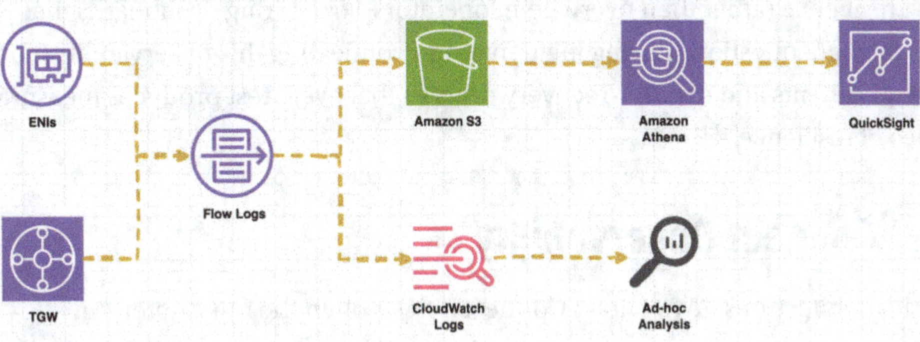

Figure 8-2. *Flow Logs Analytics Pipeline for Dashboard and Ad Hoc Investigation*

In Figure 8-2, Flow Logs from ENIs and Transit Gateway attachments can be delivered to Amazon S3 for batch analytics with Athena and QuickSight dashboards or directly to CloudWatch Logs for real-time, ad hoc querying through CloudWatch Logs Insights. This dual-path design enables both continuous observability and rapid incident investigation, giving teams a complete view of traffic behavior across Availability Zones and network boundaries.

Across all these tools, CloudWatch remains the common surface for metrics and alarms. For each critical metric—Direct Connect ConnectionState, Transit Gateway drop counters, PrivateLink resets, Network Monitor packet loss, Infrastructure Performance latency, and Flow Log-derived rates—you can define alarms that trigger when conditions persist beyond a reasonable window. Those alarms can feed **Amazon EventBridge**, which in turn can invoke **AWS Lambda**, create incidents, pause deployments, or adjust routing weights. In other words, telemetry becomes not just a reporting mechanism but a control input for automation.

At this point, the observability picture for networking starts to look complete. You have signal coverage across physical and virtual links, across backbone and edge, across data plane and control plane, and across the user's path into AWS. Each of these tools, used in isolation, is useful but limited. Combined, they form the instrumentation required to detect, understand, and respond to the behaviors described earlier in this section: partial failures, brownouts, routing drift, and path-specific degradation.

In the next part of the chapter, we will move from describing what to observe into how to use these signals effectively: using CloudWatch and designing alarms that support resilience rather than overwhelm operators, structuring dashboards that surface the right questions during incidents, and connecting this observability fabric to chaos experiments and disaster-recovery drills so that every test produces measurable evidence of resilience.

Direct Connect Observability

In hybrid architectures, AWS Direct Connect (DX) is often the most deterministic component of the network, yet also one of the most subtle when it begins to degrade. DX rarely fails in a dramatic way. Instead, it hesitates: optical power drifts, retransmissions rise, BGP reports sporadic errors, and applications begin to feel "sluggish" long before a routing session actually drops. Because the signals are so quiet, observability is the only reliable way to detect early deterioration and maintain resilience.

Direct Connect exposes its behavior through **CloudWatch metrics in the AWS/DX namespace**, and understanding these signals requires looking across three layers: physical conditions, data-plane utilization, and control-plane stability. Together, they provide a holistic view of whether DX is operating within its expected parameters.

At the **physical layer**, the earliest warning signs appear. Optical receive and transmit power (ConnectionLightLevelRx, ConnectionLightLevelTx) should remain around 0 to –10 dBm. A shift outside this envelope—whether caused by dirty fiber, aging optics, or upstream provider issues—often precedes packet loss. When the physical signal weakens, the link may remain "up," but its behavior becomes unpredictable under load. For resilient operations, deviations in light level are treated as indicators of impending instability, not mere informational metrics.

The **data-plane view** reveals how traffic is actually flowing. Counters for ingress and egress bits per second and packets per second show the real load on the circuit. A DX connection that sits consistently above 80–90% utilization does not simply run "hot"—it becomes fragile. Spikes, microbursts, or BGP reconvergence events can push it past its practical limits, resulting in jitter and loss during the moments when stability is most needed. Observability here means monitoring not just the instantaneous throughput but the utilization pattern over time.

On the control-plane side, ConnectionState provides a binary signal of Direct Connect connection health; BGP and virtual interface stability must also be validated independently, because a physical connection can remain up while routing becomes unstable. A transition to 0 indicates loss of the Direct Connect session, at which point traffic must rely on alternative connectivity paths. But equally important is ConnectionErrorCount, which rises during periods of flapping, resets, or control-plane instability on either end of the link. These nonfatal symptoms often appear long before a complete session drop—giving operators valuable time to react, rebalance workloads, or shift selected prefixes toward alternate connectivity.

Some architectures use multiple **virtual interfaces (VIFs)**, each carrying different applications or traffic classes. Because VIFs report metrics independently, it is possible for one VIF to approach saturation or experience drops even when the overall connection looks healthy. Observability at the VIF level therefore uncovers imbalances that would otherwise remain invisible and can influence the behavior of routing under stress.

Finally, route quotas are an important component of control-plane resilience. AWS Direct Connect enforces limits on how many prefixes can be exchanged over a BGP session (e.g., private and transit virtual interfaces have a default limit of 100 advertised routes). Approaching or exceeding these quotas can cause prefixes to be rejected or routing behavior to become unstable during failover. Mature teams therefore monitor advertised and received route counts and validate current limits through AWS Service Quotas as part of operational readiness.

Now, let's look at the specific metrics you should monitor for Direct Connect:

- **ConnectionState**: Alarm immediately when the value becomes 0.

- **ConnectionErrorCount**: Rising values indicate BGP churn or instability.

- **ConnectionLightLevelRx/Tx**: Detect degrading optical conditions early.

- **Bits and Packets (In/Out)**: Monitor utilization and alarm at 80–90% of circuit capacity.

- **DropCount (Blackhole/NoRoute)**: Validate that intentional blackhole routes function correctly.

- **Per-VIF metrics**: Ensure one VIF is not starving others; maintain balanced utilization.

- **Advertised and received route counts**: Stay below hard quotas to avoid control-plane failure conditions.

Direct Connect also supports controlled failover testing, allowing operators to validate how alarms, routing policies, automation, and backup paths behave during a simulated BGP withdrawal. This makes DX one of the few hybrid connectivity mechanisms where resilience can be tested in production without disrupting workloads.

In resilient architectures, Direct Connect is not simply a high-throughput link—it is a foundational dependency whose physical, data-plane, and routing characteristics must be continuously observed. When monitored correctly, DX becomes predictable and trustworthy. When ignored, it becomes one of the most fragile components of a hybrid design.

Site-to-Site VPN Observability

AWS Site-to-Site VPN is often the silent safety net beneath hybrid architectures. It is rarely the primary path, but it is almost always the fallback: the connection that carries critical traffic when Direct Connect fails or when routing policies shift during a resilience event. Paradoxically, because VPN is treated as a backup, many teams do not observe it with the same rigor as their primary paths. This is where resilience erodes. A backup path that is not operationally understood is not a backup—it is a risk.

Site-to-Site VPN exposes its health through CloudWatch metrics in the AWS/VPN namespace and through tunnel-specific telemetry. A VPN connection consists of two independent tunnels per link, providing fault tolerance. Yet the majority of operational issues arise not from complete tunnel loss but from **flapping**, **intermittent packet loss**, or **uneven tunnel utilization**. These subtle conditions are exactly what resilience instrumentation must surface.

Unlike Direct Connect, where physical impairments are often the root cause, VPN degradation typically originates in the **IPSec control plane** or in the upstream network path between the customer edge and the AWS endpoint. Tunnel negotiation issues, mismatched timers, MTU inconsistencies, asymmetric traffic patterns, or congestion in intermediate networks can all manifest as intermittent instability. Observability must therefore detect not only tunnel state but tunnel *behavior*.

The two tunnel endpoints publish a set of metrics that reveal this behavior. The most important is the **tunnel state**, which indicates whether a given IPSec tunnel is up or down. A resilient design assumes that tunnels will alternate in health: it does not require both tunnels to be up at all times, but it does assume that at least one remains consistently stable. When tunnels flap, shift states repeatedly, or spend long periods in a down state, the VPN connection becomes unreliable as a fallback mechanism.

Throughput metrics—bytes in, bytes out, packets in, packets out—reveal whether the tunnels are carrying the expected amount of traffic. During a failover from Direct Connect, these metrics should show an immediate and sustained rise. If they do not, routing may not be shifting correctly. Conversely, if tunnels show high throughput during normal operation, traffic might be unintentionally leaking onto the backup path.

Packet loss on VPN is another critical indicator. IPSec tunnels do not degrade gracefully; packet loss within the encrypted path almost always signals upstream congestion or MTU issues. A system that depends on VPN resilience must detect these deviations quickly, especially during periods where Direct Connect is unstable and traffic is poised to shift.

VPN observability also plays an important role in diagnosing hybrid routing behavior. When BGP sessions flap between customer edge and AWS, tunnel metrics reveal whether the instability is initiated from the customer side, AWS side, or an intermediate network. This clarity matters during incidents because routing oscillations on hybrid networks can cause cascading traffic instability.

Now, let's look at the key VPN signals you should observe and monitor:

- **TunnelState (Per Tunnel)**: Detect flapping, long-lasting down states, and loss of redundancy.

- **BytesIn/Out and PacketsIn/Out**: Verify expected load patterns and detect unexpected traffic shifts.

- **TunnelDataIn/Out**: Identify whether traffic is flowing through the intended tunnel or only one of the pair.

- **Tunnel down duration**: Prolonged down periods reduce resilience headroom.

- **Packet loss indicators**: Surface upstream congestion or MTU mismatches affecting encrypted paths.

- **BGP session stability**: Correlates with tunnel health to diagnose hybrid routing events.

When monitored rigorously, VPN telemetry turns a fallback mechanism into a predictable, trustworthy resilience tool. When ignored, it becomes an unknown variable during the moments when hybrid systems are under greatest pressure.

A resilient hybrid design treats Site-to-Site VPN not as an afterthought but as a measurable, observable path—one whose behavior is understood, validated, and prepared for failover conditions. VPN observability ensures that whenever the network redirects traffic to this path, the path is ready.

Transit Gateway Observability

AWS Transit Gateway (TGW) is the connective tissue of many cloud architectures: a distributed router that links VPCs, hybrid connections, and sometimes multiple regions. Because so much traffic crosses it, TGW becomes a natural point of failure if not instrumented correctly. When Transit Gateway behaves unexpectedly—when routes propagate unevenly, attachments drop packets, or control-plane updates lag—the effect is felt everywhere. Observability is therefore essential not to "monitor a router," but to ensure that resilience boundaries inside AWS behave as intended.

Transit Gateway surfaces two complementary forms of telemetry: **CloudWatch metrics** (for attachment health and packet flow) and **Flow Logs** (for sampled traffic behavior). The combination reveals whether the network fabric is coherent and whether routing changes propagate cleanly across all connected environments.

The **attachment-level CloudWatch metrics** tell you how TGW treats traffic at each ingress and egress point. Metrics such as packets in, packets out, and bytes moved provide a baseline for understanding steady-state load. More important for resilience are the **drop counters**, because they indicate mismatches between routing intent and routing reality. For example, BlackHoleDropCount increases when traffic arrives for which TGW has no valid route; NoRouteDropCount reveals propagation gaps or recently withdrawn prefixes; and AttachmentEgressDropCount often signals capacity issues or misconfigured multicast domains. These are the earliest signs that the logical topology is no longer aligned with your expectations.

The **control-plane perspective** is equally important. Transit Gateway participates in propagating routes between attachments, often across AWS Regions or hybrid boundaries. While CloudWatch provides data-plane counters, the timing and order of route propagation are exposed through CloudTrail events and AWS Network Manager's topology view. During failover, or during infrastructure-as-code deployments, propagation delays become operationally significant. A route that reaches Attachment A before Attachment B can create a brief period of asymmetric connectivity. Such moments are small, but they degrade resilience: traffic can oscillate, failover can misalign, and hybrid traffic can take unintended paths.

TGW Flow Logs complete the picture by exposing **sampled flow metadata** at the transit layer. These logs reveal which attachments communicate most heavily, which prefixes dominate traffic at the time of impact, and where rejects occur. If a single VPC begins flooding traffic unexpectedly, TGW Flow Logs show it. If traffic to a specific subnet suddenly drops, logs reveal that too. When combined with attachment counters, Flow Logs transform TGW from an opaque routing hub into an intelligible point of observability.

Now, let's look at the key TGW metrics you should monitor:

- **PacketsIn/PacketsOut (per attachment)**: Establish load patterns; catch anomalies early.

- **BytesIn/BytesOut**: Observe steady-state behavior and detect sudden changes in flow volume.

- **BlackHoleDropCount**: Detect when TGW is discarding traffic due to routing gaps.

- **NoRouteDropCount**: Indicates inconsistent propagation or missing prefixes.

- **AttachmentEgressDropCount**: Suggests congestion or configuration mismatches on an attachment.

- **PacketDropCount (general)**: Monitor for deviations from baseline during deployments or failover drills.

- **Route propagation events**: Track when routes enter or leave the control plane, and from which attachments.

- **TGW Flow Logs**: Analyze traffic by attachment, prefix, AZ, or direction to pinpoint emerging failures.

In resilient architectures, Transit Gateway plays a role similar to a regional backbone switch: it forms the network's internal fault domain boundaries. When you observe TGW carefully—both its control plane and its data plane—you catch inconsistencies before they become outages. A system with clear TGW observability has predictable failover, predictable routing behavior, and predictable blast radius containment. A system that treats TGW as a black box eventually learns that invisibility and resilience rarely coexist.

Flow Logs as a Data-Plane Signal

In any distributed system, the data plane is where truth lives. Routing may declare a path available, health checks may believe a target is responsive, and control-plane events may show everything as green—yet the packets themselves reveal what is actually happening. **Amazon VPC Flow Logs** and **Transit Gateway Flow Logs** provide this layer of truth. They do not describe configuration; they describe reality.

Flow Logs capture metadata about every sampled connection attempt: source, destination, protocol, ports, bytes, packets, and whether traffic was accepted or rejected. The more recent versions of the log format include crucial contextual fields—VPC ID, subnet ID, Availability Zone, flow direction, traffic path, and even observation points— transforming the logs from a security artifact into a resilience instrument.

What makes Flow Logs essential for network observability is not just the visibility they provide, but **when** they provide it. They surface degradation *before* metrics do. A problematic Availability Zone expresses itself first as increased retries, shortened flow durations, or a sudden rise in TCP retransmissions. A misconfigured security group reveals itself as reject spikes for a specific five-tuple. A failing downstream dependency shows up as repeated short-lived connection attempts for the same destination. These are signals that almost never reach CloudWatch alarms on their own; they appear only to systems that inspect the shape of flows over time.

Flow Logs also allow you to diagnose traffic patterns that directly affect resilience. Cross-AZ communication that unexpectedly increases, NAT or egress chokepoints that emerge without warning, and slow drifts in east–west traffic volume often explain why a system behaves differently under load. Because Flow Logs can be delivered to Amazon S3 and queried using Athena, they become a powerful forensic tool. Teams can explore what changed in the minutes leading to an incident, correlating flow anomalies with Route 53 logs, TGW metrics, or Load Balancer telemetry.

In hybrid architectures, TGW Flow Logs reveal inter-attachment communication and directional flow patterns. If traffic between on-prem and AWS decreases suddenly while TGW attachment drops increase, the logs provide clarity within seconds. If traffic destined for a failover region begins leaking into a primary region due to partial propagation, Flow Logs surface that drift long before applications report issues.

Flow Logs are not a debugging tool—they are an early detection system. They show where resilience begins to bend.

Now, let's look at the Flow Log signals and dimensions you should monitor:

- **Accept vs. Reject Disposition**: Rising rejects indicate policy drift or misconfiguration.

- **Flow Count and Churn Rate**: Spikes often reflect retries, flapping dependencies, or AZ instability.

- **Bytes and Packets per Flow**: Shrinking flows suggest retransmissions or incomplete handshakes.

- **AZ, Subnet, and VPC Identifiers**: Isolate issues to specific blast-radius boundaries.

- **Traffic-Path Tagging**: Identify flows traversing NAT, IGW, TGW, or VPC endpoints.

- **TGW Flow Logs (Per Attachment)**: Detect asymmetric routing, unexpected prefixes, and inter-VPC anomalies.

- **Short-duration, Repeated Flows**: Early sign of downstream degradation or partial network loss.

Flow Logs provide the most concrete evidence of how the network behaves under stress. They are not a replacement for CloudWatch metrics or routing telemetry—they are the lens that validates them. When Flow Logs, health checks, and routing events all point in the same direction, operators gain confidence that the system is reacting as designed. When they diverge, Flow Logs reveal which signal is lying.

A resilient network is not only one that routes traffic correctly; it is one that makes its behavior visible. Flow Logs turn visibility into something measurable, queryable, and dependable—a true data-plane foundation for resilience engineering.

Route 53 Behavior in Failover

DNS is the first control point in any global or multi-region architecture, yet it is also the least deterministic. Whether a user reaches the intended region depends not on a single authoritative answer, but on how thousands of resolvers across the internet interpret that answer, cache it, and refresh it. This introduces natural stagger, drift, and variation—which is why observability at the DNS layer is indispensable for resilience.

Amazon Route 53 exposes DNS behavior primarily through two logging mechanisms: Route 53 Resolver query logging (recursive DNS queries originating from your VPCs) and Route 53 hosted zone query logging (authoritative queries answered by your public or private hosted zones). These logs provide insight into the decisions resolvers make during steady state and during failover. Unlike metrics that simply indicate health check status or routing policy configuration, logs show the *actual* answers users receive.

During steady-state operation, query logs validate whether latency routing, geolocation routing, or weighted routing behaves as intended. They reveal which endpoints are most frequently returned to which resolver networks, how often cached responses are reused, and whether certain populations are bypassing intended routing rules due to intermediary resolvers. This matters for resilience because routing policies are not useful if the internet does not honor them.

During failover, DNS observability becomes the authoritative truth surface. Health checks inside Route 53 operate independently across multiple AWS Regions, and logs show precisely when a health check transitions from healthy to unhealthy and how quickly different resolvers adopt the new answer set. Failover is never instantaneous— resolvers honor TTLs inconsistently, some refresh aggressively, others slowly. Observability shows how the failover actually unfolds across client populations.

This visibility becomes even more important during *partial* failures. When a region is not fully down but degraded, health checks may report mixed states depending on which AWS health-check region performs the probe. DNS logs reveal whether Route 53 is returning inconsistent answers, whether only a subset of resolvers has shifted away from the impaired region, or whether traffic is "leaking" back into a problematic endpoint. These subtle patterns directly influence how a resilience event is experienced by users.

DNS behavior can also reveal misalignment between design and reality. If a system relies on short TTLs for fast failover, logs confirm whether resolvers respect them. If a multi-region architecture assumes that resolvers will choose the nearest endpoint consistently, logs expose where geographic routing is overridden by ISP infrastructure. Observability at this layer ensures that failover mechanisms behave according to design, not assumption.

Now, let's look at what you should observe and monitor in DNS telemetry:

- **Query Results Returned to Resolvers**: Confirm that intended endpoints are being selected.

- **Resolver Patterns During Failover**: Measure how quickly different networks adopt new records.

- **TTL Adherence**: Detect resolvers or ISP networks that hold onto stale answers longer than expected.

- **Health-Check Transition Timing**: Ensure that failover triggers align with actual regional conditions.

- **Mixed or Inconsistent Answers**: Detect partial failures where only part of the internet shifts.

- **Geographic or ASN-Specific Anomalies**: Identify resolver networks routing unexpectedly.

DNS is not just a lookup mechanism; it is a dynamic, probabilistic layer of the control plane. When observed carefully, it reveals how the global internet interprets your resilience design. When ignored, it turns failover into guesswork.

A resilient system aligns health checks, routing policies, and DNS observability into a coherent flow. Logs confirm that decisions are executed correctly, evenly, and with predictable timing—and they expose where resilience is compromised by caching behavior, resolver diversity, or partial impairment. DNS visibility completes the control-plane view, bridging the gap between internal health and the user's experience of failover.

Internet Monitor and External Path Health

Internal telemetry tells you how your systems behave inside AWS, but it says nothing about what happens along the path between your users and your endpoints. That path spans mobile carriers, residential ISPs, enterprise networks, regional transit providers, internet exchanges, and AWS edge locations. Most user-visible incidents originate somewhere in this chain, not in AWS itself. This is why external path observability is not optional in resilient architectures—it is the only way to measure the experience users actually have.

Amazon CloudWatch Internet Monitor provides that perspective. Instead of probing from your infrastructure inward, it measures connectivity from AWS edge locations outward, combining billions of network measurements into a continuous assessment of path health. It maps issues to **client locations**, **autonomous systems (ASNs)**, and **AWS edges**, surfacing degradations such as packet loss, latency inflation, or availability dips long before they appear in application metrics.

This outward-facing signal is particularly important because internet impairments rarely manifest uniformly. A single metropolitan area may experience congestion between a local ISP and an AWS Region. A mobile carrier may introduce packet shaping or misaligned MTU settings. A regional transit provider may reroute traffic due to maintenance, adding tens of milliseconds of latency to a particular geography but not others. Without Internet Monitor, these conditions appear as "random slowdowns" or "sporadic customer complaints"—symptoms that cannot be diagnosed with internal metrics alone.

Internet Monitor becomes especially powerful when correlated with DNS and load-balancer behavior. When a region is healthy internally but customers from a specific country experience high error rates, Internet Monitor often reveals that the impairment sits upstream: congestion on a specific ISP-to-AWS path, increased latency toward the regional edge, or a partial outage at a nearby exchange. This clarity is invaluable during incidents because it prevents teams from chasing the wrong hypothesis and allows them to communicate precisely with customers.

Internet Monitor is also a validation mechanism. After introducing a global load-balancing strategy, deploying a new region, or adding Global Accelerator or CloudFront, Internet Monitor shows whether connectivity performance actually improved. If latency or availability remains uneven across geographies, external path telemetry guides where architectural adjustments are needed.

Perhaps its most important role in resilience is detecting **partial** external impairments. Unlike a full internet outage or a major regional event, external network degradations are often subtle and geographically constrained. They affect users asymmetrically—one city may slow down while the next stays normal. Internal health checks do not catch these patterns. Internet Monitor does.

Now, let's look at what you should observe and monitor using Internet Monitor:

- **Performance Score and Its Deviation**: Measures how current user experience compares to optimal historical patterns.

- **Availability Score**: Detects packet loss and reachability issues affecting specific client networks.

- **Impacted Locations and ASNs**: Identifies where on the internet the impairment originates.

- **Latency Deviations**: Reveals upstream route changes or congestion toward AWS edges.

- **Traffic Impact Estimates**: Quantifies how much of your user base is affected.

- **Correlation with Regions and Edges**: Ensures that impairments map to external networks, not AWS infrastructure.

Internet Monitor transforms the external internet from an opaque, unpredictable medium into a measurable part of your resilience posture. It connects user experience to underlying network conditions and provides the context needed to distinguish internal failures from external ones. In doing so, it closes one of the largest gaps in cloud-native observability: the space between AWS and the customer.

A resilient system must understand external path health as deeply as it understands its own infrastructure. When combined with DNS, load-balancer telemetry, and data-plane signals, Internet Monitor provides the global view that allows teams to diagnose user-visible incidents accurately—and to improve the architecture in ways that align with real-world conditions, not just internal assumptions.

Elastic Load Balancing Observability

Elastic Load Balancing (ELB) is the first point inside AWS where user traffic converges. Whether the front end is an Application Load Balancer (ALB) or a Network Load Balancer (NLB), the behavior of the load balancer provides an immediate and highly informative view into the system's health. Because ELB sits at the boundary between the public edge and your VPC, it becomes one of the earliest indicators of Availability Zone issues, dependency failures, uneven routing, or degraded paths upstream.

ALB and NLB each expose distinct dimensions of observability, but both reflect the same underlying truth: how traffic lands, how it is distributed, and how downstream targets respond under stress. In resilience scenarios, these signals often surface anomalies before application metrics do. When an Availability Zone begins to degrade, connection attempts to targets in that AZ often slow or fail before the targets themselves become unhealthy. When DNS routing shifts traffic unevenly due to partial failover, the load balancer is the first component that sees the imbalance. And when upstream networks degrade, ELB access logs capture the pattern of retries, connection resets, and truncated requests long before internal components notice.

Metrics in the **AWS/ApplicationELB** and **AWS/NetworkELB** namespaces reveal load distribution across Availability Zones and target groups. For ALB, the number of active connections, new connections, requests per second, target response codes, and target response times tell a precise story about how traffic flows. For NLB, TCP handshake times, TLS negotiation durations, and flow completion rates offer insight into performance bottlenecks at the transport layer. These signals are critical because they reflect the real user-facing edge—the point where degraded network conditions translate directly into increased latency or reduced availability.

ALB health checks provide another dimension of resilience observability. A target becoming unhealthy in a single AZ is often an early sign of a localized issue: insufficient capacity, dependency lag, or a subtle drop in network performance that application-level health checks detect before anything else. A resilient architecture depends on predictable target health behavior; observability ensures that unhealthy transitions are caused by valid reasons, not by premature or overly sensitive configurations.

Access logs from ALB and NLB form the narrative layer of ELB observability. These logs show the exact request path taken: the client IP, the chosen AZ, the selected target, the latency breakdown between processing stages, and the final response. During incidents, these logs are invaluable: they reveal where latency originates (client, load balancer, target), whether connections are resetting prematurely, and whether certain paths consistently perform worse than others. When Flow Logs, Internet Monitor data, and ELB access logs align, the cause of user-visible degradation becomes far easier to pinpoint.

Now, let's look at the key ELB signals you should observe and monitor:

- **RequestCount/NewConnectionCount**: Observe traffic surges, shifts in AZ selection, and imbalance during failover.

- **HealthyHostCount/UnHealthyHostCount**: Detect early degradation of targets or AZ-specific instability.

- **TargetResponseTime (ALB)**: Identify slowdowns caused by application, network, or dependency issues.

- **TCP/TLS Handshake Times (NLB)**: Uncover upstream network problems or congestion at the load balancer.

- **HTTP Response Code Distribution (ALB)**: Rising 4xx/5xx responses indicate downstream failover or partial impairment.

- **SurgeQueueLength/SpilloverCount (ALB)**: Detect when load exceeds available capacity.

- **Access Logs**: Correlate user behavior, path selection, latencies, and failures with other network signals.

Load balancers form one of the most valuable layers in resilience observability because they:

- See how clients interact with your system

- Expose how AWS directs traffic across AZs

- Reflect the performance of downstream dependencies

- Reveal early signs of degraded network conditions

A resilient design does not treat ELB metrics as "application signals"—it treats them as **network signals**. They describe the real behavior of traffic across the edge, the fabric, and the targets. When observed carefully, they provide clarity about where resilience is bending, long before anything breaks.

Network Manager—Infrastructure Performance

AWS Network Manager extends observability beyond individual services and provides a coherent view of how the AWS backbone behaves across Availability Zones and Regions. While CloudWatch metrics expose the behavior of specific components such as Direct Connect or Transit Gateway, Network Manager offers something different: a continuous measurement of *AWS infrastructure latency* across the internal fabric.

This matters enormously for resilience because many failure modes begin not with packet loss but with small shifts in latency and jitter across Availability Zones. The AWS backbone normally maintains extremely stable inter-AZ and inter-region round-trip times. When these metrics begin to drift, even slightly, it often signals partial impairment, increased load on the underlying fabric, or maintenance events that temporarily alter path selection. Application telemetry rarely picks this up early; infrastructure performance metrics do.

Network Manager's Infrastructure Performance tracks latency between Availability Zones within the same region, as well as between regions. These measurements create a reliable historical baseline—the "normal operating envelope"—that resilience teams can use to detect deviation. When inter-AZ RTT increases unpredictably, internal east–west traffic may begin queuing, cross-zone flows may become unstable, and stateful components may drift further apart in time. These effects accumulate silently until visible errors emerge at higher layers.

By observing these metrics before an incident escalates, operators can identify when an Availability Zone is not functioning as expected even while it remains officially healthy. This allows for proactive mitigation: shifting traffic away from the affected AZ, delaying deployments that would increase load on the zone, or triggering resilience playbooks ahead of time. For multi-region systems, inter-region latency changes provide early signals of backbone routing shifts or increased load across a regional edge, both of which alter failover characteristics.

Infrastructure performance is not only diagnostic; it is also a validation tool. When traffic engineering changes are introduced—new Transit Gateway attachments, new Direct Connect paths, or reconfigured routing policies—the resulting behavior should align with the established baseline. If infrastructure latency increases unexpectedly after a change, Network Manager provides immediate evidence that something in the routing path has shifted and requires review.

Because this data is integrated with AWS Network Manager's topology view, teams can correlate latency deviations with network-wide events: new attachments being created, route propagations occurring at peak times, or hybrid links experiencing instability. This unified view turns complex infrastructure into an understandable, measurable system rather than a black box.

Now, let's look at what you should observe and monitor in Infrastructure Performance:

- **Inter-AZ Round-Trip Time**: Early indicator of partial Availability Zone degradation.

- **Inter-region Latency Changes**: Detect backbone path shifts or emerging congestion.

- **Latency Deviation from Baseline**: Highlight subtle impairments across the AWS fabric.

- **Geographic or AZ-Specific Anomalies**: Isolate problems to specific zones within a region.

- **Correlation with Topology Events**: Tie changes in performance to routing or attachment updates.

Infrastructure Performance fills a critical gap in resilience observability: visibility into the health of the underlying AWS network fabric. Without it, teams rely on application-layer symptoms that arise only after the degradation becomes severe.

With it, they gain an early-warning system that detects conditions long before they manifest as customer impact.

A resilient architecture does not assume the backbone is perfect—it measures it. And when measured continuously, it provides the stability and foresight needed to operate multi-AZ and multi-region systems with confidence.

Control Plane Observability (CloudTrail + EventBridge)

Data-plane metrics and logs tell you how traffic behaves. But in cloud networking, traffic behavior is often the *result* of something that happened in the control plane: a route propagation event, a changed security group, a new VPC attachment, a modified load-balancer target group, or a DNS update. If these changes are not visible, the network appears unpredictable—traffic shifts without warning, failover behaves differently from design, and teams are left diagnosing symptoms without understanding causes.

This is why **control-plane observability is as essential as data-plane observability**. Without it, you know *what* changed but not *why*. With it, you can trace network behavior back to the exact configuration events that shaped it.

AWS exposes control-plane behavior primarily through **AWS CloudTrail**, which records every API call that modifies network configuration across services such as VPC, Route 53, Transit Gateway, Network Firewall, Cloud WAN, Direct Connect, and load balancers. CloudTrail events reveal who made a change, what was modified, when it occurred, and from where. For resilience engineering, the importance of this cannot be overstated: most network-impacting incidents begin with a configuration change—intentional or accidental.

But CloudTrail on its own is not enough. The volume of events makes it impractical to monitor manually. Instead, CloudTrail becomes powerful when paired with **Amazon EventBridge**, which listens for control-plane events and routes them into alarms, workflows, automation, or incident-management systems. Together, CloudTrail and EventBridge form the backbone of automated situational awareness: they surface configuration changes in real time and connect them to operational consequences.

For example, when a new route is added to a Transit Gateway route table, CloudTrail records the API call, and EventBridge can immediately trigger a verification workflow: validating that the prefix matches the intended architecture, confirming that propagation is completed across all attachments, or running reachability tests against expected paths. During a failover event, when Route 53 health checks change state, EventBridge can detect the transition and align alarms or dashboards accordingly. When a load balancer target group shifts from healthy to unhealthy, EventBridge can initiate synthetic checks or deploy additional capacity. This ability to react to control-plane changes is what turns observability into action.

Control-plane telemetry also plays a critical role in **post-incident analysis**. When operators examine why an AZ received too much traffic or why hybrid routing diverged, CloudTrail provides the timeline of events that led to the behavior: the exact moment a route was added or removed, a NACL updated, a DX VIF reconfigured, or a DNS weight adjusted. This reconstructs causality—a requirement for meaningful resilience improvement.

Now, let's look at what you should observe and monitor from the control plane:

- **Route Table Modifications**: Changes in VPC, Transit Gateway, and Cloud WAN routing directly influence path selection.

- **Security Group and NACL Updates**: Immediate operational impact on accept/reject patterns and Flow Log signals.

- **Load Balancer Target Registration/Removal**: Affects traffic distribution and failover consistency.

- **Direct Connect and VPN Configuration Changes**: Directly influence hybrid path preference and BGP behavior.

- **Route 53 Health Check and Record Updates**: Determine how DNS shifts during failover events.

- **Attachment State Changes** (TGW, Cloud WAN): Alter blast radius boundaries and routing reachability.

- **Automation-Driven Updates**: Infrastructure-as-code pipelines that modify networking must be tracked in real time.

EventBridge makes these events operationally useful by triggering alarms, synthetic tests, policy validation, or rollback workflows. When combined with CloudTrail, it creates a living timeline of changes, providing clarity in moments when the network behaves unexpectedly.

A resilient architecture is not defined solely by how well traffic flows—it is defined by how transparent, predictable, and observable its control plane is. CloudTrail and EventBridge give teams the visibility needed to ensure that every routing change, every

DNS update, every security modification, and every attachment transition is understood, monitored, and accounted for. In this way, the control plane becomes an active contributor to resilience, not a blind spot.

Athena and Search-Driven Log Analysis

Metrics tell you *that* something is happening. Flow Logs, DNS logs, and load balancer logs tell you *what* is happening. But during a resilience event, the most important question is almost always *why* it is happening—and that answer rarely lives in a single metric or a single log stream. It emerges from patterns across many different data sources: VPC Flow Logs, Transit Gateway Flow Logs, ELB access logs, Route 53 logs, NAT or IGW records, and application-level traces.

The only practical way to correlate these at scale is through **search-driven analysis**.

This is where **Amazon Athena** becomes a central part of the observability architecture. Athena turns vast volumes of logs—stored cheaply and durably in Amazon S3—into a queryable dataset with SQL semantics. It allows engineers to slice traffic across time, space, prefix, Availability Zone, application boundary, or routing domain in seconds. It transforms raw telemetry into investigative insight.

As we briefly mentioned at the beginning of this section, in resilience engineering, timing is everything. During an incident, teams must answer questions such as:

> Did traffic shift before or after the Route 53 failover?

> Did one AZ begin producing more retries than others?

> Which prefixes were dominant right before the Direct Connect flap?

> Which attachment saw the first Transit Gateway drops?

> Did a deployment correlate with a sudden increase in 5xx responses or reset connections?

Athena answers these questions directly because the logs it queries (Flow Logs, TGW Flow Logs, ELB logs, DNS query logs) contain the chronological footprints of the event. It becomes the investigative engine that ties together all other observability tools.

Athena also enables **long-term pattern analysis**, which is fundamental for resilience. Many failure modes are not singular events but gradual drifts: increasing cross-AZ chatter, rising NAT egress volumes, or slow growth of rejects on specific traffic paths. Dashboards often miss these patterns because they are not designed for exploratory analysis. Athena lets teams inspect months of logs to understand whether an event is truly exceptional or part of a broader trend.

Because Athena queries can be saved, parameterized, scheduled, or exported into dashboards, it provides both real-time triage capability and long-term resilience intelligence. Teams can correlate metrics and logs into a single narrative: the timeline of a failure, the propagation of routing changes, the behavior of DNS resolvers, and the flow patterns that shaped the incident.

Now, let's look at what you should observe and analyze through Athena:

- **Temporal Correlations**: Understand the sequence of events leading to impact.

- **Flow-Level Anomalies**: Spikes in retries, rejects, or short-duration flows signal early degradation.

- **AZ-Level Distinctions** :Identify which Availability Zone deviated first.

- **Attachment-Level Behavior**: Pinpoint problematic Transit Gateway attachments or hybrid prefixes.

- **Prefix-Specific Patterns**: Observe which CIDRs or services dominate traffic during instability.

- **DNS Shifts Over Time**: Map which resolvers adopted failover first and where inconsistencies existed.

- **Cross-service Correlations**: Relate TGW logs, Flow Logs, ELB logs, and DNS logs into a coherent timeline.

- **Long-Term Drift**: Detect slow, resilience-eroding patterns invisible to dashboards.

Athena is not a monitoring tool. It is the **analysis engine** that turns observability into understanding.

During an incident, it explains what the metrics cannot.

After an incident, it reveals the blind spots that need to be addressed.

Over time, it becomes the institutional memory of how the network behaves—not through assumption or anecdote, but through data.

In resilient architectures, Athena plays the same role as a flight recorder in aviation. It captures everything, makes it searchable, and ensures that failures are never mysterious. Instead, they become measurable, explainable, and ultimately preventable.

Event-Driven Automation and Alerting

Observability becomes operationally meaningful only when it can drive timely and correct action. Metrics, logs, and traces provide the picture, but resilience depends on what happens next: detecting deviation, raising awareness, and triggering automated safeguards before users experience impact. In AWS, this translation layer—the point where telemetry becomes behavior—is built through **CloudWatch Alarms**, **EventBridge rules**, and **automated responses** powered by Lambda, Systems Manager, or external incident-management systems.

The goal of resilience is not to generate alerts, but to ensure that the *right things* happen when the network bends. For example, when Direct Connect utilization climbs beyond the threshold at which failover must be considered, an alarm should not merely notify engineers but initiate a verification workflow: check tunnel health on Site-to-Site VPN, confirm that backup routes are being advertised, and validate that BGP sessions remain stable. When a Transit Gateway attachment begins accumulating drops, automation can immediately query Flow Logs to determine whether the issue is caused by missing routes or escalating traffic. When Internet Monitor detects a metro-specific impairment, EventBridge can signal the need for synthetic probes from that geography, or trigger a weighted DNS adjustment if the architecture supports it.

CloudWatch Alarms provide the continuity of detection. They evaluate telemetry from ELB, Direct Connect, VPN, Transit Gateway, Route 53 health checks, Network Monitor, and more. But alarms without context are noisy. Resilient systems combine CloudWatch's detection with EventBridge's routing logic. EventBridge can decide which alarms matter, at what intensity, and under which conditions. It can suppress transient states, correlate multiple signals before escalating, or require confirmation from synthetic tests before triggering a full failover. This transforms raw alarms into structured, intelligent incident signals.

Automation does not mean eliminating humans. It means ensuring humans are engaged at the right time, with the right information. EventBridge can enrich alerts with contextual data—recent route changes recorded in CloudTrail, current tunnel status, recent DNS failover patterns, or infrastructure latency deviations—and forward these to operators. Instead of scrambling to reconstruct context during an incident, responders receive a snapshot of the network's immediate state tied to the event that triggered the alert.

Event-driven automation is also critical for **chaos testing and failover rehearsal**. When a deliberate BGP flap is initiated for Direct Connect, EventBridge should detect the resulting control-plane events, confirm the expected behavior, and verify that fallback paths carry the predicted load. When a region is deliberately marked unhealthy for DNS testing, EventBridge observes the health check transition, performs integrity checks on downstream components, and confirms that resolvers shift traffic within expected windows. In this way, the automation layer becomes part of the resilience design, not an add-on.

The final role of event-driven observability is integration: combining CloudWatch, Network Manager, DNS logs, Flow Logs, and Internet Monitor signals into coherent operational workflows. A mature resilience posture uses EventBridge to link these systems so that no signal exists in isolation.

Now, let's look at what you should monitor and automate in this layer:

- **Alarm thresholds** aligned with resilience boundaries, not just performance expectations.

- **EventBridge rules** that correlate signals (e.g., TGW drops + Flow Log rejects + route-table updates).

- **Automation workflows** that validate fallback paths before a full failover occurs.

- **Suppression logic** for transient or expected states (e.g., deployment-induced latency spikes).

- **Contextual enrichment** of alerts using CloudTrail, Flow Logs, or DNS logs.

- **Failover exercises** are automated through event-driven triggers to validate control-plane behavior in real time.

A network with strong observability but no automation is transparent but fragile. A network with automation but poor observability is fast but blind.

Resilience emerges only when the two are designed together: when telemetry informs decisions, when decisions trigger safe automation, and when automation feeds back into observability to confirm that the system behaved as intended.

Let's summarize what we learned so far...

To bring the entire observability system together, it helps to visualize how raw signals transition into meaningful action. Observability is not just an inspection surface; it is the foundation of operational decision-making. Figure 8-3 illustrates this end-to-end flow: from telemetry sources within the network, to CloudWatch ingestion, to signal evaluation through alarms, to decision routing via EventBridge, and ultimately to human operators or automated response pathways.

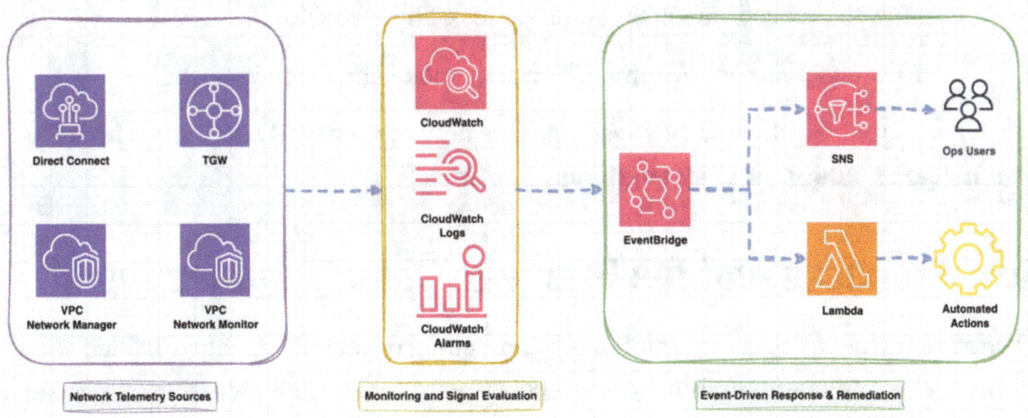

Figure 8-3. *Turning Observability into Action*

In Figure 8-3, network telemetry flows from AWS networking services (Transit Gateway, Direct Connect, VPC Network Manager, and VPC Network Monitor) into CloudWatch metrics and logs. CloudWatch Alarms feed Amazon EventBridge, which routes signals toward human operators (via SNS) or automated remediation workflows (via AWS Lambda). This event-driven control loop transforms raw telemetry into timely operational action, completing the observability–resilience feedback cycle.

The importance of this flow cannot be overstated. Without alarms, metrics remain passive. Without EventBridge, alarms remain isolated. Without automation, responses remain slow. And without operators, automation remains blind. Resilience emerges only when all these components work together: when a deviation in network conditions triggers a signal, when that signal is enriched and routed, and when the appropriate response—human or automated—is taken before the system crosses a resilience threshold.

This is the point where observability evolves from **visibility** into **capability**. Once a network can both see itself clearly and respond to what it sees, it becomes possible to test resilience in controlled conditions and to operate confidently through unexpected ones. That brings us naturally to the next section.

Now that we have built the observability fabric—metrics, logs, DNS behavior, routing drift, backbone telemetry, and event-driven action—we can explore how to turn these insights into operational practices:

- How to define meaningful alarms instead of noisy ones

- How to incorporate observability into resilience validations

- How observability becomes the backbone of chaos engineering

If observability is the nervous system of the network, **Part III focuses on how that system learns, adapts, and strengthens over time**.

Best Practices and the Bridge to Chaos Engineering

Observability becomes meaningful only when it informs action. A network filled with metrics, logs, and telemetry but lacking a clear operational model remains fragile: signals exist, but the system cannot interpret them, and operators cannot respond quickly enough to preserve resilience. The purpose of observability is not to instrument the network; it is to give the network the ability to understand itself—not in hindsight, but in real time. Best practices emerge from this principle: deliver the right signals, design the right alarms, build the right dashboards, and then test the architecture through controlled failure until every behavior is predictable.

In resilient systems, operational excellence depends on three layers working together: signal design, human interpretability, and system-level testing. If any layer is weak, the network becomes unpredictable. Too many signals and operators drown in noise; too few signals and early-warning indicators disappear. Dashboards can reflect metrics accurately yet fail to explain incidents if they are not aligned with the architecture's fault boundaries. And systems that are never tested under failure behave differently when failure arrives—even if the telemetry itself is perfect.

Strong observability is the prerequisite for meaningful chaos engineering, because chaos without insight is simply disruption. A fault injected into a system without proper telemetry produces confusion rather than confidence. Likewise, dashboards that do not map to resilience boundaries offer no interpretive value when components are intentionally stressed. Best practices, therefore, are not merely guidelines for what to monitor; they are guidelines for how to think about monitoring. They turn raw data into a coherent operational language.

A resilient network must do four things well: see early, interpret accurately, act consistently, and learn continuously. Best practices map to these four capabilities. They aim to reduce ambiguity, surface weak signals early, and unify the understanding of the system across engineering, SRE, network, and operations teams. The stronger the alignment across those teams, the faster the network can be restored to a steady state when something bends.

Designing Signals That Matter

The first best practice is to treat every metric, log, and health check as a deliberate design choice—not as a default. Signals must map cleanly to resilience boundaries: Availability Zones, routing domains, hybrid paths, private connectivity constructs, and application segments. A metric that is not tied to a boundary does not help explain failures; a log stream that cannot be correlated with others becomes noise. The craftsmanship of observability lies in selecting the signals that reveal deviation in each boundary before users notice.

Metrics like inter-AZ RTT, target availability, Transit Gateway drop counters, Direct Connect utilization, VPN tunnel health, and Internet Monitor deviations are useful precisely because they surface instability in the parts of the system that carry fault domains. They tell you how the system bends before it breaks. Best practices therefore start by identifying the resilience boundaries in the architecture and ensuring every boundary has at least one early-warning signal.

Equally important is understanding which signals *not* to use. Systems polluted with redundant metrics degrade operator confidence over time. A clear, sharp set of indicators—designed for resilience, not for exhaustiveness—produces better outcomes than hundreds of metrics that rarely matter.

Designing Alarms That Support Resilience

Alarms should reflect resilience thresholds, not performance thresholds. A system that fires alarms when latency spikes during a deployment, or when throughput exceeds nominal expectations, produces fatigue. A system that alarms when resilience boundaries are threatened—an AZ drifting, a route missing, a hybrid path saturating, DNS resolvers returning inconsistent answers—produces clarity.

Thresholds must be calibrated to the architecture, not to arbitrary values. For example, 80–90% utilization for Direct Connect is a resilience threshold, not a performance one; beyond that point, hybrid failover cannot be trusted. A Transit Gateway NoRouteDropCount rising is not a performance signal but a resilience signal: it indicates routing propagation drift. Internet Monitor availability drops are resilience signals because they reflect real user impact before the application is aware.

Best practice is to build alarms that encode intention: *alert me when the system no longer behaves according to design.* This reduces noise and strengthens operator confidence in the alarm surface.

Dashboards That Reflect How Systems Fail

Dashboards must align with failure modes, not services. Grouping metrics by "Direct Connect," "Transit Gateway," or "Load Balancer" is visually tidy but operationally useless during an incident. A failure does not ask which service owns which metric; it asks which boundary is being violated.

Best practice is to structure dashboards by **resilience question**, such as:

- What is the health of each Availability Zone?

- How is cross-zone communication behaving?

- Are hybrid paths stable and ready to receive traffic?

- Are DNS failover decisions consistent across resolvers?

- Are routing domains converged and consistent?

- What does the external internet see right now?

- Which components are drifting away from baseline?

Dashboards built this way provide interpretive power—the ability to answer *why*, not just *what*, during an incident.

Dashboards should also show trend lines, not just current values. A single data point often misleads; a 30-minute view shows where instability began and whether it is accelerating or decaying. Resilience depends on understanding movement, not snapshots.

Integrating Observability with RPO, RTO, and HA Objectives

Every metric, alarm, dashboard, and signal described in this chapter ultimately serves a single purpose: to ensure the system remains within the Recovery Point Objective (RPO), the Recovery Time Objective (RTO), and the high-availability commitments defined for the workload. Observability is not separate from resilience policy—it is the mechanism that enforces it. A system cannot meet a 30-second RTO if it cannot detect failure within seconds. A system cannot preserve a strict RPO if replication lag or cross-AZ jitter is invisible. And a system cannot maintain its HA posture if DNS, load balancing, and routing behavior cannot be observed and validated continuously.

This is why observability must be aligned directly to resilience objectives: the thresholds you alarm on, the dashboards you design, and the chaos experiments you perform must reflect the RPO/RTO boundaries you expect the system to respect. When RPO, RTO, and HA policies evolve—and they often do—the observability system must evolve with them. In a mature architecture, these are not separate processes; they form a continuous loop in which resilience policy defines what must be observed, observability reveals how the system behaves, and that behavior informs how resilience policy should evolve. Over time, the architecture becomes self-correcting: each cycle tightens the alignment between what the system promises and what it can reliably deliver.

Operational resilience checklist: Monitoring and observability at the network layer

Before moving on, the following checklist condenses the observability principles from this section into practical checks you should be able to validate in any resilient network architecture.

- **Define objectives first**

  Document SLOs and resilience targets (**RTO/RPO**) and what "impact" means (global vs. AZ vs. customer-segment).

- **Select a small set of detection signals (monitoring)**

  Alarm on symptoms that indicate approaching impact: error rate, latency, saturation, packet loss/jitter, tunnel/link state, and quota headroom.

- **Ensure dimensioned telemetry (observability)**

  Every critical signal must be explorable by **Region/AZ**, service/API, customer segment, deployment/config change, and (where relevant) **network path**.

- **Cover data plane and control plane**

  Observe traffic reality (flows, load balancer logs, DNS behavior) *and* configuration/change reality (routing, attachments, policy updates).

- **Include external/user-path visibility**

  Validate internal health with synthetics and internet-path signals; detect metro/ASN-specific impairments.

- **Correlate signals across sources**

  Use consistent identifiers (trace/request IDs, deployment IDs, resource IDs) so metrics ↔ logs ↔ traces ↔ flow records can explain the same incident.

- **Design alerts with intent and actions**

  Each alarm maps to a resilience boundary and has a clear response (notify, ticket, automate, failover, roll back).

- **Validate continuously**

  Run regular drills (AZ impairment, hybrid failover, DNS failover, path degradation) and confirm observability reduces **MTTD/MTTR** and produces evidence.

If these checks cannot be satisfied, the system may be monitored—but it will not be reliably observable under resilience stress.

Building a Feedback Loop

The last best practice I want to share is to treat observability, alarms, dashboards, and chaos experiments as a continuous feedback loop. After all, resilience is not a 1-day job or a tick of a box; it's a continuous evolution, interaction, and improvement. Incidents reveal telemetry gaps; telemetry gaps guide dashboard redesign; dashboard redesign shapes alarm tuning; alarm tuning improves chaos experiments; chaos experiments strengthen resilience.

A mature architecture does not treat observability as a one-time setup. It evolves it—improving signal quality, reducing noise, refining fault boundaries, clarifying topology, and continuously validating behavior. Over time, the network develops something akin to intuition: it knows how it should behave, recognizes when it deviates, and guides operators toward the right corrective action.

Let's now learn how to test, inject faults in a controlled manner, and learn from those data points. In the next section of this chapter, we will break things to understand how they work and react under stress, learn, and repeat, in a continuous circle.

Section 8.2: Chaos Engineering (Resilience Testing): Validating Resilience Before Disaster Hits

Resilience in cloud systems is measured not by how they behave when everything is healthy, but by how they operate when conditions deteriorate. Architectural diagrams, runbooks, and design documents describe an *intention*; resilience testing verifies the *reality*. No matter how carefully a workload is designed, it is impossible to predict with certainty how complex dependencies, distributed routing, multi-AZ paths, and global traffic flows will behave until the system is placed under real stress. Resilience testing closes this gap between theory and execution.

Modern workloads—especially those serving regulated industries or critical user journeys—sometimes rely on assumptions: this region will fail over to another; this AZ can be lost without user impact; this Direct Connect link will fail gracefully; this dependency can tolerate latency increases. These assumptions are embedded in architecture decisions, capacity planning, and operational playbooks. But unless they are tested, they remain nothing more than optimistic expectations. Resilience testing exists to convert those expectations into verified knowledge.

The first driver is the gap between architectural intent and operational reality. The second is complexity—and it is both technical and human. Modern architectures are layered systems where DNS behavior varies by geography, routing converges asynchronously, hybrid connectivity shifts based on BGP attributes, and client experience depends on ISPs, edges, and the global internet. No engineer can model this end-to-end from individual components alone. Resilience also depends on people:

operators must interpret signals correctly, follow clear runbooks, and execute failover steps with confidence under pressure. Resilience testing is the mechanism that exercises both the system and the organization, exposing hidden dependencies and unclear ownership and alerting dashboards that fail when time matters.

Resilience testing is also rapidly becoming a compliance requirement. Regulators in financial services, healthcare, and critical infrastructure demand evidence that organisations can withstand specific failure scenarios. It is not sufficient to state that a workload is multi-AZ or multi-region; organisations must demonstrate that failover occurs within the defined RTO, that data exposure is within the RPO, and that continuity of critical services can be proven through testing artifacts. In this context, resilience testing becomes a measurable control—not an optional engineering activity.

Perhaps the most important reason resilience testing matters is that failure rarely happens cleanly. Systems seldom experience a complete region drop or a hard AZ outage. More often they encounter partial impairment—rising latency in one Availability Zone, throttling or congestion on a Direct Connect path, an ISP issue affecting only certain geographies, a dependency that slows unpredictably, or a delayed Route 53 health-check transition. These "brownouts" create ambiguous signals, uneven user impact, and inconsistent failover behavior. Only testing these conditions reveals how gracefully—or unpredictably—the system behaves under imperfect circumstances.

Resilience testing bridges directly to observability. In Section 8.1, we built the observational foundation: metrics, logs, DNS decisions, network behavior, and backbone performance. Resilience tests validate whether those signals activate at the correct time, whether dashboards provide clarity during stress events, and whether alarms trigger with sufficient precision to support RTO/RPO. Observability defines what the system can see; resilience testing verifies whether what it sees is correct.

Ultimately, resilience testing matters because architecture alone does not guarantee resilience, verification does.

A system is only as resilient as the behavior that has been *demonstrated*, measured, documented, and repeated under controlled failure.

Foundations of Resilience Testing

Resilience testing or Chaos Engineering, is not random experimentation. It is a disciplined engineering practice grounded in clear definitions, safety boundaries, and measurable expectations. Before designing any experiment, the system must have a shared understanding of what "normal" looks like, what "failure" means, and how the architecture is expected to behave under stress. These foundations ensure that tests are controlled, repeatable, and meaningful rather than chaotic.

Resilience testing begins with the concept of **steady state**—the baseline operating condition of a workload when nothing is failing. Steady state is not defined by lack of errors; every system produces some background noise. Instead, steady state means that a workload is functioning within its expected parameters: acceptable latency ranges, predictable error rates, stable throughput, replication lag within tolerance, consistent behavior across Availability Zones, and alignment to RPO and RTO targets. Without a clearly defined steady state, it is impossible to determine whether a resilience test succeeds or fails.

From there, resilience testing moves to **hypothesis formulation**. Every test should begin with a clear, falsifiable statement that describes what you believe will happen when a fault occurs. For example, "If cross-AZ connectivity is disrupted, request latency remains under 150 ms and the workload continues serving traffic without errors." Or: "If we remove 40% of compute capacity, the system scales up to compensate within eight minutes." A hypothesis framed in steady-state terms provides the criteria for evaluating behavior and eliminates subjective interpretation during the experiment.

Another foundational principle is **safety**. Injecting faults into distributed systems carries inherent risk, and resilience engineering depends on controlling this risk. Safety mechanisms begin with **blast radius**—the scope of the experiment. Early-stage tests should target tightly confined components: a single node group, a single AZ, or a narrow slice of traffic. Larger or more destructive tests should only follow once smaller ones are validated. Safety also includes **stop conditions**, automated triggers— usually CloudWatch alarms—that immediately halt an experiment when a test exceeds predefined impact thresholds such as user error rates, latency, CPU saturation, or backlog growth.

Safety also means respecting the boundaries of production. Not all tests belong in production environments, particularly for immature workloads or high-risk failure modes. Many foundational tests run in staging or pre-production environments, where the blast radius is inherently limited. As the organization matures, some specific faults—unhealthy target removal, container kills, dependency throttling—may be safely promoted into production with strict traffic controls and automated rollbacks.

A foundational concept often overlooked is **dependency classification**. Modern workloads rely on dozens of internal and external systems: identity providers, payment processors, logging pipelines, analytics layers, cross-region services, shared databases, and third-party APIs. Many outages occur not because the workload itself failed, but because an upstream dependency degraded. Foundations for resilience testing include mapping these dependencies, categorizing them by criticality, and identifying which can be stress-tested directly and which must be simulated through controlled impairments.

Networking has its own foundational considerations. Distributed systems rely on DNS routing, global traffic steering, BGP propagation, cross-AZ communication, and backbone stability. These behaviors cannot be assumed; they must be tested. Foundational network testing requires identifying resilience boundaries such as AZs, subnets, routing domains, hybrid paths (Direct Connect and VPN), and edge networks. These boundaries determine the fault domains that matter and where tests should be focused.

Above all, resilience foundations must explicitly align with **RPO, RTO, and high-availability commitments**. These objectives are not abstract business numbers; they are engineering requirements. If a system has a 15-minute RTO, resilience tests must demonstrate that failover can complete within that window. If the RPO is seconds, tests must verify that data divergence stays within acceptable limits during connectivity disruption. If a service is advertised as multi-AZ, resilience tests must validate that loss of one AZ does not violate availability targets. Foundations connect resilience policy directly to engineering behavior.

Finally, resilience testing relies on a stable **observability baseline**. Section 8.1 outlined the observability fabric that makes fault injection meaningful. Without reliable metrics, logs, DNS visibility, and network telemetry, resilience tests cannot be evaluated objectively. Observability provides the instrumentation; resilience testing provides the experiments; together they form a feedback system that reveals how the architecture behaves under real-world stress.

With these foundations—steady state, hypotheses, safety, blast radius, dependency awareness, network boundaries, resilience objective alignment, and observability—you can design experiments that are not only safe and insightful, but transformative. They replace architectural assumptions with verified understanding and create the conditions for continuous improvement.

Types of Resilience Tests

Resilience testing is not a single technique but a spectrum of approaches, each serving a different purpose. Some tests are designed to reveal the unknown, others to validate the expected, and others to build organizational readiness. A well-rounded resilience program uses all of them, gradually moving from exploratory to deterministic, and from manual to automated. This progression strengthens confidence: in the architecture, in the runbooks, in the operators, and in the system's ability to maintain continuity when stress arrives unexpectedly.

Table 8-1 summarizes the major categories of resilience testing, clarifying their intent, scope, and the type of evidence they produce.

Table 8-1. *Taxonomy of Resilience Testing Approaches*

Test Type	Primary Goal	Typical Blast Radius	Key Outputs
Learning Tests	Discover unknown behaviours, hidden dependencies, and unexpected failure modes	Small and tightly scoped (single AZ slice, limited traffic, non-critical dependency)	New insights, uncovered dependencies, observability gaps, refined hypotheses
Rehearsals (Procedural)	Validate human response, runbooks, decision-making, and ownership under stress	Minimal or simulated technical impact	Team readiness assessment, runbook accuracy, ownership clarity, response-time measurements
Experiments (Hypothesis-Driven)	Validate expected resilience behaviors against a defined steady state	Controlled and explicit (single AZ impairment, defined capacity reduction, specific network path degradation)	Measured outcomes vs hypothesis, quantified MTTD/MTTR, confidence in architectural assumptions
Validation Tests	Demonstrate compliance with RTO, RPO, and HA commitments	Medium to large (full AZ loss, primary path withdrawal, controlled Regional isolation)	Evidence artefacts, recovery timelines, RTO/RPO verification, audit-ready documentation
Game Days	Exercise the full socio-technical system using realistic failure scenarios	Broad but controlled (multi-component, cross-team, staged failures)	End-to-end incident narratives, systemic weaknesses, cross-team improvements
Continuous Fault Injection	Ensure resilience does not erode as systems evolve	Very small, recurring (micro-failures, low-percentage resource or traffic impact)	Continuous assurance, early regression detection, resilience-drift prevention

Let's now explore each category in more detail.

Learning Tests—Discovering the Unknown

Learning tests are exploratory by nature. They are designed to uncover behaviors you did not predict, dependencies you did not document, and failure modes you did not expect. Their objective is not to confirm a hypothesis but to generate insight.

A learning test might inject 20% packet loss into instances within a single Availability Zone, throttle a third-party dependency, or introduce latency and packet loss **on selected EC2 instances (or their network interfaces)** to observe how **Transit Gateway–routed flows behave from the workload's perspective** under degradation. These tests often reveal surprising behaviors: retries happening earlier than expected, uneven DNS decisions, cross-AZ traffic unexpectedly increasing, or hidden calls traveling to another region.

Learning tests are most valuable early in the resilience journey because they expand your understanding of the workload's behavior under degradation. They are also the tests most likely to expose missing observability, incomplete runbooks, or misaligned RPO/RTO assumptions.

Rehearsals—Training People and Validating Process

Rehearsals exercise the *human* side of resilience. They simulate an incident and walk operators through the required steps: assessing impact, reviewing dashboards, executing a runbook, making routing or DNS changes, promoting a secondary region, or validating fallback paths.

Unlike learning tests, rehearsals need not inject faults. Their purpose is to validate

- Team coordination

- Decision-making under pressure

- Clarity of ownership

- Accuracy of runbooks

- Readiness to meet RTO

A resilience rehearsal might simulate a regional isolation event: teams declare the region impaired, begin executing failover steps, shift traffic via DNS or Global Accelerator, verify that capacity in the secondary region is sufficient, and measure the timeline from detection to restoration of service.

In networking, rehearsals can test human readiness for

- Direct Connect path failover procedures

- routing updates during a hybrid outage

- Transit Gateway attachment isolation

- DNS failover decisions when Route 53 transitions health checks

Rehearsals answer a crucial question: *Even if the architecture is sound, can the organization execute when it matters?*

Before promoting resilience testing into higher blast radius (or production), validate that the organization can execute predictably under pressure—not just that the architecture can fail over.

The checklist below provides a lightweight way to assess runbook quality and team readiness.

Operational checklist: Runbook and team readiness validation

- Clear trigger criteria

  Define what constitutes "initiate failover" (SLO breach, regional impairment, % customers impacted) and who has authority to declare it.

- Single owner and escalation path

  Identify incident commander, primary/secondary responders, and escalation contacts (network, app, database, security, third parties).

- Step-by-step runbook with verification and rollback gates

  Each step includes (1) action, (2) expected outcome, (3) how to verify, and (4) rollback/abort path.

- Resilience objectives embedded in the runbook

  Runbook explicitly references RTO/RPO and includes "time-to-complete" checkpoints (e.g., "by T+5 minutes traffic must be stabilizing").

- Pre-flight readiness checks

  Confirm secondary Region/AZ capacity, quotas, replication status, DNS/traffic policy status, and backup path health (DX/VPN).

- Observability and dashboards are incident-ready

  A defined "incident dashboard" exists and answers: affected AZ/Region, error rate, latency, dependency health, replication lag, traffic shift status.

- Alarms and stop conditions are tested

  Confirm alarms fire with the right sensitivity and that automated stop conditions prevent runaway experiments or unsafe actions.

- Communication plan and stakeholder updates

  Templates exist for internal updates, customer comms, and regulatory/compliance reporting when relevant.

- Post-exercise review is mandatory

  Every rehearsal produces: timeline, what worked/failed, runbook changes, alarm/dashboard changes, and owners with due dates.

This checklist reflects broader industry resilience best practices that emphasize procedural readiness and repeatable operational behaviors. If these checks cannot be met, treat the rehearsal as a discovery exercise and improve runbooks and ownership boundaries before increasing blast radius.

Experiments—Hypothesis-Driven Fault Injection

Experiments are more structured. You begin with a defined steady state and a concrete, testable hypothesis. For example:

- "If 40% of worker nodes are terminated, the workload should recover its baseline throughput within eight minutes."

- "If the primary Region is isolated from the backup Region, all business-critical transactions continue to operate within the primary Region."

- "If the Direct Connect primary path is withdrawn, traffic shifts to VPN within 60 seconds and user latency remains below 200 ms."

Experiments validate specific resilience characteristics and quantify how the system responds to stress. Unlike learning tests, the outcome is either aligned with the hypothesis or not. This repeatability makes experiments ideal for maturing workloads and for verifying previously identified failure modes.

AWS Fault Injection Service (FIS) is central here. It provides structured ways to inject failures in a controlled manner such as

- Instance terminations (EC2, ASG-managed capacity)

- CPU or memory saturation on compute resources

- Dependency throttling via application or OS-level controls

- Network latency or packet loss injected on customer-owned ENIs within a single AZ

- Network degradation across AZs by impairing resources participating in cross-AZ traffic

- Availability Zone impact using **AWS-provided scenarios** (e.g., **Availability Zone power interruption**), which impair **your resources in a selected AZ** rather than AWS-managed control planes

- Cross-region dependency impact simulated by blocking or degrading connectivity at the workload layer

These actions deliberately operate at the customer resource boundary—such as EC2 instances and their network interfaces—allowing teams to observe resilience behavior without attempting to impair AWS-managed networking or control planes.

Taken together, these experiments help answer a fundamental question:

Does the architecture behave the way designers expect under this specific fault?

Validation Tests—Proving That Resilience Guarantees Hold

Validation tests are deterministic and repeatable, and they directly map to resilience objectives such as RPO, RTO, and HA commitments. These tests are not exploratory; they confirm whether the system meets contractual or regulatory requirements.

Examples in the networking domain include:

- Simulating the loss of a complete Availability Zone and confirming that the workload meets its RTO without data loss beyond RPO.

- Triggering a planned DNS failover and validating that resolvers globally adopt the new endpoint within expected TTL boundaries.

- Interrupting connectivity to the primary datastore and verifying that replica promotion remains within the defined recovery window.

- Removing a Direct Connect BGP advertisement **at the hybrid edge (customer router)** and measuring how quickly traffic shifts to Site-to-Site VPN.

Validation tests become part of a predictable testing cadence—quarterly, monthly, or aligned with major releases. They form the evidentiary basis for regulated organisations to prove operational continuity, and they are often required for audits or resilience attestation.

Game Days—Realistic, End-to-End Exercises

Game days simulate real-world failures using realistic scenarios. They combine

- Technical stress

- Observational diagnosis

- Team communication

- Procedural execution

- Coordinated recovery

Unlike rehearsals (which are procedural) or experiments (which are controlled), game days recreate conditions as close to a real incident as possible. They may involve

- Multi-AZ traffic imbalance

- Partial cloud service degradation

- Dependent service slowdown

- Regional control-plane impairment

- A hybrid path flap affecting Direct Connect

Game days test the entire socio-technical system—humans, dashboards, alarms, processes, automation, and architecture—under real pressure. They reveal how the system behaves holistically, and they generate high-fidelity lessons.

Continuous Fault Injection—Making Resilience Part of Daily Life

Once a system matures, certain tests can be promoted from periodic events to continuous injection. This practice introduces small, controlled failures at regular intervals to ensure resilience remains intact as the architecture evolves.

Examples include:

- terminating a small percentage of stateless instances daily

- introducing brief latency on a non-critical dependency path weekly

- injecting packet loss on a backup hybrid link

- or temporarily isolating a microservice to test retry logic

Continuous injection is not about finding catastrophic failures; it is about guaranteeing that resilience remains an active property of the workload. It ensures that changes in deployments, dependencies, infrastructure, or scale do not silently erode the architecture's ability to operate during stress.

Continuous injection answers the question:

Does the system stay resilient every day, not just on the day we test it?

Before moving from test taxonomy into concrete experiment design, it is important to highlight common anti-patterns that undermine the effectiveness and safety of resilience testing.

Anti-Patterns in Resilience Testing

Not all resilience testing improves resilience. Certain common patterns give teams a false sense of confidence while leaving critical failure modes untested. The following anti-patterns frequently appear in immature or compliance-driven testing programs and should be avoided.

- **Testing only "hard" failures**

  Focusing exclusively on full Availability Zone or region outages ignores the most common real-world incidents: partial degradation. Latency spikes, packet loss, uneven routing, slow dependency responses, or delayed convergence often cause more user impact than clean outages. Resilience testing must include brownouts, not just blackouts.

- **Running tests without explicit stop conditions**

  Experiments that lack automated stop conditions risk escalating into real incidents. Every fault injection must define guardrails—typically CloudWatch alarms—that immediately halt the experiment when error rates, latency, backlog growth, or other safety thresholds are exceeded.

- **Testing without synthetic or controlled load**

  Running experiments against unpredictable organic traffic makes outcomes difficult to interpret. Without a stable traffic signal, it becomes impossible to distinguish failure-induced behavior from normal variation. Synthetic load provides a consistent baseline that allows routing shifts, retries, latency changes, and recovery timelines to be measured reliably.

- **Treating chaos tests as one-off events**

  A single successful test does not prove resilience. Architectures drift as code, dependencies, scale, and traffic patterns change. Resilience testing must be repeatable and continuous, not a one-time validation performed before audits or major launches.

- **Ignoring the human and process dimension**

  Testing infrastructure without validating runbooks, ownership, escalation paths, and communication flows leaves the organization unprepared for real incidents. Resilience is a socio-technical property; tests that exclude people and process validate only half the system.

- **Over-scoping experiments too early**

  Large blast-radius tests executed before smaller failures are understood increase risk without increasing insight. Effective programs progress deliberately: from narrow, low-risk faults to broader, system-level scenarios as confidence grows.

Avoiding these anti-patterns ensures that resilience testing produces actionable insight rather than false assurance, and that experiments strengthen both the architecture and the organization operating it. With these pitfalls in mind, we can now focus on how to design resilience experiments that are safe, measurable, and aligned with recovery objectives.

Designing and Running Experiments

Designing a resilience experiment begins long before any fault is injected. It starts with establishing what "normal" actually looks like. Every workload has a baseline rhythm—typical latencies, predictable throughput, healthy target distributions, replication lag that stays comfortably within tolerance, and routing behavior that remains stable across Availability Zones. This is the workload's **steady state**. Without articulating steady state in measurable terms, there is no meaningful way to determine whether a system remains resilient or quietly slips outside its recovery objectives when stressed.

Once steady state is known, you can articulate a **hypothesis**. A well-formed hypothesis transforms an experiment from curiosity into engineering. It expresses, in concrete terms, what you expect to happen when a fault is introduced. If an Availability Zone loses half its capacity, will the workload maintain its latency envelopes? If a Direct Connect circuit disappears, will traffic shift to VPN within seconds without violating user-facing SLOs? If cross-region connectivity is interrupted, will the primary region continue to operate independently rather than failing due to hidden dependencies? A hypothesis provides both direction and accountability: it makes the experiment measurable.

With a steady state and hypothesis defined, the next step is understanding **which failure mode you want to study**. Failures come in many forms—application failures, infrastructure degradation, dependency slowness, control-plane instability, or, most subtly, network impairments such as jitter in a single Availability Zone or inconsistent DNS resolver behavior during a failover. Each failure mode tells a different story, affects different components, and exposes different assumptions. The key is to choose a failure that teaches something meaningful about your architecture—especially about the boundaries where resilience is expected to hold.

Good experiments are not reckless; they are guided by carefully defined **safety boundaries**. In resilience engineering, safety begins with the **blast radius**—the scope of the experiment and how much of the system it is allowed to touch. Early tests should be as small as possible: a single node, a single subnet, or a narrow slice of traffic. As confidence grows, the blast radius can expand to include full Availability Zones or even entire regions, but only after earlier, smaller tests behave predictably. Safety also comes from automated **stop conditions**, usually CloudWatch alarms, that immediately halt an experiment if the system drifts outside acceptable impact thresholds. This ensures that tests are daring in intent but conservative in effect.

605

None of this matters, however, without visibility. **Observability** is the nervous system of resilience testing, and Section 8.1 laid the foundation for it. Before a single packet is dropped or a single node is terminated, you must confirm that you can see the system clearly: flow logs must reveal traffic behavior across subnets and Availability Zones; load balancers must surface target health and routing imbalance; DNS logs must expose resolver decisions; Direct Connect and VPN metrics must show hybrid path readiness; and inter-region or inter-AZ latency must be measurable, not assumed. Without this instrumentation, faults become indistinguishable from noise, and experiments become uninformative.

One powerful technique used in resilience experiments is the use of synthetic load. Synthetic load plays a crucial role in resilience experiments because it provides a predictable, repeatable source of traffic that is unaffected by user behavior. Real user traffic fluctuates—by geography, time of day, and client-side conditions—making it difficult to determine whether observed deviations during a fault are caused by the failure itself or simply by natural traffic variation. Synthetic load eliminates this ambiguity. By driving known request patterns at controlled rates, teams can observe how the network and application respond under precise conditions: how traffic redistributes across Availability Zones, how latency curves shift during packet loss or jitter, how retries escalate under partial failures, and how hybrid paths behave when primary routes are impaired.

Synthetic load also enables safe experimentation in environments where real user traffic cannot be risked, such as staging, pre-production, or shadow environments that mirror production but operate independently. When used alongside AWS Fault Injection Service, synthetic load becomes a powerful diagnostic tool: it highlights imbalance early, exposes routing inconsistencies, and reveals subtle network brownouts that would otherwise be invisible behind organic user behavior. In networking resilience tests— Direct Connect withdrawal, Transit Gateway route changes, DNS failover, or AZ-specific impairments—synthetic load often provides the clearest, most interpretable signal of how the architecture truly behaves.

When all these elements are in place—steady state, hypothesis, failure mode, safety boundaries, and observability—you are ready to run the experiment. This is where AWS Fault Injection Service (FIS) brings structure to the process. FIS allows you to define exactly which resources you will impair, how the fault will unfold, how long it will last, and under what conditions it must stop. It transforms chaos into choreography: a sequence of controlled actions executed with precision, backed by automated guardrails.

You can inject packet loss into a single AZ, throttle a critical dependency, disrupt cross-region communication, or simulate hybrid-path impact by degrading customer-owned components while validating that routing policies fail over as expected—all without improvisation, all with clear recovery paths.

During the experiment, the most important skill is **observation**. You compare real-time behavior to your defined steady state and hypothesis. Do latencies rise evenly or unevenly? Does traffic redistribute smoothly across AZs, or does one zone become overloaded? Do DNS resolvers converge consistently or drift unpredictably? Does hybrid traffic shift promptly when a DX path is impaired? Do retries surge? Do errors cluster? Does replication lag grow faster than your RPO allows? This is where the architecture reveals its truth—not in diagrams or intentions, but in behavior.

Finally, every experiment must end with a **coherent narrative**. You document what happened, why it happened, and how it compares to the hypothesis. A successful experiment is not one that "passes," but one that produces insight—whether that insight is that the architecture is working as intended, that thresholds must be tuned, that observability was insufficient, or that resilience objectives cannot be met without redesign. The value of the test lies in what it teaches, not in whether it validates an assumption.

The difference between theoretical resilience and operational resilience becomes clear when experiments are tied directly to recovery objectives.

Example Resilience Experiments Tied to RTO and RPO

The following examples illustrate how resilience experiments translate directly into measurable RTO and RPO validation, turning abstract objectives into observable behavior.

Example 1: Availability Zone Degradation and RTO Validation

- **Resilience objective:**

  RTO $\leq$ 5 minutes for partial AZ impairment

- **Fault injected:**

  Introduce network latency and packet loss on EC2 instances in a single Availability Zone using AWS Fault Injection Service.

- **Expected behavior:**

  Load balancers reduce traffic to impaired targets, traffic redistributes to healthy AZs, and error rates remain within tolerance.

- **Measured outcome:**

  Time from first error spike to traffic stabilization across healthy AZs is 2 minutes and 40 seconds.

- **Result:**

  RTO objective met. Observability confirms controlled failover without user-visible outage.

Example 2: Hybrid Connectivity Failure and RPO Validation

- **Resilience objective:**

  RPO $\leq$ 30 seconds during hybrid connectivity disruption

- **Fault injected:**

  Withdraw primary Direct Connect routes at the hybrid edge (customer router) and observe failover to Site-to-Site VPN.

- **Expected behavior:**

  Replication continues over backup connectivity without exceeding acceptable lag.

- **Measured outcome:**

  Replication lag peaks at 18 seconds before stabilizing.

- **Result:**

  RPO objective met. Data integrity preserved under degraded network conditions.

Example 3: Cross-Region Isolation and Combined RTO/RPO Validation

- **Resilience objective:**

  RTO $\leq$ 15 minutes, RPO $\leq$ 60 seconds for regional isolation

- **Fault injected:**

  Block cross-region connectivity at the workload layer while maintaining intra-region operation.

- **Expected behavior:**

  Primary region continues serving traffic independently; secondary
  region remains consistent and ready for promotion.

- **Measured outcome:**

  No user-visible impact in primary region; secondary region remains
  within 45 seconds of replication lag.

- **Result:**

  Both RTO and RPO objectives met. Disaster recovery assumptions
  validated under controlled isolation.

Designing and running experiments is therefore not an act of chaos; it is an act of
discipline. It is the structured process through which assumptions become knowledge,
blind spots become visible, and resilience evolves from an architectural aspiration into
a demonstrated property of the system. Having established how resilience experiments
translate into measurable recovery outcomes, the next step is to examine how these
experiments are implemented safely and repeatably using AWS-native tooling.

Implementing Resilience Testing on AWS

Resilience testing becomes most powerful when it moves from concept to practice,
and the AWS ecosystem provides the tooling needed to run controlled, repeatable,
and safe experiments across both application and network layers. What distinguishes
modern cloud resilience testing from traditional failure drills is the ability to inject
faults intentionally, observe system behavior in real time, and recover predictably—all
within a structured operational framework. AWS Fault Injection Service (FIS) is at the
center of this capability, but it is only one part of a broader ecosystem that includes
observability systems, orchestration engines, configuration management tools, and
safety mechanisms that ensure tests remain controlled and reversible.

The fundamental strength of AWS's resilience testing model lies in its **repeatability**.
A test that requires manual interaction or ad hoc infrastructure changes is not a
resilience test—it is a one-off event. True resilience testing requires the ability to run
the same experiment many times, under varying conditions, while keeping the blast
radius consistent and ensuring that safety controls are enforced automatically. AWS FIS
provides exactly this framework: it lets teams define what should fail, how it should fail,
and how the system must react.

At its core, a FIS experiment is a declarative document. It specifies which resources will be impaired, the sequence in which those impairments occur, the duration of each fault, and the conditions under which the test must stop. This structure ensures that the experiment expresses intent rather than improvisation. For example, an experiment designed to test cross-AZ resilience might terminate a percentage of EC2 instances in a single Availability Zone, inject network latency on the remaining nodes, and observe whether the load balancer correctly shifts traffic to healthy AZs. Another experiment might throttle I/O on a database volume to explore how upstream services behave when persistence slows. These experiments unfold predictably because they are defined predictably.

Where resilience testing becomes deeper—especially in networking—is in the ability to inject faults into **customer-owned AWS resources** (e.g., **EC2 instances and their network interfaces**) and observe how the workload behaves when it experiences degraded network conditions. This is where FIS can emulate impairments such as **packet loss, jitter, or added latency** as experienced by the workload, making routing decisions, retries, and failover behavior visible under stress.

Many of the most consequential resilience issues arise from conditions that never trigger a complete outage: a degraded cross-AZ link, inconsistent connectivity in a single subnet, a routing propagation delay in a Transit Gateway, or a brief period where a Direct Connect path shifts traffic unevenly. These partial failures are the most valuable to test, because they represent the majority of real-world incidents.

Through network impairment actions applied to EC2 instances and their network interfaces, FIS allows teams to model these scenarios safely, generating the conditions under which routing decisions, retries, and failover behavior become visible.

When AWS Fault Injection Service Is Not the Right Tool

AWS Fault Injection Service is designed to inject controlled faults **only within the boundary of customer-owned AWS resources**. It is intentionally scoped, and there are important scenarios where FIS is not the appropriate mechanism.

AWS FIS should not be used when:

- **The failure involves AWS-managed control planes**

  Control planes for services such as Route 53, AWS Global Accelerator, Transit Gateway routing propagation, Elastic Load Balancing, or managed service internals cannot be directly impaired. These behaviors must be validated through observation, traffic shifting, simulations, or game-day exercises rather than fault injection.

- **The dependency is external or third-party**

  SaaS providers, payment gateways, identity services, external APIs, and upstream internet networks cannot be disrupted by FIS. In these cases, failure must be simulated from the workload side (e.g., by throttling, mocking, or isolating the dependency), not by attempting to impair the provider itself.

- **The test depends on ISP, DNS resolver, or last-mile behavior**

  DNS resolver caching, ISP routing decisions, mobile networks, and internet edge behavior fall outside the control boundary of FIS. These scenarios require synthetic clients, traffic shaping, or external testing platforms.

- **The workload lacks sufficient observability or safety guardrails**

  Without reliable metrics, alarms, and automated stop conditions, fault injection becomes unsafe and uninformative. Observability maturity must precede the use of FIS.

AWS FIS excels at testing **how your architecture responds** to controlled stress. It complements—but does not replace—simulations, game days, traffic-management exercises, or dependency modelling where direct fault injection is not possible. Within these boundaries, effective resilience testing depends on how fault injection is combined with observability and orchestration to produce interpretable, actionable outcomes.

While FIS controls the fault, AWS **CloudWatch** and **X-Ray** provide the sensory system required to interpret it. During a test, observability must be real-time, complete, and correlated. Latency spikes, jitter, connection errors, health-check responses, DNS resolver behavior, and flow-log patterns must all be visible. Without this telemetry, experiments do not reveal insight. This is why organisations often pair FIS with synthetic load: synthetic requests provide a controlled, consistent stimulus that makes it easier to interpret how the network and application respond during faults, independent of natural traffic fluctuations.

To manage the orchestration around experiments, **Amazon EventBridge** plays a central role. It triggers FIS runs based on schedules, deployments, or manual workflows, and it integrates with notification systems to ensure that operators are aware when tests start, progress, or stop. EventBridge rules can chain experiments together, allowing complex multi-phase tests to unfold gradually—for example, beginning with dependency throttling, then injecting latency into a single AZ, then terminating compute capacity if the system remains within safe thresholds. This makes resilience testing feel more like a real-world incident, where failures come in stages rather than all at once.

Complementing EventBridge, **AWS Systems Manager (SSM)** provides controlled access to resources and supports test actions that require interacting with operating systems or services running on instances. For example, an experiment might use SSM commands to alter kernel parameters on a subset of instances, simulate downstream service failures, or modify application behavior temporarily. SSM becomes essential for fine-grained or system-level experiments where infrastructure actions alone are not sufficient to express the failure mode being tested.

A critical element of implementing resilience tests is ensuring that **safety conditions** are encoded directly into the experiment templates. These conditions are CloudWatch alarms configured to interrupt the experiment if the system enters an unacceptable state—rising error rates, anomalous latency, excessive traffic queuing, or rapid backlog growth. These safeguards allow organisations to test aggressively without risking user impact, especially in production environments. In regulated industries, safety controls also form part of the evidence required to demonstrate compliance: they show that experiments are intentional and controlled.

Networking-focused resilience testing introduces additional considerations. When simulating impairments to hybrid connectivity—such as a Direct Connect circuit withdrawal or BGP route change—the test must be orchestrated in a way that reflects how real routing protocols behave. Failovers must respect propagation delays, convergence times, and the retry behavior of upstream devices. Similarly, DNS failover testing must account for TTL behavior, resolver caching, and geographically distributed client behavior. These nuances are essential: resilience is not simply a matter of whether a backup path exists, but whether transitions occur smoothly, predictably, and consistently across clients and regions.

As teams mature, they begin creating **experiment templates** that capture common failure modes: AZ degradation, dependency slowdown, hybrid path withdrawal, regional isolation, database failover, or DNS failover. These templates act as codified knowledge, enabling resilience tests to become routine rather than exceptional. Some organisations integrate these tests directly into CI/CD pipelines, running them after major deployments or during off-peak windows. Others maintain a curated catalogue of fault scenarios and schedule them weekly or monthly. What matters is consistency: resilience must be validated continuously, not only when preparing for an audit or recovering from an incident.

The real power of implementing resilience testing on AWS lies not in the individual tools—FIS, EventBridge, SSM, CloudWatch—but in how they work together. FIS injects the fault. EventBridge orchestrates it. SSM modifies the environment. CloudWatch observes it. Route 53 and load balancers react to it. The network shifts. The workload adapts—or it does not. And in that behavior lies the truth of the system's resilience.

When implemented thoughtfully, resilience testing is not disruptive. It is clarifying. It reveals how systems behave when they are stressed, how they recover, and where they require reinforcement. It becomes the mechanism through which architecture evolves, observability improves, and operational maturity grows. In critical application, resilience testing is not just possible—it is expected. The tools exist not to create chaos, but to build confidence.

The architecture of AWS Fault Injection Service brings these concepts together in a cohesive workflow: experiments are defined through structured templates, authorized via IAM, executed by the FIS engine, and protected by safeguards such as CloudWatch alarms and EventBridge rules. Network, compute, storage, and database components can all be targeted in isolation or in combination, allowing engineers to model realistic failure modes while observing system behavior through AWS-native and third-party monitoring tools.

Figure 8-4 summarizes this workflow and shows how each component interacts during a resilience test.

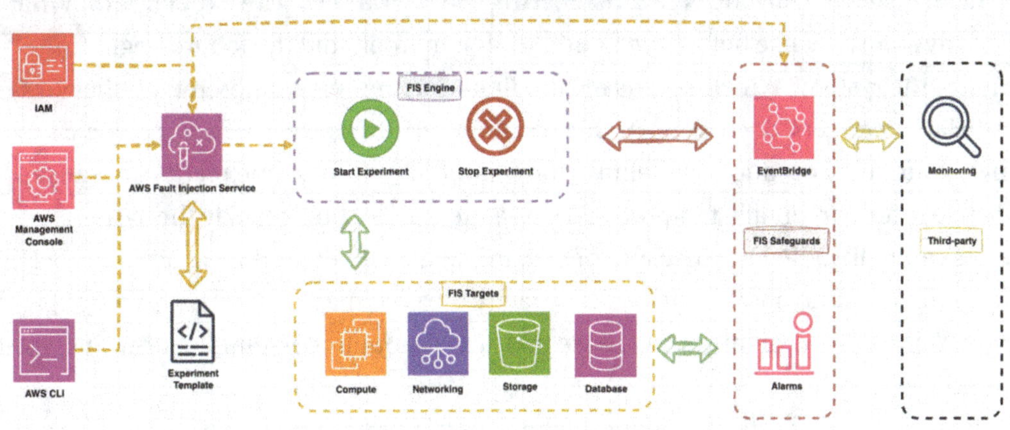

Figure 8-4. *The AWS Fault Injection Service (FIS) Workflow*

Figure 8-4 illustrates how a resilience experiment flows through the AWS Fault Injection Service ecosystem. IAM governs which users and automation pipelines can create or execute experiments. Experiment templates define the intended fault actions—such as impairing compute, networking, storage, or database resources—which are then executed by the FIS engine. CloudWatch alarms act as safety guardrails to automatically halt experiments when thresholds are breached, while EventBridge coordinates notifications, orchestration, and multi-stage scenarios. Throughout the experiment, AWS-native and third-party monitoring tools observe system behavior, enabling teams to validate failover mechanisms, routing convergence, and application recovery in controlled conditions.

Let's see now what do we learn from experimentation and testing.

Learning from Experiments

A resilience experiment has no value if it does not produce learning. Injecting a fault, watching dashboards light up, and returning the system to steady state is only the beginning. The heart of resilience testing lies in how teams interpret what happened, what they discovered about the architecture, and how those insights translate into improvements. This learning phase is where architecture matures, observability sharpens, and resilience objectives evolve from assumptions into validated, measurable properties of the system.

The first step in learning is **reconstructing the narrative of the experiment**. What did steady state look like before the fault? At what moment did the failure begin to influence the system? Which signals moved first—latency, error rates, retry behavior, load-balancer targets, or cross-AZ traffic distribution? Experiments do not produce a single truth; they produce a timeline. Understanding this timeline matters because resilience is fundamentally temporal: RTO is a measure of how quickly the system restores capability; RPO is a measure of how much data diverges during disruption; HA commitments define how much loss of capacity the system should tolerate without user impact. You cannot evaluate any of these metrics without understanding how the system behaved over time.

During the analysis, the focus should be on **deviation from expectation**, not on absolute numbers. A system that spikes in latency for 90 seconds might still be resilient if it stays within user tolerance and recovers well. A system that increases error rate by only 1% may fail resilience criteria if that 1% represents a breach of critical user journeys.

What matters is not the size of the deviation but its meaning relative to the workload's resilience objectives. A truly resilient architecture is not one without deviation—it is one in which deviations are predictable, bounded, and reversible.

Experiments often reveal **unexpected dependencies**. A service that claims to be region-isolated may quietly rely on a cross-region API. A workload designed for multi-AZ durability may rely on a dependency hosted entirely in a single AZ. Hybrid deployments may depend more heavily on a single Direct Connect link than documented. These findings are not failures; they are discoveries. They expose the operational truth of the system—how it behaves when stressed—which is often different from how teams believe it behaves. These are the moments in which resilience moves from architecture diagrams to reality.

Another crucial insight comes from **the behavior of automation**. Many modern workloads rely on auto-scaling, load balancing, health checks, DNS failover, and routing convergence as part of their resilience posture. Experiments reveal whether these mechanisms behave as expected, whether they activate too slowly, too aggressively, or inconsistently across regions or Availability Zones. For example, load balancers may continue to send traffic to impaired targets longer than documented due to staggered health-check intervals; DNS resolvers in different geographies may transition to secondary endpoints at different speeds; auto-scaling groups may take longer to recover capacity under stress than during controlled load tests. Understanding these nuances is essential because resilience often depends on how well automation reacts under non-ideal conditions.

Learning also involves evaluating **the human and procedural response**. Resilience is not solely a property of code and infrastructure; it is a property of teams. During the experiment, did operators know where to look? Did dashboards provide clarity or confusion? Did alarms fire too late or too frequently? Did ownership boundaries become unclear during the failure? Many architectural shortcomings are actually observability shortcomings in disguise—engineers cannot interpret what they cannot see. Experiments reveal whether teams have the situational awareness required to meet the workload's RTO and HA commitments.

After understanding the technical and operational narrative, the final step is **codifying improvement**. Every experiment should produce concrete actions: tuning thresholds, refining dashboards, adjusting scaling policies, restructuring dependencies, improving runbooks, or redesigning components to eliminate bottlenecks. Improvements should be mapped directly to the conditions observed. If replication lag approached RPO limits, storage policies must be revisited. If failover between hybrid paths took too long, routing attributes or backup configurations must be tuned. If DNS failover was inconsistent, TTL strategy and health-check policies must be improved. If cross-AZ traffic became imbalanced, load-balancer routing logic or target distribution needs attention.

This improvement cycle links directly back to the observability work in Section 8.1 and the architectural patterns that will follow in Section 8.3. Resilience testing acts as the bridge between the two. It tests the assumptions that observability is built to monitor, and it exposes the architectural adjustments required for reliable disaster recovery. Over time, repeated experiments produce a maturity curve: signals become clearer, thresholds become sharper, and the architecture becomes more predictable. Teams begin to trust not only the infrastructure but their ability to understand and guide it during stress.

Learning from experiments is therefore not an optional step—it is the purpose of the entire process. Faults are injected so that the system can reveal where it bends, how it heals, and what it needs to become stronger. The deeper the learning, the more resilient the architecture becomes.

Building a Continuous Resilience Testing Practice

A workload does not become resilient after a single test. It becomes resilient through repetition—through the continuous, deliberate practice of exercising failure modes, observing behavior, and reinforcing the architecture. Resilience is not a property you achieve once; it is a capability you maintain. Just as physical infrastructure deteriorates without maintenance, distributed systems drift away from their intended resilience posture unless they are tested regularly. A continuous resilience testing practice ensures that workloads evolve safely, observability stays aligned with real behavior, and architectural assumptions remain true over time.

The first step toward a continuous practice is **normalization**. Fault injection must stop being an exceptional event and become a routine part of operating a workload. Teams should view resilience tests not as disruptions but as diagnostic tools— instruments that reveal the health of the system far more reliably than dashboards alone. When experiments occur predictably, they become a natural part of the workload's lifecycle: tests run after major deployments, before peak events, during planned maintenance windows, or as part of release pipelines. A resilient architecture stands on the foundation that *if something is important enough to fail in production, it is important enough to test regularly in controlled conditions.*

Over time, organisations naturally develop a **resilience test catalogue**: a set of validated scenarios that model the failures most relevant to the workload. These scenarios often include partial AZ impairments, dependency throttling, routing changes, DNS failover tests, hybrid connectivity withdrawal, or controlled latency injections on critical microservices. Each scenario becomes a building block—a reusable test template with well-understood expectations, safety boundaries, and signals. AWS Fault Injection Service supports this pattern directly through experiment templates, which allow faults to be defined once and executed many times with consistent behavior.

A continuous practice also depends on **maturity progression**. Early in the journey, teams test isolated failures with narrow blast radius in staging environments. As confidence increases, tests expand: multi-AZ failures replace single-AZ failures, dependency impairments broaden to include entire microservice groups, and network faults become more realistic, simulating true operational conditions such as hybrid path convergence delays or incremental packet loss. Eventually, mature organisations introduce game days, then promote certain experiments into automated workflows. The direction of travel is always the same: from manual to automated, from isolated to holistic, and from rare to routine.

A key maturity marker is **integrating resilience testing into CI/CD pipelines**. Not all tests belong in automated pipelines—especially those with large blast radius or regulatory sensitivity—but many do. Container termination, dependency throttling, node-level impairments, or micro-failure scenarios can be automated safely, providing rapid validation of resilience behaviors after deployments. Over time, pipelines evolve from "does the application work?" to "does the application remain resilient?" This shift is transformative, especially for systems with stringent RTO/RPO requirements.

Resilience testing also has a growing role in **regulated industries**, where authorities expect evidence of operational continuity and recovery capability. Financial services regulators, for example, require demonstrable proof that critical services can withstand specific failure scenarios within mandated RTO/RPO boundaries. Continuous resilience testing provides exactly this evidence: timelines of failover events, measurements of recovery duration, data divergence metrics, and documented behavior across regions and Availability Zones. When combined with strong observability and structured runbooks, resilience testing becomes a compliance asset rather than an engineering burden.

One of the most overlooked aspects of continuous testing is the **feedback loop between observability and resilience engineering**. Experiments reveal gaps in metrics, dashboards, and alarms; observability improvements reveal more nuanced behaviors during the next experiment; these behaviors drive architectural refinements; and architectural changes create the need for new experiments. This loop never ends—and it should not. It is the mechanism that ensures a workload's resilience posture adapts as architecture evolves, as scale changes, and as new dependencies emerge.

Building a continuous resilience practice is as much about culture as it is about tooling. Teams must embrace the idea that faults are opportunities to learn, not events to fear. Engineers must feel empowered to question assumptions, challenge design decisions, and explore failure modes that have not yet been tested. Leadership must support regular testing by providing time, resources, and psychological safety. Organisations that cultivate this mindset find that resilience becomes embedded in the way teams think, design, build, and operate systems—not as a defensive measure, but as a form of engineering excellence.

When resilience testing becomes continuous, failures lose their power. Unknowns become known. Assumptions become validated. Weaknesses become improvements. And the system gains a form of operational confidence that cannot be achieved through design alone. A continuous resilience practice ensures that the workload can not only withstand failure, but do so predictably—with clarity, with stability, and with trust.

Bridging Toward Disaster Recovery

Resilience testing answers an essential question: *How does the system behave when it bends?* But disaster recovery asks an even more fundamental one: *What happens when it breaks?* The difference between these two domains is subtle but critical. Resilience testing focuses on disruption within the boundaries of a functioning system—an impaired Availability Zone, a degraded link, a throttled dependency, a partial loss of capacity. Disaster recovery looks beyond disruption and into discontinuity: the loss of a region, the loss of a critical data store, or the loss of an operational environment entirely.

The insights gained through resilience experiments form the foundation for disaster recovery design. Every deviation observed in an experiment, every unexpected dependency uncovered, every failover that took longer than expected, and every signal that surfaced too late becomes a data point that informs how disaster recovery must be engineered. Experiments reveal the fragility of replication paths, the behavior of routing during isolation, the speed of DNS transitions, and the real-world RTO and RPO the system achieves under stress—not the ones printed in design documents. These findings shape the strategies for failover, fallback, and reconstitution. The most valuable resilience experiments do not merely validate assumptions; they often reshape disaster recovery design by revealing which capabilities truly survive isolation.

A concrete example: When a chaos finding reshapes disaster recovery design

A common outcome of resilience testing is discovering that a workload is not as region-independent as the DR plan assumes. For example, a "regional isolation" experiment intentionally blocks cross-region connectivity at the workload boundary (or degrades the dependency path) while keeping intra-region services healthy. During one such test, the primary region continued serving traffic for most requests, but a critical user journey (login/checkout) degraded because the application still called an authentication/token endpoint hosted only in another region. The architecture was "multi-region" on paper, but the dependency graph was not.

That single finding changes disaster recovery design in a concrete way: the DR plan must treat the authentication layer as a **first-class DR dependency**. The fix is not merely "fail over faster," but **remove or redesign the cross-region hard dependency**—for example, regionalizing the auth service, adding a secondary auth endpoint in the recovery region, introducing short-lived token caching to survive isolation windows, and updating the DR runbook to explicitly validate "critical journeys" (not just infrastructure health) before declaring recovery complete. The result is a DR strategy that restores *capability*, not only *infrastructure*, and that is grounded in measured behavior observed during fault injection.

Findings like this are common in mature resilience programs and illustrate why disaster recovery cannot be designed independently of fault-injection evidence: recoverability is defined by observed behavior, not intent.

More importantly, experiments like this reveal **how recovery unfolds over time**, not just whether recovery is theoretically possible. A region may technically support replication, but experiments reveal how replication lag grows under load. A failover path may exist, but experiments show whether it activates predictably or unevenly. Network isolation tests reveal whether dependencies that were assumed to be local actually reach across regions. These time-based behaviors are essential inputs for disaster recovery planning because disaster recovery is, fundamentally, a temporal discipline—it measures how quickly and how cleanly a system can shift from an impaired state to a restored one.

In many organisations, disaster recovery planning begins with documentation: runbooks, architecture diagrams, capacity plans, and compliance requirements. But without resilience testing, these documents remain unverified hypotheses. Disaster recovery is only trustworthy when the behaviors described on paper align with the behaviors demonstrated under fault. Chaos engineering validates the mechanisms that disaster recovery depends on: scaling, promotion, routing, replication, automation, and human response. It transforms disaster recovery from a theoretical construct into a measurable capability.

As we transition into the next section, the relationship becomes clear:

Observability (8.1) gives you the ability to see.

Resilience testing (8.2) gives you the ability to understand.

Disaster recovery (8.3) gives you the ability to restore.

Together, they form a complete resilience system—one that anticipates failure, absorbs it, learns from it, and ultimately recovers from events that go beyond degradation into full disruption. The next chapter builds on everything uncovered so far and focuses on how to design a disaster recovery strategy in the cloud.

Section 8.3: Designing for Disaster Recovery

Let me start with a brief reminder of what we defined at the very beginning of this book: **Disaster recovery (DR) is defined by three constraints: scope, time, and data.**

Scope answers *what you are recovering from* (AZ loss vs. regional loss vs. logical failure such as corruption or ransomware).

Recovery Time Objective (RTO) defines *how quickly* you must restore business capability after disruption.

Recovery Point Objective (RPO) defines *how much data divergence or loss* is acceptable when you restore service.

Together, these constraints determine whether your DR strategy is backup-and-restore, pilot light, warm standby, or active/active, and whether recovery is primarily a data problem, an orchestration problem, or a networking problem.

By the time an architecture reaches disaster recovery planning, it has already travelled an important path. Observability has given the system the ability to see itself with clarity. Resilience testing has revealed how it behaves under stress, how it bends, where it hesitates, and which assumptions fail under controlled failure. These are essential disciplines—but they explain how a system endures degradation. Disaster recovery asks what happens when degradation becomes disruption, and the system must restore full capability.

Resilience and disaster recovery are related but not interchangeable. Resilience focuses on operating through imperfect conditions—brownouts, dependency degradation, partial AZ impairment—while DR addresses discontinuity such as regional loss or the need to restore a clean state after corruption or compromise (see the resilience vs. disruption distinction introduced in Section 8.2). DR is therefore not "a larger version of failover"; it introduces different failure dynamics for routing, DNS convergence, and data correctness, and it must be engineered explicitly.

Yet the practices from Sections 8.1 and 8.2 become the foundations for DR—**they provide the signals, the fault-injection evidence, and the operational muscle memory that DR depends on**. A system cannot recover successfully from a regional failure if it cannot first detect the failure through reliable signals. It cannot coordinate cross-region transition if observability does not expose the moment data divergence threatens RPO. It cannot manage failover safely if resilience testing has not validated the behavior of load balancers, DNS, routing, and application tier convergence under stress. Disaster recovery is not isolated from resilience engineering—it extends it.

Even the language of DR reflects this extension. Where resilience tests measure deviation from steady state, DR measures recovery to a new steady state. Where resilience experiments validate automation, DR validates orchestration. Where resilience tests reveal hidden dependencies, DR exposes whether those dependencies can be reattached, rehydrated, or replaced after a disruption. And where resilience defines how the system bends, DR defines how it heals.

Modern cloud disaster recovery also differs from traditional on-premises DR. In legacy environments, DR was often an infrequent, manual, expensive process—a "once a year" event, often rehearsed more than executed. In the cloud, DR becomes both more achievable and more demanding. Achievable because infrastructure can be provisioned on demand, replicated continuously, and orchestrated programmatically. Demanding because workloads evolve rapidly, dependencies spread across regions, and the system's recovery posture changes as teams deploy new features, modify data paths, or expand global footprints. DR is no longer a one-time design but an active engineering commitment.

This chapter moves beyond the question of *whether* your system survives disruption and begins to address *how* it restores its full capability after a major event. We begin with foundational concepts—the difference between high availability and disaster recovery, the nature of disasters, and the meaning of RPO and RTO in real architectures. We'll then explore the principal DR strategies available on AWS and applicable on other clouds, from backup and restore to multi-region active/active patterns. From there, we'll examine AWS-native capabilities for enabling DR at the data, compute, and storage layers, and we will devote a dedicated section to the networking behaviors that are unique to recovery events—partitioning, isolation, reunification, and cross-region connectivity under stress.

By the end of this chapter, disaster recovery will no longer be a plan on a page but a system property—something that is designed, validated, tested, and continuously improved.

Foundations of Disaster Recovery

Designing for disaster recovery requires a precise vocabulary. The term "disaster" is often used loosely in engineering conversations, but in the context of resilience architecture it has a specific meaning. A disaster is not every failure; it is the class of failures that exceed the system's ability to contain them. A single Availability Zone going offline is not a disaster for a multi-AZ architecture. A congested network path is not a disaster for a system with retries and circuit-breaking. A degraded dependency is not a disaster for a service built with graceful-degradation logic. These are resilience events—significant, but within the design margins of a well-architected system.

A disaster, by contrast, is a **loss of continuity** that exceeds the resilience envelope. It is a regional outage, a loss of data durability, a critical control-plane failure, a corruption event, or the unavailability of an entire operational environment. Disasters are rare, but they are possible, and because their impact is non-linear, they must be prepared for explicitly. Disaster recovery is the discipline of restoring capability when a system has moved beyond degradation into discontinuity.

High availability (HA) and disaster recovery (DR) address different failure envelopes, a distinction that follows directly from the resilience-versus-disruption model introduced earlier. HA focuses on continuity within a region—absorbing localized failures such as AZ impairment or infrastructure maintenance. DR applies when that envelope is exceeded and continuity must be re-established elsewhere, most commonly after regional loss or the need to restore to a clean state. As a result, a workload can be highly available yet poorly recoverable: multi-AZ design alone does not constitute disaster recovery, and cross-region replication without orchestration, routing control, and validation does not guarantee safe restoration.

To design DR effectively, teams must also understand that not all disasters are physical or infrastructure-based. AWS categorizes disasters into several types:

- **Natural or physical disasters**, affecting data centers or regional infrastructure

- **Technical disasters**, such as data corruption, misconfigurations, or software flaws that render a system inoperable

- **Cyber events**, including ransomware, unauthorized modifications, or security breaches requiring isolation of a region

- **External dependencies**, such as third-party outages that require a workload to operate elsewhere

- **Human operational errors**, which can propagate inconsistently across regions

This broader view is important because DR strategy must account for both *infrastructure failures* and *logical failures*. A workload may be deployed in two regions, but if a data corruption event replicates instantly, failover provides no protection. Disaster recovery must consider not only "where the system runs," but "how the system restores to an uncompromised state."

Central to this is the definition of **Recovery Time Objective (RTO)** and **Recovery Point Objective (RPO),** we introduced these terms at the very beginning and mentioned them many times throughout the book but let's dive into details now.

These metrics are often listed mechanically in design documents, yet they represent the core of disaster recovery.

- **RTO** defines *how long* the system can be unavailable before unacceptable business impact occurs. It governs how quickly failover mechanisms must act—how fast DNS must redirect, how rapidly the secondary region must assume traffic, how quickly data must be made available.

- **RPO** defines *how much data loss* is acceptable when restoring service. It influences replication choices, storage configuration, cross-region data flows, and the boundaries between synchronous and asynchronous replication.

RTO describes time; RPO describes divergence. Both must be defined in business terms and then translated into engineering patterns. A workload with a one-hour RPO may rely on asynchronous replication or periodic backups. One with a near-zero RPO requires continuous, multi-region replication with validated consistency guarantees. Disaster recovery is fundamentally the engineering expression of these two numbers.

But RTO and RPO do not exist in a vacuum. They depend on **Business Impact Analysis (BIA)**—the discipline of understanding which workloads are critical, how long they can be unavailable, what the financial and operational impacts are, and how recovery priorities differ by function. Some applications may require near-zero RTO, while others can tolerate hours. Some data paths require strong consistency, while others may tolerate asynchronous replay. BIA translates business requirements into technical objectives, and these objectives become the blueprint for DR architecture.

BIA also reveals the **cost of downtime**, which influences DR strategy. AWS provides multiple DR patterns—backup and restore, pilot light, warm standby, and active/active—each with increasing cost and decreasing RTO/RPO. Understanding downtime's cost allows organisations to choose intentionally rather than aspirationally. A workload with low downtime cost may not justify the expense of multi-region active/active. Conversely, a workload with extremely high downtime cost cannot rely on backup and restore. DR design is not purely technical; it is an economic decision.

The final foundation of DR is recognizing that **cloud-native disaster recovery differs fundamentally from traditional DR**. On-premises DR relied on physically duplicated environments, large capital expenditure, and manual failover processes. In the cloud, DR becomes elastic, automated, and demand-driven. Infrastructure can be provisioned only when needed; replication can be continuous; failover can be orchestrated; and validation can be frequent. This shift makes DR both more accessible and more dynamic. It also means that a DR plan must evolve continuously as workloads evolve.

Together, these foundational concepts—the distinction between resilience and disaster recovery, the nature of disasters, the meaning of RTO and RPO, the role of BIA, and the economics of downtime—form the intellectual framework for the remainder of this chapter. They allow us to move from principles to patterns, from patterns to architecture, and from architecture to execution.

AWS Disaster Recovery Strategies

Disaster recovery in AWS is built on four canonical patterns. These patterns form a continuum: from the simplest, lowest-cost approach that restores service after a disruption, to the most advanced, lowest-RTO architecture capable of surviving regional loss in real time. Understanding these strategies is essential, because every DR architecture is ultimately a variation of one of them. The right choice depends on a workload's RTO, RPO, regulatory obligations, and the cost of downtime identified during Business Impact Analysis.

Before exploring each strategy, it is useful to visualize them on a single spectrum. Figure 8-5 illustrates how the four patterns relate to one another in terms of RPO/RTO performance, complexity, and cost.

Strategy	Deployment	Typical RPO	Typical RTO	Infrastructure State (before event)	Cost Profile	Complexity	Suitable For
Backup & Restore	Passive	Hours	Hours or Days	No compute running; backups stored in secondary Region	$	Low	Non-critical workloads, archival systems, internal tools
Pilot Light	Active/Passive	Tens of Minutes	Tens of Minutes	Core infrastructure (databases, minimal services) running; application tier scaled down or off	$$	Medium	Important workloads with moderate downtime tolerance
Warm Standby	Active/Passive	Minutes	Minutes	Fully functional but scaled-down environment running continuously	$$$	Medium-High	Business-critical applications requiring rapid recovery
Multi-Site (Active/Active)	Active/Active	Near Zero	Near Zero	Fully active production environments in multiple Regions	$$$$	High	Mission-critical systems requiring zero downtime and minimal data loss

Figure 8-5. *Disaster Recovery Strategies*

Figure 8-5 serves as the summary reference for this section, mapping each disaster recovery strategy to its typical RTO/RPO envelope and operational cost. As requirements tighten—from hours, to minutes, to near-real-time—DR architectures evolve from simple restoration procedures to continuously running multi-region systems, with a corresponding increase in complexity and cost. The sections that follow expand on each pattern in detail.

Now we go through each pattern in detail.

Backup and Restore

Backup and Restore is the most foundational disaster recovery strategy—and also the simplest. It is designed for workloads where downtime and data freshness are tolerable trade-offs, and where the cost of continuously running infrastructure in a secondary region cannot be justified. In this model, the DR region contains no active compute or application services. Instead, the organization stores copies of its critical data—backups, snapshots, or periodically exported datasets—and recreates the environment only after a disruption occurs.

This approach is attractive because of its low operational overhead. No compute resources run idle. Storage costs are limited to retained backups. Cross-region replication pipelines do not require constant supervision. But the simplicity comes with a price: time. Restoration involves rebuilding the environment, redeploying application components, rehydrating data, and re-establishing identity and networking constructs. As a result, the Recovery Time Objective (RTO) is typically measured in hours, and the Recovery Point Objective (RPO) is tied directly to the frequency of backups or snapshot exports.

Backup and Restore is therefore a strong fit for workloads such as archival systems, reporting pipelines, internal tooling, dev/test environments, and other low-urgency functions. These workloads can tolerate longer restoration windows, provided that the process is predictable and well-documented.

In AWS, this pattern is implemented using services such as AWS Backup, Amazon S3 cross-region replication, Amazon RDS snapshots, EBS snapshot replication, and infrastructure-as-code templates (CloudFormation, Terraform, CDK) that reconstitute the environment. Networking plays only a supporting role because the DR environment does not exist until failover begins; however, the recovery plan must still account for DNS routing changes, load balancer creation or configuration, IAM and security perimeter updates, and any required connectivity into the DR Region.

Figure 8-6 illustrates the simplest DR approach, where backups created in the primary region—via S3 and AWS Backup—are asynchronously replicated to storage in a secondary region. No compute or database infrastructure runs in the secondary region during normal operation; the faded icons represent resources that are provisioned only after a disaster. During recovery, the environment is rebuilt from replicated backups and reconnected to restored data volumes or databases. This pattern offers the lowest cost but also the highest RPO and RTO, making it appropriate for workloads that can tolerate delayed recovery and non-current data.

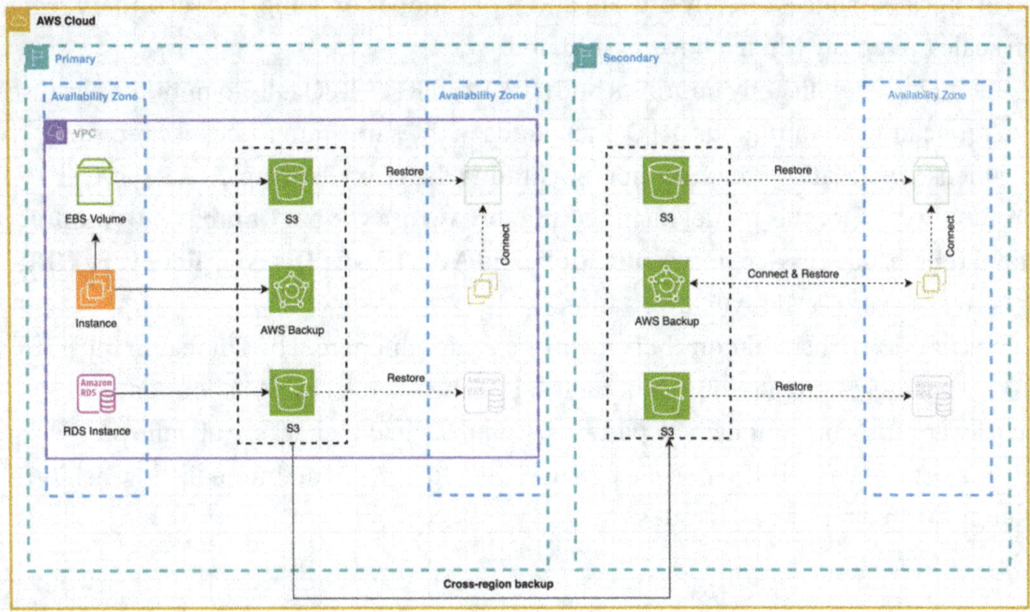

Figure 8-6. *Backup and Restore Disaster Recovery Pattern*

When to choose Backup and Restore

- Downtime of hours is acceptable and data loss is bounded by backup frequency.

- Workloads are non-customer-facing, internal, or low criticality.

- Cost sensitivity outweighs recovery speed.

- Regulatory requirements focus on data retention rather than rapid continuity.

Pilot Light

Pilot Light advances beyond **Backup and Restore** by maintaining a minimal, continuously running footprint in the secondary region. The "pilot light" refers to a small but essential set of components that stay active even when the primary region is healthy.

This typically includes cross-region–replicated databases, core storage systems, configuration repositories, or critical messaging queues. Application servers, load balancers, and most microservices remain offline until needed, but the data layer stays

warm. Because state is already present and replication is ongoing, the secondary region can scale up rapidly when failover is initiated.

Pilot Light significantly improves both RPO and RTO. RPO falls to minutes because data replication is continuous. RTO often lands in the same range because recovery now focuses on scaling compute, not rehydrating data from backups. AWS services commonly used for this model include **Amazon Aurora Global Database**, **DynamoDB global tables**, **S3 cross-region replication**, and **AWS Elastic Disaster Recovery (DRS)** for compute warm-state synchronization.

Networking considerations become more important here. The DR region must already be integrated into routing domains, DNS health checks, IAM boundaries, security groups, and connectivity patterns. Route 53 health checks, ALB failover behavior, and routing rules must be pre-designed to support an immediate transition when the primary region degrades.

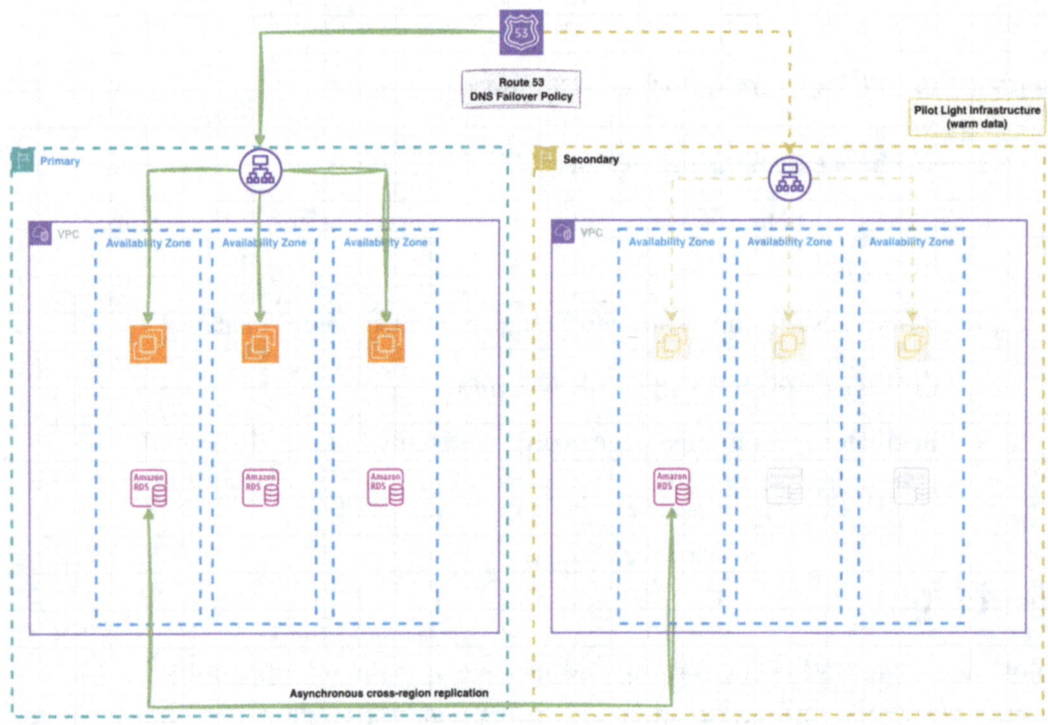

Figure 8-7. *Pilot Light Disaster Recovery Pattern*

Figure 8-7 illustrates the Pilot Light strategy, where a minimal but operational footprint is maintained in the secondary region. Route 53 directs traffic to the primary region under normal conditions, while health checks determine when to fail over to the secondary ALB. In the primary region, compute capacity and databases run fully; in the secondary region, only essential components—such as a warm database replica, pre-provisioned networking, and a standby ALB—remain in place. The **faded compute icons** represent infrastructure that exists but does not run at scale until failover is triggered. Continuous database replication keeps state warm, enabling the secondary region to scale up quickly when activated. Pilot Light offers lower RTO and RPO than Backup and Restore while still avoiding the cost of running a full parallel stack.

When to choose Pilot Light

- RTO and RPO measured in minutes rather than hours.

- Data must remain current, but full compute capacity can be provisioned on demand.

- Workloads are business-critical but do not justify full active/active cost.

- Teams can operate automated scale-up and controlled failover procedures.

Warm Standby

Warm Standby represents a major step up in readiness. In this pattern, the secondary region runs a scaled-down but fully functioning version of the workload at all times. All critical components—compute, storage, databases, caches, message buses, and supporting services—are continuously deployed and updated. They operate at reduced capacity during steady state to minimize cost.

During a disaster, the warm standby environment scales up quickly—often automatically—into the full production environment. RTO falls to minutes, and RPO approaches near-zero depending on replication mechanisms. This strategy suits business-critical workloads where downtime is unacceptable but full active/active cost is unnecessary.

In AWS, Warm Standby typically uses multi-AZ or multi-region database replication, CI/CD pipelines to synchronize infrastructure and configuration, and observability systems that allow the two regions to drift as little as possible. Networking becomes central: routing must shift cleanly, IAM must permit DR actions, and automation must scale the environment without misrouting traffic or overloading partially warmed components.

Figure 8-8 illustrates the Warm Standby strategy, where the primary region runs the full production workload across multiple Availability Zones, including fully scaled compute, active load balancing, and a writeable database. In the secondary region, a minimal but functional version of the workload is kept online: a standby ALB, a small fleet of compute instances, and a warm database replica receiving asynchronous cross-region replication. The faded compute and database icons indicate capacity that is pre-defined but not provisioned until failover. Route 53 uses DNS failover policies to direct traffic to the primary region during normal operation and shifts traffic to the secondary region when health checks detect an outage. This pattern offers significantly lower RTO and RPO than Backup and Restore while avoiding the cost of maintaining a full multi-region active environment.

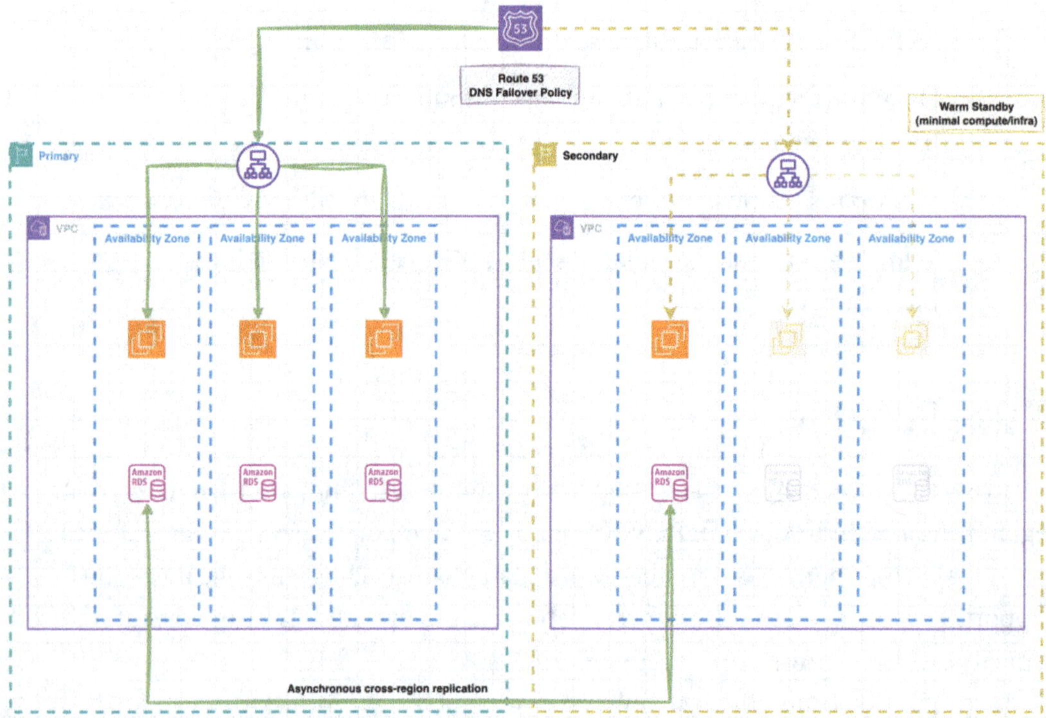

Figure 8-8. *Warm Standby Disaster Recovery Pattern*

When to choose Warm Standby

- Downtime tolerance is measured in minutes and near-zero RPO is required.

- Business impact of outage is high, but full active/active is not justified.

- Workloads require predictable, fast recovery with minimal orchestration risk.

- Organisations can sustain the cost of a continuously running secondary environment.

Multi-region Active/Active

Multi-site Active/Active is the most advanced DR strategy, delivering the strongest resilience posture. In this model, multiple regions actively serve production traffic at all times. Every core component—compute, data, routing, authentication, storage, and control plane—is live and participating in the system.

Active/active architectures can achieve near-real-time RTO and near-zero RPO **for specific data models and services**. The cost is complexity. Data replication must be continuous and consistent; routing must be globally aware; load balancing must distribute traffic across regions; and application logic must tolerate distributed state, conflict resolution, and multi-region coordination.

AWS provides several mechanisms to enable this model, including Global Accelerator, Aurora Global Database, DynamoDB global tables, multi-region API gateways, and active/active VPC patterns. At this level, networking behaviors dominate DR readiness: inter-region latency envelopes matter, routing convergence requires careful engineering, and split-brain scenarios must be prevented.

Active/active is the gold standard for mission-critical systems such as financial trading platforms, identity providers, healthcare platforms, and high-scale global applications.

Figure 8-9 illustrates a fully active/active multi-region architecture, where both regions simultaneously serve production traffic. Route 53 uses a 50/50 weighted routing policy to steer requests to ALBs in each region, ensuring that all application tiers operate in parallel. Each region maintains a complete multi-AZ deployment—compute, networking, data services, and load balancing all remain fully online.

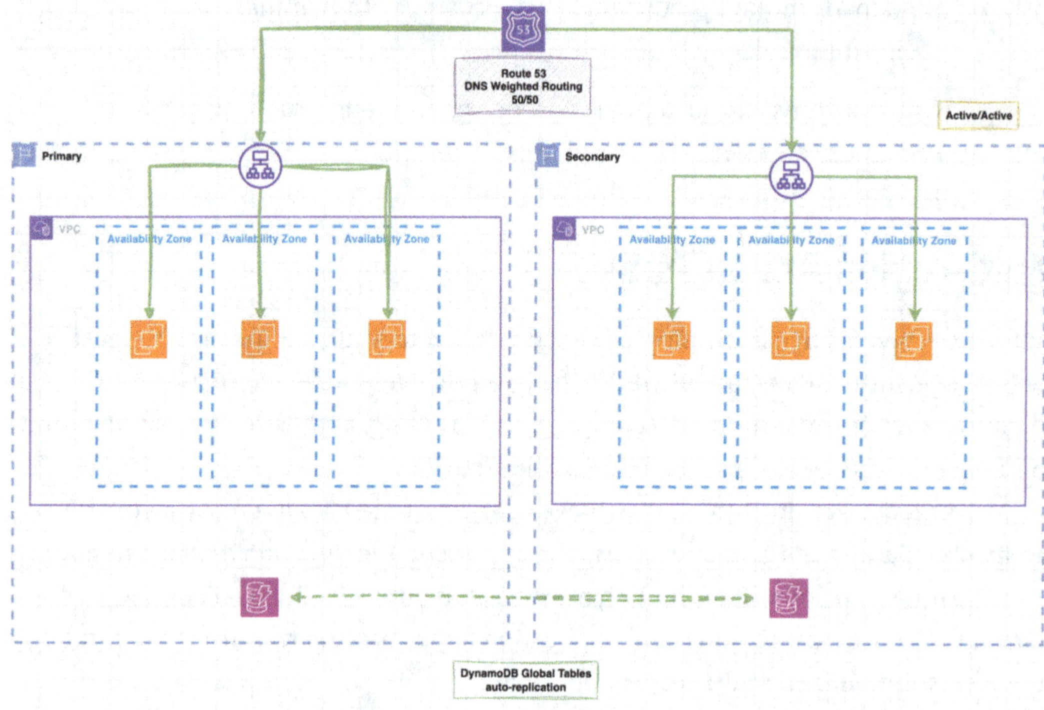

Figure 8-9. *Active/Active Disaster Recovery Pattern*

For the data layer, DynamoDB Global Tables provide multi-region, multi-writer replication with near-zero RPO, enabling both regions to accept writes independently while asynchronously propagating updates across regions. This eliminates the need for a single "primary" data source and provides continuous read/write availability everywhere.

This pattern achieves the strongest resilience posture: RTO approaches real-time and RPO is effectively zero. Because traffic never concentrates exclusively in one region, the architecture can absorb a full regional impairment without interrupting service. However, it also introduces the highest architectural complexity and operational cost, making it suitable only for mission-critical systems where uninterrupted global availability is essential.

When to choose Multi-region Active/Active

- Regulatory or contractual requirements mandate uninterrupted service (e.g., financial services, identity providers, healthcare, critical infrastructure)

- Near-zero RTO and RPO are mandatory, and any explicit failover event is unacceptable

- User experience and latency consistency matter globally, not just availability (e.g., global user bases, real-time platforms, latency-sensitive transactions)

- The workload must remain operational during regional impairment, not merely recover after it

- Applications are explicitly designed for multi-region, multi-writer operation, including conflict resolution and consistency management

- Organisations can sustain the highest level of architectural complexity and operational cost, including continuous testing, observability, and governance across regions

AWS Tools That Enable Disaster Recovery

Disaster recovery is ultimately an architectural discipline, but architectures depend on the capabilities of the platform they run on. AWS provides several native tools and services that support the four DR strategies described earlier—not as isolated products, but as building blocks that translate RTO/RPO objectives into practical recovery mechanisms. The intent of this section is not to catalogue services, but to clarify how they align with each DR strategy and what role they play in making recovery predictable. We will touch on these capabilities for context, but the emphasis of this chapter remains on the networking behaviors that ultimately determine how a system recovers across regions.

AWS Backup: Foundation for Backup and Restore

Backup and Restore relies on durable, cross-region data copies that can outlive the primary region. AWS Backup provides a unified mechanism for creating, scheduling, encrypting, and replicating backups across regions and accounts. In a Backup and Restore DR design, AWS Backup is the anchor: it ensures that data exists independently of compute, networking, or storage infrastructure. When the time comes to restore, AWS Backup integrates with CloudFormation, Terraform, or CDK templates to rebuild the environment.

Its value in DR is not operational speed but **integrity and independence**. Backups form the last line of defense when corruption, deletion, or compromise affects the primary region.

AWS Elastic Disaster Recovery (DRS): Acceleration for Pilot Light and Warm Standby

Pilot Light and Warm Standby both benefit from AWS Elastic Disaster Recovery (DRS). Unlike backup systems, DRS continuously replicates block-level data from on-premises or AWS regions into a staging area in the DR region. The replicated data remains cost-efficient until needed, but can be promoted into full EC2 instances within minutes.

DRS is powerful because it bridges the gap between simplicity and readiness:

- In **Pilot Light**, DRS maintains warm data and lets the application layer scale up only during failover.

- In **Warm Standby**, DRS ensures the standby region's instances remain current and quickly scalable.

It effectively compresses RTO by eliminating rebuild steps and compresses RPO by replicating continuously.

Cross-Region Data Replication

Disaster recovery is ultimately about restoring data, not just infrastructure. AWS offers several native replication mechanisms depending on consistency needs:

- **Amazon Aurora Global Database** and **DynamoDB Global Tables** provide continuous cross-region replication with low-latency reads and rapid failover.

- **S3 Cross-Region Replication (CRR)** replicates object storage asynchronously for immutable or semi-mutable data workloads.

- **Amazon EFS Replication** provides file system mirroring across regions.

These capabilities support Pilot Light, Warm Standby, and Active/Active strategies by ensuring the DR Region holds timely copies of application state.

The key architectural insight is that cross-region replication is not purely a storage choice—it dictates the achievable RPO. A workload's RPO tolerance tells you whether asynchronous replication is acceptable or whether a more advanced multi-region model is required.

Infrastructure-As-Code and Configuration Drift Control

A DR region must remain in sync with the primary region—not just at failover time, but continuously. Tools like **AWS CloudFormation**, **AWS CDK**, **Terraform**, and **AWS Systems Manager** enforce consistent configuration across regions and prevent the slow drift that can erode DR posture.

IaC is the glue that keeps Pilot Light and Warm Standby reliable. Without it, recovery may succeed technically but fail operationally because the environment no longer reflects production reality (IAM changes, new subnets, security adjustments, missing routing entries, etc.). DR is a configuration discipline as much as it is an infrastructure discipline.

Routing and Redirection Mechanisms

While the deeper networking behavior is covered in the next subsection, it is important to recognize that all DR strategies depend on global routing tools to realign traffic:

- **Amazon Route 53** changes authoritative DNS responses to direct clients toward the DR region.

- **AWS Global Accelerator** shifts traffic across AWS' global anycast edge with extremely fast convergence.

In Backup and Restore and Pilot Light, routing activates only during failover. In Warm Standby, routing transitions the scaled-up environment into production. In Active/Active, routing continuously distributes load across regions.

The tools we touched on give disaster recovery its machinery, but the true behavior of a system during a regional disruption is defined not by storage engines or compute orchestration, but by the network. When a region becomes unreachable—even partially—the network becomes the arbiter of what fails, what survives, and how recovery unfolds. With this in mind, we now turn to the networking patterns that shape the outcome of disaster recovery in practice.

Networking for Disaster Recovery

When disaster recovery is sketched on architecture diagrams, it often appears clean and linear: failover occurs, traffic shifts, data promotes, and the system stabilizes in the secondary region. In practice, however, the behavior of a distributed system during a regional disruption is anything but linear. Failover is not a moment; it is a negotiation. And the primary negotiator, in my opinion, is the network.

Earlier in the book we explored DNS routing, traffic engineering, Direct Connect resilience models, and the behavior of AWS routing constructs under stress. Those fundamentals remain true during a disaster, but disaster recovery introduces a different set of questions—questions about isolation, reconvergence, consistency, and what happens not only *when* a region fails, but *how* it fails. For most workloads, the decisive factor in disaster recovery is not whether infrastructure is available in a second region, but whether the network allows traffic, state, and automation to transition coherently.

Disasters rarely present themselves as clean outages. More commonly, a region becomes reachable from some parts of the world but not others; replication stalls while front-end endpoints remain up; or control-plane APIs become inconsistent while data-plane paths continue to pass traffic. This creates what is effectively a partition—a condition where components exist and run, but cannot reliably communicate across regions. For disaster recovery, partitions are more dangerous than outages because they create ambiguity. To a workload, the region is not "down"; it is "uncertain," and uncertain regions can mislead automation, DNS failover, routing convergence, and even human operators. It is also important to recognize that, despite dramatic headlines, there has never been an instance of an entire AWS Region going "down." Social media often collapses nuance into sensationalism, reporting a "region outage" when in reality the impact is usually limited to a subset of services, and often to a single cell within those services (as discussed in Chapter 6 on cell-based architectures). These impairments can be serious and widespread, but they are not regional failures; they are service-level disruptions that the architecture must be designed to absorb. Disaster recovery planning must therefore start from how failures actually manifest—gradual, uneven, and ambiguous—rather than from oversimplified narratives.

Once a system enters this ambiguous state, the primary danger is no longer loss of availability, but loss of coherence. A partitioned region may continue to accept writes, validate sessions, or serve traffic even when it is effectively isolated. The result is split brain: two regions believing they are authoritative at the same time. Databases experience it as divergent write histories; identity systems as independently validated tokens; routing and DNS as both regions continuing to respond. The real damage typically occurs not during the partition, but in the moment of reunification, when divergent states must be reconciled. Without strict safeguards, a system may recover connectivity only to discover that correctness has been compromised—an outcome far more dangerous than downtime itself.

DNS behavior during a partition magnifies this complexity, but it must be understood through authoritative DNS signals and inferred resolver behavior rather than direct visibility into recursive resolvers. While recursive resolvers operate outside AWS control, their behavior can be inferred through Route 53 health-check transitions, authoritative query volume, traffic shifts observed at load balancers or Global Accelerator, and client-side telemetry.

With Route 53 failover routing, authoritative answers change when health checks indicate the primary endpoint is unhealthy, but recursive resolvers outside AWS may continue using cached answers until TTL expiry. Some will honor the failover immediately; some will hold on to stale records until TTL expiry; others will oscillate depending on geography and local resolver logic. Seen from the perspective of users, failover is not a clean cutover—it is a gradual shift, with traffic trickling from one region to the other as caches refresh. This is why TTL strategy, health-check placement, and global testing matter far more for disaster recovery than they do for normal routing.

Transit Gateway forwarding decisions are driven by route tables and attachment state. If a route remains present while reachability degrades or becomes asymmetric, traffic can be blackholed until routing boundaries and failover controls take effect. During a partition, a route that points to an unreachable region may remain present even as the path becomes unusable. If propagation stalls or return paths become asymmetric, packets may leave one region but never return to it. Without intentional failover routing boundaries—using route table isolation, static preferences, or propagation controls— TGW architectures can inadvertently create blackholes or oscillating paths during partial regional failures.

Control-plane behavior can also become asymmetric during disruption. API calls may succeed in one region while failing or timing out in another, and automation that depends on control-plane operations can slow down or behave unpredictably under partial reachability. Additionally, some AWS services use default global endpoints (e.g., STS in certain configurations), which can create unintended single-region dependencies unless you explicitly use regional endpoints. Because DR orchestration depends on scaling, routing changes, and configuration promotion, designs should assume control-plane variability and remove avoidable global-endpoint dependencies where possible.

Yet the most delicate stage of disaster recovery is not failover—it is **reunification**. When a previously isolated region reconnects, the system must reconcile state, routes, DNS behaviors, caches, and automation. DNS resolvers may still hold the DR region's endpoint for minutes or hours. Replication pipelines may suddenly receive large backlogs of updates. Retry storms or message-queue bursts may hit newly recovered services. And if the impaired region attempts to rejoin before the system is ready, it may reintroduce stale state or prematurely attract traffic, causing secondary impact. A well-designed DR architecture controls this re-entry deliberately: validation precedes reintegration, and reintegration precedes resumption of authoritative operation.

All of these behaviors are amplified by the characteristics of **cross-region connectivity**. AWS Regions are joined by high-bandwidth, tightly controlled backbone links, while client traffic may traverse the public internet. This distinction determines the feasibility of different replication models. Synchronous replication is typically viable only within metro-level distances; across global regions, latency makes synchronous commit impractical, and asynchronous replication becomes the norm. As latency grows, so does RPO, and the system's ability to fail over without data loss becomes increasingly dependent on the behavior of replication during and after network stress.

Distributed systems built on consensus algorithms face similar constraints. Leadership changes, quorum decisions, and write durability are all network-dependent. A partition where one region cannot reliably exchange heartbeats or logs may cause leader elections, degraded write throughput, or unexpected read-staleness—even when both regions appear "up." In DR scenarios, these behaviors influence not only failover timing but also correctness guarantees after failover.

This interplay between partition, routing, DNS, consistency, and replication is why disaster recovery cannot be treated as a simple extension of high availability. DR is a fundamentally **network-shaped process**. It succeeds not when infrastructure is running in two regions, but when traffic, state, and orchestration move coherently between them under imperfect and shifting conditions.

Understanding these behaviors—and designing for them intentionally—is the difference between a failover that restores service safely and one that amplifies the failure into a second-order outage. For workloads that rely on cross-region resilience, the network is the critical determinant of whether recovery succeeds.

Before moving into operational execution, it is useful to distil the networking behaviors discussed above into the small set of failure modes that most often determine whether disaster recovery succeeds or compounds the outage.

The Networking Failure Modes That Most Often Break Disaster Recovery

Most unsafe disaster recovery outcomes are not caused by missing infrastructure, but by ambiguous or inconsistent network behavior. Three failure modes dominate real-world DR incidents:

- **Network Partition**

  Partial or asymmetric loss of connectivity between regions, services, or control planes. Partitions are more dangerous than clean outages because systems continue operating without reliable coordination, creating uncertainty rather than clear failure.

- **DNS Convergence Delay**

  DNS failover is gradual and uneven due to caching, resolver behavior, and TTL policies. Traffic shifts incrementally across geographies, often extending recovery timelines beyond theoretical RTOs.

- **Split Brain**

  Two regions simultaneously acting as authoritative. This leads to divergent writes, duplicated decisions, and correctness failures that frequently surface during reunification rather than during the outage itself.

The operational practices that follow are designed specifically to detect, contain, and sequence recovery in the presence of these conditions. In practice, this means treating uncertainty as a signal, sequencing authority deliberately, and allowing routing to converge only after state and capability are stable.

Operating a Disaster Recovery Plan

Operating a disaster recovery plan is not a matter of switching traffic from one region to another. It is a controlled, sequenced operation that must be executed with precision, awareness, and discipline. This section focuses on the *execution mechanics* of disaster recovery: detection, sequencing, routing control, and safe failback.

The first priority is establishing **reliable detection**. No disaster recovery action should begin on the basis of a single alarm or a single failing health check. Failover should be triggered only when multiple, independent signals converge: unreachable endpoints, stalled replication, rising error rates across geographies, control-plane inconsistencies, or persistent regional unreachability from external monitors. Your DR plan should define *which* signals matter, *how long* they must persist, and *who* has authority to confirm them. Acting too early creates instability; acting too late prolongs impact. The principle is simple: *failover begins when uncertainty becomes risk.*

Once failover is initiated, **sequence becomes everything**. Promote the data layer first; promote the application layer only when data is authoritative; adjust routing only when the application layer is ready. A disaster recovery plan must specify this sequence explicitly. Databases should never be promoted after routing has shifted. Caches should not begin serving traffic before they are warmed. Stateless components should not accept load before their dependencies are reachable. In well-run organisations, this sequence is not a suggestion—it is an enforced choreography.

Routing changes must be deliberate, not optimistic. DNS and Global Accelerator should move traffic only when the DR region is operationally ready, not merely "up." A mature DR plan therefore uses routing as the final step of cutover, not the first. Your recovery orchestration should include explicit readiness checks—latency thresholds, replication health, error budgets, and warm-up confirmations—before routing is allowed to converge.

During the transition, **observability becomes the stabilizer.** You should instruct teams to watch not just for green dashboards, but for the dynamics underneath: Are Availability Zones in the DR region balancing load correctly? Is replication catching up at the expected rate? Are retry storms forming under the surface? Do internal calls show rising tail latencies? Recovery is not complete when services start; it is complete when the system stabilizes under sustained load.

Failback—the return to the primary region—requires even more caution. A region becoming reachable is not the same as a region being safe to re-enter rotation. Before failback is considered, your plan should mandate:

- Consistency validation on databases and replicated state

- Confirmation that caches and configuration stores are current

- Full replication convergence

- Staged warm-up of the primary region

Traffic should be reintroduced gradually—first a small weight, then a balanced split, and only then full restoration. You can use one of the routing policies described earlier in Chapter 4, "weight," for example. Many secondary outages are caused not by the original failure, but by an over-eager attempt to failback before the system is ready.

The final best practice is the most overlooked: **no component should recover autonomously**. Auto-scaling groups, load balancers, server fleets, and even managed services should not make unilateral decisions during failover or failback. Your DR plan must centralize authority. Whether automation or humans control this orchestration, recovery must proceed according to a single, consistent plan. Autonomous recovery actions (instances restarting out of order, premature cache refills, background job restarts) are a common source of post-failover instability and must be centrally controlled.

Operating a disaster recovery plan, then, is an exercise in control. It is about ensuring the right actions happen at the right time, for the right reasons, with the right visibility. Architectures that treat DR as a simple switch inevitably encounter instability. Architectures that treat DR as a disciplined sequence—detect, confirm, promote, warm, redirect, validate—recover predictably.

If resilience engineering is about understanding how a system bends, disaster recovery is about guiding it safely back into alignment. When executed with discipline, it turns disruption into a controlled transition rather than a second failure.

Testing Disaster Recovery

Architecture diagrams and runbooks describe intended behavior during failover; controlled testing reveals how the system actually behaves. Section 8.2 established the principles of resilience testing—steady-state definition, hypothesis-driven experiments, controlled blast radius, observability readiness, and disciplined execution. Those same principles apply to disaster recovery, but DR testing introduces additional constraints: the scope is larger, the risk is higher, and the consequences of incorrect behavior are more severe. While operating a disaster recovery plan defines how recovery is executed, testing disaster recovery exists to prove that execution meets RTO, RPO, and correctness guarantees under real conditions.

Where resilience testing focuses on degradation—partial impairments, dependency failures, or network brownouts—DR testing focuses on **discontinuity**. The questions shift from "How does the system behave when a dependency slows down?" to "How does the system recover when the entire dependency must be abandoned?" DR testing is not about the system's ability to absorb impact; it is about its ability to recreate capability under pressure.

The first step is to treat DR testing as a **repeatable, hypothesis-driven exercise**, not a ceremonial simulation. A DR test must begin with a clear hypothesis: *If the primary region becomes unreachable, the workload should fail over to the secondary region within X minutes (RTO), with no more than Y seconds of data divergence (RPO), and with controlled routing convergence across clients.* Without this hypothesis, there is no objective way to assess success or failure. DR testing is not about confirming comfort—it is about measuring outcomes.

Testing begins before any failover action is taken. Just as resilience experiments cannot proceed without observability, DR tests require **full visibility into replication lag, backlog depth, cache state, routing behavior, and internal service readiness**. A DR plan that cannot be observed cannot be validated. Many organisations discover during their first DR test that they cannot quantify actual RPO, cannot see the state of replicated data, or cannot measure how quickly routing converges globally. That discovery alone proves why DR testing is essential.

The act of testing DR should follow the same discipline outlined in Section 8.2 but with **stronger safety boundaries.** You do not begin by failing over production traffic. You begin with dry runs: simulating failover without routing changes, promoting databases in isolation, validating that infrastructure can be provisioned cleanly in the DR region, and ensuring secrets, IAM roles, and configuration stores are coherent. Only when dry runs behave predictably do you expand the scope to controlled failover scenarios.

A mature DR testing practice includes **DR game days**, where cross-functional teams execute the full failover sequence: detection, confirmation, promotion, warm-up, routing adjustment, validation, and eventual failback. These are not theatrical exercises—they are operational rehearsals designed to force the plan to confront reality. During these game days, teams see how long the DR region takes to scale, how replication behaves under load, how traffic redistributes, and how user experience changes during the transition. Game days often uncover dependency chains that were invisible on diagrams, misconfigured IAM roles, stale IaC templates, or assumptions that fail at scale.

One of the most valuable aspects of DR testing is the opportunity to measure **true RTO and true RPO.** Many organisations carry theoretical numbers—an RPO of "seconds" or an RTO of "under ten minutes." In practice, the first DR test often reveals significantly higher values. Replication that appears "real time" under normal load may lag under disruption. Cache cold-start effects may stretch the recovery window. DNS convergence may take longer than laboratory estimates. Testing provides evidence, not aspiration, and DR plans must be updated to reflect what the system can actually achieve.

Testing must also address **failback**, a stage often neglected. Failback introduces its own hazards: data reconciliation, routing rebalancing, cache repopulation, and the risk of reintroducing unhealthy services prematurely. A complete DR test does not end when the DR region is serving traffic; it ends when the primary region has rejoined successfully, cleanly, and safely.

Finally, DR testing must be **continuous**, not episodic. A single annual DR exercise does not reflect the evolving nature of a cloud workload. Code changes, dependency upgrades, infrastructure modifications, IAM adjustments, and scaling behavior all alter the DR posture. DR tests should be run after major releases, prior to peak events, and on a periodic cadence determined by the workload's criticality. As with resilience experiments in Section 8.2, the value lies not in passing the test, but in the insights gained and the improvements that follow.

Disaster recovery is not proven by architecture—it is proven by behavior. Testing is the mechanism through which that behavior becomes visible, measurable, and trustworthy.

The Economics and Governance of Disaster Recovery

Disaster recovery is ultimately a business decision expressed through architecture. Every choice—synchronous replication, warm standby environments, multi-region failover capabilities—has a cost, a benefit, and a time dimension. The role of engineering is to provide the organization with clear trade-offs, not with ideals. A DR strategy that exceeds business need wastes resources; a DR strategy that underestimates business need creates existential risk. Costs and risks must be evaluated together, not independently.

The first pillar is **the cost of downtime**. A single hour of unavailability may represent lost revenue, regulatory penalties, reputational damage, operational disruption, or loss of customer trust. Understanding this cost is not optional; it defines the envelope within which RTO and RPO must fit. A workload that cannot tolerate more than a few minutes of downtime cannot live on Backup and Restore. A system that must never lose more than a few seconds of data requires cross-region replication. Governance begins with acknowledging that DR is a financial optimization problem constrained by operational and regulatory realities.

The second pillar is **the cost of readiness**. Active/active performs best but carries the highest operational cost, while Pilot Light minimizes compute expenditure but imposes higher lag during failover. AWS' elasticity helps, but costs still accumulate: cross-region data transfer, replicated storage, long-lived standby resources, and global routing layers all come with a price. Governance requires reviewing these costs periodically, adjusting strategy as workloads grow, and ensuring that the chosen architecture continues to reflect the business impact profile.

The third pillar is **compliance and auditability**. Many regulated industries—financial services, healthcare, government—require demonstrable evidence that critical systems can recover within stated timeframes. DR is not simply a technical mechanism; it is part of an organization's risk management posture. Documentation, test evidence, RTO/RPO validation reports, and failover runbooks are not administrative overhead. They are artifacts of trust. A DR plan that cannot be proven cannot be accepted by regulators, auditors, or customers. The impact of governance and economics becomes clearer when contrasting regulated and non-regulated workloads.

A regulated financial services workload—such as a payments platform or customer identity system—typically operates under explicit requirements for availability, data integrity, and recovery assurance. Supervisory frameworks often mandate defined RTO and RPO targets, regular disaster recovery testing, segregation of duties during failover, and auditable recovery evidence. In this context, disaster recovery is not an optimization exercise; it is a compliance obligation. Warm Standby or multi-region active/active architectures are frequently justified not because they are inexpensive, but because the cost of regulatory breach, prolonged unavailability, or data inconsistency far exceeds the ongoing cost of redundancy. Governance directly shapes architecture, and economics are evaluated in terms of avoided risk rather than infrastructure spend alone.

By contrast, a non-regulated workload—such as an internal analytics platform, batch processing system, or experimental service—may have no external recovery mandate beyond internal service-level expectations. Downtime of hours may be acceptable, and some data loss may be tolerable if results can be recomputed. In this case, Backup and Restore or Pilot Light strategies often represent the optimal balance. The organization consciously accepts longer recovery windows in exchange for significantly lower operational cost. Governance still exists, but it is internally defined and aligned to business impact rather than external obligation.

Both workloads may rely on the same cloud services and deployment mechanisms, yet their disaster recovery strategies diverge sharply. This illustrates the central principle of DR governance: recovery architecture is not selected purely on technical capability, but on regulatory context, risk appetite, and the real cost of downtime.

Finally, governance requires a **maturity model**, an understanding of where the organization's DR capability stands today and what improvements should be prioritized next. Immature organisations often begin with Backup and Restore and annual testing; mature ones adopt Pilot Light or Warm Standby with well-defined failover sequences; the most advanced organisations adopt active/active architectures and treat disaster recovery as a continuous state rather than a discrete event. Governance is the ongoing alignment between business risk, DR architecture, and operational discipline.

This chapter covered the fundamentals of monitoring and observability, resilience testing and disaster recovery—RPO, RTO with its four DR strategies, cross-region replication tools, failover orchestration, and the role of testing. But the heart of this book is cloud networking. We touched on these topics to the extent required for a complete understanding of resilience architectures, but each of those topics is a deep field in its own right. Each strategy, each replication model, each orchestration pattern could fill an entire book dedicated, for example, solely to DR engineering.

Our focus in this chapter remained aligned with the purpose of this book:

How networks shape resilience, how they create ambiguity during partial regional failures, how they influence routing convergence, DNS behavior, and state reconciliation and ultimately, how they determine whether a system recovers cleanly or accumulates risk under the surface.

Resilience as a whole, cannot be understood without the network, and the network cannot be understood without considering failure. The intersection of the two is where real-world architectures succeed—or fracture.

Lessons Learned

Chapter 8 brought together monitoring, resilience testing, and disaster recovery into a single resilience lifecycle.

Across these sections, a consistent theme emerged: cloud resilience is not achieved through isolated techniques, but through the interaction of observability, controlled experimentation, disciplined failover, and the networking behaviors that shape how distributed systems respond to stress. The lessons below capture the practical truths that surfaced throughout the chapter—truths that define resilient architectures in real-world cloud environments.

Observability is the foundation of resilience: A system cannot react predictably to failure if it cannot see itself clearly, across layers, regions, and network paths.

Signals only gain meaning when combined: Flow logs, metrics, health checks, and traces reveal resilience behavior only when interpreted together, not in isolation.

Steady state is the baseline against which all deviation is measured: Without a defined steady state, neither monitoring nor testing can determine whether the system remains within its resilience objectives.

Resilience testing is a discipline of controlled learning—not randomness: Experiments must be hypothesis-driven, observable, and designed to uncover hidden dependencies and behavioral gaps.

Most failures are partial, not total: Systems seldom collapse cleanly; they drift, hesitate, partition, or oscillate—behaviors that must be detected and handled intentionally.

Network partitions are more dangerous than region outages: Ambiguous reachability can mislead routing, DNS, automation, and operators, creating conditions far more complex than clean failure.

Split brain is the most severe distributed failure mode: Two regions acting authoritatively at once create correctness failures that surface only during reunification.

Failover succeeds only when executed in the correct order: Data must become authoritative before applications, and applications must stabilize before routing is shifted.

Failback requires more discipline than failover: A region becoming reachable does not make it ready—state, replication, caches, and routing must all resynchronize safely.

True RTO and RPO are discovered, not assumed: Disaster recovery testing exposes real behavior—replication lag, warm-up times, routing convergence, and global client transition.

Governance turns resilience into a repeatable capability: Runbooks, evidence, cadence, and shared responsibility turn architectural intent into steady operational practice.

Resilience is continuous, not episodic: As applications, dependencies, and regions evolve, so must observability, testing, and DR posture.

To the Final Chapter

With Chapter 8, we have completed the resilience lifecycle:

> From **observability** (how a system perceives itself)
>
> To **resilience testing** (how a system behaves under stress)
>
> To **disaster recovery** (how a system restores capability when stress becomes disruption)

But the future of resilience does not end at recovery. It extends into systems that can *predict* failure, not merely react to it; systems that shift traffic, tighten replication, or warm standby environments before conditions degrade; systems that use telemetry to forecast instability, and automation to mitigate it.

In the final chapter, we look ahead to that future, we will explore:

- **AI-driven predictive resilience and failure forecasting**

- **Emerging architectures for autonomous remediation**

- **The distant, but meaningful, role of quantum networking in long-distance coordination**

- **And a closing reflection on engineering for the inevitable outage—not as a failure of design, but as an expected state of distributed systems**

The future of resilience is not about eliminating failure.

It is about **detecting earlier, reacting smarter, and anticipating the unexpected— or, at this point, the inevitable.**

CHAPTER 9

The Next Decade of Cloud Resilience

Section 9.1: From Observability to Prediction: AIOps for Network Resilience

The Next Decade of Cloud Resilience

Operationally, the move from observability to prediction changes three things: teams stop treating alerts as *the start* of an incident, they start treating anomalies as *the start of a decision*, and they build automation that can act safely before users feel impact. Observability tells you what is happening; predictive operations tell you what is likely to happen next—and how much time you have to prevent a resilience boundary from being crossed.

Cloud networks have become too fast, too large, and too dynamic for human operators to understand in real time. The telemetry surface alone has exploded: inter-AZ latency measures, backbone probes, Direct Connect counters, flow logs across thousands of ENIs, millions of health checks, DNS queries from every corner of the planet, and a constant stream of routing decisions inside and across regions. Chapter 8 showed how to make this visible. But visibility alone is not enough. Modern networks fail in ways that are too subtle for static thresholds to catch, too interconnected for humans to correlate manually, and too fast-moving for traditional operations to intervene before users feel the impact.

AIOps emerged as a response to this scale. It is not a product category but a shift in operational philosophy: an approach where **machine learning sits on top of the observability fabric**, continuously learning what "normal" looks like, detecting

649

C. Critelli, *Cloud Networking and Resilience*, https://doi.org/10.1007/979-8-8688-2436-4_9

deviations in real time, correlating signals across layers, and triggering actions—sometimes human, sometimes automated—that prevent incidents from becoming outages. It is resilience measured not only by your recovery speed but also by your ability to **foresee instability** and steer the system away from it.

From a network engineer's perspective, AIOps is the natural evolution of everything we built so far: metrics, logs, distributed health checks, traffic steering, and failover logic. Observability explains what is happening; AIOps begins to explain **why** and, more importantly, **what will happen next** if we do nothing.

It is tempting to imagine AIOps as a futuristic, autonomous "self-healing network." That is not the goal. The purpose of AIOps in cloud networking is far more concrete:

- detect weak signals early,

- correlate disparate symptoms into a coherent story,

- forecast when a boundary (RPO, RTO, SLO, latency envelope) will be breached, and

- trigger the right remediation—automated where safe, human-led where judgment is required.

I like to think that resilience is not merely about returning to steady state; it is about preventing departures from it. AIOps is the discipline that bridges those two ideas.

Section 9.1: From Observability to Prediction: AIOps for Network Resilience

The more distributed a system becomes, the more its failures resemble weather patterns rather than discrete events. In earlier chapters, we learned how networks fail: not through sudden collapse, but through hesitation, drift, uneven latency curves, subtle congestion on one hybrid path, or resolver divergence during a DNS transition. These are not binary conditions. They are gradients—tiny deviations that accumulate long before users feel anything.

Human operators cannot see these gradients consistently. Not because humans are incompetent, but because distributed systems generate far more signals than any person, or any team, can reason about in real time. Resilience does not collapse because nobody was watching; it collapses because nobody could *notice the right deviation among thousands of others* at the moment it mattered.

This is where the operational model shifts.

Observability (Chapter 8) gives us sight.

AIOps gives us interpretation.

The leap from dashboards to prediction is the same leap from a weather station to a weather model. Both collect data; only one can project what comes next—and that projection is only useful if it changes how you operate. In the context of network resilience, the value of prediction is not academic. It is operational. Every meaningful form of resilience depends on *reaction time*:

- Routing convergence depends on how quickly drift is detected.

- DR mechanisms depend on how early replication lag is recognized.

- Hybrid failover depends on how soon a degraded path is identified.

- Application fallback logic depends on how clearly anomalies are distinguished from load.

- User experience depends on how quickly an emerging brownout is recognized, not when the outage is confirmed.

Prediction is the difference between reacting *after* the boundary is crossed and reacting *before the boundary exists at all*.

But predictive operations—AIOps—is not magic. It is not a giant black box. It is a **discipline** built on the same raw materials you already know: flow logs, RTT distributions, packet loss patterns, retransmission curves, backbone delay profiles, and DNS decision trees. The difference is scale and method. Humans spot patterns. Machines quantify them.

The role of AIOps in cloud networks is not to replace engineers but to extend the parts of engineering that do not scale linearly: the ability to observe millions of time series at once, to recognize similarities between behaviors months apart, to detect a deviation too small to cross a static alarm threshold, and to infer whether a failure mode is starting to form.

In this sense, AIOps is simply an extension of resilience engineering: it brings time into the equation. Instead of asking whether the system is healthy or unhealthy, AIOps asks whether the system is *moving toward* a state in which resilience objectives will be violated.

A near-zero RPO is meaningless if replication lag will breach it in twenty minutes.

A 30-second RTO is irrelevant if failover logic will stall under predicted conditions.

Active/active is an illusion if latency asymmetry is predicted to become unsustainable.

Prediction reframes resilience from a reactive posture ("are we within limits?") to a proactive one ("will we remain within limits long enough to avoid user impact?").

In the remainder of this section, we move beyond the marketing gloss surrounding "AI for operations" and dive into the mechanics of how predictive systems actually work when applied to cloud networking. We will examine how models learn "normal" patterns in network telemetry, how unsupervised ML extracts anomalies from multidimensional signals, how correlation engines identify the root cause of soft failures, how forecasting models anticipate when resilience thresholds will be crossed, and how these insights translate into automated or semi-automated action. Predictive operations is a broad field—far broader than we could exhaust in a single chapter—but here we will focus on the parts that matter most for resilience: the techniques that help a network anticipate stress, preserve its fault boundaries, and stay within its RPO/RTO commitments before failure becomes inevitable. The goal is simple: to show that predictive operations is not a futuristic ideal—it is the natural continuation of the observability system you already built.

The Data Substrate of AIOps

Predictive resilience begins long before any machine learning model is trained. It begins with data—not just any data, but data shaped in a way that expresses how a network behaves when it is healthy, when it is drifting, and when it is approaching a failure boundary. A cloud network generates extraordinary amounts of telemetry: packets, flows, RTT samples, health checks, routing updates, resolver logs, backbone measurements, replication lag, and retransmission curves. But none of it is immediately useful for prediction. Raw telemetry is messy, discontinuous, noisy, full of natural variability, and almost never aligned to the fault domains that matter for resilience.

This is the first challenge of AIOps in networking: **models cannot learn anything meaningful until the data is transformed into features that capture behavior, not just numbers**. This process—the quiet, unglamorous engineering behind any predictive system—is where most of the operational value actually comes from. And it requires understanding something fundamental about distributed networks: **their behavior is multidimensional, temporal, and deeply contextual**.

From Raw Signals to Interpretable Behavior

Take latency as an example. A single round-trip time measurement is meaningless in isolation. Latency fluctuates naturally with load, geography, time of day, packet size, provider conditions, and internal routing choices. A model cannot learn anything from "RTT = 5.3 ms." But it can learn from the *shape* of latency over time—the slow rise that precedes congestion, the asymmetry that suggests a failing AZ, and the sudden flattening of variance that indicates traffic has collapsed onto a single path.

This is true for every form of network telemetry. The value is never in the raw number; it is in the **pattern**, the *trajectory*, and the *relationship* between signals over time. The act of converting raw telemetry into pattern-rich signals is what makes predictive resilience possible.

Flow logs are another example. On their own, they are granular event dumps—five-tuple records that no model can digest directly. But once aggregated and transformed, they become indicators of traffic diversity, dependency relationships, retry behavior, and the emergence of unusual concentrations of flow. A subtle collapse in the diversity of destination prefixes, for instance, is often an early sign that traffic is no longer distributed as expected—a precursor to brownouts.

Routing telemetry undergoes a similar transformation. Instead of feeding models a textual "route was withdrawn," we express routing behavior as measurable transitions: the frequency of updates, the time a route takes to propagate across attachments, the divergence between routing tables that should be identical, and the convergence speed after a change. These derived features encode not just *what* happened, but *how* the control plane behaves under pressure.

Backbone health probes evolve into structured time series: the evolution of jitter, the volatility of RTT, the proportion of packets experiencing loss, and the behavior of these metrics under changing conditions. A model does not care about milliseconds; it cares whether a path is deviating from its baseline rhythm.

Even DNS logs—often overlooked in network analytics—become powerful signals when transformed. The distribution of resolver choices across geographies, the repetition of fallback patterns, the rate at which resolvers abandon a primary endpoint, and the consistency of responses across regions all hint at failover instability before any health check flips red.

What binds all of this together is the understanding that models cannot learn the semantics of the network—AZs, regions, hybrid paths, and failure domains—but they can learn **regularity**. They can learn what normal looks like, how each slice of the network usually behaves, and when the behavior deviates from expectation.

Time As the Missing Dimension

Network telemetry is not stationary. Its statistical properties drift constantly: traffic surges in the morning, falls at night, spikes at the end of billing cycles, and shifts during deployments and incident response. Any predictive system that treats network data as a static signal is doomed.

This is why predictive resilience relies heavily on temporal encoding—the act of expressing not just what the network is doing, but how it is moving through time. Rolling windows express short-term memory. Longer windows express historical behavior. Seasonality captures the difference between a Monday morning and a Saturday night. Change-point detection identifies when a system has adopted a new baseline.

These representations matter because prediction depends on context. A 10% rise in retransmission rate may be catastrophic at noon but entirely normal at 2 a.m. A sudden drop in flow volume might signal a misrouting event—unless it always happens at the start of backup windows. Temporal encoding transforms raw data into something that models can interpret with nuance.

Resilience Boundaries As the Skeleton of the Data

Resilience engineering introduces a perspective that most AIOps systems ignore: **fault boundaries**. An Availability Zone is not just a label; it is an independent failure domain with unique behavior (chapter 6). A hybrid path is not just a route; it is a distinct risk surface. A DNS failover decision is not just a response; it is a potential point of divergence.

A model does not need to understand what these constructs are. But the data pipeline must respect them. Instead of munging all telemetry into a single dataset, predictive systems align their features along resilience boundaries. Latency patterns are learned per AZ pair. Flow diversity is measured per hybrid path. Routing convergence is tracked per routing domain. DNS divergences are monitored per geographic resolver cluster.

This turns the network's architecture into the **implicit structure** of the data. Even unsupervised models—models with no explicit labels—begin to learn clusters that map naturally to the system's fault domains. When an AZ begins to drift, its metrics separate from the cluster the model has learned. When a hybrid link begins to degrade, its behavior becomes distinguishable from its peers. This is not magic; it is the result of shaping data in a way that mirrors the system's real fault surfaces.

This fault-boundary-first approach is what differentiates resilience-focused AIOps from generic AIOps: the goal is not to predict anomalies in isolation but to detect and forecast drift relative to the failure domains—Availability Zones, hybrid paths, routing domains, and regions—that determine blast radius and recovery outcomes.

Why This Foundation Matters

Predictive failure avoidance is often mischaracterized as an advanced capability—something that requires exotic models, deep learning, or expensive AI pipelines. But the truth is far simpler: prediction begins with representation. A system can only forecast what it can understand, and it can only understand the patterns that its data substrate allows it to express.

Once telemetry has been transformed into feature-rich time series aligned with resilience boundaries, the network gains a new form of introspection. It can begin to express questions that were previously invisible:

- Does this AZ's latency curve resemble the early stages of last year's brownout?

- Is this hybrid path starting to follow the same degradation trajectory that preceded the last incident?

- Are these DNS responses diverging in a way that suggests unstable failover behavior?

- Is replication lag drifting toward a point where RPO will be breached?

- Does this routing domain exhibit the same misalignment pattern that once caused a subtle but long-lived connectivity hole?

These questions are powerful not because of the algorithms that answer them, but because of the **structure encoded in the data**. Even so, this is also where many AIOps initiatives fail in practice. Before we move into the models themselves, it is worth calling out the most common ways predictive systems break—not in theory, but in real operations.

Predictive Resilience Anti-Patterns: What Breaks Predictive Systems

Predictive systems rarely fail because of model choice. They fail because the data substrate does not reflect how the network behaves under normal variability and under stress. Three anti-patterns appear repeatedly:

Poor feature shaping.

Feeding models raw events instead of behavioral signals. Single RTT samples, isolated packet-loss counters, or unaggregated flow records do not express system dynamics. Predictive models need distributions, trajectories, and relationships over time—not individual measurements.

Boundary ignorance.

Pooling telemetry across fault domains such as Availability Zones, hybrid paths, or routing domains. When signals from independent failure surfaces are averaged together, early drift disappears into noise. Prediction works best when features are aligned to the resilience boundaries the architecture depends on.

Static baselines.

Treating network behavior as stationary. Traffic patterns shift with time of day, deployments, and user geography. Systems that rely on fixed "normal" profiles either generate constant false positives or miss slow-moving degradation.

Avoiding these anti-patterns does not require sophisticated models. It requires shaping telemetry to express behavior, preserving fault-boundary context, and designing for non-stationary data.

Taken together, these failure modes reinforce the same point: predictive resilience is less about advanced algorithms and more about disciplined representation of how the network actually behaves.

With this substrate in place, the chapter can now move to the next part:

how models—supervised, unsupervised, and forecasting-based—learn, detect, and predict resilience drift.

How Predictive Models Learn Behaviors a Human Could Never See

Machine learning enters the resilience story at the moment observability reaches its natural limit. In earlier chapters, we built an instrumentation system capable of describing how the network behaves. But description alone does not create foresight. A system can be perfectly observable and still experience outages simply because nobody noticed the right signal soon enough. ML becomes relevant not as a buzzword, but as a necessity: the only mechanism capable of ingesting thousands of concurrent time series, correlating them across regions, and recognizing the latent structure in the network's behavior.

To understand how ML does this, we must start with a simple truth:

the network does not label its own failures.

There is no field in a log that says "this is the beginning of a brownout" or "this routing change will cause partial reachability in eight minutes." Failures in distributed systems are gradual and ambiguous; by the time the symptoms are clear enough for a human observer, the system has already crossed a resilience boundary.

So the first question any predictive system must answer is not "what kind of failure is this?" It is more primitive, more foundational:

"Is this behavior still consistent with what the network normally does?"

Unsupervised Learning: Discovering Normality in a System That Never Sits Still

Classical monitoring systems assume that network behavior is stable enough to measure through thresholds. This assumption fails immediately in a cloud environment. A link may be lightly used at 3:00 a.m. and congested at 3:00 p.m., without implying failure in either case. Cross-AZ latency may rise gently during monthly billing runs and drop sharply when streaming platforms finish their nightly ingestion. DNS traffic may double during an app release, stabilize in an hour, then oscillate as caches refresh globally. None of this is anomalous; it is simply behavior.

Unsupervised learning is the only model family that can understand such behavior without prior labels. Instead of starting with definitions of "good" and "bad," unsupervised systems attempt to map the *manifold* of normal operations. They observe tens of thousands of signals—latency distributions, jitter patterns, flow-volume profiles, DNS decision trees, replication lag curves—and infer the invisible geometry that connects them.

When these signals are healthy, they trace a narrow, predictable shape in this high-dimensional space. The shape is not specified by humans; it is discovered by the model. It becomes the mathematical representation of "this is how the system behaves when it is fine."

Failures reveal themselves not as spikes, but as **departures from this shape**.

A Zone drifting from its manifold.

A hybrid link departing from its usual rhythm.

DNS resolvers splitting into sub-clusters instead of moving as one.

Replication lag sliding into a region of the space it rarely occupies.

This approach is perfectly aligned with resilience engineering because resilience itself is defined as preservation of boundaries. Unsupervised ML discovers those boundaries empirically, from behavior, not configuration.

Supervised Learning: Giving Meaning to Deviation

Detection without interpretation is not enough. When the system begins to drift, operators need to understand whether the drift resembles something dangerous. But unlike in application-level ML, we cannot train a classifier on millions of historical labels. Network failures are too infrequent, too diverse, and too dependent on topology and sequencing.

Yet some patterns *do* recur.

A very specific pre-failure jitter signature may appear on a Direct Connect link hours before a carrier issue. An AZ entering a brownout may display a recognizable asymmetry in the p95–p99 latency distribution. DNS failover instability may always begin with a distinct stagger in resolver choice distributions across a handful of ISP clusters. Routing propagation errors often produce a characteristic "flicker pattern" in flow entropy before converging into a stable failure.

These recurring shapes are not common, but they are informative.

Supervised learning is used not to build a classifier of all failures but to recognize **the few precursor signatures that history has made familiar**.

The labeled data does not come from textbooks or research repositories; it comes from **your own incidents, chaos experiments, DR drills, and near misses**. A supervised model trained on this corpus provides a second layer of insight: when an anomaly matches a previously observed failure trajectory, the system can say so.

This transforms predictive operations from a generic "something is drifting" into a targeted "this looks like the beginning of the hybrid link saturation pattern we saw three months ago." That shift cuts hours of investigation into minutes—sometimes seconds— and fundamentally changes how operators reason about network health.

Forecasting Models: Predicting the Moment of Boundary Violation

Even interpretation is not enough for true resilience.

What matters most is **knowing whether a boundary will be crossed before it is crossed;** this is the domain of forecasting models.

Unlike anomaly detection systems, which compare present behavior to the past, forecasting systems project future behavior based on past dynamics. They do not simply ask whether a signal is drifting; they ask where the drift leads if nothing changes. That distinction is profound in resilience engineering because every resilience objective— RPO, RTO, MTTR, latency SLOs, and failover thresholds—is a boundary defined in time.

Forecasting models treat network telemetry as evolving sequences. They look at the slope of replication lag, not just its current value. They examine the second derivative of jitter across AZs, not just its mean. They model cross-AZ latency as a time series with seasonality, structural breaks, and long-term trends. They analyze backbone RTT volatility as an evolving distribution rather than a point metric.

In doing so, they can answer questions that static monitoring can never express:

- Replication lag is 1.3 seconds now but is accelerating toward your 5-second RPO in the next 18 minutes.

- Cross-AZ latency in us-east-1c has not violated thresholds yet but is on a trajectory that historically precedes brownouts.

- Hybrid link B is drifting into the same slope we observe before saturation events during end-of-quarter spikes.

- DNS failover paths will bifurcate within the next 15 minutes unless health checks stabilize.

This is a prediction in the strict, mathematical sense; the model is not guessing the future but extrapolating behavior based on learned structure.

In a distributed system that fails gradually rather than suddenly, forecasting is the only way to move from reactive mitigation to proactive adaptation.

Why All Three Models Matter—Together

Taken individually, each class of model solves a different problem:

- Unsupervised learning discovers when the system stops looking like itself.

- Supervised learning recognizes whether the deviation resembles a known pre-failure pattern.

- Forecasting models determine whether the deviation is taking the system toward a resilience boundary.

Together, they form a layered cognitive system: detection ➤ interpretation ➤ anticipation. Table 9-1 summarizes how each layer contributes a distinct operational capability, from detecting novelty to interpreting meaning to anticipating boundary violations.

***Table 9-1.** Predictive Resilience Model Stack*

Capability	Core Question	Typical Signals	Output you can act on
Unsupervised anomaly detection	*Is the network still behaving like itself?*	Drift across latency, jitter, and loss distributions; flow-entropy shifts; DNS decision patterns; routing-state dynamics	Anomaly score or risk index per path, Availability Zone, Region, or attachment
Correlation (system-level inference)	*Which deviations are related, and which component is most likely upstream?*	Temporal ordering of symptoms, topology constraints, and dependency behavior fingerprints	Correlated anomaly groups with likely origin and estimated blast radius
Supervised pattern recognition (interpretation layer)	*Does this correlated deviation resemble a known pre-failure pattern?*	Labeled signatures from past incidents, DR drills, chaos experiments, and near misses	Match confidence against known failure trajectories and expected impact type
Forecasting (time-to-impact)	*When will a resilience boundary be crossed if nothing changes?*	Trends, seasonality, and change points in utilization, replication lag, latency envelopes, or error rates	Time-to-breach estimate and probability of crossing a defined threshold

Individually, none of these capabilities is sufficient; together, they turn raw observability into foresight that can be acted on before resilience objectives are breached. This is not abstract theory; it is resilience engineering translated into mathematics.

In a cloud network, no human operator—regardless of skill or intuition—can observe all signals, correlate all behaviors, and reason about future risk with this degree of breadth and depth. But models can, because they operate not through intuition but through structure. They make the implicit patterns of the network explicit.

And once the network can articulate its own patterns, it can finally articulate its own warnings.

How Correlation Engines Identify the Root of Soft Network Failures

Detecting an anomaly in a cloud network is straightforward; everything emits metrics, and many of them move constantly. The hard part is understanding *why* a deviation appeared. In a distributed system, dozens of signals change at the same time for reasons that have nothing to do with failure. A deployment pushes slightly different traffic patterns. A cache warms up. A client population shifts geography. Even the global Internet adjusts its routes continuously. If you simply look for metrics that "spike together," everything correlates with everything, and nothing explains the problem.

Predictive systems address this by learning how the network behaves as a *system*, not as a collection of independent counters. Instead of looking at one metric at a time, they analyze how signals relate to each other under normal conditions: which ones typically move first, which ones respond shortly after, and which ones only shift when a specific dependency is under stress. This lets the system distinguish between random noise and meaningful patterns. When a deviation appears, the model checks whether the pattern resembles known behavior that historically preceded real issues.

The first ingredient is timing. Failures rarely hit all components at once; they unfold in sequences. A small increase in inter-AZ jitter may appear long before an ALB shows elevated latency, and retries may begin rising before anyone sees user-visible errors. Models learn these temporal offsets by analyzing large amounts of historical telemetry. When multiple anomalies arise, the system checks whether the ordering matches any of the known sequences associated with previous degradations. This prevents the classic human error of blaming the metric that moved last simply because it is the most visible.

The second ingredient is topology. A cloud network enforces strict boundaries: some components influence each other directly; others cannot possibly interact. A Transit Gateway propagation delay cannot cause packet loss between two EC2 instances sitting in the same subnet. A degraded Direct Connect link cannot explain DNS resolver drift in another region. Predictive systems build an internal representation of these dependencies by observing long-term traffic patterns, routing behavior, and replication flows. That topology model acts as a filter: if two anomalies originate in components that never interact, they are dismissed as unrelated regardless of how similar their metric graphs look. This dramatically reduces false correlations.

The final ingredient is dependency behavior. Every distributed system has characteristic reactions to stress. If a database replica slows down, API latency does not spike immediately—it rises in a gradual, recognizable curve. If an Availability Zone begins to struggle, ALBs shift traffic away in a very specific pattern. If a hybrid link degrades, applications relying on it show a distinctive retry pattern that differs from local connectivity issues. Predictive systems learn these behavioral fingerprints implicitly through their model weights. When similar patterns reappear, the system can infer which upstream component is likely causing the downstream symptoms.

With these three dimensions—timing, topology, and behavioral fingerprints—a correlation engine can separate cause from effect. Instead of saying "many things look wrong," it can estimate which component is most likely responsible and with what level of confidence. In practice, this might look like identifying that a subtle rise in global API latency is most consistent with a cross-AZ path beginning to degrade, rather than with a database or compute bottleneck. Humans can perform this reasoning, but it takes time, and during an incident, time is a luxury. Predictive systems compress that thinking into seconds.

For resilience, this capability matters because most failures are not outages—they're drifts. They're the slow erosion of a fault boundary: inter-AZ latency shifting outside its usual range, a hybrid path becoming slightly unstable, a subset of DNS resolvers making inconsistent choices, or a routing update taking longer than expected to propagate. None of these triggers a traditional alert on its own. All of them, however, can accumulate into conditions that push a system beyond its RPO or RTO commitments. Correlation engines detect these early, not because any one metric is alarming, but because the *pattern* of deviations matches known precursors to real degradation.

What you gain is time—minutes or sometimes hours—to rebalance traffic, shift routing preferences, scale out proactively, or simply avoid crossing a threshold that would otherwise lead to user-visible impact. That timing difference is often the margin between graceful degradation and a full incident.

This is the role of correlation engines in predictive resilience: turning a stream of ambiguous, noisy signals into early, actionable understanding of where the system is bending, why it is bending, and whether it is about to break.

Forecasting Resilience Drift: Predicting When the Network Will Cross Its Thresholds

If correlation engines explain *why* something is happening, forecasting models answer a different question: *when will this become a problem?*

In cloud networking, most failures do not appear as sudden breaks. They emerge gradually, often invisibly at first, as slow drifts in behavior that remain technically "within limits" until the moment they are not. This is where forecasting becomes essential. A system that can detect a problem is good; a system that can see a problem coming is resilient.

Forecasting models work by learning the shape of normal behavior over time—its trends, its seasonality, and its acceptable ranges. Networks, like mechanical systems, have rhythms. Traffic ebbs and flows throughout the day. Hybrid paths heat up during business hours and cool during the night. Inter-AZ latency rises predictably during peak periods, then stabilizes. Even error rates have patterns. Humans sense these rhythms intuitively after years of experience, but humans cannot watch thousands of metrics continuously. Predictive models can.

The simplest form of forecasting is boundary estimation: determining whether a signal is likely to breach a meaningful threshold in the near future. For example, if Direct Connect utilization has been rising steadily for the last thirty minutes and the slope of the increase is consistent, the model can project when the link will hit saturation— perhaps in seven minutes, perhaps in twenty. The exact time is less important than the advance warning. Saturation on a hybrid link does not appear suddenly; it is usually the last stage of a trend that began long before. Forecasting brings that trend into focus early enough that operators or automated systems can react before the boundary is crossed.

More advanced models look beyond a single signal. They observe the relationships between metrics as they evolve. Consider inter-AZ latency: it rarely increases in isolation. When a single AZ begins drifting, you often see packet retransmissions rise shortly afterward, followed by uneven load balancer distribution, followed eventually by application latency. A model trained on historical patterns learns that once the first two symptoms appear, the third is likely to follow within a predictable time window. This transforms anomaly detection into early-stage prediction. Instead of alerting when latency is *already too high*, the system alerts when latency is *moving toward* a breach.

In hybrid networking, forecasting becomes even more valuable. Degradation of an on-premises link or intermediate provider path often begins with tiny, nearly invisible increases in jitter or loss that humans would never notice. Models trained on long-term telemetry can detect that the jitter profile has shifted into a pattern that historically preceded partial outages. They cannot guarantee that failure will occur, but they can assign a probability that such a pattern leads to impact. In a resilience context, probability is enough to adjust routing weights, warm up alternate paths, or slow down deployments that would otherwise stress the system at the worst possible moment.

Another subtle but important aspect of forecasting is its ability to detect when *recovery* is unlikely. After a network impairment, metrics often oscillate as the system tries to stabilize. A model trained on healthy recovery patterns can identify when a recovery curve is diverging rather than converging. This gives operators early warning that the system is not healing as expected and may require manual intervention. In resilient architectures, knowing that a recovery is failing is as important as predicting the failure in the first place.

Forecasting is not magic, nor is it perfect. Models can misinterpret noise as a trend or overlook slow-moving changes that have no historical precedent. But the value is not in precision forecasting; it is in directional insight. A predictive system does not need to know exactly when a link will saturate; it only needs to know that saturation is *coming*. It does not need to know the precise moment when inter-AZ latency will breach its envelope; it only needs to know that the curve is bending the wrong way. These early signals enable architecture and operations teams to act before resilience boundaries are violated.

Ultimately, forecasting shifts resilience from reactive to proactive. Instead of waiting for failures to trigger alarms, the system highlights where failures are likely to emerge. It gives operators time. It gives automation context. It gives the architecture a chance to preserve continuity *before* the crisis arrives. And in distributed systems—where recovery takes time, replication can stall, and routing changes propagate gradually—that time is often the difference between a smooth failover and a broad, user-visible disruption.

Closing the Loop: Turning Predictions into Safe, Automated Action

Prediction has no value unless it changes what the system does.

A model that forecasts an impending saturation event or identifies the early signature of an Availability Zone drift is only useful if that insight flows into decision-making—either by informing operators or by triggering automated corrective steps. But closing this loop is where predictive resilience becomes difficult. Automation can protect a system; it can also destabilize one if it reacts too aggressively, too often, or without understanding the broader context. The challenge is to build automation that is anticipatory but not impulsive, decisive but not brittle.

The first principle is that predictive signals must feed into a *decision framework*, not directly into actuators. In cloud networking, every action—shifting routing weight, initiating cross-region failover, or draining an impaired AZ—carries consequences. A naive automation pipeline that immediately reacts to a forecasted threshold crossing would create more incidents than it prevents. Instead, predictions are treated as early warnings that elevate system attention. The automation layer may validate the signal with additional checks, correlate it with recent deployments, or compare it with independent telemetry sources. When prediction and verification align, the system transitions from observation to action.

These actions usually fall into two categories: **protective** and **preparatory**. Protective actions reduce the likelihood of failure by modifying traffic patterns or redistributing load—for example, adjusting the weight of a Direct Connect path predicted to saturate or slowly draining traffic from an Availability Zone showing early drift. These actions operate within the existing architecture and do not change the system's topology. Their purpose is to keep the system within its resilience envelopes long enough for operators to intervene if required.

Preparatory actions, on the other hand, adjust the system's readiness. If the model predicts rising instability in a region, automation may warm up resources in another region, accelerate checkpointing, increase replication frequency, or pre-scale the compute layer. These steps do not assume that failure is inevitable; they simply position the architecture to tolerate it with minimal impact if it does occur. This is one of the most powerful aspects of predictive resilience: it allows the system to shift into a more defensive posture *before* the incident materializes.

Closing the loop also requires guardrails that prevent automation from making the situation worse. For example, if a forecasting model predicts cross-AZ degradation, blindly shifting traffic away might overload the remaining zones or trigger unintended cascading effects. To avoid this, automated actions must be bounded by capacity models, dependency graphs, and the same resilience boundaries discussed earlier in the book. In practice, this means defining "safe" and "unsafe" actions for each predicted scenario, along with the conditions under which automation may proceed or must defer to human oversight. Predictions are probabilistic; safeguards must be deterministic. A useful rule of thumb is this: automation may act as long as it adjusts reversible parameters within a single fault domain and the predicted outcome remains bounded. The moment an action would irreversibly change topology, expand blast radius, or consume scarce shared capacity across domains, the decision must shift to a human operator. In other words, automation can rebalance, bias, or prepare—but actions that commit the system to a new failure mode require human judgment.

Another essential component is acknowledging that predictions themselves can fail. A model may misread a pattern, interpret deployment noise as instability, or overlook a novel failure mode. Mature predictive systems incorporate feedback loops that adjust model behavior based on how well predictions matched reality. After a predicted event is averted—or after one unexpectedly materializes—the system compares the outcome to the model's expectations and adapts its parameters. This continual learning tightens the alignment between prediction and actual system behavior over time.

Finally, predictive automation must be observable and explainable. Operators need to understand *why* the system is preparing to shift load or warm up a failover region, not simply that it has done so. Explanations do not need to be mathematically detailed; they need to be operationally meaningful. When automation is explainable, operators trust it. When it is opaque, they override it—and a system that is constantly overridden is not resilient.

Putting this all together, closing the loop transforms predictive analytics from an advisory capability into an operational one. The system senses early signals of drift, verifies them, and takes measured action to remain within RPO, RTO, and HA commitments. It does not replace human operators; it buys them time and reduces the cognitive load required during the early minutes of an incident. And because the actions are bounded by fault-domain awareness and embedded safeguards, predictive automation strengthens stability rather than compromising it.

Predictive resilience is not about letting machines run the system. It is about letting machines notice what humans cannot see soon enough and enabling the architecture to defend itself before conditions deteriorate. In a world where most failures grow slowly before they break suddenly, that head start is often the most powerful form of resilience any network can have.

From Prediction to Prevention: How AIOps Reshapes Incident Response Models

Traditional incident response assumes a simple sequence: something breaks, an alarm fires, humans investigate, and the system is stabilized. This model worked when infrastructure moved slowly, when topologies were fixed, and when the blast radius of failure was narrow. But cloud networking behaves differently. Failures emerge gradually, propagate unevenly, vary by client geography, and grow at speeds that surpass the pace of human-only diagnosis. In a distributed, multi-region environment, waiting for an alarm means the resilience boundary has already been crossed.

Predictive systems change this dynamic by shifting the inflection point of an incident. Instead of treating resilience as a process that starts after failure, predictive resilience begins before the system drifts into danger. Once anomaly detection, correlation, and forecasting are integrated into operations, the familiar sequence of "detect ➤ diagnose ➤ mitigate" becomes "anticipate ➤ prepare ➤ adjust." The shape of incidents changes because the architecture begins defending itself proactively.

The first practical impact is that incidents start earlier on the timeline—at the moment the system detects a precursor, not at the moment of failure. In a network context, this might be when inter-AZ jitter moves into an unusual pattern, when hybrid return-path asymmetry begins to emerge, or when DNS resolvers in a specific geography start choosing different endpoints than expected. None of these is a failure on its own. But predictive systems recognize these as early signs of strain. For the operations team, the "start of incident" becomes the moment the model identifies a dangerous trajectory, not when user-facing errors appear.

The second impact is that mitigations become smaller, safer, and more reversible. In a reactive model, adjustments are large because they must be decisive: shifting all traffic out of an impaired AZ, disabling an entire routing path, and failing over to another region. These interventions carry high risk and significant operational cost, but they are necessary when the system is already degraded. Predictive systems allow interventions to be subtle. Instead of failing over, the system gradually drains a fraction of traffic from an AZ showing drift. Instead of switching routing entirely, weights are nudged to buy headroom on a path projected to saturate. Instead of triggering a full DNS failover, a region is quietly prepared for activation while the system continues functioning normally. The result is a gentler, more controlled operational posture.

The third change is cognitive: operators no longer enter an incident in a state of incomplete information. When predictive models surface early indicators, they bring context with them. They show which parts of the architecture are deviating from baseline, which metrics are expected to deteriorate next, and which past incidents had similar signatures. This shortens the investigative phase dramatically. Instead of sifting through dashboards to determine whether the issue is networking, compute, DNS, or a dependency, operators start with a ranked hypothesis built from the system's own history.

Most importantly, predictive operations upgrade the role of humans from firefighters to decision-makers. Instead of spending the first twenty minutes discovering what is wrong, teams spend those twenty minutes deciding what to do about it—whether to allow automation to continue, whether to override it, or whether to initiate a controlled failover. This redirection of attention—from diagnosis to strategy—is one of the most significant cultural shifts in resilient engineering.

None of this eliminates failure. Networks will still degrade, links will still saturate, resolvers will still diverge during rare DNS events, and dependencies will still behave unpredictably. But the shape of these failures changes. Instead of sudden, explosive outages, organizations experience slow-approaching conditions that can be managed while the system remains within its resilience boundaries. Instead of entering an incident with too little information, operators enter with more than they need. Instead of reacting when users are already impacted, the system stabilizes itself long before the customer notices.

This is the promise of predictive resilience: it does not make failures impossible, but it makes them uneventful. It reduces drama, reduces blast radius, and replaces surprise with preparedness. It does not replace the need for architecture, observability, or chaos testing; it amplifies their value by using their signals to anticipate what comes next.

To make this more tangible, and to close this section, I want to show how these ideas can be assembled into a real architecture using AWS-native building blocks. This is not theory; it is a pattern I see customers and partners explore in my role at AWS today.

A Reference Architecture for Predictive Network Resilience on AWS

So far in this chapter, predictive resilience has been described as a collection of capabilities: anomaly detection, correlation, forecasting, and safe automation layered on top of the observability foundation you built in Chapter 8. Before moving to the final section, it is worth grounding these ideas in a concrete form—a reference architecture showing how these capabilities can be implemented today using AWS-native services.

How to read Figure 9-1: treat it as a left-to-right pipeline. Signals enter on the left as raw telemetry and change events, are shaped in the middle into features aligned to fault boundaries, and exit on the right as bounded operational decisions. The ML layer converts history into risk signals (anomaly scores and time-to-impact forecasts), and those signals re-enter operations as ordinary metrics and events that can trigger either reversible automation or a human decision. Read it once as "signal ➤ insight ➤ decision," then come back for the service-by-service detail.

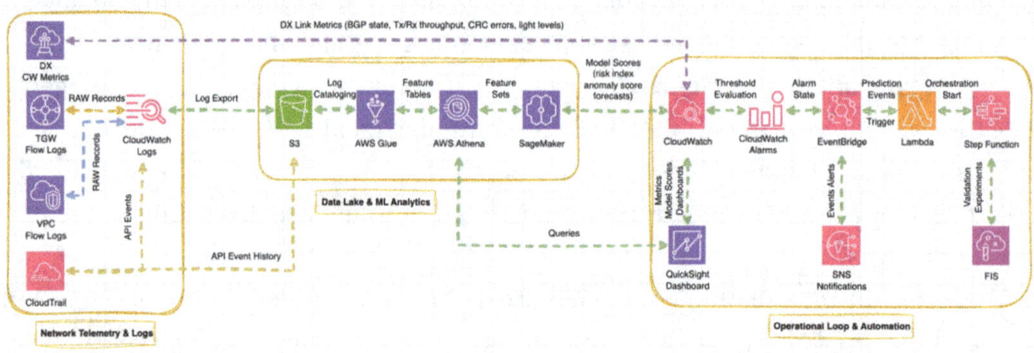

Figure 9-1. *Reference architecture for predictive network resilience on AWS*

Figure 9-1 summarizes this closed-loop architecture in three domains: telemetry, analytics, and operational response.

Signals from AWS Transit Gateway, Direct Connect, Site-to-Site VPN, load balancers, and Route 53 health checks are surfaced through CloudWatch metrics and health probes—covering availability, throughput, error patterns, and control-plane behavior—while path characteristics such as RTT and loss are typically inferred from health checks, synthetic probes, or time-series analysis of observed behavior. VPC Flow Logs and Transit Gateway Flow Logs provide packet-level context, delivered either to CloudWatch Logs or directly into Amazon S3. AWS CloudTrail captures every configuration and API event across these networking components, creating an immutable timeline of what changed and when. Together, these systems form the factual baseline of how the network behaves over time.

These raw facts are then shaped into something models can learn from. S3 serves as the central data lake for historical telemetry, while AWS Glue infers schemas and maintains the data catalog. Amazon Athena queries this telemetry into structured feature sets—for example, per-AZ latency distributions, per-link utilization time series, health-check deviation patterns, or error-rate histories for specific Transit Gateway attachments. Lightweight AWS Lambda functions enrich this data by aligning timestamps, normalizing units, and attaching topology identifiers such as region, Availability Zone, or VIF/attachment IDs. At this stage, the network is no longer just emitting logs; it is producing numerical histories suitable for machine learning.

The predictive layer sits on top of this foundation, typically implemented in Amazon SageMaker. Here, models learn what "normal" looks like along each boundary. Time-series models forecast utilization, latency, or jitter envelopes for critical paths, while anomaly-detection models identify when multi-dimensional telemetry begins drifting into patterns that historically preceded impairments. These models may run as real-time SageMaker endpoints for continuous scoring or as scheduled batch jobs at fixed intervals. Their outputs are numerical scores—indicators that a given path is statistically unsafe or trending toward breaching resilience thresholds.

These predictions are then reintroduced into operations. Prediction scores are published back into CloudWatch as **custom metrics** using the PutMetricData API, allowing CloudWatch Alarms to evaluate them just as they would any native metric. In parallel, structured prediction events are emitted to Amazon EventBridge, annotated with context such as region, path ID, severity, and predicted time-to-impact. At this point, predictive signals sit alongside traditional operational signals, and EventBridge becomes the routing layer for decisions.

Automation lives here. AWS Lambda functions validate predictions, cross-check them against independent telemetry, enforce guardrails, and perform low-risk adjustments such as nudging Route 53 routing weights or biasing Global Accelerator endpoint weights. More elaborate multi-step orchestration—such as draining an impaired Availability Zone, preparing a secondary region for activation, or executing a staged traffic shift—is implemented in AWS Step Functions. These workflows provide transparency, auditability, branching logic, and optional human approval. And because automation must be validated, the same Step Functions workflows can invoke AWS Fault Injection Service actions to test whether alternate paths behave exactly as expected, closing the resilience loop.

1. Network Telemetry and Logs (Left Column)

Telemetry from AWS Direct Connect, Transit Gateway, Site-to-Site VPN, load balancers, and Route 53 health checks is surfaced through CloudWatch metrics and health probes—covering availability, throughput, error patterns, and control-plane behavior—while path characteristics such as RTT and loss are typically inferred from health checks, synthetic probes, or time-series analysis of observed behavior.

VPC Flow Logs and **Transit Gateway Flow Logs** supply packet-level evidence of traffic patterns, delivered either to **CloudWatch Logs** or stored directly in **Amazon S3**.

AWS CloudTrail records configuration, routing, and API activity across these networking services, providing the authoritative timeline of changes.

Together, these sources form the factual substrate of how the network behaves and evolves over time.

2. Data Lake and ML Analytics (Center Column)

Amazon S3 acts as the long-term telemetry lake. **AWS Glue** maintains a unified catalog of flow logs, CloudTrail events, and exported metrics. **Amazon Athena** transforms these datasets into structured feature tables—for example, per-AZ latency distributions, Direct Connect utilization histories, link-level anomaly baselines, and enriched flow aggregates.

Amazon SageMaker trains two classes of models on these feature sets:

- **Anomaly-detection models**, which learn what "normal" looks like across multidimensional signals

- **Forecasting models**, which predict when utilization, RTT, or error rates will breach resilience thresholds

Model outputs—risk indices, anomaly scores, early-warning divergence measures, or short-term forecasts—are published back into **CloudWatch** as **custom metrics** and emitted as structured events into **EventBridge**.

Dashboards in **Amazon QuickSight** query Athena to visualize both the raw telemetry and the ML-derived insights, giving operators interpretive context.

3. Operational Loop and Automation (Right Column)

CloudWatch Alarms evaluate both traditional metrics and SageMaker-generated prediction metrics. When a prediction metric crosses a risk threshold, the alarm state emits an EventBridge event.

Amazon EventBridge becomes the decision router: it forwards prediction events—annotated with region, path, and severity—to **AWS Lambda** for first-layer validation. Lambda enforces guardrails, cross-checks predictions against independent signals, and decides whether intervention is required.

For complex mitigations, Lambda triggers **AWS Step Functions**, which orchestrate multi-step workflows such as

- Draining an Availability Zone

- Adjusting routing bias (Route 53 or Global Accelerator)

- Warming up a secondary region

- Reconfiguring hybrid paths or attachments

Where appropriate, Step Functions can also invoke **AWS Fault Injection Service**, performing controlled impairments to confirm that backup paths, routing domains, and failover mechanisms behave correctly under stress.

Finally, **SNS notifications**, CloudWatch Dashboards, and QuickSight visualizations keep operators informed and in control, ensuring humans remain part of the decision loop even when automation is active.

Together, these components form a closed predictive-resilience loop: telemetry becomes insight, insight becomes action, and action is continuously validated. The architecture demonstrates how AWS-native services can be assembled today to anticipate network drift, detect degradation before it becomes failure, and take controlled corrective steps while operators remain fully informed.

With this reference architecture, predictive resilience stops being theoretical and becomes a practical capability. It does not replace human expertise—it amplifies it with earlier signals, clearer context, and safer automation. It also strengthens the architectural principles established throughout this book and sets the stage for the final section, which looks beyond today's tools toward the future of global networking.

Having built a predictive architecture around the protocols we rely on today, the natural question becomes: what happens when those protocols reach their limits? The next section looks beyond BGP and into the emerging ideas shaping the future of resilient networking.

Section 9.2: Beyond BGP: Path-Aware and Quantum Networks

I know you are wondering... "Why Talk About Quantum Networking in a Book About Cloud Network Resilience?"...

At first glance, quantum networking looks like something that belongs in a physics lab, not in a book about cloud networking and resilience. Today, no production AWS VPC is running over entangled photons, and no routing table in your environment is programmed by a quantum algorithm. The internet still runs on fiber, routers, and BGP—just as it has for decades.

So why devote space in the final chapter to a topic that, for most practitioners, feels years or even decades away? There are three reasons.

First, **classical networking has hard limits**. We have spent the entire book working inside those constraints: speed-of-light latency across regions, BGP convergence delays after failures, the risk of partitions between metros, and the fragility of key exchange and encryption in a world where compute continues to grow. Path-vector protocols like BGP are extraordinarily successful, but they are also known to converge slowly and can get stuck in pathological states when policies interact badly. Many of the resilience problems we wrestle with are not misconfigurations; they are consequences of how classical routing and physics work.

Second, **quantum technologies are no longer purely theoretical**. AWS has a dedicated Center for Quantum Networking (CQN), actively researching how quantum-secured communication and entanglement-based networks might underpin future cloud infrastructure, and has already run metropolitan quantum-secured communication pilots with customers. Governments and telecom operators are building early quantum key distribution (QKD) networks and long-distance entanglement testbeds. These are not yet general-purpose "quantum internets," but they are concrete experiments that target exactly the domains we care about: **security, integrity, and resilience of critical networks**.

Third, and most importantly, **quantum networking forces us to revisit core assumptions about failure and resilience**. In classical networks, we duplicate packets, cache state, and replay messages. In quantum systems, the no-cloning theorem forbids copying unknown quantum states, quantum repeaters behave differently from routers, and entanglement-based links fail in probabilistic ways that don't map neatly to "packet drops." Even if you never work directly with quantum hardware, the design questions it raises are the same ones you already face today: how to define isolation boundaries, how to reason about trust, and how to build systems that remain correct when the underlying transport behaves in unfamiliar ways.

This section is not an attempt to turn you into a quantum physicist, nor to predict the exact shape of a "quantum internet." Entire shelves of books are devoted to those topics, and more will come. Instead, my goal is narrower and more practical:

- To explain, in plain engineering terms, **what "quantum networking" actually means**—beyond marketing slides.

- To explore **how quantum communication and QKD might intersect with the kind of cloud backbones and multi-region architectures** we've discussed so far.

- To show **how the resilience principles you've learned in this book still apply**, even when the transport layer changes radically.

To manage expectations, it helps to separate these ideas by time horizon. Some technologies discussed here—such as quantum key distribution and path-aware routing overlays—are already being piloted or approximated in production environments today. Others, particularly entanglement-based networking and quantum repeaters, remain long-term research efforts that may reshape networking fundamentals over the coming decades rather than the next deployment cycle.

We cannot possibly cover the full breadth of quantum networking in a single section, and we should not try. What we can do is focus on the parts that matter most for you as a cloud and network engineer: where classical networking is reaching its limits, what quantum research is realistically exploring as "next," and how those ideas might reshape the way we think about resilience, security, and global routing in the long term.

In the next subsection, we'll start by looking at the constraints of the world you already know—classical networks and BGP—and use those constraints as the stage on which quantum networking enters the picture.

The Limits of Classical Networking (and Why They Matter for Resilience)

Before we can understand what quantum networking brings to the table, we need to confront the boundaries of the world we operate in today. Not theoretical boundaries, but the ones you feel every time you architect a multi-region system: the limits of physics, the limits of routing protocols, and the limits of distributed consistency. These constraints are the reason outages propagate, the reason recoveries are never instantaneous, and the reason resilience is an ongoing discipline rather than a solved problem.

The first and most unavoidable boundary is **speed of light latency**. When you replicate data between Frankfurt and Oregon, the minimum one-way propagation time is dictated by fiber distance and refractive index—there is no amount of optimization, caching, or clever routing that makes information travel faster than physics allows. This constraint forces every multi-region architecture to choose between consistency and availability, because synchronous replication across continents simply cannot maintain tight latency budgets. We compensate with asynchronous replication, conflict resolution strategies, and carefully partitioned data domains, but the underlying reason is always the same: nothing moves faster than light in glass.

The second constraint emerges from the behavior of **BGP**, the protocol that quite literally holds the global internet together. BGP is a path-vector protocol built on incremental update propagation, local decision-making, and implicit trust in neighbors. It converges eventually, but "eventually" can mean seconds or minutes during volatile events. During that window, global routing is neither consistent nor predictable. Some networks see the new path first; others lag; some flap between alternatives as updates ripple through the internet. The result is familiar: asymmetric paths, intermittent reachability, and the partial failures that dominate real-world incidents. These are not implementation bugs—they are how BGP works. When a link fails in a continent-spanning backbone, convergence is not instantaneous; it is smeared across geography and time.

What makes this even more relevant for resilience is how **policy-driven** BGP is. Two networks may prefer completely different paths even when the "shortest" path is available, because routing decisions are shaped by business agreements, traffic engineering constraints, and local preferences—not global optimization. This decentralized autonomy is what makes the internet robust at a planetary scale, but it also means that during failures, no single operator can predict exactly how traffic will reroute. Convergence is not just slow; it is path-dependent, policy-dependent, and non-deterministic. For multi-region cloud architectures, this manifests as sporadic reachability issues, inconsistent DNS resolver behavior across geographies, and cross-region failover sequences that do not activate uniformly. Classical routing gives us resilience through diversity, but it also gives us unpredictability through decentralization.

A second consequence of BGP's design is that **failures propagate differently** than inside tightly controlled cloud networks. When a fiber cut happens in a metropolitan area, some upstream networks may withdraw prefixes immediately, some may hold onto stale routes, and others may briefly oscillate as multiple alternatives compete. The propagation of these updates across tens of thousands of autonomous systems takes time and unfolds unevenly. This explains why an outage affecting only a single backbone path can create globally inconsistent symptoms: some users see the service; others do not; some oscillate between working and failing. These partial failures are often the hardest to diagnose because they are rooted in the mechanics of global convergence, not local misconfiguration.

The third classical limitation is the fragility of **cryptographic trust anchored in computational hardness**. Today's encryption rests on the difficulty of factoring large numbers or solving discrete logarithms. Quantum computers, if they reach sufficient scale, threaten these assumptions. This is not an operational outage in the traditional sense—but it is a resilience event of a different kind, one that undermines the trust layer on which all secure communication relies. Post-quantum cryptography will help, but it is a software solution layered over the same physical channels and routing behaviors that remain vulnerable to interception, manipulation, or compromise during misconfigurations or hijack attempts. In other words, the channels are classical and therefore inherit classical risks.

Finally, classical networks are fundamentally designed around copying data to preserve it, caching it to accelerate it, and replaying it to recover it. These behaviors— duplication, buffering, and retransmission—form the backbone of TCP/IP reliability. They also create the conditions for failure amplification: queues fill, retries snowball, congestion collapses links, and routing oscillates under stress. The very mechanisms that make classical networks reliable in the small can make them fragile in the large.

Why spend time on these limits? Because the entire topic of quantum networking emerges precisely here—at the points where classical systems show that they cannot improve without fundamentally new tools. Quantum networks do not erase these challenges, but they reshape them: they offer new primitives for trust, new models for communication, and new ways of thinking about what "connectivity" means when information isn't just a packet moving through a router but a quantum state distributed across space.

In the next subsection, we will look at the first of these primitives: **quantum key distribution (QKD)**—the most mature and practical application of quantum communication today, and the one closest to impacting how cloud providers think about secure, resilient backbone connectivity.

Quantum Key Distribution: The First Practical Step Toward Quantum Networking

If quantum networking sounds distant from the day-to-day realities of cloud architecture, QKD is the exception—the bridge between frontier research and what operators are already beginning to deploy in critical networks. It is the first quantum technology that addresses a real and urgent constraint in classical resilience: the fragility of encryption built on computational hardness. Every secure session, every cross-region replication stream, every VPN tunnel, and every TLS handshake ultimately depends on the assumption that certain mathematical problems are difficult enough to keep adversaries out. For decades this assumption has held, but it rests on shifting ground. As quantum computing advances, the security of those primitives becomes more fragile— not catastrophically today, but no longer unassailable. QKD enters precisely at this intersection: it reinforces the trust fabric that modern cloud networks depend on, and it does so using mechanisms that behave in ways classical systems never could.

Despite what the name suggests, QKD is not about transmitting quantum data. It is, at its heart, a method for generating shared symmetric keys with a very specific property: if anyone attempts to observe the key while it is being created, the endpoints know. The detection is not heuristic or statistical; it is a direct result of quantum physics. Any measurement performed by an eavesdropper disturbs the quantum states used for the exchange, changing the error characteristics of the signal in ways that the communicating parties can quantify. If the disturbance stays below a threshold, the extracted key is considered safe; if it exceeds it, the key is discarded, the channel is deemed compromised, and the system falls back to classical negotiation modes. In a world where most security failures are silent until it is too late, this kind of built-in tamper detection brings a fundamentally new capability: visibility into the trust layer itself.

This is why QKD fits naturally into a discussion about resilience. Throughout this book, we framed resilience as the discipline of maintaining a system's intended behavior under stress. Normally, that stress is operational—network congestion, cross-AZ jitter, routing instability, dependency outage—but the integrity of cryptographic keys is just as foundational. A system that continues forwarding traffic while its keys have been intercepted has not remained resilient; it has simply failed in a way no metric or alarm will detect. QKD transforms key exchange from a silent vulnerability into a monitored, observable process. A spike in the quantum bit error rate becomes the cryptographic analogue of rising packet loss on a fiber link: an early warning that the path is no longer trustworthy. In conventional networks, we discover such compromises long after the fact, if at all. In quantum-assisted networks, detection is intrinsic. Operationally, this turns trust into a monitored signal: a measurable degradation that can trigger the same escalation paths as latency or loss in classical networks.

Another reason QKD belongs in a resilience conversation is its failure behavior. Classical links typically fail in binary fashion: up or down, reachable or unreachable. Even brownouts—while subtle—still map to measurable patterns of loss, jitter, or latency. QKD links behave differently. Their failure modes are probabilistic. As fiber length increases or environmental noise fluctuates, the quantum error rate rises gradually, reducing key generation throughput long before the link becomes unusable. For operators, this is more than a curiosity: it provides advance notice that a backbone segment is degrading even if the classical transport on the same fiber looks healthy. This makes QKD-monitored links behave almost like their own sensor layer, exposing physical-layer conditions that traditional observability cannot see. Long before a carrier circuit experiences visible disruption, the trust channel signals that it is under strain.

Far from being futuristic speculation, these technologies are already being piloted in real networks. For example, telecommunications operators across Europe and Asia have deployed metro-scale QKD systems between datacenters and exchange points, securing fiber spans in cities such as Paris, Berlin, and Tokyo.

Government networks are testing quantum-secured communication for high-sensitivity workloads. The European Commission has launched a continent-wide program (EuroQCI) aimed at building a quantum-secured backbone. And AWS itself, through the Center for Quantum Networking, is conducting research on how quantum links may eventually integrate into cloud-scale infrastructure. None of these deployments replace existing internet routing, and none of them change how applications send packets. They are additive: classical data paths protected by quantum-generated keys.

Integrating QKD into a cloud or hybrid environment is more pragmatic than it sounds. A typical deployment places quantum transmitters and receivers at the physical ends of a fiber span—perhaps between two metro datacenters or a customer facility and a carrier meet-me room. Those devices generate symmetric keys continuously, feeding them into existing encryption layers such as MACsec, IPSec, or TLS. The traffic itself remains classical; only the key negotiation changes. From a cloud architect's perspective, this becomes yet another input into the resilience posture of a cross-region or hybrid path. If the quantum channel remains healthy, key generation is steady and trust boundaries are strong. If the error rate begins to drift, the system can prepare: rotate to classical post-quantum algorithms, reroute traffic to alternate links, or initiate a controlled failover before the situation escalates.

Seen through this lens, QKD does not compete with the resilience techniques discussed throughout this book—it complements them. Just as observability gives you awareness of network behavior, QKD gives you awareness of trust integrity. Just as chaos engineering validates failover readiness, QKD validates the security of the underlying channel in real time. And just as redundancy in classical networks mitigates physical failure, redundancy in key-exchange methods mitigates cryptographic failure. It is simply another layer of early detection, another dimension of failure isolation, another mechanism through which a system can anticipate rather than react.

This is why we discuss QKD here—not because it will replace BGP or magically solve latency, but because it reshapes one of the most fragile assumptions in distributed systems: that the keys used to secure long-distance communication are unobservable by adversaries. QKD challenges that assumption directly and provides a new operational signal that resilience engineers can act upon.

In the next subsection, we shift from trust to routing. If QKD strengthens the secrecy of communication, the next frontier—path-aware networking—aims to improve the *control* of communication. Together, they outline what a post-classical networking landscape may eventually look like and how cloud-scale systems might evolve when both the trust plane and the routing plane begin to incorporate new primitives.

Path-Aware Networking: Rethinking Routing in a Post-BGP Era

If QKD strengthens the trust foundation of networks, path-aware networking represents the next evolution in how networks decide *where* traffic goes. One of the themes running through this book is that routing—more than CPUs, storage, or application code—is often the real origin of resilience issues. Not because routing protocols are poorly designed, but because they were built for a very different world: one where networks evolved slowly, where topologies were largely static, and where policy was simple because the internet was small.

BGP still carries the global internet, and for all its imperfections, it has proved astonishingly robust. But its fundamental design choices create behaviors that make resilience harder than it should be. Routes propagate incrementally, influenced by local decisions rather than global understanding. Convergence happens eventually, but the path to convergence is unpredictable, often chaotic, and varies by geography. When failures occur, routing does not heal instantly—it drifts toward correctness, sometimes through several transient states. These transient states are where real-world outages live: asymmetric paths, intermittent black holes, strange pockets of reachability, and the especially confusing moments when a service works from some countries but not others.

Path-aware networking begins as an answer to these limitations. It starts from a simple premise: that endpoints, applications, or administrative domains should not be blind to the paths their traffic takes. Instead of the traditional model—where the network chooses a path and the application merely accepts it—path-aware networks expose path properties explicitly and allow endpoints to express intent. Latency, geographic location, trust relationships, provider identity, and security posture become attributes the application can select from, rather than mysteries buried deep in ISP routing policies.

This shift sounds subtle, but its implications are profound. In a path-aware model, routing is not merely reactive; it becomes descriptive. The network doesn't just advertise reachability; it advertises characteristics. The endpoint doesn't just accept whatever path BGP announces first; it chooses the one that aligns with its requirements. That choice might be to avoid an untrusted jurisdiction, to prefer a path with low jitter, or to route replication traffic through links with stable latency envelopes. A path becomes more than a sequence of AS hops; it becomes a verifiable object with metadata, provenance, and predictable behavior.

This is not science fiction. The SCION architecture—alongside related work emerging from the IETF Path-Aware Networking (PAN) Working Group—has already demonstrated how endpoints can select paths with explicit cryptographic guarantees about their structure. SCION has been deployed in production research and government networks, providing path selection with cryptographic verification of each routing segment. While SCION itself is not used inside public cloud fabrics today, its core ideas already surface in operational cloud environments through controlled backbones and routing overlays. Services such as Amazon Global Accelerator, traffic steering with Route 53 routing policies, and application-level path selection logic all reflect the same principle: reducing reliance on opaque internet convergence by choosing paths based on intent, health, and trust rather than accepting whatever BGP happens to deliver. In these systems, a path is assembled from verifiable segments, each belonging to a specific administrative domain, forming something closer to a signed contract than a blind bet.

An endpoint does not simply trust that a route is safe because a BGP speaker announced it; it knows who signed each segment and can choose alternatives if a segment becomes degraded or geopolitically undesirable.

These ideas matter for cloud networks because modern applications increasingly span multiple regions, multiple clouds, and multiple connectivity models. When the health of a service depends on transcontinental replication, routing drift becomes a resilience risk, not an operational curiosity. When identity providers operate in active/active mode, asymmetric paths can create subtle inconsistencies in session validation. And when thousands of microservices communicate across Availability Zones, even small routing instabilities can produce cascading retries and emergent congestion. Path awareness gives operators and applications the control to avoid these pitfalls by selecting paths that reflect their own resilience requirements, rather than relying on the network's best guess.

Importantly, path-aware networking also reframes how we think about failure domains. In a traditional topology, a single fiber cut might be just one of many events BGP must absorb. In a path-aware system, an endpoint can see that a specific geographic segment has degraded and proactively choose a different one—not because routing has failed, but because the path no longer fits the application's intent. This transforms resilience from a passive property ("wait for convergence") into an active practice ("avoid convergence failures altogether"). Instead of asking the network to heal itself invisibly, path-aware architectures allow applications to route around trouble before the system enters instability.

For cloud providers, these ideas point toward a future where networks become more transparent, more programmable, and less hostage to slow global reconvergence. Amazon Global Accelerator already hints at this direction: traffic is steered through the AWS backbone in ways that mask external internet instability, abstracting path selection away from BGP and toward a controller that understands the health of the global network. It is not yet a path-aware protocol in the academic sense, but it is a real-world expression of the same idea: control the path with intent, not hope.

We are still at the beginning of this transition. Path-aware networking is not a drop-in replacement for BGP, nor does it eliminate the need for the decentralized, fault-tolerant properties that make BGP resilient. Instead, it layers additional intelligence above the routing substrate, allowing endpoints, applications, and cloud fabrics to choose paths based on semantics rather than chance. In that sense, path-aware networking occupies an important middle ground: it is more realistic and near-term than quantum entanglement but more visionary than incremental tweaks to BGP.

682

And with this perspective in place—as both a complement to, and an evolution beyond, today's routing—we can finally turn to the question at the edge of the horizon: what happens when the transport itself changes? If QKD enhanced security and path-aware networking improved control, the next development goes further still. It challenges the very notion of a "path" by introducing communication that does not travel through routers in the classical sense at all.

To understand that shift, we need to examine the next frontier: entanglement-based networks—moving from technologies that can augment cloud resilience in the near to medium term to those that remain firmly in the research domain but may redefine networking assumptions in the long run.

Quantum Networking: Entanglement, Quantum Repeaters, and the Future of Connectivity

If QKD is the first practical step toward quantum-enhanced networking, entanglement-based communication is the step that forces us to rethink the very meaning of "connectivity." It is the point where networking ceases to be about sending information through a path and becomes instead about *establishing correlations* between distant endpoints—correlations so strong that changing the state of one system influences the other, no matter how far apart they are, without anything physically travelling between them. This is not faster-than-light messaging—no usable information is transmitted in this way—but entanglement gives us a new kind of link: a link defined not by propagation but by shared structure.

To understand why this matters, we need a simple, grounded notion of what a *quantum state* actually is. In classical systems, a state is just a value: a bit is either 0 or 1; a packet is either here or not; a link is either up or down. Quantum systems behave differently. A quantum state represents the full set of probabilities defining how a particle will behave when measured. Before measurement, it is not "somewhere" or "something" in the classical sense—it is in a superposition, a weighted combination of possibilities. What entanglement adds is correlation: two particles become linked in such a way that their combined state must be described as a whole, even when the particles are separated. Measuring one instantaneously defines the outcome of the other, not because a signal has travelled, but because the state itself is shared. This is the object that quantum networks manipulate: not packets or frames, but patterns of correlation distributed across space.

The challenge is not whether entanglement exists—it has been demonstrated in laboratories for decades and deployed across metropolitan fiber networks for years. The challenge is how to create it reliably, maintain it across distance, and move it from one pair of endpoints to another without destroying it. Classical networks overcome distance with amplifiers and regenerators; quantum networks cannot, because the no-cloning theorem forbids copying unknown quantum states. Instead, quantum networks depend on an entirely different construct: **quantum repeaters**. These devices do not amplify signals. They generate entanglement on adjacent spans and use teleportation protocols to stitch those spans together, extending entanglement across many kilometers without ever copying the underlying state.

This architecture introduces failure behavior that does not match anything in classical networking. In a classical link, attenuation manifests as loss, jitter, or latency. In a quantum link, degradation shows up as a reduced probability that entanglement can be established with sufficient fidelity. It is not that the link "goes down"; it is that the *quality* of entanglement declines until it becomes unusable. This produces a kind of soft-failure mode that precedes any visible degradation of the classical fiber. Long before a traditional network would raise alarms, the entanglement generation rate begins to fall. From an operational perspective, this behaves like a new class of brownout: the link remains nominally available, but its ability to support secure coordination degrades progressively and predictably rather than failing outright. In a future hybrid environment—where classical transport is overlaid with quantum trust channels—these early signals could become a new observability axis, revealing physical-layer stress long before customers feel the impact.

Research groups across the world—including MIT, Delft, the Chicago Quantum Exchange, and AWS's own Center for Quantum Networking—are actively exploring these architectures. Their work goes well beyond physics. It touches the concerns that cloud network engineers already recognize: how to coordinate distributed resources, how to schedule link operations, how to verify the integrity of a path, and how to blend quantum and classical control planes into something that behaves predictably. In many ways, a quantum network behaves less like an internetwork of routers and more like a distributed operating system, allocating entanglement as a resource, consuming it, refreshing it, and routing it where applications need it most.

For multi-region cloud architectures, quantum networking will not replace the data plane for the foreseeable future. Routing will continue to run on classical protocols, and packets will not "travel by entanglement." Applications will still replicate asynchronously across oceans, using the same physical constraints and routing mechanisms that exist today.

But quantum networking could fundamentally reshape trust and coordination. It could allow endpoints to share cryptographic material with properties that classical systems cannot match, synchronize distributed components in ways that are provably secure, or validate the integrity of long-distance communication without relying solely on computational assumptions. Even if the data continues to flow at the speed of light, the certainty with which systems can coordinate might evolve dramatically.

This section intentionally blended technologies that vary in maturity—from QKD, which is already being piloted in operational networks, to entanglement distribution and quantum repeaters, which remain in early stages of research. The purpose is not to claim imminent disruption but to explore the art of the possible. Throughout this book we have looked at the limits of current architectures and the engineering practices required to stay ahead of failure. Quantum networking offers a glimpse of what comes next: a world where trust is physical, where routing is intentional, and where coordination spans great distances without relying entirely on classical transmission.

In the next section, we step back from both the present and the future to look at the discipline that connects them. Whether networks are classical, quantum, or a mixture of both, the question remains the same: **what does it mean to build systems that expect failure, absorb it, and continue to serve?** Section 9.3 brings this book to its final destination—not with speculation about technology, but with a perspective on resilience that endures regardless of how the transport evolves.

Section 9.3: Final Thoughts: Building for the Inevitable Outage

Everyone who designs or operates distributed systems eventually learns a hard truth: systems fail, and they rarely fail loudly. I began this book with that reality, and I want to end with it.

They fail softly and inconveniently—in the dead zones between what dashboards show and what humans immediately perceive. A hint of cross-AZ jitter. A Direct Connect path returning retransmits. A resolver favoring an endpoint that should have been deprioritized. Nothing is "down," but something is undeniably wrong.

And in these moments, the strength of the architecture—not the cloud provider—determines what happens next.

It is tempting to believe that because we run on hyperscale cloud platforms, resilience is implicit. After all, providers operate vast backbones, redundant facilities, globally distributed control planes, and fleets of automated repair systems. AWS, Azure, Google Cloud, OCI, etc.—these platforms are engineering achievements of staggering complexity. And yet, despite their scale, despite their sophistication, they cannot make your architecture resilient on your behalf. **This is the central distinction of cloud resilience:**

> cloud providers are responsible for the resilience *of* the cloud

> but you are responsible for the resilience *in* the cloud

They cannot decide which workloads must survive a regional impairment. They cannot choose your consistency boundaries or recovery models. And they cannot ensure your recovery path actually works when you need it. Cloud providers give you highly available and resilient infrastructure. **But you have to architect for resilience in what you build on top of it.**

Throughout this book, we've examined how failures unfold in the real world— not as dramatic blackouts, but as gradual degradations that accumulate until they cross a resilience boundary. The architecture you design determines whether those degradations stay invisible or explode into user-visible incidents. A well-designed system absorbs damage and keeps serving; a brittle system collapses long before an alarm ever fires.

This leads us to a question that is uncomfortable precisely because it is necessary: **What if the region fails?**

Full regional failures are extraordinarily rare, and many "region down" headlines collapse nuance into a single phrase. But resilience engineering does not design only for what has already happened. Its purpose is to design beyond the historical record—for the outage you hope never occurs.

A resilient system is not defined by how it behaves when everything is healthy, but by how it behaves when the environment becomes hostile. Can it reroute around impaired hybrid paths without destabilizing? Can it maintain state coherence when network partitions emerge? Can it shift traffic smoothly to a secondary region without amplifying the failure? Can it keep delivering the experience your users expect, even when the underlying world is unstable?

The core message is simple but demanding:

This is the responsibility that comes with resilience in the cloud.

And it applies everywhere—whether your workloads run on AWS, Azure, GCP, OCI, edge environments, or a hybrid of all of them.

That is why resilience engineering is ultimately a discipline; it is feature number 1 and should be embedded everywhere in your architecture. It asks you to test your recovery capabilities relentlessly—not once a year for an audit, but continuously, until the recovery environment becomes as familiar and trustworthy as the production one. It asks you to tier your applications based on business impact—not every workload requires multi-region active/active, but some absolutely do. It asks you to troubleshoot your recovery paths with the same intensity that you apply to your primary ones—because an untested recovery environment is indistinguishable from *no* recovery environment.

Most importantly, it asks you to build systems that continue to serve even when something else is breaking—to hide chaos behind intention.

In this final section, the goal is not to overwhelm you with yet another list of best practices. Instead, it is to offer clarity:

after everything we've explored—the architectures, the routing behaviors, the traffic patterns, the observability signals, the DR models, the predictive systems—what should you do next?

How do you turn all of this into an operational posture you can trust on the worst day of the year? What are the calls to action and lessons I want you to take home after journeying with me throughout this book?

The next subsection begins that journey.

And the final subsection closes the loop: how to build for the failure you hope never happens and how to ensure that when it comes, you meet it with preparation rather than panic.

The Practical Roadmap: What You Should Do on Monday Morning

Everything you've learned so far—routing behavior, failover patterns, recovery models, observability, chaos testing, predictive analytics—becomes irrelevant unless you validate it continuously. Resilience is not a feature. It is not a configuration. And it is absolutely not a box you tick once and forget. **Resilience is a continuous practice**, a cycle of testing, observing, correcting, and repeating. If you stop, your system drifts. If you drift, you fail.

So here is what you must do next, what I want you to take away with you, apart from all the technical domains we discussed—not in theory, but in your actual environment.

Your first responsibility is to **tier your applications** based on real business impact. Do it bluntly and honestly. Identify which workloads must survive a regional impairment, which must survive an AZ failure, and which can tolerate being restored from backup. Make these decisions with business leaders, not just engineers. If everything is Tier 0, you are lying to yourself. Tiering determines your DR model, your routing strategy, your observability boundaries, and your testing cadence. It is step zero for everything that follows.

Once you know what truly matters, your next task is to validate how your system behaves under stress—both in place and during recovery. This means deliberately injecting controlled impairments: degrading an Availability Zone, simulating packet loss or jitter on critical paths, disrupting Direct Connect return traffic, or delaying route propagation. Observe how the system responds, not just whether alarms fire.

At the same time, treat the DR region as a first-class production environment. Deploy into it regularly. Inspect its routing tables. Validate IAM alignment, load balancer listeners, database replicas, and CIDR allocations. A recovery region you haven't exercised under stress is not a recovery region—it is a liability disguised as readiness.

Next, test the full recovery process end-to-end, repeatedly, until failover becomes routine rather than ceremonial. Perform real failover drills. Measure true RTO. Inspect every step that consumes time. Validate that the Route 53 cutover behaves as expected, load balancers rebalance smoothly, and hybrid connectivity converges cleanly. Fail back—and do it again.

Each drill should feed directly into improvement. Remove unnecessary dependencies. Harden automation. Simplify what does not need to be complex. Fast recovery is rarely achieved by adding features; it is achieved by removing friction. Your recovery path should be the smoothest operational surface in the system.

And now the part most architects forget: **resilience is continuous**. It is not a one-day job. It is not something you implement once per quarter or once per audit. The moment you stop testing, your system begins to decay. Infrastructure evolves, code changes, dependencies shift, teams rotate—and your resilience posture erodes quietly in the background.

To prevent this, build a **continuous loop** into your operating model. After all, if you remember, resilience is the expression of High Availability (HA), Disaster Recovery (DR), and continuous testing and continuous improvements:

The Continuous Resilience Loop

1. **Test**: Inject controlled failure and perform scheduled DR drills

2. **Observe**: Use telemetry and baselines to understand behavior under stress

3. **Validate**: Confirm that failover mechanisms, routing, and state replication behave as intended

4. **Adjust**: Refine architecture, alarms, automation, and runbooks based on what you learned

5. **Repeat**: Restart the cycle before drift accumulates

If you stop at step 1 or step 2, you are not doing resilience.

If you execute the full cycle consistently, you will build a system that behaves predictably under degradation—a system that absorbs impact without visible failure.

These actions are not optional. They are what turn the ideas in this book into operational truth. They are the difference between merely "running in the cloud" and engineering for survival. They are what allow you to face a sudden regional impairment or a major network brownout with confidence instead of panic.

In the final section, we confront the reality every architect must accept: failures are not hypothetical. They *will* come—and your preparation determines whether those failures become lessons or catastrophes.

Final Thoughts: Building for the Inevitable Outage

If there is one lesson that runs like a thread through every chapter of this book, it is that **resilience is neither accidental nor automatic**. It does not emerge from the cloud provider on its own, nor from hardware redundancy, nor from the illusion that "distributed" means "invulnerable." Resilience is a property you cultivate deliberately— through architecture, observation, preparation, and the willingness to engage honestly with failure.

Across all of computing history, systems have failed for the same fundamental reasons: limits of physics, limits of coordination, limits of design, and limits of human cognition. Whether your workload runs on-premises, on AWS, on Azure, on GCP, or across all of them, these limits persist. Even the most advanced cloud infrastructure cannot override the reality that distributed systems behave unpredictably under stress and that your application's behavior under impairment is the only behavior that matters to your users.

This book has shown you that outages are rarely singular events. They are sequences—subtle degradations, partial partitions, routing asymmetries, replication delays, control-plane inconsistencies, and dependency failures that amplify each other. The most consequential incidents in modern distributed systems do not begin with a dramatic "region down." They begin with a drift: a few milliseconds of latency, a misaligned health check, a slow convergence event, or a stale DNS cache in the wrong geography. Catastrophe grows quietly until it touches the fault boundary you failed to reinforce.

Which leads to the foundational truth of resilient engineering:

> **You do not control when failure arrives, but you fully control how prepared you are when it does.**

Cloud platforms have become astonishingly reliable, but they cannot make decisions on your behalf. They cannot classify your critical workloads. They cannot test your recovery plan. They cannot validate your routing architecture during a shift. They cannot confirm that your failover path is trustworthy. That responsibility sits with you—the architect who understands the business impact, the engineer who knows the system's weak points, and the team who must be ready when the conditions turn hostile.

Resilience is ultimately a discipline of anticipation rather than reaction. When you test your recovery environment, when you inject controlled faults, when you rehearse failover, when you measure true RTO, and when you map your resilience boundaries to actual telemetry, you begin to understand your system in a way diagrams can never express. You no longer rely on intention; you rely on behavior. And once you rely on behavior, you remove the element of surprise from failure.

The future of cloud resilience will not be defined by eliminating outages—that would be a fantasy—but by **making outages less meaningful**. The systems that endure will be the ones that continue serving even when individual components, links, regions, or clouds behave unpredictably. The organizations that thrive will be the ones that treat resilience not as a project but as an operating philosophy.

As we look ahead to the next decade—to predictive operations, path-aware networks, quantum-secured communication, and architectures that reason about their own behavior—the role of the architect becomes more, not less, essential. The tooling will evolve; the patterns will evolve; the technology will evolve. But the core responsibility remains unchanged: design with failure in mind, operate with clarity, and test until confidence is earned rather than assumed.

Before you close this book, I want you to take away one final message:

Resilience is not built on perfection—it is built on preparation.

It is the quiet, continuous work of strengthening the places where the system bends. It is the discipline of validating recovery paths until they are routine. It is the honesty to confront where your architecture is weak and the resolve to improve it before stress exposes it for you.

If you apply the principles in these chapters—if you observe deeply, test relentlessly, design intentionally, and prepare continuously—then your systems will not only survive the inevitable outage; they will behave with grace and predictability when it matters most.

And that is the true measure of resilient engineering:

Not that failure never happens, but that failure never defines you.

Epilogue

Resilience is ultimately about protecting what matters.

Every architectural pattern in this book—every routing decision, every replication strategy, every failover path, and every chaos experiment—exists so that when the environment becomes unpredictable, the systems we build continue to serve the people who rely on them. Beneath all the technical detail, the goal is simple: **preserve what is valuable, even when conditions deteriorate.**

For me, that idea is not abstract.

It is tied to Ade.

I placed him on the cover so that a part of him continues forward—seen, remembered, and carried into the work I leave behind.

Losing him taught me something no distributed systems textbook ever could: that failure can arrive abruptly, without warning, and that some losses cannot be engineered away. Ade's quiet resilience—the way his presence brought calm even during difficult moments—shaped how I think about *life* before it shaped how I think about systems. It taught me that resilience is not merely a technical property; it is a way of approaching uncertainty with steadiness, intention, and care.

That lesson carried into my engineering work, but it began long before any architecture decision or routing pattern. And that is what I hope you take with you as you leave this book: the understanding that resilience is a human discipline as much as a technical one.

Design architectures that assume impairment.

Deploy workloads that expect isolation.

Test failover paths until they are predictable.

Observe your systems until their behavior under stress feels familiar, not foreign.

But above all, remember that the purpose of all this engineering is to protect something meaningful—people, trust, continuity—the same way we strive to protect what matters in our personal lives.

C. Critelli, *Cloud Networking and Resilience,* https://doi.org/10.1007/979-8-8688-2436-4

You now have the technical foundations: the fault domains, the routing models, the recovery mechanisms, the testing loops, and the predictive signals. What remains is to apply them with the same intention and care that true resilience requires.

Thank you for reading, and wherever your work takes you next, in every architecture you design, **build something as steady as the companions who teach us what resilience really means.**

Epilogas

Atsparumas — iš esmės, tai apsauga to, kas svarbu.

Kiekvienas šios knygos architektūros šablonas — kiekvienas maršruto sprendimas, kiekviena replikavimo strategija, kiekvienas perjungimo kelias ir kiekvienas chaoso eksperimentas — egzistuoja tam, kad aplinkai tapus nenuspėjamai mūsų kuriamos sistemos toliau tarnautų žmonėms, kurie jomis pasikliauja. Už visų techninių detalių slypi paprastas tikslas: išsaugoti tai, kas vertinga, net kai sąlygos blogėja.

Man ši mintis nėra abstrakti.

Ji neatsiejama nuo Ade.

Įamžinau jį viršelyje, kad dalis jo keliautų toliau — matoma, prisimenama, atsispindinti darbuose, kuriuos paliksiu po savęs.

Jo netektis išmokė mane to, ko niekada neišmokytų joks paskirstytųjų sistemų vadovėlis: kad sąlygos gali suprastėti staiga, be jokio įspėjimo, ir kad kai kurių praradimų neįmanoma pašalinti jokiais inžineriniais sprendimais. Tylus Ade atsparumas — tai, kaip jo buvimas nešdavo ramybę net sunkiausiomis akimirkomis — suformavo mano požiūrį į gyvenimą, dar prieš suformuodamas požiūrį į sistemas. Jis parodė, kad atsparumas — tai ne vien techninė savybė; tai būdas pasitikti nežinią ramiai, sąmoningai ir rūpestingai.

Ši pamoka įkvėpė mano inžinerinį darbą, bet gimė kur kas anksčiau — dar prieš bet kokį architektūrinį sprendimą ar maršrutizavimo šabloną. Ir būtent tai tikiuosi liks jumyse perskaičius šią knygą: supratimą, kad atsparumas yra tiek pat žmogiška, kiek ir mokslo sritis.

Kurkite architektūras, kurios yra pasiruošusios gedimams.

Diekite sistemas, paruoštas izoliacijai.

Testuokite perjungimo kelius tol, kol jie tampa nuspėjami.

Stebėkite savo sistemas tol, kol jų elgsena įtampos metu tampa pažįstama, o ne svetima.

Bet visų svarbiausia — prisiminkite, kad visos šios inžinerijos tikslas yra apsaugoti tai, kas turi prasmę: žmones, pasitikėjimą, tęstinumą — taip, kaip stengiamės apsaugoti tai, kas mums brangu asmeniniame gyvenime.

C. Critelli, *Cloud Networking and Resilience*, https://doi.org/10.1007/979-8-8688-2436-4

Dabar turite techninius pagrindus: gedimų sritis, maršrutizavimo modelius, atkūrimo mechanizmus, testavimo ciklus ir nuspėjamuosius signalus. Belieka juos taikyti su tokiu pačiu sąmoningumu ir rūpesčiu, kokio reikalauja tikras atsparumas.

Ačiū, kad skaitėte. Kad ir kur toliau jus nuves jūsų darbas, kiekvienoje kuriamoje architektūroje kurkite kažką tokio pat tvirto, kokie buvo bendražygiai, mokę mus, ką iš tiesų reiškia atsparumas.

Epilogo

La resilienza, in fondo, riguarda una sola cosa: proteggere ciò che conta davvero.

Ogni scelta architetturale in questo libro—ogni decisione di routing, ogni strategia di replica, ogni percorso di failover e ogni esperimento, chaos engineering—esiste affinché, quando l'ambiente diventa imprevedibile, i sistemi che costruiamo continuino a servire le persone che dipendono da essi. Dietro tutta la tecnica c'è un obiettivo semplice: preservare ciò che è prezioso, anche quando tutto si complica.

Per me, questo non è teorico.

È legato ad Ade.

L'ho voluto sulla copertina perché una parte di lui potesse andare avanti—vista, ricordata, e custodita in ciò che lascio dietro di me.

Perderlo mi ha insegnato qualcosa che nessun manuale sui sistemi distribuiti avrebbe mai potuto insegnarmi: che il fallimento può arrivare all'improvviso, senza preavviso, e che alcune perdite non possono essere "risolte". La resilienza silenziosa di Ade—il modo in cui portava calma anche nei momenti difficili—ha formato il mio modo di vedere la vita, prima ancora di influenzare il mio modo di architettare sistemi. Mi ha mostrato che la resilienza non è solo una proprietà tecnica; è un modo di affrontare l'incertezza con fermezza, intenzione e cura.

Quella lezione è arrivata poi nel mio lavoro di ingegneria, ma è nata molto prima—ben prima di qualsiasi scelta architetturale o pattern di routing. Ed è ciò che spero portiate con voi chiudendo questo libro: la consapevolezza che la resilienza è una disciplina umana tanto quanto tecnica.

Progettate architetture che presuppongono un disservizio.

Disegnare sistemi in isolamento.

Testate i vostri processi di failover finché non diventano affidabili.

Osservate i vostri sistemi finché il loro comportamento sotto stress non diventa familiare, non estraneo.

Ma soprattutto ricordate che lo scopo di tutta questa ingegneria è proteggere qualcosa di significativo—persone, fiducia, continuità—proprio come proteggiamo ciò che conta nelle nostre vite personali.

© Cristian Critelli 2026

C. Critelli, *Cloud Networking and Resilience*, https://doi.org/10.1007/979-8-8688-2436-4

Ora avete le basi tecniche: fault domains, modelli di routing, meccanismi di recupero, cicli di test, segnali predittivi. Ciò che rimane è applicarli con la stessa intenzione e attenzione che richiede la vera resilienza.

Grazie per aver letto questo libro. Ovunque vi porti il vostro lavoro, in ogni architettura che progetterete: costruite qualcosa di solido come coloro che ci hanno insegnato cosa significa davvero essere resilienti.

Index

B

L

M

N

O

P

Q

R

S

SD-WAN
overlay path selection, 426, 435, 437, 457, 534
real-time link scoring, 422, 426
SEEMS model
excessive latency, 8
excessive load, 8
misconfiguration and bugs, 8
shared fate, 9
single point of failure (SPOF), 8, 30
Shared services
centralized DNS, 366
centralized logging, 379
service VPC, 366
Shuffle sharding
failure containment, 328
isolation improvement, 330
Site-to-Site VPN observability
failover readiness, 570
flapping detection, 567, 569
packet loss in IPSec, 569
throughput verification, 569
tunnel health, 585, 589
Software-Defined Networking (SDN)
centralised control plane, 61
data plane separation, 59
intent-based networking, 54, 63
OpenFlow, 62
Split-horizon DNS
internal *vs.* external answers, 123
risk of inconsistent views, 123
State management
consistency boundaries, 274, 278, 285, 301
regional state replication, 265, 298
Static stability

AWS VPC data plane behaviour, 61
control-plane impairments, 61, 67

T, U

Time-to-Live (TTL)
alignment with RTO objectives, 173, 194, 204, 209, 213, 217, 218, 255
recovery time trade-offs, 170, 255
Traffic engineering
deterministic failover, 422, 457, 499
egress control, 422, 465
ingress control, 422
path predictability, 425, 453
Transit Gateway (TGW)
association route tables, 366
attachment isolation, 366
propagation boundaries, 366
routing domains, 350, 366, 368
Transit Gateway observability
attachment metrics, 562–565, 570–573, 580, 583, 585, 637
drop counters, 562, 565, 570, 589
Flow Logs at transit layer, 561, 562, 564, 565, 570–573, 583–585
route propagation events, 563, 570

V, W, X, Y, Z

Virtual Private Cloud (VPC)
route table segmentation, 366, 396, 403
subnet scoping, 331, 350, 396, 403
VPC-level isolation, 366
Virtualisation
commodity hardware adoption, 53, 56
DPUs and SmartNICs, 57
hypervisors (KVM, VMware), 55, 63
Intel DPDK, 57